T0156114

Lecture Notes in Artificial Intelligence 13613

Subseries of Lecture Notes in Computer Science

More information about this subseries at https://link.springer.com/bookseries/1244

Obdulia Pichardo Lagunas ·
Juan Martínez-Miranda ·
Bella Martínez Seis (Eds.)

Advances in Computational Intelligence

21st Mexican International Conference on Artificial Intelligence, MICAI 2022
Monterrey, Mexico, October 24–29, 2022
Proceedings, Part II

Editors
Obdulia Pichardo Lagunas
Instituto Politécnico Nacional
Mexico, Mexico

Bella Martínez Seis
Instituto Politécnico Nacional
Mexico, Mexico

Juan Martínez-Miranda
Centro de Investigación Científica y de
Educación Superior de Ensenada
Ensenada, Baja California, Mexico

ISSN 0302-9743 ISSN 1611-3349 (electronic)
Lecture Notes in Artificial Intelligence
ISBN 978-3-031-19495-5 ISBN 978-3-031-19496-2 (eBook)
https://doi.org/10.1007/978-3-031-19496-2

LNCS Sublibrary: SL7 – Artificial Intelligence

This Springer imprint is published by the registered company Springer Nature Switzerland AG
The registered company address is: Gewerbestrasse 11, 6330 Cham, Switzerland

Preface

The Mexican International Conference on Artificial Intelligence (MICAI) is a yearly international conference series that has been organized by the Mexican Society for Artificial Intelligence (SMIA) since 2000. MICAI is a major international artificial intelligence (AI) forum and the main event in the academic life of the country's growing AI community.

MICAI conferences publish high-quality papers in all areas of AI and its applications. The proceedings of the previous MICAI events have been published by Springer in its Lecture Notes in Artificial Intelligence (LNAI) series (volumes 1793, 2313, 2972, 3789, 4293, 4827, 5317, 5845, 6437, 6438, 7094, 7095, 7629, 7630, 8265, 8266, 8856, 8857, 9413, 9414, 10061, 10062, 10632, 10633, 11288, 11289, 11835, 12468, 12469, 13067, and 13068). Since its foundation in 2000, the conference has both grown in popularity and improved in quality.

The proceedings of MICAI 2022 are published in two volumes. The first volume, Advances in Computational Intelligence (Part I), contains 34 papers structured into three sections:

– Machine and Deep Learning
– Image Processing and Pattern Recognition
– Evolutionary and Metaheuristic Algorithms

The second volume, Advances in Computational Intelligence (Part II), contains 29 papers structured into two sections:

– Natural Language Processing
– Intelligent Applications and Robotics

The two-volume set will be of interest to researchers in all fields of artificial intelligence, students specializing in related topics, and the general public interested in recent developments in AI.

The conference received for evaluation 137 submissions from authors in 20 countries: Belgium, Bolivia, Brazil, Colombia, Cuba, Ecuador, France, Ireland, Japan, Kazakhstan, Mexico, Morocco, The Netherlands, Pakistan, Peru, Russia, Serbia, Spain, the UK and the USA. From these submissions, 63 papers were selected for publication in these two volumes after a peer-reviewing process carried out by the international Program Committee, with each paper receiving a minimum of 2 reviews. The acceptance rate was 46%.

The international Program Committee consisted of 112 experts from 14 countries: Brazil, China, Colombia, France, Iran, Ireland, Japan, Kazakhstan, Malaysia, Mexico, Pakistan, Portugal, Russia, and the UK.

Three workshops were held jointly with the conference:

- WILE 2022: 15th Workshop on Intelligent Learning Environments
- HIS 2022: 15th Workshop of Hybrid Intelligent Systems
- CIAPP 2022: 4th Workshop on New Trends in Computational Intelligence and Applications

The authors of the following papers included in this volume received the Best Paper Awards based on the papers' overall quality, significance, and originality of the reported results:

- "Diachronic Neural Network Predictor of Word Animacy" by Vladimir Bochkarev, Andrey Achkeev, Anna Shevlyakova, and Stanislav Khristoforov, Russia
- "A Novel Hybrid Endoscopic Dataset for Evaluating Machine Learning-based Photometric Image Enhancement Models" by Carlos Axel García Vega, Ricardo Abel Espinosa Loera, Gilberto Ochoa Ruiz, Thomas Bazin, Luis Eduardo Falcón Morales, Dominique Lamarque, and Christian Daul, Mexico/France
- "Towards an interpretable model for automatic classification of endoscopy images" by Rogelio García-Aguirre, Luis Torres-Treviño, Eva María Navarro-López, and José Alberto González-González, Mexico/UK

We want to thank all the people involved in the organization of this conference: the authors of the papers published in these two volumes – it is their research work that gives value to the proceedings, the reviewers for their great effort spent on reviewing the submissions, the Track Chairs for their hard work, and the Program and Organizing Committee members.

We are grateful to all the executive members at Tecnológico de Monterrey: David Garza Salazar, President; Juan Pablo Murra Lascurain, Rector General; Guillermo Torre Amione, Vice President of Research; Neil Hernández Gress, Director of Research; Mario Adrián Flores Castro, Vice President of North Region; Manuel Zertuche Guerra, Dean of Engineering; and Luis Ricardo Salgado Garza, Director of the Computer Science Department, for the invaluable support to MICAI and providing the infrastructure for the keynote talks, tutorials, and workshops.

We are also grateful to the personnel of Tecnológico de Monterrey for their warm hospitality and hard work, as well as for their active participation in the organization of this conference. We greatly appreciate the generous sponsorship provided by the Monterrey government via the Tourism Office.

We deeply grateful to the conference staff and to all members of the Local Organizing Committee headed by José Carlos Ortiz Bayliss. We gratefully acknowledge the support received from the following project: FI-NEXT, Europe – CONACYT Project 274451.

The entire submission, reviewing, and selection process, as well as preparation of the proceedings, was supported by the EasyChair system (www.easychair.org). Last but not least, we are grateful to Springer for their patience and help in the preparation of these volumes.

October 2022

Obdulia Pichardo Lagunas
Juan Martínez-Miranda
Bella Martínez Seis

Conference Organization

MICAI 2022 was organized by the Mexican Society for Artificial Intelligence (SMIA, Sociedad Mexicana de Inteligencia Artificial) in collaboration with the Tecnológico de Monterrey.

The MICAI series website is www.MICAI.org. The website of the Mexican Society for Artificial Intelligence, SMIA, is www.SMIA.mx. Contact options and additional information can be found on these websites.

Conference Committee

General Chair

Hiram Calvo	Instituto Politécnico Nacional, Mexico

Program Chairs

Obdulia Pichardo Lagunas	Instituto Politécnico Nacional, Mexico
Juan Martínez-Miranda	Centro de Investigación Cienífica y de Educación Superior de Ensenada, Mexico
Bella Martínez Seis	Instituto Politécnico Nacional, Mexico

Workshop Chair

Noé Alejandro Castro-Sánchez	Centro Nacional de Investigación y Desarrollo Tecnológico, Mexico

Tutorials Chair

Roberto Antonio Vázquez Espinoza de los Monteros	Universidad La Salle, Mexico

Doctoral Consortium Chairs

Miguel González Mendoza	Tecnológico de Monterrey, Mexico
Francisco Javier Cantú Ortiz	Tecnológico de Monterrey, Mexico

Keynote Talks Chair

Sabino Miranda-Jiménez	Centro de Investigación e Innovación en Tecnologías de la Información y Comunicación, Mexico

Publication Chair

Hiram Ponce	Universidad Panamericana, Mexico

Financial Chairs

Hiram Calvo	Instituto Politécnico Nacional, Mexico
Lourdes Martínez-Villaseñor	Universidad Panamericana, Mexico

Grant Chair

Félix A. Castro Espinoza	Universidad Autónoma del Estado de Hidalgo, Mexico

Local Organizing Committee

José Carlos Ortiz Bayliss	Tecnológico de Monterrey, Mexico
Luis Ricardo Salgado Garza	Tecnológico de Monterrey, Mexico
Héctor Gibrán Ceballos Cancino	Tecnológico de Monterrey, Mexico
Ivan Mauricio Amaya Contreras	Tecnológico de Monterrey, Mexico
Neil Hernández Gress	Tecnológico de Monterrey, Mexico
Joanna Alvarado Uribe	Tecnológico de Monterrey, Mexico
Luis Alberto Muñoz Ubando	Tecnológico de Monterrey, Mexico
Miguel González Mendoza	Tecnológico de Monterrey, Mexico
Sergio Camacho León	Tecnológico de Monterrey, Mexico
Laura Hervert Escobar	Tecnológico de Monterrey, Mexico
Gilberto Ochoa Ruiz	Tecnológico de Monterrey, Mexico
Francisco Javier Cantú Ortiz	Tecnológico de Monterrey, Mexico

Track Chairs

Natural Language Processing

Grigori Sidorov	Instituto Politécnico Nacional, Mexico
Sabino Miranda-Jiménez	Centro de Investigación e Innovación en Tecnologías de la Información y Comunicación, Mexico

Machine Learning

Alexander Gelbukh	Instituto Politécnico Nacional, Mexico
Navonil Majumder	Singapore University of Technology and Design, Singapore

Deep Learning

Hiram Ponce — Universidad Panamericana, Mexico

Evolutionary and Metaheuristic Algorithms

Roberto Antonio Vázquez Espinoza de los Monteros — Universidad La Salle, Mexico

Soft Computing

Miguel González Mendoza — Tecnológico de Monterrey, Mexico
Félix A. Castro Espinoza — Universidad Autónoma del Estado de Hidalgo, Mexico

Image Processing and Pattern Recognition

Lourdes Martínez-Villaseñor — Universidad Panamericana, Mexico

Robotics

Gilberto Ochoa Ruiz — Tecnológico de Monterrey, Mexico

Intelligent Applications and Social Network Analysis

Iris Iddaly Méndez Gurrola — Universidad Autónoma de Ciudad Juárez, Mexico

Other Artificial Intelligence Approaches

Nestor Velasco Bermeo — University College Dublin, Ireland
Gustavo Arroyo Figueroa — Instituto Nacional de Electricidad y Energías Limpias, Mexico
David Eduardo Pinto Avendaño — Benemérita Universidad Autónoma de Puebla, Mexico

Program Committee

Iskander Akhmetov — Institute of Information and Computational Technologies, Kazakhstan
José David Alanís Urquieta — Universidad Tecnológica de Puebla, Mexico
Giner Alor Hernandez — Instituto Tecnologico de Orizaba, Mexico
Joanna Alvarado-Uribe — Tecnológico de Monterrey, Mexico
Miguel Alvarez Carmona — Centro de Investigación Científica y de Educación Superior de Ensenada, Mexico
Maaz Amjad — Instituto Politécnico Nacional, Mexico
Gustavo Arroyo Figueroa — Instituto Nacional de Electricidad y Energías Limpias, Mexico

Ignacio Arroyo-Fernández	Universidad Tecnológica de la Mixteca, Mexico
Ramon Barraza	Universidad Autonoma de Ciudad Juarez, Mexico
Ari Yair Barrera-Animas	Tecnológico de Monterrey, Mexico
Ildar Batyrshin	Instituto Politecnico Nacional, Mexico
Gemma Bel-Enguix	Universidad Nacional Autónoma de México, Mexico
Vadim Borisov	National Research University, Russia
Monica Borunda	Instituto Nacional de Electricidad y Energías Limpias, Mexico
Alexander Bozhenyuk	Southern Federal University, Russia
Ramon F. Brena	Tecnológico de Monterrey, Mexico
Davide Buscaldi	Université Paris 13, France
Sabur Butt	Instituto Politécnico Nacional, Mexico
Ruben Carino-Escobar	Instituto Nacional de Rehabilitación, Mexico
Heydy Castillejos	Universidad Autónoma del Estado de Hidalgo, Mexico
Felix Castro Espinoza	Universidad Autónoma del Estado de Hidalgo, Mexico
Hector Ceballos	Tecnológico de Monterrey, Mexico
Jaime Cerda Jacobo	Universidad Michoacana de San Nicolás de Hidalgo, Mexico
Haruna Chiroma	Federal College of Education (Technical) Gombe, Malaysia
Elisabetta Crescio	Tecnológico de Monterrey, Mexico
Laura Cruz	Instituto Tecnológico de Ciudad Madero, Mexico
Nareli Cruz Cortés	Instituto Politécnico Nacional, Mexico
Jorge De La Calleja	Universidad Politécnica de Puebla, Mexico
Omar Arturo Domínguez-Ramírez	Universidad Autónoma del Estado de Hidalgo, Mexico
Andrés Espinal	Universidad de Guanajuato, Mexico
Karina Figueroa	Universidad Michoacana de San Nicolás de Hidalgo, Mexico
Denis Filatov	Sceptica Scientific Ltd, UK
Dora-Luz Flores	Universidad Autónoma de Baja California, Mexico
Sofia N. Galicia-Haro	Universidad Nacional Autónoma de México, Mexico
Vicente Garcia	Universidad Autónoma de Ciudad Juárez, Mexico
Claudia Gomez	Instituto Tecnológico de Ciudad Madero, Mexico
Pedro Pablo Gonzalez	Universidad Autónoma Metropolitana, Mexico
Miguel Gonzalez-Mendoza	Tecnológico de Monterrey, Mexico
Gabriel Gonzalez-Serna	Centro Nacional de Investigación y Desarrollo Tecnológico, Mexico

Fernando Gudiño	Universidad Nacional Autónoma de México, Mexico
Rafael Guzman Cabrera	Universidad de Guanajuato, Mexico
José Alberto Hernández	Universidad Autónoma del Estado de Morelos, Mexico
Yasmín Hernández	Centro Nacional de Investigación y Desarrollo Tecnológico, Mexico
Betania Hernandez-Ocaña	Universidad Juárez Autónoma de Tabasco, Mexico
Laura Hervert-Escobar	Tecnológico de Monterrey, Mexico
Miguel Hidalgo-Reyes	Instituto de Ecología A.C., Mexico
Olga Kolesnikova	Instituto Politécnico Nacional, Mexico
Angel Kuri-Morales	Instituto Tecnológico Autónomo de México, Mexico
Virginia Lagunes	Universidad Veracruzana, Mexico
Carlos Lara-Alvarez	Centro de Investigación en Matemáticas, Mexico
José Antonio León-Borges	Universidad de Quintana Roo, Mexico
Victor Lomas-Barrie	Universidad Nacional Autónoma de México, Mexico
Gerardo Loreto	Instituto Tecnológico Superior de Uruapan, Mexico
Jerusa Marchi	Federal University of Santa Catarina, Brazil
Aldo Márquez Grajales	Universidad Veracruzana, Mexico
Carolina Martín Del Campo Rodríguez	Instituto Politécnico Nacional, Mexico
Lourdes Martínez	Universidad Panamericana, Mexico
Bella Citlali Martinez Seis	Instituto Politécnico Nacional, Mexico
Jose Martinez-Carranza	Instituto Nacional de Astrofísica, Óptica y Electrónica, Mexico
Juan Martínez-Miranda	Centro de Investigación Científica y de Educación Superior de Ensenada, Mexico
Iris Iddaly Méndez-Gurrola	Universidad Autónoma de Ciudad Juárez, Mexico
Efrén Mezura-Montes	Universidad de Veracruz, Mexico
Sabino Miranda	Centro de Investigación e Innovación en Tecnologías de la Información y Comunicación, Mexico
Daniela Moctezuma	Centro de Investigación en Ciencias de Información Geoespacial, Mexico
Saturnino Job Morales Escobar	Universidad Autónoma del Estado de México, Mexico
Guillermo Morales-Luna	Centro de Investigación y de Estudios Avanzados del Instituto Politécnico Nacional, Mexico

Alicia Morales-Reyes	Instituto Nacional de Astrofísica, Óptica y Electrónica, Mexico
Masaki Murata	Tottori University, Japan
Nikita Murzintcev	Institute of Geographical Sciences and Natural Resources Research, China
Antonio Neme	Universidad Nacional Autónoma de Mexico, Mexico
César Núñez	Instituto Politécnico Nacional, Mexico
Gilberto Ochoa-Ruiz	Tecnológico de Monterrey, Mexico
C. Alberto Ochoa-Zezatti	Universidad Autónoma de Ciudad Juárez, Mexico
Juan Carlos Olivares Rojas	Instituto Tecnológico de Morelia, Mexico
José Luis Oliveira	University of Aveiro, Portugal
Jesús Patricio Ordaz Oliver	Universidad Autónoma del Estado de Hidalgo, Mexico
José Carlos Ortiz-Bayliss	Tecnológico de Monterrey, Mexico
Ismael Osuna-Galán	Universidad Politécnica de Chiapas, Mexico
Abigail Pallares-Calvo	Instituto Politécnico Nacional, Mexico
Obed Pérez Cortés	Universidad Autónoma del Estado de Hidalgo, Mexico
Humberto Pérez-Espinosa	Centro de Investigación Científica y de Educación Superior de Ensenada, Mexico
Obdulia Pichardo-Lagunas	Instituto Politécnico Nacional, Mexico
Garibaldi Pineda García	University of Sussex, UK
David Pinto	Benemérita Universidad Autónoma de Puebla, Mexico
Hiram Ponce Espinosa	Universidad Panamericana, Mexico
José Federico Ramírez Cruz	Instituto Tecnológico de Apizaco, Mexico
Tania Aglaé Ramírez Del Real	Universidad Politécnica de Aguascalientes, Mexico
Jorge Reyes	Universidad Autónoma de Yucatán, Mexico
Elva Lilia Reynoso Jardón	Universidad Autónoma de Ciudad Juárez, Mexico
Katya Rodriguez-Vazquez	Universidad Nacional Autónoma de México, Mexico
Alberto Rosales	Instituto Politécnico Nacional, Mexico
Horacio Rostro Gonzalez	Universidad de Guanajuato, Mexico
Angel Sanchez	Universidad de Veracruz, Mexico
Luis Humberto Sánchez Medel	Instituto Tecnológico de Orizaba, Mexico
Eddy Sánchez-Delacruz	Instituto Tecnológico Superior de Misantla, Mexico
Alejandro Santiago	Instituto Politécnico Nacional, Mexico
Grigori Sidorov	Instituto Politécnico Nacional, Mexico
Juan Humberto Sossa Azuela	Instituto Politécnico Nacional, Mexico
Ramon Soto de la Cruz	Universidad de Sonora, Mexico

Antonio Tamayo	Universidad de Antioquia, Colombia
Eric S. Tellez	Centro de Investigación e Innovación en Tecnologías de la Información y Comunicación, Mexico
David Tinoco Varela	Universidad Nacional Autónoma de México, Mexico
Nasim Tohidi	K. N. Toosi University of Technology, Iran
Aurora Torres	Universidad Autónoma de Aguascalientes, Mexico
Diego Uribe	Instituto Tecnológico de la Laguna, Mexico
Genoveva Vargas Solar	Laboratoire d'Informatique en Image et Systèmes d'Information, France
Roberto Antonio Vázquez Espinoza	Universidad Lasalle, Mexico
Nestor Velasco Bermeo	University College Dublin, Ireland
Luis M. Vilches-Blázquez	Instituto Politécnico Nacional, Mexico
Juan Villegas-Cortez	Universidad Autónoma Metropolitana, Mexico
Yenny Villuendas-Rey	Instituto Politécnico Nacional, Mexico
Saúl Zapotecas Martínez	Instituto Nacional de Astrofísica, Óptica y Electrónica, Mexico

Additional Reviewers

Rogelio Florencia
Daniel Flores Araiza
Ivan Reyes-Amezcua
Mirna Patricia Ponce Flores
J. David Terán-Villanueva
Alejandro Humberto Garcia Ruiz
Francisco López Ramos
Nelson Rangel-Valdez
Patricia Sánchez
Ricardo Espinosa Loera
Francisco Lopez-Tiro
Marco Sotelo-Figueroa
Francisco López-Orozco
Jesus German Ortiz Barajas
Carlos Aguilar
Juan Vásquez
Valery Solovyev

Contents – Part II

Best Paper Award

Intelligent Applications and Robotics

Contents – Part I

31. Kumar, P., & Kiran, V. R.: A hybrid named entity recognition system for south Asian languages. In: Proceedings of The IJCNLP-08 Workshop on ner For South And South East Asian Languages, pp. 83–88 (2008)
32. Mikolov, T., Chen, K., Corrado, G., Dean, J.: Efficient estimation of word representations in vector space. arXiv preprint arXiv:1301.3781(2013)
33. Pennington, J., Socher, R., Manning, C.D.: Glove: global vectors for word representation. In: Proceedings of the 2014 Conference on Empirical Methods In Natural Language Processing (EMNLP), pp. 1532–1543 (2014)
34. Bojanowski, P., Grave, E., Joulin, A., Mikolov, T.: Enriching word vectors with subword information. Trans Assoc. comput. Linguist. **5**, 135–146 (2017)

Natural Language Processing

Urdu Named Entity Recognition with Attention Bi-LSTM-CRF Model

Fida Ullah[1], Ihsan Ullah[2], and Olga Kolesnikova[3](✉)

[1] Beijing University of Chemical Technology, Beijing, China
[2] Department of Robotics Engineering, Daegu Gyeongbuk Institute of Science and Technology (DGIST), Daegu 42988, South Korea
[3] Centro de Investigación en Computación (CIC), Instituto Politécnico Nacional (IPN), 07320 Mexico City, Mexico
kolesolga@gmail.com

Abstract. The named entity recognition (NER) task is a challenging problem in natural language processing (NLP), especially for languages with very few annotated corpora such as Urdu. In this paper we proposed an Attention-Bi-LSTM-CRF method and applied it to the MK-PUCIT Corpus which is the latest NER dataset available for the Urdu language. In addition to word-level embedding, we used an embedding-level focus mechanism. The output of the embedding layer was fed into a bidirectional-LSTM encoder unit, accompanied by another self-attention layer to boost the system's accuracy. Our Attention-Bi-LSTM-CRF model demonstrated an F1-score of 92%. The cumulative findings of the experiments show that our approach outperforms existing methods, thus yielding a new UNER (Urdu Named Entity Recognition) state-of-the-art performance.

Keywords: Natural language processing · Named entity recognition · Deep learning · Attention mechanism · Word embedding

1 Introduction

Named Entity Recognition (NER) is one of the most fundamental natural language processing (NLP) tasks, also referred to as entity naming. Urdu is a blend of different languages because it derives from various languages including Persian, Sanskrit, Hindi, Turkish, and Arabic. Identifying and classifying named entities (NEs) from English text has significantly benefited from capitalization, precise POS tagging, and massive gazetteers' accessibility. Furthermore, quality word tokenizers and strong grammatical rules played a major part in effective English NER methods development. On the contrary, NER in the Urdu language is a challenging task due to a lack of capitalization, context-sensitivity, and agglutination.

The main contribution of our paper is an Attention Bi-LSTM-CRF model. We applied it to the MK-PUCIT Corpus and our model outperformed state of the art methods. We used Bi-LSTM-CRF techniques combined with a self-attention mechanism with three types of word embeddings, namely, Word2Vec, GloVe, and fastText.

O. Pichardo Lagunas et al. (Eds.): MICAI 2022, LNAI 13613, pp. 3–17, 2022.
https://doi.org/10.1007/978-3-031-19496-2_1

2 Related Work

The research on NER was initialized in 1996 with the rule-based approach defined as entity tagging or entity extraction. All proper nouns in text were identified and classified into categories such as person, location, organization, etc. [1]. Among many NLP tasks, e.g. question answering, machine translation, and information retrieval, NER is considered the most important initial step, thus playing a significant role in processing and extracting intelligent information from text [2]. Several NER techniques have been developed, especially for Western languages, and mostly for English [3].

NER techniques have been advancing significantly in many virtual assistants like Samsung's Bixby, Microsoft's Cortana, Apple's Siri, and Amazon's Alexa [4]. The English NER shows excellent results due to the abundance of available research data. However, the NER experiments in Urdu are not that strong. This can be attributed to the complexity of Urdu. Furthermore, if deep learning is used, the lack of available datasets becomes a major research issue. Urdu is Pakistan's dominant language, spoken by 75% of the population in this country and easily understood in some states of India. Urdu speakers live worldwide, particularly, in the United States, Norway, the United Kingdom and in some other European countries.

Early 1990s various NER development techniques can be in general classified into three major categories: (1) rule-based, (2) statistical, and (3) hybrid approaches. Among these categories, statistical methods have played a very significant role, with introduction of such techniques as the hidden Markov model, maximum entropy, maximum entropy Markov model, and semi-Markov model [5]. In the following subsections we give a brief description of the three categories mentioned above.

2.1 Rule-Based Techniques

Various NLP tasks are performed using a rule-based technique based on patterns. Concerning the Urdu language, rules are defined on stems of words [6, 7]. The Urdu stemmer called Assas band [23] removes inflections while maintaining an affix exception list. Firstly, the prefix is removed from a word, and the stemmer returns a stem postfix sequence. After that, the stem is extracted by taking out the postfix.

Another rule-based method is application of XML tags and readability contents for NER; experiments with this method were performed on the Becker-Riaz dataset showing that NER gives best results using statistical learning with a recall of 90.7% and a precision of 91.5% [24, 25].

Cucerzan et al. [22] used semantic and morphological data for five languages, including English, Greek, Romanian, Turkish, and Hindi, to establish a language-independent NER structure for Hindi. However, Hindi NER methods perform poorly, as shown in another work [7] with an F1-score of 41.70%, a recall of 27.84%, and an accuracy of about 85%.

By expanding the twelve tags from IJCNLP2008, Singh et al. [26] proposed a rule-based solution recognizing thirteen entities in offline plain Urdu text. The rules were tested using test data gathered from news outlets and grouped into two sets of 12,032 and 150,243 tokens, respectively. An accuracy of 74.09% was reached across all thirteen tags.

2.2 Statistical Techniques

Statistical learning techniques are currently the most dominant methods in NLP. Models based on statistical learning are able to induce rules from training data and are essentially important for analyzing large datasets. For instance, Borthwick et al. [9], working on English NER, applied the maximum entropy approach and achieved an F1-score of 84.22%. For the Hindi language, Li et al. [27] proposed a conditional random field (CRF) method and got an accuracy of 71.50%. These authors constructed features automatically by providing the platform of a large lexical test array. However, this method still fails to find the best feature to improve the accuracy of the NER system [9].

By classifying 100 named entities, Nadeau et al. [10] proposed a semi-supervised method to implement an English NER scheme. The method achieved an F1-score in the range of 78–87%. For the Hindi language, Saha et al. [28] used a maximum entropy-based NER scheme. Using feature reduction strategies focused on word filtering and word clustering, the method obtained an F1-score of 80.01%.

Statistical Conditional Random Field (CRF) model was developed by Ekbal et al. [11] for NER system on South and Southeast Asian languages including Bengali, Hindi, Telugu, Oriya, and Urdu. The system classified named entities into 12 classes by implementing different contextual information and features. Except for the Bengali and Hindi languages, language-independent features were utilized for all available languages. For the Bengali and Hindi languages, the gazetteer lists were also used. The system showed the following values of F1-score: 59.39% for Bengali, 33.12% for Hindi, 28.71% for Oriya, 4.74% for Telugu, and 35.52% for Urdu.

Goyal [29] developed a NER system for the Hindi language also based on CRF. To train the system, the NLPAI machine learning contest 2007 data was used. The system included three modules: the first module, NER, recognized named entities in text, the second module identified the types of the recognized named entities, and the third module classified nested named entities. The following NER tags were used in the experiments: individual, place, measure, time, number, domain-specific terms, abbreviations, titles, among others.

For three scarcely resourced languages, Hindi, Bengali, and Telugu, Ekbal and Saha [1] created a multi-objective simulated annealing-based classifier ensemble NER method. Their method showed the following results: for Bengali, recall, accuracy, and F1-score values were 93.95%, 95.15%, and 94.55%, respectively; for Hindi, they were 93.35%, 92.25%, and 92.80%, respectively; and for Telugu, they were 84.02%, 96.56%, and 89.85%, respectively. In [13], different models based on independent language features were built using Conditional Random Field (CRF), Maximum Entropy (ME), and Support Vector Machine (SVM). A sufficient weight of vote for each output class in each classifier was determined using an ensemble scheme.

2.3 Hybrid Techniques

The hybrid technique combines both rule-based and statistical techniques such as in the work of Biswas et al. [12]. The authors integrated the maximum entropy and hidden Markov model (HMM) approaches and improved the accuracy of NEs recognition. Also, Saha et al. [13] developed a NER system for Hindi, Bengali, Telugu, Oriya, and Urdu languages using ME together with transliteration. Bikel et al. [14] worked with English and Spanish extracting named entities and categorizing them into four sections, including names, times, dates, and numerical quantities, using a hybrid approach and achieved an accuracy of 90.44%.

Gali et al. [30] proposed a hybrid scheme which combined tailor-made principles with CRFs. However, their device generated an F1-score of only 43.46% due to a lack of training. Kumar and Kiran [31] developed a hybrid NER scheme that combined CRFs and HMMs with customized heuristics.

Chaudhuri and Bhattacharya [15] proposed a NER technique for the Indian language. Their method included a three stage procedure built on a dictionary-based, rule-based, and left–right co-occurrences statistics approaches. Srivastava et al. [16] proposed a hybrid technique for the Hindi Language. To solve the optimization problem of machine learning models for complex morphological languages like Hindi, these scientists developed a model based on maximum entropy, part-of-speech features, and orthography features.

3 Our Proposal

This section addresses our proposed Urdu NER (UNER) model based on Bi-directional LSTM with self-attention and conditional random field (CRF) layers. Figure 1 presents the architecture of the network that implements our model. The network includes four layers: an embedding layer, a Bi-LSTM module, a self-attention layer, a dense layer with ReLU activation, and a CRF layer. We used drop-out between the embedding layer and the Bi-LSTM module. In subsections that follow we describe the layers of our network in detail.

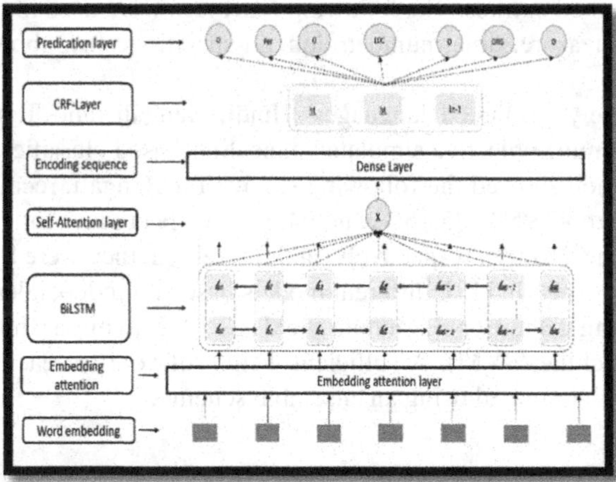

Fig. 1. Architecture of our network

3.1 Embedding Layer

We used pre-trained embeddings to create a distributed representation of terms which captured a variety of syntactic and semantic relationships. Such embeddings are called fixed constants and perform better than learnable parameters. In this work we used such embeddings as Word2Vec [32], GloVe [33], and fastText [34]. These embeddings were concatenated in the embedding layer with the intention to improve the model generalization power. The output of the embedding layer was fed into the Bi-LSTM module to process the sequence in both forward and backward directions, then the hidden states of both directions were concatenated. Furthermore, the output of the Bi-LSTM module was passed to the self-attention layer.

3.2 Bi-LSTM Module

The Long Short-Term Memory (LSTM) network provides the ability to learn long-term dependencies. The LSTM can delete or add information to the cell state, which is controlled by gates. The equations for updating an LSTM unit at time t are as follows:

$$i_t = \sigma(W_i|x_t; h_{t-1}| + b_i), \tag{1}$$

$$f_t = \sigma\left(W_f|x_t; h_{t-1}| + b_f\right), \tag{2}$$

$$o_t = \sigma(W_o|x_t; h_{t-1}| + b_o), \tag{3}$$

$$\hat{c} = \tanh(W_c|x_t; h_{t-1}| + b_c), \tag{4}$$

$$c_t = f_t \cdot c_{t-1} + i_t \cdot \hat{c}, \tag{5}$$

$$h_t = o_t \cdot \tanh(c_1) \tag{6}$$

In the above equations, σ is element-wise sigmoid, $\cdot$ is element-wise matrix multiplication, x_t is the input vector at time t, and h_t represents the hidden state. Weights W_i, W_f, W_o, W_c and biases b_i, b_f, b_o, b_c are learnt parameters.

Both past and expected inputs are defined for a given time when interpreting a sequence of terms, allowing for an optimal use of features in both the right and left directions. Bidirectional LSTM (Bi-LSTM) is the name given to this variant of the LSTM [17]. To capture both the left and right context of the expression, the input is provided to forward and backward LSTMs. The final representation is obtained by concatenating the left context h_t^l and the right context h_t^r.

3.3 Attention Layer

The purpose of implementing the attention mechanism is to give terms high or low weight depending on their contribution to the context of the sentence [18, 19]. The attention layer is used after the encoding layer to encode an arbitrary size sentence into a fixed size embedding with self-attention methodology. The output is not transferred directly to the prediction layer. As seen in Eq. 7, it passes through a function that takes the whole Bi-LSTM concealed states H_z as input and outputs a vector of attention weights A_z:

$$A_z = \text{softmax}(W_{s2} \tanh(W_{s1} \cdot H_z)). \quad (7)$$

In Eq. 7, W_{s2} is a vector of parameters $W_{s2} \in \mathbb{R}^d$ and W_{s1} is a weight matrix of the format $W_{s2} \in \mathbb{R}^{d \times 2u}$, where d is a randomly set hyperparameter. To ensure that all measured focus weights can be added up to one, the softmax function is used. The weighted A_z obtains the sentence vector as a weighted total of the LSTM hidden layer given the attention vector A_z. The sentence embedding matrix is the output of this procedure.

3.4 Encoder Layer

The embedded sequence is input to the encoder which is composed of the concatenated embeddings. The Bi-LSTM module collects forward and backward data by processing the input sequence either forward or backward in two separate hidden states. We start with a sentence with m tokens expressed by a set of word embeddings S. The Bi-LSTM is used to encrypt the tokens in our encoder layer. The composition of the forward LSTM and backward LSTM reads the tokens in sentences in a forward manner, from token 1 to token m, and in a backward manner, from token m to token 1, respectively.

3.5 Conditional Random Field (CRF)

We initially evaluate the MK-PUCIT dataset using a CRF-based approach, widely used in sequence classification problems. The CRF proposed by [20] for modelling sequential data such as word labels in a given input sentence offers several advantages for sequence segmentation and labelling tasks. It is useful to consider the relationship between surrounding labels and jointly decode the most suitable chain of labels for an input sentence. Another advantage of using CRF is its rich feature sets, e.g., overlapping features using conditional probability. So given an input sentence $X = x_1, x_2, \ldots, x_n$ and sequence of named entity tags $Y = y_1, y, \ldots, y_n$, CRF defines the conditional probability $Y|X$ as follows:

$$Y|X \propto \exp\Big(w^T f(y_n, y_{n-1}, x)\Big). \quad (8)$$

In Eq. 8 w is a weight vector $w = (w_1, w_2, \ldots, w_m)$ that maps the entire input sequence X and Y into $\mathbb{R}^d$ as a log-linear model with the parameter vector $w \in \mathbb{R}^d$. The regularization log-likelihood function is defined as follows:

$$\sum_{i=0}^{n} \log \mathrm{P}\Big(y^i|x^i; W\Big) - \frac{\lambda_2}{2}\|w\|_2^2 - \lambda_1\|w\|_1. \quad (9)$$

The vector parameters are forced to be trivial by the terms $\frac{\lambda_2}{2}\|w\|_2^2$ and $\lambda_1\|w\|_1$ in normalization; the vector parameter w^* is estimated as

$$w^* = \text{argmax } x_{w\in\mathbb{R}} dL(W). \tag{10}$$

After the estimation of w^*, the most likely tag of y can be found by

$$S^* = argmax\ x_S P(Y|X; w^*). \tag{11}$$

3.6 Prediction Layer

The CRF constructed on top of the dense layer effectively models many hard constraints while still taking into account dependencies between output labels. In light of the CRF broad description, let $x = (x_1, x_2, \ldots, x_t)$ and $y = (y_1, y, \ldots, y_t)$ represent observed input tokens and the corresponding output labels, respectively. A linear-chain CRF distribution $p(y|x)$ is given by

$$p(y|x) = \frac{1}{Z(X)} \prod_c f_c(y, x), \tag{12}$$

where $Z(X)$ is a normalization function defined by the formula

$$Z(X) = \sum_y \prod_c f_c(y, x). \tag{13}$$

The CRF layer knows only the transition probability of the outcome prediction because the hidden layer on top of the attention layer provides the performance matrix P for a given sequence.

Table 1 gives a summary of the proposed model layers and parameters.

Table 1. The proposed model layers and parameters

Layer Type	Number of parameters
Input layer	0
Embedding layer	9,348,600
Drop-out	0
Bidirectional LSTM	140,400
Self-Attention layer	6,465
Dense layer	5,050
CRF	354
Total	9,500,869

4 Experimental Setup

In this section, we describe our dataset and the experiment design.

4.1 Data

The proposed model was evaluated on the MK-PUCIT dataset [21], a large-scale and open-source text collection[1] compiled for named entity recognition in Urdu. The MK-PUCIT dataset contains 926,776 tokens and 99,718 named entities. The data was collected from news websites related to such topics as entertainment, sports, and religious highlights. This dataset was a part of UNER (Urdu Named Entity Recognition) two-year (2016–17) project and it was published in 2019. The MK-PUCIT dataset is the largest dataset currently available for the evaluation of newly developed named entity recognition methods.

4.2 Experiments

The proposed technique was implemented in Python 3.7 in the Jupyter Notebook. The experiments were executed on Intel (R) core™ i7-8750H CPU with 8.0 GBs of memory. NVidia GeForce GTX 1050Ti, a high-speed graphical processing unit (GPU) of 8 GB memory, was used. The computation computability of the used GPU was 6.1, being suitable enough for processing text-based dataset. To perform training, the batch size was set to 512 samples per iteration. The experiments were performed on 20 epochs. The training accuracy of the dataset achieved its maximum and became linear starting from the 18th epoch. The maximum learning rate was set to 75 as being a suitable length of reviewing.

To evaluate the performance of our model, we used tenfold cross-validation technique, 70% of the dataset was set for training, 10% for validation, and 20% for testing. The total number of trainable parameters of the proposed model was 9,500,869, see Table 1. In the embedding layer, 300 dimensions of GloVe embeddings were trained on 21,776 samples and validated on 2,420 samples. Word2Vec and fastText embeddings were trained and validated similarly.

For both Bi-LSTM-CRF and Attention Bi-LSTM-CRF layers, a drop-out with 20% probability was used for regularization. The ReLU activation function was used after the self-attention layer, and a softmax classifier was used in the output layer. Drop-out was used as an additional measure to monitor the inputs in the LSTM network and combat overfitting. Among various optimization functions, RMSprop showed the best outcome for our model. We tested various values for the number of epochs, varying from 5 to 20, and the best result was obtained for 20 epochs.

4.3 Evaluation Metrics

To evaluate the performance of our model, we used precision (P), recall (R), and F1-score (F1) calculated according to the following formulas:

$$\mathrm{P} = \frac{\text{count of correctly classified NEs: true positive}}{\text{count of NEs in the output: true positive + false positive}}, \tag{14}$$

[1] https://www.kaggle.com/datasets/safiakanwal/mkpucit-ner-dataet.

$$R = \frac{\text{count of correctly classified NEs: true positive}}{\text{count of NEs in the test data: true positive + false negative}}, \quad (15)$$

$$F1 = \frac{2PR}{P+R} \quad (16)$$

5 Results

In the experimental stage we suggested a variety of approaches to look for the best performing option. For comparison, we chose methods in previous research that is similar to ours, i.e., using the same dataset and evaluation metrics. We compared our proposed method with unsupervised methods, namely, maximum entropy Markov model (MEMM), CRF, and with deep learning-based methods such as neural network (NN), recurrent neural network (RNN), and Bi-LSTM CRF, the results are in Table 10 and in Fig. 2. Bi-LSTM CRF without using any embeddings outperforms the unsupervised methods, NN, and RNN methods [21].

Our proposed Attention Bi-LSTM model was tested against the NN and RNN models for Urdu named entity recognition. The task was to predict such named entities as Person, Location, Organization, and Other. Our model outperformed the other models by a significant margin.

In the first experiment, we combined Bi-LSTM with CRF, which is an unsupervised method, and ran it on our dataset. The result is shown in Table 2. In the second experiment, we added Word2Vec embeddings, which significantly improved the model's performance, as shown in Table 3. In the third and fourth experiments we used fastText and GloVe embeddings, respectively, to further improve the model's performance, the results are in Tables 4 and 5. In the fifth experiment, we placed the self-attention layer below the encoder and ran several tests to fine-tune the system's parameters and assess its prediction validity, the result is presented in Table 6.

Table 2. The performance of Bi-LSTM CRF

Named Entity	Precision	Recall	F1-score
Location	0.860	0.873	0.871
Person	0.870	0.893	0.886
Organization	0.780	0.676	0.718
Other	0.980	0.985	0.985
Average	0.873	0.857	0.865

Finally, above the word-level embedding layer, we added the embedding attention layer and the self-attention layer below the encoder unit. This showed a significant change in the model's efficiency. Table 6 presents the results of attention Bi-LSTM-CRF; Tables 7, 8, and 9 show the results of attention Bi-LSTM-CRF with three different types of embeddings: Word2Vec, fastText, and GloVe, respectively. To the best of our knowledge, no method in the literature has used Bi-LSTM CRF and Attention BiLSTM CRF with word embeddings.

In addition, based on these results, we make the following observations:

1. The embedding attention layer mechanism improves the system's performance significantly. There is no simultaneous computation of word embeddings in this process. It does, however, dynamically decide how much information is needed from the word-level embedding, allowing it to select the best representation from any embedding.
2. Finally, using an attention layer and word embedding in our model improves sequence labeling predictions, resulting in state-of-the-art results on the UNER task.

Table 3. The performance of Bi-LSTM CRF with Word2Vec embeddings

Named Entity	Precision	Recall	F1-score
Location	0.900	0.900	0.888
Person	0.892	0.929	0.909
Organization	0.826	0.777	0.796
Other	0.989	0.988	0.990
Average	0.902	0.899	0.896

Table 4. The performance of Bi-LSTM CRF with fastText embeddings

Named Entity	Precision	Recall	F1-score
Location	0.881	0.895	0.886
Person	0.902	0.914	0.908
Organization	0.833	0.735	0.775
Other	0.988	0.988	0.990
Average	0.901	0.883	0.890

Table 5. The performance of Bi-LSTM CRF with GloVe embeddings

Named Entity	Precision	Recall	F1-score
Location	0.885	0.883	0.883
Person	0.872	0.938	0.904
Organization	0.844	0.778	0.798
Other	0.987	0.988	0.990
Average	0.897	0.892	0.894

Table 6. The performance of Attention Bi-LSTM CRF

Named Entity	Precision	Recall	F1-score
Location	0.890	0.890	0.880
Person	0.900	0.900	0.900
Organization	0.790	0.780	0.780
Other	0.980	0.970	0.980
Average	0.890	0.885	0.880

Table 7. The performance of Attention Bi-LSTM CRF with Word2Vec embeddings

Named Entity	Precision	Recall	F1-score
Location	0.930	0.920	0.920
Person	0.930	0.940	0.940
Organization	0.880	0.866	0.860
Other	0.990	0.990	0.990
Average	0.930	0.929	0.920

Table 8. The performance of Attention Bi-LSTM CRF with fastText embeddings

Named Entity	Precision	Recall	F1-score
Location	0.910	0.930	0.920
Person	0.900	0.950	0.920
Organization	0.850	0.870	0.860
Other	0.990	0.980	0.990
Average	0.913	0.933	0.923

Table 9. The performance of Attention Bi-LSTM CRF with GloVe embeddings

Named Entity	Precision	Recall	F1-score
Location	0.890	0.910	0.900
Person	0.910	0.930	0.920
Organization	0.810	0.800	0.810
Other	0.990	0.990	0.990
Average	0.900	0.908	0.905

Table 10. Comparison of our proposed technique and state of the art methods

Methods	Embedding	Precision	Recall	F1-score
MEMM	–	0.740	0.540	0.610
CRF	–	0.780	0.620	0.690
NN	Word2Vec	0.760	0.750	0.750
	fastText	0.750	0.720	0.730
	GloVe	0.760	0.710	0.730
RNN	Word2Vec	0.760	0.790	0.770
	fastText	0.750	0.780	0.760
	GloVe	0.740	0.770	0.750
Bi-LSTM CRF	–	0.873	0.857	0.865
Bi-LSTM CRF	Word2Vec	0.902	0.899	0.896
	fastText	0.901	0.883	0.890
	GloVe	0.897	0.892	0.894
Attention Bi-LSTM CRF (Our proposal)	–	0.890	0.885	0.880
Attention Bi-LSTM CRF (Our proposal)	Word2Vec	0.930	0.929	0.920
	fastText	0.913	0.933	0.923
	GloVe	0.900	0.908	0.905

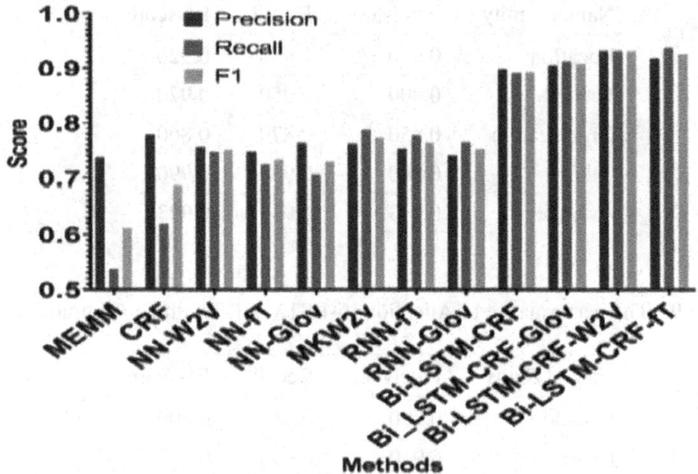

Fig. 2. Comparison of the proposed technique with state of the art methods, this diagram is visualization of the results in Table 10

6 Conclusions

In this work we proposed a Bi-LSTM neural network model with a discriminative model called Conditional Random Field (CRF) to recognize Urdu named entities (NE) as a labeling prediction task. The Attention Bi-LSTM-CRF paradigm combines an attention layer with a Bi-LSTM model and CRF. The self-attention layer is used above the encoder layer to improve the model efficiency by concentrating on more concepts which helps with the labeling prediction task. This is the first-ever attempt to thoroughly evaluate the performance of deep learning techniques using three types of word embeddings, namely, Word2Vec, GloVe, and fastText in the context of Urdu named entity recognition (UNER). Our proposed model achieved a high result showing an F1-score of 92% on the MK-PUCIT corpus, thus surpassing the existing approaches including feature-based methods and neural network-based methods such as MEMM, CRF, NN, RNN, NN with embeddings, RNN with embeddings, Bi-LSTM, and Bi-LSTM with embeddings for UNER by a notable margin.

Acknowledgements. The authors appreciate the support of Mexican Government which made it possible to complete this work: SNI-CONACYT, BEIFI-IPN, SIP-IPN: grant 20221627.

References

1. Ekbal, A., Saha, S.: Weighted vote-based classifier ensemble for named entity recognition: a genetic algorithm-based approach. ACM Trans. Asian Lang. Inf. Process. (TALIP) **10**(2), 1–37 (2011)
2. Patil, N., Patil, A. S., Pawar, B. V.: Survey of named entity recognition systems with respect to Indian and foreign languages. Int. J. Comput. Appl., 134(16) (2016)
3. Patawar, M.L., Potey, M.A.: Approaches to named entity recognition: a survey. Int. J. Innovative Res. Comput. Commun. Eng. **3**(12), 12201–12208 (2015)
4. Gandomi, A., Haider, M.: Beyond the hype: Big data concepts, methods, and analytics. Int. J. Inf. Manag. **35**(2), 137–144 (2015)
5. Wibawa, A.S., Purwarianti, A.: Indonesian named-entity recognition for 15 classes using ensemble supervised learning. Procedia Comput. Sci. **81**, 221–228 (2016)
6. Daud, A., Khan, W., Che, D.: Urdu language processing: a survey. Artif. Intell. Rev. **47**(3), 279–311 (2017)
7. Naz, S., Umar, A.I., Shirazi, S.H., Khan, S.A., Ahmed, I., Khan, A.A.: Challenges of Urdu named entity recognition: a scarce resourced language. Res. J. Appl. Sci., Eng. Technol. **8**(10), 1272–1278 (2014)
8. Khan, W., Daud, A., Alotaibi, F., Aljohani, N., Arafat, S.: Deep recurrent neural networks with word embeddings for Urdu named entity recognition. ETRI J. **42**(1), 90–100 (2020)
9. Borthwick, A., Sterling, J., Agichtein, E., Grishman, R.: Exploiting diverse knowledge sources via maximum entropy in named entity recognition. In: Sixth Workshop on Very Large Corpora (1998)
10. Nadeau, D., Turney, P. D., Matwin, S.: Unsupervised named-entity recognition: Generating gazetteers and resolving ambiguity. In: Conference of the Canadian society for computational studies of intelligence, pp. 266–277. Springer, Berlin, Heidelberg (2006). https://doi.org/10.1007/11766247_23

11. Ekbal, A., Haque, R., Bandyopadhyay, S.: Named entity recognition in Bengali: a conditional random field approach. In: Proceedings of the Third International Joint Conference on Natural Language Processing: Volume-II (2008)
12. Biswas, S., Mohanty, S., Mishra, S. P.: A hybrid Oriya named entity recognition system: Integrating HMM with MaxEnt. In: 2009 Second International Conference on Emerging Trends in Engineering & Technology, pp. 639–643. IEEE (2009)
13. Kumar Saha, S., Sarathi Ghosh, P., Sarkar, S., Mitra, P.: Named entity recognition in Hindi using maximum entropy and transliteration. Polibits **38**, 33–41 (2008)
14. Bikel, D. M., Miller, S., Schwartz, R., Weischedel, R.: Nymble: a high-performance learning name-finder. arXiv preprint cmp-lg/9803003 (1998)
15. Chaudhuri, B. B., Bhattacharya, S.: An experiment on automatic detection of named entities in Bangla. In: Proceedings of the IJCNLP-08 Workshop on Named Entity Recognition for South and South East Asian Languages (2008)
16. Srivastava, S., Sanglikar, M., Kothari, D.C.: Named entity recognition system for Hindi language: a hybrid approach. Int. J. Comput. Linguist. (IJCL) **2**(1), 10–23 (2011)
17. Graves, A., Schmidhuber, J.: Framewise phoneme classification with bidirectional LSTM and other neural network architectures. Neural Netw. **18**(5–6), 602–610 (2005)
18. Gupta, V., Lehal, G.S.: Named entity recognition for Punjabi language text summarization. Int. J. Comput. Appl. **33**(3), 28–32 (2011)
19. Ramage, D., Hall, D., Nallapati, R., Manning, C. D.: Labeled LDA: a supervised topic model for credit attribution in multi-labeled corpora. In: Proceedings of the 2009 Conference on Empirical Methods in Natural Language Processing, pp. 248–256 (2009)
20. Lafferty, J., McCallum, A., Pereira, F. C.: Conditional random fields: probabilistic models for segmenting and labeling sequence data (2001)
21. Kanwal, S., Malik, K., Shahzad, K., Aslam, F., Nawaz, Z.: Urdu named entity recognition: corpus generation and deep learning applications. ACM Trans. Asian Low-Resour. Lang. Inf. Process. (TALLIP) **19**(1), 1–13 (2019)
22. Cucerzan, S., Yarowsky, D.: Language independent named entity recognition combining morphological and contextual evidence. In: 1999 Joint Sigdat Conference on Empirical Methods in Natural Language Processing and Very Large Corpora (1999)
23. Naseer, A., Hussain, S. Assas-Band, an affix-exception-list based Urdu stemmer. In: Proceedings of the 7th Workshop on Asian Language Resources (ALR7), pp. 40–47 (2009)
24. Becker, D.: A study in Urdu corpus construction. In: Proceedings of the 3rd Workshop on Asian Language Resources and International Standardization at the 19th International Conference on Computational Linguistics (2002)
25. Riaz, K.: Rule-based named entity recognition in Urdu. In: Proceedings of the 2010 Named Entities Workshop, pp. 126–135 (2010)
26. Singh, U., Goyal, V., Lehal, G.S.: Named entity recognition system for Urdu. In: Proceedings of COLING 2012, pp. 2507–2518 (2012)
27. Li, W., McCallum, A.: Rapid development of Hindi named entity recognition using conditional random fields and feature induction. ACM Trans. Asian Lang. Inf. Process. (TALIP) **2**(3), 290–294 (2003)
28. Saha, S. K., Sarkar, S., Mitra, P.: A hybrid feature set based maximum entropy Hindi named entity recognition. In: Proceedings of the Third International Joint Conference on Natural Language Processing: Volume-I (2008)
29. Goyal, A.: Named entity recognition for south Asian languages. In: Proceedings of the IJCNLP-08 Workshop on Named Entity Recognition for South and South East Asian Languages (2008)
30. Gali, K., Surana, H., Vaidya, A., Shishtla, P. M., Sharma, D. M.: Aggregating machine learning and rule based heuristics for named entity recognition. In: Proceedings of the IJCNLP-08 Workshop on Named Entity Recognition for South and South East Asian Languages (2008)

Impact Evaluation of Multimodal Information on Sentiment Analysis

Luis N. Zúñiga-Morales[1(✉)], Jorge Ángel González-Ordiano[1], J.Emilio Quiroz-Ibarra[2], and Steven J. Simske[3]

[1] Departamento de Estudios en Ingeniería para la Innovación, Universidad Iberoamericana Ciudad de México, Mexico City, Mexico
luis.zuniga@correo.uia.mx, jorge.gonzalez@ibero.mx

[2] Instituto de Investigación Aplicada y Tecnología, Universidad Iberoamericana Ciudad de México, Mexico City, Mexico
jose.quiroz@ibero.mx

[3] Department of Systems Engineering, Colorado State University, Fort Collins, CO, USA
steve.simske@colostate.edu

Abstract. Text-based sentiment analysis is a popular application of artificial intelligence that has benefited in the past decade from the growth of digital social networks and its almost unlimited amount of data. Currently, social network users can combine different types of information in a single post, such as images, videos, GIFs, and live streams. As a result, they can express more complex thoughts and opinions. The goal of our study is to analyze the impact that incorporating different types of multimodal information may have on social media sentiment analysis. In particular, we give special attention to the interaction between text messages and images with and without text captions. To study this interaction we first create a new dataset in Spanish that contains tweets with images. Afterwards, we manually label several sentiments for each tweet, as follows: the overall tweet sentiment, the sentiment of the text, the sentiment of the individual images, the sentiment of the caption, if present, and—in cases where a single tweet has several images—the aggregate sentiment of all images present in the tweet. We conclude that incorporating visual information into text-based sentiment analysis raises the performance of the classifiers that determine the overall sentiment of a tweet by an average of 25.5%.

Keywords: Sentiment analysis · Multimodal information · Social networks

1 Introduction

Digital social networks have become one of the most useful platforms for people to express their opinions and sentiments around different topics. The idea to massively analyze them proved to be of great interest to both academia and industry since they represent a nearly unlimited amount of information that can help

O. Pichardo Lagunas et al. (Eds.): MICAI 2022, LNAI 13613, pp. 18–29, 2022.
https://doi.org/10.1007/978-3-031-19496-2_2

provide tools that learn from data and, as a result, improve the process of decision making. Early efforts on sentiment analysis focused on textual information sources like emails, web pages, blogs, and micro-blogging social networks [14]. Nowadays, social networks users can combine different types of information like text, images, videos, GIFs, polls, or live streams to enhance the opinion-sharing experience. As a result, users are able to express more complex ideas in a single post.

Most of the existing research on sentiment analysis focuses on working on a single modality (image, text, or video). Despite their popularity, unimodal systems have certain limitations regarding their accuracy, reliability, and robustness [4]. Hence the need to explore systems that incorporate multiple modalities of information to enhance traditional sentiment analysis.

The main goal of multimodal sentiment analysis is to propose techniques that can learn multi-view relationships from complex multimodal data [20]. Multi-view relationships focus on modeling view-specific dynamics and cross-view dynamics between information. View-specific dynamics refer to the interactions within a particular modality, like the interaction between words in the text of a tweet. On the other hand, cross-view dynamics focus on capturing the interactions between different modalities, e.g., how an image affects the meaning of the text of a tweet. Multimodal systems are more efficient in recognizing the sentiment of a user than unimodal systems [1]. Furthermore, multimodal information can provide more clues, thus resulting in better classifiers than those obtained using only text-based sentiment analysis [11].

Recent studies focus on the fusion of audio and visual modalities [5,6,25]; text and audio modalities [12]; text, audio, and video modalities [16–18,29]; and information fusion methods [1]. Currently, multimodal sentiment analysis is centered on video blogs [17,18], a popular video format that consists on recording the speaker's upper body as they recite their speech, usually giving an analysis or critique about popular topics.

This trend is reflected by the available datasets to study multimodal sentiment analysis. Wollmer et al. [29] collected 370 movie reviews on YouTube and ExpoTV. Perez-Rosas et al. [19] built the Multimodal Opinion Utterances Datasets (MOUD), made up of 80 product analysis videos and recommendations on YouTube in Spanish. The Multimodal Opinion-level Sentiment Intensity (MOSI) [30] contains 2199 utterances collecting opinions from 93 videos with 89 speakers in English. The Interactive Emotional Dyadic Motion Capture Database (IEMOCAP) [3] contains 12 h of audiovisual information including video, voice, facial motion capture and English text transcriptions.

As shown by the previous examples, the majority of datasets are built with information in English. For this reason, it is clear that there is a need to build datasets in other languages, such as Spanish; the third most used language on the internet[1]. Also, more general social media publications and its multimodal components are not studied in detail. Recently, Kumar and Garg [10] proposed a method that combines text and images, including images with captions, to

[1] https://www.internetworldstats.com/stats7.htm.

predict the sentiment of Twitter publications with great success. However, when analyzing the interaction between the images and text of different social media publications, we noticed the need for a finer annotation scheme to describe the impact that different types of information (isolated and in combination with others) have on sentiment analysis.

Our work aims to: 1) present a new dataset in Spanish for multimodal sentiment analysis, 2) propose a new annotation scheme to label multimodal datasets that better reflect the impact of each modality, and 3) study the impact of incorporating multimodal data to text-based sentiment analysis.

The paper is organized as follows: Sect. 2 describes the dataset used in the study; Sect. 3 explains the proposed analysis framework; Sect. 4 covers the experimental results and its discussion; and Sect. 5 concludes the paper.

2 Dataset

For this study, we built a new dataset[2] with the help of the Twitter API v2[3]. In particular, we requested tweets with media elements like images or videos about two different sport events that involved Mexican boxer Saúl "Canelo" Álvarez. The requested fields and their descriptions are shown in Table 1.

Table 1. Requested information to the Twitter API v2 for the construction of the dataset. Note that at the time of writing this paper, the API was unable to return full video elements. Instead, it returned only the corresponding preview thumbnails.

Field	Description
text	Text of the tweet.
has:media	Return tweets with media elements. Between 1 to 4 different images or 1 video/GIF thumbnail.
lang	Tweet language. Set to Spanish.
place_country	Specify the country where tweets are gathered. Limited to Mexico.
tweet.fields	Author id, creation date, and public metrics.
media.fields	Media URL.
date	2021/11/08 - 2021/09/24, 2022/05/12 - 2022/05/02

The dataset consists of 674 tweets that were manually labeled into four different categories: +1 for a positive sentiment, -1 for a negative sentiment, 0 for a neutral sentiment, and 2 for spam. The fourth category helps us identify tweets that do not contribute to the current task due their unconnected nature to the main topic of the study. Despite this, spam tweets should be considered in future works as they represent a natural component of digital social networks [24].

[2] The dataset can be downloaded here: https://github.com/lzun/mssaid.

[3] https://developer.twitter.com/en/docs/twitter-api.

Table 2. Proposed sentiment label annotation scheme for each tweet.

Sentiment Label	Description
Text Sentiment	Sentiment in the text element of a tweet.
Text in Image Sentiment	Sentiment expressed by the text that is considered relevant in an image.
Image Sentiment	Sentiment expressed by each individual image/video thumbnail.
Overall Image Sentiment	Sentiment expressed in conjunction by all the media elements of a tweet.
Overall Tweet Sentiment	Final sentiment of a tweet considering text and media

To label the dataset, we propose a labelling scheme for each tweet that facilitates the analysis of incorporating different types of information to the classifier. Moreover, since we consider the impact of the cross-view dynamic of text present in visual elements, we incorporate the extracted text as an additional element to label. Table 2 shows a summary of the labeling scheme.

A particular element present in some tweets is a specific type of visual content created by users: images with captions (e.g., memes). These images help express intertextual references where the text usually indicates a joke or critique associated with a popular event [28]. An example of such images can be seen in Fig. 1a[4]. Given the above definition, it can be hard to discern which images belong to this category since there are some instances where a caption within an image does not transmit any opinion or thought (e.g., Fig. 1b). Images with relevant captions were selected from the dataset to work with separately.

The idea that different information modalities carry different sentiments is supported by the sentiment distributions shown in Fig. 2. Furthermore, Fig. 3 shows a Sankey diagram that helps visualize how the sentiment of the tweets change when we not only consider text, but also other modalities of information (i.e. overall sentiment). This supports the claim that the inclusion of other information modalities (e.g., images) results—in some cases—in a different sentiment than the one we would perceive when considering only text.

3 Method

To perform the analysis, we propose a model that takes into account text and image modalities of a tweet to determine its overall sentiment. For each tweet, we first determine the modality types, that is, whether an element is text, image, or image with caption. Further processing is done depending on the modality type.

[4] Note that in this paper we used as examples images of our own authoring instead of the ones contained within the dataset to avoid any violations of the original authors' copyright.

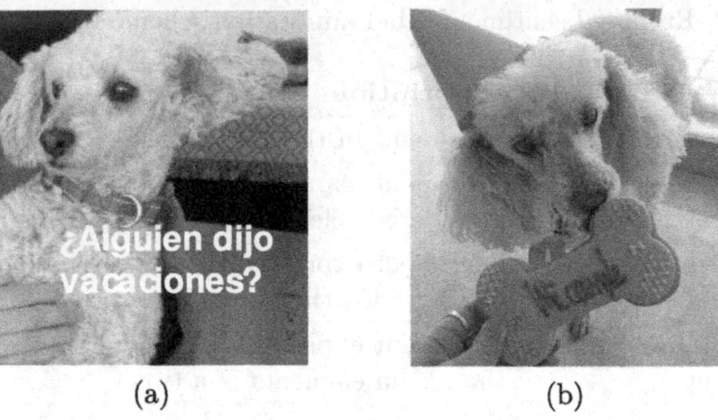

Fig. 1. (a) Example of an image with a caption that expresses a joke or opinion. Text translation: "Did someone say vacations?". (b) Example of a regular image with text that does not contribute with a useful opinion or thought (i.e. text in the cookie).

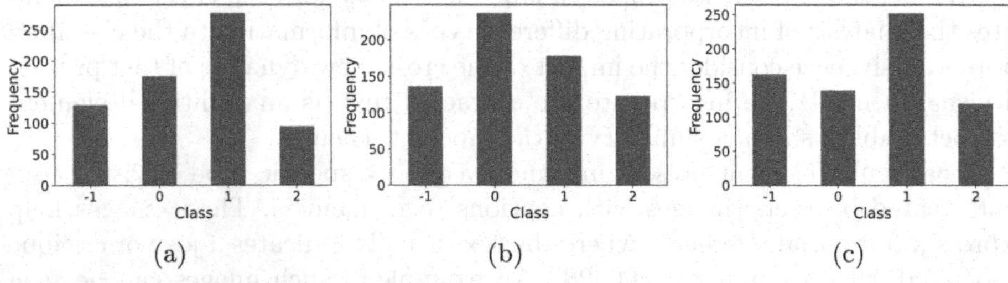

Fig. 2. Dataset distribution for the main sentiment labels: a) tweet text sentiment, b) tweet overall image sentiment, c) overall tweet sentiment.

Figure 4 shows the proposed work pipeline. The individual steps of the pipeline are described in the following subsections.

3.1 Text Processing and Feature Extraction

To process text elements of a tweet, we follow what is considered a common processing framework when working with social network data [13]. During the prepossessing step, we remove Twitter specific tags like user names, hashtags, and cashtags. Then, we get rid of stand alone numbers and URLs. Finally, we remove punctuation marks and reduce the number of consecutive repeating letters to two in cases where a word contains more than two consecutive repeating letters.

After this step, the resulting text undergoes a processing step whose goal is to normalize and reduce the vocabulary size of the document collection. First, the text is tokenized and transformed to lower case to perform stop word removal. To reduce spelling mistakes, a spelling checker program is used. Finally, stemming is performed on the text.

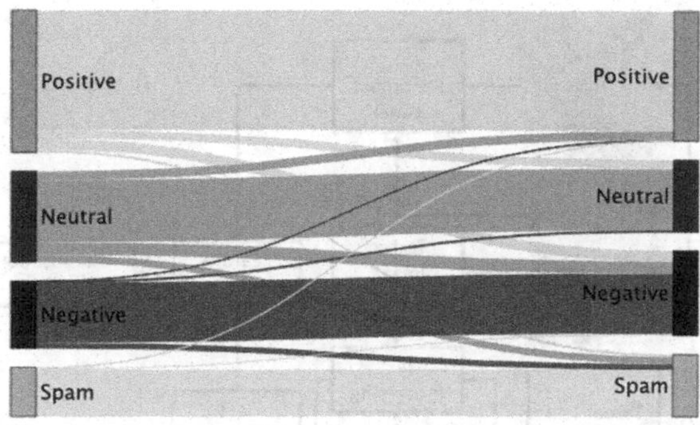

Fig. 3. Sentiment polarity transitions in the dataset. Left: tweet sentiment considering only text. Right: tweet sentiment considering all information modalities (i.e. overall sentiment)

Text features are extracted with different word embedding models. We consider Bag-of-Words (BoW) and Term Frequency - Inverse Document Frequency (TF-IDF) [21] models with different n-grams combinations [2], i.e. unigrams and bigrams (1–2 n-grams) or unigrams, bigrams, and trigrams (1–3 n-ngrams). The reason for selecting these models is that we believe they are a good starting point for our research, due to their simplicity and ease-of-use (specially compared to more complex deep learning methods).

The text preprocessing and processing step is implemented with NLTK 3.7 on Python 3.8.9, while for BoW and TF-IDF, we use Scikit-learn 1.1.1 [15].

3.2 Emoji Processing

Emojis are a widely adopted form of media content used by users in various digital social media sites [8]. They represent a second case of a cross-view dynamic: the interaction of a visual element within text. To incorporate them to our analysis, we consider a keyword approach which consists of translating each emoji to its Spanish equivalent within the text with the help of Python library Emoji[5]. This way, we extract features using n-grams with the emoticons, as explained in the Text Processing and Feature Extraction section.

3.3 Text in Image Detection

For the text-in-image detection module, we use a variation of You Only Look Once (YOLO) v3 [23], a fast and accurate object detection architecture originally proposed by Redmon et al. [22]. Since the task of identifying text in an image is similar to that of object detection performed by YOLO, we can apply transfer learning.

[5] https://github.com/carpedm20/emoji/.

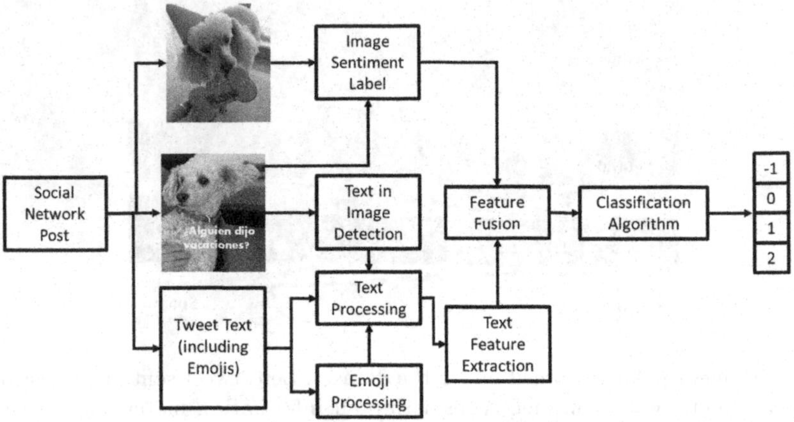

Fig. 4. Proposed multimodal sentiment analysis pipeline.

First, text-in-image regions were manually labeled to determine the bounding box coordinates for each image in the training set. Then, each image goes into a processing pipeline that resizes the image to a new size of 416×416 pixels (even the images with different width and height) and applies grayscale transformation. The bounding box coordinates are fed to the YOLO architecture to fine-tune its parameters. Note that, due to the limited amount of images with captions available at the moment of writing this paper, we trained the YOLO network using all images with captions in our dataset. Once trained, this network is able to identify if an image has text according to our definition, or if the image has no text at all. Figure 5 shows an example of how the ideal output of the text detection module should look like. When text is detected, the region box coordinates are used to make a sub-image that is fed into an Optical Character Recognition (OCR) engine to extract the identified text. An image processing pipeline is applied to this sub-images: we transform them to grayscale, normalize pixel values between 0 and 1, and apply histogram equalization. In this work we use the keras-ocr engine[6]. Finally, the extracted text undergoes the same processing steps described in the text processing subsection.

To perform the transfer learning pipeline, YOLO v3 was trained with Keras 2.8.0 and Tensorflow 2.8.0. Image processing is done with scikit-image 0.19.2 [27].

3.4 Image Sentiment Label

To fully analyze the proposed sentiment analysis model, we must consider the best possible performance of the image sentiment labeling module. In order to achieve this, we use the manually labeled sentiment fields of the images as the "output" values of the module. We opted to do this to avoid missclassified instances since mistakes here would affect the final results. The values we utilize

6 https://github.com/faustomorales/keras-ocr.

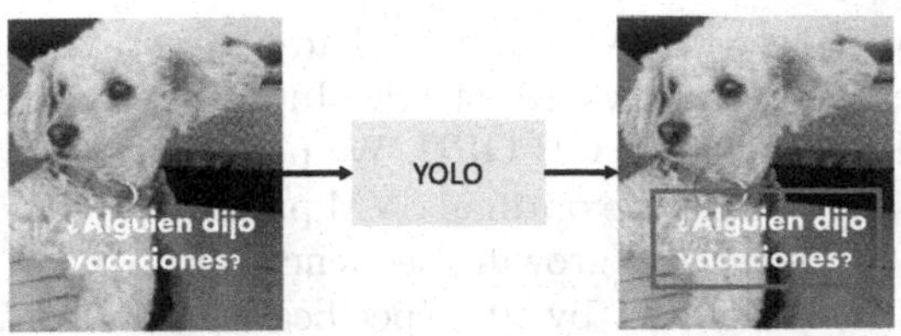

Fig. 5. Example of how the ideal output of the text detection module should look like. After the detection, the highlighted region is extracted and fed into the OCR module.

are the overall image sentiment polarity. In the future, this step would consist of an image sentiment classifier.

3.5 Feature Fusion

To fuse the information of each modality, we select an early fusion based model. This model consists in concatenating the features of each modality into a single vector [1]. In our case, we concatenate text features, and the overall image sentiment label (without checking if the sentiment of the text and the image match beforehand). The text obtained from the emojis, as well as the text obtained from the images is added to the text of the tweet, so that all that information is processed together during the text processing step.

3.6 Classification Algorithm

To determine the overall sentiment label of a tweet, we use a Support Vector Machine (SVM) [26] with a radial basis function (RBF) kernel. As shown in Fig. 2, we are working with an imbalanced dataset. To counter this problem we use Cost-Sensitive Training. This technique uses a penalized learning algorithm that increases the cost of classification mistakes of each class according to a specified weight vector [7]. To evaluate the performance of the model, we use the balanced accuracy metric (as defined in the scikit-learn package[7]), which avoids inflated performance estimates on imbalanced datasets. If y_i is the true value of the i-th class, $\hat{y}_i$ is the predicted value, and w_i is the corresponding penalization weight, the balanced accuracy metric for the multiclass problem is defined as follows :

$$\text{balanced accuracy}(y, \hat{y}, w) = \frac{1}{\sum \hat{w}_i} \sum_i 1(\hat{y}_i = y_i)\hat{w}_i \tag{1}$$

where

$$\hat{w}_i = \frac{w_i}{\sum_j 1(y_j = y_i) w_j}. \tag{2}$$

[7] https://scikit-learn.org/stable/modules/model_evaluation.html#balanced-accuracy-score.

To train the (penalized) SVM model we had access to a computer with the following specifications: Windows 10 64 bits, Intel Xeon W-2295 3.00 GHz, 64 GB RAM, and a RTX A4000 16 GB GPU. We perform cross-validation with 10 folds and a grid-search to find the optimal SVM parameters (C, γ). The approach we take considers exponentially growing sequences of C and γ to identify good initial parameters, as suggested by [9]. Specifically, $C = 2^k, k \in [-5, 16]$ and $\gamma = 2^k, k \in [-15, 4]$. Once we obtain an optimal value of C, γ in the initial grid-search, we progressively refine the search by looking at the neighborhood of the parameters simply by adding or subtracting small increments of 0.25 to their value of k, iteratively, until a tolerance threshold in the balanced accuracy result of 1×10^{-4} is met.

4 Experimental Results

Table 3 shows the classification results obtained from using the different language models, as well as the combination of different information modalities (i.e. text, text + image, text + emojis, text + emojis + image, text + image + image text, and text + image + image text + emojis). The best classifier, with a 74.7% balanced accuracy score, considers text and overall image sentiment features with a BoW model with unigrams, bigramas, and trigrams. However, considering the standard deviation values for the classifiers, we can argue that, for each feature combination block, the performance of the BoW and TF-IDF models are similar. Thus, they represent good starting models to perform sentiment analysis.

Regarding the classifier parameters (C, γ), we can argue that the SVM is not sensitive to γ due the overall small values seen in the results. For C, which has the exponential form 2^k, we can observe a region between $k \in [1.5, 6.5]$ that outputs the best results.

We can also notice the sensitivity of the classification scheme when we incorporate emojis. Despite their constant use, they do not represent a general performance improvement for any of the classifiers. The same applies to the addition of text from images. Therefore, future works should investigate other ways of incorporating this information, as the one described herein.

Finally, the addition of visual sentiment (images) as an additional classification feature to determine the overall sentiment of a tweet outperforms text-based only classifiers by an average 25.5%. This supports the idea that exploring the semantic relationships between visual and text elements might provide important information to help the sentiment analysis task applied to digital social networks.

Table 3. Classification results. The values shown for C and γ are the value of k from the exponential function 2^k. For the classification features, T indicates text, I indicates image, E indicates emoji, and IT indicates image text. The best result is highlighted in bold.

Balanced Accuracy	Standard Deviation	C	γ	Language Model	Classification Features
0.4631	0.0679	12.75	-15.75	BoW, 1–2 ngrams	T
0.4532	0.0663	15.5	-13.75	BoW, 1–3 ngrams	T
0.4935	0.0598	13.75	-15.75	TF-IDF, 1–2 ngrams	T
0.4942	0.0678	9.5	-11.25	TF-IDF, 1–3 ngrams	T
0.7437	0.0604	5.75	-10.5	BoW, 1–2 ngrams	T+I
0.7474	**0.0621**	**6**	**-11**	**BoW, 1–3 ngrams**	**T+I**
0.7359	0.0566	6.25	-7.5	TF-IDF, 1–2 ngrams	T+I
0.7312	0.0560	1.75	-2	TF-IDF, 1–3 ngrams	T+I
0.4630	0.0679	12.75	-15.75	BoW, 1–2 ngrams	T+E
0.4532	0.0663	15.5	-13.75	BoW, 1–3 ngrams	T+E
0.4935	0.0598	13.75	-15.75	TF-IDF, 1–2 ngrams	T+E
0.4942	0.0678	9.5	-11.25	TF-IDF, 1–3 ngrams	T+E
0.7260	0.0613	6.25	-11	BoW, 1–2 ngrams	T+E+I
0.7279	0.0637	6.5	-11.5	BoW, 1–3 ngrams	T+E+I
0.7359	0.0566	6.25	-7.5	TF-IDF, 1–2 ngrams	T+E+I
0.7349	0.0498	1.5	0	TF-IDF, 1–3 ngrams	T+E+I
0.7270	0.0543	2.5	-7	BoW, 1–2 ngrams	T+I+IT
0.7258	0.0565	6.5	-11.5	BoW, 1–3 ngrams	T+I+IT
0.7367	0.0508	2	-2.5	TF-IDF, 1–2 ngrams	T+I+IT
0.7342	0.0491	1.5	0	TF-IDF, 1–3 ngrams	T+I+IT
0.7270	0.0543	2.5	-7	BoW, 1–2 ngrams	T+I+IT+E
0.7258	0.0565	6.5	-11.5	BoW, 1–3 ngrams	T+I+IT+E
0.7367	0.0508	2	-2.5	TF-IDF, 1–2 ngrams	T+I+IT+E
0.7342	0.0491	1.5	0	TF-IDF, 1–3 ngrams	T+I+IT+E

5 Conclusions and Future Work

In this paper, we explored the effect of including other information modalities to traditional text-based sentiment analysis to determine the overall sentiment polarity of a tweet. We also trained a text-detection module to identify what we defined is relevant text in an image. Additionally, we showed a framework to work with multimodal information, as well as how to proceed with imbalanced dataset classification and parameter optimization. We conclude that incorporating multimodal information to text features enhances traditional text-based sentiment analysis, in particular image sentiment. Furthermore, the labelling scheme helped us see how the information provided by images affected the overall sentiment polarity of some tweets.

Despite not having a bigger impact in the presented results, the incorporation of cross-view dynamics (text-in-image and emojis) should not be completely abandoned. In the presented results, the pipeline showed in Fig. 4 can be expanded to work with each feature separately given we gather enough information to train each feature this way and test more appropriate feature fusion approaches.

Our future work will focus on the different ways to expand the framework, especially: a) the construction of a dedicated module to work with different types of images present in the dataset, b) explore deep learning classification techniques for both image and text classification, c) to focus on how text in images interact with the visual elements around them, and d) expand the proposed dataset with future and past events to enhance the tweet analysis.

Acknowledgements. This work was supported by the Universidad Iberoamericana Ciudad de México and the Institute of Applied Research and Technology.

References

1. Abdu, S.A., Yousef, A.H., Salem, A.: Multimodal video sentiment analysis using deep learning approaches, a survey. Inf. Fusion **76**, 204–226 (2021)
2. Broder, A.Z., Glassman, S.C., Manasse, M.S., Zweig, G.: Syntactic clustering of the web. Computer Networks and ISDN Systems 29(8), 1157–1166 (1997). https://www.sciencedirect.com/science/article/pii/S0169755297000317, papers from the Sixth International World Wide Web Conference
3. Busso, C., et al.: IEMOCAP: interactive emotional dyadic motion capture database. Lang. Resour. Eval. **42**, 335–359 (2008)
4. Chandrasekaran, G., Nguyen, T.N., D., J.H.: Multimodal sentiment analysis for social media applications: a comprehensive review. WIREs Data Min. Knowl. Discov. 11(5) (2021)
5. Chen, L., Huang, T., Miyasato, T., Nakatsu, R.: Multimodal human emotion/expression recognition. In: Proceedings Third IEEE International Conference on Automatic Face and Gesture Recognition, pp. 366–371 (1998)
6. Datcu, D., Rothkrantz, L.J.M.: Semantic audio-visual data fusion for automatic emotion recognition. Euromedia (2008)
7. Ganganwar, V.: An overview of classification algorithms for imbalanced datasets. Int. J. Emerg. Technol. Adv. Eng. **2**(4), 42–47 (2012)
8. Guibon, G., Ochs, M., Bellot, P.: From emojis to sentiment analysis. In: WACAI 2016. Lab-STICC and ENIB and LITIS, Brest, France (2016). https://hal-amu.archives-ouvertes.fr/hal-01529708
9. Hsu, C.W., Chang, C.C., Lin, C.J.: A practical guide to support vector classication. National Taiwan University, Tech. rep. (2016)
10. Kumar, A., Garg, G.: Sentiment analysis of multimodal twitter data. Multimedia Tool. Appl. **78**(17), 24103–24119 (2019). https://doi.org/10.1007/s11042-019-7390-1
11. Liu, B., et al.: Context-aware social media user sentiment analysis. Tsinghua Sci. Technol. **25**(4), 528–541 (2020)

12. Metallinou, A., Lee, S., Narayanan, S.: Audio-visual emotion recognition using gaussian mixture models for face and voice, pp. 250–257 (2008)
13. Oliveira, N., Cortez, P., Areal, N.: Stock market sentiment lexicon acquisition using microblogging data and statistical measures. Decis. Support Syst. **85**, 62–73 (2016)
14. Pang, B., Lee, L., Vaithyanathan, S.: Thumbs up? Sentiment classification using machine learning techniques. In: Proceedings of the 2002 Conference on Empirical Methods in Natural Language Processing (EMNLP 2002), pp. 79–86. Association for Computational Linguistics (2002). https://aclanthology.org/W02-1011
15. Pedregosa, F., et al.: Scikit-learn: machine learning in Python. J. Mach. Learn. Res. **12**, 2825–2830 (2011)
16. Poria, S., Cambria, E., Gelbukh, A.: Deep convolutional neural network textual features and multiple kernel learning for utterance-level multimodal sentiment analysis. Association for Computational Linguistics, pp. 2539–2544 (2015). https://www.aclweb.org/anthology/D15-1303
17. Poria, S., Cambria, E., Hazarika, D., Mazumder, N., Zadeh, A., Morency, L.P.: Context-dependent sentiment analysis in user-generated videos. In: Proceedings of the 55th Annual Meeting of the Association for Computational Linguistics, pp. 873–883 (2017)
18. Poria, S., Majumder, N., Hazarika, D., Cambria, E., Gelbukh, A., Hussain, A.: Multimodal sentiment analysis: Addressing key issues and setting up the baselines (2018)
19. Pérez-Rosas, V., Mihalcea, R., Morency, L.P.: Utterance-level multimodal sentiment analysis. In: Proceedings of the 51st Annual Meeting of the Association for Computational Linguistics, pp. 973–982 (2013)
20. Rajagopalan, S.S., Morency, L.-P., Baltrušaitis, T., Goecke, R.: Extending long short-term memory for multi-view structured learning. In: Leibe, B., Matas, J., Sebe, N., Welling, M. (eds.) ECCV 2016. LNCS, vol. 9911, pp. 338–353. Springer, Cham (2016). https://doi.org/10.1007/978-3-319-46478-7_21
21. Rajaraman, A., Ullman, J.D.: Data Mining, pp. 1–17. Cambridge University Press, Cambridge (2011)
22. Redmon, J., Divvala, S., Girshick, R., Farhadi, A.: You only look once: unified, real-time object detection (2015)
23. Redmon, J., Farhadi, A.: YOLOv3: an incremental improvement (2018)
24. Rodrigues, A.P., et al.: Real-time twitter spam detection and sentiment analysis using machine learning and deep learning techniques. Computat. Intell. Neurosci. (2022)
25. Silva, L.D., Miyasato, T., Nakatsu, R.: Facial emotion recognition using multimodal information, pp. 397–401. IEEE (1997)
26. Vapnik, V., Cortes, C.: Support-vector networks. Mach. Learn. **20**, 273–297 (1995)
27. Van der Walt, S., et al.: The Scikit-image contributors: Scikit-image: image processing in Python. PeerJ 2, e453 (2014). https://doi.org/10.7717/peerj.453
28. Wiggins, B.E.: The discursive power of memes in digital culture: ideology, semiotics, and intertextuality. Routledge, 1st edn. (2019)
29. Wöllmer, M., et al.: Youtube movie reviews: sentiment analysis in an audio-visual context. IEEE Intell. Syst. **28**, 46–53 (2013)
30. Zadeh, A., Zellers, R., Pincus, E., Morency, L.P.: Multimodal sentiment intensity analysis in videos: facial gestures and verbal messages. IEEE Intell. Syst. **31**, 82–88 (2016)

Improving Neural Machine Translation for Low Resource Languages Using Mixed Training: The Case of Ethiopian Languages

Atnafu Lambebo Tonja(✉), Olga Kolesnikova, Muhammad Arif, Alexander Gelbukh, and Grigori Sidorov

Instituto Politécnico Nacional (IPN), Centro de Investigación en Computación (CIC), Mexico City, Mexico
atnafu.lambebo@wsu.edu.et, kolesolga@gmail.com, {mariff2021,gelbukh,sidorov}@cic.ipn.mx

Abstract. Neural Machine Translation (NMT) has shown improvement for high-resource languages, but there is still a problem with low-resource languages as NMT performs well on huge parallel data available for high-resource languages. In spite of many proposals to solve the problem of low-resource languages, it continues to be a difficult challenge. The issue becomes even more complicated when few resources cover only one domain. In our attempt to combat this issue, we propose a new approach to improve NMT for low-resource languages. The proposed approach using the transformer model shows 5.3, 5.0, and 3.7 BLEU score improvement for Gamo-English, Gofa-English, and Dawuro-English language pairs, respectively, where Gamo, Gofa, and Dawuro are related low-resource Ethiopian languages. We discuss our contributions and envisage future steps in this challenging research area.

Keywords: Machine translation · Low-resource machine translation · Neural machine translation · Ethiopian languages · Mixed training

1 Introduction

Natural Language Processing (NLP) is a branch of artificial intelligence which employs computational techniques for the purpose of learning, understanding, and producing human language content [1]. Machine Translation (MT) is one of the widely used NLP applications that carries out the automatic translation from one language to another in order to facilitate communication between people who speak different languages [1]. There are different MT approaches that are being proposed by different researchers and industries to facilitate this task:- from these approaches, Neural Machine Translation (NMT), also known as corpus-based/data-driven machine translation is a current state-of-the-art technique that uses neural networks [2]. NMT is trained on a large corpus of language segments and their respective translations, usually containing hundreds of thousands or even millions of translation units [2].

O. Pichardo Lagunas et al. (Eds.): MICAI 2022, LNAI 13613, pp. 30–40, 2022.
https://doi.org/10.1007/978-3-031-19496-2_3

Researchers have shown that NMT can perform much better than other machine translation models [3]. The quality of NMT as a data-driven approach, massively depends on the quantity, quality, and relevance of the training dataset [2,4]. NMT currently achieved promising results for high-resource languages [4–7], however, it is still inadequate for low-resource conditions [4]. NMT for languages that have low and limited resources is currently one of the research directions in the area of NLP and MT to enable under resource languages to be presented in digital space and to help language speakers to access the current advancement in technologies.

1.1 High vs Low Resource Languages

Currently, in the NLP community there is no single way of defining a language as low resource, researchers have proposed various criteria to distinguish high and low resource languages. Joshi et al. [8] created a language resource availability classification based on the amount of existing labeled and unlabeled data. The scale goes from 0 (lowest resources) to 5 (highest resources). One of the details in determining the amount of data is how a data unit is defined. For example, MT data is measured by a number of parallel sentences. The authors also added that high resource languages are characterized by a dominant online presence, it implies massive industrial and government investments in the development of resources and technologies for such languages. On the other hand low resource languages have been suffering from a lack of new language technology designs. When the resources are limited and a little amount of unlabeled data is available, it is very hard to reach a true breakthrough in creating powerful novel methods for language applications.

This paper discusses a new method to improve the performance of NMT for low-resource languages by mixing their data in different scenarios using four languages spoken in Ethiopia as an example. The paper is organized as follows: Sect. 2 describes the previous research related to this study, Sect. 3 gives an overview of the dataset statistics and language description, Sect. 4 explains the methodology adopted in this study, Sect. 5 presents the experimental results and discussion. Finally, Sect. 6 concludes the paper and sheds some light on possible future work.

2 Related Work

Mechanization of translation is one of the human beings oldest dream, it became a reality in the 20th century, in the form of computer programs capable of translating a wide variety of texts from one natural language into another [9]. There are different approaches used by researchers for machine translation, some of these are rule-based MT [10,11], statistical MT [12,13], hybrid MT [14] and neural MT [15–17]. Among these approaches neural MT is most efficient current state-of-the-art [2,3] trained on huge datasets containing sentences in a source language and their equivalent target language translations. Basically, NMT takes advantage of huge translation memories with hundreds of thousands or even millions of translation units [16]. However, NMT for low-resource languages [18] still under-preforms due to scarcity of parallel datasets.

A lot of research has been done to solve machine translation problems in low-resource languages, most of them are focused on training a model on high-resource language data and applying transfer learning methodology to low-resource texts. The model trained on a high-resource language pair is called the parent model, then some of the learned parameters are transferred to low-resource pairs (the child model) to initialize and constrain training. During the experiments in [19], the authors used French as the parent source language, and Hausa, Turkish, Uzbek, and Urdu with English as the target language to build the child model. The authors used 300 million English tokens to train French-English parent model and 1.8 million tokens for each of the low-resource languages. As result of transfer learning, they improved the baseline Syntax Based Machine Translation (SBMT) model by an average of 5.6 BLEU on the four low-resource language pairs still leaving room for improvement by selecting parent languages that are more similar to child languages. Concerning the context of our work there are two very important details to note in [19]. First, the researchers used 1.8 million tokens for their selected low-resource languages, however, comparing to our case of Ethiopian languages, such a dataset can be called big. Second, the authors performed experiments in only one direction, i.e., from a low-resource language to English, but not vice versa.

Feng et al. [20] also presented a transfer learning method which improved the BLEU score of the low-resource machine translation. They used an encoder-decoder framework with attention mechanism to train one NMT model for a high resource (French-English) pair, then employed some parameters of the trained model to initialize another NMT model for the Vietnamese-English pair with less parallel corpora compared to the parent French-English model. For the French-English case a 2 million parallel dataset to train NMT as the parent model was used. For the low-resource Vietnamese and Mongolian languages, 133K and 67K sentence pairs were used, respectively. On the Vietnamese-English translation task, their model improved the translation quality by an average of 1.55 BLEU score. Besides, they also got an increase of 0.99 BLEU score translating from Mongolian to Chinese [20].

Slim et al. [21] worked on a transfer learning approach for low-resource NMT applied to the Algerian Arabic dialect. The authors used a fine-tuning transfer learning strategy to transfer knowledge from the parent model(multi-dialects Arabic) to the child model(Algerian dialect). They used a 52K dataset to train the parent model and 12.8K parallel dataset to train the child model using Seq2Seq and attentional-Seq2Seq techniques. The researchers compared the performance of these techniques before and after transfer learning showing that transfer learning improves the BLEU score for the Seq2Seq model from 0.3 to more than 34.56, and for the Attentional-Seq2Seq model from 16.5 to 35.87 for Algerian-English translation.

The above transfer learning approaches showed improvements in low-resource languages but they still use a high-resource language as parent language. In this paper we explore the way of improving NMT performance for low-resource languages without using high-resource language data.

3 Dataset

For our experiments we used four related Ethiopian languages spoken in the Southern part of Ethiopia, which are categorized under the same language group and family. Ethiopia is a linguistically and ethnically heterogeneous country with more 80 officially recognized languages [22]. Four languages chosen for our study, namely Wolaita, Gamo, Gofa and Dawuro; are grouped under the Omotic language group which is one of the six language families within the Afro-Asiatic phylum, predominantly spoken in the region between the lakes of the Southern rift valley and the Omo River [23]. The languages in the large Omotic group are classified together as an agenetic unit because their phonology, grammar and lexicon are quite close.

Parallel datasets used in this study are borrowed from the NMT research conducted by [24], they belong to the religious domain available in digital form. Table 1 shows parallel dataset distribution of the four languages in this study. It can be observed in Table 1, that English has less type count than Ethiopian languages. This demonstrates the morphological complexity of Ethiopian languages. The number of sentences in the Wolaita-English pair is bigger than in the others, due to the fact that, the Wolaita-English parallel dataset contains both the Old and New-Testaments of the Bible, whereas the rest contain only the New Testament of the Bible.

Table 1. Parallel dataset distribution

Languages	Sentences	Tokens	Types	Average words in a sentence
English	26,943	703,122	12,131	26
Wolaita		469,851	42,049	17
English	7,866	177,410	11,078	23
Gamo		125,509	23,589	16
English	7,928	175,727	8,769	22
Gofa		119,289	25,301	15
English	7,804	207,954	4,368	27
Dawuro		126,734	17,392	16

4 Methodology

This section describes the proposed model and data processing used for our proposed approach. For our NMT approach we employed the transformer model, the current state-of-the-art deep learning model occupied primarily in the fields of natural language processing after its first introduction in [25]. Like Recurrent Neural Networks (RNNs), transformers are designed to handle sequential input data, e.g., natural language texts, for tasks such as translation and text summarization. However, unlike RNNs, transformers do not necessarily process the data in order. Rather, the attention mechanism provides context for any token position in the input sequence [25].

4.1 Data Pre-processing

Before training the NMT model with the datasets described previously, we preprocessed them to facilitate training by converting text data into a format suitable for our model. This phase includes removing duplicate entries, characters that are not in Latin scripts, removing digits, and converting each sentence into lower case.

4.2 Model

Our NMT model based on the transformer architecture contains both Encoder and Decoder blocks with six layers, input embedding(subword embedding), output embedding (subword embedding), positional encoding, linear classifier, and the final Softmax layer for output probabilities. Figure 1 shows the proposed transformer-based model architecture for low-resource NMT. As shown in Fig. 1, our proposed model has a dataset block and a transformer block. The dataset block contains datasets of four languages. To mix the data, we developed the procedure which we will explain here for the Dawuro language as an example. We take the data of the three datasets except Dawuro. Then we split the Dawuro-English dataset into training, validation, and test subsets, combine the training

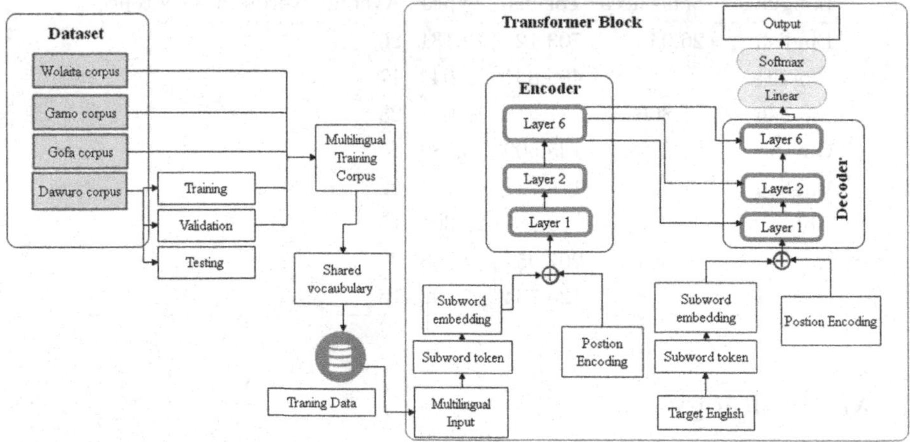

Fig. 1. Proposed transformer-based model for low-resource NMT

and validation subsets with the data of the three(Gamo, Gofa and Wolaita) languages for training and further on apply the Dawuro-English test subset to evaluate the model performance. Such procedure is used to train NMT for the other three languages. The source and target parallel sentences are converted into subword tokens using Byte Pair Encoding (BPE) representation [26] and further to subword embedding as input to the positional encoder block.

5 Experiments and Results

This section describes the experimental settings, dataset split strategies and performance of the models and comparison with the previous studies.

5.1 Experiments

We trained our translation models using an open source ecosystem for neural machine translation and neural sequence learning toolkit called OpenNMT [27] with tensorflow version and transformer [25]. To conduct the study we used OpenNMT-tf [27] in Google colab pro + [28] with Graphical processing Unit(GPU). We used transformer [25] and BPE [26] subword tokenization which is a simple form of data compression algorithm in which the most common pair of consecutive bytes of data is replaced with a byte that does not occur in that data. The BPE representation was chosen in order to remove vocabulary overlap during dataset combinations. Table 2 shows the parameters used to train our proposed model.

Table 2. Parameters used for training and evaluation of the proposed NMT model

Parameters	Values
Encoder layers	6
Decoder layers	6
Model-dim	512
Learning rate	0.0001
Drop out	0.3
Optimizer	Adam
Batch size	3072
Batch type	Tokens

5.2 Dataset Split

In order to carry out our experiments we divided the datasets into training, validation and test set. As shown in the Table 3 except for Experiment(1) we used Wolaita-English dataset without splitting in other experiments. For Experiment

(1) (2) and (4) we used the same splitting method for three (Gamo, Gofa, and Dawuro) language pairs. For Experiment (3) we used Wolaita- English dataset for training and three language pairs for validation and testing.

Table 3. Training, validation and test set split for the experiments. The numbers indicates the amount of parallel sentences used in each split

Experiments	Language Pair	Training set	Validation set	Test set
Exp-1	Wolaita-English	21,555	5,388	-
	Dawuro-English	4,996	1,248	1,560
	Gamo-English	5,035	1,258	1,573
Transfer Learning	Gofa-English	5,077	1,267	1,584
Exp-2	Wolaita-English	26,943	-	-
	Dawuro-English	4,996	1,248	1,560
	Gamo-English	5,035	1,258	1,573
	Gofa-English	5,077	1,267	1,584
Exp-3	Wolaita-English	26,943	-	-
	Dawuro-English	-	1,561	6,243
	Gamo-English	-	1,574	6,293
	Gofa-English	-	1,584	6,335
Exp-4	Wolaita-English	26,943	-	-
	Dawuro-English	4,996	1,248	1,560
	Gamo-English	5,035	1,258	1,573
	Gofa-English	5,077	1,584	1,267

5.3 Results

We conducted four experiments for low-resource NMT. In **Experiment (1)** we trained the model using a transfer learning approach, for this experiment we first trained the parent (Wolaita - English) model on the Wolaita-English parallel dataset and fine-tuned it on the resting three language pairs. In **Experiment (2)** we trained the NMT model by combining the Wolaita - English dataset with one of the resting language pairs. In **Experiment (3)** we trained the model by combining the Wolaita -English dataset with two language pairs, validated and tested the performance of the model with the unused language pair. In **Experiment (4)** we trained the model by combining the Wolaita - English dataset with three language pairs and tested the performance on each of the language pairs.

As shown in Table 4, using English as a target language, combining two or more low-resource languages(**Experiment 2 & 4**) gives better results than using low-resource languages as parent languages for the transfer learning approach (**Experiment 1**) and testing on unused language pairs (**Experiment 3**). This shows the possibility of improving NMT performance for low-resource languages by:-

Table 4. Low-resource NMT experimental results using English as the target language

Language	Exp1			Exp2			Exp3			Exp4		
	BLEU	TER	chrF2++	BLEU	TER	chrF2++	BLEU	TER	chrF2++	BLEU	TER	chrF2++
Gamo-English	1.4	106.2	20.4	6.5	88	22.8	4.8	94.4	22.2	9.4	83.6	26.9
Dawuro-English	3.9	92.5	21.5	6.2	87.2	23.1	2.2	101.7	20.9	7.3	83.5	26.5
Gofa-English	5.6	99.3	22.4	7.2	86.8	25.1	5.4	93.1	25.6	9.5	83.3	27.1

Table 5. Low-resource NMT experimental results using English as source languages

Language	Exp1			Exp2			Exp3			Exp4		
	BLEU	TER	chrF2++	BLEU	TER	chrF2++	BLEU	TER	chrF2++	BLEU	TER	chrF2++
English - Gamo	-	-	-	2.0	100.7	21	-	-	-	1.5	103.2	20.7
English - Dawuro	-	-	-	2.6	97.7	21.4	-	-	-	1.8	101.4	21.2
English - Gofa	-	-	-	2.9	97.5	22.3	-	-	-	2.1	100.5	21.2

- Combining two related languages, one with more resources and the other with fewer resources for training and using less resource language for validation and testing.
- Combining more than two related languages one with more resources and the others with fewer resources for training and using less-resource language for testing and validation.

As shown in Table 5 using English as a source language gives poor results compared to using English as the target language in Table 4, because the model favors the English data over the Ethiopian data due to the morphological richness and complexity of the Ethiopian languages. In addition to this, when English is used as the source language, the translation is challenged by many-to-one alignment.

Table 6. Comparison of the proposed approach with previous studies

Methods	Languages	BLEU score	
		English-*	*-English
Tonja et al. [24]	Gamo*	2.2	4.1
	Gofa*	2.4	4.5
	Dawuro*	2.1	3.6
Yigezu et al. [29]	Gamo*	-	3.4
	Gofa*	-	4.5
	Dawuro*	-	2.5
Our proposed approach(Exp2)	Gamo*	2.0	**6.5**
	Gofa*	**2.9**	**7.2**
	Dawuro*	**2.6**	**6.2**
Our proposed approach(Exp4)	Gamo*	1.5	**9.4**
	Gofa*	2.1	**9.5**
	Dawuro*	1.8	**7.3**

In Table 6 and Fig. 2, we compared our proposed approaches with previous studies [24,29] that used the same datasets and languages. It can be seen that the results of our **Experiments 2** and **4** show improvement over previous works on the same language pairs with English as a target language. This evidences that using a combination of more than two related low-resource languages for training improves the performance of NMT for low-resource languages without using high-resource languages in one direction. Besides, a combination of two related low-resource languages improves translation in both directions.

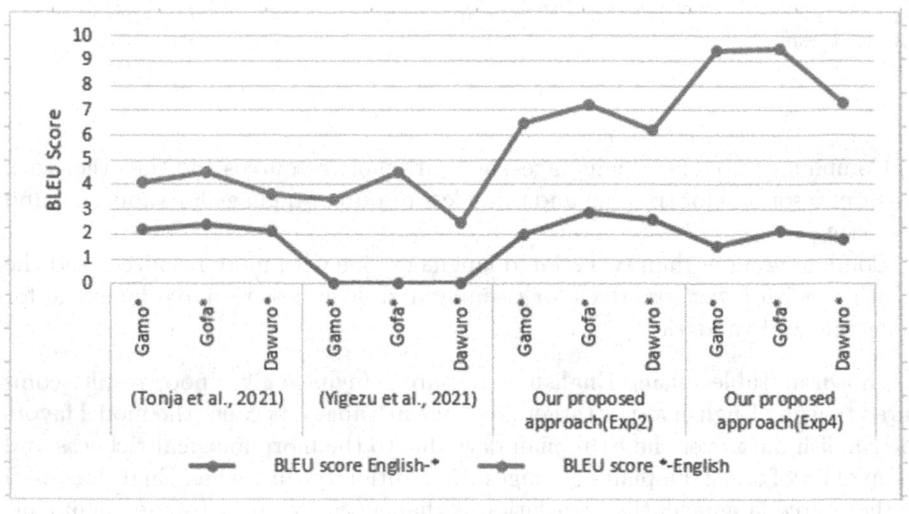

Fig. 2. Comparison of the proposed approach with previous research works

6 Conclusions and Future Work

In this paper, we proposed and discussed a new approach to improve neural machine translation for low-resource languages using a transformer-based model. Combining two or more low-resource languages for training and validating, then testing the performance on another language shows result improvements when English is used as the target language. Our proposed model showed better results compared to previous experiments in the same languages and datasets without using high-resource languages.

In future work, we will apply the proposed approach for other related low-resource languages and compare the performance of the proposed approach with other suggested NMT approaches for low- resource languages. Also, we plan to add more domains and investigate the effect of domain for low-resource languages in machine translation.

Acknowledgments. The work was done with partial support from the Mexican Government through the grant A1S-47854 of CONACYT, Mexico, grants 20220852,

20220859, and 20221627 of the Secretaría de Investigación y Posgrado of the Instituto Politécnico Nacional, Mexico. The authors thank the CONACYT for the computing resources brought to them through the Plataforma de Aprendizaje Profundo para Tecnologías del Lenguaje of the Laboratorio de Supercómputo of the INAOE, Mexico and acknowledge the support of Microsoft through the Microsoft Latin America PhD Award.

References

1. Julia, H., Manning, C.D.: Advances in natural language processing. Science **349**(6245), 261–266 (2015)
2. Forcada, M.L.: Making sense of neural machine translation. Transl. Spaces **6**(2), 291–309 (2017)
3. Mohamed, S.A., Elsayed, A.A., Hassan, Y.F., Abdou, M.A.: Neural machine translation: past, present, and future. Neural Comput. Appl. **33**(23), 15919–15931 (2021). https://doi.org/10.1007/s00521-021-06268-0
4. Benyamin, A., Dorr, B.J.: Augmenting neural machine translation through round-trip training approach. Open Comput. Sci. **9**(1), 268–278 (2019)
5. Alexandre, B., Kim, Z.M., Nikoulina, V., Park, E.L., Gallé, M.: A multilingual neural machine translation model for biomedical data. arXiv preprint arXiv:2008.02878 (2020)
6. Markus, F., Firat, O.: Complete multilingual neural machine translation. arXiv preprint arXiv:2010.10239 (2020)
7. Khaled, S., Rafea, A., Moneim, A.A., Baraka, H.: Machine translation of English noun phrases into Arabic. Int. J. Comput. Process. Oriental Lang. **17**(02), 121–134 (2004)
8. Pratik, J., Santy, S., Budhiraja, A., Bali, K., Choudhury, M.: The state and fate of linguistic diversity and inclusion in the NLP world. arXiv preprint arXiv:2004.09095 (2020)
9. Hasibuan, Z.: A comparative study between human translation and machine translation as an interdisciplinary research. J. Eng. Teach. Learn. Issue. **3**(2), 115–130 (2020)
10. Dubey, P.: Study and development of machine translation system from Hindi language to Dogri language an important tool to bridge the digital divide (2008)
11. Okpor, M.D.: Machine translation approaches: issues and challenges. Int. J. Comput. Sci. Issue. (IJCSI) **11**(5), 159 (2014)
12. Lopez, A.: Statistical machine translation. ACM Comput. Surv. (CSUR) **40**(3), 1–49 (2008)
13. Philipp, K.: Statistical Machine Translation. Cambridge University Press (2009)
14. Sergei, N., Somers, H.L., Wilks, Y.A.: A Framework of a Mechanical Translation between Japanese and English by Analogy Principle, pp. 351–354 (2003)
15. Philipp, K.: Neural machine translation. arXiv preprint arXiv:1709.07809 (2017)
16. Stahlberg, F.: Neural machine translation: a review. J. Artif. Intell. Res. **69**, 343–418 (2020)
17. Wu, Y., et al.: Google's neural machine translation system: bridging the gap between human and machine translation. arXiv preprint arXiv:1609.08144 (2016)
18. Robert, Ö., Tiedemann, J.: Neural machine translation for low-resource languages. arXiv preprint arXiv:1708.05729 (2017)
19. Barret, Z., Yuret, D., May, J., Knight, K.: Transfer learning for low-resource neural machine translation. arXiv preprint arXiv:1604.02201 (2016)

20. Tao, F., Li, M., Chen, L.: Low-resource neural machine translation with transfer learning. In: LREC 2018 Workshop, p. 30 (2018)
21. Amel, S., Melouah, a., Faghihi, u., Sahib, k.: Improving neural machine translation for low resource Algerian dialect by transductive transfer learning strategy. Arab. J. Sci. Eng. **47**, 10411–10418 (2022)
22. Hirut, W.: Language planning challenged by identity contestation in a multilingual setting: the case of gamo. Oslo Stud. Lang. **8**(1) (2016)
23. Azeb, A.: The Omotic Language Family. Cambridge University Press (2017)
24. Atnafu Lambebo, T., Woldeyohannis, M.M., Yigezu, M.G.: A parallel corpora for bi-directional neural machine translation for low resourced Ethiopian languages. In: 2021 International Conference on Information and Communication Technology for Development for Africa (ICT4DA), pp. 71–76. IEEE (2021)
25. Ashish, V., et al.: Attention is all you need. In: Advances in Neural Information Processing Systems, vol. 30 (2017)
26. Gage, P.: A new algorithm for data compression. C Users J. **12**(2), 23–38 (1994)
27. Guillaume, K., Kim, Y., Deng, Y., Senellart, J., Rush, A.M.: OpenNMT: open-source toolkit for neural machine translation. arXiv preprint arXiv:1701.02810 (2017)
28. Michael, C., Bragança, L., Paranaiba Vilela Neto, O., Nacif, J.A., Ferreira R.: Google colab cad4u: hands-on cloud laboratories for digital design. In: 2021 IEEE International Symposium on Circuits and Systems (ISCAS), pp. 1–5. IEEE (2021)
29. Yigezu, M.G., Woldeyohannis M.M., Tonja, A.L.:Multilingual neural machine translation for low resourced languages: Ometo-English. In: 2021 International Conference on Information and Communication Technology for Development for Africa (ICT4DA), pp. 89–94 (2021). https://doi.org/10.1109/ICT4DA53266.2021.9671270

Machine Translation of Texts from Languages with Low Digital Resources: A Systematic Review

Hermilo Benito-Santiago[1(✉)], Diana Margarita Córdova-Esparza[1], Noé Alejandro Castro-Sánchez[2], and Ana-Marcela Herrera-Navarro[1]

[1] Facultad de Informática, Universidad Autónoma de Querétaro, Queretaro, Mexico
hsantiago13@alumnos.uaq.mx, {diana.cordova,mherrera}@uaq.mx

[2] Centro Nacional de Investigación y Desarrollo Tecnológico, Cuernavaca, Mexico
noe.cs@cenidet.tecnm.mx

Abstract. This research conducted a systematic review of related works on machine translation of languages with low digital resources. First, we carried out the information search in the databases: ScienceDirect, IEEE Xplore, ACM Digital Library. Eighteen articles were collected following inclusion and exclusion criteria, considering a search period from 2016 to 2022. Subsequently, we analyzed and classified these articles according to the libraries developed and/or used based on machine learning, statistics, or grammar. The results indicate that pre-training and morphological segmentation techniques with finite state machines and machine learning techniques improve the translation of languages with low digital resources. In addition, according to the articles compiled in the specialized databases, in Mexico, unlike other countries that we analyzed, there are few publications on the translation of languages with low digital resources, and we mostly found research papers published in international conferences.

Keywords: Machine translation · Parallel corpus · Languages with low digital resources

1 Introduction

Languages with low digital resources are those languages that do not have a large amount of written or digitized documentation. It may also be the case that this documentation exists but is not published. The reduced number of language speakers means no documentation is generated about it. These languages represent a significant challenge in Artificial Intelligence knowledge, particularly in natural language processing, for two main reasons: the first refers to the scarcity of corpus since, to carry out the experimentation, a set of data is required. With a considerable size that can be processed to obtain results; the second refers to rethinking and adapting existing methods that have been used with languages with characteristics different from languages that are considered to have low digital resources [1].

O. Pichardo Lagunas et al. (Eds.): MICAI 2022, LNAI 13613, pp. 41–56, 2022.
https://doi.org/10.1007/978-3-031-19496-2_4

According to Hedderich et al. [2] low-resource languages can be divided into:

- The availability of task-specific labels.
- Availability of untagged or domain-specific language.
- Availability of auxiliary data.

In this research work, we performed a literature review on the latest trends regarding machine translation methods for languages with limited digital resources. We considered specialized databases such as ScienceDirect, IEEE Xplore, ACM Digital Library, analyzing journal articles, book chapters, and proceedings.

This article aims to quantitatively and qualitatively analyze the state-of-the-art for automatic translation of languages with low digital resources. The quantitative analysis was carried out to have a perspective on the number of articles published by year, country, and by areas of knowledge. In contrast, the qualitative analysis categorizes articles with characteristics in common regarding the methodology they implement and the resources used.

This paper contains the following sections. Second we present, the method with the following phases, documentary search in databases, description of criteria used for select works, analysis, and categorization of works, and discussion. Third, we present conclusions and future work after reviewing works.

2 Method

In this work, we carried out a mixed systematic review, for which the information is analyzed quantitatively and qualitatively from the works that have been developed in the literature on machine translation of low-resource languages.

To carry out the systematic review, we adopted the phases of Palacios-Díaz and Escudero-Nahón [3]. Next, we detail each of the phases that make up this work's methodology.

2.1 Phase 1: Documentary Search

We carried out the documentary search in the databases: ScienceDirect, IEEE Xplore, and ACM Digital Library, selecting journal articles, book chapters, and conference proceedings. Words that include machine translation and languages of limited resources were taken into account due to the main focus of finding articles related to machine translation.

In the case of the term low-resources languages, we considered different ways that these languages can be named. According to the author Singh [4], they can be identified as less-studied languages, languages of scarce resources, less computerized languages , and less privileged languages. Other terms that Cieri mentions [5] are: low density, less taught, scarce resources, less resources, low resources, critical languages, and in danger of extinction.

Taking into account the terminologies mentioned above, we considered the following keywords: minority languages, fewer resources, languages in danger of extinction, language, and dialect; to find research with these characteristics. We replicated the following query in each database: *machine translation AND (low resource OR scarce resource OR poor OR minoritized OR lesser resourced OR endangered) AND (dialect OR languages).*

According to the results obtained by entering the query string and following the selection criteria detailed below, we identified relevant articles related to machine translation of low-resource languages.

2.2 Phase 2: Description of Selection Criteria

In the searches in ScienceDirect, we obtained 1,592 results, in IEEE Xplore 259 results, in ACM Digital Library 395 results, in Proceedings (ACL Anthology) 3130 results, in the COMTEL Conference we found one, and in the ADHO Conference, we found one as well. We accepted 18 articles in total, considering the following criteria that allowed each to be selected.

Inclusion Criteria

- Articles whose methodology has developed and implemented machine translation of languages with low digital resources or distant languages since this systematic review focuses on analyzing the translation methods used for these languages.
- Articles whose title, abstract, and keywords contain the terms: machine translation, low-income languages, and dialect or lingo.
- Articles with publication data from 2016 to 2022.
- Works that are open access and that belong to indexed, refereed journals and conference publications.
- Articles written in English and Spanish.
- Articles from the areas of engineering, computer science, artificial intelligence, and language translation.
- Research articles, short communications, conferences or congresses, magazines, and book chapters.
- An advanced search was performed in the ScienceDirect database in the title, abstract, or author fields with the query string to obtain relevant results.
- In the ScienceDirect database, the filter <<types of articles>> was selected for the following: Review articles, research articles, and book chapters.
- In the ScienceDirect database in areas of knowledge, the following were selected: Medicine and Dentistry, Computer Science, and Engineering.
- Transactions journal articles on Asian and Low-Income Language Information Processing (TALLIP) were selected from the ACM Library database.
- In the ACM database, we used the filter <<Journals>> in the publications section.

Exclusion Criteria

- Articles that do not contain the keywords in the title, abstract, or whose methods are not related to the machine translation of low-resource languages.
- Works of automatic translation of high-resource languages, for example, English-Spanish, French-Spanish, and Spanish-Portuguese.

– After applying the inclusion and exclusion criteria of the articles, we analyzed them in-depth and categorized the results following the phase described below.

2.3 Phase 3: Analysis and Categorization

We performed a quantitative and qualitative analysis of the collected articles in this phase. The first allowed us to analyze the information based on numerical data, while the second allowed us to identify the common characteristics shared by the research works. Each one is detailed below:

Quantitative Analysis
In this quantitative analysis, we took into account the total number of publications that have been made in a period from 2016 to 2022, the countries that have carried out translation work, the areas of knowledge in which these publications are made, what languages of low digital resources have been published and finally the metrics that are implemented in the translation to evaluate the results of the investigations.

Next, Table 1 shows the research questions that we took into account for the quantitative analysis of the collected articles are presented.

Table 1. Questions for the quantitative analysis and motivation.

Questions	Motivations
What is the number of publications that have been made from 2016 to 2022?	Identify publications relevant pear year
What are the countries that publish on the machine translation of low-resource languages?	To identify countries that publish on the machine translation of low-resource language
What areas of knowledge have published articles on the machine translation of languages with low digital resources?	To analyze and identify areas of knowledge that have published articles on the machine translation
In which languages with low digital resources have machine translation been developed?	To identify and show languages with low digital resources where machine translation has been developed
What metrics are implemented in the evaluation of translations from languages with low digital resources?	To identify and analyze metrics implemented in the evaluation of translations from languages with low digital resources
What score did they obtain in the evaluation of the investigations?	To analyze score obtained in the evaluation of the investigation

Results From the Quantitative Analysis
According to the quantitative analysis, the number of publications per year is as follows: in 2016, a total of three documents were obtained; in 2017, no results related to machine

translation were produced; in 2018 and 2019, one article. In 2020 five works were developed; in 2021, seven documents were obtained, and finally, to date, in 2022, there is one article.

Regarding the publications by country, the countries with publications on machine translation of languages with low digital resources are: Germany at 5%, Burma 5%, Canada 5%, China 11%, United States 11%, Finland 5%, Japan 17%, Malaysia 6%, Mexico 17%, Pakistan 6%, South Africa 6%, Tunisia 6%.

According to the systematic review of the articles and the observation of the topics in which they are published in the databases and conferences, we took the following areas of knowledge into account with their respective number of published articles: Medicine and dentistry with zero works, Engineering zero, Computer Science 11, Computational Linguistics six, Social Sciences and Humanities with one. The data indicates that most publications are made in Computer Science and Computational Linguistics. At the same time, no articles related to the translation of languages with low digital resources are reported in the area of Medicine.

Qualitative Analysis

In the qualitative analysis, we took into account the techniques implemented for the translation, the corpus used in the translation works, the scenarios that arise when translating with languages with low digital resources, and the significant results that have been obtained in the investigations, and finally the problems they face when translating these languages. The research questions taken into account for the qualitative analysis of the set of articles collected are shown in Table 2.

Based on the research questions for the qualitative analysis previously mentioned, the following categorization of the works related to machine translation was carried out.

- Translation based on libraries that apply machine learning techniques

Table 2. Questions for qualitative analysis.

Questions	Motivations
What techniques are used in machine translation of low-resource languages?	Identify and categorize techniques used in machine translation of low-resource languages
What kind of corpus are used in a low digital resource environment?	Identify the type of corpus used in a low digital resource environment
What translation scenarios have been used for languages with low digital resources?	Analyze and identify the translation scenarios with existing parallel, monolingual, and not existing corpus
What tools or software are used in the automatic translation of languages with low digital resources?	To categorize tools or libraries used in the automatic translation of languages with low digital resources
What challenges are faced in a translation environment with languages with low digital resources?	To identify challenges in a translation environment with languages with low digital resources

- Translation based on libraries that use statistics.
- Translation based on libraries that make use of grammar rules
- Combination of translation libraries
- Taking into account the classification of the articles below, a brief description of each category is made.

1. Translation Based on Libraries that Apply Machine Learning Techniques
This section describes the works developed using machine learning techniques. Table 3 shows the works whose contents have implemented libraries using machine learning techniques for translation.

In the article by Zacarías and Meza [6], the JoeyNMT[1] library is implemented for automatic translation between the Ayuuk and Spanish languages[2]. For its development, the following steps were followed: automatic alignment, tokenization, orthographic normalization of the corpus, and training with the JoeyNMT tool. A BLEU (Bilingual Evaluation Understudy) above 5.0 was obtained. BLEU is a method of automatic evaluation of machine translation, quickly and language-independent. BLEU measures the quality of translation with respect to a reference [24].

In the work of Knowles et al. [7] highlight the translation of Spanish, Wixárika, Nahuatl, Rarámuri, and Guarani. The Sockeye[3] library was implemented in the translation experiments. The results were validated with the ChrF metric (character n-gram F-score) obtained in Guaraní (gn) 0.258, Wixarika (hch) 0.262, Nahuatl (nah) 0.252, Raramuri (tar) 0.134. ChrF is a technique for the measure of machine translation with the use of the character n-gram F-score. ChrF is language-independent, and tokenization-independent of language [25].

In the work of Mager et al. [8] propose shared tasks for the translation of parallel corpora in the languages Quechua-Spanish, Wixarika-Spanish, Shipibo-Konibo-Spanish, Asháninka-Spanish, Rarámuri-Spanish, Nahuatl-Spanish, Otomí-Spanish, Aymara-Spanish, Guarani-Spanish, and Bribri-Spanish. Researchers can choose to use the baseline that was developed with the FairSeq[4] tool or implement whatever techniques they deem appropriate. The Helsinki method is used, and the results are validated with the ChrF metric of the languages Aymara (aym) 28.3, Bribri(bzd) 16.5, Ashaninka (cni) 25.8, 33.4, Wizarika (hch) 30.04, Nahuatl (nah) 26.6, Otomí 14.7, Quechua (quy) 34.6, Shipibo-Konibo (shp) 32.9, Raramuri (tar) 18.4.

In the article by Vazquez et al. [9], they report a machine translation system based on the OpenNMT[5] tool in combination with pre-training and back-translation. The languages taken into account are Ashaninka, Wixarika and Shipibo-Konibo. The results are validated with the ChrF2 metric obtaining for: Ashaninka(cni) 0.258, Aymara(aym) 0.283, Bribri (bzd) 0.165, Guaraní (gn) 0.336, Hnahñu (oto) 0.147, Nahuatl (nah) 0.266, Quechua (quy) 0.343, Rarámuri (tar) 0.184, Shipibo-Konibo (shp) 0.329, Wixarika (hch) 0.304.

---
1 https://github.com/joeynmt/joeynmt

2 https://github.com/DelfinoAyuuk/corpora_ayuuk-spanish_nmt

3 https://github.com/awslabs/sockeye

4 https://github.com/facebookresearch/fairseq

5 https://opennmt.net

The work presented by Zheng et al. [10] highlights the implementation of the FairSeq library for translation between the languages Aymara, Bribri, Asháninka, Guarani, Wixarika, Nahuatl, Hñähñu, Quechua, Shipibo-Konibo, Rarámuri, Bulgarian, English, French, Irish, Korean, Latin, Spanish, Sundanese, Vietnamese, and Yoruba. Pre-training was performed with mBart-multilingual encoder-decoder (sequence-to-sequence), Tokenization with SentencePiece, and training with FairSeq. Regarding the results, a BLEU of 1.64 and a ChF of 0.0749 were obtained.

The authors Ahmadnia et al. [11] propose machine translation with neural networks in combination with alignment and filtering for Persian-Spanish languages. The bilingual texts used during the training process were taken from the Tanzil corpus, which contains 67 thousand pairs of Persian-Spanish sentences. The use of these filtering techniques considerably improves the results of the translation process. A BLEU of 26.02 was obtained.

Ghafoor et al. [12] report translation using the Google Translate API tool in combination with error analysis. Translations were done between the languages English, Urdu, German, and Hindi. Regarding the results, it was obtained that the accuracy of the English language using SVM (Support vector machine) is 90.45%, and the German data set is 90.01%. In the Urdu language with SVM, an accuracy of 87.26% was obtained, while in the Hindi language with the use of a Bi-LSTM, an accuracy of 85.99% was achieved.

Nekoto et al. [13] publicize machine translation with a community of researchers who share growth strategies, knowledge exchange, and the development of translation models in more than 30 African languages. The JoeyNMT library was implemented in the translation experiments. The evaluation of the translation tool with the support of human experts is highlighted. As future works stand out, to continue with the compilation of parallel corpora, to carry out developments for other areas of natural language processing, and support the tool's implementation for other languages. The following results were obtained using the BLEU metric: Dendi (ddn) 22.30, Pigdin (pcm) 23.29, Fon (fon) 31.07, Luo (luo) 34.33, Hausa (ha) 41.11, Igbo (ig) 34.85, Yoruba (yo) 38.62, Shona (sn) 30.84, Kiswahili (sw) 48.94.

The authors Imankulova et al. [14] translate between Russian, Japanese, French and Malagasy, German and English languages. The OpenNMT library was used for the translation experiments. They propose unsupervised translation to generate bilingual resources to be reused in supervised tasks. They emphasize that the accuracy of the results depends on the length and quality of the training. In future works, the proposal can be trained with the same domain and corpus size, and reinforcement learning can be incorporated. It was obtained with the French-Malagasy with the metric AAS (Average Alignment Similarity) 16.87, Japanese-Russian a BLEU 13.20 was obtained. German-English BLEU 24.13.

2. Translation Based on Libraries that Use Statistics

This section describes the articles whose contents implemented translation libraries with statistics. Table 4 shows the most significant works that were taken into account for this category.

Table 3. Translation with machine learning libraries.

Authors and references	Problem-solving technique	Libraries used	Challenges in language translation	Metrics
Zacarías y Meza [6]	Neural networks	JoeyNMT	Orthographic normalization, Shortage of corpus	BLEU
Knowles et al. [7]	Neural networks	Sockeye	Dialectal and orthographic variety	ChrF
Mager et. al. [8]	Neural networks	FairSeq	Shortage of corpus, Orthographic rules and normalization, Dialectal variety	ChrF
Vazquez et al. [9]	Pre-training, Back translation, Neural networks	OpenNMT	Shortage of corpus, Orthographic normalization	ChrF2
Zheng et al. [10]	Pre-training, Neural networks,	FairSeq	Scarcity of resources, Morphological complexity	ChrF
Ahmadnia et al. [11]	Neural networks	Library not specified	Scarcity of corpus, Morphological complexity	BLEU
Ghafoor et al. [12]	Neural networks	Google Translate API	Scarcity of corpus	Precision
Nekoto et al. [13]	Neural networks, evaluation by human expert	JoeyNMT	Shortage of corpus, language standardization, Difficult adaptation of existing methods, Infrastructure and time limitations	BLEU
Imankulova et al. [14]	Neural networks	OpenNMT	Scarcity of corpus	AAS, BLEU

In the work of Mager et al. [15], Translation between the Wixarika languages and Spanish was developed. The use of the Moses[6] library with the probability technique in combination with morphological segmentation is highlighted. It faces the problem of morphological complexity of the Wixarika language. The result was obtained with WER (Word Error Rate) 38, TER (Translation Error Rate) 0.84. TER measures the amount of

[6] http://www2.statmt.org/moses/

correcting a human expert would have to modify the output to match a reference [25]. On the other hand, WER [26] reduces the word error rate in textual summaries of spoken languages.

Pa et al. [16] highlight the implementation of the Moses tool in translation. Translation comparisons were performed with probability techniques and hierarchical phrase strategies. The latter helps in reordering the words during translation. In addition to the language syntax technique that is built into Moses. The parallel corpus is written in the languages Lao, Myanmar, and Thai. It was obtained with BLEU metric Myanmar-English 21.65, Thai-English 36.98, Lao-English 31.47.

Table 4. Translation with statistics libraries.

Authors and references	Problem-solving technique	Libraries used	Challenges in language translation	Metrics
Mager et al. [15]	Probability technique	Moses	Morphological complexity, Orthographic normalization, Scarcity of corpus	WER, TER
Pa et al. [16]	Probability technique	Moses	No challenges specified	BLEU

3. Translation with Libraries Based on Grammar Rules

The article by [17] discloses the translation with grammatical rules for Arabic languages. The Apertium tool is implemented in the translation since the Apertium[7] library already has the language incorporated in its translation. Future works include continuing to add data to the bilingual dictionary, combining the method with statistics, and adding more semantic rules. In the evaluation, it was obtained with the metrics WER 23.28%, TER 23.85%, and BLEU 55.22.

Table 5. Translation based on grammar rules.

Authors and references	Problem-solving technique	Libraries used	Challenges in language translation	Metrics
Sghaier y r Zrigui [17]	Grammatical rules	Apertium	Morphological and lexical disambiguation	WER, TER, BLEU

[7] https://wiki.apertium.org/wiki/Main_Page

4. Combination of Translation Libraries
Maimaiti et al. [18] proposed the implementation of the THUMT[8] neural network library in combination with transfer learning and word embedding (Word Embeddings of the English language). Applying this combination to low-resource languages helps to find better performance. This method can be applied to other areas of Natural Language Processing (NLP) and other languages as it is language and architecture-independent. It was obtained with BLEU with Azerbaijani and Uzbek languages 4:94 and 4:84.

In the work of [19], they disclose the machine translation with the unsupervised neural network with the Marian[9]library and Moses statistical translation. The corpus that they generated with unsupervised neural translation was reused for supervised tasks. Using supervised and unsupervised neural networks considerably improves the translation quality compared to previous works. In this work, tests were carried out in 5 languages: English, French, German, Indonesian, and Japanese. Regarding the evaluation for Japanese-English languages, a BLEU of 3.9 was obtained, while the Japanese-Indonesian of 0.3.

Yeong et al. [20] propose the use of the Moses library in English-Malay translation experiments in combination with an English language stemmer to improve the translation. Future work highlights the implementation of the Giza++ tool for automatic alignment at the word level. It was obtained with Malay-English BLEU 12.90.

In the article by [21], they expose a scenario with low-resource languages in which there is not a large amount of parallel data and easy access. Neural machine translation training with the OpenNMT library and statistical machine translation with the Moses library in combination with the multidomain corpus were performed. In the evaluation with the BLEU metric with the Gnome corpus, the following results were obtained: Moses 20.54, OpenNMT 15.49, Moses adapted 17.26, OpenNMT adapted 18.76. With the Subtitles corpus, the following scores were obtained: Moses 18.82, OpenNMT 18.62, Moses adapted 19.51, OpenNMT adapted 22.54, respectively.

In the work of [22], they perform the translation between the Chinese and Vietnamese languages. They propose the use of back-translation in combination with the OpenNMT neural network library and Moses statistical translation. Future works include adding more data to the corpus and incorporating transfer learning. According to the results with a focus on Chinese-Vietnamese characters with the METEOR metric with statistical techniques 30.29 and neural networks 25.32.

In the work of Mager and Meza [23], they highlight a comparison between scenarios, on the one hand, those that use the Moses library based on the probability technique. On the other hand, there is the scenario with neural networks with the OpenNMT library. These two libraries were combined with automatic word alignment with the Giza++ library. It faced the challenges of scarce digital resources; languages have morphological complexity, and they do not have orthographic normalization. In this work, experiments were carried out with 5 indigenous languages, Wixarika, Nahuatl, Yorem Nokki, Purépecha, and Mexicanero. Regarding the results, the BLEU metric was obtained with neural networks in the following languages: Mexicanero-Spanish 2.95,

[8] https://github.com/THUNLP-MT/THUMT
[9] https://marian-nmt.github.io

Nahuatl-Spanish 3.04, Purépecha-Spanish 0, Wixarika-Spanish 0, Yorem Nokki-Spanish 0. On the other hand, with the probability technique with the languages: Mexicanero-Spanish 23.47, Nahuatl-Spanish 10.14, Purépecha-Spanish 5.38, Wixarika-Spanish 0, Yorem Nokki-Spanish 2.44.

Table 6. Combination of translation libraries.

Authors and references	Problem-solving technique	Libraries used	Challenges in language translation	Metrics
Maimaiti et al. [18]	Neural networks	THUMT		BLEU
Marie y Fujita [19]	Neural networks, probability techniques	Moses, Marian	Corpus shortage	BLEU
Yeong et al. [20]	Probability techniques, English language lemmatizer	Moses	Corpus shortage	BLEU
Ahmadnia y Dorr [21]	Neural networks, Probability techniques	OpenNMT, Moses	Corpus shortage	BLEU
Li, Sha y Shi [22]	Neural networks and probability techniques	OpenNMT, Moses	Corpus shortage	METEOR
Mager y Meza [23]	Probability techniques and neural networks	OpenNMT, Moses	Scarcity of resources, Morphological complexity, Orthographic normalization	BLEU

2.4 Phase 4: Discussion

According to the results of the analysis of the articles and the characteristics that they share in common, these works were categorized into the following categories:

- Translation with machine learning libraries
- Translation with statistics libraries
- Translation with libraries based on grammar rules
- Combination of translation libraries

According to the analysis of the articles, the following challenges or limitations were generally identified:

- The scarcity of the corpus. It refers to the fact that there is not a considerable amount of digital corpus to support automatic translation tasks.
- Orthographic normalization or standardization in languages. It refers to the fact that languages with low digital resources do not have documentation of the common writing standards for all the variants of the language, which causes inconveniences when translating these languages.
- The morphological complexity of languages. It refers to the fact that languages with low digital resources have many morphemes that can cause difficulties when dealing with these languages.
- The complexity of existing techniques. It refers to the fact that the libraries and tools that already exist for machine translation to apply to languages with low digital resources require an adaptation of the existing tools to languages with low digital resources.
- Computational infrastructure and time. It is mentioned that sometimes there is not enough computer equipment that supports translation tasks, mainly computers, memories, GPUs, and hard drives. In addition to the time limitation, sometimes there is not enough time for machine translation tasks with languages with low digital resources.

Table 3 shows the articles related to translation with machine learning libraries. In the work of Zacarías and Meza [6] in the evaluation, a BLEU above 5.0 was obtained. The translation focuses only on the languages Spanish and Ayuuk. This work used a corpus size of more than 6000 phrases. In this article, we only worked with the corpus of the San Juan Güichicov variant. The authors point out that it is easier to translate from Spanish to Ayuuk than vice versa. The work highlights that the use of Transformers neural networks in low-resource languages yields results, although they point out that the results are low compared to machine translation standards. In the future works of this article, it is highlighted to continue with the compilation of the corpus of other Ayuuk variants, to incorporate the morphological analysis to support the translation, and to continue with the orthographic normalization. However, a high score was obtained in the article by Ahmadnia et al. [11] with a BLEU value of 26.02; this indicates that the quality of the translation and the scores are close to the reference translation, in addition to the fact that in this last article the size of the training corpus is 67K sentence pairs are greater than in the work of Zacarías and Table [6]. On the other hand, the tool implemented in the translation is not mentioned since its own development was carried out with neural network techniques. In this work, he focuses on the Persian and Spanish languages.

In the work of Mager et al. [8] highlight the implementation of the FairSeq library in the translation of low-resource languages in America. Regarding the results with the ChrF metric, the following scores were obtained: Aymara (aym) 0.157, Bribri (bzd) 0.68, Ashaninka (cni) 0.102, Guaraní (gn) 0.193, Wixárika (hch) 0.126, Nahuatl (nah) 0.157, Otomí 0.054, Quechua (quy) 0.304, Shipibo-Konibo (shp) 0.121, Raramuri (tar) 0.039.

The corpus[10] size used is 228275 sentence for training, 9122 sentence for validation and 10018 sentence for test. Although the work presented by Zheng et al. [10] highlights better results with the ChrF metric in the Aymara 0.209, Bribri 0.131, Asháninka 0.214, Guaraní 0.254, Wixarika 0.229, Nahuatl 0.238, Hñähñu 0.133, Quechua 0.33, Shipibo-Konibo 0.175 and Rarámuri 0.123 languages, respectively. In this article, the FairSeq library was implemented for translation and the corpus size used is 13 GB monolingual phrases data, 140 MB phrases of parallel corpus. The authors attribute the improvement of the score to the use of pre-training of the language model, which allowed learning of the languages involved before adjustments. In future works, they propose pre-training using the dictionary augmentation technique, pseudo-monolingual data, and experiments with a probabilistic morphological segmenter of finite states. On the other hand, with the ChrF metric, outstanding scores are obtained in the article by Vázquez et al. [9] in the languages Aymara 0.283, Bribri 0.165, Ashaninka 0.258, Guarani 0.336, Wixárika 0.304, Nahuatl 0.266, Otomí 0.147, Quechua 0.343, Shipibo-Konibo 0.329, Raramuri 0.184. The results improve with the implementation of the OpenNMT translation library, pre-training, and corpus data filtering. In this work, the corpus size is 228274 sentences for training and 9122 sentences for development.

In the article, Knowles et al. [7] highlight the translation with the Sockeye library in languages with low digital resources, in this case, Guaraní, Wixarika, Nahuatl, and Rarámuri. Therefore, this article only focuses on these four languages. Regarding the results with the ChrF metric, the following scores were obtained: Guaraní 0.258, Wixarika 0.262, Nahuatl 0.252, and Rarámuri 0.134. The improvement of scores is tokenization, pre-training, and translation memories. The size corpus used is 65863 sentence pairs for training and 3656 sentence pairs for development.

In the work of Nekoto et al. [13] with the COVID corpus in the HBLEU metric, the following scores were obtained: Dendi (ddn) 0.27, Pidgin (pcm) 3.03, Fon (fon) 15.43, Luo (luo) 0, Hausa (ha) 26.96, Igbo (ig) 11.94, Yoruba (yo) 85.92, Shona (sn) 31.31, Kiswahili (sw) 0 while the following scores were obtained with the TED corpus with the HBLEU metric: Dendi (ddn) 0, Pidgin (pcm) 9.76, Fon (fon) 0, Luo (luo) 7.90, Hausa (ha) 20.42, Igbo (ig) 33.74, Yoruba (yo) 49.22, Shona (sn) 0, Kiswahili (sw) 60.47. These data indicate that in the COVID corpus in the Fon and Igbo languages, the scores are close to each other, while the TED corpus in the Dendi, Fon and Shona languages do not mention the scores obtained. In this work, he focuses on African languages. The corpus size used is 2528078 sentences for training[11].

Table 4 shows the automatic translation works with statistical libraries. Mager et al. [15] present the first translation tool in the Wixarika language with the Moses library. In this work, he focuses on the Wixarika and Spanish languages. Future works include improving the translator with bilingual lexical extraction and continuing with the compilation of the corpus. Regarding the evaluation, it was obtained with WER metrics (without morphological segmentation 38, with morphological segmentation 25, segmentation with labeling 21) and with TER metrics (segmentation 0.84, with morphological segmentation 0.46, segmentation with labeling 0.46) these results indicate that the use

[10] https://github.com/AmericasNLP/americasnlp2021/tree/main/data

[11] https://github.com/masakhane-io/masakhane-mt

of morphological segmentation and labeling considerably improve the results since the error score is lower when implementing these techniques.

On the other hand, the work of Pa et al. [16] explore statistical machine translation in Myanmar, Thai, Lao, and English languages. In the evaluation with the BLEU metric with a statistical technique based on phrases, the following scores were obtained: English-Lao 20.87, Lao-English 31.41, English-Myanmar 10.71, Myanmar-English 21.65, English-Thai 37.33, Thai-English 36.98 while using the hierarchical phrase-based technique, English-Lao 18.94, Lao-English 30.73, English-Myanmar 12.53, Myanmar-English 20.95, English-Thai 38.60, Thai-English 35.45 were obtained. According to these scores, the Thao-English and English-Thao languages received outstanding scores. However, with the translation technique based on hierarchical phrases, the minimum score was 12.53 in the English-Myanmar languages. The corpus size used in Myanmar is 13042 sentence pairs and Lao 35125 words.

Table 5 shows the machine translation jobs with grammar rules. In the article by Sghaier and Zrigui [17], they report the results of the translation with the Apertium library in the Tunisian dialect to Arabic. The following scores were obtained in the evaluation: WER 23.28%, TER 23.85%, and BLEU 55.22. According to the authors, the scores indicate that the error rate was acceptable since it is below 30%, and the BLEU metric indicates that the performance was good since it was a percentage above 50. In this work, the corpus size is 763 words for test and 805 words for reference corpus.

Table 6 shows the jobs that perform the combination of libraries. In the article by Ahmadnia and Dorr [21], they report the results of machine translation in a multi-domain scenario for languages with low digital resources. It focuses on the performance of the Moses library and OpenNMT. In the evaluation with the BLEU metric with the Gnome corpus with Moses 20.54, OpenNMT 15.49, Moses adapted 17.26, OpenNMT adapted 18.76, while with the Subtitles corpus with Moses 18.82, OpenNMT 18.62, Moses adapted 19.51, OpenNMT adapted 22.54. These data indicate that better results are obtained with Moses than with OpenNMT. Although Moses and OpenNMT adapted to a specific domain, the latter's results improved. The corpus sized was 5213125 sentences.

In the work by Mager and Meza [23], they present the advances in machine translation for five low-resource languages. In this work, they compare the Moses and OpenNMT libraries. They emphasize that using morphological segmentation improves the results with both libraries. In the evaluation with the BLEU metric with the Moses library, the following values were obtained: Mexicanero-Spanish 23.47, Nahuatl-Spanish 10.14, Purépecha-Spanish 5.38, Wixárika-Spanish 2.44, Yorem Nokki-Spanish 0, while with the OpenNMT library the following values were obtained: obtained the following scores: Mexicanero-Spanish 2.95, Nahuatl-Spanish 3.04, Purépecha-Spanish 0, Wixárika-Spanish 0, Yorem Nokki-Spanish 0. The data indicate that the results of the Moses library are better than the OpenNMT library because they are trained with a small corpus. Furthermore, the Mexicanero and Nahuatl languages performed better than the Wixarika language, considering that the Wixarika language has a greater number of morphemes per word than Nahuatl. The corpus size used is 985 sentence pairs.

3 Conclusions

According to the searches carried out in databases such as ScienceDirect, ACM Library, and IEEE, there are few articles on machine translation of low-resource languages in Mexico. According to the review, most of them have been published at international conferences, in addition to the fact that, in Mexico, there are few works on rule-based machine translation with languages with low digital resources due to the complexity of creating language rules. Also, through the systematic review, we identified that in the area of medicine, articles on the automatic translation of languages with low digital resources were not published, making it difficult to accurately communicate information on the health of patients from indigenous communities. So this area may be an area of opportunity in future work. In Mexico's machine translation advances were identified for the following indigenous languages: Nahuatl, Wixarika, Otomí, Raramuri, Ayuuk, Yorem Nokki, Purépecha, and Mexicanero. According to our research in databases and conferences, there are no automatic translation works on Mixteco, Amuzgo, Tlapaneco, Chatino, among others.

References

1. Gutierrez-Vasques, X., Vilchis-Vargas, E., Cerbon-Ynclan, R.: Recopilación de un corpus paralelo electrónico para una lengua minoritaria: el caso del español-náhuatl. In: Primer Congreso Internacional el Patrimonio Cultural y las Nuevas Tecnologías. Ina. (2015)
2. Hedderich, M.A., Lange, L., Adel, H., Strötgen, J., Klakow, D.: A survey on recent approaches for natural language processing in low-resource scenarios. In: Proceedings of the 2021 Conference of the North American Chapter of the Association for Computational Linguistics: Human Language Technologies, pp. 2545–2568 (2021)
3. Palacios-Díaz, R., Escudero-Nahón, A.: Revisión sistemática de los desafíos del uso de tecnología digital en la formación de investigadores. Educatcconciencia **26**(27), 147–178 (2020)
4. Singh, A.K.: Natural language processing for less privileged languages: where do we come from? Where are we going? In: Proceedings of the IJCNLP-08 Workshop on NLP for Less Privileged Languages, pp. 7–12, January 2008
5. Cieri, C., Maxwell, M., Strassel, S., Tracey, J.: Selection criteria for low resource language programs. In: Proceedings of the 10th International Conference on Language Resources and Evaluation, Lr. 2016, pp. 4543–4549 (2016)
6. Zacarías Márquez, D., Meza Ruiz, I.V.: Ayuuk-Spanish neural machine translator, pp. 168–172 (2021)
7. Knowles, R., Stewart, D., Larkin, S., Littell, P.: NRC-CNRC machine translation systems for the 2021 AmericasNLP shared task. In: Proceedings of the 1st Workshop on Natural Language Processing for Indigenous Languages of the Americas 2021, pp. 224–233 (2021)
8. Mager, M., et al.: Findings of the AmericasNLP 2021 shared task on open machine translation for indigenous languages of the Americas, pp. 202–217 (2021)
9. Vázquez, R., Scherrer, Y., Virpioja, S., Tiedemann, J.: The Helsinki submission to the AmericasNLP shared task. In: Proceedings of the 1st Workshop on Natural Language Processing for Indigenous Languages of the Americas 2021, pp. 255–264 (2021)
10. Zheng, F., Reid, M., Marrese-Taylor, E., Matsuo, Y.: Low-resource machine translation using cross-lingual language model pretraining, pp. 234–240 (2021)

11. Ahmadnia, B., Dorr, B.J., Aranovich, R.: Impact of filtering generated pseudo bilingual texts in low-resource neural machine translation enhancement: the case of Persian-Spanish. Procedia CIRP **189**, 136–141 (2021)
12. Ghafoor, A., et al.: The impact of translating resource-rich datasets to low-resource languages through multi-lingual text processing. IEEE Access **9**(2), 124478–124490 (2021)
13. Nekoto, W., et al.: Participatory research for low-resourced machine translation: a case study in African languages, pp. 2144–2160 (2020)
14. Imankulova, A., Sato, T., Komachi, M.: Filtered pseudo-parallel corpus improves low-resource neural machine translation. ACM Trans. Asian Low Resour. Lang. Inf. Process. **19**(2), 1–16 (2019)
15. Mager Hois, J.M., Barrón Romero, C., Meza Ruiz, I.V.: Traductor estadístico wixarika-español usando descomposición morfológica. COMTEL, pp. 63–68 (2016)
16. Pa, W.P., Thu, Y.K., Finch, A., Sumita, E.: A Study of statistical machine translation methods for under resourced languages. Procedia Comput. Sci. **81**, 250–257 (2016)
17. Sghaier, M.A., Zrigui, M.: Rule-based machine translation from Tunisian dialect to modern standard Arabic. Procedia Comput. Sci. **176**, 310–319 (2020)
18. Maimaiti, M., Liu, Y., Luan, H., Sun, M.: Enriching the transfer learning with pre-trained lexicon embedding for low-resource neural machine translation. Tsinghua Sci. Technol. **27**(1), 150–163 (2022)
19. Marie, B., Fujita, A.: Iterative training of unsupervised neural and statistical machine translation systems. ACM Trans. Asian Low Resour. Lang. Inf. Process. **19**(5), 1–21 (2020)
20. Yeong, Y.L., Tan, T.P., Mohammad, S.K.: Using dictionary and lemmatizer to improve low resource English-Malay statistical machine translation system. Procedia Comput. Sci. **81**, 243–249 (2016)
21. Ahmadnia, B., Dorr, B.J.: Low-resource multi-domain machine translation for Spanish-Farsi: neural or statistical? Procedia Comput. Sci. **177**, 575–580 (2020)
22. Li, H., Sha, J., Shi, C.: revisiting back-translation for low-resource machine translation between Chinese and Vietnamese. IEEE Access **8**, 119931–119939 (2020)
23. Mager, M., Meza, I.: Hacia La Traducción Automática De Las Lenguas Indígenas De México. Digital Humanities 2018, México City, pp. 1–7 (2018)
24. Papineni, K., Roukos, S., Ward, T., . Zhu, W.: BLEU: a method for automatic evaluation of machine translation. In: Proceeding of the 40th Annual Meeting of the Association for Computational Linguistics, pp. 311–318 (2002)
25. Papovic, M.: chrF: chareacter n-gram F-score for automatic MT evaluation. In: Proceedings of the Tenth Workshop on Statistical Machine Translation, pp. 392–395 (2015)
26. Snover, M., Dorr, B., Schwartz, R., Micciulla, L., Makhoul, J.: A study of translation edit rate with targeted human annotation. In: Proceedings of the 7th Conference of Association for Machine Translation in the Americas: Technical papers, Cambridge, Massachsetts, USA, pp. 223–231 (2006)
27. Zechner, K., Waibel, A.: Minimizing word error in textual summaries of spoken language. In: Proceedings of the 1st North American Chapter of the Association for Computational Linguistics Conference, pp. 186–193 (2000)

Comparison Between SVM and DistilBERT for Multi-label Text Classification of Scientific Papers Aligned with Sustainable Development Goals

Roberto Carlos Morales-Hernández[1], David Becerra-Alonso[2], Eduardo Romero Vivas[1], and Joaquín Gutiérrez[1](✉)

[1] Centro de Investigaciones Biológicas del Noroeste, S.C., Av. Instituto Politécnico Nacional 195, Playa Palo de Santa Rita, 23096 La Paz, B.C.S, México
joaquing04@cibnor.mx

[2] Department of Quantitative Methods, Universidad Loyola Andalucía, 41704 Seville, Spain

Abstract. The scientific articles identification with the 17 sustainable development goals of the UN 2030 Agenda is a valuable task for research and educational institutions. Finding an efficient and practical multi-label classification model using machine or deep learning remains relevant. This work refers to the performance comparison of a text classification model that combines Label Powerset (LP) and Support Vector Machine (SVM) against a transfer learning language model such as DistilBERT in 5 different imbalanced and balanced dataset scenarios of scientific papers. A proposed classification process was implemented with performance metrics, which have confirmed that the combination LP-SVM continues to be an option with remarkable results in multi-label text classification.

Keywords: Multi-label text classification · Label powerset · Support vector machine · Transfer learning · DistilBERT · Sustainable development goals

1 Introduction

For research centers and universities, identifying their scientific production with sustainable goals or policies becomes crucial to assess their contribution and influence. In this context, Natural Language Processing (NLP) through Machine or Deep Learning enables large-scale data handling for text classification. Text classification is a technique of text analysis to categorize data into different types, forms, or any other distinct predefined class [1]. According the number of classes, classification problems can be grouped in three types: Binary, Multi-class, and Multi-label.

In supervised learning, Multi-label Text Classification (MLTC) refers to models that learn from training data, to classify new instances by assigning a correct class label to each of them [2]. Binary classification algorithms, such as Support Vector Machine (SVM), Naive Bayes (NB), Random Forest (RF) or Logistic Regression (LR), need methods to transform the multi-label instances into a set of binary or multi-class datasets [3].

O. Pichardo Lagunas et al. (Eds.): MICAI 2022, LNAI 13613, pp. 57–67, 2022.
https://doi.org/10.1007/978-3-031-19496-2_5

Problem transformation methods like Binary Relevance (BR), Label Powerset (LP), or Classifier Chains (CC) remain convenient to this day to help binary algorithms for MLTC [4–8].

While in machine learning a combination of problem transformation method with a classification algorithm is a traditional model, in deep learning, transfer learning models such as BERT are pre-trained methods with the state-of-art performance in classification [9]. However, this pre-trained model could have the problem of consuming high computational resources, making it difficult to adopt. Nevertheless, more and more methods develop to create models to consume less resources based on BERT (DistilBERT [10], DocBERT [11], LegalDB [12], or TinyBERT [13]).

This paper aims to evaluate two MLTC models. One model, more traditional by combining LP with SVM, and the second one, by implementing a light and small pre-trained model, DistilBERT [10]. The database is a collection of scientific articles from the domain of knowledge in Organic Agriculture 3.0 aligned to the 17 Sustainable Development Goals (SDG) of the United Nations 2030 Agenda [14]. Likewise, the performance of the classification models is tested by proposing five scenarios with different balances and imbalances of the dataset.

The contributions of this project are as follows:

- Dataset creation with 31,434 scientific papers from year 2018 with title and abstract from organic agriculture 3.0 domain, labeled with the 17 SDG classification.
- LP-SVM results a competitive traditional model under the five dataset scenarios with balanced and imbalanced SDG labels.
- DistilBERT with a *minimum* configuration, evaluated under the five dataset scenarios of scientific papers with sustainable developments labels.

This research quantifies the performance of two MLTC models, comparing the LP-SVM and DistilBERT models to classify scientific articles (title and abstract) under the domain of organic agriculture.

2 Related Work

MLTC have different ways of being implemented. This section shows two widely used ways, a traditional machine learning combining a problem transformation method with a single-label classification algorithm, and a transfer learning model with a pre-trained method: DistilBERT.

2.1 Problem Transformation Method and Classification Algorithm

Unlike binary or multiclass text classification, MLTC presents more challenges because each text document can have multiple labels. It can find solutions through so-called multi-label learning methods such as Problem transformation, Problem Adaptation, and Ensemble [15, 16]. Problem transformation techniques change to one (or more binary) or multi-class datasets to be managed by single-label or multi-class classification algorithms [17].

LP is a problem transformation method. LP [18] transforms multi-labels from each instance into one single-label. This approach converts the multi-label problem in a multi-class classification. With this transformation, a single-label classifier such as SVM can perform the needed classification. LP has the advantage of taking label correlations into account albeit increasing the number of label classes, where most of them represent few or very few instances.

SVM is a linear classification model that maximizes the margin between data instances and a hyperplane, acting as a division boundary [19]. Some studies maintain the experimentation and performance evaluation with acceptable results of SVM as a multi-label classifier [20–22].

2.2 Transfer Learning Model

For NLP, another relevant area of study with an influence and paradigm change has been transfer learning where different types of word embeddings and pre-trained language models are proposed. Transfer learning refers more specifically to pre-trained language representations [1]. NLP has two types of pre-trained languages representations: feature-based and fine-tuning models. The first are often used to initialize the first layer of a neural network, the latter are fine-tuned as an entire model for a specific downstream task [9].

To create a lighter version of BERT, in DistilBERT the token-type embeddings and the pooler are removed from the architecture, thus reducing the number of layers by a factor of 2 [23]. Knowledge distillation is a compression technique in which a compact model - the student - is trained to reproduce the behavior of a larger model - the teacher - or an ensemble of models [10].

Comparison studies between SVM and a pre-trained model for classification continue to be carried out, which is why SVM performance evaluations remain current in a wide variety of scenarios, beyond the performance level that pre-trained models generally present [21, 24–27].

3 Methodology

3.1 Framework for Multi-label Text Classification

The proposed framework to classify scientific articles into 17 SDG multi-label data classes is described in Fig. 1. It shows a typical MLTC pipeline to apply classification methods in four condensed phases: Information Retrieval and Dataset Creation, Data Analysis and Preprocessing, Model Building, and Model Evaluation.

Information Retrieval and Dataset Creation. A first phase where data collection is attained from bibliographic resources. The dataset used here was obtained from Dimensions, a bibliographic database produced by the company Digital Science, who offers a feasible categorization scheme in scientific papers for the seventeen SDG [28]. Scientific articles had three features: Title, Abstract and labels of the 17 SDGs of the UN 2030 Agenda (Table 1). For this study, year 2018 was selected to create dataset from the dominion organic agriculture 3.0.

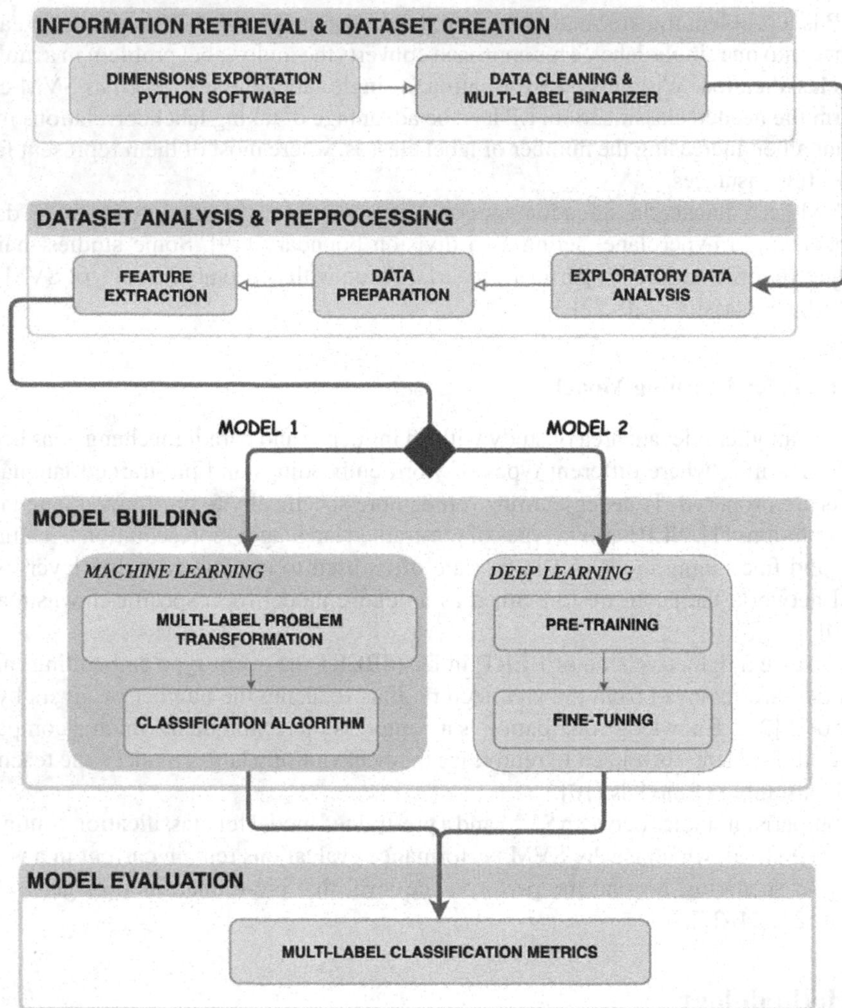

Fig. 1. Framework for the comparison experiment of text classification models

Data Analysis and Preprocessing. In this second phase, a relevant dataset preprocessing involves the extraction of text to create clean word sequences. Also, in this stage, datasets are created and adjusted in label distribution for classification model evaluation according to experimental requirements. Stop-word elimination, stemming and tokenization are pre-processing tools. Term Frequency-Inverse Document Frequency (TF-IDF) is used as a feature extraction method. TF-IDF can describe how important the word is in a text and is applied as a weighting factor in text mining [29].

Table 1. Sustainable development goals from United Nations Agenda 2030.

Sustainable Development Goals (SDG) from UN Agenda 2030		
SDG1 No Poverty	**SDG7** Affordable and Clean Energy	**SDG13** Climate Action
SDG2 Zero Hunger	**SDG8** Decent Work and Economic Growth	**SDG14** Life Below Water
SDG3 Good Health and Well-being	**SDG9** Industry, Innovation, and Infrastructure	**SDG15** Life on Land
SDG4 Quality Education	**SDG10** Reducing Inequality	**SDG16** Peace, Justice, and Strong Institutions
SDG5 Gender Equality	**SDG11** Sustainable Cities and Communities	**SDG17** Partnerships for the Goals
SDG6 Clean Water and Sanitation	**SDG12** Responsible Consumption and Production	

Model Building. This is a stage where classification models are established, configured, and run. According to Fig. 1, Model 1 is constructed with LP as the problem transformation method to convert the multi-label to multi-class classification from SVMV as classification algorithm. Scikit-multilearn is a multi-label classification software module that builds on top of the scikit-learn python framework with transformation methods such as LP. SVM algorithm is implemented through scikit-learn, a tool for predictive data analysis.

In Model 2, the pre-training phase refers to distilbert-base-uncased model as a distilled version of the BERT [9] base model to tokenize the data (distilbert-base-uncased has 66 million parameters against 110 million for BERT-base). For the model construction, maximum length Bert tokenizer, learning rate, batch size, epochs, its loss, and an optimizer are parameters to be defined in this step. For this project, in the fine-tunning stage, a training function is defined to train the neural network on the training dataset via pytorch. Parameters are default values, and none of their respective hyperparameters are optimized in both models. This criterion enables a fair comparison among the methods.

Model Evaluation. Three multi-label classification metrics are selected to evaluate the experiment multi-label classification models: Accuracy, F1-Score (micro), and Hamming loss. Accuracy is defined as the ratio of observations predicted correctly to the total number of observations. Hamming loss refers to an average binary classification error [30] represented by the fraction of labels that are incorrectly predicted. F1-Score (micro) is the harmonic mean (weighted) of Recall (the ratio of true positives to the sum of true positives and false negatives across all labels) and Precision (refers to the percentage of predicted labels that are relevant) [30].

4 Model Experiments

This section presents several experiments with different dataset scenarios to find performance for the two multi-label text classification models, according to Fig. 1.

4.1 Dataset

For this experiment, dataset creation was produced from Dimensions with organic agriculture 3.0 as a knowledge domain from 2018. Total instances collected with SDG labels: 31,434. This study proposed five different dataset scenarios described in Table 2. These dataset scenarios let discover the performance for both proposed MLTC models. For the SC2, SC3, and SC4 scenarios, six SDG tags were discarded for having less than 1,000 instances and being considered noisy tags (SDG 1, 5, 8, 9, 10, and 17). Scenario 4 (SC4) involved creating, in turn, 11 datasets. In each one, a label has the number of instances equal to the sum of the remaining 10 labels. In SC4, classification models are applied to each dataset and the average is the result presented.

Table 2. 2018 Dataset scenarios for classification models performance evaluation.

Five Dataset Scenarios	Instances		
	Total	Train 66%	Test 33%
SC1. Imbalanced with all 17 SDG labels	31,434	20,745	10,687
SC2.Imbalanced with 11 SDG labels greater than 1,000 examples	30,480	20,098	10,353
SC3. Balanced with equal number of instances in 11 SDG labels	13,623	7,791	4,014
SC4. *Extreme* imbalanced (10 to 1) from one label vs other 10 labels	5,310*	3,540	1,770
SC5. Instances with only one SDG label (multi-class)	27,400	18,084	9,316
*Average			

4.2 Data Preprocessing

The dataset undergoes feature selection implemented with libraries, such as: Re (for symbol filtering), NLTK (for stop words removal), NumPy (for rows randomization), and scikit-learn (for tokenization). The feature extraction was made vectorizing with TF-IDF from scikit-learn. Databases were split for training and test with a 2:1 ratio.

4.3 Models Building

In Model 1, the LP-SVM model is configured with default values and none of its hyperparameters are optimized, both for the problem transformation method LP and the classification algorithm SVM.

For Model 2, the transfer learning model, DistilBERT pre-trained features are selected using the distilbert-base-uncased model, i.e., the distilled version of the BERT base model [9] to tokenize the data. For the training/fine-tunning stage, the PyTorch library defines a series of minimal standard parametrizations that shape and control the data pre-processing and its passage to the neural network: batch size (4), maximum length (128), optimizer (Adam), learning rate (1-e-15), and epochs (3).

4.4 Model Evaluation

Scikit-learn library in Python offers a series of reports for the quantitative model evaluation for classification. Accuracy, F1-Score (micro) and Hamming loss are the performance metrics relevant for this experiment.

5 Results and Discussion

This section discusses in detail the results obtained for the individual models. Table 3 presents the accuracy, F1 (micro), and Hamming loss results for both classification models under five dataset scenarios.

In SC1, in accuracy, LP-SVM had a better performance with respect to DistilBERT by less than 2%. It is remarkable that LP-SVM achieves 81% in accuracy with standard parameters provided by the scikit-learn library. SC1 features the closest performance between both models.

Eliminating noisy labels in SC2, SC3, and SC4, yields slight improvements on both models. However, LP-SVM had a higher enhancement than DistilBERT (Fig. 2). For instance, in F1 (micro), while in DistilBERT the improvement is around 2%, for LP-SVM the improvement was 5%.

Table 3. Comparison of Accuracy, F1 and Hamming loss scores of DistilBERT and LP-SVM on the five Dataset Scenarios

Metric	Model	Dataset Scenarios				
		SC1	SC2	SC3	SC4	SC5
Accuracy	DistilBERT	0.791	0.813	0.787	0.736	0.875
	LP-SVM	**0.809**	**0.868**	**0.833**	**0.756**	**0.893**
F1-score (micro)	DistilBERT	0.855	0.874	0.858	0.826	0.892
	LP-SVM	0.855	**0.901**	**0.870**	**0.834**	**0.893**
Hamming loss	DistilBERT	0.018	0.024	0.028	**0.032**	0.019
	LP-SVM	0.018	**0.022**	**0.025**	0.034	**0.013**

In SC3, with balanced instances, both models had an acceptable performance with few differences between them.

SC4 has the worst performance for both models due to the low number of instances.

Finally, in SC5 (multi-class dataset) both models had the best performance in accuracy, LP-SVM with 89% and DistilBert with 88%.

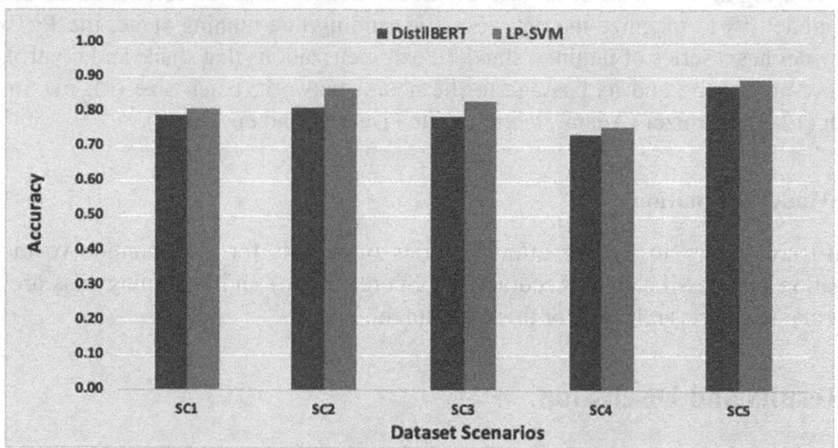

Fig. 2. Accuracy comparison of DistilBERT and LP-SVM in five dataset scenarios.

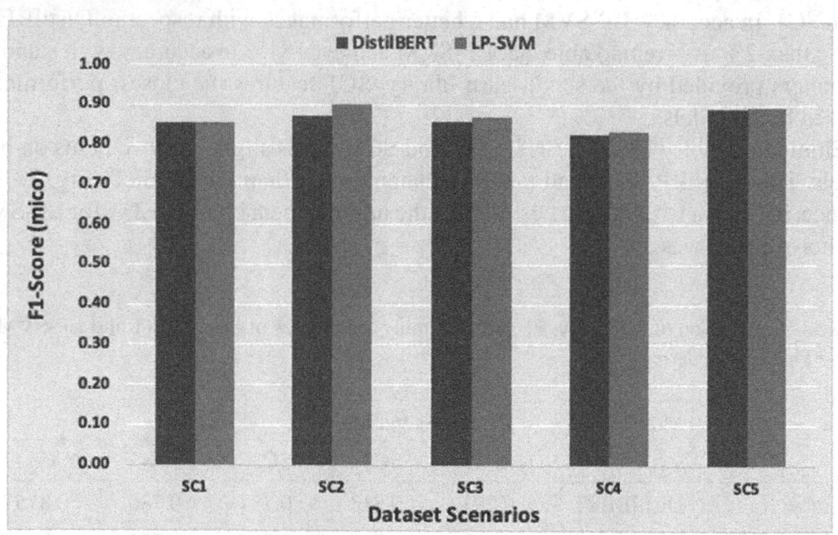

Fig. 3. F1-Score (micro) comparison of DistilBERT and LP-SVM in five dataset scenarios.

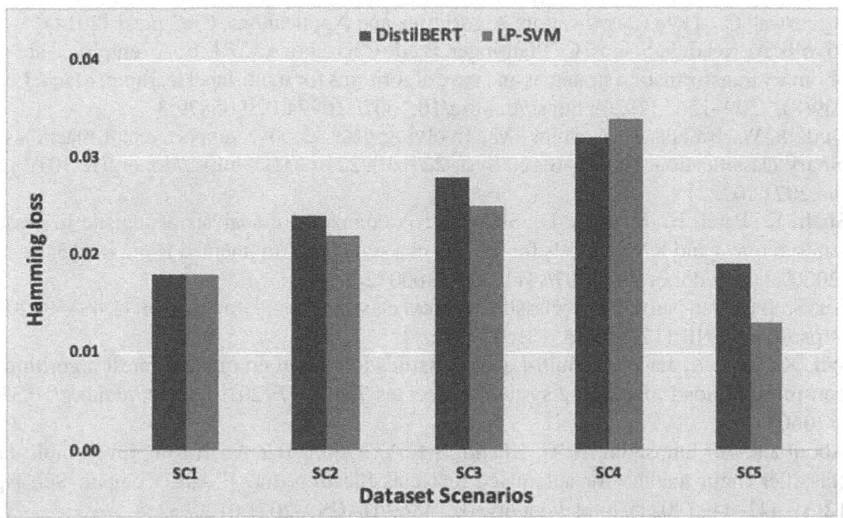

Fig. 4. Hamming loss comparison of DistilBERT and LP-SVM in five dataset scenarios.

6 Conclusion and Future Work

This study presented a comparison review of multi-label text classification models based on their performance. The results support the framework that implemented a combination of transformation methods with classification algorithms and a pre-trained model with acceptable classification performance.

LP-SVM, even with default parameters, had a remarkable result from almost all scenarios.

DistilBert, with similar results compared to the other model, has the disadvantage of requiring more computer resources and this is a disadvantage for some institutions that wish to implement the recognition of their academic products aligned with the SDGs. Thus, this study confirms the complexity of pre-trained models and the need to deepen the tuning of the model. Future work includes defining adjustments to hyperparameters in both models and quantifying performance improvements.

Institutions with little computing resource capacity can implement LP-SVM to classify their scientific production with respect to the SDG.

For future work, the dataset with organic agriculture 3.0 as a dominant theme could be a promising source of information. Topic modeling and recognition of emerging trends could bring opportunities for data mining and knowledge management applying artificial intelligence.

References

1. Medina, S.R., Niamir, A., Dadvar, M.: Multi-Label Text Classification with Transfer Learning for Policy Documents The Case of the Sustainable Development Goals. Uppsala University (2019)

2. Aggarwal, C. .:Data Classification: Algorithms and Applications. CRC press (2014)
3. Rivolli, A., Read, J., Soares, C., Pfahringer, B., de Carvalho, A.C.P.L.F.: An empirical analysis of binary transformation strategies and base algorithms for multi-label learning. Mach. Learn. **109**(8), 1509–1563 (2020). https://doi.org/10.1007/s10994-020-05879-3
4. Dudzik, W., Nalepa, J., Kawulok, M.: Evolving data-adaptive support vector machines for binary classification. Knowl.-Based Syst. **227**, 107221 (2021). https://doi.org/10.1016/j.knosys.2021.107221
5. Shah, K., Patel, H., Sanghvi, D., Shah, M.: A comparative analysis of logistic regression, random forest and KNN models for the text classification. Augmented Hum. Res. **5**(1), 1–16 (2020). https://doi.org/10.1007/s41133-020-00032-0
6. Xu, S.: Bayesian Naïve Bayes classifiers to text classification. J. Inf. Sci. **44**(1), 48–59 (2018). https://doi.org/10.1177/0165551516677946
7. Wu, X., Gao, Y., Jiao, D.: Multi-Label classification based on random forest algorithm for non-intrusive load monitoring system. Processes **7**(6), 337 (2019). https://doi.org/10.3390/pr7060337
8. Abdullahi, A., Samsudin, N.A., Khalid, S.K.A., Othman, Z.A.: An improved multi-label classifier chain method for automated text classification. Int. J. Adv. Comput. Sci. Appl. **12**(3), 442–449 (2021). https://doi.org/10.14569/IJACSA.2021.0120352
9. Devlin, J., Chang, M.-W., Lee, K., Toutanova, K.: BERT: pre-training of deep bidirectional transformers for language understanding. In: Proceedings of the 2019Conference of the North American Chapter of the Association for Computational Linguistics: Human Language Technologies, pp. 4171– 4186 (2019). Available: http://arxiv.org/abs/1810.04805
10. Sanh, V., Debut, L., Chaumond, J., Wolf, T.: DistilBERT, a distilled version of BERT: smaller, faster, cheaper and lighter. In: Proceedings of the 5th Workshop on Energy Efficient Machine Learning and Cognitive Computing (EMC2) co-located with the Thirty-third Conference on Neural Information Processing Systems (NeurIPS 2019), pp. 1–5 (2019). Available: http://arxiv.org/abs/1910.01108
11. Adhikari, A., Ram, A., Tang, R., Lin, J..: DocBERT: BERT for document classification. In: Proceedings of the 5th Workshop on Representation Learning for NLP, pp. 72–77 (2020). Accessed: 26 Jun 2022. [Online]. Available: https://aclanthology.org/2020.repl4nlp-1.10.pdf
12. Bambroo P., Awasthi, A.: LegalDB: long distilbert for legal document classification. In: Proceedings of the 2021 1st International Conference on Advances in Electrical, Computing, Communications and Sustainable Technologies, ICAECT 2021 (2021). https://doi.org/10.1109/ICAECT49130.2021.9392558
13. Jiao, X., Hui, K., Sun, L., Sun, Y.: TinyBERT: distilling BERT for natural language understanding. In: Findings of the Association for Computational Linguistics: EMNLP 2020, pp. 4163–4174 (2020). Accessed: 26 May 2022 [Online]. Available: https://aclanthology.org/2020.findings-emnlp.372.pdf
14. United-Nations, "Resolution 70/1. Transforming our world: the 2030 Agenda for Sustainable Development," United Nations (2015)
15. Madjarov, G., Kocev, D., Gjorgjevikj, D., Džeroski, S.: An extensive experimental comparison of methods for multi-label learning. Pattern Recogn. **45**(9), 3084–3104 (2012). https://doi.org/10.1016/j.patcog.2012.03.004
16. Tsoumakas, G., Katakis, I.: Multi-Label classification: an overview. Int. J. Data Warehouse. Min. **3**(3), 1–13 (2007). https://doi.org/10.4018/jdwm.2007070101
17. Read, J.: Advances in Multi-label Classification (2011)
18. Tsoumakas, G., Vlahavas, I.: Random k-labelsets: an ensemble method for multilabel classification. In: Kok, J.N., Koronacki, J., Mantaras, R.L.D., Matwin, S., Mladenič, D., Skowron, A. (eds.) Machine Learning: ECML 2007. Lecture Notes in Computer Science (Lecture Notes in Artificial Intelligence), vol. 4701, pp. 406–417. Springer, Heidelberg (2007). https://doi.org/10.1007/978-3-540-74958-5_38

19. Cortes, C., Vapnik, V.: Support-vector networks. Mach. Learn. **20**(3), 273–297 (1995)
20. Cervantes, J., Garcia-Lamont, F., Rodríguez-Mazahua, L., Lopez, A.: A comprehensive survey on support vector machine classification: applications, challenges and trends. Neurocomputing **408**, 189–215 (2020). https://doi.org/10.1016/j.neucom.2019.10.118
21. Hana, K.M., Adiwijaya, S., Faraby, A., Bramantoro, A.: Multi-label classification of Indonesian hate speech on Twitter using support vector machines. In: 2020 International Conference on Data Science and Its Applications (ICoDSA), pp. 1–7 (2020). https://doi.org/10.1109/ICoDSA50139.2020.9212992
22. Saeed, S., Ong, H.C.: Performance of SVM with multiple kernel learning for classification tasks of imbalanced datasets. Pertanika J. Sci. Technol. **27**(1), 527–545 (2019)
23. Büyüköz, B., Hürriyetoğlu, A., Özgür, A.: Analyzing ELMo and DistilBERT on socio-political news classification. In: Proceedings of the Workshop on Automated Extraction of Socio-political Events from News 2020, pp. 9–18 (2020). Available: https://www.aclweb.org/anthology/2020.aespen-1.4
24. Clavié, B., Alphonsus, M.: The unreasonable effectiveness of the baseline: discussing SVMs in legal text classification. Front. Artif. Intell. Appl. **346**, 58–61 (2021). https://doi.org/10.3233/FAIA210317
25. Menger, V., Scheepers, F., Spruit, M.: Comparing deep learning and classical machine learning approaches for predicting inpatient violence incidents from clinical text. Appl. Sci. (Switzerland) **8**(6), (2018). https://doi.org/10.3390/app8060981
26. Alammary, A.S.: BERT models for Arabic text classification: a systematic review. Appl. Sci. **12**(11), 5720 (2022). https://doi.org/10.3390/app12115720
27. Lagutina, K.: Topical text classification of Russian news: a comparison of BERT and standard models. In: 2022 31st Conference of Open Innovations Association (FRUCT), pp. 160–166 (2022). https://doi.org/10.23919/FRUCT54823.2022.9770920
28. Wastl, J., Porter, S., Draux, H., Fane, B., Hook, D.: Contextualizing sustainable development research. Digit. Sci. (2020). Available: https://doi.org/10.6084/m9.figshare.12200081
29. Mishra, A., Vishwakarma, S.: Analysis of TF-IDF model and its variant for document retrieval. In: 2015 International Conference on Computational Intelligence and Communication Networks (CICN), pp. 772–776 (2015). https://doi.org/10.1109/CICN.2015.157
30. Nasierding, G., Kouzani, A.Z.: Comparative evaluation of multi-label classification methods. In: Proceedings - 2012 9th International Conference on Fuzzy Systems and Knowledge Discovery, FSKD 2012, pp. 679–683 (2012). https://doi.org/10.1109/FSKD.2012.6234347

A Hybrid Methodology Based on CRISP-DM and TDSP for the Execution of Preprocessing Tasks in Mexican Environmental Laws

Yessenia Díaz Álvarez[1], Miguel Ángel Hidalgo Reyes[1](✉), Virginia Lagunes Barradas[1], Obdulia Pichardo Lagunas[2], and Bella Martínez Seis[2]

[1] Instituto Tecnológico Superior de Xalapa (ITSX), Subdirección de Posgrado e Investigación, Maestría en Sistemas Computacionales, Xalapa, Veracruz, México
{217000013,miguel.hidalgo}@itsx.edu.mx, virginia.lb@xalapa.tecnm.mx

[2] Unidad Profesional Interdisciplinaria en Ingeniería y Tecnologías Avanzadas (UPIITA), Instituto Politécnico Nacional (IPN), Ciudad de México, México
{opichardola,bcmartinez}@ipn.mx

Abstract. This article focuses on the one hand, on showing some techniques applied during the preprocessing of texts represented by environmental laws of Mexico. The need to carry out this type of analysis is due to several factors such as: the large number of existing legislative documents such as laws, programs, regulations, etc., the modifications that are made to the legal system due to reforms and decrees, and especially, to those possible contradictions that may arise among one or more laws. On the other hand, certain tasks of the CRISP-DM methodology were selected and, specifically, for the data preparation phase in the generic tasks of selection, cleaning, transformation, and formatting. This was done using the NLTK library through text preprocessing techniques of tokenization, segmentation, denoising and normalization. Among the most remarkable results there is a combination between CRISP-DM and Team Data Science Process by Microsoft oriented to the preprocessing of Mexican federal environmental laws. In addition, this article shows a detailed application of the hybrid methodology with the execution of a specialized task related to the extraction of text from a pdf file using the PyPDF2 and Pdfplumber libraries.

Keywords: Text mining · Preprocessing · Environmental laws · Methodologies · NLTK

1 Introduction

Based on the idea that relevant information and, therefore, practical knowledge for better decision making can be obtained from adequate data processing, this research focused on analyzing the importance of generating an adequate methodology for one of the phases prior to data mining. This phase, generically called data preprocessing, is made up of several tasks that must be carried out using a methodological guide.

O. Pichardo Lagunas et al. (Eds.): MICAI 2022, LNAI 13613, pp. 68–82, 2022.
https://doi.org/10.1007/978-3-031-19496-2_6

The fundamental purpose of preprocessing or data preparation is to manipulate and transform raw data so that the information content enfolded in the data set can be exposed or made easily accessible [1]. Without proper data preparation, the return on the resources invested in data mining could be a waste of time.

This project has paid attention on both local news and academic work. In the case of the news already published, they claim the development of sustainable public policies [2] under assumption that environmental legislation needs to be analyzed to detect possible flaws or inconsistencies and, also, to seek the application of such laws to guarantee the protection of ecosystems from risks and threats [3].

An important example is the case of La Paila, Municipality of Alto Lucero, Veracruz, where substantive sections of environmental laws have been ignored, such as the prevention of environmental impact assessment by the authority, and therefore, environmental protection and sustainable development, as dictated by our laws, have been disregarded [4].

In the academic context, work has been presented in computational learning seminars on the application of artificial intelligence in favor of the environment [5]. Also, the Data Science team of the Interdisciplinary Professional Unit in Engineering and Advanced Technologies of the National Polytechnic Institute (UPIITA-IPN) in liaison with the Institute of Ecology (INECOL), have recognized some challenges, such as the lack of uniformity in the structure of Mexican legislation and the need to develop computational tools to assist in the syntactic and semantic analysis of legislative documents on environmental matters [6].

These are just two examples of many others where the lack of precision among the federal and general laws might produce ambiguity in the decision-making process.

The research presented in this paper makes use of the features of two methodologies that guide the life cycle of the data mining project, (CRoss Industry Standard Process for Data Mining) CRISP-DM, (Team Data Science Process) TDSP, and an additional step oriented to the validation of the data preparation phase. Consequently, this paper proposes a hybrid methodology applied to the preprocessing of Mexican environmental laws.

After analyzing some research related to the topic of study, IBM has a white paper that mentions a 10-step methodology in which it recognizes the incorporation of text analytics as a way of using text information into predictive models. It emerges as an iterative process capable of providing a strategy, independent of the technologies, data volumes or approaches involved [7]. Additionally, IBM extended CRISP-DM in its deployment phase and added activities related to project management and operational and proposed a methodology called Analytics Solution Unified Method (ASUM) [8].

Unlike IBM, Microsoft created TDSP as a data science methodology focused on collaborative work and the use of industry-recognized best practices. Among the components it defines we find interesting its standardized project structure and the resources for data science projects [9].

In [10] the authors conducted a systematic literature review on the adaptations of data mining methodologies. It is noteworthy to highlight that in this work ASUM appears as the latest methodology that combines CRISP-DM with another approach, in this case, agile implementation.

Another finding shows that in the period 2008 - 2018 the application of CRISP-DM methodology as it is, fell to 32%, with respect to the period 1997 - 2007. This downward trend shows that CRISP-DM seeks to adapt to specific project needs.

In summary, CRISP-DM adaptations considered three categories: modification, extension, and integration. Among these adaptations, and for the purposes of this research, the update of CRISP-DM with respect to big data technologies, environments and infrastructure stands out.

In [11] the authors performed a study on the extension and adaptation of data mining processes for the financial services industry. From among the papers analyzed, they grouped six categories into 18 perceived gaps. The category identified as process refers to those enablers that are absent and are related to data, code, tools, and infrastructure, i.e., the technical context for a data mining project.

With the purpose of generating a methodology focused on the preprocessing of Mexican environmental laws, this paper proposes a hybrid methodology that takes advantages of certain elements of CRISP-DM and TDSP to obtain a structured corpus ready to be analyzed by means of natural language processing techniques.

Therefore, this article defines in Sect. 2 the conceptualization of the hybrid methodology, then develops its application in a use case with a generic data preparation task in Sect. 3, and in Sect. 4 the results obtained such as the problems identified, and their proposed solution are presented.

2 Methodology Conceptualization for the Preprocessing of Legislative Documents

The CRISP-DM process model was introduced at the end of 1996 as an industry initiative to apply the data mining process to the business operations of companies [12]. However, this methodology is still widely used within organizations conducting a data mining/science project as stated by some polls published in web portals [13].

By 2008, the CRISP-DM 2.0 special interest group was created with the intention of updating the process towards a more adaptable version, however, the main results have not been reported in the community to date. Since 2009, Marbán et al., recognized that data mining should adopt the engineering path, because CRISP-DM did not cover tasks and processes as in the case of software engineering and, therefore, it was necessary to borrow ideas from this area to generate a comprehensive process model for data mining [14].

In 2019, Martínez-Plumed et al., published an analysis, 20 years after the emergence of CRISP-DM [15], asking to what extent is CRISP-DM still applicable to data science projects. One of the insights of this work is that data science presents new activities, and it is necessary to define exploratory trajectories according to the nature of each type of project.

On the one hand, previous works make it clear that the data being generated today has new properties such as velocity, variability, and volume, widely presented in the big data paradigm, and on the other hand, these data are part of the types of data science projects that use, for example, audio, text, images, maps, among others.

For this research, the data of interest are the legislative documents on environmental matters and the development of this project has also required collaborative work with policy experts, lawyers, and specialists in the field. Among the initial tasks carried out with the group of experts, one of these consisted of recognizing the different categories that legislative documents have, for example, federal laws and general laws, regulations, among others. Based on a previous selection of legislative documents, the selected laws for this research are presented in Sect. 3.1.

In the following subsections we describe the preprocessing methodology and its application to specialized tasks for text preprocessing.

2.1 Methodology Description

There are works that have taken advantage of specific data mining methodologies and have proposed a combination of these. For example, Fois et al. [16] carried out a comparative analysis of TDSP and Analytics Solutions Unified Method for Data Mining (ASUM-DM), highlighting that both adopt an agile approach, despite some conceptual differences and their different forms of application.

The hybrid methodology proposed in this article combines specific elements of CRISP-DM, TDSP and the experimental process defined by McGeoch [17]. The integration of the proposed methodologies allows CRISP-DM to be extended to the specific needs of this research, according to experts who have used it in practice.

CRISP-DM remains successful because it is based on practical, real-world experience, thanks to its hierarchical process, consisting of phases and generic tasks. In that sense, this project follows the phases established by the model, however, in this proposal we use the first three phases due to the main objective of obtaining a specialized corpus of Mexican environmental laws.

The phases and generic tasks used in this project are shown in Fig. 1, and they compliant with the main objective mentioned on previous paragraph. It is important to mention that generic data preparation tasks indicated by CRISP-DM are oriented to tabular data, where records represent the raw data from which it is possible to derive new attributes or integrate records from different sources.

In the case of this project, environmental laws are examples of data whose cleaning and formatting are not fully described by CRISP-DM and, therefore, it is necessary to select one generic task but to customize its treatment towards the performance of specialized tasks and to adopt exploratory approaches such as TDSP.

This means that documents require specific data preprocessing and CRISP-DM requires an extension to successfully execute projects related to natural language processing and based on a specialized domain corpus.

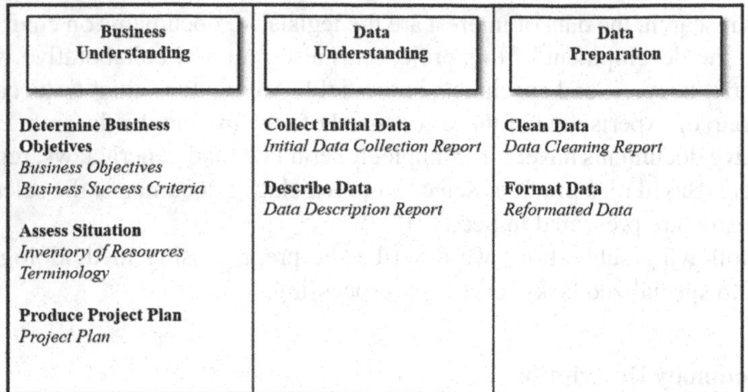

Business Understanding
Data Understanding
Data Preparation
Determine Business Objetives
Business Objectives
Business Success Criteria
Assess Situation
Inventory of Resources
Terminology
Produce Project Plan
Project Plan
Collect Initial Data
Initial Data Collection Report
Describe Data
Data Description Report
Clean Data
Data Cleaning Report
Format Data
Reformatted Data

Fig. 1. Phases accompanied by generic tasks (bold) and outputs (italic) [3]

Regarding the TDSP methodology and analyzing its description from Microsoft's official website [9], we find that it handles similar elements to CRISP-DM, such as phases and tasks. In addition, it defines other novel components such as roles and artifacts. However, the most attractive contribution of TDSP for this research is found in the recommendations for structuring and standardizing the project, the definition of the organization of the code and the templates for documenting the project.

Another advantage of TDSP is that it uses an infrastructure that can be implemented through different types of tools that allow the automation of certain tasks, such as the creation of the repository, cloning the project repository, among others.

In our project, the infrastructure begins with a local directory structure and, later we plan to migrate that structure to the cloud. The storage of the information considers both, the data in original or raw format (PDF format) and pre-processed, in plain text and JSON (JavaScript Object Notation) format.

Figure 2 shows the folder structure and templates required for project documentation. The folders and templates are distinct artifacts that are associated with the deliverables defined in Fig. 1 of this section.

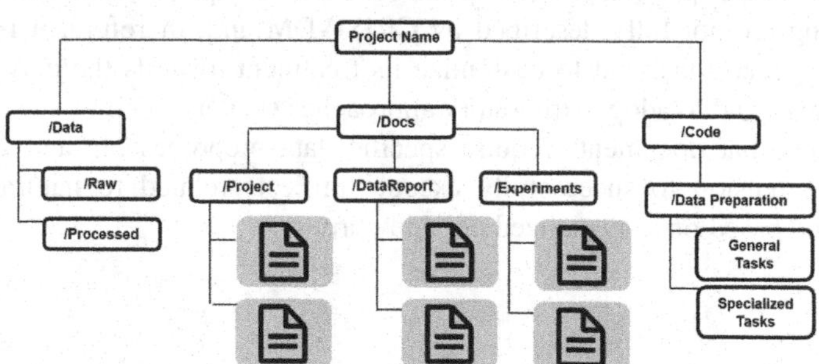

Fig. 2. Directory structure for project management.

The directory structure already defines standard names and locations; however, we created a directory called *experiments* that includes the configuration scripts and the experimental results report. About the deliverables for our phases, 5 of them are contemplated for the business understanding, 2 for the data understanding and 2 for the data preparation.

TDSP focuses on collaboration and teamwork as well. In this sense, this project intends to cover various roles in the category of individual project collaborators, e.g., policy experts, environmental specialists, among others.

Lastly, this project includes a phase related to the validation of the data preparation phase by means of an experimental process with the aim of systematically plan and execute testing strategies, for example, programming libraries specially coded for text mining and natural language processing. McGeoch's experimental guide is shown in Fig. 3.

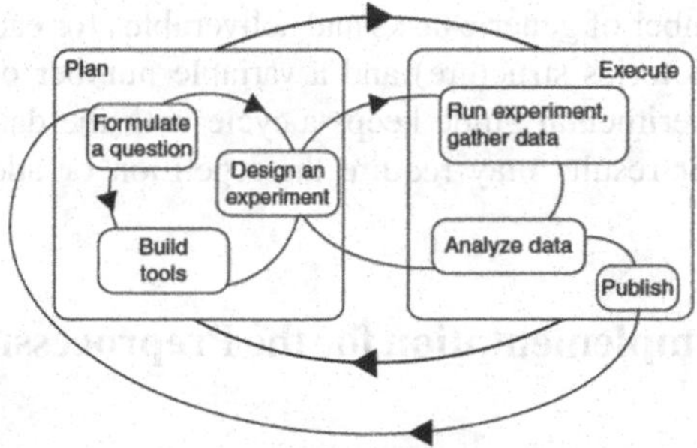

Fig. 3. The experimental process proposed by Catherine McGeogh [5].

Figure 3 shows two stages of an experiment. The first one is the planning of the experiment, where we start with the formulation of a question and build or use tools (programming scripts, software packages) that allow us to design a specific experiment (variables to be measured, size of documents). Then, in the execution stage, the experiment is run, and the collected data are analyzed and published within academia and research.

The cycles included in the figure indicate that, in the planning stage, the steps can be performed in any order; on the other hand, the analyzed data may suggest further questions that cause alternating between these two phases and starting a new experiment.

Hence, the hybrid methodology is presented in Fig. 4.

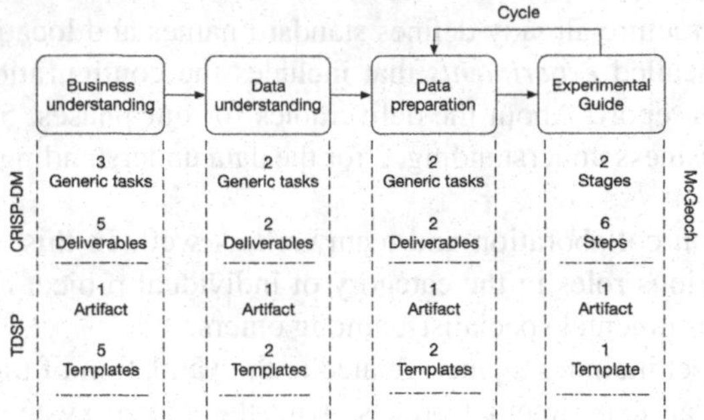

Fig. 4. Hybrid methodology with interaction between CRISP-DM, TDSP and McGeoch for the preprocessing of environmental laws.

The figure above shows the hybrid methodology, composed of the 3 phases of CRISP-DM, as well as the number of generic tasks and deliverables for each phase. TDSP adds a general artifact (directories structure) and a variable number of templates for each phase. Finally, the experimental guide keeps a cycle with the data preparation phase, as the analysis of their results may require the repetition or addition of specialized preprocessing tasks.

3 Methodology Implementation for the Preprocessing of Legislative Documents

This section shows the application of the hybrid methodology in the preprocessing of laws within the Mexican environmental domain.

3.1 Judiciary of Mexico

The Mexican state has a division of government authorities, namely the executive, the legislative and the judiciary. Each of these authorities has its own sphere of action, its own organizational structure and a set of functions and responsibilities [18].

The legislative authority is placed in the Congress of the Union, which is composed of the Deputies Chamber and the Senators Chamber. The Congress oversees issuing laws that regulate the internal structure and functioning of the Mexican Republic.

When talking about legislative documents, we start with the Federal Constitution or the Political Constitution of the United Mexican States. However, there are other important documents such as laws, regulations, norms, plans, programmes, strategies, agreements, and guidelines. In this project, and with the support of a group of expert researchers in public policies, nine environmental laws have been chosen for the case of Mexico.

The laws, which are the object of analysis for this research, are the following [19]:

1. General Law on Ecological Equilibrium and Environmental Protection (LGEEPA).
2. Law on National Waters (LAN).

3. Law on Sustainable Rural Development (LDRS).
4. General Law on Fishing and Sustainable Aquaculture (LGPAS).
5. General Law on Wildlife (LGVS).
6. General Law on Sustainable Forestry Development (LGDFS).
7. General Law for the Prevention and Integrated Management of Waste (LGPGIR).
8. Federal Law on Biosafety of Genetically Modified Organisms (LBOGM).
9. General Law on Climate Change (LGCC).

3.2 Text Preprocessing Use Case for Environmental Laws

Based on Fig. 4 (Sect. 2.1) the interaction between CRISP-DM, TDSP and the experimental process, is shown in Table 1:

Table 1. Hybrid methodology application.

Generic Task	Deliverable	Description	Artifacts directory	Template
Business understanding phase				
Determine business objectives	Business objectives	Describe the primary goal of the customer from a business point of view	/Docs/Project	Business goals
	Business success criteria	Describe the criteria for a useful outcome to the project from the business perspective	/Docs/Project	Business success criteria
Assess situation	Inventory of resources	Hardware, software, and human resources	/Docs/Project	Resources inventory
	Terminology	Concepts from Mexican legislation, natural language processing and text mining	/Docs/Project	Terminology
Produce project plan	Project Plan	List resources required, roles, responsibilities and costs and benefits	/Docs/Project	Initial project plan

(*continued*)

Table 1. (*continued*)

Generic Task	Deliverable	Description	Artifacts directory	Template
Data understanding phase				
Collect initial data	Initial data collection report	List documents together with their location and procedure to access them	/Data/Raw	Initial data collection report
Describe data	Data description report	Describe the data that has been acquired, including it format, quantity, and fields' identities	/Docs/Data	Data description report
Data preparation phase				
Clean data	Data cleaning report	Describe transformations of the data for cleaning purposes	/Docs/Data	Data cleaning report
Format data	Reformatted data	Describe syntactic changes made to satisfy the business goal	/Docs/Data	Data reformatted report
Experimental Process				
Formulate a question	Questions to gain insight	Informal or directed questions based on raw data	/Docs/ Experiments	Goals Questions report
Build tools	Software and hardware tools	Select programming IDE, text mining or NLP libraries and test environment	/Docs/ Experiments	Tools report
Design exp	Experiment plan	Review parameters to be measured, input sizes and statistical model strategy	/Docs/ Experiments	Experiment plan

(*continued*)

Table 1. (*continued*)

Generic Task	Deliverable	Description	Artifacts directory	Template
Run exp	Experiment tests	Execute a fixed or variable number of runs	/Data/ Processed	Processed data
Analyze data	Data efficiency analysis	Testing of the hypotheses generated from the questions, efficiency analysis, version and error control	/Docs/ Experiments	Data efficiency report
Publish	Test results	Results publication and start the process over again	/Docs/ Experiments	Test report

4 Validation of the Results

Considering the interactions resulting from the above methodologies, their implementation is divided into the subsections according to the phases and showing an extract of their deliverables.

4.1 Business Understanding Deliverables

Business Objective: Generating a specialized corpus from nine federal laws, to perform a set of analyses using text mining and NLP techniques.

Business Success Criteria: Corpus of Mexican environmental laws validated by policy experts and natural language processing researchers.

Inventory of Resources: Nine federal and environmental laws; Software: Python programming language, NLTK, PyPDF2 and pdfplumber libraries; Hardware: HP laptop computer, Intel Celeron 1.60 GHz ×64 Processor, 3 GB RAM, 500 GB HD and Windows 10 operating system; Experts: a public policy researcher, 4 NLP and text mining researchers; 1 environmental attorney.

Terminology: Commonly concepts include token, vector, corpus, preprocessing, generic task, specialized task, law, title, chapter, article, content, tagging, entity, formatting, etc.

Project Plan: A detailed document with the following topics: resources required, roles and responsibilities, costs and benefits.

4.2 Data Understanding Deliverables

Initial Data Collection Report: The laws can be found on the website https://www.diputados.gob.mx. In the section called "Parliamentary Information" choose the option "Federal Laws in Force". On the new page, type the key words of the law in a search box, e.g., ecological balance. Then, the process returns all the entries where the terms ecological balance appears and the law found is accompanied by a numerical identifier, its full name, the date of the last reform and the current downloadable text.

Data Description Report: The downloaded documents have PDF and Word formats, and for Android/iOS mobile devices, are only in PDF format. Based on the General Law on Ecological Balance and Environmental Protection, the word file contains 142 pages and 56,143 words. Each page has a header with the following elements: Name of the law, date of the last reform, three text labels that read, respectively: Chamber of Deputies of the Congress of the Union, General Secretariat and Secretariat of Parliamentary Services, and the national coat of arms in the upper left corner. Regarding its structure, this law has a name, a title (composed of number and name), chapters (composed of number and name), articles (composed of number and text), transitory articles of reform decrees.

4.3 Data Preparation Deliverables

The first specialized data preparation task consists of extracting text from the 9 selected laws (see Fig. 5).

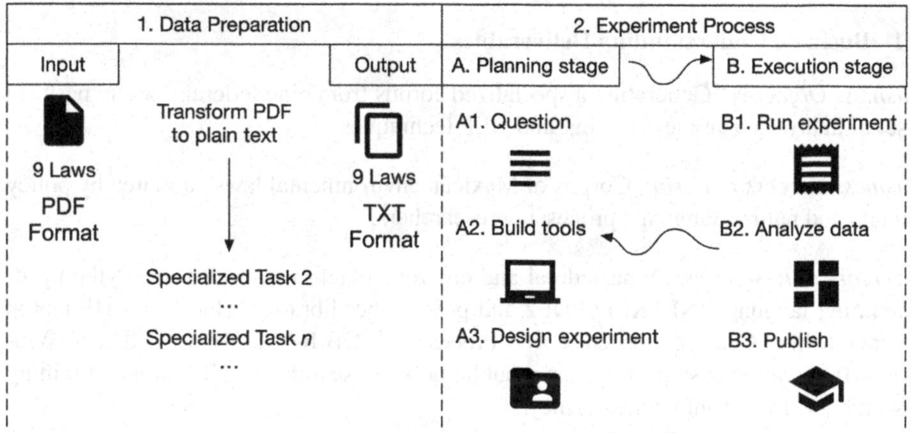

Fig. 5. Interaction between the data preparation phase and the experimental process applied to a specialized task.

On the left side is the data preparation phase and the specialized tasks that require input data and get an output. For example, for the specialized task of transforming the law PDF format to plain text format, the 9 laws are required as input and 9 plain text files are generated.

Data Cleaning Report: Texts are transformed into structured or semi-structured representation, empty words are removed and then, the text is segmented into tokens.

Reformatted Data: A transformation from pdf file format to plain text format.

4.4 Experimental Process Deliverables

Experimental process is linked to the data preparation phase and when performing the experiment, it is important to note that the 6 deliverables correspond to the planning and execution stages.

Questions to Gain Insight: Are there any libraries that could perform text extraction from pdf files? What kind of problems might occur using such libraries?

Software and Hardware Tools: The programming IDE used is a software system for application design that combines common developer tools in a single graphical user interface. The test environment uses windows 10, a command-line interface and the libraries mentioned in Subsect. 4.1.

Experiment Plan: Measure the execution time by using a text extraction library for each of the laws separately. Then run all 9 laws as a batch process.

Experiment Tests: Run the individual and batch experiments 30 times collecting the run time results.

Data Efficiency Analysis: Apply descriptive statistics and correlation analysis to determine whether there is a correlation between the size of the law, measured in pages or tokens, and the duration of text extraction measured in milliseconds.

4.5 Experimental Process Results

The versions used in the execution of the preprocessing task (text extraction from the pdf file) are Python 3.10, pdfplumber 0.1.2, pypdf2 2.10.3 and fitz 0.0.1.dev2.

In general, some unforeseen situations arose with the use of the Fitz and pdfminer3 libraries. For example, text that doesn't display or print correctly after converting documents; text that appears blended with characters overlapping and text indecipherable, illegible, or replaced by unusable characters.

In particular, the problems encountered with the use of NLTK were that it only recognizes a limited number of stop words. Another problem was the preprocessing of Spanish text since the Python libraries work with English terms and there exist a truncation of them. For example, "ambient" is the truncated word for the Spanish term "ambiente".

In the case of noise removal, the above libraries don't remove text file headers, footers, or labels. However, PyPDF2 and Pdfplumber libraries for the extraction of pdf to txt proved to be adequate in the results. Table 2 below shows the results of the execution time for the text extraction preprocessing task.

Table 2. Execution time measurement for 9 laws using PyPDF2 and pdfplumber.

LAW	PDF file size	Number of pages	PyPDF2 Time (s)	Pdfplumber Time (s)
LGEEPA	976 KB	128	**0.004640**	0.006640
LAN	1,036 KB	112	0.005790	0.006790
LDRS	597 KB	73	0.002003	0.003003
LGPAS	754 KB	71	0.003885	0.004095
LGVS	655 KB	72	0.027638	0.028638
LGDFS	592 KB	50	0.006040	0.008040
LGPGIR	584 KB	56	0.002121	0.002321
LFBOGB	532 KB	49	**0.000538**	**0.000538**
LGCC	609 KB	64	0.002277	0.004176

Time measurements showed a positive correlation, that is, when the number of pages of a law increase, so does the execution time. Only in the case of the LFBOGB law, both libraries reported the same execution time, in all other cases the PyPDF2 library was superior to pdfplumber. Nevertheless, time measurements can depend on many factors unrelated to program performance and need a detailed analysis.

Some of the project links are as follows:

Initial project structure: https://github.com/YesseniaD/CRCPMT-Project

Environmental laws text: https://github.com/YesseniaD/CRCPMT-Project/tree/main/Data/Raw/DP2.%20Limpieza%20de%20Datos

Data cleaning: https://github.com/YesseniaD/CRCPMT-Project/tree/main/Data/Raw/DP2.%20Limpieza%20de%20Datos

Next questions that arise when analyzing the results of the first experiment are the following:

- What is the memory consumption for text extraction?
- Are the results like those of the runtime?
- Is it possible to compare the tokenization and segmentation results for each law?

The specialized data preparation task used as an example showed that each result obtained need to be validated through an experimental process and that the analysis of the results generates new questions that allow to start the process again.

5 Conclusions

This paper shows that it is feasible to develop a methodology for the preprocessing of environmental laws, thanks to the combination of elements taken from CRISP-DM,

Team Data Science Process (TDSP) and an experimental stage to validate the results of the data preprocessing.

Thanks to the support of public policy and natural language processing experts, this project has a team with well-defined roles and responsibilities. Generic and specialized text preprocessing tasks use the Python programming language and libraries such as NLTK, PyPDF2 and Pdfplumber to extract text from pdf format. However, there are more specialized tasks that are already identified and need to be planned and executed, for example, entity identification, text labeling and formatting of laws to a JSON structure.

The execution of the text extraction preprocessing task yielded predictable results with respect to the number of pages of each law and its execution time. Additionally, we observed few significant differences in the libraries used. Nevertheless, this experiment showed the importance of integrating CRISP-DM with TDSP in order to enrich the technical context of this text mining project.

The conceptualization of the hybrid methodology will help to define the trajectory in the generation of specialized corpora for different types of legislative documents.

Finally, a remarkable contribution of this work consists in the identification of generic tasks, deliverables, artifacts, and templates, which are linked to the phases established by CRISP-DM, also, this combination of elements favors the development of data-oriented projects of an exploratory nature.

References

1. Pyle, D.: Data Preparation for Data Mining, 1st edn. Morgan Kaufmann Pub, Burlington (1999)
2. Medina Palmeros, F.: Leyes ambientales son letra muerta, acusa biólogo. Diario de Xalapa (2017)
3. Flores, D.: Exigen ejecutar leyes ambientales. Diario de Xalapa (2019)
4. Narave Flores, H., Cházaro Basañez, M.J., Arzaba Villalba, C.: La Paila un proyecto ambientalmente inviable: necesidad de fortalecer legislación de protección Ambiental. In: Aguilar López, M., Canales Espinosa, M., Domínguez González, N., Ojeda Jimeno, A., (eds.) En defensa del patrimonio natural y cultural de Veracruz. El caso del proyecto de la Mina La Paila, Municipio de Alto Lucero, Veracruz, Secretaría de Medio Ambiente del Estado de Veracruz/Universidad Veracruzana, pp. 29–40 (2018)
5. Hidalgo Reyes, M.A.: Ayudando al medio ambiente con inteligencia artificial. In: 4° Seminario de aprendizaje computacional, pp. 31–32 (2018)
6. Pichardo Lagunas, O., Martínez Seis, B.C., Carrera Trejo, V.: Interrogando datos en legislación Ambiental. Suplemento Científico de La Jornada Veracruz: El Jarocho Cuántico, no. 14, p. 6 (2020)
7. Rollins, J.B.: Metodología Fundamental para la Ciencia de Datos (2015)
8. IBM: IBM Analytics Solutions Unified Method (ASUM) (2015). http://i2t.icesi.edu.co/ASUM-DM_External/index.htm#cognos.external.asum-DM_Teaser/deliveryprocesses/ASUM-DM_8A5C87D5.html
9. Microsoft: What is the Team Data Science Process? (2015). https://docs.microsoft.com/en-us/azure/architecture/data-science-process/overview
10. Plotnikova, V., Dumas, M., Milani, F.: Adaptations of data mining methodologies: a systematic literature review. Peer J. Comput. Sci. **6**, 1–43 (2020)

11. Plotnikova, V., Dumas, M., Milani, F.P.: Applying the CRISP-DM data mining process in the financial services industry: elicitation of adaptation requirements. Data Knowl. Eng. **139**, 102013 (2022)
12. Chapman, P., et al.: CRISP-DM 1.0 Step-by-step data mining guide (2000)
13. Nuggets, K.D.: What main methodology are you using for your analytics, data mining, or data science projects? kdnuggets.com (2014). https://www.kdnuggets.com/polls/2014/analytics-data-mining-data-science-methodology.html
14. Marbán, O., Mariscal, G., Segovia, J.: A data mining & knowledge discovery process model. In: Ponce, J., Karahoca, A., (eds.) Data Mining and Knowledge Discovery in Real Life Applications, Vienna, p. 438. I-Tech, Austria (2009)
15. Martínez-Plumed, F., et al.: CRISP-DM twenty years later: from data mining processes to data science trajectories. IEEE Trans. Knowl. Data Eng. **33**(8), 3048–3061 (2021)
16. Fois, G, Agüero Crovella, G.A., Britos, P.V.: Evaluación comparativa de las metodologías Team Data Science Process TDSP y Analytics Solutions Unified Method for Data Mining ASUM-DM desde la perspectiva de la ciencia de datos. In: Cuarta, E. Serna M., (Ed.) Investigación Formativa en Ingeniería, Medellín - Antioquia: Editorial IAI, pp. 264–270 (2020)
17. McGeoch, C.C.: A Guide to Experimental Algoritmics, 1st edn. Cambridge University Press, Cambridge (2012)
18. Lagunas Rivera, A.R., del Alcalde, M.: Colección del Poder Judicial del Estado de Oaxaca. Escuela Judicial - Consejo de la Judicatura (2016)
19. de Diputados, C.: Leyes Federales Vigentes. LXV Legislatura (2022). https://www.diputados.gob.mx/LeyesBiblio/index.htm

News Intention Study and Automatic Estimation of Its Impact

Cesar Macias[1(✉)], Hiram Calvo[1], and Omar Juárez Gambino[2]

[1] Centro de Investigación en Computación, Instituto Politécnico Nacional, CIC-IPN, Mexico City 07738, Mexico
{cmaciass2021,hcalvo}@cic.ipn.mx

[2] Escuela Superior de Cómputo, Instituto Politécnico Nacional, ESCOM-IPN, Mexico City 07738, Mexico
jjuarezg@ipn.mx
https://www.cic.ipn.mx

Abstract. Since the invention of the Internet, and with the rise of social networks, information is available to all users quickly and in large quantities. One of the main sources of information on social networks is news. Among the possible options available for users to express their opinion or comment about some topic Twitter is a great tool for its users' to express their thoughts, this makes tweets the source of data and one of the central points of this work. The content of these opinions is highly emotionally charged. By analyzing user's comments about a news item, it is possible to determine its polarity and in turn use it as an indicator of the controversy of the news. Controversy tells us how the news affected its consumers, since if the responses are highly controversial it means that the readers opinions differed greatly, and that there was no common agreement on the news. Since there was no consensus in the responses, it can be inferred that there was a heated discussion in the comments. Those heated discussions are striking because they indicate which types of news generate more conflicts among readers and which do not.

Keywords: Sentiment analysis · News controversy · Natural language processing

1 Introduction

Internet has become one of the main tools for consulting and disseminating information. With the development and exponential growth of social networks the way in which human beings relate to each other has undergone some changes since interacting using social networks has become part of our daily lives, to such an extent that we even maintain interpersonal relationships solely through the use of online platforms, moreover, the recent pandemic of COVID-19 led to an accelerated evolution of this phenomenon, since we have been forced to interact using online platforms exclusively. According to the publication "Digital 2021"[1]

[1] https://datareportal.com/reports/digital-2021-october-global-statshot.

O. Pichardo Lagunas et al. (Eds.): MICAI 2022, LNAI 13613, pp. 83–100, 2022.
https://doi.org/10.1007/978-3-031-19496-2_7

approximately 57% of the worlds population actively uses social networks such as Facebook or Twitter and on average 2 h 27 min are spent daily in this activity. Online platforms are increasingly involved in public discourse. Their algorithms help citizens join social groups, sort through the noise of public discourse, and stay abreast of current events [4].

With the ease of access to social networks, users' can easily share their favorite posts with hundreds of their contacts in the blink of an eye. In general, social networks are a great tool for both posting and commenting on news, and Twitter is a great case of study because according to Kwak et al. [13] classifying trending topics on Twitter showed that the vast majority of tweet topics (over 85%) are headlines or persistent news.

Twitter posts can be about any topic; furthermore, there are very few restrictions on the content of the posts (e.g. news, comments, etc.). This is one of the main reasons for users' to use this platform, as they feel free to express themselves and their opinions. By analyzing Twitter comments, Li et al. [14] realized that the content of the comments is usually emotionally charged. This emotional charge is useful for identifying users' points of view (positive, negative or neutral), or in other words, the polarity of the text.

This paper focuses on the study of the intention of news in social networks and the estimation of its impact and controversy by analyzing news headlines in Spanish and their comments posted on Twitter. This is achieved by implementing a multi-label classification model in Twitter API V.2[2], to classify each of the comments in the conversation of the original publication as negative, neutral or positive; in addition, a search and classification of the comments and conversations corresponding to the 'quoted tweets" is performed to obtain the polarity of the news from the reader's perspective. Once the polarity is obtained, we proceed to cluster the data to see the general behavior of the polarity during its propagation.

Rest of the paper is organized as follows: Sect. 2 describes the state of the art; Sect. 3 describes the methodology and describes the solution to the problem; Sect. 4 describes the experiments performed, the results obtained from those experiments and its analysis; finally in Sect. 5 the conclusions are presented.

2 State of the Art

Sentiment Polarity. Automatic opinion analysis is part of the field of study known as sentiment analysis. Sentiment polarity is a subtask of this field [11]

In 2009, Bhowmick [7] mentions that emotions can be analyzed from two different perspectives: the writer's perspective and the reader's perspective. This paper focuses on the analysis of sentiment polarity from the reader's perspective. The polarity of a text indicates whether the response of the writer (e.g. the comment in a tweet) is negative, positive or neutral. From the multinomial approach, the probability of the text belonging to each of the mentioned classes

[2] https://developer.twitter.com.

can be obtained. Another approach is the multi-label classification problem in which it is considered that a person can express more than one sentiment at a time in the same comment.

In that same year, Winston et al. [20] address the problem of contextual polarity at the sentence level by introducing the use of a lexicon of "clues". In the first stage of the classification task, they use both the lexicon and the corpus to identify all instances of lexicon cues in the corpus, then polarity instances are obtained by passing the corpus with the annotations through a "neutral-polar" classifier that classifies each instance as neutral or polar (negative or positive); finally the polar instance is passed to a classifier that disambiguates the contextual polarity of each polar instance.

In 2014, Anjaria and Guddeti [2] proposed a high-level system using supervised machine learning features for text-based sentiment classification; In addition, they used Multinomial Naïve Bayes (Multi NB), Support Vector Machine (SVM), Maximum Entropy (MaxEnt) and an Artificial Neural Network (ANN) as classifiers. Features were extracted from tweets using unigram, bigram and a hybrid method.

In 2018, Jianqiang et al. [12] applied a convolution algorithm to perform sentiment analysis on Twitter. They first used the GloVe model that expresses sentiment as embeddings that can be represented as semantic features of the tweet. Then they concatenated this word representation with the polarity score. These sets of features were used to feed a deep convolutional neural network and train it to predict the categorical sentiment labels of the tweet.

Later, in 2021 Arasteh et al. [3] used sentiment polarity to predict the general polarity of first-order replies to an english source tweet with a deep learning approach, they also created a public dataset "ReTweet" for sentiment prediction of first-order Twitter replies.

Retweet or Quote Tweet Trees. The use of retweet trees has been proposed for two main purposes, to study the propagation of the tweets and its retweets and to obtain the most influential nodes in the propagation process.

In 2010 Kwak et al. [13] used the trees to determine how fast and deep retweets travel in Twitter. They developed an information dissemination tree. In their experiments they found that most of the retweet trees have first or second level breaks, and in addition no tree has more than six levels of retweets, considering that the first level is the original tweet, the second level is the retweet of the original tweet and so on. Their analysis of the tree showed how retweets propagate and how many tweets are involved in the process.

In 2018 Bhowmick et al. [6] built influence trees with sequences of temporal retweets, this sequences exhibit strengths for accurately modeling the tree of a cascade. They developed CasCon, a lightweight unsupervised learning model to build the trees, the model is able to identify the most influential node in a neighborhood of "friendships". With the influence trees they proposed two perspectives: (a) to discover the relationship between the retweet intervals and the formation of trees representing the influence of the most influential node and (b) to provide the ground truth for the validation of the trees built with the CasCon model.

Later, in 2022 Roth et al. [17] built non trivial quote trees for a root-tweet, considering recursive cascades of tweets. The experiments showed that the tree size follows a heterogeneous law where 75% of all the generated trees have 2 or maximum three levels, and by computing the average depth of trees, the results showed that 90% of trees only have an average depth of 1, indicating the absence of secondary quotes or quotes of quotes.

Polarity and Clustering. Clustering has been used in combination with sentiment analysis to improve the scores of a sentiment classification model, or to observe the polarity trend of tweets.

In 2014, Coletta et al. [9] first used an SVM classifier to perform the task of sentiment analysis of tweets, then used a set of clusters to refine the SVM classifier results and increase their quality. They performed experiments on four different tweet datasets. The experiments showed that the combination of SVM classifier and clustering improves the polarity classification task in tweets.

Later, in 2017, Ahuja and Dubey [1] used the AFINN Dictionary lexicon and TextBlob which is a natural language processing library for Python. They used TextBlob's polarity and subjectivity scores and AFINN's polarity to create two sparse data graphs, which they then grouped using clustering methods to determine the classes to which the polarity of each tweet belongs.

Finally in 2021, Shamrat et al. [18] used Python TextBlob library to calculate the polarity and subjectivity of the tweets, and once they obtained the polarity score, a supervised classification using a K-nearest Neighbor (KNN) algorithm was performed to the score to obtain the final classification of the polarity of the tweet.

2.1 Difference of This Proposal with Respect to the State of the Art Presented Above

Based on the study of the works presented above, the following observations can be made.

- Most of the cited works perform sentiment analysis as the main or only task of the work. On the other hand sentiment analysis is complex. The task of using the polarity of a tweet and its tree of quote tweets to observe the trend of polarity on a macroscopic scale to use it as the estimate of the tweet's impact has not been explored in the aforementioned work.
- The works that use retweet trees only use them to explore the propagation of a tweet through Twitter, or to obtain the most influential nodes of a tree. In comparison, the use of trees to obtain the polarity of the quote tweets and their comments has not been explored in the works presented above.

In this work we explore the possibility of using a sentiment analysis model together with a quote tweets tree and a clustering algorithm. This helps to improve the classification of tweets and their trend at the macro level of polarity to estimate te impact of a news item. Moreover, the sentiment analysis task to obtain the polarity of the comments is performed in Spanish.

3 Solution Development

We proposed to use the Logistic Regression (MaxEnt), multinomial Naïve Bayes (Multi NB) and Support Vector Machine (SVM) classifiers from the Scikit-learn [15] library for Python, and a BERT (Bidirectional Encoder Representations from Transformers) [10] model trained on a big Spanish corpus known as "BETO" [8]; and train them with features extracted from the corpus of the Semantic Analysis Workshop at International Conference of Spanish Society for Natural Language Processing (SEPLN) [19] to obtain the polarity of a text (tweet post). The classifier with the best results is then selected according to the evaluation metrics proposed in Sect. 3.3. In addition, we propose to implement the best model already trained to classify the polarity of news tweets in Spanish, using the news headline, main conversation of the news post, quote tweets and their conversations obtained from the Twitter API v2. Finally, the extracted polarity data from the Twitter API is clustered using unsupervised learning clustering methods to observe how the polarity generated in a news tweet post tends to be from a macroscopic point of view.

3.1 Description of the Solution

To estimate the impact of the news on its readers, a system composed of three main stages is proposed as shown in Fig. 1.

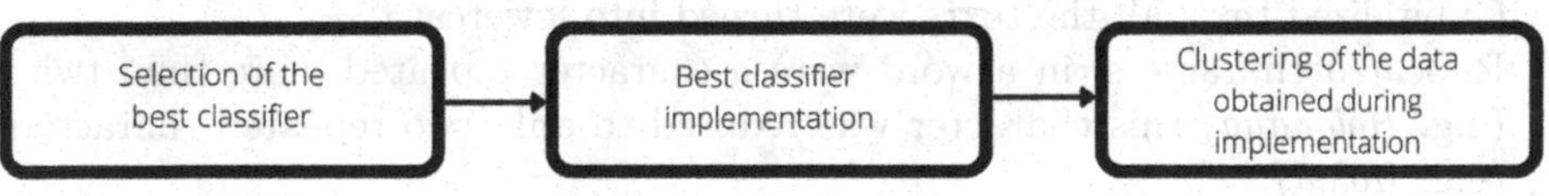

Fig. 1. Main system stages

The following is a description of the subtasks to be performed in each of the stages proposed in Fig. 1.

Selection of the Best Classifier This stage is divided into the subtasks shown in Fig. 2. These subtasks are described below.

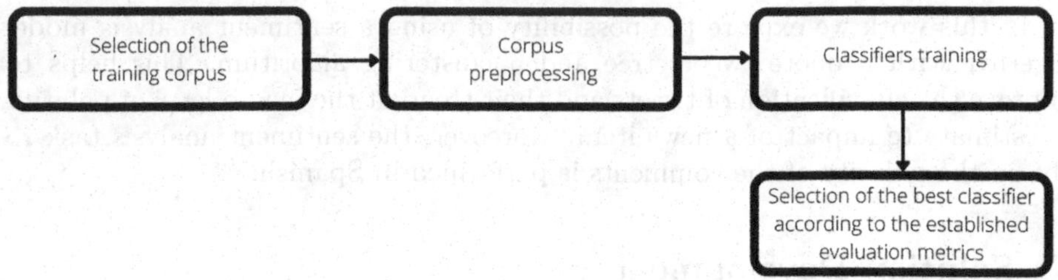

Fig. 2. Subtasks for the selection of the best classifier

Selection of the Training Corpus. The selected training corpus is the corpus of the Semantic Analysis Workshop at SEPLN (TASS) [19]. This corpus contains 60, 798 tweets written in Spanish, published between November 2011 and March 2012. The corpus was selected as it has a large number of comments, all written in Spanish. Each tweet is labeled with the overall polarity of the tweet in four levels: negative (N), neutral (NEU), positive (P) and an extra label (NONE) for those tweets that do not reflect any kind of polarity. For the purposes of this paper, the tweets labeled as neutral (NEU) and (NONE) were all considered within the neutral category (NEU) because from the authors point of view, if a comment does not reflect any polarity, then it remains neutral to the situation it is commenting on.

Corpus Preprocessing. To obtain the feature vectors, the corpus was preprocessed to clean up the texts. The details of the cleaning performed are described below.

- Usernames: the usernames identified by an @ or *_USER_* at the beginning were removed.
- URLs: all the URLs were removed
- Capitalized text: all the texts were turned into lowercase.
- Repeated characters: in a word were a character repeated more than twice (e.g. *Holaaaaa*) this character was reduced to only two repeated characters (e.g. *Holaa*).
- Stop words: the stop words were removed using the NLTK Spanish stopwords corpus.
- Alphanumeric characters: the alphanumeric characters were removed.
- Special characters: all the special characters were removed.
- Emojis: The emojis were transformed to text using an Emoji dictionary.

An example of clean text is shown below.

Raw text.

. _USER_ nada más peligroso que un presidente que cree que sólo responde ante la historia (y no ante sus ciudadanos) .

Clean text.
mas peligroso presidente cree solo responde historia ciudadanos

Unigrams were used as the method of feature extraction for experimental purposes. Once the data were cleaned, the number of negative (N), positive (P) and neutral (NEU) labels composing the corpus was obtained. The values are shown in Table 1.

Table 1. Number of labels per class in the corpus

Label	Amount
Negative (N)	15,844
Neutral (NEU)	22,721
Positive (P)	22,233

Classifiers Training. The supervised learning algorithms Logistic Regression (MaxEnt), Multinomial Naïve Bayes (Multi NB) and Support Vector Machine (SVM) from the Scikit-learn [15] Python library; and the pre-trained BETO model [8] were used.

1. Logistic Regression (MaxEnt): The Logistic Regression classifier has a generalization for the multi-class scenario known as Maximum Entropy (MaxEnt). It is a technique that has been used in a large number of natural language processing applications according to [5]. The model representation is the following.

$$Pw(y|x) = \frac{exp\ (w^T f(x, y))}{\Sigma_{y'} exp\ (w^T f(x, y'))} \tag{1}$$

   where x denotes the context (tweet), y denotes the class label of context x, $w \in \mathbb{R}^n$ is the weights vector; a vector function $f(x, y) \in \mathbb{R}^n$ denotes the extracted features of the context x and the class label y. The normalization function is a characteristic/class function for $f(x, y')$ and is defined as follows:

$$f(x, y') = \begin{cases} 1 \text{ if } n(x) > 0 \text{ and } y' = y \\ 0 \text{ otherwise} \end{cases} \tag{2}$$

   The weight vectors decide the importance of the features in the classification. A higher weight indicates that a feature is more representative for a class and vice versa.
2. Multinomial Naïve Bayes (Multi NB): The Multinomial Naïve Bayes classifier is a probabilistic learning method. This classifier is suitable to perform classification with discrete features (e.g. word counts for text classification). Multinomial probability usually requieres integer counts; but it has been observed that in practice, fractional counts such as tf-idf also work. The probability that a document d is classified in c is computed as:

$$P(c|d) = P(c) \prod_{1 \leq k \leq n_d} P(t_k|c) \tag{3}$$

where $P(t_k|c)$ is the conditional probability that the term t_k occurs in the document (tweet) of class c. $P(t_k|c)$ is interpreted as the measure of how much the evidence for t_k contributes to c being the correct class. $P(c)$ is the prior probability of a document (tweet) occurring in class c. If the terms of a document (tweet) do not provide clear evidence for one class with respect to another, the one with higher prior probability is chosen. $\langle t_1, t_2, \ldots, t_{n_d} \rangle$ are the tokens in d that are part of the vocabulary used for the classification and n_d is the number of those tokens in d. If one wants to know the best class for the document (tweet), the one with the highest a posteriori probability or maximum given by c_{map} defines the polarity of the tweet and its given by:

$$c_{map} = arg\ max_{c \in C}\ P(c|d) \tag{4}$$

3. Suport Vector Machine (SVM): For multi-class classification the SVC class of the Scikit-learn [15] Python library implement the "one versus one" approach. Mathematically a SVM constructs a hyper-plane or set of hyper-planes in a high dimensional space, those planes can be used for classification. Given training vectors $x_i \in \mathbb{R}^p$ and a vector $y \in \{1, -1\}^n$ the objective is to find $w \in \mathbb{R}^p$ and $b \in \mathbb{R}$ such that the prediction given by $sign\ w^T \phi(x) + b$ is correct for most samples.
The main problem to solve is the following.

$$\begin{gathered} \min_{w,b,\zeta} \frac{1}{2} w^T w + C \sum_{i=1}^{n} \zeta_i \\ \text{subject to} \\ y_i \left(w^T \phi(x_i) + b \right) \geq 1 - \zeta_i, \\ \zeta_i \geq 0,\ i = 1,\ \ldots,\ n \end{gathered} \tag{5}$$

The goal is to maximize the margin by penalizing when a sample is misclassified or within the margin boundaries. Because problems are not always perfect, some samples are allowed to be at a distance ζ_i from their correct margin boundary. The penalty term C controls the strength of the penalty. Once the optimization problem is solved the output of the decision function for a sample x is:

$$\sum_{i\ inSV} y_i \alpha_i K(x_i, x) + b \tag{6}$$

and the predicted class corresponds to its *sign*.
4. BETO: BETO [8] is a BERT [10] model trained on a large Spanish corpus. BETO is similar in size as the BERT base and was trained with the technique whole word masking.

Selection of the Best Classifier. To select the best classifier, the metrics established in Sect. 3.3 are compared for each of the classifiers proposed above and the one with the best performance is selected.

Best Classifier Implementation. During the implementation stage, the model with the best performance selected in the previous stage is implemented in conjunction with a search algorithm developed to obtain the tweet from a news item (original tweet) and its content (comments in the conversation and a list of quoted tweets); from the quoted tweets the following is obtained: (*1*) the text of the tweet, which usually contains an opinion about the original tweet; (*2*) the comments of the conversation of the quoted tweet (in case there is a conversation) and (*3*) a list of the tweets that quote the tweet quoting the original tweet and so on in case there is another level of quoted tweets. This algorithm makes use of the Twiiter API v2. The implementation of this algorithm is justified since in this way it is possible to obtain the polarity from the reader's perspective for a complete thread of conversation of a news publication (tweet) and is not only limited to obtain the polarity of the comments in the original tweet. The general operation of the algorithm is shown in Fig. 3.

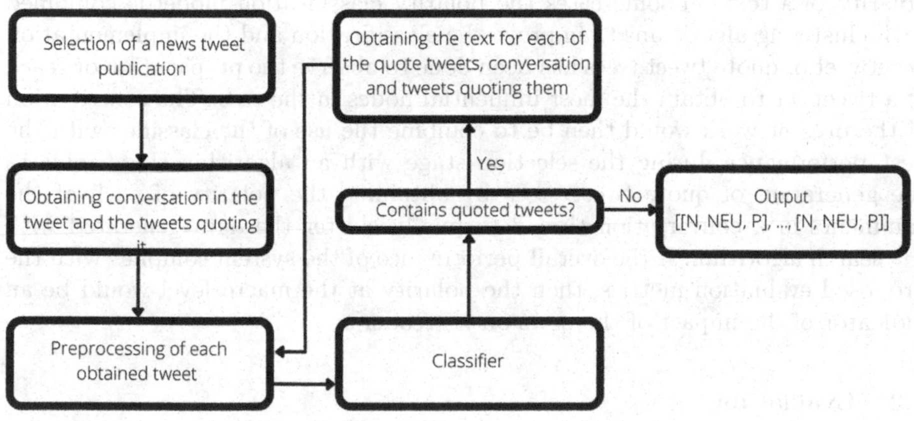

Fig. 3. Search algorithm

The output of the model is an array containing the polarity vectors obtained for each of the classified texts of the original tweet.

Clustering of the Data Obtained During Implementation. In the final stage, the polarity data contained in the output array of the previous stage algorithm are clustered using the k-means algorithm [16]. The k-means algorithm is an unsupervised learning classification algorithm, this means that the data is not labeled and performs the classification task by clustering objects into k groups based on their characteristics. The grouping is performed by minimizing the sum of the distances between the samples and the centroid of their group cluster. The k-means algorithm is described below.

```
1. The number of clusters k is selected
2. Centroid coordinates are initialized randomly
3. Each of the samples is assigned to a cluster
4. Cluster centroids are recalculated
5. Steps 3 and 4 are repeated until halt criterion is reached
```

The halt criterion could be when the centroids are no longer changing, when the samples cease to change groups or when a limit of iterations is reached. The k-means algorithm was chosen since the output data of the previous stage algorithm (polarity of comments) is not labeled. By using the clustering algorithm it is possible to observe the behavior of the polarity of a news item from the reader's perspective at the macroscopic level.

3.2 Scientific Novelty

The proposed system involves three main stages explained in Sect. 3.1. The works cited in Sect. 2 mostly perform the training of several models for predicting the polarity of a text, in some cases the polarity classification model is combined with clustering algorithms to improve the classification and the implementation of retweet or quote tweet trees has been done to observe the propagation or reach of a tweet, or to obtain the most influential nodes in the tree. The contribution of the present work would then be to combine the use of the classifier with the best performance during the selection stage with an algorithm that emulates the generation of quote tweet trees by obtaining the polarity of each of the comments in a conversation thread to finally cluster the data generated with the search algorithm. If the overall performance of the system complies with the proposed evaluation metrics, then the polarity at the macro level would be an indicator of the impact of the news on its reader's.

3.3 Evaluation

The metrics to be used to compare the classifiers proposed on the first stage of the system are F1 score, precision and recall.

4 Experiments and Results

In this section, a detailed description of the experiments performed is given according to the stages described in the Fig. 1 in Sect. 3.1.

Selection of the Best Classifier

In order to evaluate the tweets corresponding to the news headlines and their dispersion across the different classes, it is first necessary to perform the training of the dataset described in Sect. 3.1 with the different models that have been proposed. To achieve this goal, the following was taken into account:

- The data set was divided into 80% for training and 20% for testing.
- In order to make the experiment replicable, seed 42 for the machine learning models and the default seed for the pre-trained BETO model [8] were used for data partitioning which was performed with the function *train_test_split*() from the Scikit-learn [15] library.

The objective of this experiments is to obtain the classifier with the best performance, so it then can be implemented in the search algorithm. The selection depends on the metrics established in Sect. 3.3.

Tables 2, 3, and 4 show the results obtained from the machine learning classifiers. On the other hand, in Table 5 the results obtained for the BETO model [8] are shown.

Table 2. Logistic regression metrics result.

	Precision	Recall	F1-score
Negative	0.79	0.49	0.61
Neutral	0.69	0.51	0.58
Positive	0.88	0.63	0.73
Average	0.79	0.55	0.65

Table 3. Multinomial NB metrics result.

	Precision	Recall	F1-score
Negative	0.83	0.29	0.43
Neutral	0.79	0.22	0.34
Positive	0.84	0.55	0.67
Average	0.82	0.36	0.48

From these results it can be observed that the performance of the classifiers is not very favorable, which could affect the predictions in the later stages. Precision is a metric that expresses the ratio of correctly predicted positive observations to the total of predicted positive observations, in the following stage, this is very important because we want to use the classifier that gets the most correct positive predictions. Taking into account the precision metric as a performance indicator, the best of the classifiers selected to be implemented in posterior stages is Multinomial Naïve Bayes.

Table 4. SVM metrics result.

	Precision	Recall	F1-score
Negative	0.80	0.50	0.61
Neutral	0.72	0.48	0.57
Positive	0.88	0.63	0.73
Average	0.80	0.54	0.64

Table 5. BETO metrics result.

	Precision	Recall	F1-score
Negative	0.77	0.69	0.73
Neutral	0.78	0.80	0.74
Positive	0.78	0.83	0.80
Average	0.78	0.77	0.76

Best Classifier Implementation

Given the above results, the Multinomial Naïve Bayes classifier was chosen to be implemented in the process involving the search algorithm. At this stage 60 trees of quote tweets were obtained. Figure 4 shows an example of the obtained trees, the information it contains was reduced for a better appreciation. The process to generate the quote tweet trees is the one described in Sect. 3.1. The goal of this stage is to obtain the polarity data for the whole conversation thread of a news tweet, and with this data, perform a final classification with the clustering algorithm.

An explanation of the information observed in Fig. 4 is as follows. The parent node contains the news headline and an array including the probability of the analyzed text to belong to each class (negative, neutral, positive). The array represents a weighted average of the probabilities for the news headline and the conversation tweets belonging to that publication. Child nodes contain the "tweet id" of the quoted tweet, and an array that includes the polarity probability scores for each class. This polarity is a weighted average of the quote tweet text and the conversation (if it exists) generated in that quote tweet. A total of 50 quoted tweets per each iteration is requested from the Twitter API, the amount of quoted tweets depends on the response obtained from the API.

Clustering of the Data Obtained During Implementation

Once the polarity data is obtained for the conversation thread of a news tweet, the clustering algorithm described in Sect. 3.1 is implemented to perform a final classification of the polarity data with the intention of obtaining a macroscopic vision of the thread's polarity behavior. By assigning a final classification, the total of negative, neutral and positive posts is obtained so it is possible to observe how the news impact its reader's. The obtained results are summarized in a graph as shown in Fig. 5. This graph shows the total o negative, neutral and positive texts analyzed for the news tweet.

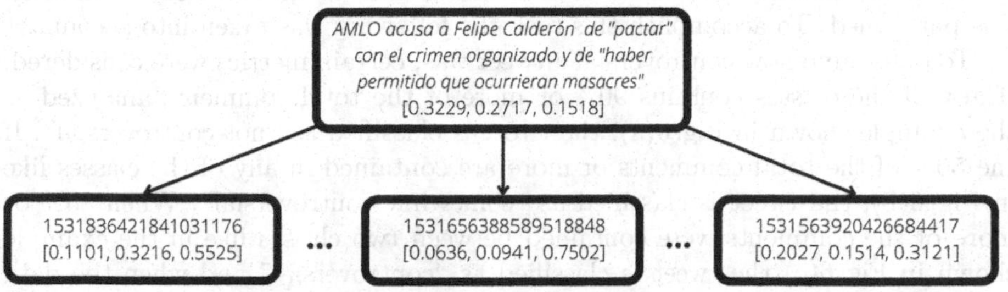

Fig. 4. Example of the obtained trees

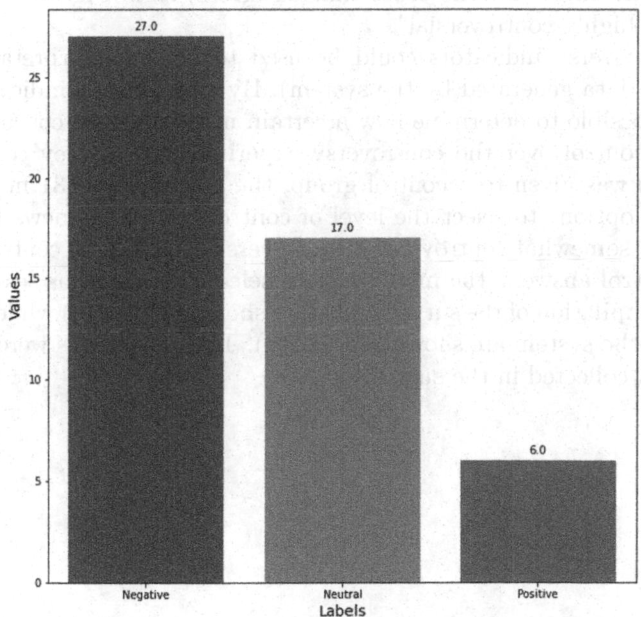

Fig. 5. Example of the results after clustering

Controversy. The controversy is an indicator of how polemical the tweet was, in other words, if the general opinion of the reader's tends to have the same polarity, the tweet may not be controversial or somewhat controversial and viceversa. If the general opinion tends to be partitioned then the tweet may be controversial or highly controversial. This is a novelty introduced to the system to obtain some preliminary results.

With the polarity count for each of the labels, the controversy estimation was performed. To accomplish this task the following was taken into account.

To determine how controversial a tweet was, certain metrics were considered. If any of the classes contains 90% or more of the total comments analyzed as the example shown in Fig. 6(a), the tweet is classified as "not controversial". If the 50% of the total comments or more are contained in any of the classes like in Fig. 6(b), the tweet is classified as "somewhat controversial". When 80% or more of the comments were contained between two classes like in the example shown in Fig. 6(c) the tweet is classified as "controversial" and when the data is balanced between the three classes like in Fig. 6(d) or in a special case where 80% of the comments or more are contained between the positive and negative classes (this can be interpreted as a heated discussion between to parts, one that agrees with the tweet and the other that disagrees) as in Fig. 6(e) the tweet is classified as "highly controversial".

This controversy indicators could be used to get an interpretation of the polarity (the data generated by the system). By assigning an indicator to each tweet, it is possible to determine how a certain news affect its consumers.

To have control over the controversy experiments, a survey containing 60 news headers was given to a control group, the participants (31 in total) have four possible options to select the level of controversy of the news header: not controversial, somewhat controversial, controversial and highly controversial. To label the control answers, the most frequent selected option was selected as the class. The compilation of the survey labels are shown in Fig. 7(a) while the classes predicted by the system are shown in Fig. 7(b). The predictions were made over the 60 tweets collected in the survey.

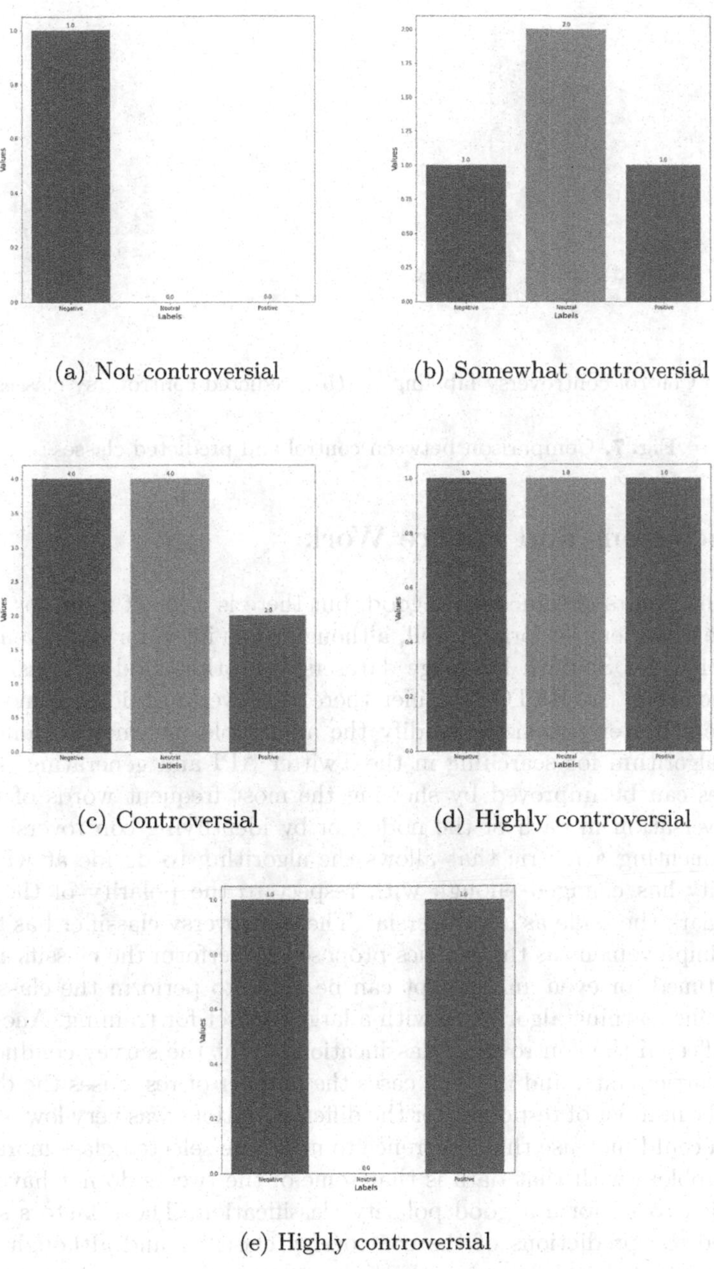

(a) Not controversial

(b) Somewhat controversial

(c) Controversial

(d) Highly controversial

(e) Highly controversial

Fig. 6. Examples of controversy classification

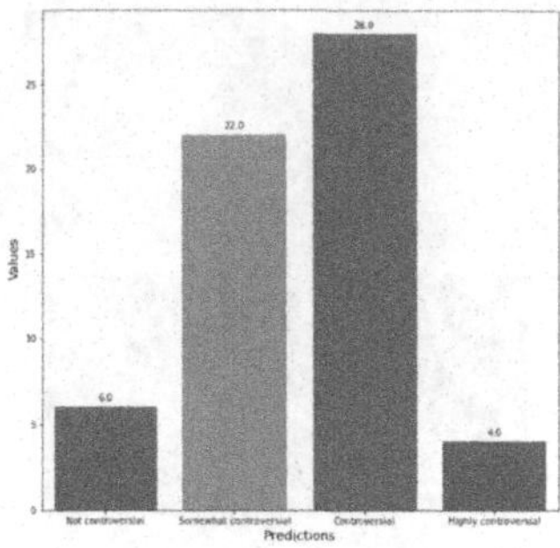

(a) Control controversy labeling

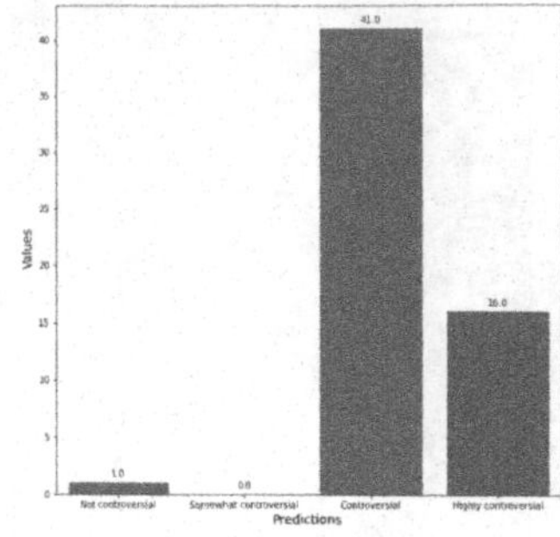

(b) Predicted controversy classes

Fig. 7. Comparison between control and predicted classes

5 Conclusions and Future Work

Overall, the results obtained were good, but there is a lot of room for improvement. The classifiers performed well, although some ideas for improvement are: to try with other Spanish language datasets, use other kind of classifiers or a combination. For the BETO classifier there are several options, some of them are to use a better tokenizer, modify the adjustable parameters, among others. The algorithm for searching in the Twitter API and generating the quote tweet trees can be improved by showing the most frequent words of the analyzed conversation in each of the nodes, or by identifying controversial nodes, i.e., implementing a metric that allows the algorithm to decide at what point the polarity has changed enough with respect to the polarity of the original tweet to mark the node as controversial. The controversy classifier has the most room for improvement as the metrics proposed to perform the classification can be finely tuned, or even an attempt can be made to perform the classification with machine learning algorithms with a large dataset for training. Another factor that affected the controversy classification is that the survey conducted had very few participants, and in some cases the number of responses the difference between the number of responses for the different options was very low, so having more data could increase that difference to make the selected class more robust, another problem with that data is that some of the tweets do not have enough conversation to perform a good polarity classification. Those factors somehow determined the predictions of the controversy classifier and although the tendency of most of the tweets towards the controversial class is observed in both control and prediction data, the difference between them for the other classes is representative.

Finally, even though there were some obstacles to obtain a better performance during the experimental stage, the reward was worth it since the results are promising as they indicate that by further refining, this system and the methods implemented here, a good indicator of controversy for news could be obtained.

This indicator is useful because it allows us to observe both macroscopically and particularly the behavior of reader's when faced with a news item, how they are polarized and how controversial a news item can be.

References

1. Ahuja, S., Dubey, G.: Clustering and sentiment analysis on twitter data. In: 2017 2nd International Conference on Telecommunication and Networks (TEL-NET), pp. 1–5 (2017). DOI: https://doi.org/10.1109/TEL-NET.2017.8343568
2. Anjaria, M., Guddeti, R.M.R.: A novel sentiment analysis of social networks using supervised learning. Soc. Netw. Anal. Min. **4**(1), 181 (2014)
3. Arasteh, S.T., et al.: How will your tweet be received? predicting the sentiment polarity of tweet replies. In: 2021 IEEE 15th International Conference on Semantic Computing (ICSC), pp. 370–373 (2021). https://doi.org/10.1109/ICSC50631.2021.00068
4. Bastick, Z.: Would you notice if fake news changed your behavior? an experiment on the unconscious effects of disinformation. Comput. Hum. Behav. **116**, 106633 (2021). https://doi.org/10.1016/j.chb.2020.106633
5. Berger, A.L., Pietra, V.J.D., Pietra, S.A.D.: A maximum entropy approach to natural language processing. Comput. Linguist. **22**(1), 39–71 (1996)
6. Bhowmick, A.K., Sai Bharath Chandra, G., Singh, Y., Mitra, B.: Constructing influence trees from temporal sequence of retweets: an analytical approach. In: 2018 IEEE International Conference on Big Data (Big Data), pp. 624–633 (2018). https://doi.org/10.1109/BigData.2018.8622315
7. Bhowmick, P.K.: Reader perspective emotion analysis in text through ensemble based multi-label classification framework. Comput. Inf. Sci. **2**(4) (2009)
8. Cañete, J., Chaperon, G., Fuentes, R., Ho, J.H., Kang, H., Pérez, J.: Spanish pre-trained BERT model and evaluation data. In: PML4DC at ICLR 2020 (2020)
9. Coletta, L.F.S., da Silva, N.F.F., Hruschka, E.R., Hruschka, E.R.: Combining classification and clustering for tweet sentiment analysis. In: 2014 Brazilian Conference on Intelligent Systems, pp. 210–215 (2014). https://doi.org/10.1109/BRACIS.2014.46
10. Devlin, J., Chang, M.W., Lee, K., Toutanova, K.: Bert: pre-training of deep bidirectional transformers for language understanding. arXiv preprint arXiv:1810.04805 (2018)
11. Gambino, J.O.J.: Sentiment polarity prediction of Twitter users' opinions to national newspapers news. Ph.D. thesis, Centro de Investigación en Computación (2019)
12. Jianqiang, Z., Xiaolin, G., Xuejun, Z.: Deep convolution neural networks for twitter sentiment analysis. IEEE Access **6**, 23253–23260 (2018). https://doi.org/10.1109/ACCESS.2017.2776930
13. Kwak, H., Lee, C., Park, H., Moon, S.: What is twitter, a social network or a news media? In: Proceedings of the 19th International Conference on World Wide Web, WWW 2010, pp. 591–600. Association for Computing Machinery, New York, USA (2010). https://doi.org/10.1145/1772690.1772751
14. Li, X., Peng, Q., Sun, Z., Chai, L., Wang, Y.: Predicting social emotions from readers' perspective. IEEE Trans. Affect. Comput. **10**(2), 255–264 (2019). https://doi.org/10.1109/TAFFC.2017.2695607

15. Pedregosa, F., et al.: Scikit-learn: machine learning in Python. J. Mach. Learn. Res. **12**, 2825–2830 (2011)
16. Piech, C.: K means (2012). https://stanford.edu/cpiech/cs221/handouts/kmeans.html
17. Roth, C., St-Onge, J., Herms, K.: Quoting is not citing: disentangling affiliation and interaction on Twitter. In: Benito, R.M., Cherifi, C., Cherifi, H., Moro, E., Rocha, L.M., Sales-Pardo, M. (eds) Complex Networks and Their Applications X. COMPLEX NETWORKS 2021. Studies in Computational Intelligence, vol. 1015. Springer, Cham (2022). https://doi.org/10.1007/978-3-030-93409-5_58
18. Shamrat, F.M.J.M., et al.: Sentiment analysis on twitter tweets about Covid-19 vaccines using NLP and supervised KNN classification algorithm. Indonesian J. Elec. Eng. Comput. Sci. **23**(1), 463–470 (2021)
19. Villena-Román, J., Lana-Serrano, S., Martínez-Cámara, E., González-Cristóbal, J.C.: Tass - workshop on sentiment analysis at sepln. procesamiento del lenguaje natural, 50. https://journal.sepln.org/sepln/ojs/ojs/index.php/pln/article/view/4657 (2013)
20. Wilson, T., Wiebe, J., Hoffmann, P.: Recognizing contextual polarity: an exploration of features for phrase-level sentiment analysis. Comput. Linguist. **35**(3), 399–433 (2009). https://doi.org/10.1162/coli.08-012-R1-06-90

Evaluation of a New Representation for Noise Reduction in Distant Supervision

Juan-Luis García-Mendoza[1(✉)], Luis Villaseñor-Pineda[1], Davide Buscaldi[2], Lázaro Bustio-Martínez[3], and Felipe Orihuela-Espina[1,4]

[1] Instituto Nacional de Astrofísica, Óptica y Electrónica (INAOE), Puebla, Mexico
{juanluis,villasen}@inaoep.mx
[2] Université Sorbonne Paris Nord, LIPN, Villetaneuse, France
davide.buscaldi@lipn.univ-paris13.fr
[3] Universidad Iberoamericana, DEII, CDMX, Mexico
lbustio@ibero.mx
[4] University of Birmigham, Birmingham, UK
f.orihuela-espina@bham.ac.uk

Abstract. Distant Supervision is a relation extraction approach that allows automatic labeling of a dataset. However, this labeling introduces noise in the labels (e.g., when two entities in a sentence are automatically labeled with an invalid relation). Noise in labels makes difficult the relation extraction task. This noise is precisely one of the main challenges of this task. Until now, the methods that incorporate a previous noise reduction step do not evaluate the performance of this step. This paper evaluates the noise reduction using a new representation obtained with autoencoders. In addition, it was incoporated more information to the input of the autoencoder proposed in the state-of-the-art to improve the representation over which the noise is reduced. Also, three methods were proposed to select the instances considered as real. As a result, it was obtained the highest values of the area under the ROC curves using the improved input combined with state-of-the-art anomaly detection methods. Moreover, the three proposed selection methods significantly improve the existing method in the literature.

Keywords: Noise reduction · Distant supervision · Adversarial autoencoders · Data representation

1 Introduction

The goal of the Relation Extraction (RE) task is the extraction and classification of the relations existing between two entities of interest in a sentence [24]. Several approaches for solving this task have been proposed, which can be consulted in [6,8,13,21,29].

O. Pichardo Lagunas et al. (Eds.): MICAI 2022, LNAI 13613, pp. 101–113, 2022.
https://doi.org/10.1007/978-3-031-19496-2_8

One of these approaches is Distant Supervision (DS) [21]. DS allows the automatic labeling of a dataset based on existing knowledge about a specific domain [28]. This knowledge is generally stored in knowledge bases such as Freebase[1]. The labeling is performed following the idea proposed in [21]. Mintz et al. expressed that "if two entities participate in a relation, any sentence that contains those two entities might express that relation". That is, given two entities in a sentence, these entities are searched in the knowledge base. If there is a relation between these entities, the sentence is labeled with this relation. Otherwise, it is labeled with "Not a relation" ($\mathcal{NA}$) (see Fig. 1). This idea is the most commonly used in automatic labeling.

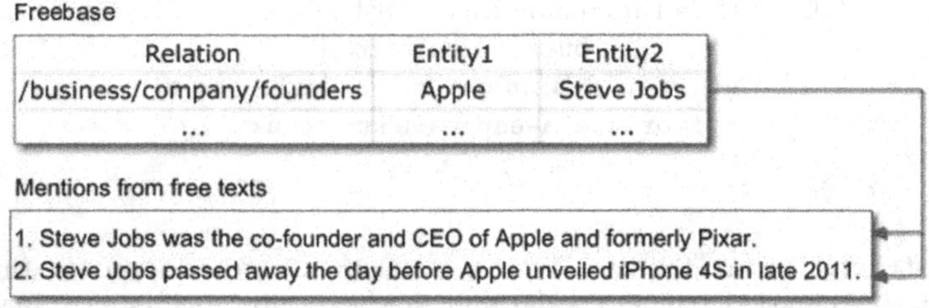

Fig. 1. In this example, two sentences with the same pair of entities are automatically labeled with the same relation. Considering the *founders* relation, the first one will be correctly labeled while the second will not [33].

In [25], the idea proposed by Mintz et al. in [21] was relaxed because all sentences with the same pair of entities do not necessarily express the relation. Therefore, Riedel et al. concluded that "if two entities participate in a relation, at least one sentence that mentions these two entities might express that relation". Despite this, it may happen that no sentence expresses the relation. This idea is frequently used in the heuristics of methods for solving DS task.

Automatic labeling in DS introduces instances with noise in the labels due to following the idea proposed by Mintz et al. in [21]. These noisy instances are considered false positives. For example, in Fig. 1, the second sentence is considered as a false positive. This is because this sentence is labeled with the relation *founder* and it does not actually express such relation. This noise is precisely one of the problems of DS [28]. The late problem has been addressed in two ways. The first one is the inclusion of a noise tolerance mechanism within the proposed methods [12,16,21,25,31–33]. While the second one includes a previous noise reduction step [7,26,30]. However, none of the previous work that incorporates a previous noise reduction step evaluates the performance of that step.

Therefore, the aim of this paper is to evaluate the noise reduction on the representations obtained with autoencoders (AE). This evaluation is performed considering the area under the ROC curves (AUC). The ROC curves are obtained as

[1] https://developers.google.com/freebase/.

a result of applying state-of-the-art anomaly detection methods to the obtained representations. For this purpose, a dataset was used for the RE task because the noise can be controlled. In DS datasets, the noise introduced by automatic labeling is not known a priori and cannot be controlled.

In addition, it was proposed to add more information to the input of the AE reported in [7] to improve the representation used in noise reduction. Finally, three methods were proposed to select instances used in the adversarial autoencoders (AAE) to obtain the a priori known distribution.

2 Related Work

According to [28], DS can be divided, into three categories. However, these methods are not exclusive to each category. In this work, noise handling is used as a division criterion. Based on this criterion, two groups are formed: *noisy label tolerant methods* [12,16,25,31–33] and *noisy label cleaning methods* [7,26,30]. On the one hand, *noisy label tolerant methods* incorporate a mechanism to handle noise within the method itself. For example, in the approach reported in [21], features from several sentences were combined into an enriched vector that was able to tolerate noise. Based on the idea proposed in [25], a multi-instance learning approach was used in several neural networks [12,16,32,33]. The main idea is to consider a bag of instances containing the same pair of entities. In addition, some mechanisms have been added to these networks at the word level [11], at the sentence level [16], at the entity level [12], at the intra-bag level [34] and the intra-bag level and inter-bag level [32]. Finally, several papers included information from knowledge bases such as entity type and relations alias [31] and entity label, entity alias, entity description and the entity type [2].

On the other hand, *noisy label cleaning methods* incorporate a previous noise reduction step. In [30], negative patterns were used to remove noisy labels. Elements such as the syntactic tree path between the two entities are considered if it does not exceed 4 steps. Later, in [26], an algorithm calculates the semantic similarity between text fragments is used to reduce noisy labels. The idea here is to compute the semantic similarity that exists between the triplet stored in the knowledge base representing the relation and the dependency phrase between the two entities. Finally, in [7], architectures based on classical and adversarial AE are used to obtain data representations that allow noise reduction. These representations are obtained by training different AE for each relation. After the noise reduction step, new datasets with less noise were obtained, which can be used by classifiers and will obtain better performance/result. In the revised state-of-the-art papers, the classifiers performance is evaluated using precision-recall curves and precision at N elements obtained. Nevertheless, the performance of the representations used in noise reduction was not evaluated. In [7], the input of the AE and AAE is the vector of the complete sentence. This vector is calculated with pretrained embeddings proposed in [1,4].

AAE is one of the most common AE to obtain representations using unsupervised approaches. AAE uses an adversarial training procedure to force the generated vectors to fit a known prior distribution [20]. The known prior distribution is generated in [7] from randomly selected instances.

3 Methodology

Anomaly detection, according to [22], "is referred to as the process of detecting data instances that significantly deviate from the majority of data instances". In the following, we formally define this problem in the DS task.
Let:

- A set of sentences $\mathcal{S} = \{s_i | i = 1 \ldots |S|\}$.
- A set of entities $\mathcal{E} = \{e_z | z = 1 \ldots |\mathcal{E}|\}$.
- A set of relations $\mathcal{R} = \{r_j | j = 1 \ldots J\}$. One of these relations is the $\mathcal{NA}$ relation.
- A set of observations $\mathcal{X} = \{x_k | x_k = (s_i, e_h, e_t, r_j) \in \mathcal{S} \times \mathcal{E} \times \mathcal{E} \times \mathcal{R}\}$.
- A subset of observations $\mathcal{X}_n \subseteq \mathcal{X}$ where the relation r_j is noisy (the relation is not expressed).
- An *encoder* function to obtain data representation where $\mathcal{V} = \{v_i | v_i \in \mathbb{R}^n\}$ is the vector representation of each sentence s_i.

$$\begin{aligned} \mathit{encoder} : \mathcal{S} &\rightarrow \mathcal{V} \\ (s_i, v_i) \end{aligned} \tag{1}$$

- A *noisy* function that determines whether the sentence s_i is noisy or not from its v_i representation.

3.1 Dataset

One of the main datasets in DS task, New York Times 2010 (NYT2010)[2] was automatically labeled by Riedel et al. [25]. This labeling results in instances with noise in the labels that are not known a priori. Because of this, noise cannot be controlled during the experiments. An alternative to this problem is to use a dataset of the RE task. SemEval-2010 Task 8 (*semeval2010*) [9] dataset was released as part of Task 8 of the SemEval-2010 event [9]. It has 10 relations, including "Other" which represents $\mathcal{NA}$. Nine of these relations are represented in a bidirectional way becoming 18 relations, which when adding $\mathcal{NA}$ are a total of 19. In the training and test partitions there are 8000 and 2717 instances respectively. We take as *inlier* all instances with a relation different from $\mathcal{NA}$ (6590 instances in train partition and 2263 in test). Those belonging to $\mathcal{NA}$ are taken as *outliers* or *noisy* (1410 instances in train partition and 454 in test).

---

[2] Available in http://iesl.cs.umass.edu/riedel/ecml/.

3.2 Baseline of Representation Learning Methods

In this section it is defined the baseline of representation learning methods. These methods are the *encoder* function defined in the Eq. 1.

Bag-of-Words Based Methods. In this approach it was used bag-of-words (BoW) and bag-of-characters (BoC) methods to represent the texts using a vector. In both cases it was used unigrams and bigrams. These functions were named *f_ bow_ 1* and *f_ boc_ 1* for unigrams. For the case of bigrams, the functions were named as *f_ bow_ 2* and *f_ boc_ 2*. Finally, the union of unigrams and bigrams were named *f_ bow_ 12* and *f_ boc_ 12*. For the comparisson, it were selected the 10 000 most frequent terms.

TF-IDF Based Methods. The frequency-based methods (TF-IDF) of words and characters was used for representing texts as a vector. It was calculated the TF-IDF representation for unigrams and bigrams. These functions were named as *f_ tfidf_ 1* and *f_ tfidf_ char_ 1* for unigrams. For the case of bigrams, they were named as *f_ tfidf_ 2* and *f_ tfidf_ char_ 2*. Finally, the union of unigrams and bigrams was named as *f_ tfidf_ 12* and *f_ tfidf_ char_ 12*. As with BoW and BoC, it were selected the 10 000 most frequent terms.

Pretrained Embeddings Based Methods. Pretrained embeddings were used to obtain a vector from all text. The pretrained embeddings used in this work were RoBERTa [18], DAN [4], TRANSF [4] and LASER [1]. These functions were named as *f_ roberta*, *f_ dan*, *f_ transf* and *f_ laser* respectively.

3.3 Unsupervised Representation Learning Methods

Inputs Used in Unsupervised Methods. For the input of these methods, one input representation is used and another is proposed. Both inputs use the functions *f_ dan*, *f_ transf*, *f_ laser* and *f_ roberta* as pretrained embeddings. The inputs *f_ dan*, *f_ transf* and *f_ laser* are used in [7], while *f_ roberta* is included in this work. The inputs are:

- original input: This input was proposed in [7]. It consists of the vector obtained with pretrained embeddings from all the text.
- improved input: This input is proposed in this research. The improved input consists of a concatenation of the vectors obtained from the entities, the text between the two entities including them, and the full text. As in the original input, these vectors are obtained with pretrained embeddings.

Autoencoder Based Methods. The use of AE was proposed to obtain unsupervised text representations (see Fig. 2(a)). This method is based on [7]. The architecture is composed of two dense layers in the encoder and the decoder, with 768 dense units and a ReLu-like activation function. These AE-based functions were named *f_ ae_ roberta*, *f_ ae_ dan*, *f_ ae_ transf* and *f_ ae_ laser* according to the function with which the input vectors are obtained.

Adversarial Autoencoders Based Methods. AAE, as AE, was used to obtain unsupervised text representations (see Fig. 2(b)). It was proposed as *encoder* AAE under the assumption that if an observation (s_i, r) is noisy, then the observation will not fit the distribution of the rest of the observations, and it will remain far away. As in the AE, this paper is based on the architecture proposed in [7]. The AAE's input is composed of two elements: the *instance representations* and *data distribution*. On the one hand, the instance representations are the vectors obtained from the $\mathcal{X}_{train}$ partition with original or improved input. On the other hand, *data distribution* is an essential element of the AAE. This distribution is obtained from instances considered as real. They are represented by vectors obtained using an AE with the same architecture as the AAE encoder. The real instances are essential because the latent space z of *instance representations* is tried to fit the distribution obtained from them. These AE-based functions were named as *f_aae_roberta*, *f_aae_dan*, *f_aae_transf* and *f_aae_laser* according to the function with which the input vectors are obtained.

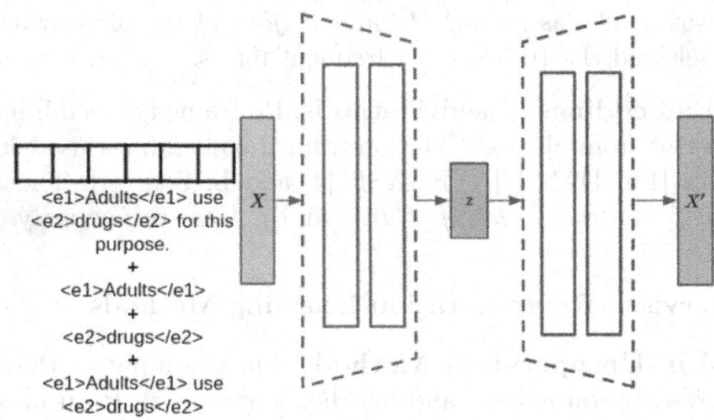

(a) AE with dense layers and improved input

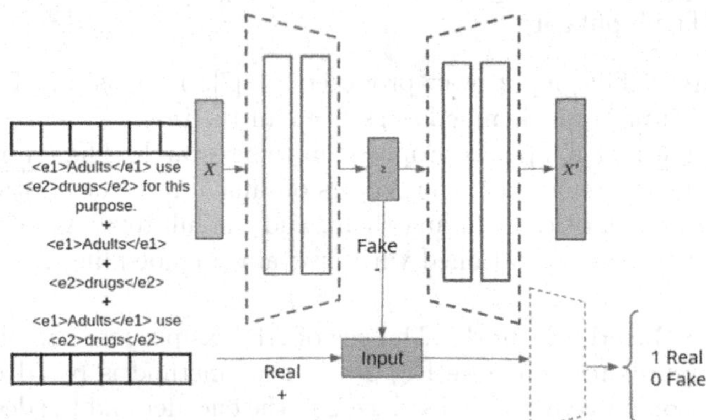

(b) AAE with dense layers and improved input

Fig. 2. Architectures with dense layers and improved input.

In [7], the authors randomly selected one-third of the total of instances as real. In this work, three methods are proposed to select these instances.

- *Random*: It consists of selects randomly the 30% of the total number of instances as real. This method was proposed in [7].
- *Gaussian*: This method generates random instances fitted to the Gaussian distribution as real.
- *k-Means* clustering algorithm [19]: This algorithm was trained on the complete train partition to create 2 clusters. Then, those that belong to the cluster with the largest number of instances were selected as real instances. This decision is given because the number of noisy instances is generally a small percent of the total number of instances. The representation $\mathcal{V}$ used to train this algorithm was the functions *f_roberta*, *f_dan*, *f_transf* and *f_laser* output.
- *DBScan* [5]: This algorithm constructs the groups based on the density of the points. It only requires defining the number of points (min_pts) to consider a region as dense and the distance (eps) to consider the neighborhood of a point. The points considered real (real instances) are the cores of each built group. In this work, we try to get the number of core points between 10 and 50 of the total number of points.

3.4 Anomaly Detection Methods

Anomaly detection methods can be grouped into *proximity-based*, *linear model*, *ensembles* and *neural networks* among other categories [22]. The functions *noisy* of the *proximity-based* group used were Local Outlier Factor (*lof*) [3], k Nearest Neighbors (*knn*) [22] and Subspace Outlier Detection (*sod*) [15]. In addition, in the *linear model* group are Principal Component Analysis Outlier Detector (*pca_od*) [27]. Also, Variational Autoencoder Outlier Detector (*vae_od*) [14] belong to the *neural networks* group. Finally, Isolation Forest (*iforest*) [17] and Lightweight On-line Detector of Anomalies (*loda*) [23] are in group *ensembles*.

3.5 Experimental Design

First Experiment. To determine the best $< encoder, noisy >$ pair for each group of representation learning methods, it were performed 5 iterations. The 10 best *encoder* functions with their associated *noisy* functions were chosen from these results. Then, the performance of these functions was evaluated based on 20 replications of each of these pairs $< encoder, noisy >$. The number of replications (sample size) was determined using ANOVA One Way test for a desired significance level of 0.05, statistical power of $\beta = 0.95$ and assuming an effect size of F distribution $= 0.4$. From the results of the replications, the ANOVA One Way test is applied to know if there are significant differences between the results achieved by the pairs. Finally, if there were significant differences, pairwise comparisons were made to observe which pair showed differences. The two-by-two comparisons were made with t-test and Holm Correction [10]. The

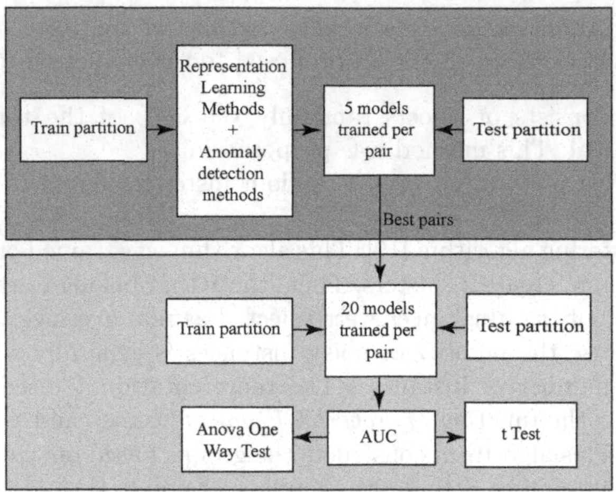

Fig. 3. Methodology followed in the current experiment.

significance threshold was set at $\alpha = 5\%$. Figure 3 summarizes the above experimental design.

Second Experiment. In addition, it was analyzed the performance of the original input proposed in [7] with respect to the improved input proposed in this work. To analyze the performance, the 10 best $< encoder, noisy >$ pairs were considered, and run 5 replications with each input. Then, it was analyzed if there were variations in the ranking for each replication with Friedman test.

Third Experiment. Finally, the performance of the four methods was evaluated to select the instances considered as real in the AAE. To do so, all results with the same method were pooled to select without considering the pretrained embeddings with which the input vectors are obtained. The *noisy* functions are also not taken into account.

4 Experiments and Evaluation

First Experiment. The first 10 $< encoder, noisy >$ pairs with highest AUC after 5 iterations in the *semeval2010* dataset were selected. Table 1 summarizes the AUC of this 10 best $< encoder, noisy >$ pairs after 20 iterations in the *semeval2010*. Significant differences were found between all pairs (ANOVA: $F(9, 190) = 24.34, p < 2e^{-16}$). In the case of pairwise comparisons with t-test, the pair $< f\_ae\_transf, knn >$ presents significant differences with the rest, except with $< f\_ae\_roberta, lof >$ and $< f\_ae\_dan, knn >$.

Table 1. AUC of the 10 best < *encoder*, *noisy* > pairs using the *semeval2010* dataset after 20 iterations.

encoder	*noisy*	AUC
f_ae_transf	knn	0.580 ± 0.007
f_ae_roberta	lof	0.576 ± 0.005
f_ae_dan	knn	0.573 ± 0.011
f_aae_roberta (gaussian)	lof	0.561 ± 0.021
f_ae_transf	sod	0.555 ± 0.012
f_ae_dan	sod	0.554 ± 0.014
f_tfidf_12	lof	0.552 ± 0.000
f_aae_roberta (kmeans)	lof	0.551 ± 0.009
f_aae_roberta (random)	lof	0.549 ± 0.011
f_dan	knn	0.548 ± 0.000

The obtained results indicate that architectures based on AE and AAE combined with anomaly detection methods obtain the highest AUC. Eigth of the 10 best pairs have an *encoder* functions based on AE and AAE. Only the functions *f_tfidf_12* and *f_dan* are not based on these architectures. Among these first pairs, architectures *f_ae_transf* and *f_ae_dan* stand out, appearing twice each with different anomaly detection methods. Also, the architecture *f_aae_roberta* with the instance selection methods *gaussian*, *kmeans* and *random* are present. This suggests that the AAE is able to adjust the latent space z independently of the instances considered as real. Among the anomaly detection methods, *lof* appears the half of the time.

Second Experiment. Table 2 summarizes the AUC with the improved input and original input in the *semeval2010* dataset. The *encoder* functions *f_tfidf_12* and *f_dan* do not depend on the previous inputs. However, it was decided to keep them in the analysis as baseline since their results should not vary considerably. In this way, it can be observed how the other functions behave with respect to these 2 functions. All methods increased their AUC with the improved input relative to their performance with the original input. Further, and more critically here, the order of the methods in terms of their performance varied significantly (Friedman: $\chi^2(2) = 108.37$, $p < 2.2e^{-16}$). This confirms that the addition of the elements to the input of the AE and AAE, proposed in this work, increased the AUC concerning the input used in [7].

Third Experiment. Table 3 shows the AUC values of the AAE architecture considering the 4 methods to select the instances considered as real. It was found significant differences between all ways to select (ANOVA: $F(3, 556) = 7.52, p < 6.12e^{-05}$). In the case of pairwise comparisons with t-test, all methods have significant differences with the *random* method. The obtained results indicate

Table 2. AUC of the ROC curves after 5 replications with improved input and original input.

improved input			original input		
encoder	*noisy*	AUC	*encoder*	*noisy*	AUC
f_ae_transf	knn	0.581 ± 0.009	*f_tfidf_12*	lof	0.552 ± 0.000
f_ae_roberta	lof	0.577 ± 0.006	*f_dan*	knn	0.548 ± 0.000
f_aae_roberta (kmeans)	lof	0.560 ± 0.013	*f_ae_transf*	sod	0.544 ± 0.011
f_ae_dan	knn	0.559 ± 0.003	*f_ae_dan*	knn	0.542 ± 0.007
f_aae_roberta (random)	lof	0.555 ± 0.014	*f_ae_transf*	knn	0.541 ± 0.007
f_tfidf_12	lof	0.552 ± 0.000	*f_ae_dan*	sod	0.532 ± 0.015
f_aae_roberta (gaussian)	lof	0.552 ± 0.042	*f_aae_roberta (kmeans)*	lof	0.529 ± 0.013
f_ae_dan	sod	0.551 ± 0.007	*f_ae_roberta*	lof	0.524 ± 0.002
f_dan	knn	0.548 ± 0.000	*f_aae_roberta (random)*	lof	0.522 ± 0.005
f_ae_transf	sod	0.547 ± 0.016	*f_aae_roberta (gaussian)*	lof	0.515 ± 0.006

that the three methods for selecting real instances proposed in this paper improve the *random* selection method reported in [7].

Table 3. Performance of the methods to select the instances considered as real after 5 iterations.

AAE with method to select	AUC
aae_gaussian	0.510 ± 0.023
aae_dbscan	0.506 ± 0.023
aae_kmeans	0.506 ± 0.027
aae_random	0.496 ± 0.032

5 Conclusions

In this paper it was evaluated the noise reduction performance of several methods to obtain unsupervised text representations. The best representation for noise reduction are obtained with the AE and AAE architectures using the improved input proposed in this work. The input consists of a concatenation of the entity vectors, the text between the two entities including them and the full text. Moreover, using the improved input results in higher AUC values compared to using the *original* input. The obtained results confirm the importance of adding more information as input to the AE and AAE.

The obtained results demonstrate that the three methods to select the instances considered as real that are proposed in this work improve significantly the AUC of the random selection method. However, no significant differences were found between the three methods. Because of this, it is considered that the *gaussian* method may be a good choice considering its low computational cost compared to the other two.

As future work, the next step is proposing an approach that improves the representations by adding more input information. Also it is worth to investigate how to combine the input information. Finally, use of other types of layers such as long short-term memory (LSTM) will be evaluated.

Acknowledgements. The present work was supported by CONACyT/México (scholarship 937210 and grant CB-2015-01-257383) and Labex EFL through EFL mobility grants. Additionally, the authors thank CONACYT for the computer resources provided through the INAOE Supercomputing Laboratory's Deep Learning Platform for Language Technologies.

References

1. Artetxe, M., Schwenk, H.: Massively multilingual sentence embeddings for zero-shot cross-lingual transfer and beyond. Trans. Assoc. Comput. Linguist. **7**, 597–610 (2019)
2. Bastos, A., et al.: RECON: relation extraction using knowledge graph context in a graph neural network. In: Proceedings of the Web Conference 2021, pp. 1673–1685 (2020)
3. Breunig, M.M., Kriegel, H.P., Ng, R.T., Sander, J.: LOF: identifying density-based local outliers. In: Proceedings of the 2000 ACM SIGMOD international conference on Management of Data, pp. 93–104 (2000)
4. Cer, D., et al.: Universal Sentence Encoder. arXiv:1803.11175v2 [cs.CL] p. 7 (2018)
5. Ester, M., Kriegel, H.P., Sander, J., Xu, X.: A density-based algorithm for discovering clusters in large spatial databases with noise. In: Proceedings of Second International Conference on Knowledge Discovery and Data Mining (KDD-1996), vol. 96(34), pp. 226–231 (1996)
6. Etzioni, O., Fader, A., Christensen, J., Soderland, S.: Mausam: open information extraction: the second generation. Int. Joint Conf. Artif. Intell. **11**, 3–10 (2011)
7. García-Mendoza, J.L., Villaseñor-Pineda, L., Orihuela-Espina, F., Bustio-Martínez, L.: An autoencoder-based representation for noise reduction in distant supervision of relation extraction. J. Intell. Fuzzy Syst. **42**(5), 4523–4529 (2022)
8. Hearst, M.A.: Automatic acquisition of hyponyms from large text corpora. In: Proceedings of the 14th Conference on Computational Linguistics (COLING-1992), pp. 539–545 (1992)
9. Hendrickx, I., et al.: SemEval-2010 task 8: multi-way classification of semantic relations between pairs of nominals. In: Proceedings of the 5th International Workshop on Semantic Evaluation, ACL 2010, pp. 94–99 (2010)
10. Holm, S.: A simple sequentially rejective multiple test procedure. Scand. J. Stat. **6**(2), 65–70 (1979)
11. Jat, S., Khandelwal, S., Talukdar, P.: Improving distantly supervised relation extraction using word and entity based attention. In: 6th Workshop on Automated Knowledge Base Construction, AKBC@NIPS 2017 (2017)
12. Ji, G., Liu, K., He, S., Zhao, J.: Distant supervision for relation extraction with sentence-level attention and entity descriptions. In: Proceedings of the Thirty-First AAAI Conference on Artificial Intelligence (AAAI-2017), pp. 3060–3066 (2017)
13. Kim, J.T., Moldovan, D.I.: Acquisition of semantic patterns for information extraction from corpora. In: Proceedings of 9th IEEE Conference on Artificial Intelligence for Applications, pp. 171–176 (1993)

14. Kingma, D.P., Welling, M.: Auto-encoding variational bayes. In: International Conference on Learning Representations (ICLR) (2014)
15. Kriegel, H.-P., Kröger, P., Schubert, E., Zimek, A.: Outlier detection in axis-parallel subspaces of high dimensional data. In: Theeramunkong, T., Kijsirikul, B., Cercone, N., Ho, T.-B. (eds.) PAKDD 2009. LNCS (LNAI), vol. 5476, pp. 831–838. Springer, Heidelberg (2009). https://doi.org/10.1007/978-3-642-01307-2_86
16. Lin, Y., Shen, S., Liu, Z., Luan, H., Sun, M.: Neural relation extraction with selective attention over instances. In: Proceedings of the 54th Annual Meeting of the Association for Computational Linguistics, pp. 2124–2133 (2016)
17. Liu, F.T., Ting, K.M., Zhou, Z.H.: Isolation forest. In: Eighth IEEE International Conference on Data Mining, pp. 413–422. ICDM 2008 (2008)
18. Liu, Y., et al.: RoBERTa: A Robustly Optimized BERT Pretraining Approach. arXiv:1907.11692(2019)
19. Lloyd, S.P.: Least squares quantization in PCM. IEEE Trans. Inf. Theory **28**(2), 129–137 (1982)
20. Makhzani, A., Shlens, J., Jaitly, N., Goodfellow, I., Frey, B.: Adversarial autoencoders. In: International Conference on Learning Representations (ICLR) Workshop (2016)
21. Mintz, M., Bills, S., Snow, R., Jurafsky, D.: Distant supervision for relation extraction without labeled data. In: Proceedings of the 47th Annual Meeting of the ACL, pp. 1003–1011 (2009)
22. Pang, G., Shen, C., Cao, L., Van den Hengel, A.: Deep learning for anomaly detection: a review. ACM Comput. Surv. **1**(1), 3569–3570 (2020)
23. Pevný, T.: LODA: lightweight on-line detector of anomalies. Mach. Learn. **102**(2), 275–304 (2016)
24. Piskorski, J., Yangarber, R.: Information extraction: past, present and future. In: oibeau, T., Saggion, H., Piskorski, J., Yangarber, R. (eds.) Multi-source, Multilingual Information Extraction and Summarization. Theory and Applications of Natural Language Processing, pp. 23–49. Springer, Heidelberg (2013). https://doi.org/10.1007/978-3-642-28569-1_2
25. Riedel, S., Yao, L., McCallum, A.: Modeling relations and their mentions without labeled text. In: Balcázar, J.L., Bonchi, F., Gionis, A., Sebag, M. (eds.) ECML PKDD 2010. LNCS (LNAI), vol. 6323, pp. 148–163. Springer, Heidelberg (2010). https://doi.org/10.1007/978-3-642-15939-8_10
26. Ru, C., Tang, J., Li, S., Xie, S., Wang, T.: Using semantic similarity to reduce wrong labels in distant supervision for relation extraction. Inf. Process. Manage. **54**(4), 593–608 (2018)
27. Shyu, M.L., Chen, S.C., Sarinnapakorn, K., Chang, L.: A Novel Anomaly Detection Scheme Based on Principal Component Classifier. Technical report (2003)
28. Smirnova, A., Cudré-Mauroux, P.: Relation extraction using distant supervision: a survey. ACM Comput. Surv. **51**(5), 1–35 (2018)
29. Soderland, S.: Learning information extraction rules for semi-structured and free text. Mach. Learn. **34**, 233–272 (1999)
30. Takamatsu, S., Sato, I., Nakagawa, H.: Reducing wrong labels in distant supervision for relation extraction. In: Proceedings of the 50th Annual Meeting of the Association for Computational Linguistics, pp. 721–729 (2012)
31. Vashishth, S., Joshi, R., Prayaga, S.S., Bhattacharyya, C., Talukdar, P.: Reside: improving distantly-supervised neural relation extraction using side information. In: Proceedings of the 2018 Conference on Empirical Methods in Natural Language Processing, pp. 1257–1266 (2018)

32. Ye, Z.X., Ling, Z.H.: Distant supervision relation extraction with intra-bag and inter-bag attentions. In: Proceedings of the 2019 Conference of the North American Chapter of the Association for Computational Linguistics: Human Language Technologies, pp. 2810–2819 (2019)
33. Zeng, D., Liu, K., Chen, Y., Zhao, J.: Distant supervision for relation extraction via piecewise convolutional neural networks. In: Proceedings of the 2015 Conference on Empirical Methods in Natural Language Processing, pp. 1753–1762 (2015)
34. Zhou, P., Xu, J., Qi, Z., Bao, H., Chen, Z., Xu, B.: Distant supervision for relation extraction with hierarchical selective attention. Neural Netw. **108**, 240–247 (2018)

Automatic Identification of Suicidal Ideation in Texts Using Cascade Classifiers

María del Carmen García-Galindo[1(✉)], Ángel Hernández-Castañeda[1,2], René Arnulfo García-Hernández[1], and Yulia Ledeneva[1]

[1] Autonomous University of the State of Mexico, Instituto Literario 100, Col. Centro. C.P., 50000 Toluca, Mexico State, Mexico
marycarmeng142@gmail.com, angelhc2305@gmail.com, renearnulfo@hotmail.com, yledeneva@yahoo.com

[2] Cátedras CONACyT, Av. Insurgentes Sur 1582, Col. Crédito Constructor. C.P., 03940 Mexico City, Mexico

Abstract. According to the 2021 World Health Organization report, suicide is a universal phenomenon that causes about 703,000 deaths per year, being among the first five causes of unnatural death. Suicide mainly affects young people between 15 and 29 years old, who are also the main users of social media. It is noteworthy that these digital platforms play a dual role in suicide issues, on the one hand, by allowing access to dangerous sites that can provide pro-suicide information and, on the other hand, by allowing clues of suicidal ideations to be detected through shared content. To address this health concern, this study presents a computational method based on a cascade classification that first detects the distribution of latent emotions in text and uses this output to identify signs of suicidal ideation. Our experimental results show that the cascade architecture proves to be more robust than direct classification when there are no explicit signs of suicidal ideation. In addition, unlike direct classification, our proposed approach automatically provides information about the emotions that influence a person with suicidal thoughts.

Keywords: Suicide ideation · Social networks · Sentiment analysis · Natural language processing

1 Introduction

Suicide is not a new topic, on the contrary, it is a universal human phenomenon that has always existed, being mentioned since aancient Greece in the writings of Plato and Aristotle, to the present day [12,15,20].

The term suicide coming from the Latin expressions "sui" (oneself) and "caedere" (to kill) [15,22]. Nonetheless, its meaning varies according to the principles of each culture [15]. For this reason, in this study we adopt a simple but

O. Pichardo Lagunas et al. (Eds.): MICAI 2022, LNAI 13613, pp. 114–126, 2022.
https://doi.org/10.1007/978-3-031-19496-2_9

concise definition given by Echeburúa [8], who defines suicide as the death produced by oneself as a result of the execution of a plan/action, whose precise intention is to put an end to one's own life.

According to the American Foundation for Suicide Prevention - AFSP [1], suicide is an event that involves three main steps:

- Suicidal ideation: The person begins to have thoughts and desires to intentionally take his or her own life [22].
- Planning: The individual defines methods, artifacts, to achieve the goal (killing oneself) [1].
- Attempt/Consummate suicide: Attempt suicide is potentially self-injurious behavior with a non-fatal outcome. However, it may end in a consummate suicide [20,22].

In the latest report from World Health Organization (WHO) in 2021, it is mentioned that around 703,000 people commit suicide every year [28] and for each commit suicide there are many more attempts [7,12,15]. Previous studies indicate that suicide rates have increased globally by up to 60% in the last 45 years [2,9].

As a result of the increase in suicide deaths, suicide is considered among the first five most frequent causes of unnatural death [8,22,28], mainly in young people aged 15–29 years [4,12,28].

There is a great diversity of reasons why a person decides to commit suicide, however, some of the protective factors have been identified are high self-esteem, good relationships with family/friends/ partners, distraction in hobbies (for example, in social media), religion and good regulation of emotions [1,12,13].

Nowadays, the Internet and social media are preferred by young people to express themselves [3]; however, Durkee et al. [7] indicates that these means play a dual role in the ideation suicide (risk or protective factor).

On the one hand, the inappropriate use of these platforms could allow users to access pro-suicide content [18,27]. Furthermore, social media facilitate the dissemination of suicidal ideas, suicide pacts or the obtaining the material means to make an attempt [9].

On the other hand, previous studies claims that the contents of social media can be used as a protective and preventive factor, because they allow identifying patterns that frequently appear in text with suicidal ideation [6,21].

The extensive use of social media to share suicidal thoughts is commonly due to the possibility of remaining anonymous [18]. Anonymity increases the possibility that individuals will freely confess and discuss their thoughts and emotions related to suicide, leading to the publication of suicide notes [19,27]. In this sense, Luxton et al. [16] mentions that, in many cases, people who attempt suicide prefer to post it on social media instead of calling health services or asking their relatives for help.

In this study, we analyze the performance of a cascade classification method to automatically identify texts with content of suicidal intent, based on their distribution of latent emotions. A first classifier determines the distribution of emotions present in each text; then, a second classifier identifies probable cases of suicidal ideation based on the result of the first classifier.

2 Related Works

Over the years, several strategies have been implemented in different fields of study with the aim of preventing and reducing suicide deaths. Recently, these prevention strategies have focused mainly on the study of social media and the Internet, due to its influence on young people.

In the computational area, machine learning and natural language processing techniques have been used mainly for the task of detecting notes with suicidal ideation content.

In this regard, Seah and Shim [25], by applying the latent Dirichlet allocation (LDA) algorithm, find fourteen latent topics related to depression and suicide in the social media Reddit. According to this study, knowledge of latent topics can help understand the contexts in which conversations about depression and suicide events occur. These contexts do not necessarily explain the direct causes of suicidal acts, however, they provide clues about the events that a suicidal person faces.

Tadesse et al. [26] examined the potential of combined model of Long Short-Term Memory (LSTM) and Convolutional Neural Network (CNN) to recognize suicidal ideation texts on the social network Reddit. The authors conclude that suicidal people make greater use of words with connotations of death, in contrast to non-suicidal people who predominantly use words describing happy moments, positive attitudes and feelings. Their proposed model shows an F1 of 92.6%; however, the authors mention that the dataset used was very small.

Other works address the impact of emotions related to suicide. In this sense, Sarsam et al. [23] use the NRC Affect Intensity Lexicon and SentiStrength resources to identify emotions related to suicide on Twitter. The authors apply the YATSI (Yet Another Two-Stage Idea) semi-supervised learning classifier to perform the classification and argue that suicidal tweets are largely associated with negative emotions such as fear and sadness. In contrast, the set of non-suicidal tweets reflects a greater presence of positive emotions. This proposed approach shows an accuracy of 86.97%.

Desmet and Hoste [5] proposes an automatic emotion detection system using 15 binary support vector machine (SVM) classifiers. Each classifier assigns a specific emotion for a given text according to a threshold. The authors consider the combination of 7 lexico-semantic feature representation sets. The most informational models, in this proposal, are trigram, lemma bags-of-words and subjectivity clues achieving an 68.86% F-score.

Identification of regular language patterns in social media texts is also applied to recognize suicidal tendencies. For instance, Jain et al. [14] examine posts and comments, from subreddits "r/Depression" and "r/SuicideWatch", to understand the difference in linguistic terms between a person with suicidal ideation and someone who is depressed. The authors apply different machine learning algorithms to find out which one provides the best performance for suicide note detection. As a result, the Logistic Regression algorithm obtains the best performance with an accuracy of 77.29%.

According to current standards, different works have been developed to automatically identify suicide notes using Natural Language Processing (NLP) techniques and machine learning algorithms, giving promising results. However, standard and robust datasets are not usually available to validate and compare results in new proposals. Furthermore, most of these studies apply direct classification and focus on explicit linguistic terms that characterize suicide notes.

Consequently, methods based on direct classification may not be useful in the detection of texts with non-explicit suicidal content, due to this kind of texts do not present specific linguistic terms related to suicide. This makes it difficult to identify suicidal ideation by simple approaches; instead, the cascade methodology can address this weaknessess, as mentioned by Tadesse et al. [26].

Therefore, in this study, we propose a cascade classification that first automatically detects the distribution of latent emotions in texts, and then determines whether the text has suicidal content based on that obtained distribution. One of the main advantages of this approach is that it can consider more than the words that characterize suicidal texts (e.g. kill, suicide, life, die); instead, our proposed method focuses on a person's emotional state to identify non-explicit suicidal ideation.

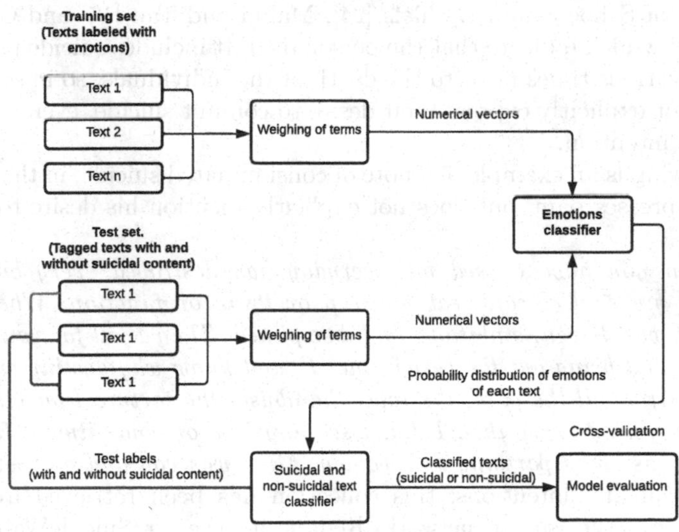

Fig. 1. General scheme of the proposed method.

3 Proposed Method

To detect the presence of suicide ideation, in this study, an ensemble of classifiers is performed. Our proposed method takes the output vectors of the first classifier (latent emotional distribution) as the input vectors of the second classifier that determine whether the text has suicidal content.

Figure 1 shows a general overview of our proposed method described as follows. The first stage consists of term weighting in which each text is converted into a numerical fixed-length vector. Then the emotional distribution of each text is determined with the first classifier. Next, the emotional distribution feed the second classifier that determines, based on that input, which text is suicidal. To validate our results, a 5 fold cross-validation procedure was performed.

3.1 Datasets

A suicide note is usually written moments before an attempt is made. The suicide note provides insight into the emotional state, motivations, thoughts, desires, etc, of the suicidal person linked to the moment when they carry out their death.

To the best of the authors' knowledge, there is no robust, open access corpus of suicide notes, making it difficult to validate our proposed method. Therefore, three different datasets were created in this work, which are detailed below.

- Notes of consummated suicide: this collection consists of the notes used in the study of Schoene and Dethlefs [24], Malini and Tan [17] and Gunn and Lester [10], which indicate that the person died. It includes suicide notes published at various times prior to the death of the individuals, so in some cases they do not explicitly express their desire to commit suicide, even when they have that intention.
  The following is an example of a note of consummated suicide, in the note the person expresses pain, but does not explicitly mention his desire to commit suicide.
  "The pain you have caused me everyday has destroyed every bit of me, destroyed my soul. I can't eat or sleep or think or function. When I first met you I was driven, ambitious and disciplined. Then I fell for you, a love I thought would bring out the best in me. I don't know why destiny brought us together. After all the pain, the rape, the abuse, the torture I have seen previously I didn't deserve this. I didn't see any love or commitment from you. Your life was about partying and women. Mine was you and my work".
- Notes of suicidal intentions: this collection has been retrieved from public posts on the social network Reddit in the "r/SuicideWatch" and "r/Depression" subreddits. It was manually created by searching for words and expressions related to suicide, example: suicide, suicidal ideation, attempted suicide, best death, failed attempt, etc. These texts mark a clear difference between people who explicitly express their intention to die, versus others who have the same desire, but do not express it openly.

The following is an example of a note of suicidal intention in which the person uses suicide-related terms.
"I wish I was allowed to commit suicide. I hate how suicide is so stigmatized by society, and how much guilt-tripping there is surrounding the issue. I am not "mentally ill" for being suicidal, rather my wish is a product of rational choice. I no longer believe that life is worth living and I am not interested in living it. I have little interest in "improving" either myself or the world, as both things turn to dust in the final analysis, along with any accomplishments I or anyone else might make. I just want this whole pointless existence to be over already, as I see literally no point in it continuing".

- Non-suicide notes: this collection was manually created from public posts on the social network Reddit in the "r/culture", "r/economy", "r/politics", "r/music", "r/food" and "r/sports" subreddits.

For a deeper analysis of involved emotions in cases previous to death, we also used a set of notes of final statements made by death row inmates executed in the state of Texas[1]. Thus, an analysis is made of the linguistic and emotional differences of people who take their own lives compared to people who have been convicted, who do not exactly have a desire to die.

One of the steps of our proposal requires provide a distribution of latent emotions presented by each text in the suicide notes collection. For this purpose, the CEASE (Corpus of Emotion Annotated Suicide notes in English) was used. This collection consists of 1,001 sentences, labeled with 13 emotions, distributed as follows: abuse (12), anger (79), blame (47), fear (29), forgiveness (24), guilt (74), peacefulness (38), hopefulness (169), hopelessness (85), love (85), pride (16), sorrow (305) and thankfulness (38).

Our first dataset consists of 155 notes of consummated suicide, the second has 453 notes of suicidal intentions, the third 255 non-suicidal notes, and the last 453 final statements made by death row inmates. Table 1 shows the basic statistics of each corpus.

Table 1. Description of the corpus used.

Class	No. of Docs	Tokens avg. per Doc
Consummated suicide	155	11
Suicidal intentions	453	67
Not-suicide notes	255	56
Written by people sentenced	453	50

As a preprocessing step, we lowercase words and remove punctuation marks, stop words, special symbols, and all URLs.

[1] https://www.tdcj.texas.gov/death_row/dr_executed_offenders.html.

3.2 Weighing of Terms

Feature vectorization is performed to transform the original text into numerical vectors. Specifically we focus on three feature sources: Term frequency - Inverse document frequency (TF-IDF), LDA and Doc2Vec (D2V).

These methods were chosen, because they have shown competitive results in the current research and, on the other hand, because they cover different levels of language (lexical and semantic); for example, TF-IDF provides features related to the importance of words in a text collection, LDA provides semantic features and D2V provides semantic features considering the context of the words [11].

3.3 Cascade Classification

The proposed approach consists of two classifiers set up in a cascading architecture. The first classifier is in charge of obtaining latent emotions from text and the second classifier take the emotions to identify suicide texts.

Therefore, to obtain the distribution of emotions from the suicide dataset, a classifier with the CEASE (Corpus of Emotion Annotated Suicide notes in English) is trained. Then, with the model obtained, suicidal and non-suicidal texts are classified. Because the CEASE is labeled with 13 emotions, 13-dimensional vectors are obtained. Each dimension represents the extent to which each emotion is present in each classified text (suicidal or non-suicidal).

The output of the first classifier are those vectors with the emotional distribution of each text in the suicide dataset. Thus, these vectors feed a second classifier that makes the final decision. The final classification decides if a text is a suicidal note. To estimate the performance of the second classifier, a 5 fold cross-validation model is used.

The classifiers analyzed in this study are support vector machine (SVM), naive Bayes Multinomial(NB) and Multilayer Perceptron (MLP) which is a feed-forward artificial neural network (FANN) model. This network is trained using Backpropagation.

The configuration of the hyperparameters of the SVM consists of lineal kernel with control error of one for each misclassified data point, The curvature weight of the decision boundary was defined as one over the number of features.

FANN architecture consists of two hidden layers, where the first layer has four neurons, while the second layer has two neurons. The activation function was specified as 'tahn', the maximum number of interations was determined in 10000 epochs.

4 Experimentation and Results

In this study, we implement and compare two approaches:

- Direct classification: It is the most used in current approaches that consist of representing texts as vectors (using some mapped method) and performing classification. This approach serves as a point of comparison to validate our proposed approach.

- Cascade classification: This is the proposed approach, in which the output of the first classifier (emotional distribution) is used to train the second classifier to determine if a text is a suicide note. According to our experimental results, cascade classification, unlike the direct classification, is capable to detect signs of suicidal risk when people do not explicitly express it.

In the first experiment, we analyzed the explicit notes obtained from Reddit and the final statements of those sentenced to death. This classification allows knowing the performance of the proposed method when the study texts have the same domain (death topics), although different in intention (some want to die voluntarily and other are forced to die).

Table 2. Results of the classification of explicit content notes vs. final statements of those sentenced to death.

Approach	Method	Precision	Recall	F1
Direct	TF-IDF + SVM	97.21%	98.46%	97.79%
	TF-IDF + ANN	98.03%	96.92%	**97.9%**
	TF-IDF + NB	95.97%	99.12%	97.46%
Cascade	D2V + SVM	96.37%	96.9%	**96.57%**
	LDA + ANN	51.16%	41.45%	92.04%
	TF-IDF + NB	79.59%	92.71%	84.18%

Table 2 shows the results obtained from both approaches (direct and cascade classification). As can be seen, direct classification obtained the best result with 97.9% of F1 using TF-IDF and ANN, while cascade classification obtained 96.57% of F1 using D2V and SVM. This results is in agreement with to our inference because the Reddit texts have several explicit words about suicide that lead the direct classification to have high performance.

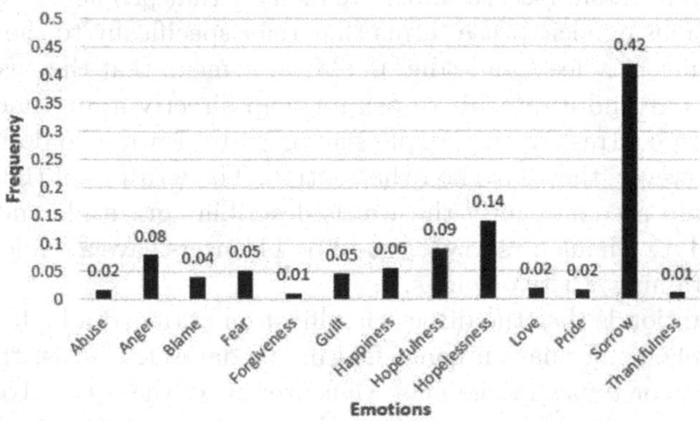

Fig. 2. Distribution of emotions in explicit notes from Reddit.

To obtain a deeper analysis of the emotional distribution between the intentional and forced death, the sum of all vectors in each corresponding dataset is averaged. This resultant average (see Fig. 2) shows that people who wants to die are more influenced by negative emotions such as: sorrow (0.42%), hopelessness (0.14%) and anger (0.08%). However, suicide notes do not only consist of negative emotions, but positive emotions are present to a lesser extent.

In contrast, texts written by people sentenced to death show more diversity between positive and negative emotions as shown in Fig. 3. Those sentenced to death show in their notes high sense of hopelfulness (0.34%) compared to those who wish to die by choice (0.09%). In addition, the emotions of love, sorrow and thankfulness have a 0.14% probability of belonging to these texts. According to the distribution obtained, those sentenced express more positive emotions.

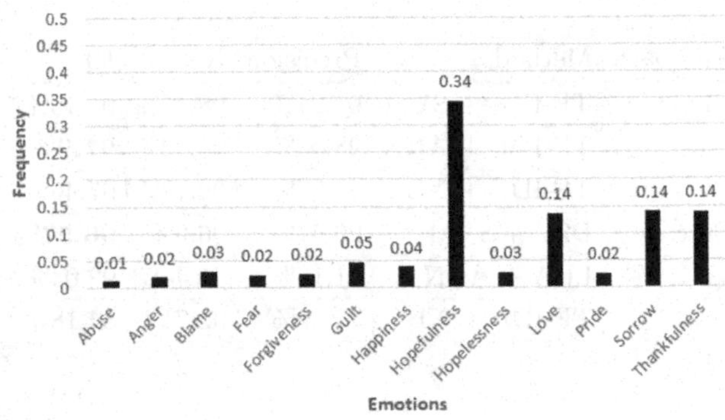

Fig. 3. Distribution of emotions of people sentenced to death.

The datasets (explicit notes and writings by people sentenced) were examined to compare dissimilarities in the lexicon. We selected the top ten frequent terms from each class to examine their nature and connection to the topic of death, in different intent (see Table 3). We identify that people who express their suicidal intentions explicitly, use terms that refer specifically to the intention to die ("life", "suicide", "feel" and "die"). This may mean that they want someone to help them, but find it difficult to ask for help directly from someone in their family circle. In contrast to the people sentenced to death who do not precisely wish to die, however, they have no other option. The writings of those sentenced to death contain predominantly the words describing gratitude and repentance ("love", "family", "thank", "sorry", "good"). The users have a tendency to strive towards maintaining positive spirits.

Our assumption is that the direct classification obtained a high performance due to the explicit information contained in the dataset; that is, there are predominant words or topics in one class that are not in the other. To confirm the assumption, we conducted a second experiment where we classified the suicide notes consummated and notes not related to suicide. Table 4 shows the results

Table 3. Most frequent words in the explicit notes and writings of those sentenced to death.

No	Explicit notes		Writings of those sentenced to death	
	Word	Frequency	Word	Frequency
1	im	600	**love**	816
2	want	416	**family**	371
3	**life**	366	know	356
4	like	324	**thank**	331
5	know	304	**sorry**	285
6	**suicide**	280	want	257
7	**feel**	238	like	255
8	even	236	**god**	247
9	people	203	say	200
10	**die**	193	**life**	174

obtained. In this case, on the one hand, the direct classification obtained 90.85% of F1 using DV2 and SVM. On the other hand, the cascade classification obtained the best result with 94.84% of F1 using D2V and NB.

Table 4. Results of the classification of suicide notes consummated vs. non-suicide notes.

Approach	Method	Precision	Recall	F1
Direct	D2V + SVM	85.76%	92.26%	**90.85%**
	D2V + ANN	83.33%	88.39%	89.19%
	D2V + NB	85.33%	90.97%	87.66%
Cascade	D2V + SVM	81.61%	90.71%	88.98%
	LDA + ANN	79.11%	88.69%	85.78%
	D2V + NB	95.96%	90.69%	**94.84%**

Table 4 shows that the direct classification decrese its perfomance when there is no explict terms for suicide. In contrast, the cascade classification performance increased. Therefore, it can be inferred that the direct approach is not robust to classify notes where suicidal thoughts are not directly exposed, but are latently.

D2V being a context-sensitive mapping technique, provide useful features to detect suicide and achieve the best performance in the cascade approach. It is important to detect these signs of risk to prevent suicide attempts or completed suicide.

The datasets (suicide notes consummated and notes not related to suicide) were examined to compare dissimilarities in the lexicon. We examine the top ten frequent terms from each class to examine their connection with suicide ideation (see Table 5). The word count allows us to identify, that in the consummated suicide notes the use of terms that refer to their suicidal intentions does not stand out. In contrast to the explicit notes previously analyzed (see Table 3) where use different terms that refer specifically to the intention to die.

Table 5. Most frequent words in the suicide notes consummated and notes not related to suicide.

No	Consummated notes		Non-suicide notes	
	Word	Frequency	Word	Frequency
1	never	22	people	169
2	**time**	19	**like**	136
3	**love**	18	get	94
4	know	17	one	87
5	said	15	dont	80
6	**life**	14	even	76
7	much	14	would	73
8	**feel**	13	really	69
9	would	12	**time**	65
10	get	12	good	63

Overall results indicate that it is not enough to analyze the linguistic terms present in a suicide note to define whether there is an intention to die. Latent distribution of emotions is relevant information, in which not only the emotions present are known, but also the percentage of presence of each one is shown.

5 Conclusions

Suicide is a relevant phenomenon that can be prevented analyzing the notes shared in the social media by people with this tendency. It is therefore important to improve the systems for detecting suicidal notes that are expressed explicitly and not explicitly, because not all people who have these thoughts say it openly.

In this paper, a cascade method was proposed to first analyze the emotional distribution presented by each study text and with the emotional distribution determine which text focuses on suicide. We used different data representation techniques to cover different levels of language.

Based on our experiments, the proposed method considerably improves the detect of suicide notes with non-explicit content. In contrast to a direct classification; In which certain terms related to the topic of death ("suicide", "want die", "die", "suicide ideation", "wish die", "want kill", etc.) must be present, to make a correct division between the classes. The main reason the cascade method is more robust and outperforms the direct classification, is that not depend exclusively on the words of the suicide notes. First, it takes advantage of the latent emotional distribution. Second, it uses the emotional distribution to classify which text is related to suicide.

Through the analysis of the information obtained in this study, we observed that the negative emotions are more predominant in people who want to die voluntarily, however, positive emotions also exist less frequently. In comparison with the final statements of people sentenced to death, who express great diversity between the positive and negative polarity of their emotions. Another interesting observation is found in the use of linguistic terms used by those who wish to die voluntarily and those who are forced. In the first case, the presence of certain terms referring to death is observed, making visible this tendency to die. On the contrary, people sentenced to death make greater use of positive terms.

Acknowledgements. We thank Autonomous University of the State of Mexico and CONACYT.

References

1. AFSP American Foundation for Suicide Prevention: https://afsp.org/risk-factors-protective-factors-and-warning-signs, Last Accesed 23 Oct 2021
2. Arroyo Fernández, A., Bertomeu Ruiz, A.: Métodos suicidas e internet. Revista Española de Medicina Legal **38**(4), 143–148 (2012)
3. Bohórquez López, C., Rodríguez Cárdenas, D.E.: Percepción de amistad en adolescentes: el papel de las redes sociales. Revista Colombiana de Psicología **23**(2), 325–338 (2014)
4. Borges Guilherme Orozco, R., Benjet, C., Medina-Mora, M.E.: Suicidio y conductas suicidas en méxico: retrospectiva y situación actual. Salud Pública de México **52**(4), 292–304 (2010)
5. Desmet, B., Hoste, V.: Emotion detection in suicide notes. Expert Syst. Appl. **40**(16), 6351–6358 (2013)
6. Dieu, F., Kahan, E.: Cibersuicidio en adolescentes. Universidad de la República, Facultad de Psicología, Trabajo final de grado (2018)
7. Durkee, T., Hadlaczky, G., Westerlund, M., Carli, V.: Internet pathways in suicidality: a review of the evidence. Int. J. Environ. Res. Public Health **8**(10), 3938–3952 (2011)
8. Echeburúa, E.: Las múltiples caras del suicidio en la clínica psicológica. Terapia psicológica **33**(2), 117–126 (2015)
9. Fehling, K.B., Selby, E.A.: Suicide in DSM-5: current evidence for the proposed suicide behavior disorder and other possible improvements. Front Psychiatry **11**, 499980 (2021)
10. Gunn, J.F., Lester, D.: Twitter postings and suicide: an analysis of the postings of a fatal suicide in the 24 hours prior to death. Suicidologi **17**(3), 28–30 (2012)
11. Hernández-Castañeda, Á., García-Hernández, R.A., Ledeneva, Y., Millán-Hernández, C.E.: Extractive automatic text summarization based on lexical-semantic keywords. IEEE Access **8**, 49896–49907 (2020)
12. Hernández Soto, P.A., Villarreal Casate, R.E.: Algunas especificidades entorno a la conducta suicida. MEDISAN **19**(08), 1051–1058 (2015)

13. Holman, M.S., Williams, M.N.: Suicide risk and protective factors: a network approach. Arch. Suicide Res. **26**(1), 137–154 (2022)
14. Jain, P., Srinivas, K.R., Vichare, A.: Depression and suicide analysis using machine learning and NLP. J. Phys: Conf. Ser. **2161**(01), 012034 (2022)
15. Jiménez Treviño, L., Sáiz Martínez, P.A., Bobes García, J.: Suicidio y depresión. Humánitas, Humanidades médicas **09**, 1–21 (2006)
16. Luxton, D.D., June, J.D., Kinn, J.T.: Technology-based suicide prevention: current applications and future directions. Telemedicine J. E-health **17**(1), 50–54 (2011)
17. Malini, N., Tan, V.: Forensic linguistics analysis of Virginia Woolf's suicide notes. Int. J. Edu. **9**(1), 53–58 (2016)
18. Murcia Sanabria, C.M., Brillyth, V.Y.K.: Factores relacionados al suicidio en adolescentes. Trabajo final de grado, Institución Universitaria Politécnico Grancolombiano, Facultad de Ciencias Sociales (2020)
19. O'Dea, B., Larsen, M., Batterham, P., Calear, A., Christensen, H.: Talking suicide on Twitter: linguistic style and language processes of suicide-related posts. Eur. Psychiatry **33**, S274 (2016)
20. Ortega González, M.: Comportamiento Suicida. Reflexiones críticas para su estudio desde un sistema psicológico. Qartuppi, S. de R.L. de C.V., Hermosillo, Sonora 83220 México, 1era edn. (2018)
21. Parrott, S., Britt, B.C., Hayes, J.L., Albright, D.L.: Social media and suicide: a validation of terms to help identify suicide-related social media posts. J. Evid. Based Soc. Work **17**(5), 624–634 (2020)
22. de salud, M.: Programa nacional de prevención del suicidio - orientaciones para su implementación. Norma General Administrativa (027) (2013)
23. Sarsam, S.M., Al-Samarraie, H., Alzahrani, A.I., Alnumay, W., Smith, A.P.: A lexicon-based approach to detecting suicide-related messages on Twitter. Biomed. Signal Process. Control **65**, 102355 (2021)
24. Schoene, A.M., Dethlefs, N.: Unsupervised suicide note classification. In: Proceedings of WISDOM Workshop (WISDOM'18), vol. 4, p. 9. ACM, NY, USA (2018)
25. Seah, J.H.K., Jin Shim, K.: Data mining approach to the detection of suicide in social media: a case study of Singapore. In: 2018 IEEE International Conference on Big Data (Big Data), vol. 10–13, pp. 5442–5444. Research Collection School Of Computing and Information Systems, Seattle, WA (2018)
26. Tadesse, M.M., Lin, H., Xu, B., Yang, L.: Detection of suicide ideation in social media forums using deep learning. Algorithms **13**(1), 7 (2020)
27. Tam, J., Tang, W., Fernando, D.: The internet and suicide: a double-edged tool. Eur. J. Intern. Med. **18**(6), 453–455 (2007)
28. WHO Organización Mundial de la Salud: https://www.who.int/es/news-room/fact-sheets/detail/suicide, Last Accesed 17 Jun 2021

Web Crawler and Classifier for News Articles

Consuelo-Varinia García-Mendoza and Omar Juárez Gambino(✉)

Instituto Politécnico Nacional, ESCOM, Lindavista, G.A. Madero, 07738 Mexico City, Mexico
{cvgarcia,jjuarezg}@ipn.mx

Abstract. In this work, we present a crawler that collects news articles and a classifier that identifies the section to which these articles belong. Due to a large number of available sources of information, a tool for gathering and filtering news articles about specific interests is necessary. For instance, a person might be interested in news about sports or science, and it could be necessary to check several websites to obtain this kind of news finally. Therefore, in this work, we propose a web application that uses a crawler to collect news articles from different websites automatically, then a classifier determines the section of each news article, and finally, the news articles that match the section of interest are displayed in the web application.

Keywords: Web crawling · Text classification · Machine learning

1 Introduction

The use of websites as a means of communication is increasing, which makes it possible to consult news from different sites such as electronic newspapers; their information as well as that of traditional newspapers is divided into sections to facilitate consultation, however, this division tends to vary in each website, even with the same content. News articles can be retrieved by search engines using special tags and markers, such as sections of news articles (sport, science, culture, politics, etc.), but when this information is not available or is wrong, retrieving these documents becomes a difficult task.

Crawlers automatically obtain web pages by following a list of hyperlinks. The visited web pages are downloaded and the process continues with the next set of hyperlinks [1]. There have been important advances in web crawling techniques like focused web crawler which refines the collected web documents by searching predefined keywords in the documents, and only those that contain the keywords are downloaded [2]. Although it is possible to retrieve documents based on keywords, as was explained above, some documents may be relevant despite not having the specified keywords and would not be retrieved. Therefore, we propose an additional step that can analyze the content of the documents to

O. Pichardo Lagunas et al. (Eds.): MICAI 2022, LNAI 13613, pp. 127–136, 2022.
https://doi.org/10.1007/978-3-031-19496-2_10

verify if it is relevant for the users. For this last step we follow a text classification approach.

Text classification is used to organize documents in predefined groups. This task can be done using supervised and unsupervised approaches [3]. Unsupervised approach is an interesting field of research, but in this paper we have decided to follow a supervised approach based on the good results obtained in the state of the art [4,5].

Authors in [6] collected 2,000 news articles from Indian websites. The corpus was splitted into two datasets, 80% for training and 20% for testing. Several classifiers were used, but the best results was obtained by Random Forest with 85.92% of precision. In [7] authors collected 4,027 news articles from three different Mexican Newspapers. The newspapers have several predefined sections which are different between them. By following a supervised approach, three classifiers were trained, one for each newspaper. A 10-fold cross-validation was applied and 83% of average accuracy was obtained. The authors in [8] used an Artificial Neural Network (ANN) to classify news articles into 5 sections. 542 news articles were collected, then an Autoencoder was used to extract features. The ANN was trained with 386 news articles and tested with 156 news articles, obtaining 83% of accuracy.

In this work a web application was created to collect news articles from 7 sources of information using a crawler, and then a classifier groups the gathered articles into sections. Finally, the news articles that match the section previously selected in the web application are displayed. In the following section the crawling process is described (Sect. 2); then the classification process is explained (Sect. 3); after that details of the developed web application are given (Sect. 4); and finally conclusions and future work are discussed (Sect. 5).

2 Web Crawling and Corpus Creation

There are many websites that publish news articles. In order to provide good sources of information, we verify different reports, published by *Reuters Institute*[1] *El Economista*[2] and *comScore*[3], about users confidence level and websites popularity in Mexican media. Based on these reports we have selected the sources of information shown in Table 1. This variety of media allows for greater plurality in the collected information.

The selected media organize the information in sections. Some of the sections are similar but others are different between them. After analyzing the content of each media section, we standardized them into 5 general sections:

- Politics
- Sports
- Science and technology

[1] https://reutersinstitute.politics.ox.ac.uk/.
[2] https://www.eleconomista.com.mx/.
[3] https://www.comscore.com/.

Table 1. Selected sources of information

Name	Type of media	Webpage
La Jornada	News paper	www.jornada.com.mx
El Economista	News paper	www.eleconomista.com.mx
La Prensa	News paper	www.la-prensa.com.mx
Proceso	Political maganize	www.proceso.com.mx
Aristegui Noticias	News website	www.aristeguinoticias.com
Sopitas	News website	www.sopitas.com
Azteca Noticias	Television network	www.tvazteca.com/aztecanoticias

- Economy
- Culture

The created crawler access the websites and download the web documents of each media. Then an extraction process was used. In this process the following information was obtained:

- URL
- Headline
- Author
- Date
- News content

It is important to mention that two versions of the crawler were created. The first version was used to collect articles for the training corpus, while the second was used in the web application. The first crawler was executed during three months every 4 days, and 7,707 news articles were collected in total from the 7 websites. Figure 1 shows the number of the downloaded news per section.

The information extracted from the downloaded documents needs to be pre-processed. Documents were tokenized and then a lemmatization process was carried out with NLTK toolkit [9] to reduce data sparsity. After that, repeated news articles were eliminated. We remove HTML tags, special characters and emojis that do not provide useful data for classification. Finally, only news articles with at least 180 words were integrated in the corpus. Figure 2 shows the number of news articles per section after pre-processing the documents.

Unbalanced datasets has different number of instances per class, and are a great challenge for classifiers [10,11]. Techniques like undersampling and oversampling and variations of them have been used to balance highly imbalance datasets with interesting results [12,13]. Considering that class imbalance is present in our corpus, but not to a great extent, we have decided to randomly select 700 news articles of each section to create a balanced corpus of 3,500 news articles and use it to train the classifier explained in the following section.

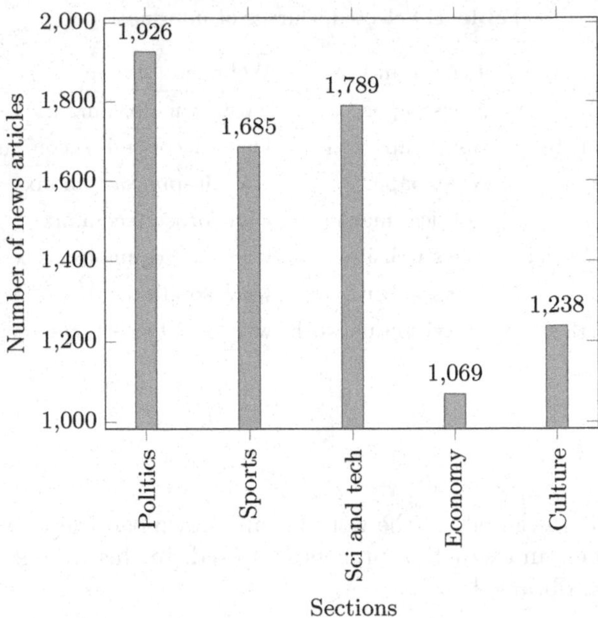

Fig. 1. Downloaded news per section

3 Classifier

Classifiers use features to discriminate between instances. In this work we use words from the news articles as features and they are mapped in a vector space model. A tokenization and lemmatization process were applied to the text and no stopwords were removed. Three variations of text representation were tested: term occurrences, binary term occurrences and TF-IDF. The binary term occurrences obtained the best results and was selected to be used.

Considering the results obtained in the state of the art, the following classifiers were selected:

- Naïve Bayes (NB)
- Logistic Regression (LR)
- Random Forest (RF)
- Support Vector Machines (SVM)

Classifiers have sensible parameters that need to be adjusted in order to provide good results. In particular, for SVM it is very important to select an appropriate kernel and a penalty parameter value usually called C. We use Scikit-learn toolkit [14] to run multiple tests with variations in the parameters of the four classifiers and the best results are shown in Table 2. As can be seen, SVM obtained the best result using a radial base kernel and a penalty parameter C = 100.

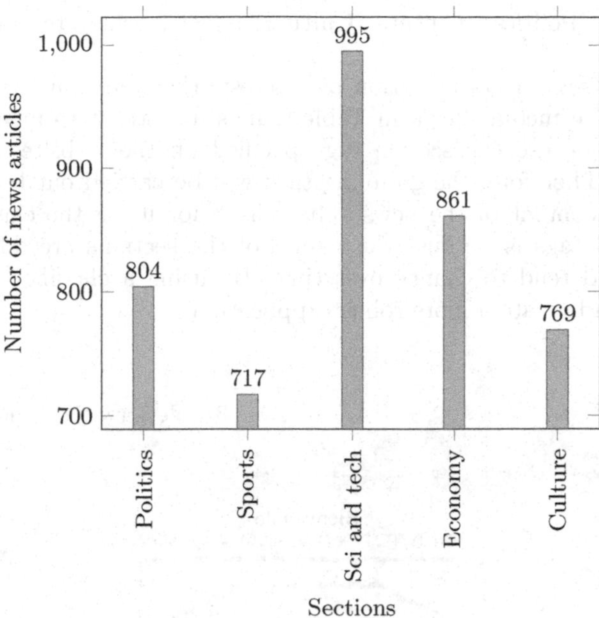

Fig. 2. Pre-processed news per section

Table 2. Best results after parameter adjustment

Classifier	Accuracy
SVM	0.869
LR	0.868
RF	0.861
NB	0.851

We followed a ten-fold cross-validation strategy using the best classifier with the tuned parameters, the classifier obtained an average accuracy of 0.89 that we consider a very good result when compared to related works reported in Sect. 1. After that, the final model was trained with the full corpus (3,500 news articles). This model will be used by the web application.

4 Web Application

The last stage of this work was the creation of a web application in which users search for news articles from specific sections. This web application uses a modified version of the crawler created in the Sect. 2 and the final classifier model trained in the previous section. Figure 3 shows the home page of the web application with the predefined sections Deportes (Sports), Economía (Economy), Política (Politics), Cultura (Culture) and Ciencia y tecnología (Science and technology).

Once the user selects a section of interest, the web crawler collects news articles from the media shown in Table 1. It is important to mention that the crawler does not use the section tag specified on the websites to group the news articles. Therefore, the grouping task will be carried out by the classifier analyzing the content of the news. The reason for using the classifier instead of the sections tags is because the names of the sections are different among the media[4] and tend to change over time. By using a classifier we avoid this dependency and create a more robust application.

Fig. 3. Home page of the web application

The collected news articles are pre-processed (see Sect. 2) and then represented in the same vector space model explained in Sect. 3. Then, the trained model is used to classify news articles in sections and only those articles of the selected section are displayed by the web application. Figure 4 shows two news articles collected and classified in section Economy. The first article is about money for infrastructure in Mexico, and the second one is about domestic gasoline sales in Mexico. Both news articles are clearly related to economy topics. The web application can display the news published not only from the current day, but from one, two and even three or more days ago. Figure 5 shows some news articles published the day before the search was made and classified in the section Economy, from left to right "Cuáles son los nuevos impuestos que se plantean para 2020 en CDMX?" (Wich are the proposed new taxes for Mexico city in 2020?), "Audi recortará 9,500 empleos en Alemania" (Audi to cut 9,500 employees in Germany) and "Proteja sus tarjetas al comprar en línea y evite fraudes" (Protect your cards when you buy online and avoid fraud).

[4] For instance, the Economy section is called Finanzas (finance) in some websites.

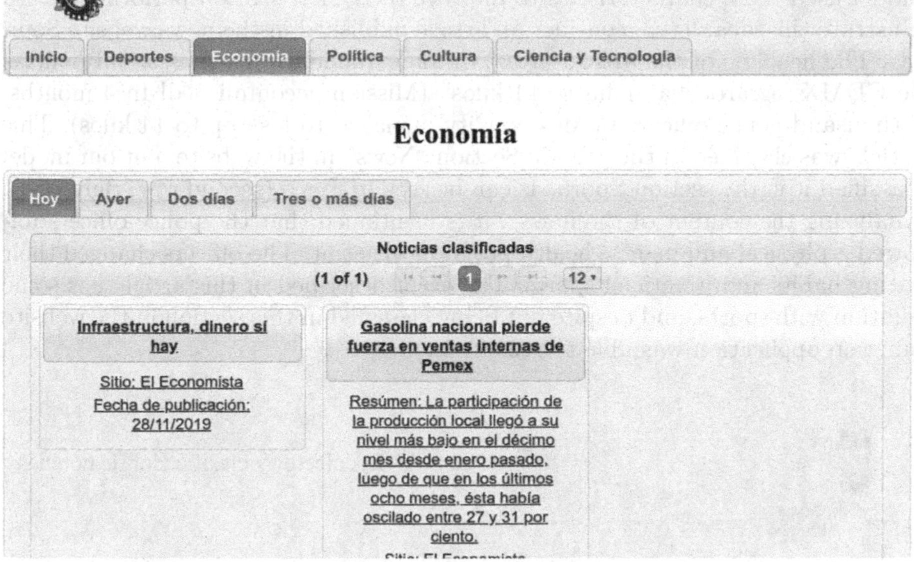

Fig. 4. Collected and classified news articles of the Economy section

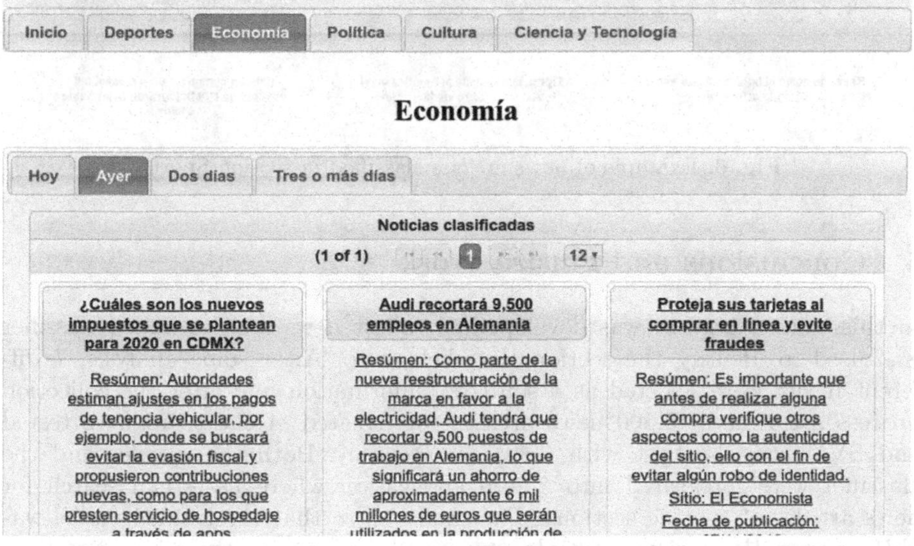

Fig. 5. News articles collected and classified from the Economy section one day ago

The use of multiple sources of information as well as the differences in writing styles of the selected media made our corpus richer. Results suggest that the model used these characteristics to improve the generalization performance. To illustrate this idea, let us consider an article published in the news website Sopitas. The headline of the article says "Misión cumplida! En 4 meses, mil policias de CDMX lograron bajar hasta 14 kilos" (Mission accomplished! In 4 months, a thousand police officers in Mexico City managed to lose up to 14 kilos). This article was classified in the general Section "News" in the website, but our model classified it in the section Sports as can be seen in Fig. 6 (second row, right end). Analyzing the content of the news[5], it is mentioned that the police officers followed a physical and mental health program to get fit. The officers changed their eating habits and practiced sports. The event described in this article has some relation with sports, and despite not being classified in this section in the website our web application was able to recover it.

Fig. 6. Example of news articles classified in section Sports

5 Conclusions and Future Work

In this work a crawler was developed to collect news articles and a classifier was used to identify the section they belong to. After some analysis, 7 different media were selected as a source of information and after the collection process a corpus of 3,500 news articles was created. 4 classifiers were tested and SVM was the best with 0.89% of accuracy. Both the crawler and the classifier were integrated into a web application where users can search for news articles of specific sections. The results show that the trained model was able to correctly retrieve multiple news articles related to the selected section.

[5] https://www.sopitas.com/noticias/policia-saludable-peso-ssc-cdmx/.

The use of the crawler in conjunction with the classifier makes the web application more robust, as it does not rely on tags, but analyzes the content when searching for news articles. More media could be added in the future to increase the variety of information sources, as well increasing the size of the corpus. Other approaches like Artificial Neural Networks could be explored to improve accuracy of classification.

Acknowledgments. No acknowledgments given We thank the support of Insituto Politécnico Nacional (IPN), ESCOM-IPN, SIP-IPN projects numbers: SIP-20220620, SIP-2083, SIP-20220925 COFAA-IPN, EDI-IPN and CONACyT-SNI.

References

1. Kumar, M., Bhatia, R., Rattan, D.: A survey of web crawlers for information retrieval. WIREs Data Min. Knowl. Disc. **7**, e1218 (2017)
2. Agre, G.H., Mahajan, N.V.: Keyword focused web crawler. In: 2015 2nd International Conference on Electronics and Communication Systems (ICECS), pp. 1089–1092 (2015)
3. Aggarwal, C.C.: Machine Learning For Text. Springer, Cham (2018). https://doi.org/10.1007/978-3-030-96623-2
4. Gambino, O.J., Ortega-Pacheco, J.D., Mendoza, C.V.G., Felix-Mata, M.: Automatic detection and registration of events by analyzing email content. Res. Comput. Sci. **130**, 35–43 (2016)
5. Wu, X., Wu, G.Q., Xie, F., Zhu, Z., Hu, X.G.: News filtering and summarization on the web. IEEE Intell. Syst. **25**, 68–76 (2010)
6. Rao, V., Sachdev, J.: A machine learning approach to classify news articles based on location. In: 2017 International Conference on Intelligent Sustainable Systems, pp. 863–867 (2017)
7. García-Mendoza, C.-V., Gambino Juárez, O.: News article classification of Mexican newspapers. In: Mata-Rivera, M.F., Zagal-Flores, R. (eds.) WITCOM 2018. CCIS, vol. 944, pp. 101–109. Springer, Cham (2018). https://doi.org/10.1007/978-3-030-03763-5_9
8. Farias, G., Vergara, S., Fabregas, E., Hermosilla, G., Dormido-Canto, S., Dormido, S.: Clasificador de noticias usando autoencoders. In: 2018 IEEE International Conference on Automation/XXIII Congress of the Chilean Association of Automatic Control (ICA-ACCA), pp. 1–6 (2018)
9. Bird, S., Klein, E., Loper, E.: Natural Language Processing with Python: Analyzing Text with the Natural Language Toolkit. O'Reilly Media, Inc., Sebastopol (2009)
10. Roy, A., Cruz, R.M., Sabourin, R., Cavalcanti, G.D.: A study on combining dynamic selection and data preprocessing for imbalance learning. Neurocomputing **286**, 179–192 (2018)
11. Fernández, A., García, S., Galar, M., Prati, R.C., Krawczyk, B., Herrera, F.: Learning from Imbalanced Data Sets. Springer, Cham (2018). https://doi.org/10.1007/978-3-319-98074-4

12. Yap, B.W., Rani, K.A., Rahman, H.A.A., Fong, S., Khairudin, Z., Abdullah, N.N.: An application of oversampling, undersampling, bagging and boosting in handling imbalanced datasets. In: Proceedings of the First International Conference on Advanced Data and Information Engineering (DaEng-2013), pp. 13–22 (2014)
13. Lin, W.C., Tsai, C.F., Hu, Y.H., Jhang, J.S.: Clustering-based undersampling in class-imbalanced data. Inf. Sci. **409–410**, 17–26 (2017)
14. Pedregosa, F., et al.: Scikit-learn: machine learning in Python. J. Mach. Learn. Res. **12**, 2825–2830 (2011)

Sentiment Analysis in the Rest-Mex Challenge

Jessica-Alejandra Castillo-Montoya, Jonathan-Fernando Gómez-Pérez, Tania Rosales-Onofre, Marco-Antonio Torres-López, and Omar J. Gambino(✉)

Escuela Superior de Cómputo, Instituto Politénico Nacional, ESCOM-IPN, J.D. Batiz e/M.O. de Mendizabal s/n, 07738 Mexico City, Mexico
jjuarezg@ipn.mx

Abstract. In this paper, we describe our participation in the Rest-Mex 2022 forum for the Sentiment Analysis task. The objective of the task was to create a model capable of predicting the polarity of the sentiment expressed by a tourist's opinion, as well as the type of attraction visited. For this task, we followed two different approaches: a lexicon-based approach and a Machine Learning approach. In the lexicon-based approach, we use a dictionary with words that have a numerical value that specifies the association with some emotions or attractions. We trained a logistic regression model for the Machine Learning approach to predict sentiment polarity and attractions. Our proposal obtained a combined score for both tasks of 0.85, which is only 0.03 away from the best reported result.

Keywords: Sentiment analysis · Emotion lexicon · Machine learning

1 Introduction

Online platforms have allowed people to share opinions with other users about their experiences. In opinions, users express polarity about certain topic in the form of likes or dislikes, agreement or disagreement. These opinions are a valuable resource for many economic activities, because opinions can influence people's decisions [1]. Tourism is one of these economic activities in which opinions are important because people tend to express the experience they had when they visited a place, which may impact people interested in visiting the same site.

Given the above, efforts have been made to propose models that can automatically analyze opinions and determine the polarity expressed by users. Two main approaches have been followed to determine sentiment polarity: lexicon-based and Machine Learning.

Lexicon-based approach are usually based on lexical resources like sentiment lexicons, which are a list of words with sentimental attachment. Taboada et al.

O. Pichardo Lagunas et al. (Eds.): MICAI 2022, LNAI 13613, pp. 137–147, 2022.
https://doi.org/10.1007/978-3-031-19496-2_11

[2] created dictionaries of words annotated with their semantic orientation or polarity for classifying the polarity of different users' reviews. Each word in those reviews was compared to the words in the dictionaries in order to find a match; if they matched, the polarity of the words was used to determine the global polarity of the review. In [3] a lexicon for determining sentiment polarity in Urdu language was used. The authors classify opinions as positive, negative or neutral with 89.03% of accuracy. Authors in [4] proposed a method for sentiment analysis considering aspects in opinions. They used two methods to generate lexicons for aspect-based problems—using a statistical method and a genetic algorithm—and obtained an improvement of 7.4% points of F-measure when compared with baseline method reported in [5].

The Machine Learning approach considers the task a classification problem, where classes are the polarities of the expressed opinions (i.e., positive or negative opinions). Algorithms are used to learn from data examples and then apply the learned model to unseen data. In [6] Naïve Bayes, Maximum Entropy and Support Vector Machine algorithms were used to classify sentiment polarity on a corpus of movie reviews in English. Even though the experiments obtained 82% of accuracy, the authors pointed out that the applied algorithms were not able to achieve results comparable to those reported for standard topic-based categorization, concluding that sentiment polarity is a more difficult problem than text categorization. On the other hand, hybrid approaches propose using lexicons and Machine Learning methods to classify sentiment polarity. In [7] the authors used two Spanish emotion lexicons combined with a Naïve Bayes classifier. The features provided by the lexicons allowed the classifier to increase the baseline accuracy, demonstrating that the combination of both approaches can lead to better performance.

In order to encourage the develop of computational models for Natural Language Processing in Spanish, IberLEF@sepln 2022[1] proposed an evaluation forum called Rest-Mex. The forum stated that using Machine Learning and Natural Language Processing can help promote tourism by generating mechanisms to identify the polarities of tourists' opinions. This paper describes our participation in the Rest-Mex forum for the Sentiment Analysis task. We developed two models, one using a lexicon and the other using a Machine Learning method. In the following section, the corpus and task are described (Sect. 2); then the method used is explained (Sect. 3); after that, we present the experiments and results (Sect. 4); and finally, conclusions and future work are discussed (Sect. 5).

2 Corpus and Task Description

The Rest-Mex forum provided a corpus for training models. There are 30,212 opinions, and the structure of the content is as follows:

- Title. Title of the opinion.
- Opinion. Opinion expressed by the user.

[1] https://sepln2022.grupolys.org/eventos/.

- Polarity. Sentiment polarity of the opinion.
- Attraction. Place visited by the user.

The corpus was collected from tourists who shared their opinion on TripAdvisor between 2002 and 2021.

The forum had two objectives. The first was to predict the polarity of opinion expressed by tourists traveling to a place in Mexico. The second objective was to predict the type of place visited by tourists (attractions). Polarity can have the following values: Very negative (VN), Negative (N), Neutral (NEU), Positive (P), Very positive (VP). The places visited by the tourist can be Hotel (H), Restaurant (R), and Attractive (A).

For the contest, the corpus was divided into a training set with 30,212 opinions and a test set with 12,938 opinions. Figure 1 shows the class distributions for both tasks, sentiment polarity and attractions in the training corpus[2]. As can be seen, the class distribution for sentiment polarity is unbalanced, with almost 69% of the opinions labeled as very positive. On the other hand, the distribution of attractions is also unbalanced, but to a lesser extent.

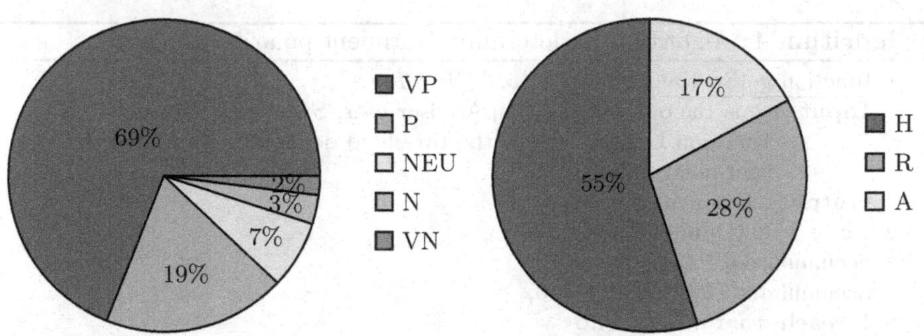

Fig. 1. Class distribution of sentiment polarity (left figure), class distribution of attractions (right figure)

Machine Learning methods have problems with unbalanced classes and this problem affects performance. This situation is described in Sect. 4.

3 Method

We used two approaches in the contest. One is based on a lexicon, and the other is based on Machine Learning algorithms. In this section, both approaches are described.

[2] Distributions of classes in the test set were not provided by the forum organizers.

3.1 Lexicon-Based Approach

To determine sentiment polarity we can use a dictionary of words attached to emotions. For English, numerous lexicons have been created over the years, for instance: SentiWordnet [8], OpinionFinder [9], Harvard inquirer [10] and LIWC [11]. Some English lexicons have been translated to Spanish and used for sentiment analysis in this language [8,10]. Authors in [12] created a dictionary composed of 2,036 words called Spanish Emotion Lexicon (SEL). For every word, the dictionary calculates the probability factor for affective use (FPA for its acronym in Spanish). This value indicates how often a word is used to express the following emotions: Joy, Surprise, Anger, Fear, Disgust, and Sadness. A word can be related to more than one emotion. This lexicon was selected for determining the polarity of opinions.

We follow a procedure based on the algorithm described in [7] to calculate the polarity. The first step was to tokenize the opinions; then, the text was lemmatized using Freeling [13]. The pseudocode to determine the sentiment polarity is described in Algorithm 1.

Algorithm 1: Algorithm to determine sentiment polarity using SEL

```
function getSentimentPolarity (o, SEL, PT);
Input  : o is the opinion of a TripAdvisor user, SEL is the Spanish
         Emotion Lexicon, PT is the threshold defined to determine the
         sentiment polarity
Output: sentiment polarity
words = getOpinionWords(o);
accumulatedFPAPositive = 0;
accumulatedFPANegative = 0;
foreach word in words do
    if word in SEL then
        fpaValues, emotion = getFPAValues(word);
        if emotion in positiveEmotions then
            accumulatedFPAPositive = accumulatedFPAPositive +
            fpaValues;
        else
            accumulatedFPANegative = accumulatedFPANegative +
            fpaValues;

end
emotionDifference = accumulatedFPAPositive - accumulatedFPANegative;
sentimentPolarity = getSentimentPolarity (emotionDifference, PT);
```

As can be seen, the pseudocode takes an opinion, the lexicon SEL, and a polarity threshold. Words in the opinion are separated and looked up in the lexicon. If the word is founded, the FPA values are obtained for the related emotions (Joy, Surprise, Anger, Fear, Disgust, and Sadness). These values are accumulated for each word. Then, we obtain the difference between the FPA values of positive and negative emotions. For this, we consider the emotions Joy and Surprise as positive and the rest as negative. Finally, the sentiment polarity is obtained using a threshold. The threshold establishes the value ranges that the differences in emotions can have to be considered in the five possible polarities. The threshold values were empirically determined and using evolutionary computation. Both procedures are described in Sect. 4.

For the second task—places visited by tourists—we do not use the lexicon approach, so the description of the method used can be found below.

3.2 Machine Learning Approach

Sentiment analysis can be tackled as a text classification problem. A classifier uses a labeled dataset to train a model that learns from the data. In the Rest-Mex corpus each opinion is labeled with five different sentiment polarities, and these are considered the classes that the model should predict. As with the lexicon-based procedure, the opinions were tokenized and lemmatized. No stop words were removed. The text must be represented appropriately so that Machine Learning methods can use it. We tried different text representation like bag of words and TF-IDF. These representations were used to train a Logistic Regression classifier. Details of the experiments are described in Sect. 4.

A similar procedure was followed to determine the places visited by tourist, but the classes were the three different attractions (i.e., Hotel, Restaurant and Attractive) considered in the corpus. The following Section describe the experiments performed for this task.

4 Experiments and Results

We created a development set from the training corpus to perform the experiments. The development set had 80% (24,170 opinions) of data for training and 20% (6,042 opinions) for testing, instances of both sets were randomly selected. The corpus has the attributes title and opinion related to the sentiment expressed by users, so we concatenated them into a sentence and used it to determine sentiment polarity

4.1 Experiments with the Lexicon-Based Approach

As was explained in Sect. 3.1, our method uses the emotion difference between positive and negative emotions to determine sentiment polarity. The experiments performed are explained below.

Empirical Threshold Adjustment. Algorithm 1 uses different threshold values to determine sentiment polarity. The ranges of initial values were defined experimentally. Subsequently, information from the confusion matrix was used to determine the classes that generated the most errors and, based on this, the thresholds were modified. We tested with different ranges of values and calculated the accuracy obtained with the test set. We changed the ranges until the accuracy no longer improved. In Table 1 we show the results of the experiments. The difference (df) between positive and negative emotions (see line 13 of Algorithm 1) was used to determine different values of the sentiment polarity. As can be seen, experiment 3 obtained the best accuracy.

Table 1. Results of empirical threshold adjustment

Experiment	Threshold	Sentiment polarity	Accuracy
1	$df \geq 1$	VP	0.61
	$0.5 \leq df < 1$	P	
	$-1 \leq df < 0.5$	NEU	
	$-2 \leq df < -1$	N	
	$df < -2$	VN	
2	$df \geq 1$	VP	0.62
	$-1.3 \leq df < 1$	P	
	$-1 \leq df < -1.3$	NEU	
	$-2.6 \leq df < -1$	N	
	$df < -2.6$	VN	
3	$df \geq 0$	VP	0.67
	$-1.3 \leq df < 0$	P	
	$-1.8 \leq df < -1.3$	NEU	
	$-2.6 \leq df < -1.8$	N	
	$df < -2.6$	VN	
4	$df \geq 0.5$	VP	0.66
	$-0.7 \leq df < 0.5$	P	
	$-1.8 \leq df < -0.7$	NEU	
	$-2.6 \leq df < -1.8$	N	
	$df < -2.6$	VN	
5	$df \geq 0.5$	VP	0.66
	$0 \leq df < 0.5$	P	
	$-1.8 \leq df < 0$	NEU	
	$-2.6 \leq df < -1.8$	N	
	$df < -2.6$	VN	

Threshold Adjustment Using Evolutionary Algorithms. The adjustment of threshold values can be considered an optimization problem. Evolutionary algorithms have been used to solve optimization problems with good results [14]. The advantage of this type of algorithms is that the tuning process automatically tries different threshold values that improve accuracy instead of the manual tuning performed in previous experiments. There are several evolutionary algorithms such as particle swarm optimization, ant colony optimization, and genetic algorithm. Specifically, for the sentiment analysis task, evolutionary algorithms have been used for creating adaptive sentiment lexicons [15]. In [16], the authors used particle swarm optimization to label the words of a lexicon. In this work, we decided to use a genetic algorithm.

The genetic algorithm is inspired by Charles Darwin's theory of natural evolution. This theory establishes the survival of the fittest individual. The main elements of genetic algorithms are chromosome representation, fitness selection and operators [17]. For the implemented genetic algorithm[3] we set the following parameters.

- Number of generations: 50
- Crossover type: single point
- Mutation type: random

In Table 2 we show the results of the experiments. As can be seen, we obtained a 2% improvement in accuracy compared to the empirical approach. The threshold values were all negative, implying that the accumulated positive values are less than the negative ones. We consider this because the words used in the comments are more likely to match a negative emotion since there are four possible ones, while the positive ones are only 2.

Table 2. Results of genetic algorithm threshold adjustment

Threshold	Sentiment polarity	Accuracy
$df \geq -0.1$	VP	
$-1.09 \leq df < -0.1$	P	0.69
$-2.68 \leq df < -1.09$	NEU	
$-3.37 \leq df < -2.68$	N	
$df < -3.37$	VN	

4.2 Experiments with the Machine Learning Approach

We tested three text representations for the Machine Learning approach: bag of words with word frequency, binarized bag of words (presence or absence of

[3] We thank Gustavo-Alain Peduzzi-Acevedo, Edgar-Josue Varillas-Figueroa, Juan-Daniel Del-Valle-Pérez and Francisco-Javier Aragón-González for their help in implementing this algorithm.

a word), and TF-IDF. We used logistic regression as a classifier. After several experiments, the binarized version of the bag of words was selected because it obtained the best results.

In Fig. 1, we show that the class distribution of sentiment polarity is imbalanced. Of the five polarity classes in the corpus, 69% of the opinions have the VP polarity, while 31% of the remaining opinions have one of the other four classes. This situation usually affects the learning process of classifiers because the algorithms are biased toward the majority class examples while the minority classes are not well modeled [18]. Some algorithms help classifiers to deal with unbalanced data sets. Resampling methods—like undersampling and oversampling—are one the most used for this purpose [19]. Undersampling reduces the data by eliminating instances belonging to the majority class while oversampling replicates or generates new instances belonging to the minority class. In our experiments, we tested both resampling methods, and undersampling was selected because it obtained the best results. The resampling methods were implemented using the Imbalanced learn library [20].

The logistic regression classifier using the selected text representation and resampling method obtained 0.74% accuracy. Compared to the lexicon-based approach, the Machine Leaning approach had a 5% improvement; therefore, this model was selected for use with the test set. However, it is important to mention that the comparison is unfair because the classifier takes advantage of training examples while the first approach does not use this information.

The second task, which consists of determining the destination visited by the tourist, was also treated as a classification problem. The opinions were also tokenized and lemmatized. The selected text representation was a binarized bag of words. As shown in Fig. 1, the class distribution of attractions is unbalanced. Resampling methods did not improve accuracy and therefore were not used in the final model. We believe that resampling methods did not help because there are fewer classes (3) in the opinion polarity (5) and, in addition, the imbalance is smaller between classes. We used a Logistic Regression classifier and obtained 97% accuracy.

The contest rules allowed for two runs in the test set. We decided to create two versions of the trained model by making slight variations. Specifically, we changed the number of instances removed by the subsampling algorithm. We tried to generate a more balanced corpus in the first run by removing more instances labeled with the majority class. In contrast, in the second run, fewer instances were removed to reduce the imbalance but trying to preserve a similar distribution.

The final models for both tasks were used in the test set composed of 12,938 opinions. In the sentiment polarity task, the best run of our model obtained 73.52% of accuracy and 96.39% for the attraction prediction. In Table 3 we show the results of all participants of the contest. The results of our model are marked in bold. As can be seen, the second run that removed fewer instances had better performance than the first run in which more instances were removed. We believe eliminating instances to balance the corpus is helpful but may be too restrictive.

Forcing the corpus to be fully balanced does not allow the model to learn from the natural distribution of classes. On the other hand, reducing the imbalance to a lesser extent reduces the impact of bias in the classifier but preserves classes with a higher presence from which the trained model can learn.

Table 3. Official results of Rest-Mex 2022

Team	Final rank	Polarity acc	Attraction acc
UMU-Team-Run-1	0.8923	75.9854	98.9642
UC3M-Run1	0.8907	76.2523	98.8481
CIMAT MTY-GTO-Run1	0.8899	75.7845	98.8406
MCE_Team-Run2	0.8891	75.8503	98.8790
MCE_Team-Run1	0.8870	76.2909	98.6239
UMU-Team-Run-2	0.8855	74.1536	98.8483
GPI_CIMAT-Run1	0.8854	75.7072	98.1913
CIMAT2020_beto-Run1	0.8826	75.9740	97.8432
DCI-UG-Run1	0.8753	75.7690	96.5527
UCI-UC-CUJAE-Run2	0.8721	74.5284	97.9050
UCI-UC-CUJAE-Run1	0.8691	73.6858	97.4412
CIMAT2020_botextautoaugment-Run2	0.8690	73.9795	97.8432
DCI-UG-Run2	0.8662	74.6096	96.5527
ESCOM-IPN-IIA_run2	**0.8596**	**73.5275**	**96.3904**
GPI_CIMAT-Run1	0.8442	75.0734	92.4640
ESCOM-IPN-LCD_run2	0.8400	69.2456	94.7364
ESCOM-IPN-IIA_run1	**0.8341**	**72.9247**	**92.9741**
UPTC_UDLAP-Run1	0.8273	67.6147	96.5527
SENA Team	0.8029	65.2882	93.1133
DevsExMachina-Run1	0.7035	64.9868	82.021
DevsExMachina-Run1	0.6668	56.2528	84.6885
ESCOM-IPN-LCD_run1	0.5956	49.8144	67.1896
UPTC_UDLAP-Run2	0.5422	58.6489	47.4339
Majority class (baseline)	0.4568	70.0262	54.8771

According to the results in Table 3, our model ranked 14th out of 24[4] The final rank was calculated with a metric that combines results of both tasks; details of this metric can be found in the official web page[5]. As can be seen,

[4] Results were published in the official web page https://sites.google.com/cicese.edu.mx/rest-mex-2022/results?authuser=0.

[5] https://sites.google.com/cicese.edu.mx/rest-mex-2022/data-and-evaluation?authuser=0.

the difference between our model and the best-ranked one was only 0.03. We consider that, despite the simplicity of our model, it was very competitive.

5 Conclusions and Future Work

In this paper we reported our participation in the Rest-Mex forum. We explored two approaches for the sentiment polarity task. The first approach used a lexicon to determine five different polarities based on a threshold. Values of the threshold were calculated experimentally and using a genetic algorithm. The second approach used a Machine Learning method to classify polarity of the opinions. The latter approach performed best in the development set and was chosen for use in the test set. The same approach was used for determining the kind of place visited by the tourist. Our results placed us 14th out of 24 in the competition, with a difference of only 0.0327 points compared to first place. For future work, we propose the use of other evolutionary algorithms to improve the lexicon-based approach, as well as the use of a hybrid approach combining lexicon-based and Machine Learning methods. Further research on the use of methods for dealing with class imbalance is also proposed as well as the use of Deep Learning techniques.

Acknowledgments. We thank the support of Insituto Politécnico Nacional (IPN), ESCOM-IPN, SIP-IPN projects numbers: SIP-20220620, SIP-2083, SIP-20220925 COFAA-IPN, EDI-IPN and CONACyT-SNI.

References

1. Cheung, C.M., Lee, M.K., Rabjohn, N.: The impact of electronic word-of-mouth: The adoption of online opinions in online customer communities. Internet Res. (2008)
2. Taboada, M., Brooke, J., Tofiloski, M., Voll, K.D., Stede, M.: Lexicon-based methods for sentiment analysis. Comput. Linguist. **37**, 267–307 (2011)
3. Mukhtar, N., Khan, M.A.: Effective lexicon-based approach for Urdu sentiment analysis. Artif. Intell. Rev. **53**, 2521–2548 (2020)
4. Mowlaei, M.E., Abadeh, M.S., Keshavarz, H.: Aspect-based sentiment analysis using adaptive aspect-based Lexicons. Expert Syst. Appl. **148**, 113234 (2020)
5. Hu, M., Liu, B.: Mining opinion features in customer reviews. In: AAAI 2004, pp. 755–760. AAAI Press (2004)
6. Pang, B., Lee, L., Vaithyanathan, S.: Thumbs Up?: sentiment classification using machine learning techniques. In: Proceedings of the ACL-02 Conference on Empirical Methods in Natural Language Processing, vol. 10, Association for Computational Linguistics (2002)
7. Gambino, O.J., Calvo, H.: A comparison between two Spanish sentiment lexicons in the twitter sentiment analysis task. In: Montes-y-Gómez, M., Escalante, H.J., Segura, A., Murillo, J.D. (eds.) IBERAMIA 2016. LNCS (LNAI), vol. 10022, pp. 127–138. Springer, Cham (2016). https://doi.org/10.1007/978-3-319-47955-2_11

8. Baccianella, S., Esuli, A., Sebastiani, F.: SentiWordNet 3.0: an enhanced lexical resource for sentiment analysis and opinion mining. In: LREC, European Language Resources Association (2010)
9. Wilson, T., et al.: OpinionFinder: a system for subjectivity analysis. In: Proceedings of Human Language Technology Conference and Conference on Empirical Methods in Natural Language Processing (HLT/EMNLP-2005) Companion Volume (software demonstration) (2005)
10. Stone, P.J.: The General Inquirer: A Computer Approach to Content Analysis. The MIT Press, Cambridge (1966)
11. Tausczik, Y.R., Pennebaker, J.W.: The psychological meaning of words: LIWC and computerized text analysis methods. J. Lang. Soc. Psychol. **29**, 24–54 (2010)
12. Rangel, I.D., Guerra, S.S., Sidorov, G.: Creación y evaluación de un diccionario marcado con emociones y ponderado para el español. Onomázein **29**, 31–46 (2014)
13. Padró, L., Stanilovsky, E.: FreeLing 3.0: towards wider multilinguality. In: Proceedings of the Language Resources and Evaluation Conference, Istanbul, Turkey, ELRA (2012)
14. Bartz-Beielstein, T., Branke, J., Mehnen, J., Mersmann, O.: Evolutionary algorithms. WIREs Data Min. Knowl. Disc. **4**, 178–195 (2014)
15. Keshavarz, H., Abadeh, M.S.: ALGA: adaptive lexicon learning using genetic algorithm for sentiment analysis of microblogs. Knowl. Based Syst. **122**, 1–16 (2017)
16. Machová, K., Mikula, M., Gao, X., Mach, M.: Lexicon-based sentiment analysis using the particle swarm optimization. Electronics **9**, 1317 (2020)
17. Sourabh, K., Singh, C.S., Vijay, K.: A review on genetic algorithm: past, present, and future. Multimed. Tools App. **80**, 8091–8126 (2021)
18. Fernández, A., García, S., Galar, M., Prati, R.C., Krawczyk, B., Herrera, F.: Learning from Imbalanced Data Sets. Springer, Cham (2018). https://doi.org/10.1007/978-3-319-98074-4
19. Estabrooks, A., Jo, T., Japkowicz, N.: A multiple resampling method for learning from imbalanced data sets. Comput. Intell. **20**, 18–36 (2004)
20. Lemaître, G., Nogueira, F., Aridas, C.K.: Imbalanced-learn: a python toolbox to tackle the curse of imbalanced datasets in machine learning. J. Mach. Learn. Res. **18**, 1–5 (2017)

A Bibliometric Review of Methods and Algorithms for Generating Corpora for Learning Vector Word Embeddings

Beibarys Sagingaliyev[1], Zhuldyzay Aitakhunova[1], Adel Shaimerdenova[1], Iskander Akhmetov[1,2(✉)], Alexander Pak[1,2], and Assel Jaxylykova[2,3]

[1] Kazakh-British Technical University, Almaty, Kazakhstan
{b_sagingaliyev,z_aitakhunova,a_shaimerdenova}@kbtu.kz
[2] Institute of Information and Computational Technologies, Almaty, Kazakhstan
i.akhmetov@ipic.kz
[3] Al-Farabi Kazakh National University, Almaty, Kazakhstan

Abstract. Natural Language Processing (NLP) problems are among the hardest Machine Learning (ML) problems due to the complex nature of the human language. The introduction of word embeddings improved the performance of ML models on various NLP tasks as text classification, sentiment analysis, machine translation, etc. Word embeddings are real-valued vector representations of words in a specific vector space. Producing quality word embeddings that are then used as input to downstream NLP tasks is important in obtaining a good performance. To accomplish it, corpora of sufficient size is needed. Corpora may be formed in a multitude of ways, including text that was originally electronic, spoken language transcripts, optical character recognition, and synthetically producing text from the available dataset. The study provides the most recent bibliometric analysis on the topic of corpora generation for learning word vector embeddings. The analysis is based on the publication data from 2006 to 2022 retrieved from Scopus scientific database. A descriptive analysis method has been employed to obtain statistical characteristics of the publications in the research area. The systematic analysis results show the field's evolution over time and highlight influential contributions to the field. It is believed that compiled bibliometric reviews could help researchers gain knowledge of the general state of the scientific knowledge, its descriptive features, patterns, and insights to design their studies systematically.

Keywords: Corpora · Data augmentation · Word embedding · NLP downstream tasks · Descriptive analysis · Natural language processing

NLP word embedding models can now preserve semantic and syntactic features in generated data from large collections of unlabeled texts known as corpora. The collection of rules used to analyze a language can choose and process it. Corpora may be formed in various ways, including text that was originally electronic, transcripts of spoken language, and optical character recognition. There

O. Pichardo Lagunas et al. (Eds.): MICAI 2022, LNAI 13613, pp. 148–162, 2022.
https://doi.org/10.1007/978-3-031-19496-2_12

are previously familiar methods, such as Word2vec, GloVe, and fastText, which improved the NLP tasks to upgrade. The latest modified models are Bert, Gpt-3 which are relatively new for the industry, developed by Google in 2018. This bibliometric review will illustrate investigating models in word embedding methods with data augmentations on NLP tasks.

1 Introduction

Word embedding is a term in Natural Language Processing, which refers to the language modeling and representing the words and whole sentences in a vector format [17]. There has been an ultimate rise in several downstream tasks such as question answering, text classifications, and sentiment analysis [12–14]. Nowadays, word embedding models can preserve semantic and syntactic features in generated data from an enormous unlabeled collection of texts called corpora. It is selected and processed by the set of rules leveraged to study a language [1]. The term corpora can be created in various methods, including text that was initially electronic, transcripts of spoken language, and other optical character recognition [3,15].

Bibliometrics is an analysis of books, articles and other publications using statistical methods, emphasizing scientific content in terms of objectivity and quantity. Bibliometric methods are widely used in librarianship, and informatics [4]. There are several outlining advantages of bibliometrics. First is organizing specific data from related works [10]. The second advantage is that it requires very little time to make and be used [9]. Thirdly, it is adaptable. It can be revised individually in institutional, national, and worldwide levels. Finally, the approaches are easy to deal with because they are based on simple counting. Because their use may be automated, several approaches have become extremely simple in the digital age [11].

Bibliometric analysis has been widely used in various fields to assess the quality and productivity of academic results, and it has proven to be highly effective over time. Relevant studies primarily focus on revealing statistical aspects of publications, discovering and exploring the collaborative relationship [6].

As a result, this study aims to analyze works related to generating corpora for learning vector word embeddings using bibliometric methodologies. To be more explicit, bibliometric data retrieved from Scopus, with the area of search in learning vector word embeddings downloaded and analyzed via descriptive analysis [2].

2 Methodology

We will analyze the bibliometrics by the following methods to get more insight into research related to word embedding methods with data augmentations on NLP tasks. Data retrieved from Scopus, with the search area in learning vector word embeddings.

2.1 Methods

Descriptive analysis. Descriptive analysis is the statistical method of statistical analysis by describing certain coefficients, which gives a brief explanation of the data. It could be a more general analysis or specific. Statistical measures derived from the descriptive analysis include standard deviation, mode, mean, skewness of the curve, etc. And variables are depicted in terms of graphs, charts, or tables, which gives a more visually informative understanding of statistical measures. Thus, it will help us gather knowledge on published research related to word embeddings and data augmentation tasks. It aims to generalize the large data set and give insightful features.

Here, we want to employ descriptive analysis to acquire statistically proven information on publications, citations, and authors. Also, their inter-relations and dependencies will be key points to analyze in this study. By analysis, we want to get the distribution of publications, citations, and average citations each year. Additionally, we will analyze publications by country, area of research, and journal. Thus, the objective is to get a clear analytical description of publications related to our research area.

2.2 Materials

Scopus is the main database for collecting the necessary information on publications related to corpora generation for learning word vector embeddings (the paper's topic). Scopus is considered a highly reputed and easily navigated multidisciplinary Elsevier citation database with high-quality peer-review and a large research base.

2050 rows of data, including publication authors, title, keywords, abstract, year, source journal, citation amount, etc., were retrieved from the database using "learning vector word embedding", "word embedding" and "text augmentation" keywords. The publication year of collected papers is between 2006 and 2022.

A list of publication information was downloaded in a CSV file format and analyzed in Python programming language using libraries such as pandas, NumPy, Matplotlib.

The descriptive analysis presented in the paper is based on information on the aforementioned 2050 publications. Figure 1 demonstrates publication distribution by subject areas: Engineering, Mathematics, Social Sciences, Decision Science, Medicine, Computer Science and etc. The top 3 areas are Computer Science, which contributes 43.6% of total publications, Engineering (13,3%), and Mathematics (10.7%). Table 1 and Figs. 2, 3, 4 and 5 present a statistical overview of collected publications. Results show that a total of 2050 publications are related with 2148 unique affiliations and 4894 unique authors. The average number of citations per publication is 11.95, the average number of authors is 3.51, and the average number of references is 33.46. An expanded analysis on the subject area, country/region, and affiliation can be found in the next section of the paper.

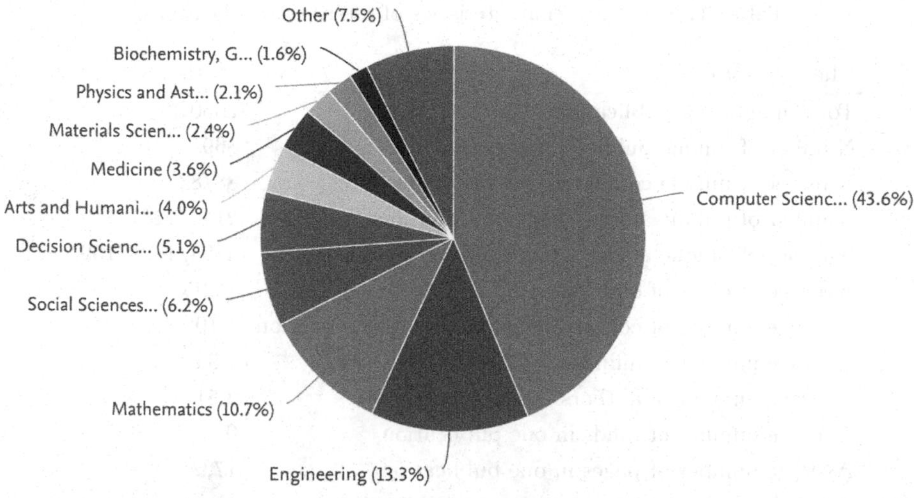

Fig. 1. Publication distribution by subject areas.

3 Results

3.1 Publications and Citations by Year

A descriptive analysis of the distribution of publication and citation by year is demonstrated in Fig. 6. The analysis results depict a bell-shaped distribution for total citation and a steadily increasing trend for total publications on word embedding and text augmentation research.

A total citation shows an upward increase until 2017 and then a gradual decline up to 2022. It can be explained by the fact that newer publications had less time to generate citations than older ones. Overall, it demonstrates that citations and interest by researchers in the area of NLP are increasing if we compare the total number of citations in the first and second halves of the 2006–2022 time frame. A total of 28235 citations were recorded from 2006 to 2022 and peaked at 5326 citations in 2017. As of May 10, 2022, word embedding and text augmentation publications were cited 170 times.

In 2006, two papers were published in the word embeddings research area. From then, the number of publications increased significantly, where the peak recorded in 2021 with 414 papers. In 2022, the published paper quantity is currently 110, but the year's total quantity is not yet final.

Figure 7 shows the average number of citations by each year in the period 2006–2022. It is calculated by dividing total publications by total citations. The peak result corresponds to publications made in 2013, where three articles collected 789 citations, which averages to approximately 263 citations per paper. After the climax in 2013, average citations sharply declined in the proceeding year. In 2017, we had 5326 citations, and the average citation was 28. As of May 2022, citation per paper is 1.55 (110 publications cited 170 times).

Table 1. Statistical characteristics of retrieved publications.

Characteristics	Statistics
Total number of publications	2050
Number of unique publication sources	869
Number of unique countries/first countries	88/83
Number of unique affiliations/first affiliations	2148/1237
Number of unique authors/first authors/last authors	4894/1629/1595
Average number of citations	11.95
Average number of countries/regions in one publication	1.19
Average number of affiliations in one publication	1.94
Average number of authors in one publication	3.51
Average number of funds in one publication	0.52
Average number of pages in one publication	17.94
Average number of references in one publication	33.46
Average number of author keywords	4.95
Average number of words/characters in title	10.34/81.57
Average number of words/characters in abstract	196.00/1,347.51

Additionally, we constructed a regression analysis based on the collected data. As independent variables, we picked $year/1000$ and $(year/1000)^2$, and the quantity of publications is assigned as the dependent variable. Our estimated regression model is: ($\hat{y} = 14903004 - 14833349 * (year/1000) + 3691000 * (year/1000)^2$). R^2 of the resulting model equals 0.958. In 2017 we had 415 publications, and the regression model predicted 397 publications.

Figure 8 shows Spearman correlation between four variables. It is observed that there exists moderate relation between Year and Total publication by year. As R^2 metric of the constructed regression model tells, the number of publications is explained by year by 95.8%. A positive correlation means that the number of publications rises each subsequent year.

3.2 Top Conferences and Journals

We analyzed total publications, total citations, and averages by conferences and journals and selected the top ten of them as the most contributing sources. Table 2 lists the top 10 conferences and journals that generated the most citations per publication (ACP). Two papers presented at the 52nd Annual Meeting of the Association for Computational Linguistics in 2014 were cited 905 times, resulting in 452.5 citations per paper for the conference. Article [16] titled "Learning Sentiment-Specific Word Embedding for Twitter Sentiment Classification" from

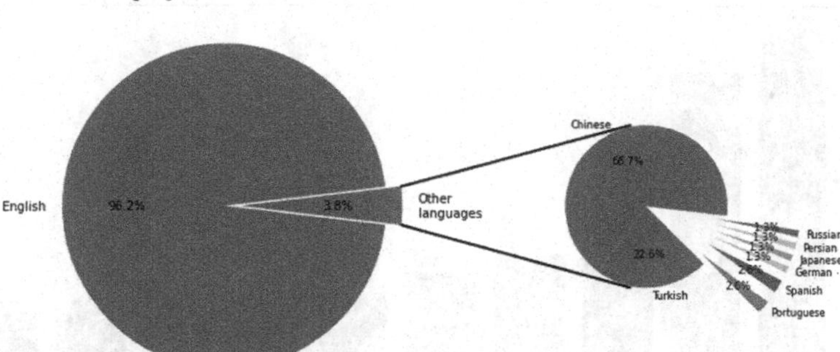

Fig. 2. Language distribution and most frequent words in the retrieved articles (in keywords, titles, and abstracts).

this conference was cited 837 times. Among journals, the Journal of Chemical Information and Modeling, with 177 citations, is worth noting. The article titled "Mol2vec: Unsupervised Machine Learning Approach with Chemical Intuition" by Sabrina Jaegar et al. [8] was the top performing article in that journal.

3.3 Top Institutions and Funding Organizations

The Paper also analyzes institutions and funding organizations that help researchers publish papers in NLP related to word embedding and text augmentation. The results are illustrated in Fig. 9. In the top six, we observe only Chinese institutions and organizations; out of six, three are Chinese universities: Beijing University, Tsinghua University, and Peking University. The three universities have made a total of 88 publications in the period 2006–2022. Another interesting observation is that the list of top 10 institutions and organizations consists of only Asian universities and organizations, seven of which are from China, two from India, and one from Hong Kong SAR.

Next, Fig. 10 contains the top 10 foundations involved in investing in and sponsoring research paper publications. In the top 3 are two Chinese foundations: the National Natural Science Foundations of China and the National Key Research and Development Program of China. In total, they made contributions to the publication of 300 research papers. Besides Chinese organizations, in the top 10, we see two United States foundations: National Science Foundation and European Commission. In total, these two foundations have sponsored 109 paper publications.

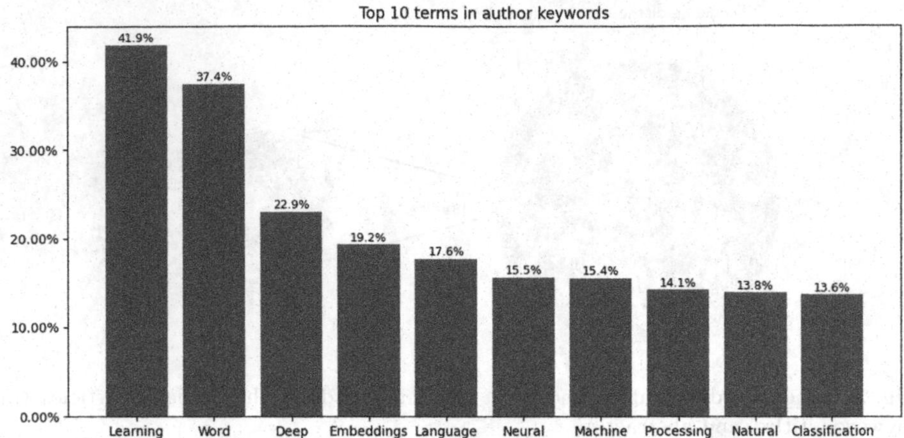

Fig. 3. Language distribution and most frequent words in the retrieved articles (in keywords, titles, and abstracts).

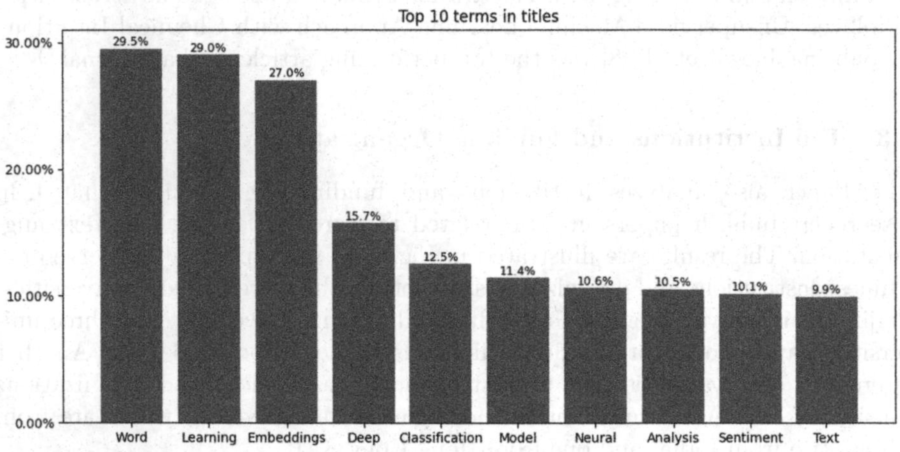

Fig. 4. Language distribution and most frequent words in the retrieved articles (in keywords, titles, and abstracts).

3.4 Top Influential Publications

Citations measure the success of the publications and their garnered interest. The more citations paper acquires, the more successful and influential it can be considered. Citation information from the dataset was analyzed, and the top 10 publications with the most citations were identified. Table 3 lists paper titles, authors' names, publication year, and total citations of the 10 most influential publications. A research paper titled 'Supervised learning of universal sentence

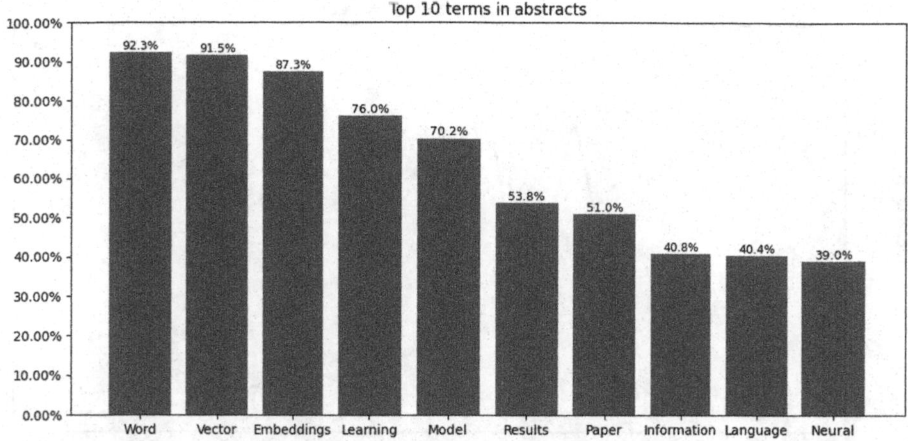

Fig. 5. Language distribution and most frequent words in the retrieved articles (in keywords, titles, and abstracts).

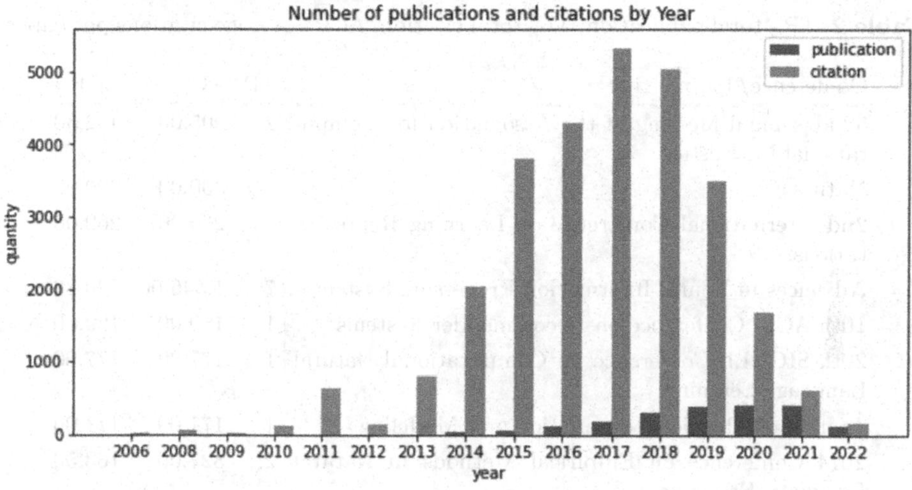

Fig. 6. Total publications and total citations distribution in 2006–2022 period.

representations from natural language inference data' by Conneu et al. [5], published in 2017, is the most influential work with a total of 909 citations. The top 10 is concluded with an article by Bordes, A. et al. and has 416 citations.

After further analysis, we found that there are 256 publications with more than 20 citations, 112 with more than 50 citations, and 56 papers with more than 100 citations from 2006 to 2022.

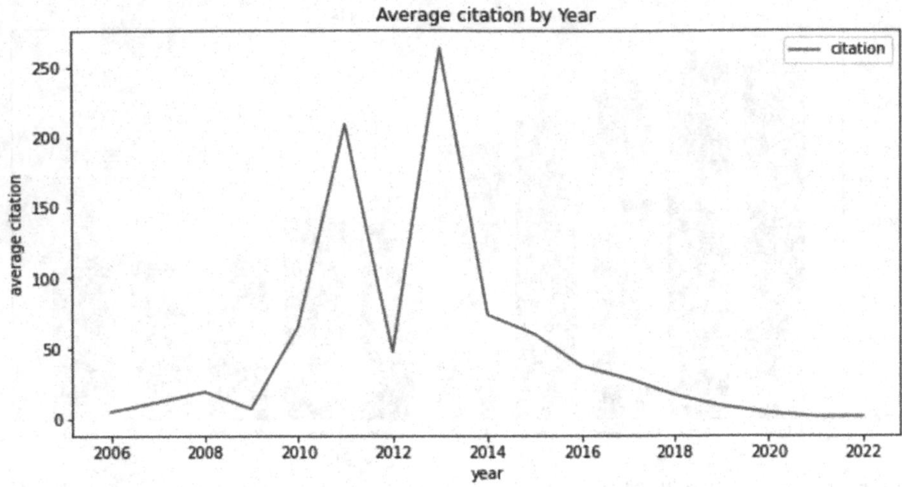

Fig. 7. Average citation per publication from 2006 to 2022.

Table 2. TP - total publication, TC- total citation, ACP - average citations per paper.

Conference/Journal title	TP	TC	ACP
52nd Annual Meeting of the Association for Computational Linguistics	2	905.00	452.50
Nature	1	300.00	300.00
2nd International Conference on Learning Representations,	1	260.00	260.00
Advances in Neural Information Processing Systems	7	1,546.00	220.86
10th ACM Conference on Recommender Systems	1	189.00	189.00
20th SIGNLL Conference on Computational Natural Language Learning	1	177.00	177.00
Journal of Chemical Information and Modeling	1	171.00	171.00
2014 Conference on Empirical Methods in Natural Language Processing	2	327.00	163.50
Synthesis Lectures on Human Language Technologies	2	312.00	156.00
2017 IEEE International Conference on Software Quality, Reliability and Security	1	155.00	155.00
2015 Conference of the North American Chapter of the Association for Computational Linguistics: Human Language Technologies, Proceedings of the Conference	4	601.00	150.25

3.5 Top Countries by Publications

An analysis of the number of publications by country was performed. In Fig. 11, bar chart depicts top-10 countries by paper publication quantity. 87 different

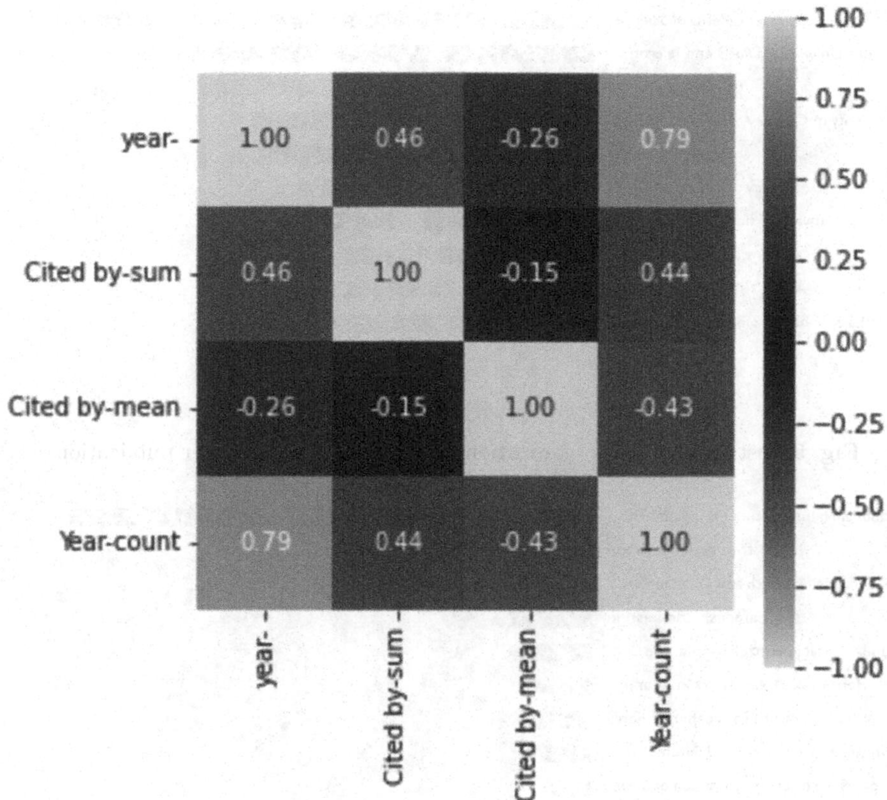

Fig. 8. Spearman correlation matrix of four variables. Correlation values range in [−1,1]. −1 and 1 correspond to the highest negative and positive correlations. In the figure, a high correlation between 'year' and 'Year-count' variables is observed. year - year of publications, Year-count is total publications by year, Cited by-mean - average citation value by year, Cited by-sum - total citation by year.

countries published two thousand fifty papers, and Kazakhstan has two publications among these. It is observed that China is in the leading position with more than 500 publications. This result is consistent with other analyses presented earlier, i.e., in influential publications, institutions, and funding organizations ranking, China is also holding the top position. The USA's next position is owned by the list, contributing 350 publications from 2006 to 2022. And India comes in 3rd place with 215 papers.

In the most influential publication list, papers published by China appear four times in the top 7. With a total of 2423 citations, it results in an average of 606 citations per paper.

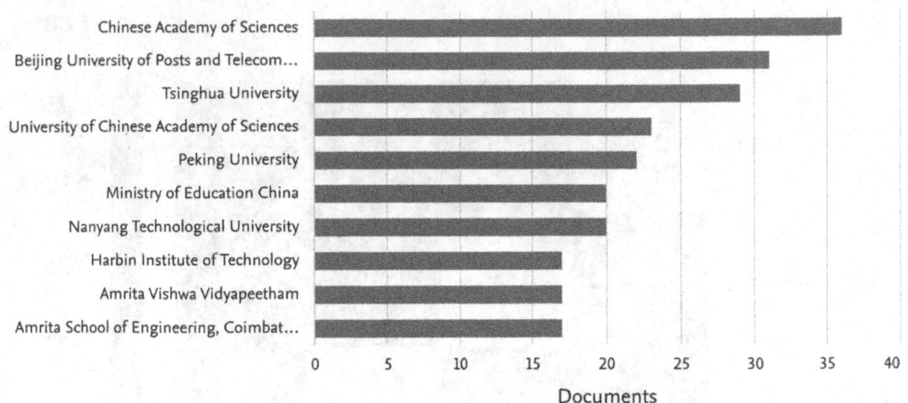

Fig. 9. Institutions and organizations listed in top 10 on paper publications.

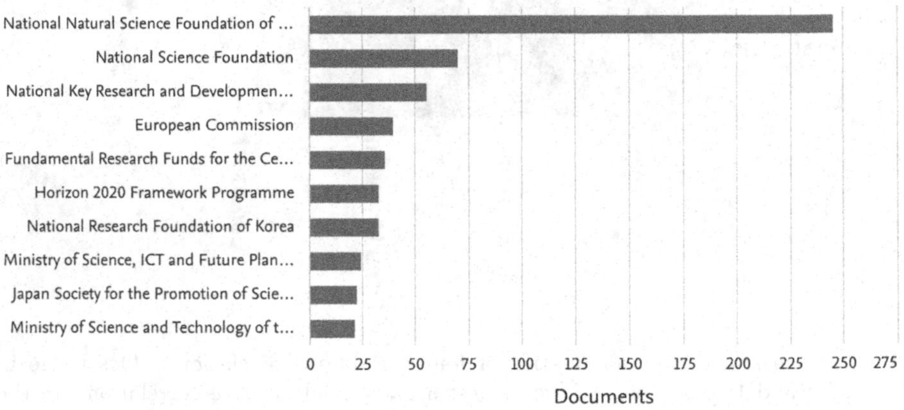

Fig. 10. Top 10 foundations sponsoring paper publications. The horizontal axis represents the number of publications sponsored by the foundation.

4 Discussion

The study provides the most recent bibliometric analysis on the topic of corpora generation for learning word vector embeddings. The research is based on the publication data from 2006 to 2022 retrieved from Scopus scientific database. Key findings are included in this section.

There is an upward trend in the number of publications made in the research area of the paper. In 2006, which corresponds to the lowest value of the metric, 2 papers were published. Since then, it has been on a steady rise, and 2021 corresponds to the peak number of publications which equals 414.

However, the average number of citations does not portray a significant upward trend from 2006 to 2022 because both the number of citations and the number of publications are increasing simultaneously, although at different rates.

Table 3. Top 10 influential publications based on total citations.

Title	Author	Year	Citations
Supervised learning of universal sentence representations from natural language inference data	Conneau, A. et al.	2017	909
Learning sentiment-specific word embeddings for Twitter sentiment classification	Tang, D. et al.	2014	837
Zero-shot learning through cross-modal transfer	Socher, R. et.al	2013	743
Graph embedding techniques, applications, and performance: A survey	Goyal, P. et al.	2018	698
Is Man to computer programmer as woman is to homemaker? Debiasing word embeddings	Bolukbasi, T. et.al	2016	658
PTE: Predictive text embeddings through large-scale heterogeneous text networks	Tang, J. et.al	2015	475
Deep Sentence embeddings using long short-term memory networks: Analysis and application to information retrieval	Palangi, H. et.al	2016	453
A simple but though-to-bit baseline for sentence embeddings	Arora, S. et.al	2017	437
Learning deep representations of fine-grained visual descriptions	Reed, S. et.al	2016	417
Learning structured embeddings of knowledge bases	Bordes, A. et.al	2011	416

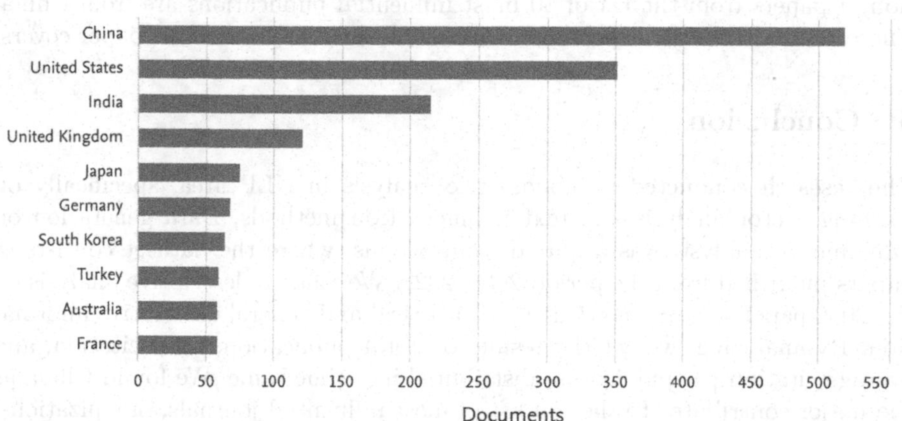

Fig. 11. Top 10 countries by publications. The horizontal axis represents the number of publications for each country from 2006 to 2022.

Instead, its graph demonstrates fluctuations, and a peak value of 263 citations in 2013 is easily noticeable.

Key statistical characteristics show that collected 2050 publications come from 869 unique sources, and 4894 unique authors with 2148 unique affiliations have contributed to the publications.

Top 3 most influential publications sources (conferences and journals) include *52nd Annual Meeting of the Association for Computational Linguistics*(ACP 452.5), *Nature* (ACP 300), and *2nd International Conference on Learning Representations* (ACP 260). Such high values of average citations are explained by the small number of articles (range in 1–7) from the sources and high citation numbers of the articles in the top-10 publication sources.

The most influential publication in terms of citations was 'Supervised learning of universal sentence representations from natural language inference data' by Conneu et al. [5], and it was cited 909 times. The number of citations in the top 15 most influential papers (published between 2011 and 2019) ranges between 260 and 909. Ten of the articles from the list were written in collaboration between 4 and more authors (up to 9 authors). Only one article titled"Neural Network Methods for Natural Language Processing" was written by a single author [7].

Another interesting observation was made by comparing the results of analyses conducted to identify the top institutions and funding organizations and top countries by publications, presented in Sects. 3.3 and 3.5, respectively. The top 6 institutions and organizations from the list of most influential institutions are from China. Also, 2 foundations from China are among the top 10 paper publications sponsoring foundations, placed first and third. And these results are consistent with the ranking of 87 countries by publications. China leads the list with more than 500 (out of 2050) publications made from 2006–2022. In addition, 4 papers from the list of 10 most influential publications are from China. These results show the expertise of China in the research area this paper covers.

5 Conclusion

The research conducted is bibliometric analysis in NLP area, specifically on learning vector analysis and text augmentation methods. Data generation on bibliometric analysis was acquired from Scopus, where the dataset consists of papers published from the period 2006–2022. We made a descriptive analysis on the 2050 paper to gain knowledge on statistical and general descriptive information. By analyzing, we get the results on total publication, total citation, and average citation per publication distributed in a timeframe. We found China as the major contributor to the top list of most influential journals, organizations, publications, and institutions.

In the end, we believe that the compiled bibliometric research would help researchers to get knowledge on general descriptive features, patterns, and insights to systematically design their studies and get the best results on research.

Acknowledgments. This research is conducted within the Committee of Science of the Ministry of Education and Science of the Republic of Kazakhstan under the grant number AP09260670 "Development of methods and algorithms for augmentation of input data for modifying vector embeddings of words."

References

1. Bojanowski, P., Grave, E., Joulin, A., Mikolov, T.: Enriching word vectors with subword information. CoRR arXiv:abs/1607.04606 (2016)
2. Bullinaria, J.A., Levy, J.P.: Extracting semantic representations from word co-occurrence statistics: a computational study. Behav. Res. Methods. **39**, 510–526 (2007)
3. Chakma, K., Das, A.: CMIR: a corpus for evaluation of code mixed information retrieval of hindi-english tweets. Computacion y Sistemas. **20**, 425–434 (2016). https://doi.org/10.13053/CyS-20-3-2459
4. Chiu, W.T., Ho, Y.S.: Bibliometric analysis of tsunami research. Scientometrics **73**, 3–17 (2007). https://doi.org/10.1007/s11192-005-1523-1
5. Conneau, A., Kiela, D., Schwenk, H., Barrault, L., Bordes, A.: Supervised learning of universal sentence representations from natural language inference data. CoRR arXiv:abs/1705.02364 (2017)
6. Geng, Y., et al.: A bibliometric review: Energy consumption and greenhouse gas emissions in the residential sector. J. Clean. Prod. **159**, 301–316 (2017). https://doi.org/10.1016/j.jclepro.2017.05.091
7. Goldberg, Y.: Neural Network Methods in Natural Language Processing. Morgan & Claypool Publishers, San Rafael (2017)
8. Jaeger, S., Fulle, S., Turk, S.: Mol2vec: unsupervised machine learning approach with chemical intuition. J. Chem. Inf. Model. **58**(1), 27–35 (2018). https://doi.org/10.1021/acs.jcim.7b00616. pMID: 29268609
9. Merigo, J.M., Gil-Lafuente, A., Yager, R.: An overview of fuzzy research with bibliometric indicators. Appl. Soft Comput. **27**, 420–433 (2015). https://doi.org/10.1016/j.asoc.2014.10.035
10. Merigó, J.M., Gil-Lafuente, A.M., Yager, R.R.: An overview of fuzzy research with bibliometric indicators. Appl. Soft Comput. **27**(C), 420–433 (2015). https://doi.org/10.1016/j.asoc.2014.10.035
11. Neuhaus, C., Daniel, H.D.: Data sources for performing citation analysis: an overview. J. Document. **64**, 193–210 (2008). https://doi.org/10.1108/00220410810858010
12. Ojo, O.E., Ta, T.H., Gelbukh, A., Calvo, H., Sidorov, G., Adebanji, O.O.: Automatic hate speech detection using deep neural networks and word embedding. Computacion y Sistemas. **26**(2), 1007–1013 (2022). https://doi.org/10.13053/CyS-26-2-4107
13. Sasaki, S., Suzuki, J., Inui, K.: Subword-based compact reconstruction for open-vocabulary neural word embeddings. IEEE/ACM Trans. Audio Speech Lang. Process. **29**, 3551–3564 (2021). https://doi.org/10.1109/TASLP.2021.3125133
14. Shekhar, S., Sharma, D., Beg, M.: An effective BI-LSTM word embedding system for analysis and identification of language in code-mixed social media text in English and roman Hindi. Computación y Sistemas. **24**, 1415–1427 (2020). https://doi.org/10.13053/cys-24-4-3151

15. Singla, K., Bose, J., Varshney, N.: Word embeddings for IoT based on device activity footprints. Computación y Sistemas. **23**, 1043–1053 (2019). https://doi.org/10.13053/cys-23-3-3276
16. Tang, D., Wei, F., Yang, N., Zhou, M., Liu, T., Qin, B.: Learning sentiment-specific word embedding for Twitter sentiment classification. In: Proceedings of the 52nd Annual Meeting of the Association for Computational Linguistics (Volume 1: Long Papers), pp. 1555–1565. Association for Computational Linguistics, Baltimore, Maryland, June 2014. https://doi.org/10.3115/v1/P14-1146
17. Zhang, X., Zhao, J.J., LeCun, Y.: Character-level convolutional networks for text classification. CoRR arXiv:abs/1509.01626 (2015)

Evaluating the Impact of OCR Quality on Short Texts Classification Task

Oxana Vitman[1(✉)], Yevhen Kostiuk[1], Paul Plachinda[2], Alisa Zhila[1,2,3], Grigori Sidorov[1], and Alexander Gelbukh[1]

[1] Instituto Politécnico Nacional, Centro de Investigación en Computación, Mexico City, Mexico
ovitman2021@cic.ipn.mx

[2] Idaho National Laboratory, 83415 Idaho Falls, ID, USA
paul.plachinda@inl.gov

[3] Ronin Institute for Independent Scholarship, Montclair, USA
alisa.zhila@ronininstitute.org

Abstract. The majority of text classification algorithms have been developed and evaluated for texts written by humans and originated in text mode. However, in the contemporary world with an abundance of smartphones and readily available cameras, the ever-increasing amount of textual information comes from the text captured on photographed objects such as road and business signs, product labels and price tags, random phrases on t-shirts, the list can be infinite. One way to process such information is to pass an image with a text in it through an Optical Character Recognition (OCR) processor and then apply a natural language processing (NLP) system to that text. However, OCR text is not quite equivalent to the 'natural' language or human-written text because spelling errors are not the same as those usually committed by humans. Implying that the distribution of human errors is different from the distribution of OCR errors, we compare how much and how it affects the classifiers. We focus on deterministic classifiers such as fuzzy search as well as on the popular Neural Network based classifiers including CNN, BERT, and RoBERTa. We discovered that applying spell corrector on OCRed text increases F1 score by 4% for CNN and by 2% for BERT.

Keywords: NLP · OCR · Text classification · Multi-class classification · CNN · BERT · RoBERTa · Fuzzy search · Short texts

1 Introduction

As of today, Optical Character Recognition (OCR) systems produce a significant amount of texts in all sorts of modern activities and businesses. Think of scanned documents, store receipts, and texts of any kind that come from the camera of a smartphone with built-in OCR, the latter becoming an ever-increasing mode of OCR text data generation. The text produced by OCR – referred to in this paper as OCRed text – needs to be processed in many automated tasks, just

O. Pichardo Lagunas et al. (Eds.): MICAI 2022, LNAI 13613, pp. 163–177, 2022.
https://doi.org/10.1007/978-3-031-19496-2_13

like regular human-typed text. The automation of text processing lies in the core goal of Natural Language Processing (NLP) domain. Nevertheless, so far the majority of research and applications in NLP have focused on texts directly typed by humans, and, hence, there is still little systematic evidence on how the quality of OCRed text affects the downstream NLP tasks and what methods are best to mitigate any negative effects.

For example, previously authors conducted research on OCR for NER [1,2]. Others looked into analysis of OCR quality and provided recommendations for improving OCRed documents [16]. In the research [14] the authors looked at classification of news articles into five classes. Other experiments have been performed on data corrupted by OCR to measure the impact of its quality on such NLP tasks as sentence segmentation, NER, dependency parsing, topic modelling [18] and part of speech tagging [12].

To the best of our knowledge, the previous research on the effect of OCRed text in NLP has not addressed one large area of NLP, namely, multi-class classification of short texts. This task is frequently encountered in a variety of real-world applications, in particular, e-commerce and consumer recommender systems, which is why it is an important subject and an impactful problem to study. In this paper, we compare various approaches to multi-class classification of short OCRed text ranging from deterministic fuzzy search to classification based on neural network with CNN, BERT, and RoBERTa as well as propose and analyze methods for classification improvement.

For this, we created a dataset of 6642 short OCRed texts obtained as a result of OCR-processing of beauty products images sourced from the publicly available data collected by Open Beauty Facts project[1]. The targets for our multi-class classification are 73 unique brands corresponding to the beauty products in the set.

Our study shows that training on the OCRed text decreases the performance of CNN-based classifier in comparison to training on the human-typed data (F1-score is equal to 0.69 for training on OCR and 0.99 for training on human-typed text) , introducing spell checking on the OCRed texts can actually increase the classification performance.

We also showed that applying spell checking on the OCRed texts improves experiment results for our baseline method - fuzzy search, as well as BERT and RoERTa classifiers.

Our paper contributes the following:

- we form a dataset of short OCRed texts annotated for multi-class classification;
- comparative analysis of various approaches –deterministic and ML-based– to multi-class classification of short OCRed text;
- comparative analysis of the effect of training data quality for the same task;
- analysis of the effect of spell checker application as a means for improvement of the classification task at hand.

[1] https://world.openbeautyfacts.org/.

This paper is organized as follows. The next section presents a brief survey of relevant research works in the literature. Section 3 describes data prepossessing steps. In Sect. 4 we present classification approaches. Section 5 presents experiments and results, general conclusions, and a short discussion.

2 Related Work

The importance of OCR cannot be overstated. OCR'd texts are most commonly used in search and mining operations on digital collections. Unfortunately, OCR'd texts often contain errors.

The research [2] reports on experiments on improving OCR quality of historical text by performing correction steps and measuring the impact on named entity recognition (NER) task. They used such correction steps as removing hyphens at the end of lines and correcting *f* letters to *s* if they were a "long s" in the original document. Suggested steps improved OCR error rate by 12%, however, they didn't use spell checking.

In [16] the authors analyzed OCR quality of various prints and manuscripts of different languages and eras of history by conducting interviews with a wide range of researchers. Authors formed nine broad recommendations for improving OCR documents, declaring that researchers should develop and distribute tools for training and adapting OCR post-correction models as well as perform quantitative evaluations of the effect of OCR errors on commonly used text-analysis methods.

The paper [1] is focused on the quality of historical text digitized through OCR and how it affects text mining and NER in the context of mining big data. Experiments were performed on data extracted from historical documents by Trading Consequences project. Results show that OCR errors decrease the number of correct commodity mentions recognized: in a random sample of documents picked from several historical text collections, 30.6% of false negative commodity and location mentions and 13.3% of all manually annotated commodity and location mentions contain OCR errors.

Van Strien [18] measured the impact of OCR quality on various NLP tasks, such as sentence segmentation, NER, dependency parsing, and topic modeling. They used datasets drawn from historical newspaper collections and based their tests and evaluation on OCR'd and human-corrected versions of the same texts. According to their findings, the performance of the examined NLP tasks was affected to various degrees, with NER progressively degrading and topic modeling diverging from the "ground truth", with the decrease of OCR quality. The study demonstrated that there is still a lack of knowledge on the effects of OCR errors on this type of application, and emphasized the importance of discovering accurate methods for measuring OCR quality.

In [12] experiments were performed on Part of Speech Tagging on data corrupted by OCR as well as using artificial experiments on data representation quality. Results indicate that already a small drop in OCR quality significantly increases the error rate both on English and German data. On the contrary, the research [17] discovered that even a relatively high level of errors in the OCRed documents does not significantly affect stylistic classification accuracy.

In research [14] authors perform automatic text classification for English newswire articles to study the impact of OCR errors on the experiment accuracies. Five categories of articles (acq, crude, earn, grain, trade) were selected from Reuters-21578 text benchmark collection[2] for English text classification, 150 articles per category. Statistical classification techniques were applied such as absolute word frequency, relative word frequency, and their power transformations. The study reveals that classification rates of OCR texts decreased with increase in OCR errors, however, transformed features improved the performance of all used classifiers. Nonetheless, Support Vector Machine (SVM) method outperformed other techniques, such as linear discriminant function and the Euclidian distance. The text classification rates for the latest were more rapidly deteriorated.

3 Dataset

As a data source for our dataset creation, we used data and images from Open Beauty Facts[3]. Open Beauty Facts is a community-driven collaborative open project that stores data about cosmetics products. The data along with the uploaded images are gathered by volunteers from 150 countries and is available under Open Database License.

The original source data contained 27.5K entries with 15,830 entries labeled with a corresponding brand.

3.1 Selection of Classification Categories

For the sake of simplicity, we focused on the task of brand classification from the text printed on the label of a beauty jar. This setting is quite straightforward as the vast majority of beauty products clearly show their brand right on the package of a product or a jar or tube itself. The feature that interested us most was that brands are often printed in a variety of sophisticated and unusual fonts that might be tricky for OCR to read correctly. An illustrative example is depicted in Fig. 1.

There were nearly 4,000 unique brands with the 90% having 6 or fewer entries. As the sparse data distribution could create unnecessary technical difficulties for ML-based classifiers, and overcoming these difficulties is not the main goal of this paper, we dropped brands with fewer than 20 entries.

This left us with 73 unique brands, transformed into 73 categorical classes. The resulting dataset contained 6,642 entries correspondingly annotated with 73 unique brands.

---

[2] https://archive.ics.uci.edu/ml/datasets/reuters-21578+text+categorization+collection.

[3] https://world.openbeautyfacts.org/data.

3.2 Obtaining OCRed Text

The remaining entries contained URLs of corresponding beauty product images taken by volunteers. First, we fetched the images from Open Beauty Facts database. An example is shown in Fig. 1.

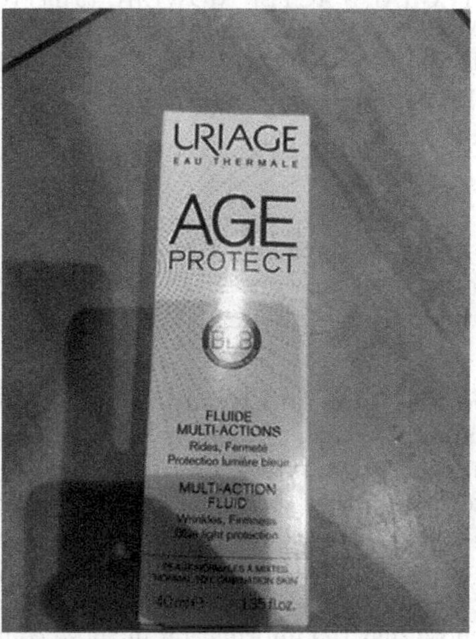

Fig. 1. Example of an image fetched from the Open Beauty Facts database. The corresponding brand is *Uriage*.

Further, we processed these images through native Apple OCR[4], thus, obtaining corresponding OCRed texts for all 8,456 annotated entries. A sample of these OCRed texts is provided in Table 1.

3.3 The Human Typed Text and Its Approximations

As the aim of this work is to analyze the effect that training of ML-based multiclass classifiers on OCRed text produces on the resulting quality of classification compared with the training on originally typed text, we needed to obtain reasonable originally typed equivalents for the OCRed texts. The authors admit that the ideal approach would be manual correction of the results of OCR processing. However, at a scale of 8,456 strings, it was not feasible within the resources of this research.

[4] https://developer.apple.com/documentation/vision/vnrecognizetextrequest.

Table 1. Illustration of OCRed text.

#	OCRed text examples
1	Smooth on Sioin PALMOLIVE NATURALS AOOr CAMELLIA OIL & ALMOND EL OE ROOCRONON
2	NIVEA Deme 100 ml
3	Tdi Signal® INTEGRAL S ACTER MOWEAU (94nt) (CO) EXPERT SENSIBILITE Arocne don oeto aca pone toude to botcne CHnE UTICACITE CLINIQUEMENT PROUVEE • SOIN APAISANT
4	P YVES ROCHER Pomme Rouge Red Apple E MUINS • HAND CREAN
5	Baby talc Peaux délicates Atuchan

Therefore, we proposed and implemented 2 approaches that served as approximations of originally typed text. By design, these approaches bear varying levels of spelling errors introduced by OCR.

Concatenated Product Name and Brand. The Open Beauty Fact database has multiple columns representing various characteristics of a beauty product. While some of them, e.g., `city`, `store`, are irrelevant for our purpose, others contained textual information that corresponded to some extent to the information provided on the label of the product. After thorough analysis of the fields, we concluded that concatenating fields `name` and `brand` would serve as the best available approximation to what is actually typed on the product face.

We would like to note that the information in those columns has been typed in by the volunteers. Therefore, it includes only as many words corresponding to the label as the volunteer provided. A few examples of the resulting texts and the corresponding OCRed texts are provided in Table 2.

Table 2. Examples of HTT texts.

OCRed text	Human Typed Text (HTT) text
NIVEA comon protect & Care 4 PROTECTION A COL CEETATU	Nivea Protect & Care - Déodorant anti-transpirant 48h
compressé compressé Dove OFFRE invisible dry LOT to c 48h x2 clean touch anti traces bipe vtoot	Dove Dove Déodorant Femme Spray Anti Transpirant Invisible Dry Compressé 100ml Lot de 2
Monsavon au lait y/ Fleur Goton Go wute l6gère Vion Geste raschd 48-8	Monsavon Monsavon Déodorant Anti-transpirant Spray Femme Fleur de Coton 200ml
NOUVEAU Sc warz. opf SMOOTH'N SHINE SOIN HUILE HYDRATANT ue Huiles 4Moringa O Olive t slmot el Caraseed	Schwarzkopf,Smooth'n shine Soin huile hydratant
WELEDA After Shave Balsam pflegt und beruhigt natürlich frisch Ganzheitliche Naturkosmetik	Weleda After Shave Balsam

While the texts in the HTT dataset variant are not properly spelled, they were typed by humans. Therefore, we assume that the distribution of spelling errors is different from the type of distortion introduced by OCR. Our goal is to analyze whether and how the performance of classifiers differs for HTT texts from OCRed texts.

Spell-corrected OCRed Texts. Another approximation to "humanizing" the OCRed text consisted in passing it through a spelling corrector. For spell correction, we employed FuzzyWuzzy[5] library, version 0.18.0. This library uses Levenshtein Distance to calculate the differences between sequences of characters. The spell checker relies on the `difflib.ratio`. This function returns a measure of the sequences' similarity (float in [0,1]). Where T is the total number of elements in both sequences, and M is the number of matches, the matching score is calculated as is $\frac{2*M}{T}$. Note that this is 1 if the sequences are identical, and 0 if they have nothing in common. For each word, it scans over the user-provided dictionary and returns the string in which each token is replaced by a word from the user-provided dictionary if the similarity score obtained from `fuzz.ratio` is higher than 0.75. We used the list of unique brands as our user-provided dictionary.

The illustration of resulted texts is provided in Table 3.

Table 3. Examples of spell-corrected OCRed texts.

OCRed text	Spell-corrected OCRed text
GARNICR Ultra DOUX CORPS	garnier Ultra DOUX CORPS
LSEVE HULE	elseve HULE
WVELEDA Depuis 1921 Bébé CALENDULA	weleda Depuis 1921 Bebe CALENDULA

As a result, we obtained 3 variants of the annotated dataset with varying degree of text distortion introduced by OCR:

1. "as-is" OCRed texts directly from an OCR processor;
2. a spell-checked version of the OCRed texts;
3. human typed texts approximately lexically equivalent to the OCRed text.

To provide numerical evaluation of the degree of distortion introduced by OCR, we calculated the aggregated numbers of exact brand string matches for each dataset and then computed the decrease (in percent) of exact match as compared to the Human Typed Text, see Table 4. As expected, the spell correction procedure removes certain fraction of the distortion placing the spell-checked OCRed variant between the OCRed one and HTT, slightly closer to the OCRed text.

[5] https://pypi.org/project/fuzzywuzzy/.

Table 4. Aggregated counts of exact substring match of a brand string in text entries for each dataset variant. The last column evaluates the distortion introduced by OCR as the decrease of matched brand strings as compared to the Human Typed Text.

Test set	# of entries with exact match	% of dataset size	% decrements from HTT
OCR	727	54.7	−27.6
SC OCR	837	63.0	−16.7
HTT	1004	75.5	0

3.4 Train/Test Split

The dataset was split into train and test parts, leaving 80% for the train part, which is equal to 5313 samples, and 20% for the test part, which equals 1329 samples accordingly. The train and test parts contain same row IDs across all variants ensuring fair comparison in our experiments.

The resulting dataset including three variants and the train-test split has been made publicly available[6].

4 Classification Approaches

We performed the analysis for several popular classifiers based on neural networks such as CNN, BERT-based classifier, RoBERTa-based classifier. For each of the classifiers, we first performed hyper-parameter tuning to determine the configuration that worked best for each variant of text. In particular, for CNN we validated input text representation via different embeddings, FastText, $\text{GloVe}_{\text{Wiki}}$, and $\text{GloVe}_{\text{CommonCrawl}}$. For BERT and RoBERTa we checked the cased and uncased models as well as base and large versions.

We also included a deterministic "classifier" based on fuzzy substring search in our analysis.

4.1 Fuzzy Substring Search

Substring search can be considered a deterministic form of a classifier. If a given brand string is found within a given text, it may be considered a "hit". Of course, it happens that more than one brand string may be found within the same text. To resolve these conflicts, we use a score provided by the fuzzy search algorithms.

Similar to the spell correction procedure described in Sect. 3.3, we used `FuzzyWuzzy` library, version 0.18.0, and Levenshtein Distance to provide a score for a potential match.

The fuzzy search relies on the `fuzz.partial_token_sort_ratio` function. It attempts to account for similar strings without regard to the token order. It sorts tokens in each string and then calls `fuzz.partial_ratio`, which in turn calls `fuzz.ratio` using the shortest string (length n) against all n-length substrings of the larger string and returns the highest score.

[6] https://github.com/Wittmann9/DataImpactOCRQuality.

This returns best matching brand as a substring of the OCRed text string, alongside with the matching score.

4.2 CNN

In this paper, we used the Convolutional Neural Network (CNN) architecture after [10]. The majority of the hyperparameters were set as proposed in [21].

CNN takes as its input text representation via vector embeddings. Commonly, popular word embeddings such as Glove [15] and FastText [9] are used. As those embeddings have been trained on different kinds of text corpora ranging from Wikipedia to CommonCrawl Corpus[7], they may have different initial information that may be helpful to a different degree for the task at hand. One can argue,for example, that while Wikipedia may contain articles on the majority of famous beauty brands, it's unlikely that it has information on all possible products produced by these brands and, hence, sufficient exposure to the vocabulary used on beauty jar labels.

On the other hand, Common Crawl Corpus is a huge corpus of a large chunk of the Internet, and the corresponding embeddings have been built from an extremely assorted vocabulary that is likely to have included beauty products.

In this paper, we have conducted preliminary experiments with different embeddings to select the optimal representation for OCRed texts in beauty product domain.

For out-of-vocabulary words the embeddings were initialized randomly (random vector sampled from U[-0.25, 0.25]).

The overall architecture can be described as follows. The padded embedded sentences are processed via the CNN cells. Next, the ReLU activation function and Max Pooling are applied. The concatenated outputs from the previous step are processed by linear layers to produce final class distribution.

Text Preprocessing. Before classification, all texts in all three dataset variants were preprocessed by converting them to lower case and standardizing Unicode symbols by applying `unidecode` package[8] for Python. It takes a Unicode character and represents it as an ASCII character mapping between two character sets in such a way that a human with a US keyboard layout would choose. For example, é → e.

GloVe Embeddings. As mentioned earlier, GloVe has various versions trained on different text corpora and varying in word vector dimension length. In particular, one version of GloVe embeddings was trained on Wikipedia and an archive of English newswire text named Gigaword 5 which contains 6 billion tokens. This version is commonly used in research. Another version is GloVe Common Crawl, 300-dimensional word vectors trained on 42 billion tokens. We compared which

[7] https://nlp.stanford.edu/projects/glove/.
[8] https://pypi.org/project/Unidecode/.

of the versions would provide the best results for our dataset which belongs to a beauty product domain.

FastText. We have experimented with FastText pretrained word vectors [4], trained on 600 billion tokens from the Common Crawl corpus.

The results of training with various word embeddings are shown in Table 5. For all variants of texts, GloVe vectors for word representation trained on Common Crawl corpus (GloVe_{CC}) outperformed or were at par with the others. Therefore, we further used the CNN trained using this particular word vector representation.

Table 5. Choosing among various word vector representations for CNN-based classifier.

Test	$\text{Model}_{\text{train}}$	FastText				GloVe_{CC}				$\text{GloVe}_{\text{Wiki}}$			
		Acc	F1	P	R	Acc	F1	P	R	Acc	F1	P	R
OCR	CNN_{OCR}	0.74	0.66	0.73	0.64	**0.76**	**0.69**	**0.76**	**0.67**	0.70	0.60	0.68	0.58
	CNN_{SC}	0.72	0.63	0.69	0.63	0.74	0.68	0.75	0.65	0.70	0.60	0.64	0.59
	CNN_{HTT}	0.53	0.43	0.57	0.43	0.66	0.62	0.72	0.61	0.40	0.27	0.36	0.31
SC OCR	CNN_{OCR}	0.77	0.66	0.72	0.65	0.77	0.70	0.77	0.68	0.71	0.60	0.67	0.59
	CNN_{SC}	0.76	0.67	0.72	0.66	**0.79**	**0.73**	**0.80**	**0.71**	0.73	0.63	0.67	0.62
	CNN_{HTT}	0.55	0.44	0.55	0.44	0.69	0.64	0.73	0.64	0.42	0.28	0.36	0.32
HTT	CNN_{OCR}	0.17	0.15	0.29	0.14	0.88	0.80	0.82	0.80	0.16	0.14	0.28	0.13
	CNN_{SC}	0.15	0.15	0.27	0.14	0.88	0.81	0.85	0.80	0.17	0.15	0.26	0.14
	CNN_{HTT}	0.98	0.97	0.98	0.97	**0.99**	**0.99**	**0.99**	**0.99**	0.98	0.96	0.96	0.96

4.3 BERT

Bidirectional Encoder Representations from Transformers (BERT) [6] is a very powerful transformer-based [19] deep learning model suitable for a variety of NLP tasks including short text classification [3,8,22].

Unlike the CNN, which we trained from scratch in this paper using the previously trained word embeddings from existing work, BERT model is a contextual representation model that has been pre-trained on large text corpora, BooksCorpus [23] and English Wikipedia, and comes with pre-trained weights.

To use it in our tasks of multi-class classification on short texts, we applied fine-tuning. BERT model is initialized with its pre-trained weights, and new additional classification layers (a linear layer on top of the pooled BERT output) are initialized with random weights. After that, we trained the model for each of our labeled training sets.

BERT model exists in various configurations: (1) as trained on cased or uncased text; (2) in a base size and large size that differ in the number of layers and, consequently, parameters. The larger model has been shown generally to outperform the BERT-base model [6]. Therefore, we perform our experiments on this version.

In our research, we used transformers python package [20], which provides pre-built transformers tokenizers and models. The preprocessing pipelines, which are required for the model are also included. We used these pipelines for the training and testing.

To choose between the cased or uncased versions of BERT, we performed the configuration experiments shown in Table 6. We observed that while the cased version performs better on spell-checked OCRed text as well as Human-typed texts, the OCRed text slightly benefits from using the uncased version as compared to the cased version. Therefore, we use the corresponding best-performing results for the final analysis in Table 7.

Table 6. Experiments with cased and uncased BERT model to choose the optimal settings for each variant of the dataset.

Test set	$\text{Model}_{\text{Train}}$	**Cased**				**Uncased**			
		Acc	F1	P	R	Acc	F1	P	R
OCR	BERT_{OCR}	**0.8021**	**0.7263**	**0.7776**	**0.7097**	**0.8043**	**0.7287**	**0.7948**	**0.7093**
	BERT_{SC}	0.4680	0.3517	0.4211	0.3643	0.1993	0.1891	0.2956	0.1878
	Bert_{HTT}	0.4266	0.3538	0.4090	0.3902	0.2151	0.0936	0.1198	0.1116
SC	BERT_{OCR}	0.6049	0.4640	0.5258	0.4710	0.3265	0.1947	0.2367	0.2100
	BERT_{SC}	**0.8073**	**0.7483**	**0.7968**	**0.7306**	0.7456	0.6965	0.7737	0.6691
	BERT_{HTT}	0.4070	0.3549	0.4182	0.3957	0.179	0.0740	0.1082	0.0795
HTT	BERT_{OCR}	0.5921	0.4265	0.4961	0.4580	0.1316	0.1261	0.3280	0.1050
	BERT_{SC}	0.5665	0.6399	0.6399	0.5277	0.1091	0.1040	0.2886	0.0881
	BERT_{HTT}	**0.9962**	**0.9938**	**0.9953**	**0.9934**	0.4236	0.2675	0.3604	0.2711

4.4 RoBERTa

A Robustly Optimized BERT Pretraining Approach (RoBERTa) [11] is an even better performing modification of BERT trained longer with bigger batch size and a number of other modifications. RoBERTa was shown to achieve superior results in various NLP tasks. In particular, recent works [5,7,13] demonstrate RoBERTa's highest results in text classification. Therefore, we included this model in our comparison to see whether it proves more stable against the spelling errors intrinsic to OCR as opposed to human text typing.

For the experiments, we used the RoBERTa large version of the model.

5 Experiments and Results

We have trained CNN and BERT classifiers on three sets of data: human-typed text, spell-corrected OCR text, and OCR text so that we could observe how our classifiers perform on texts of different quality. Each model we then evaluated on the same three types of texts.

5.1 Evaluation Metrics

For evaluation, we use Accuracy, macro-averaged F1, Precision, and Recall as implemented in scikit-learn metrics package[9]. Macro-average metrics calculate the designated value for each label and find their unweighted mean.

5.2 Experiments

For the purpose of analyzing the impact of the degree of distortion introduced by OCR on the multi-class classification task, we conducted a series of experiments. For each of the classifiers outlined in Sect. 4 apart from the fuzzy search, for each variant of the dataset with varying degrees of distortion introduced by OCR described in Sect. 3, we first trained the classifier on the training part of the dataset variant for those classifiers where training applies and then inferred the classes for the testing parts of all dataset variants.

As fuzzy search is a deterministic classifier and, hence, does not require any training, it was applied directly to the test parts of our dataset.

The results of our experiments are presented in Table 7.

Table 7. Impact of OCRed texts on the performance of various classifiers. The columns correspond to the test parts of the dataset variants with corresponding level of text distortion introduced by OCR. SC stands for spell-corrected OCRed text.

$\mathbf{Model_{train}}$	**Test OCR**				**Test SC OCR**				**Test HTT**			
	Acc	F1	P	R	Acc	F1	P	R	Acc	F1	P	R
Fuzzy	0.059	0.013	0.01	0.02	0.060	0.014	0.01	0.022	**0.065**	**0.016**	**0.03**	**0.02**
CNN_{OCR}	**0.76**	**0.69**	**0.76**	**0.67**	0.77	0.70	0.77	0.68	0.88	0.80	0.82	0.80
CNN_{SC}	0.74	0.68	0.75	0.65	**0.79**	**0.73**	**0.80**	**0.71**	0.88	0.81	0.85	0.80
CNN_{HTT}	0.66	0.62	0.72	0.61	0.69	0.64	0.73	0.64	**0.99**	**0.99**	**0.99**	**0.99**
$BERT_{OCR}$	**0.80**	**0.73**	**0.79**	**0.71**	0.47	0.35	0.42	0.36	0.43	0.35	0.41	0.39
$BERT_{SC}$	0.60	0.46	0.53	0.47	**0.81**	**0.75**	**0.8**	**0.73**	0.41	0.35	0.42	0.40
$BERT_{HTT}$	0.59	0.43	0.50	0.46	0.57	0.64	0.64	0.53	**0.99**	**0.99**	**0.99**	**0.99**
$RoBERTa_{OCR}$	**0.82**	**0.76**	**0.81**	**0.75**	0.70	0.58	0.63	0.58	0.58	0.70	0.73	0.72
$RoBERTa_{SC}$	0.59	0.47	0.57	0.47	**0.78**	**0.70**	**0.77**	**0.69**	0.68	0.57	0.67	0.58
$RoBERTa_{HTT}$	0.46	0.43	0.51	0.46	0.37	0.36	0.44	0.40	**0.99**	**0.99**	**0.99**	**0.99**

From Table 7, we observe that while fuzzy search generally performs poorly on the multi-class classification compared to the NN-based methods, it gets least confused by the human-typed text, and its performance increases from OCRed text to HTT.

For all learning-based models, we observe that the best results are achieved for the same distribution as the model was trained on, e.g., the model trained on OCRed text performs best on the OCRed test. Interestingly, CNN shows smaller

[9] https://scikit-learn.org/stable/modules/model_evaluation.html.

variance for a given test set across training on texts with varying OCR distortion level (that is, looking at the results column-wise in Table 7) compared to the BERT-based models. However, both BERT and RoBERTa achieve higher results for the OCR test set. Interestingly, for the SC OCR while BERT is showing the best performance, CNN classifier managed to outperform RoBERTa. The HTT set was trivial to learn from for all the models.

One of the main takeaways of this analysis is that adding spell correction as a pre-processing for the OCRed text tends to improve classification, at least for CNN and BERT. In particular, F1 metric has increased by 4% for CNN and by 2% for BERT.

In general, our analysis suggests that in order to obtain better performance for classification of OCRed texts, it has to be processed to reduce the distortion introduced by OCR.

Acknowledgments. The work was done with partial support from the Mexican Government through the grant A1-S-47854 of CONACYT, Mexico, grants 20220852 and 20220859 of the Secretaría de Investigación y Posgrado of the Instituto Politécnico Nacional, Mexico. The authors thank the CONACYT for the computing resources brought to them through the Plataforma de Aprendizaje Profundo para Tecnologías del Lenguaje of the Laboratorio de Supercómputo of the INAOE, Mexico and acknowledge the support of Microsoft through the Microsoft Latin America PhD Award.

References

1. Alex, B., Burns, J.: Estimating and rating the quality of optically character recognised text. In: Proceedings of the First International Conference on Digital Access to Textual Cultural Heritage, pp. 97–102 (2014)
2. Alex, B., Grover, C., Klein, E., Tobin, R.: Digitised historical text: does it have to be mediocre? In: KONVENS, pp. 401–409 (2012)
3. Amjad, M., et al.: Urduthreat@ fire2021: shared track on abusive threat identification in Urdu. In: Forum for Information Retrieval Evaluation, pp. 9–11. FIRE 2021, Association for Computing Machinery, New York, NY, USA (2021). https://doi.org/10.1145/3503162.3505241
4. Bojanowski, P., Grave, E., Joulin, A., Mikolov, T.: Enriching word vectors with subword information. Trans. Assoc. Comput. Linguist. **5**, 135–146 (2017)
5. Briskilal, J., Subalalitha, C.: An ensemble model for classifying idioms and literal texts using BERT and RoBERTa. Inf. Process. Manage. **59**(1), 102756 (2022)
6. Devlin, J., Chang, M.W., Lee, K., Toutanova, K.: BERT: pre-training of deep bidirectional transformers for language understanding. In: Proceedings of the 2019 Conference of the North American Chapter of the Association for Computational Linguistics: Human Language Technologies, Volume 1 (Long and Short Papers), pp. 4171–4186. Association for Computational Linguistics, Minneapolis, Minnesota, June 2019. https://doi.org/10.18653/v1/N19-1423
7. Guo, Y., Dong, X., Al-Garadi, M.A., Sarker, A., Paris, C., Aliod, D.M.: Benchmarking of transformer-based pre-trained models on social media text classification datasets. In: Proceedings of the The 18th Annual Workshop of the Australasian Language Technology Association, pp. 86–91. Australasian Language Technology Association, Virtual Workshop, December 2020. https://aclanthology.org/2020.alta-1.10

8. Jiang, H., He, P., Chen, W., Liu, X., Gao, J., Zhao, T.: SMART: Robust and efficient fine-tuning for pre-trained natural language models through principled regularized optimization. In: Proceedings of the 58th Annual Meeting of the Association for Computational Linguistics, pp. 2177–2190. Association for Computational Linguistics, July 2020. https://doi.org/10.18653/v1/2020.acl-main.197, https://aclanthology.org/2020.acl-main.197
9. Joulin, A., Grave, E., Bojanowski, P., Mikolov, T.: Bag of tricks for efficient text classification. arXiv preprint arXiv:1607.01759 (2016)
10. Kim, Y.: Convolutional neural networks for sentence classification. In: Proceedings of the 2014 Conference on Empirical Methods in Natural Language Processing, EMNLP 2014, 25–29 October 2014, Doha, Qatar, A meeting of SIGDAT, a Special Interest Group of the ACL, pp. 1746–1751 (2014). https://aclweb.org/anthology/D/D14/D14-1181.pdf
11. Liu, Y., et al.: RoBERTa: a robustly optimized BERT pretraining approach (2019). arxiv.org/abs/1907.11692
12. Mieskes, M., Schmunk, S.: OCR quality and NLP preprocessing. In: WNLP@ ACL, pp. 102–105 (2019)
13. Murarka, A., Radhakrishnan, B., Ravichandran, S.: Classification of mental illnesses on social media using RoBERTa. In: Proceedings of the 12th International Workshop on Health Text Mining and Information Analysis, pp. 59–68. Association for Computational Linguistics, April 2021. https://aclanthology.org/2021.louhi-1.7
14. Murata, M., Busagala, L.S.P., Ohyama, W., Wakabayashi, T., Kimura, F.: The impact of OCR accuracy and feature transformation on automatic text classification. In: Bunke, H., Spitz, A.L. (eds.) DAS 2006. LNCS, vol. 3872, pp. 506–517. Springer, Heidelberg (2006). https://doi.org/10.1007/11669487_45
15. Pennington, J., Socher, R., Manning, C.D.: Glove: global vectors for word representation. In: Proceedings of the 2014 Conference on Empirical Methods in Natural Language Processing (EMNLP), pp. 1532–1543 (2014)
16. Smith, D.A., Cordell, R.: A research agenda for historical and multilingual optical character recognition, p. 36. NULab, Northeastern University (2018). https://ocr.northeastern.edu/report
17. Stein, S.S., Argamon, S., Frieder, O.: The effect of OCR errors on stylistic text classification. In: Proceedings of the 29th Annual International ACM SIGIR Conference on Research and Development in Information Retrieval, pp. 701–702 (2006)
18. Van Strien, D., Beelen, K., Ardanuy, M.C., Hosseini, K., McGillivray, B., Colavizza, G.: Assessing the impact of OCR quality on downstream NLP tasks (2020)
19. Vaswani, A., et al.: Attention is all you need. In: Guyon, I., et al. (eds.) Advances in Neural Information Processing Systems, vol. 30. Curran Associates, Inc. (2017). https://proceedings.neurips.cc/paper/2017/file/3f5ee243547dee91fbd053c1c4a845aa-Paper.pdf
20. Wolf, T., et al.: Transformers: state-of-the-art natural language processing. In: Proceedings of the 2020 Conference on Empirical Methods in Natural Language Processing: System Demonstrations, pp. 38–45. Association for Computational Linguistics, October 2020. https://doi.org/10.18653/v1/2020.emnlp-demos.6, https://aclanthology.org/2020.emnlp-demos.6
21. Zhang, Y., Wallace, B.: A sensitivity analysis of (and practitioners' guide to) convolutional neural networks for sentence classification. arXiv preprint arXiv:1510.03820 (2015)

22. Zhao, Z., Zhang, Z., Hopfgartner, F.: SS-BERT: mitigating identity terms bias in toxic comment classification by utilising the notion of "subjectivity" and "identity terms". CoRR abs/2109.02691 (2021). arxiv.org/abs:2109.02691
23. Zhu, Y., et al.: Aligning books and movies: Towards story-like visual explanations by watching movies and reading books. In: 2015 IEEE International Conference on Computer Vision (ICCV), pp. 19–27 (2015). https://doi.org/10.1109/ICCV.2015.11

Techniques for Generating Language Learning Resources: A System for Generating Exercises for the Differentiation of Literal and Metaphorical Context

Ericka Ovando Becerril(✉) and Hiram Calvo

Centro de Investigación en Computación (CIC-IPN), Mexico City, Mexico
{eovandob2021,hcalvo}@cic.ipn.mx

Abstract. Automatic generation systems for language learning, as well as computer-assisted language learning (CALL) systems have evolved according to the demands of teachers and students. For those systems, it is important to review Natural Language Processing (NLP) techniques aimed at that task, considering other disciplines such as Computational Sciences, Computational Linguistics and Creativity for teaching and learning other languages. This work is twofold. First, it presents an effort to review the main characteristics, methods and techniques used for its implementation, relevance and profitability of the systems developed in recent years; considering the importance to develop the abilities to recognize literal use of language as well as its non literal use, particularly metaphorical expressions in the natural process of learning a new language. For the second part, it presents a system that, based on the Trofi dataset (Gao G. et al. 2018), is able to generate different exercises to strengthen the students' abilities to read and recognize the use of some verbs in literal and non-literal contexts.

Keywords: Automatic generation systems for language learning · Natural language processing · Literal · Metaphorical

1 Introduction

Automatic generation systems for language learning have become important in recent years. Although its formal development began only in the 90's years [2] computer-assisted language learning systems (CALL), that are defined as the "search and study of the application of the computer in the teaching and learning of Languages" [3], have made it possible to evolve the teaching process, facilitating the teacher's task and supporting the student, achieving better results in the area of teaching.

O. Pichardo Lagunas et al. (Eds.): MICAI 2022, LNAI 13613, pp. 178–192, 2022.
https://doi.org/10.1007/978-3-031-19496-2_14

Natural Language Processing (NLP) has been essential in the development of automatic generation systems for language learning, this task being considered by some as a hybridization of both Computation, Creativity and the Educational use of NLP, since the automatic generation of exercises can offer acceptable options saving time for teachers, designers of textbooks or study material, it can also be useful for self-study. In this respect, it is necessary to limit the implication of linguistic processes in language learning.

Returning to the ideas of William Horton (2000) [6], students require certain skills to carry out their work successfully, overcoming the various challenges that current conditions impose; on the other hand, teachers, aware of the situation, have been forced to use new teaching methods and tools. For this task, various techniques and methods are used, most of them typical of NLP, such as machine-readable dictionaries (MRD), corpora, lexical data sets, grammar books and thesauri that have given rise to the development of new tools for learning many languages, putting at our disposal the possibility of becoming polyglots from anywhere in the world, particularly improving syntax or grammar [7].

In language terms, Literal and Non-literal language, particularly metaphorical, is a phenomenon of language approached by intellectuals such as Chomsky, Ricoeur, Jakobson and Veale to mention some academics on the subject. The relevance of the metaphor not only in linguistic but also in cognitive terms allows us to understand the importance of the development of this ability and, in general, the study of literal and non-literal language. The ability to differentiate between a literal and a metaphorical text in the framework of language teaching is an indicator of language proficiency, although it is a characteristic skill of native speakers, certainly it is an element to consider within the learning process of a language and in computational terms, that has been little explored. Finally when learning a language we learn a new way of thinking, and metaphorical language is part of this.

The objective of this work is to review some of the main characteristics of automatic generation systems for language learning, as well as the methods around this task and to propose a system that allows evaluating and developing new skills and, in particular, to propose an automatic generation system for learning English, through exercises focused particularly on developing skills around the differentiation of literal language and metaphorical language.

Finally, it's important to highlight the relevance of reconsidering the way in which a language is learned and taught, in this case the English language, and to rethink, in a particular way, the awareness that the speaker acquires in this process about the use of non-literal language and its importance for language proficiency. Another point to consider is the importance of implementing these automatic generation systems from the computational cognitive and linguistic area and including them in the educational field due to their profitability, quality and the number of exercises that can be generated, and making them available to students and teachers either by digital means or through educational institutions. It's our responsibility to evaluate the use of computational tools for language learning considering.

2 Characteristics of Automatic Generation Systems for Learning

In general, an automatic exercise generation system has four relevant points [2] as general characteristics:

1. Supported language: which refers to the language that it aims to teach the user.
2. Types of exercises they generate, that is, the type of questions or texts they generate for language practice.
3. Authoring sources such as the web resources, corpus of some language or type of text, dictionaries or databases etc.
4. The objective aspect of learning can be lexical or grammatical and is the particular objective of the system.

To these four fundamental points it should be consider a fifth: the techniques and methods used for its implementation, on which the functionality, the results and particularly the profitability of the system in economic and particularly computational terms will largely depend. On the other hand, some of the tasks or factors considered in general for the automatic generation of language resources are:

The extraction of linguistic knowledge automatically "from online machine-readable dictionaries and thesauri, datasets, simple and annotated corpora, grammar books. From these resources, we can automatically extract various elements such as collocations, co-occurrences, conceptual relationships, semantic similarities, contextual similarities, selection restrictions, the definition and the actual use of the vocabulary" [7]. This allows for very broad and diverse material that otherwise could not be studied and in turn helps the student's learning to be enriched; this makes available to the teacher or educator an enormous amount of material to reinforce the student's knowledge.

The automatic generation of questions, from the previously selected material "various types of questions and answers are automatically or semi-automatically produced. These questions will be stored in a question data set" [7]. This allows the student to be evaluated in a comprehensive way, and in turn, this variety helps to better practice the language.

The human interfaces, "designed for students, tutors and designers. For students, they can rate these tools by their degree of satisfaction, and give some suggestions that may be useful to improve the system. For tutors or teachers, they can check the question base and edit it, assign some important syntactic patterns and select particular fonts that are used to generate questions, answers and explanations as is possible. Designers, in turn, can make the system more user-friendly and extend their applications to other areas or languages" [7]. The success of Computer Based Learning Systems is the collaboration between tutors, students, teachers and designers to help the student in the best way, the interfaces helps the user to take advantage of the generated exercises in the best way.

Personalized Tracking. One of the main advantages is that "student models offer an efficient, time-saving method of tracking each student's progress and registering each student with test scores and items of their learning grade. The student-of-a-learner model can help the system generate individual-oriented learning material and organize individual learning sequences that enable each student to achieve her learning goals" [7]. This represents an evolution because it would allow learning tools to be provided according to the model of each student, thus the teaching task will be much more comprehensive for the teacher and the student could advance in a better way.

2.1 NLP Tasks at Automatic Generation Systems for Language Learning

In this context, two of the main tasks associated with Natural Language Processing for language learning are [8]:

1. The tools focused on analyzing the language of the learner, that is words, sentences or texts produced by language learners.
2. The analysis of the native language. This includes finding native language reading material for language learners, developing relevant examples from native language corpora, or generating exercises, games and quizzes from native language materials.

From these two subtasks it is possible to understand the scope of these systems and the interaction between the learner, the system and the native speakers. The relationship between these three elements is fundamental, since the efficiency and use of an automatic exercise generation system will depend on these fundamentals. Among the most common exercises to generate that are recorded in the literature are [2]:

1. Column Relation: The student is offered two columns with placement parts in random order. A student has to match the first part of the collocation with the second part of the given list with the aim of increasing lexical proficiency.
2. Multiple choice the student has to fill in the blanks in the sentence. 4 options are generated and only one answer is correct.
3. Blank questions: the student must fill in the gaps with an appropriate complete answer. No options are given for answers.
4. Word Bank: the student must fill in the gaps with an appropriate answer. From a list of response options.
5. Word formation. A student has to fill in the gaps with the letters or the answers given by the system.

Although they are not the object of study in this work, it is worth considering that there are other tools proposed by computer-assisted language learning (CALL) systems, such as spelling correction of texts for students, the generation of readings and support in the drafting of new languages; the variety of proposed tools, although in this work the main ones found in the literature are mentioned, the development of this type of resources is very varied and related to the creativity of its creators.

2.2 Creation Sources

As already mentioned, there are various sources for language learning. We can consider dictionaries, corpus, thesauri, word lists or data sets according to the focus and task of the automatic generation systems for language learning, another point to consider is the level in which the student is.

One of the relevant issues in this regard is the demand for the available vocabulary [14] which can be divided into three levels:

- Level 1: Everyday Conversations
- Level 2: General Academic Words
- Level 3: Words from specific domains

Given the above, some of the efforts for the selection of support texts in language teaching or the selection of texts to form a corpus for this task contemplate the accessibility or understanding of a text according to its linguistic properties that determine that a text be more or less accessible. In this sense, they are considered predictors of the grade or range of the text: primary, secondary, preparatory or certain morphological and syntactic properties of the text [9].

Another option used with the aim of enriching the vocabulary available to the student is the consideration of words and mutual information. Mutual information is [11] a "measure for evaluating word association norms" [7].

Another tool is the "Vital Semantic Similarity to generate questions and/or their answers for many question types" by using WordNet as a tool that measures the semantic similarities between two words or phrases. WordNet is a lexical database organized on [10] psycholinguistic principles. It has a thesaurus-like structure in which lexical information about nouns, verbs, adjectives, and adverbs is expressed in terms of words [7]. It allows obtaining a value of 0 for related words and 1 for antonyms.

Likewise, the Selection Constraint (SR) governs a semantic relationship that occurs between the constituents of a phrase or sentence. It can be expressed a semantic constraints in the process of semantic interpretation. SR is a semantic restriction imposed on lexical items in forming a sentence [7]. These considerations allow the selection of sentences that may be useful for vocabulary learning, and rule out sentences, for example, that are not literal or more complex.

Taking as an example the work of Fenogenova et al. (2006) [2] can be considered support in English-language corpora aimed at Russian speakers, such as:

- The British Academic Corpus of Written English (BAWE) [12] is an English corpus of academic written texts. The BAWE corpus contains approximately 6,700,000. The texts are evenly distributed in four disciplines: Arts and Humanities, Social Sciences, Life Sciences and Physical Sciences and through four levels of difficulty, thirty-five disciplines are represented in total. The corpus is freely available online for academic purposes to researchers who agree to the terms of use.

– British National Corpus (BNC) [13] is a 100 million word collection of written and spoken British English texts from the late 20th century. The collection includes excerpts from regional and national newspapers, trade magazines for all ages and interests, academic and popular fiction books, school and college essays, and many other texts. Corpus is available online and can be freely downloaded for academic purposes as well.

Another example of the use of this type of resource is Agirrezabal M. et al. (2014) [5] that uses WordNet, and extracts a corpus from the fantastic narrative of Project Gutenberg, which has 57,000 electronic books freely available on 67 languages. ImageNet is also mentioned as support for the exercises and illustrations of the proposed systems.

Unquestionably, before choosing the resource, the language and the objective of the exercises to be generated should be considered. There are many resources already considered and developed mainly in majority languages that have contributed to the development of automatic generation systems for language learning. As an area of opportunity is the development of sources of linguistic resources for minority languages, in order to develop more tools around their learning and diffusion.

2.3 Technical and Methodological Aspects of Automatic Generation Systems for Learning

Throughout this work, the general characteristics of an automatic generation system for language learning have already been mentioned. In this sense, the techniques and methods related to Natural Language Processing should be considered as crucial for the development of these systems, being fundamental in the preprocessing of the text [source], the generation of exercises, their evaluation and the personalized follow-up of each user.

The linguistic aspects treated by NLP are mainly lexical, morphological and syntactic aspects of language, on the other hand, aspects of meaning, discourse and the relationship with the extralinguistic context have become increasingly studied in the last decade [8].

This section will present methods and techniques used to understand the evolution and development of automatic generation systems for language learning and its relationship with the NLP.

2.4 Text Preprocessing

Once the text has been selected (corpus, dictionaries, thesauri, web, etc.) from which it is planned to automatically generate the language learning exercises, the preprocessing of the text should be contemplated from four basic tasks of the NLP [5]:

Tokenization: process of dividing sequences of characters into minimums in significant units. In the tokenization process, texts are divided into words, numbers, acronyms or punctuation marks according to the language of the text.

Lemmatization: involves removing word inflection to return the dictionary form or lemma of a word. The lemma is the basis of our experimentation, since we create the transformations based on it. Consequently, an unknown or incorrect lemma can lead to errors in the following processes, or confusion in the exercises and thus make learning difficult.

Tagging: of parts of speech: it consists of assigning a grammatical category to each one of the cards. In this process, both linguistic knowledge (rules) and statistical methods are combined. This process is important for understanding sentence structure and semantic relationship.

Word Sense Disambiguation (WSD): aims to identify the [real] or secondary meaning of a word in a sentence within a context.

Although these tasks are simple within the NLP, they are mentioned in a general way because the preprocessing of the text is essential for automatic generation systems for language learning, not being clear about this process can generate a system that far from helping the user. learning generates confusion in the user, in addition to allowing the extraction of the relevant elements according to the objective of the system.

3 An Automatic Generation System for Learning the English Language: Literal Language and Metaphorical Language

Once the main concepts of automatic generation systems for language learning have been reviewed, it is possible to propose in this work an automatic generation system for learning the English language focused on the distinction between literal and non-literal language, particularly: the metaphor.

The complexity of language is reflected in the various resources that we use in thought, argumentation and communication in general. Non-literal language that results from different meanings than those formally established words or phrases. The metaphor, considered a figure of speech, makes an implicit comparison between unrelated things that, however, have certain characteristics in common [15]. In accordance with the above, and in a general way, we can understand metaphor as the exercise of extrapolating a word from one semantic to another. In a particular way according to [16] the metaphor can be considered conceptual; when it is not limited to functioning in a signed system, but is present in the way we understand the world, the associations that we generate naturally and in the various sign systems that surround us.

The metaphor allows us, in the first place, to make of something strange something more familiar or understandable, on the other hand, in poetic terms, the metaphor allows the opposite effect, to make the familiar strange or rarefied in the language. From a cognitive perspective, the human brain has the ability to decode the implicit message in the metaphor and mentally link semantically unrelated concepts through their similarities [17]. In this sense, it is important to highlight the evolutionary nature of metaphorical expressions according to time, culture and society [18]. In this sense, it is through the language learning process that the student gradually develops this ability in the new language, which is not limited to the linguistic part but also to the cognitive part an in that work for this task it relation to Computational Linguistics and Computational Cognitive Science.

The metaphor can be understood as a stretching of linguistic conventions to cover new concepts or to generate linguistic innovations. In particular, the interpretation of the metaphor depends on the ability of a system to recognize these conventions and understand in a parallel way the exceptional meaning that each metaphorical expression conveys. Within the teaching process, practice is a fundamental point to successfully develop the skills of identification and interpretation of literal and non-literal language; Therefore, it is considered that the impact of this project is relevant in the area of English language teaching and allows considering new areas to explore within the field of teaching, NLP and Cognitive Computational area.

3.1 Corpus Selection

For this project, the TroFi database is used because that is a reference in the study of metaphorical language within computational linguistics. The corpus is writed in english, it contains 3737 Literal and Non-Literal or metaphorical sentences. The Corpus does not contain a particular training and test set and is composed of snippets from the Wall Street Journal Corpus for the years 1987–1989. It focuses on grouping sentences about the use of 50 verbs, using three labels:

- L (literally)
- N (not literal)
- U (No Annotations)

This corpus makes it possible to clearly exemplify the use of literal and non-literal language, and from this the system generate different exercises all very interesting for the type of material and its size.

The TroFi Example Base contains literal/non-literal clusters for the following verbs:

absorb	drink	flow	**pass**	sleep	assault	drown	
fly	plant	smooth	attack	eat	grab	play	step
besiege	escape	grasp	plow	stick	cool	evaporate	
kick	pour	strike	dance	examine	kill	pump	
destroy	fill	knock	rain	target	stumble	die	fix
lend	rest	touch	dissolve	flood	melt	ride	
vaporize	drag	flourish		miss	roll	wither	

3.2 System Development: General Preprocessing

Using Python 3.9, each sentence was separated and three lists of sentences were formed according to their corresponding tag:

- 1592 sentences with L (Literal)
- 2145 sentences N (Not literal)
- 2699 sentences U (No annotations)

3.3 System Development: Exercises

Once the automatic language generation systems have been studied, the aforementioned linguistic, cognitive and technical elements have been considered for this project. According to the above, there are three main types of exercises proposed for this project:

Labeling Exercise: a random selection of 3 literal sentences and 2 metaphorical sentences is randomly generated. According to the above, the student must correctly label each sentence with: L if the sentence is literal or N if the sentence is metaphorical.

Blank Spaces with Answer Options: two sentences are randomly selected from each of the categories, the sentence is lemmatized and tokenized, and a syntactic analysis is performed to detect the verbs. Blank spaces are generated in the place of verbs. The options for the answer will consist of the verbs in the infinitive corresponding to the correct answers and two additional verbs, the student must write in the blank space the answer in the correct conjugation. The three sentences with their blank space and their corresponding label should be shown to the student; and the five suggested verbs for the answer.

Word Bank: a sentence is randomly selected, tokenized and blank spaces are generated according to the length of the sentence, finally the answer bank is created and the student must fill in the blank spaces with the appropriate answer.

These three proposed exercises allow you to explore metaphorical and literal language from three different perspectives, particularly the use of verbs and the way the language is structured. Undoubtedly, the ability to distinguish between literal and non-literal language corresponds to a skill developed by reaching a good level of English.

This project concentrates its efforts on proposing functional exercises for the linguistic process of learning English as a second language, but also highlighting the relevance of exploring other perspectives in teaching with a computational perspective; and demonstrating the importance in the linguistic process of the distinction between literal and non-literal language.

4 Results

Below are some examples of the exercises developed, two examples of each type of exercise proposed.

The exercises 1 and 2 are two examples Labeling exercise:

Exercise 1

Directions: Read the following five sentences carefully. Label L if you consider the sentence a literal text or N if you consider it a non-literal or metaphorical text.

___ The Federal Home Loan Bank Board, as expected, adopted a resolution intended to reassure Wall Street firms that have lent about $ 12.6 billion to the thrift unit of troubled Financial Corp. of America

___ What is missing is a general investor demand for physical gold, which would be the "swing" factor, he said

___ The plant, the company's second-largest, has annual slitting and rolling capacity of about 120, 000 tons

___ Now, in a suit filed in State Supreme Court in Manhattan, Claiborne alleges that Avon failed to keep an agreement to continue filling orders for the former venture, which had 1987 sales of about $ 27 million

___ Oil prices continued to fall yesterday in trading torn by rumors and growing evidence that Saudi Arabian crude is pouring into the market

Answers: L, N, L, L, N

Exercise 2

Directions: Read the following five sentences carefully. Label L if you consider the sentence a literal text or N if you consider it a non-literal or metaphorical text.

___ Israel deported eight Palestinians to Lebanon and ordered the expulsion of 12 others, including six from the West Bank village where an Israeli teen-ager and two Palestinian youths were killed last week.

___ Pravda said an Azerbaijan metalworker went on trial for murder for his part in February ethnic riots that killed at least 32 in the Soviet republic.

___ "This is serious because the financial community is getting flooded with these things, "said Robert Siller, an FBI agent investigating the Ohio incidents.

___ At the same time, Coleco's diversification plan – which industry analysts approve of as a way to smooth out the company 's ups and down of the past – has been disappointing so far.

___ But the Nazis didn't occupy Hungary, and kill half a million Jews, until 1944.

Answers: L, L, N, N, L

The exercises 3 and 4 are two examples Blank spaces with answer option:

Exercise 3

Instructions: Read the following sentences carefully and fill in the blanks with the corresponding verb correctly conjugated. Five possible verbs are proposed.

Literal: When sentencing a criminal, the chief justice of the country's Supreme Court ___ into consideration whether the felon has atoned for his sins by drinking sakau with the victim's family

No-Literal: Judges often can't ___ voluminous fee applications as they pour in.

Undefined: A lot of times, I ___ afraid to go to sleep for fear I wouldn't wake up. "

Box of proposed verb: sleep, take, review, flow, dance, be

Answers: takes, review, was

Exercise 4

Instructions: Read the following sentences carefully and fill in the blanks with the corresponding verb correctly conjugated. Five possible verbs are proposed
Literal: In the letter, Tom Matthews, Eastern's senior vice president of human resources, asked the mediation board to begin a 30-day countdown after which the machinists union would be free to strike – and Eastern free to impose unilaterally the cost – saving contract that it ___.
No-Literal: Mr. Reagan's speech was designed to ___ off a triumphant final year in office, but a new poll suggests that his standing in public opinion hasn't recovered from the dive it took after the disclosure of the Iran-Contra affair.
Undefined: I've been ___ better lately than I've been ___ in a long, long time.
Box of proposed verb: destroy, want, lend, play, kick, sleep
Answers: wants, kick, sleeping

The exercises 5 and 6 are two examples Word bank:

Exercise 5

Instructions: Read the following sentence carefully and fill in the blanks with the options from the answer bank.
No Literal sentence: The load factor, or ___ of seats ___, for the month declined to 54.6 ___ from ___ ___ a ___ earlier.
answer bank: 55.7, %, filled, year, percentage
Answer: The load factor, or percentage of seats filled, for the month declined to 54.6 % from 55.7 % a year earlier.

Exercise 6

Instructions: Read the following sentence carefully and fill in the blanks with the options from the answer bank.
Literal sentence: ___ Rail ___ said ___ agreed to pay $ ___ ___ to settle ___ claims ___ on behalf of 16 ___ killed in a 1987 train collision
answer bank: outstanding, people, Corp., it, 58, million, Consolidated, all
Answer: consolidated Rail Corp. said it agreed to pay $ 58 million to settle all claims outstanding on behalf of 16 people killed in a 1987 train collision.

4.1 The Exercises Generated and Their Validation

According to the English levels of the Common European Framework of Reference, the basic levels A1 and A2 include language skills for everyday situations, expressions of common use and basic vocabulary; For its part, level B1 and B2 focus on the development of the necessary ability to communicate without problem with native speakers; and levels C1 and C2 are for expert or advanced users of the language.

The sentences resulting from the proposed system at this work are perfectly coherent sentences and are related to the material of the corpus, which are fragments of journalistic texts. The exercises focus on the use of verbs in different tenses, consider different grammatical structures including passive and active voice, vocabulary is not limited to everyday situations and puts the student in contact with various semantic fields. Due to the above, the proposed system focuses mainly on intermediate students B1 and B2, or as review exercises for levels C1 and C2.

The indicators consider for this work of the skills required for reading comprehension are [19]:

- Understanding of scientific-technical vocabulary
- Interpretation of the content offered by the written text.
- Application of inference strategies to distinguish the use of verbs according to the context and the central idea of the sentence.
- Determination of central and secondary ideas of the written text, in this case of the sentence.
- Critical evaluation of the written text that allows the recognition of the literal and non-literal text.

According to these, the proposed exercises allow the student to develop and reinforce these linguistic skills and advance in their learning of the English language.

5 Conclusion

Nowadays it is important highlight the importance of automatic generation systems for language learning, its value within teaching and the relevance of continuing to investigate and propose new techniques and data sets for its development from Natural Language Processing, Computational Sciences and Sciences Computational cognitive. Likewise, the interdisciplinarity of these systems since their creation, use and evaluation allows proposing systems with new approaches according to the demands of teaching.

The use of conditional tools, smooth, web resources, and deep learning as well as various language models and NLP techniques, highlight the importance of the generation of these systems and their complexity from the computational area. Becoming aware of the processes involved in the generation of these resources makes it possible to propose new projects in the future and identify areas of opportunity for the teaching of majority languages and promote the use of these resources in minority languages. It is clear that, at an economic and social level, this type of system can make it possible to profitably learn new languages, generate a large number of learning resources that would be impossible using traditional methods, and adapt these resources to each user or learner, supporting teachers in the work of teaching and evaluation. The impact of machine-generated language learning systems makes self-learning of languages available to all by democratizing education, including for minority groups.

The three proposed exercises allow strengthening English language skills by proposing to pay attention to a purely linguistic ability, the distinction between metaphorical and literal language. This work proposes a new perspective within the development of computational tools, particularly automatic generation systems for language learning. Its real application in the world of education involves providing perfectly functional exercises for teachers and students. As future work, it is proposed to explore other corpus for the generation of exercises, focused on literal and non-literal language such as MOH-X and VUA, as well as the development of an interface that allows easy exploration of its content.

In general, this work allows us to consider three fundamental points: the methodological and technical needs of automatic generation systems for language learning, its impact at a social, educational and economic level due to its great scope in these three areas, the development of exercises for language learning with a new linguistic-computational approach and the consideration of non-literal language within learning and as a reference of language proficiency.

References

1. Gao, G., Choi, E., Choi, Y., Zettlemoyer, L.: CorMet: Neural Metaphor Detection in Context. University of Washington (2018)
2. Fenogenova, I., Kuzmenko, E.: Automatic generation of lexical exercises (2016)
3. Levy, M.: Computer-Assisted Language Learning: Context and Conceptualization. Oxford University Press, Oxford (1997)
4. Horton, R.: Principios de bioquímica, 4ta edn. Prentice Hall Person, México (2008)
5. Agirrezabal, M., Altuna, B., Gil-Vallejo, L., Goikoetxea, J., Gonzalez-Dios, I.: Creating vocabulary exercises through NLP (2014)
6. Horton, W.: Designing Web-Based Training. Robert Ipsen (2000)
7. Zhang, Y., Liu, J.: Natural language processing for foreign languages learning as computer-based learning tools. Mod. Appl. Sci. **1**(3) (2009)
8. Meurers, D.: Natural language processing and language learning. In: Encyclopedia of Applied Linguistics (2012)
9. Jurstein, J., Sabatini, J., Shore, S., Moulder, B., Lentin, J.: A user study: technology to increase teachers' linguistic awareness to improve instructional language support for English language learners (2013)
10. Miller, G., Beckwith, B., Fellbaum, C., Gross, D., Miller, K.: Introduction to WordNet: an on-line lexical database (1990)
11. Church, K.W., Hanks, P.: Word association norms, mutual information, and lexicography. Comput. Linguist. **16**(1), 22–29 (1990)
12. Alsop, S., Nesi, H.: Issues in the development of the British Academic Written English (BAWE) corpus (2009)
13. Leech, G.: Corpora and theories of linguistic performance. In: Startvik, J. (ed.) Directions in Corpus Linguistics, pp. 105–122. Mouton de Gruyter, Berlin (1992)
14. Beck, I., McKeown, M., Kucan, L.: Robust Vocabulary: Frequently Asked Questions and Extended Examples (2008)

15. Shutova, E.: Models of metaphor in NLP. In: 48th Annual Meeting of the Association for Computational Linguistics, pp. 688–697. Association for Computational Linguistics (2010)
16. Kövecses, Z.: Metaphor, Oxford (2010)
17. Rapp, A., Leube, D., Erb, M., Grodd, W., Kircher, T.: Neural correlates of metaphor processing. Cogn. Brain Res. **20**(3), 395–402 (2004)
18. Ottolina, G., Palmonari, M., Alam, M., Vimercati, M.: On the impact of temporal representations on metaphor detection (2021)
19. Llerena, I.: Sistema de ejercicios para el desarrollo de la compresión lectora en idioma inglés en estudiantes de Derecho de la Universidad de Ciego de Ávila. República de Cuba (2017)

Exploratory Data Analysis for the Automatic Detection of Question Paraphrasing in Collaborative Environments

Tania Alcantara(✉) and Hiram Calvo

Centro de Investigación en Computación, Instituto Politécnico Nacional, Mexico City, Mexico
{talcantaram2020,hcalvo}@cic.ipn.mx

Abstract. Internet searches are a daily occurrence, but we must be aware that more than one person searches the same topic with different words, this is called paraphrasing. Paraphrasing involves syntactic changes and the overlapping of words, linked to the rules of the language in which we work. The identification is a problem of great importance for natural language processing (NLP), especially paraphrasing questions with the same intention. In addition, it has been found that for the study of similarities, some features are not taken into account, which makes the identification yield lower results. In this paper, we address the problem of automatic paraphrase identification in the *Quora Question Pair* (QQP) dataset, paying special attention to data's shape through exploratory data analysis (EDA). This is in order to obtain better results in the identification tasks, as well as to compare different classifiers in collaborative environments where resources are limited.

1 Introduction

Paraphrase identification (PI) is a mechanism to detect different linguistic expressions with the same intention or similarity, this can be at different textual levels (document level, paragraph level, sentence level, word level or a combination between words) (Arase and Tsujii 2019). Paraphrasing requires a process of syntactic and semantic comprehension, which makes the task a topic of interest within natural language processing (NLP) (Dong et al. 2021).

Paraphrase example:

- **Original**: The purpose of art is to embody the secret essence of things, not to copy their appearance" said Aristotle.
- **Paraphrase**: According to Aristotle, art has the mission of embodying the hidden essence of reality, instead of simply copying its appearance.

Identification in pairs of sentences is a central problem in the natural language understanding, but when we speak about pairs of sentences, we only think of

O. Pichardo Lagunas et al. (Eds.): MICAI 2022, LNAI 13613, pp. 193–211, 2022.
https://doi.org/10.1007/978-3-031-19496-2_15

paragraphs and not in questions. Questions are a type of paragraphs that has been explored poorly and is what we find ourselves every day, for example, daily Internet searches that have already been done by other users, the set of *Quora Question Pairs* (QQP) provides us with this case study, with a wide variety of questions and paraphrasing within the questions.

Some models have already been tested, such as language inference (Prabhumoye et al. 2018) whose main objective is to predict the relationships between sentences by analyzing them in an integral way, using natural language preprocessing methods. As a clear example, the models that produce results from the use of tokens (Rajpurkar et al. 2016).

There are other architectures for specific tasks, such as ELMo (Embeddings for Language Models), which includes pre-trained representations and are used as additional features (E. Peters et al. 2018). There are models that are previously trained and generally can be adjusted and improved, such as BERT.

BERT *(Bidirectional Encoder Representations from Transformers)*, is a representation model of the language and is designed to previously train the representations in a bidirectional way (from left to right or from right to left). The difference between BERT and other models is the design for training, which performs a preliminary to deep bidirectional representations of unlabeled text. The result of all this concludes that BERT is capable of training itself by adding an additional layer for complex tasks (Devlin et al. 2021).

Given the robustness of these models, their use in conventional hardware becomes a complicated issue; In order to carry out these models in the most efficient way and with the best results, two things must be taken into account: One, carry out a study of the data in depth, this through an *Exploratory Data Analysis* (EDA), this in order to ensure the correct optimization of the model that will be used, without wasting resources and knowing the behavior of the data; Two, regarding the use of computer resources in a physical way it becomes complex, for which the use of collaborative environments becomes paramount, such as the one designed by Google called Collaboratory or Colab, which allows programming and run Python cells in a browser, which makes it accessible anywhere, with limited hardware, requires no configuration, and gives access to free GPUs.

In this article, the QQP dataset will be explored and different solutions will be reflected to solve the paraphrase detection problem, through natural language processing techniques within collaborative environments to improve system performance.

2 Theorical Framework

Paraphrase

Before starting the study, there are different theoretical foundations on which the research will be based. The first concept is paraphrase. According to Flores (2014), there are 7 paraphrase techniques.

Antes de comenzar con el estudio, existen diferentes fundamentos teóricos en los que se basará la investigación. El primer concepto es paráfrasis. De acuerdo con Flores (2014), existen 8 tècnicas de paráfrasis.

Technique 1: Change the grammatical function of some words.

Original: Professor of medicine John Swanson argues that global changes influence the spread of disease.

Paraphrase: According to John Swanson, a professor of medicine, changes around the globe cause diseases to spread (James 2004).

Technique 2: Use of synonyms.

Original: A US government spokesman stated that the AIDS crisis...

Paraphrase: A United States government spokesman announced that AIDS....

Paraphrase: Every year, more than a million people die from malaria (Angier 2001)...

Technique 3: Change word order (e.g., change from active to passive voice and move modifiers to different positions).

Original: Angier (2001) reported that malaria kills more than a million people annually...

Paraphrase: Every year, more than a million people die from malaria (Angier 2001)...

Technique 4: Use different structures for definitions.

Original: Lyme disease is an inflammatory disease caused by bacteria transmitted by ticks (small blood-sucking arachnids...)

Paraphrase: Lyme disease—an illness that causes swelling and redness—is caused by bacteria that transmit a small arachnid known as a tick...

Technique 5: Use different attribution indicators.

Original: "This disease could have reached our farms in different ways," said veterinarian Mark Walters in his recent book The Six Modern Plagues.

Paraphrase: According to Mark Walters (as cited in Peterson 2004), a veterinarian who is the author of the book The Six Modern Plagues, the disease could have reached the country's farms in different ways.

Technique 6: Change the structure of the sentence and use different connectors.

Original: Although only about a tenth of the world's population lives there, sub-Saharan Africa remains the hardest hit region...

Paraphrase: Approximately 10% of the world's population lives in sub-Saharan Africa. However, thisarea of the world has the highest percentage of AIDS-related illnesses...

Technique 7: Do not change key terms or proper names.

Original: In the northeastern United States, people make their homes near forests, where ticks that carr'y Lyme disease latch onto deer. Also, in Africa, hunters bring back meat from animals that scientists believe may carry Ebola, a usually fatal disease that causes massive bleeding in its victims.

Paraphrase: In the United States, residential areas are built near forested areas in the Northeast. These areas are also home to ticks that carry Lyme disease. In addition', according to scientists, hunters in Africa kill animals that may be carriers of the Ebola virus (a generally fatal virus that causes massive bleeding).

Exploratory Data Analysis

It is not easy to see a stack of books and say which one is the best, or to look at a set of data in an excel table, it is difficult for us to understand what it is about, recognizing possible patterns or recognizing distributions that could help.

Exploratory Data Analysis (EDA) is a useful tool for this type of analysis, since it involves a deep exploration of the information, and the objective is to explore and find different patterns in the data to find the most appropriate models (Camizuli and Carranza 2018).

EDA studies are born from statistics, developed in 1977 by John Tukey, who explained that theobjective of this is to "observe" the data to see what they look like Beyer (1981), to visualizeand extract the information on which is less obvious to our eyes. The core of this approach comes from descriptive statistics, supported by graphical tools for better visualization.

EDA also allows us to visualize the structure of the data and identify different patterns and outliers (errors, peculiarities or anomalies); In addition, keys and/or clues are sought that can lead to the identification of patterns, since the exploration of the variables is carried out in a different way, first one by one, then two by two and then on larger sets, it is an iterative process.

There are some questions to understand this:

- How many records are there?
- Are there binary distributions?

- Can the dataset be reduced?
- Is this a supervised task?
- What is the form of the data?
- Is the distribution skewed?
- Does the data have specific patterns?
- Are there outliers or unusual points?
- Does the data have temporal data?

W hat do we get with the EDA?

It is a more than valid question for this type of study, for raw or processed data it is possible to obtain:

- An approach to first-hand data
- Know if the data is sufficient or not
- Identify initial data patterns
- If the variable under study is measurable or not
- Probabilistic type distributions
- Most frequent and infrequent values
- Usual and unusual patterns

For the data already processed, exactly the same characteristics can be obtained, and additional characteristics can be created from those already observed, for example, the distances between each variable at the rate of a similarity.

BERT

BERT is an Artificial Intelligence (AI) based system developed for *Google Search* algorithms to better understand the language used for searches. This model uses the *transformers mechanism*, which is an attention mechanism that learns the context relationships between words in a given sentence or text.

The transform methods include two mechanisms: An encoder, which reads the text input, and a decoder, which produces a prediction for the task. BERT only uses the coding part, since its main function is to generate models of the language.

The difference between BERT and other models is that the transformers read it bidirectionally. This allows the model to learn the context of a word.

The model uses 2 steps: pretraining and fine tuning.

The model initializes with all its parameters pretrained and fine-tuned, using the labeled data in subsequent tasks. Each of the subsequent tasks have separate fine-tuning models, although they are initialized with the same previously trained parameters. The same architectures are used for pretraining, such as fine tuning. The parameters of the previously trained model are used to initialize models for later tasks. During the fine tuning, all the parameters are precisely adjusted, this can be visualized within Fig. 1 (Devlin et al. 2021).

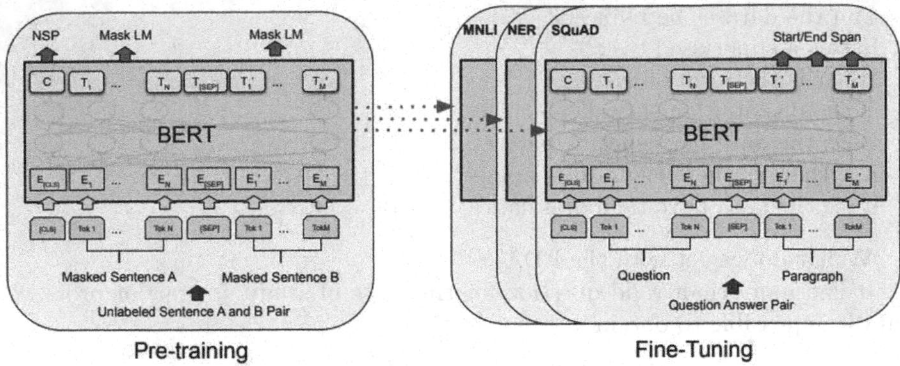

Fig. 1. General procedures, previous preparation and settings for BERT (Devlin et al. 2021).

Operation: The system model needs an input and output representation to handle the variety of tasks. The input must be an unambiguous sequence (whether one or a pair of sentences is used). The sequence must be a sequence of tokens (in NLP tokenization is the separation of a sentence into words and can be assigned a numerical value). Sentence pairs are packed into a unique sequence. Sentences can be differentiated in two ways; First, the spaces are separated by a special token *([SEP])*; Second, an embedding is added to each token to indicate whether the token belongs to sentence A or sentence B.

Pre-training: BERT uses 2 main tasks:

Task 1: Masked Language Modeling (MLM): The mask tokens feed a soft mask output on the vocabulary, Typically 15% of all tokens are masked and only predict the words masked instead of reconstructing the entire input, which allows obtaining a pre-trained bidirectional model. The training data generator chooses 15% of the positions at random for the prediction, if possible the i-th token is chosen, we replace the i-th token with (1) the token [MASK] 80% of the time (2) a random token 10% of the time (3) the i-th token unchanged 10 The time denoted as Ti will be used to predict the original token with cross-entropy, loss (Devlin et al. 2021).

Task 2: Prediction of the next sentence: To train the model that understands the relationships between sentences, the task is prepared in a binary way, this to make the prediction of the next sentence and it can be generated trivially from any monolingual corpus. BERT passes the values to initialize the model parameters of the final task. Figure 2 shows the input embeddings, the sum of the token embeddings, the segmentation embeddings and the position embeddings (Devlin et al. 2021).

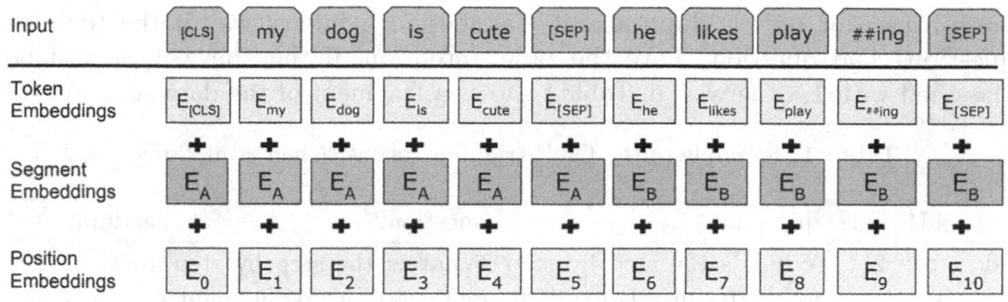

Fig. 2. BERT input representation (Devlin et al. 2021).

Dataset for Pre-training: Before continuing, it is important to know that BERT has a training with a previous dataset. The model uses Books Corpus (Kiros et al. 2015) and Wikipedia in English—Wikipedia contains 2.5 billion words—. For wikipedia only text passages were extracted, lists, tables and headings were ignored.

Fine-Tuning: This is the most important section, since it is a fine adjustment that, through the selfattention mechanism, unifies these two stages, helps to code a pair of concatenated texts and effectively includes bidirectional cross-attention between two sentences.

For each task the specific inputs and outputs to BERT are introduced and all the parameters are adjusted. In the input sentence A, and sentence B from the pretraining are analogous to (1) the pairs of sentences in the paraphrase, (2) the pairs of premise hypotheses in the link, (3) question-answer pairs, (4) a pair of texts deformed in the classification or labeling of sequences. At outputs, these representations are fed to the output layer for the selected tasks.

Quora Question Pair: Quora Question Pairs (QQP): Quora is an online platform for questions and answers, where the same questions are often asked but worded differently. From this Quora Question Pair or QQP is born, which is a dataset made up of pairs of questions. Within the dataset you can find similar questions and others that are not.

QQP consists of more than 400,000 separate question between training and test data. Within the training data, the pairs of questions that are paraphrases of the other are binary labeled with a 1, and if they are not, they are labeled with a 0.

According to Chen et al. (2018), the inspiration behind the creation of the dataset by Quora, is due to the similarity of questions from the people who visit their site, in addition to multiple questions with the same intention causing loss of time in addition to not finding the best answer to the question. Quora canonically rates questions because they provide better experiences for writers and seekers.

The dataset provides the opportunity to train and test models. The training part in a .csv format with 6 columns: ID, identifies the pair of questions; qid1 and qid2, contains the identifier of each of the questions linked to the question1 and question2 columns; question1 and question2, contains each of the questions paraphrased or not; is duplicate, it classifies in a binary way if the texts in question1 and question2 have the same intention, if they have it, it will be classified with 1, otherwise 0. Table 1 shows a fragment of the data set.

Table 1. Example of the QQP training corpus (Chen et al. 2018)

id	qid1	qid2	question1	question2	is_duplicate
0	1	2	What is the step by step guide to invest in share market in india?	What is the step by step guide to invest in share market?	0
1	3	4	What is the story of Kohinoor (Koh-i-Noor) Diamond?	What would happen if the Indian government stole the Kohinoor (Koh-i-Noor) diamond back?	0

The test part is in a .csv format with 3 columns: ID, identifies the pair of questions; *id1* and *qid2*, contains the identifier of each of the questions and is linked to the question1 and question2 columns; question1 and question2, contains each of the questions paraphrased or not. Table 2 shows a fragment of the test data set.

Table 2. Example of the QQP test corpus (Chen et al. 2018)

test_id	question1	question2
0	How does the Surface Pro himself 4 compare with iPad Pro?	Why did Microsoft choose core m3 and not core i3 home Surface Pro 4?
1	Should I have a hair transplant at age 24? How much would it cost?	How much cost does hair transplant require?

3 State of the Art

Entailment as Few-Shot Learner (Wang et al. 2021). They focus on EFL, which can convert small LMs to improve learning in a few triggers. The key idea, is to reformulate the NLP task, into a linking task and refining it with 8 examples. They show that the method improves deep learning methods by 12%.

Charformer: Fast Character Transformers via Gradient-Based Subword Tokenization (Tay et al. 2021). They propose a new inductive bias model, which learns a tokenization of subwords with the smooth gradient (GBST). The main approach is the path of high-performance tokenless models.

Transformer Likes Residual Attention (He et al. 2020). This paper focuses on RealFormer, a simple and generic technique for creating transformer networks in the residual attention layer, which can modify transformers such as BERT with the broad spectrum of tasks.

FNet: Mixing Tokens with Fourier Transforms (Lee-Thorp et al. 2021). Through the attention layers, it performs mixtures of the input tokens, the feed-forward layers demonstrate to be proficient at modeling semantic relationships. layers prove to be proficient at modeling semantic relations, this through a standard fourier transform encoded through the standard transform.

Data2vec: A General Framework for Self-supervised Learning in Speech, Vision and Language (Baevski et al. 2022). This model proposes data2vec, a framework that uses the same learning method for speech. This helps predict specific targets, in this case words.

StructBERT: Incorporating Language Structures into Pre-training for Deep Language Understanding (Wang et al. 2019). They propose an extension of BERT to a new model: Struct BERT, which proposes linguistic structures in pre-training, with two auxiliary tasks to make the most of the order. In pre-training, with two auxiliary tasks to take full advantage of the order.

Quora Question Pairs. (Chen et al. 2018) the detection of duplicate questions, they use a neural network, the model is the Manhattan LSTM (Long-Short Term Memory), through the fusion of two neural networks performs the final classification, to finally evaluate the performance through the logarithmic loss between the predicted values and the reality.

Identification of Duplication in Questions Posed on Knowledge Sharing Platform Quora Using Machine Learning Techniques. (Rishickesh et al. 2019) through the extraction of context features such as bag-of-words features, Count-Vectorizer and TFIDF-Vectorize, is able to perform similarity predictions with machine learning modeling methods like XGBoost and TFIDF.

Siamese Neural Networks with Random Forest for Detecting Duplicate Question Pairs (Godbole et al. 2018). In this article they used a siamese adaptation of closed recurrent units (GRU), in a bidirectional mode, this with a combination of a Random Forest Classifier, for the QQP set.

What Do Questions Exactly Ask? MFAE: Duplicate Question Identification with Multi-Fusion Asking Emphasis. (Zhang et al. 2020) uses a transformer mechanism called BERT, this will help to obtain the embeddings of the words dynamically. Then it elicits an upward emphasis of attention and self-attention. When one word interacts more with another, the more important it becomes. Finally, an eight-way combination is used for question identification.

Transfer Fine-Tuning: A BERT Case Study (Arase and Tsujii 2019). They propose to inject phrase paraphrase relations into BERT in order to generate suitable representations for semantic equivalence evaluation instead of increasing the size of the model.Experiments on standard natural language comprehension tasks confirm that the method effectively improves the base BERT model while maintaining the size. The generated model exhibits superior performance compared to a larger BERT model in semantic equivalence evaluation tasks.

3.1 Scientific Novelty and Difference with the State of the Art

Current developments have focused on applying different algorithms, novel and modern, but they have left aside the analysis of the data; what are the patterns that follow the questions, how many repetitions exist in my set, what grammatical rules are the most used? These are just a few questions that, when answered through EDA analysis, will make the application of algorithms obtain better results than those applied without analysis. In addition, this analysis and modeling can be applied to other tasks such as sentence prediction, question answering and, with this study, automatic text generation.

4 Solution Development

4.1 Initial EDA

Number of Classes: The first step is data recognition, in other words, we need to know type of classes, the Fig. 3, represent the question distribution. The **35.9%** of the pairs of questions are duplicated (1); the **63.08%** the pairs of questions are not duplicated (0).

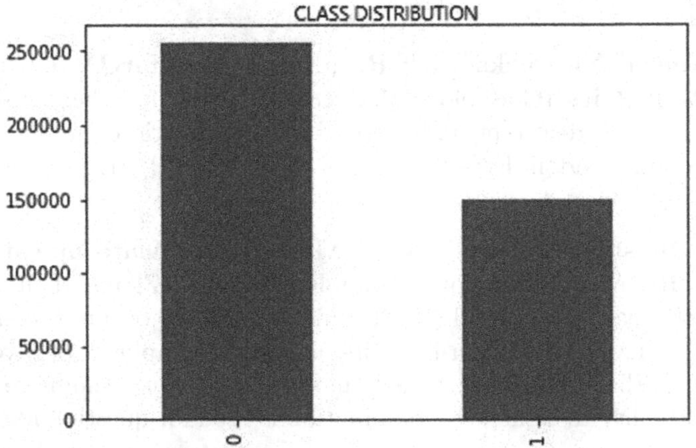

Fig. 3. Duplicate question and not duplicate distribution

Repeated Questions: We analyzed whether there was repetition of questions in the dataset, for example, whether question 1 or 2 were used in more than one comparison; the figure shows the distribution of unique questions; one question is repeated 157 times, which makes it the highest number of repetitions (Fig. 4).

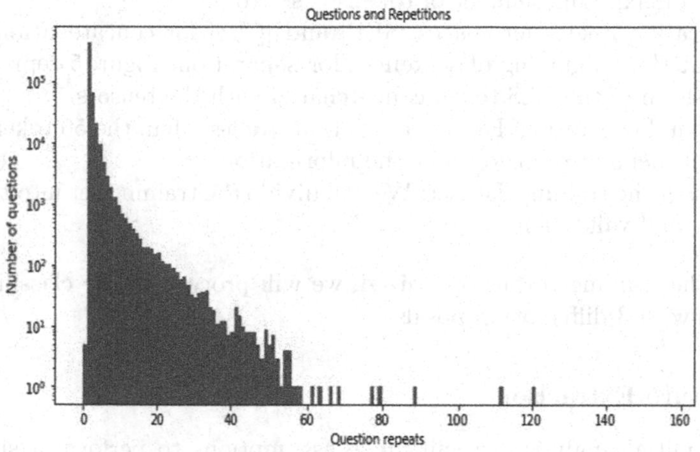

Fig. 4. Question distribution vs each repetition.

4.2 Preprocessing

Homogeneous Data: For best results, it is necessary that the data set is homogenized, for example, that there is no disparity in the representation of the same concept.

1. Data from uppercase to lowercase.
2. Quantities to letters: e.g., quantities ending in ",000" up to ",999" will be replaced by a "k", quantities with "000, 000" up to "999, 999" will be replaced by an "m".
3. Conversion of single quotation marks.
4. Data contractions: Contractions in words are removed, e.g. *wont't* changes to *will not.*
5. Special characters of prices or percentages changed: They are changed to text, example: The euro symbol, € is changed to *euros*.

Lemmatization: The process of lemmatization of a text is a technique, in which morphological variants of words will be reduced to the most basic form or lexeme, in order to improve the task, for example: - **Originals:** We will work, work, worked, worked, work -**Lexeme:** Work

Tokenization: The tokenization process is a NLP technique, where the sequence of words is converted into sections or parts of it, according to the task. During this process the tokenizer proposed by BERT will be used (Devlin et al. 2021).

- Configure the tokenizer to generate the Tensorflow dataset: Tokenization is performed with *WordPiece* system, in which a word can be converted into a conventional token or a word can be multiple tokens precisely adjusted, this can be visualized within Fig. 1 (Devlin et al. 2021).
- Limitation of tokens: Since there are long questions and they must be homogenized, a maxi mum number of tokens is set to 50.
- Identification tokens for spaces [SEP] and [CLS] for concatenation: This is added at the be ginning of sentences for separation. Figure 5 represents the anteposition of the CLS token concatenated with the tensors.
- Data complementation: For sentences that are less than the 50 tokens, it will be supplemented to homogenize the information.
- Division of the training dataset: We will divide the training set into two parts, training and validation.

With the training corpus optimized, we will proceed to the classification of our model with 3 different proposals:

4.3 Feature Extraction

From the initial analysis, we will make assumptions to perform a specialized EDA to the data set:

1. Number of letters
2. Number of words
3. Total of new words
4. Similarities the first word
5. Similarities the last word
6. Unique words
7. Unique words without stop words

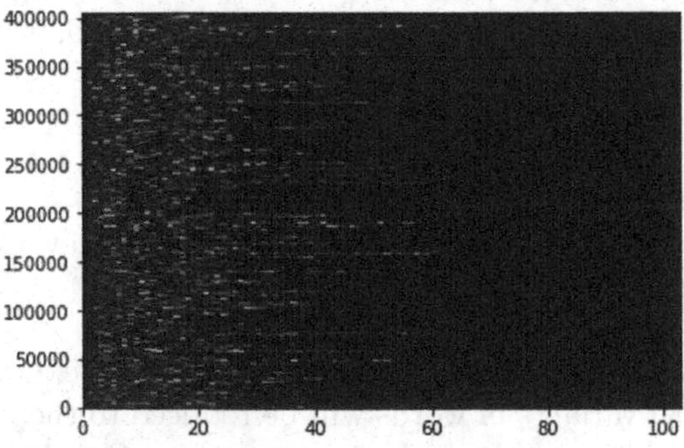

Fig. 5. Anteposition of the CLS token concatenated with the tensors

4.4 Analysis of Preprocessed Data

EDA it is an important step between classifier and pure data, though Sanjay (2021), you can see the recommended features for QQP.

After the data preprocessing, an EDA analysis with features is started, in order to know extensively the different patterns and behaviors of the data and to choose the best classifier. For the analysis, questions 1 and 2 are taken into account respectively, making the analysis focused on this one.

Total Words. It represents the word count between question 1 and question 2, the Fig. 6 represents that word count.

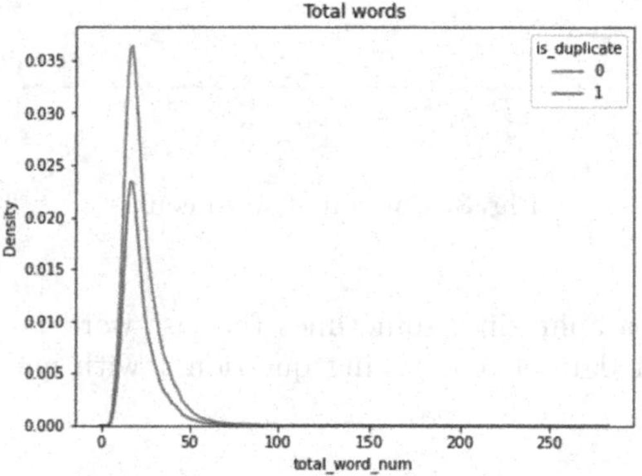

Fig. 6. Total words

Absolute Difference. The original and the paraphrased question generally do not include the same number of words, the Fig. 7 represents that word count.

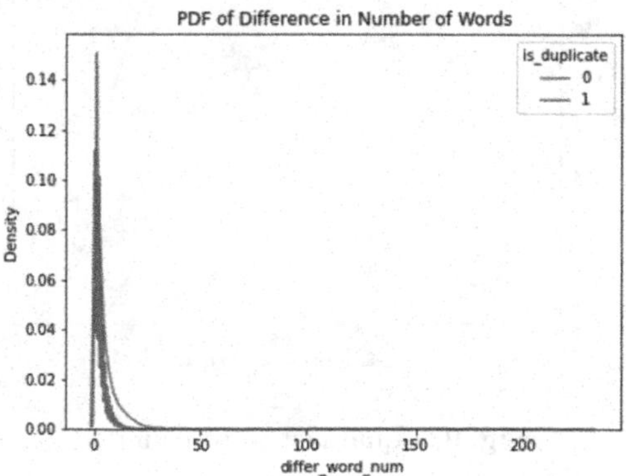

Fig. 7. Absolute difference between the number of words

First Word. In some paraphrasing techniques, it is common for the first word to be shared. In the Fig. 8 is visualized from our dataset, comparing question 1 with question 2.

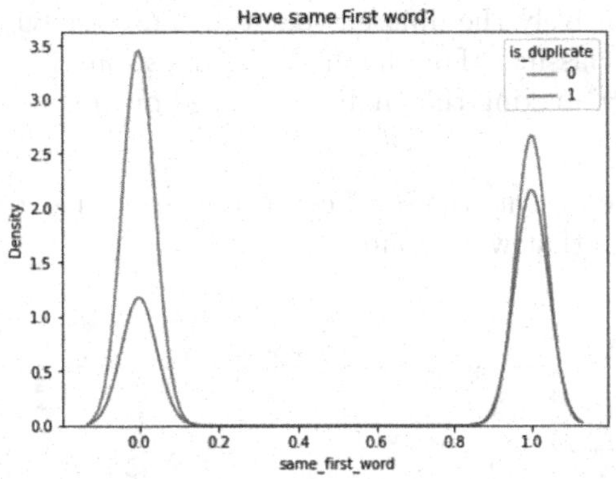

Fig. 8. Equal first word count

Last Word. In paraphrasing, sometimes the last word is shared. Figure 9 is displayed from our dataset, comparing question 1 with question 2 in the last word (Fig. 10).

Word Repetition. It is common that the words still exist in both sentences, they have only been moved from passive to active voice and vice versa. Figure 11 shows the repetition of these words, without considering the stop words.

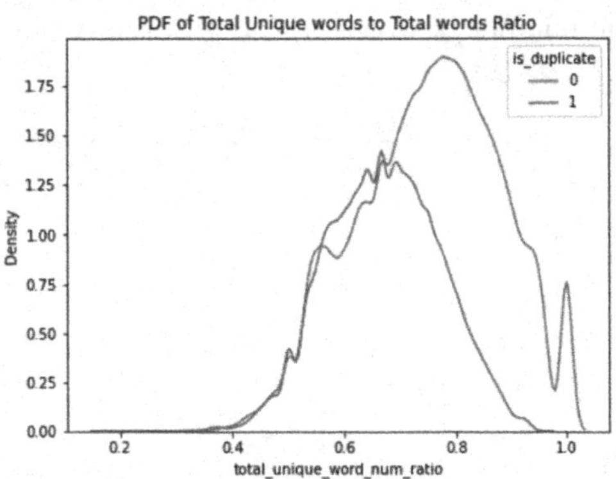

Fig. 9. Equal last word count

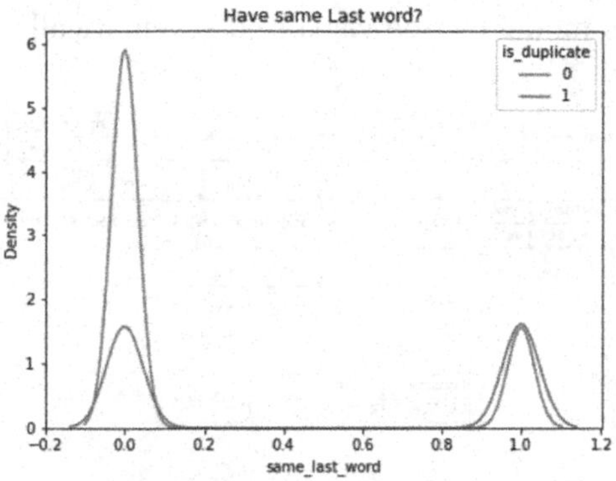

Fig. 10. Last word

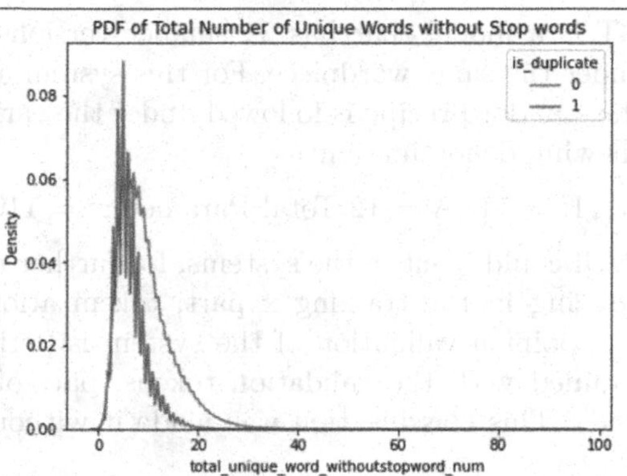

Fig. 11. Word repetition without stopwords

4.5 Classifier Models

The identification in pairs of questions will be performed by means of a classification model. In this configuration the kernel of the model is defined from the keras library, in it the outputs of the number of classes with a maximum length sequence were predicted. The function will return the encoder and the classifier. The conditions of our configuration will be: Attention dropout prob ability, 0.1; hidden dropout probability, 0.1; hidden size, 768; intermediate size, 3072; maximum position of *embeddings*, 512; number of *head-attention*, 12. For this case, the classifier has three inputs and one output. In the Fig. 11 this model can be visualized schematically.

In the Fig. 12 this model can be visualized schematically.

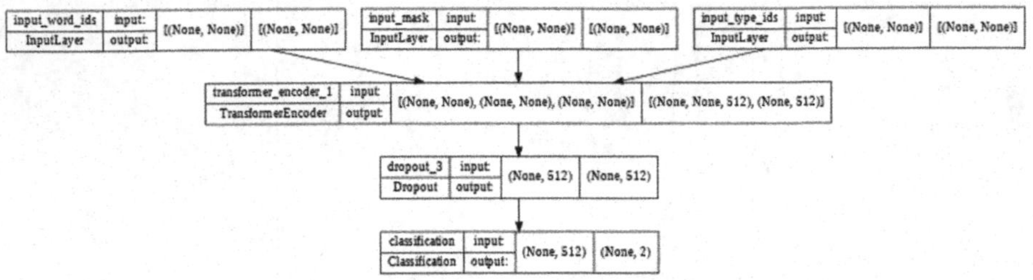

Fig. 12. Classifier 3 inputs 1 output

Bert Training

Bert Training BERT is a model that has 24 smaller versions (only trained in English), trained under the same wordpiece. For this system and taking advantage of its power, the standard recipe is followed under the variant named *Small BERT*, with the following denomination:

Small Bert: $\mathrm{L} = 4\,\mathrm{H} = 512\,\mathrm{A} = 12$ Total Parameters = 110M

The model by itself could identify the systems, for further results the encode part is used, introducing in the training x part, tokenization of the training dataset, at this same point a validation of the system is performed, for a validating "x", it is trained with the validation tokens, part of the training set (previously separated). This classification was made it without EDA, to try it scope.

Random Forest

As a second classification model for the QQP problem, a random forest(RF) is an estimator based on decision tree that classifies on lots sub-samples of the data set.

RF predicts accuracy and helps to control overfitting. The parameters of the classifier are 200 estimators, 5 samples split and a maximum depth of 50.

XGBoost

As a third model, an XGBoost classifier was implemented that uses the regularization gradient augmentation to attack this problem, where the first thing that is required is to separate the training data from its indexes since these will help for it's addition to the labels and thus to know its correlation, then it is necessary to define the model where in this case a logistic binary classification will be used as objective, as metric the loss function and as augmenter the reinforced decision tree.

Subsequently, a separation of training data is performed and we proceed to train and test with 500 epochs, making a jump every 20 epochs. As a result, it can be observed how throughout the 500 epochs the loss function decreases, demonstrating that the model is reaching its convergence point. For best results, XGBoost was trained with two different configurations.

4.6 Model Comparison

The results from the SVM, XGBoost and SmallBERT models indicate that the SmallBERT model based on transformers is better compared to other models, we found that (Tables 3 and 4):

Table 3. F1 results for classifier models

id	Model	Accuracy
1	**XGBoost 1**	**90.2%**
2	**XGBoost 2**	**90.11%**
3	EFL	89.2%
4	Charformer-tall	88.5%
5	**XGBoost 1**	**88.70%**
6	RealFormet	88.28%
7	FNet-Large	85%
8	**Random forest**	**82.60%**
9	StrucBERTRoberta ensemble	74.4%

Table 4. Accuracy results for classifier models

id	Model	Accuracy
1	**SmallBERT**	**91.4%**
2	data2vec	92.4
3	SmallBERT	91.3
4	Charformer-tall	91.4
5	RealFormet	91.34
6	StrucBERTRoberta ensemble	90.7
7	**XGBoost 2**	**90.48%**
8	**XGBoost 1**	**88.70%**
9	**MVP**	**83.28%**

5 Conclusions and Future Work

Research has been described for the question paraphrase identification task, using the Quora Question Pairs dataset, for the identification of two questions using collaborative environments.

It can be concluded that the key to the results of the classifiers is the correct exploratory data analysis (EDA), since by making use of it, patterns visualized help in the extraction of characteristics; this shows us that the transformers do generate better results, but by making better use of the EDA, good results can be obtained with less processing power. XGBoost2 obtained in F1 90.2%, above systems that have used transformers and very similar to ours.

References

Arase, Y., Tsujii, J.: Transfer fine-tuning: a BERT case study, pp. 5393–5404 (2019)

Arase, Y., Tsujii, J.: Transfer fine-tuning of BERT with phrasal paraphrases. Comput. Speech Lang. **66**, 101164 (2021)

Ayala, M.: Paráfrasis. lifeder.com (2021)

Baevski, A., Hsu, W., Xu, Q., Babu, A., Gu, J., Auli, M.: data2vec: a general framework for self-supervised learning in speech, vision and language. CoRR, abs/2202.03555 (2022)

Barrron, A., Marti, A., Vila, M., Rosso, P.: Plagiarism meets paraphrasing: insights for the next generation in automatic plagiarism detection. Comput. Lingüistics **39**, 917–947 (2013)

Beyer, H.: Tukey, John W.: Exploratory Data Analysis. Addison-Wesley Publishing Company, Reading, Mass.—Menlo Park, Cal., London, Amsterdam, Don Mills, Ontario, Sydney 1977, XVI, 688 s. Biometr. J. **23**(4), 413–414 (1981)

Camizuli, E., Carranza, E.J.: Exploratory data analysis (EDA) (2018)

Chen, Z., Zhang, H., Zhang, X., Zhao, L.: Quora question pairs. Universityof Waterloo (2018)

Chopra, A., Agrawal, S., Ghosh, S.: Applying transfer learning for improving domain-specific search experience using query to question similarity (2020)

Correa, B., Londoño, C.: Los 5 tipos de plagio más frecuentes (2018)

Deng, L., Liu, Y.: Deep Learning in Natural Language Processing, 1st edn. Springer, Singapore (2018). https://doi.org/10.1007/978-981-10-5209-5

Devlin, J., Chang, M.-W., Lee, K., Toutanova, K.: BERT: pre-training of deep bidirectional transformers for language understanding. In: Proceedings of the 2019 Conference of the North American Chapter of the Association for Computational Linguistics: Human Language Technologies, Volume 1 (Long and Short Papers) (2021)

Dong, Q., Wan, X., Cao, Y.: ParaSCI: a large scientific paraphrase dataset for longer paraphrase generation, pp. 424–434. CoRR, abs/2101.08382 (2021)

E. Peters, M., Neumann, M., Iyyer, M., Gardner, M., Clark, C., Lee, K., and Zettlemoyer, L. (2018). Deep contextualized word representations. Proceedings of the 2018 Conference of the North American Chapter of the Association for Computational Linguistics: Human Language Technologies, Volume 1 (Long Papers)

Flores, R.: Citas y referencias. recomendaciones y aspectos básicos del estilo APA, biblioteca de la universidad de lima. Principios para citar parafrasear y resumir; Cómo evitar el plagio accidental (2014)

Godbole, A., Dalmia, A., Sahu, S.K.: Siamese neural networks with random forest for detecting duplicate question pairs. CoRR, abs/1801.07288 (2018)

He, R., Ravula, A., Kanagal, B., Ainslie, J.: RealFormer: transformer likes residual attention. CoRR, abs/2012.11747 (2020)

Hermann, M., Frank, K., Bilal, Z.: Plagiarism - a survey. J. Univ. Comput. Sci. **08**(25), 1050–1084 (2006)

Kiros, R., et al.: Skip-thought vectors, vol. 28 (2015)

Lan, W., Qiu, S., He, H., Xu, W.: A continuously growing dataset of sentential paraphrases, pp. 1224–1234 (2017)

Lee-Thorp, J., Ainslie, J., Eckstein, I., Ontañón, S.: FNet: mixing tokens with Fourier transforms. CoRR, abs/2105.03824 (2021)

Mota-Montoya, M., Cunha-Da, I., López-Escobedo, F.: Un corpus de paráfrasis en español: metodología, elaboración y análisis. RLA: Revista de Lingüistica Teórica y Aplicada (54) (2016)

Prabhumoye, S., Tsvetkov, Y., Salakhutdinov, R., Black, A.-W.: Style transfer through back-translation. In: Proceedings of the 56th Annual Meeting of the Association for Computational Linguistics (Volume 1: Long Papers) (2018)

Rajpurkar, P., Zhang, J., Lopyrev, K., Liang, P.: SQuAD: 100,000+ questions for machine comprehension of text. In: Proceedings of the 2016 Conference on Empirical Methods in Natural Language Processing (2016)

Rishickesh, R., Ram Kumar, R.P., Shahina, A., Nayeemullah Khan, A.: Identification of duplication in questions posed on knowledge sharing platform quora using machine learning techniques. Int. J. Innov. Technol. Explor. Eng. (IJITEE) **8**(12), 2444–2451 (2019)

Roig, M.: Avoiding plagiarism, self-plagiarism, and other questionable writing practices: a guide to ethical writing. States Department of Health & Human Services, Office of Research Integrity (2019)

Sanchez-Perez, M.A., Gelbukh, A., Sidorov, G.: Adaptive algorithm for plagiarism detection: the best-performing approach at PAN 2014 text alignment competition. In: Mothe, J., et al. (eds.) CLEF 2015. LNCS, vol. 9283, pp. 402–413. Springer, Cham (2015). https://doi.org/10.1007/978-3-319-24027-5_42

Sanjay, C.: The quora question pair similarity problem (2021). https://towardsdatascience.com/the-quora-question-pair-similarity-problem-3598477af172. Accessed 25 Aug 2022

Segura, M.: N-gramas sintácticos para el reconocimiento de paráfrasis (2014)

Segura-Olivares, A., Garcia, A., Calvo, H.: Feature analysis for paraphrase recognition and textual entailment. Res. Comput. Scie. **70**, 119–144 (2013)

Tay, Y., et al.: Charformer: fast character transformers via gradient-based subword tokenization. CoRR, abs/2106.12672 (2021)

Thompson, V.: Methods for detecting parpharse plagiarism. Department of Computer Science, University of Sunderland (2017)

Lin, W.-Y., Peng, N., Yen, C.-C., Lin, S.-D.: Online plagiarism detection through exploiting lexical, syntactic, and semantic information. In: Proceedings of the ACL 2012 System Demonstrations (2012)

Wang, S., Fang, H., Khabsa, M., Mao, H., Ma, H.: Entailment as few-shot learner. CoRR, abs/2104.14690 (2021)

Wang, W., et al.: StructBERT: incorporating language structures into pre-training for deep language understanding. CoRR, abs/1908.04577 (2019)

Wang, Z., Hamza, W., Florian, R.: Bilateral multi-perspective matching for natural language sentences, pp. 4144–4150 (2017)

Zhang, R., Zhou, Q., Wu, B., Li, W., Mo, T.: What do questions exactly ask? MFAE: duplicate question identification with multi-fusion asking emphasis, pp. 226–234 (2020)

Zubarev, D., Schonkov, I.: Pharaphrased plagiarism detection using sentence similarity. Conference Paper (2017)

Best Paper Award

Diachronic Neural Network Predictor of Word Animacy

Vladimir Bochkarev(✉), Andrey Achkeev, Anna Shevlyakova, and Stanislav Khristoforov

Kazan Federal University, 420008 Kazan, Russia
vladimir.bochkarev@kpfu.ru

Abstract. The paper considers the problem of automatic recognition of animacy in the Russian language. We propose a recognizer that is based on the analysis of co-occurrence with the most frequent words and is trained on data from the Russian subcorpus of Google Books Ngram. The obtained recognition accuracy of animacy is 94.3% on the test sample. We also consider the application of the trained recognizer to diachronic data. The performed analysis shows that high recognition accuracy can be obtained even using the data extracted from the corpus for one single year. This allows one, firstly, to diachronically investigate changes in perception of words for which variability of animacy/inanimacy is observed. Secondly, the considered examples show that change in perception of an object as animate or inanimate can serve as a marker of semantic change and, in particular, emergence of new meanings of a word denoting this object. This makes the recognizer a good tool for studies of language evolution.

Keywords: Animacy · Neural networks · Lexical semantics change detection · Diachronic corpus

1 Introduction

Word semantics is changeable which has given rise to multiple surveys in the field of word meaning change. Creation of large text corpora and modern data processing methods have contributed much to this research area.

Large text corpora are used to study various properties of words which presence or change may indicate changes in word semantics. Various computational methods for detecting these changes are also being developed.

The well-known distributive hypothesis says that changes in semantics are quantified in terms of changes in distribution of words. The hypothesis is based on the idea that distributional similarity correlates with meaning similarity [1–3]. There are different algorithms of distributional meaning acquisition. Early works mainly used representations based on co-occurrence vectors [4–6]. A new impetus to research was given in 2013 by the appearance of an improved word embeddings technique [7]. Various applications of word embeddings to the study of semantic change have been proposed in

O. Pichardo Lagunas et al. (Eds.): MICAI 2022, LNAI 13613, pp. 215–226, 2022.
https://doi.org/10.1007/978-3-031-19496-2_16

[8–10]. Presently, the most commonly used methods are based on vector models of neural networks. However, simpler representations based on explicit word vectors are also employed in natural language processing [11].

In some papers, other ways of solving the problem of lexical semantic change detection are considered. For example, [12] presents three algorithms for detecting semantic change. One of these methods, called by the authors [12] the syntactic method, is based on tracing frequency of a word used as a particular part of speech. Part-of-speech change is associated in [12] with the appearance of new meanings of a studied word. That is, some grammatical properties of a word can, without using the lexical-semantic analysis (even in its context), indicate a change in word meaning. This approach is developed in [13], where it is shown that grammatical profiling of a word can be more informative than methods based on word embedding in semantic change studies.

One of the grammatical categories relevant to the study of semantic change is the category of animacy, which shows whether we percept an object as a living or non-living thing. Our perception may depend on various factors such as subconscious perception of entities or deliberate consideration of an object as animate or inanimate thing. The latter factor, in turn, can be associated with both a stylistic effect and semantic change. In this article, we will also study this property of a word.

The issue of animacy detection has been studied in linguistics and related fields. [14, 15]. It is important to note that this category is not considered fixed but depends on the context of use and human perception [16]. Besides linguistics, the category of animacy is also studied in in natural language processing to address various issues [17–19]. One such works devoted to the study of animacy is [20]. It surveys in detail the cases of atypical animacy and examines scenarios in which typically inanimate objects, specifically machines, are given animate attributes.

Speaking about NLP and creating animacy recognizers, it is worth noting that morphosyntactic analyzers make decisions depending on the context in which some word is used [21, 22]. As contrasted with such works, the present work objective was to create an animate/inanimate noun recognizer that makes decisions based on the co-occurrence statistics of a word in a large corpus and which could be used to reveal new meanings of words. A marker for the emergence of a new meaning would be a sharp transition from animate objects to inanimate ones (and vice versa).

A similar technique of searching for changes in a word semantics was used in [23]. It used the method of co-occurrence with the most frequent words (CFW) to determine whether a word is used as a proper or common noun, and the transition from one specified category to another was interpreted as a change in the word semantics. The data on co-occurrence of the studied words was taken from the English version of the Google Books Ngram corpus (GBN).

The present study uses the Russian subcorpus of GBN which is based on the texts of more than one million books with a total size of 89.4 billion words, published between 1486–2019 [24]. Today it is the largest diachronic corpus of Russian texts.

2 Data and Method

We used the Open Corpora dictionary [25, 26] to determine whether the noun is animate or inanimate. Then, the nouns that are marked in this dictionary as animate or inanimate were extracted from the GBN corpus for the period 1920–2019.

The words that are precepted only as animate or inanimate things were selected. In other words, the sample did not include nouns that, according to the dictionary, has two homonymous forms represented both by animate and inanimate nouns. Such choice allows one to avoid ambiguities.

The sample also did not include very infrequent words. More precisely, the sample consisted of:

- words that occur in the GBN corpus at least 50 times in 1920–2019;
- words that are a part of 3 unique bigrams found in the corpus.

We determined 239,196 word forms belonging to 60,683 lemmas (taking into account homonymy) that satisfied the described conditions. The proportion of the obtained animate nouns was 28.71%.

We used two different vector representations of words. The main results were obtained using explicit word vectors. To construct a vector representation of a particular word, we used data on the word co-occurrence statistics in a large corpus. The method of co-occurrence with the most frequent words (CFW) is described in detail, for example, in [27, 28]. According to this method, a vector that represents a word is constructed from the frequency values of all possible bigrams of the form Wx and xW, where W is a target word and x is one of the context words. In the CFW approach, a given number of the most frequent words is selected as context words. In this work, the number of context words is 20,000, so the dimension of the vector representation of words is 40,000. In [29], it was proposed to build vectors from the corresponding pointwise mutual information (PMI) values instead of the frequencies themselves. We will use its regularized version instead of PMI:

$$\log_2\left(\frac{f_{wx}}{f_w f_x} + 1\right)$$

Here f_{wx} is a relative frequency of the bigram consisting of a target word W and a context word x, and f_w and f_x are relative frequencies of both words.

Bigram frequencies were extracted from the Google Books Ngram [24] corpus. The interval 1920–2019 was chosen for the analysis. There are two reasons for such choice. Firstly, there are great number of texts published in this period and included in the corpus (the summed size of texts is 86.7 billion words from the total amount of 89.4 billion). Secondly, choosing this period, we avoid problems associated with the spelling reform of 1918.

For comparison, we also implement a recognizer that uses pre-trained fasttext vectors as input. The fasttext algorithm, including various enhancements to word embeddings, was introduced in [30]. The authors also provided free access to the vectors pre-trained on the Common Crawl corpus by using this algorithm (for 157 languages) [31].

The neural network model is a four-layer perceptron with a sparse input layer of dimension 40000, three dense layers of dimension 128, and an output layer of dimension 2. The dimension of the output layer corresponds to the number of target classes: one class includes animate nouns and the other one consists of inanimate nouns. The softmax function was used as the activation function of the output layer, which makes it possible to interpret the values of the outputs as a probability distribution on the target classes. The RELU [32] activation function was used for the input and inner layers. To regularize the model, a dropout [33] with a 5% parameter was applied to the inner layers.

To determine the optimal configuration of the model, experiments were carried out with a change in the dimension of the inner layers and their number, training rate, training algorithm and the dropout parameter The number of the inner layers varied from one to five, and their dimensions varied from 16 to 256. When using one and two inner layers, the accuracy of the model on the test set decreased. Also, a drop in the accuracy was observed when the dimension of the inner layers was less than 64. With an increase in the dimension of the inner layers above 128, the training time increased greatly, however, no increase in the accuracy was observed. The same effect was observed with increasing network depth.

Categorical cross-entropy was used as a loss function. The Adam, Nesterov Accelerated Gradient and Stochastic Gradient Descent algorithms [34] were tried as training algorithms with different training rates. The first two algorithms provided a similar result. Stochastic Gradient Descent allows one to achieve slightly higher accuracy (by 0.5–0.6%) with a higher training rate.

For a model using pre-trained fasttext vectors, a neural network of the same configuration was used, except for the number of inputs, which in that case was 300. The list of words used to train and test the model was also different. In total, the authors of [31] provided free access to the vectors for 2 million Russian words. However, the list of 239,196 selected word forms has many infrequent words that are not included in this number. Therefore, the list of words employed for training and testing the model using fasttext vectors included 164,353 nouns.

TensorFlow [35] and Keras [36] libraries were used to train the neural network models.

3 Results

At the first stage, we trained the recognizer on synchronous data. All 239,196 word forms were divided into a training and a test sets in a ratio of 2 to 1 (two thirds for the training set and one third for the test set).

To do this, the entire set of words was divided into six non-overlapping groups. The division was performed so that all word forms belonging to any lemma, as well as homonymous words, were included only to one of these groups. Except for this condition, the division was random, so the percentage of infrequent and frequent words was about the same in all groups.

The training was performed in turn on the selected four groups (out of 6), and the rest ones were used to test the resulting model. Thus, 15 models were trained (the number of combinations is 4 out of 6). The described procedure allows cross-checking of the obtained results. However, the main goal was to get evidence-based estimates for the widest possible range of vocabulary. For any given word from the initial list, there are five models for which this word is included in the test set. With regard to word embeddings, necessity of multiple training of the model was noted in [37, 38]. Resampling of the training samples was used in [38] to consider the influence on reproducibility of the results of such factors as the use of stochastic optimization algorithms in the training process, as well as random selection of texts for the training sample. The same factors play a significant role in the case considered in this paper. The presence of several independently trained models allows one to estimate the standard deviation of the model outputs and, thus, control the reliability of the results for each example.

The average accuracy for the trained 15 models on test sets was 92.07%. Similarly, a set of recognizers was trained using the pre-trained fasttext vectors. In that case, the average accuracy was 98.12%. When comparing these values, it should be taken into account that the latter was obtained using a narrower list of words, from which, as mentioned above, some of the most infrequent words were excluded. The average recognition accuracy by the CFW method on the same sample, which was used to test the fasttext recognizer, was 94.36%. Thus, under equal conditions, the use of the pre-trained fasttext vectors provides significantly higher accuracy. However, the CFW method has an advantage - it can easily be adapted to diachronic data extracted from the Google Books Ngram corpus.

At the second stage, the recognizer was trained on diachronic data. We extracted data for a certain year of the period 1920–2019 from the GBN. If the frequency of some word was below 10 in the selected year and the number of unique bigrams containing this word was less than 3, then such a vector was not included in the sample. In total, the sample included 9,604 thousand vectors, each of which characterized a certain word in a given year. After additional selection, some of the most infrequent words were excluded from the sample. In total, the resulting sample contained 213,945 words.

The average accuracy of the 15 models trained on annual vectors was 96.55%. It may come as some surprise that this value is higher than the value given above for the synchronous model. In fact, as explained above, some of the vectors for less frequent words were not included in the sample, which causes this effect. If meanings of a word do not change over time, we would like to get some general answer based on the diachronic model for the word we are interested in, and not a series of answers for each year. For example, we can feed the model input with a vector constructed from the data of the entire considered interval 1920–2019. In this case, the obtained accuracy is 91.85%. The second possibility that immediately comes to mind is to take the answers of the model for all the years and make a decision depending on the most frequent answers. Thus, the obtained average accuracy for words is 93.62%. However, a different solution provides a slightly better result. Using the output layer with the softmax activation function allows one to interpret the outputs of the neural network as the probabilities of a word belonging to a particular class. As stated in [23], the logarithm of the ratio of the outputs of the network y_1 and y_2, respectively, can be interpreted as the logarithm of the likelihood ratio:

$$L = \log_2 \frac{y_1}{y_2}$$

In accordance with the criterion of maximum likelihood, we decide that the word is animate if:

$$\sum_t L(t) > 0$$

For words, this rule provides an average accuracy of 93.75%. To further increase the accuracy, one can average the values of the likelihood ratio L(t) not only over years, but also over a set of independently trained models. In this case, to make a decision, we use the value calculated by the formula:

$$\sum_i \sum_t L^{(i)}(t)$$

Here i is the model number, and the summation is performed over all models where the target word belongs to the test set. Averaging over 5 models increases the average accuracy for words to 94.28%. Similarly, averaging the likelihood ratio on 5 independently trained models allows increasing accuracy estimation on annual vectors of up to 97.11%. Thus, averaging the estimate over the set of independently trained models makes it possible to further improve the accuracy.

Comparing the described values with the above-mentioned recognizer accuracy based on the pre-trained fasttext vectors, it should be taken into account that the latter was tested on a narrower sample, from which a significant proportion of the most infrequent words was excluded. Counting on a sample narrowed to 164,353 words provides the accuracy of 95.73% for best version of the CFW recognizer.

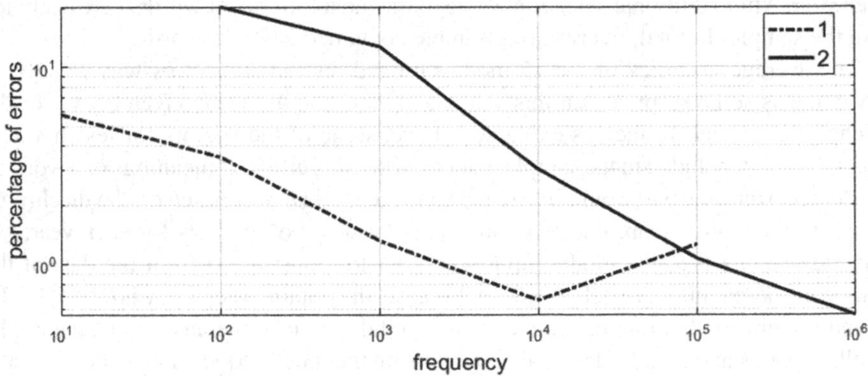

Fig. 1. Percentage of recognition errors depending on frequency. The dash-dotted line (1) is for annual vectors depending on the annual frequency, the solid line (2) shows the percentage of errors for words depending on their total frequency for 1920–2019

To conclude this section, let's consider how recognition accuracy depends on word frequencies. We divided words into frequency classes - from 10 to 99 (for the mentioned period 1920–2009), from 100 to 999, and so on; and separately calculated the percentage of recognition errors for each class. The results are shown in Fig. 1 (solid line). We also calculated the percentage of recognition errors by annual vectors, in this case the frequency class was determined depending on frequency of a word in a given year. The results are shown in the figure by a dash-dotted line. The figure shows the results for the classes that include at least a thousand cases.

The graph illustrates a quite natural improvement in accuracy as word frequency increases. Only the last point on the dashed-dotted curve is outlined from this dependence. For this class (with frequencies from 105 to 106 per year), there are 282 errors per 22,226 vectors. Considering the number of errors as a random variable with a binomial distribution, it is easy to calculate that the relative error in estimating the recognition error probability for a given class does not exceed 6%. Thus, the effect is certainly statistically significant. The question of why the recognizer worser copes with the most frequent examples requires additional research. Nevertheless, the recognizer accuracy should be assessed as high. As one can see from the graph, even for cases where the word has a frequency of 10 to 99 uses per year, the recognition accuracy for the annual vector is 94.23%.

At the end of this section, we present a summary of the obtained results (see Table 1).

We compare the following models:

- CFW model initially trained on synchronous data (according to total frequencies for 1900–2019);
- Diachronic CFW model trained on annual frequency vectors;
- Model using pre-trained fasttext vectors and feedforward neural networks.

We report accuracy on four test datasets:

- Large sample of 239,196 words;
- Its subset of 213,945 words, for which annual vectors are available;
- Its subset of 164,353 words, for which pre-trained vectors are presented in [31];
- Directly on the set of 9,604 thousand annual vectors.

Table 1. Accuracy of the compared models on different test sets

Model	239K words	214K words	164K words	Annual vect.
CFW, synchronic	92.07%	93.32%	94.36%	94.93%
CFW, diachronic	–	94.28%	95.73%	97.11%
fastText + FNN	–	–	98.12%	–

As can be seen from the table, it is more reasonable to train the model immediately on diachronic data.

The obtained accuracy is quite high (see, for example, [21, 22]). However, a direct comparison with the accuracy of traditional recognizers will be incorrect, since fundamentally different problems are solved in this work and in [21, 22]. In [21, 22], recognition is considered for a specific word in the context of a sentence. In contrast, our recognizer determines (without using source texts) how a word is predominantly used in a large corpus.

4 Case Study

Let us show by examples how change of animacy/inanimacy of a word in diachrony serves as a marker semantic change.

As mentioned above, for each word (out of the 239,196 selected words) there are five trained models for which this word belongs to the test set. For the target word, we average the log likelihood ratio $L^{(i)}(t)$ from the output of these five neural networks:

$$\langle L(t)\rangle = \sum_i L^{(i)}(t)$$

Sudden jumps $\langle L(t)\rangle$ can indicate changes in the perception of the word as denoting an animate or inanimate object. We can use one of the many change-point detection algorithms that have been recently developed to detect the time of change of average meaning [39–41]. Here we follow the change point detection technique described in [23], which uses the frequency vector resampling procedure proposed in [42] to detect significant changes.

Out of 239,196 selected words, 1,442 words were found that show significant jumps $\langle L(t)\rangle$, and the sign of $\langle L(t)\rangle$ before and after the jump is different. As a manual check shows, for a significant percentage of these words, a real change in animacy/inanimacy is observed. All of them can be divvied into two large groups. The first one includes words for which variability of the specified category is observed, justified by the perception of the speaker. Semantics of such words does not change radically. Gradual transition from one category to another may even be explained by cultural reasons. This group of words includes biological terms such as *robot, microbes, embryos, streptococcus* (see Fig. 2,a). Initially, these words are percepted as animate objects, however, they become inanimate over time. For example, the word *streptococcus* is initially is percepted as an animate object. In the 1970s years, $\langle L(t)\rangle$ decreases and it is percepted mostly as inanimate one.

The second group includes words that have transferred from one category to another due to a change in semantics. Often these are homonymous forms of the common noun/proper noun type. For example, the word *triton* (see Fig. 2,b) denotes an animal, a Greek god, and the name of a satellite of the planet Neptune. Other examples include the words *grant* (see Fig. 2,c), *show, polygraph,* etc. There is also homonymy of the type common/common noun. For example, the word *mot* (see Fig. 2,d) refers to a person who wastes money and means a *coil of rope*. *Gadi* denotes both reptiles and people. The last word shows a tendency to transfer to the category of inanimate nouns.

The graph shows the transition of the word *kop* from a group of inanimate nouns to animate ones. Let's analyze semantics of this word. *Kop* (see Fig. 2,e) is an abbreviation for the word *kopeika (kopek),* which is an inanimate noun. The transfer to the category of animate nouns is associated with a change in semantics. In particular, this word has gained a new meaning "police officer". The meaning was borrowed from American English.

Thus, it has been once again confirmed that semantics of a word and its animacy are interrelated parameters. And identification of a change in the category of animacy/inanimacy can be interpreted as one of the markers of semantic change.

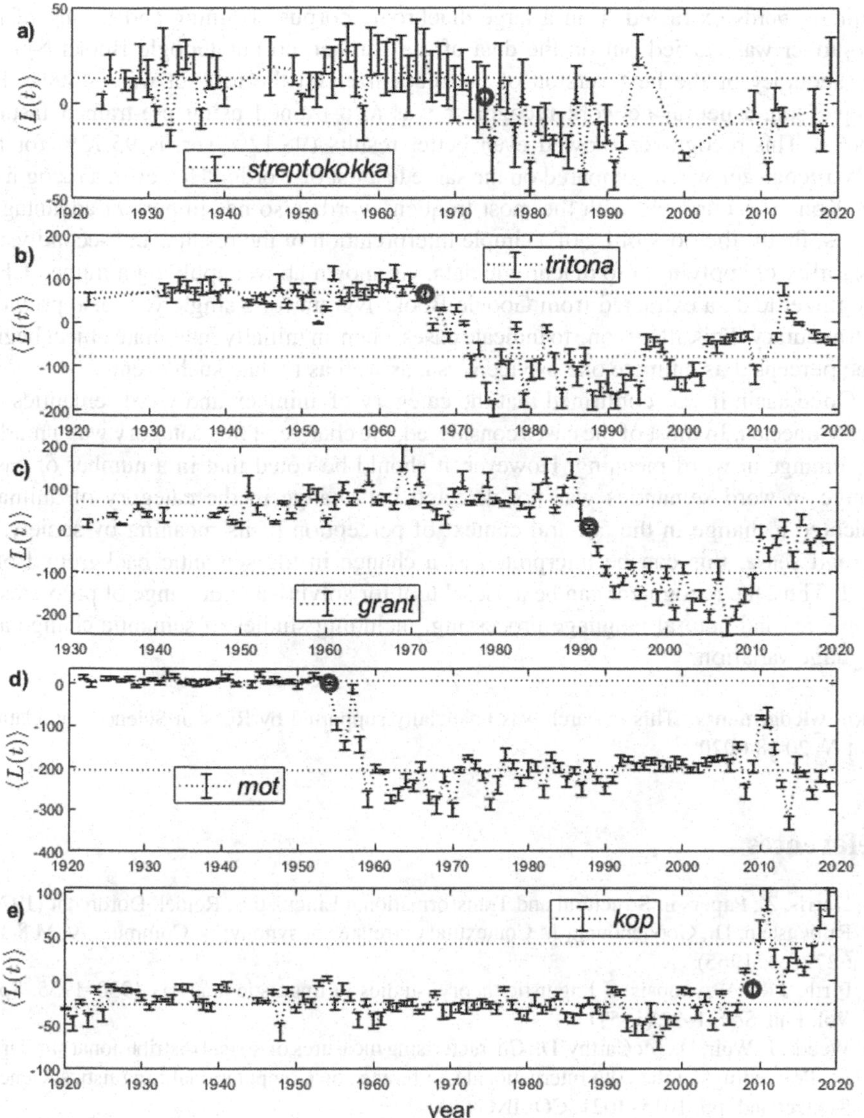

Fig. 2. Changes in $\langle L(t) \rangle$ over time for the word forms *streptokokka, tritona, grant, mot, kop (streptococcus, triton, grant, spender/skein* and *cop/kopek)*. For each point, the boundaries of the 95% confidence interval are determined. The circle indicates the change-point found by the algorithm. The dotted lines show the average levels of $\langle L(t) \rangle$ before and after the change-point

5 Conclusion

We have created a recognizer to detect animacy/inanimacy of Russian nouns. A tagged list of 239,196 words was selected using the OpenCorpora morphological dictionary. Recognition is performed according to the statistics of co-occurrence with the most frequent words extracted from a large diachronic corpus. Training and testing of the recognizer was carried out on the data of the Russian corpus Google Books Ngram. The accuracy of the best version of the recognizer on the test set was 94.28%. For comparison, a neural network recognizer was also trained using pre-trained fasttext vectors. This recognizer showed even better results (98.12% versus 95.73% for the CFW recognizer when compared on the same test list of words). However, a recognizer based on co-occurrence with the most frequent words also has important advantages. This is, firstly, the possibility of a simple interpretation of the results, and secondly, the possibility of applying it to diachronic data. As shown above, applying a trained CFW recognizer to data extracted from Google Books Ngram for a single year also provides high accuracy. This allows one to indicate cases when an initially inanimate object begins to be percepted as animate one or vice versa, as well as to date such events.

Once again it was confirmed that the category of animacy and word semantics are interconnected. In most of the cases considered, the change of this category was a marker of a change in word meaning. However, it should be noted that in a number of cases change in word semantics was not detected but change in the category of animacy indicated a change in the cultural context of perception of its meaning by society. In a broad sense, this can be interpreted as a change in the semantic background of a word. Thus, the recognizer can be a useful tool for solving a wide range of problems in linguistics and natural language processing, including studies of semantic change and language variation.

Acknowledgements. This research was financially supported by Russian Science Foundation, grant № 20-18-00206.

References

1. Harris, Z.: Papers in Structural and Transformational Linguistics. Reidel, Dordrecht (1970)
2. Rubenstein, H., Goodenough, J.: Contextual correlates of synonymy. Commun. ACM **8**(10), 627–633 (1965)
3. Firth, J.R.: A synopsis of linguistic theory, studies in linguistic analysis 1930–1955. Spec. Vol. Phil. Soc. 1–32 (1957)
4. Weeds, J., Weir, D., McCarthy, D.: Characterising measures of lexical distributional similarity. In: Proceedings of the 20th International Conference on Computational Linguistics, Geneva, Switzerland, pp. 1015–1021. COLING (2004)
5. Pantel, P.: Inducing ontological co-occurrence vectors. In: Proceedings of the 43rd Conference of the Association for Computational Linguistics, pp. 125–132. Association for Computational Linguistics, USA (2005)
6. Bullinaria, J., Levy, J.: Extracting semantic representations from word co-occurrence statistics: a computational study. Behav. Res. Methods **39**, 510–526 (2007). https://doi.org/10.3758/BF03193020
7. Mikolov, T., Sutskever, I., Chen, K., Corrado, G., Dean, J.: Distributed representations of words and phrases and their compositionality. In: Advances in Neural Information Processing Systems, vol. 26, pp. 3111–3119. Curran Associates, Inc. (2013)
8. Kim, Y., Chiu, Y.-I., Hanaki, K., Hegde, D., Petrov, S.: Temporal analysis of language through neural language models. In: Proceedings of the ACL 2014 Workshop on Language Technologies and Computational Social Science, pp. 61–65. ACL (2014)

9. Frermann, L., Lapata, M.: A Bayesian model of diachronic meaning change. Trans. Assoc. Comput. Linguist. **4**, 31–45 (2016)
10. Yao, Z., Sun, Y., Ding, W., Rao, N., Xiong, H.: Dynamic word embeddings for evolving semantic discovery. In: Proceedings of the Eleventh ACM International Conference on Web Search and Data Mining, WSDM 2018, pp. 673– 681. ACM (2018)
11. Tang, X.: A state-of-the-art of semantic change computation. Nat. Lang. Eng. **24**(5), 649–676 (2018)
12. Kulkarni, V., Al-Rfou, R., Perozzi, B., Skiena, S.: Statistically significant detection of linguistic change. In: Proceedings of the 24th International Conference on World Wide Web, Florence, Italy, pp. 625–635 (2015)
13. Giulianelli, M., Kutuzov, A., Pivovarova, L.: Grammatical profiling for semantic change detection. In: Proceedings of the 25th Conference on Computational Natural Language Learning, pp. 423–434. Association for Computational Linguistics (2021)
14. Vihman, V.-A., Nelson, D.: Effects of animacy in grammar and cognition: introduction to special issue. Open Linguist. **5**(1), 260–267 (2019)
15. Gao, T., Scholl, B., McCarthy, G.: Dissociating the detection of intentionality from animacy in the right posterior superior temporal sulcus. J. Neurosci. Off. J. Soc. Neurosci. **32**, 14276–14280 (2012)
16. Nieuwland, M., van Berkum, J.: When peanuts fall in love: N400 evidence for the power of discourse. J. Cogn. Neurosci. **18**(7), 1098–1111 (2005)
17. Lee, H., Chang, A., Peirsman, Y., Chambers, N., Surdeanu, M., Jurafsky, D.: Deterministic coreference resolution based on entity-centric, precision-ranked rules. Comput. Linguist. **39**(4), 885–916 (2913)
18. Orasan, C., Evans, R.: NP animacy identification for anaphora resolution. J. Artif. Intell. Res. **29**, 79–103 (2007)
19. Chen, J., Schein, A., Ungar, L., Palmer, M.: An empirical study of the behavior of active learning for word sense disambiguation. In: Proceedings of the Main Conference on Human Language Technology Conference of the North American Chapter of the Association of Computational Linguistics, pp. 120–127. Association for Computational Linguistics (2006)
20. Coll Ardanuy, M., et al.: Living machines: a study of atypical animacy. In: Proceedings of the 28th International Conference on Computational Linguistics, Barcelona, Spain, pp. 4534–4545. International Committee on Computational Linguistics (2020)
21. Karsdorp, F., van der Meulen, M., Meder, T., van den Bosch, A.: Animacy detection in stories. In: Proceedings of the 6th Workshop on Computational Models of Narrative, Saarbrücken/Wadern, Germany, pp. 82–97. Dagstuhl Publishing (2015)
22. Jahan, L., Chauhan, G., Finlayson, M.: A new approach to animacy detection. In: Proceedings of the 27th International Conference on Computational Linguistics, Santa Fe, New Mexico, USA, pp. 1–12. Association for Computational Linguistics (2018)
23. Bochkarev, V.V., Khristoforov, S.V., Shevlyakova, A.V., Solovyev, V.D.: Neural network algorithm for detection of new word meanings denoting named entities. IEEE Access **10**, 68499–68512 (2022). https://doi.org/10.1109/ACCESS.2022.3186681
24. Lin, Y., Michel, J.-B., Aiden, E.L., Orwant, J., Brockman, W., Petrov, S.: Syntactic Annotations for the Google Books Ngram Corpus. In: Li, H., Lin, C.-Y., Osborne, M., Lee, G.G., Park, J.C. (eds.) 50th Annual Meeting of the Association for Computational Linguistics 2012, Proceedings of the Conference, Jeju Island, Korea, vol. 2, pp. 238–242. Association for Computational Linguistics (2012)
25. Bocharov, V.V., Alexeeva, S.V., Granovsky, D.V., Protopopova, E.V., Stepanova, M.E., Surikov, A.V.: Crowdsourcing morphological annotation. In: Computational Linguistics and Intellectual Technologies. Papers from the Annual International Conference "Dialogue", vol. 12, no. 1, pp. 109–115. RGGU, Moskow (2013)

26. OpenCorpora, n.d. http://opencorpora.org/dict.php. Accessed 14 July 2022
27. Xu, Y., Kemp, C.: A computational evaluation of two laws of semantic change. In: Proceedings of the 37th Annual Meeting of the Cognitive Science Society, CogSci 2015, Pasadena, California, USA, 22–25 July 2015
28. Khristoforov, S., Bochkarev, V., Shevlyakova, A.: Recognition of parts of speech using the vector of bigram frequencies. In: van der Aalst, W.M.P., et al. (eds.) AIST 2019. CCIS, vol. 1086, pp. 132–142. Springer, Cham (2020). https://doi.org/10.1007/978-3-030-39575-9_13
29. Bullinaria, J.A., Levy, J.P.: Extracting semantic representations from word co-occurrence statistics: Stop-lists, stemming, and SVD. Behav. Res. Methods **44**(3), 890–907 (2012)
30. Joulin, A., Grave, E., Bojanowski, P., Mikolov, T.: Bag of tricks for efficient text classification. In: Proceedings of the 15th Conference of the European Chapter of the Association for Computational Linguistics, Valencia, Spain, vol. 2, Short Papers, pp. 427–431. Association for Computational Linguistics (2017)
31. Grave, E., Bojanowski, P., Gupta, P., Joulin, A., Mikolov, T.: Learning word vectors for 157 languages. In: Proceedings of the Eleventh International Conference on Language Resources and Evaluation (LREC 2018), European Language Resources Association (ELRA), Miyazaki, Japan (2018)
32. Dubey, S.R., Singh, S.K., Chaudhuri, B.B.: Activation functions in deep learning: a comprehensive survey and benchmark. Neurocomputing **503**, 92–108 (2022)
33. Srivastava, N., Hinton, G., Krizhevsky, A., Sutskever, I., Salakhutdinov, R.: Dropout: a simple way to prevent neural networks from overfitting. J. Mach. Learn. Res. **15**(1), 1929–1958 (2014)
34. Sun, S., Cao, Z., Zhu, H., Zhao, J.: A survey of optimization methods from a machine learning perspective. IEEE Trans. Cybern. **50**(8), 3668–3681 (2020)
35. Abadi, M., Agarwal, A., Barham, P., Brevdo, E., Chen, Z., et al.: TensorFlow: large-scale machine learning on heterogeneous systems (n.d.). https://www.tensorflow.org/. Accessed 28 July 2022
36. Chollet, F.: Keras (n.d.). https://keras.io. Accessed 28 July 2022
37. Antoniak, M., Mimno, D.: Evaluating the stability of embedding-based word similarities. Trans. Assoc. Comput. Linguist. **6**, 107–119 (2018)
38. Bochkarev, V.V., Maslennikova, Yu.S., Shevlyakova, A.V.: Testing of statistical significance of semantic changes detected by diachronic word embedding. J. Intell. Fuzzy Syst. 1–13 (2022). https://doi.org/10.3233/JIFS-212179
39. Poor, H., Hadjiliadis, O.: Quickest Detection. Cambridge University Press, Cambridge (2008)
40. Lavielle, M.: Using penalized contrasts for the change-point problem. Signal Process **85**(8), 1501–1510 (2005)
41. Killick, R., Fearnhead, P., Eckley, I.A.: Optimal detection of changepoints with a linear computational cost. J. Amer. Statist. Assoc. **107**(500), 1590–1598 (2012)
42. Bochkarev, V., Shevlyakova, A.: Calculation of a confidence interval of semantic distance estimates obtained using a large diachronic corpus. J. Phys. Conf. Ser. **1730**, 012031 (2021)

Sequential Models for Sentiment Analysis: A Comparative Study

Olaronke Oluwayemisi Adebanji, Irina Gelbukh, Hiram Calvo(✉), and Olumide Ebenezer Ojo

Instituto Politécnico Nacional, Natural Language and Text Processing Laboratory, Centro de Investigacion en Computación, CDMX, Mexico
i.gelbukh@nlp.cic.ipn.mx, hcalvo@cic.ipn.mx

Abstract. Sentiment analysis has been a focus of study in Natural Language Processing (NLP) tasks in recent years. In this paper, we propose the task of analysing sentiments using five sequential models and we compare their performance on a Twitter dataset. We used the bag of words, as well as the tf-idf, and the Word2Vec embeddings, as input features to the models. The precision, recall, f1 and accuracy scores of the proposed models were used to evaluate the models' performance. The Bi-LSTM model with Word2Vec embedding performs the best against the dataset, with an accuracy of 84%.

Keywords: Sentiment analysis · Sequence modeling · Word embedding · Machine learning algorithm · Deep learning algorithm

1 Introduction

Sentiment analysis is an open research area in the field of Natural Language Processing (NLP). The use of sequential modeling techniques in sentiment analysis research has increased considerably. Many language models have been developed to help in the automatic processing and understanding of text in order to properly interpret the sentiments in text. These language models receive a sequence of data as input, examines each element of the sequence, then output the data in a sequence. Textual data has a structure that is based on the order of individual characters or words, which can be decoded as a sequence. There have been several examples of complex sequences being represented using machine learning algorithms. Sequence-to-sequence problems are being solved using a number of machine learning techniques which involves learning task-specific, nonlinear, and more abstract feature representations from raw data and has shown to be an excellent achievement for human language understanding.

Twitter is a rapidly developing and influential social media network that allows users to send and receive short messages known as tweets. As an integral part of the online community, it is one of the most widely used social media platforms in the world. Tweets contain opinions on a wide range of topics in

O. Pichardo Lagunas et al. (Eds.): MICAI 2022, LNAI 13613, pp. 227–235, 2022.
https://doi.org/10.1007/978-3-031-19496-2_17

different fields of life. Text in tweets is one of the most popular forms of sequence data. Although seen as a string of letters or a string of words, sequence data can be passed into sequential models for sentiment analysis. Previous sentiment analysis research looked at the efficacy of several classifiers [1,5,13,16], including transformer models [8], on a variety of datasets.

In this study, we analyze the sentiments in tweets using well-known machine learning and neural network techniques. More importantly, we publish the results of our own experiments on the same dataset using multiple approaches, allowing for direct comparison. The investigation was conducted in the context of processing sequential data by employing sentiment 140 datasets [5] containing 1,600,000 tweets extracted from Twitter where there are 800,000 tweets annotated as negative and 800,000 positive tweets. Following our inquiry, we evaluated the well-known algorithms in order to show that the proposed sequential models are effective in predicting sentiments in text. The following are the other sections that make up the paper: Sect. 2 gives a quick overview of sentiment analysis research, and Sect. 3 discusses the technique for cleaning and processing the datasets, as well as the algorithms used in this experiment. Section 4 provides a detailed explanation and analysis of our findings, while Sect. 5 summarizes the conclusion and future plans.

2 Literature Review

Different traditional machine learning techniques [13,14,19], as well as neural network models [1,3,6,11,15,16] have been utilized in the past to learn how to predict the sentiments in text. In the task of analysing sentiments, the Naive Bayes Algorithm, Decision Tree Classifier, Logistic Regression, Support Vector Machines and other machine learning classifiers in [13,14,19] with varied parameters (n-gram size, corpus size, number of sentiment classes, balanced vs. unbalanced corpus, multiple domains) performed well. Different pre-processing methods were applied, with the use of multiple classifiers in the experiments resulting in a more efficient evaluation than any single classifier.

The effectiveness of deep neural network models of varied complexity was leveraged on in [1] to automatic detect aggression in social media posts. The trials were carried out using models ranging in complexity from CNN, LSTM, BiLSTM, CNN-LSTM, LSTM-CNN, CNN-BiLSTM, and BiLSTM-CNN to BiLSTM-CNN. The models were able to perform better in classes where there are more training examples, but not in other classes.

An experiment was conducted in [3] to detect the use of violent threat language in YouTube comments to individuals and groups. The investigation was conducted using two text representations: bag of words (BOW) and pretrained word embedding such as GloVe and fastText. Deep learning classifiers such as 1D-CNN, LSTM, and bidirectional LSTM (BiLSTM) were applied, and it was discovered that deep learning outperforms other methods.

S. Poria et al. [16] were successful in analyzing features from short texts using a deep Convolutional Neural Network (CNN) based on multiple kernel learning.

In this case, a faster variant of their technique was developed based on decision-level fusion, which includes assigning a weight to the classifier, and was able to improve the performance of the multimodal sentiment analysis framework. The authors in [11] employed a neural architecture based on recurrent neural networks to maintain the track of each individual party's status during a conversation and used that knowledge for emotion analysis. This scalable technique examines each incoming utterance in light of the speaker's attributes, thereby giving the utterance a richer context.

The interpretations in these studies were based on real dataset inputs that maximized each output with respect to an input sequence. These sentimental tweets are important in a range of fields, including health [2], economics [13, 14] and political campaign news [4]. We compared the performance of multiple machine learning and neural network models for sentiment analysis using well-known methods of processing sequential inputs.

3 Experimental Setup

We apply different machine learning and deep learning classifiers for the task of tweets classification into positive and negative classes. The accuracy of the various algorithms proposed were obtained and compared. We computed each model's performance scores and drew inferences from them.

Dataset. The proposed techniques were applied to the Sentiment140 dataset [5] to predict the positive and negative classes and evaluated using the precision, recall, f1 and accuracy scores. The Sentiment140 dataset was created using the sentiment140 corpus, which contains 1.6 million tweets stripped of emoticons, 50% of which are positive and 50% of which are negative. The data was cleaned by removing information that isn't relevant to the analysis and tokenized to turn raw data into usable data that can be digested by the models. The bag of words with the term frequency-inverse document frequency (tf-idf) method [17] was used to rescale the data. We also represented the document vocabulary using Word2Vec representations as an embedding, which aids the deep learning algorithm in automatically understanding word analogies. The pre-processed data is separated into two groups, with the training data accounting for 80% of the total dataset and the test data accounting for 20%. The statistics of the data is as shown in Table 1.

Table 1. Statistics of the dataset

Dataset	No. of tweets
Training data	1,280,000
Testing data	320,000

Models. In this section, we propose to explain the various sequential models used for sentiment analysis in this task. Word2Vec [12] is a model architecture for learning word embeddings from huge datasets. The bag of words (with tf-idf) and word embedding (with Word2Vec) features were extracted as input into the machine learning and deep learning algorithms used.

Some machine learning techniques that has performed well in some sentiment analysis tasks [7,9,10,13,20] were proposed, which includes the Naive Bayes Algorithm (NBA), Random Forest Classifier (RFC), Support Vector Machines (SVM), and Logistic Regression Model (LRM). The deep learning approach implemented is the bidirectional long-short term memory (Bi-LSTM) network [18] with the Word2Vec embedding used as input into it. These machine learning and deep learning models have been thoroughly evaluated for different sentiment analysis tasks and have shown consistently good results when working with a variety of dataset types. The Word2Vec-learned embeddings combined with the Bi-LSTM method outperformed the other learning algorithms in this natural language processing task of sentiment analysis.

4 Results and Discussion

In this paper, we present a comparison of multiple sequential models in a sequence labeling task applied on Twitter dataset. The logistic regression model (LRM), support vector machine (SVM), naive bayes algorithm (NBA), and random forest classifier (RFC) were the machine learning techniques applied to the dataset. The Bi-LSTM model with Word2Vec embedding was used to analyse the sentiments in the data for better and quicker decision making as a deep learning method, and we were able to compare the output of all the approaches proposed. The datasets were used as input into the algorithms in order to predict sentiments and classify them accordingly. Table 2 shows the features applied and the class of the dataset. The precision, recall, f1 and accuracy scores of the different models used were also presented. Among the models, the Bi-LSTM model with Word2Vec embedding performs the best with an accuracy of 84%. The accuracy score was our assessment metric since our dataset has an equal amount of positive and negative tweets. We also plotted the Confusion Matrix to see how our model performed against the dataset. Our analysis was able to show that the word embeddings was able to learn bigger dimensions quickly from enormous corpora of text (Figs. 1, 2, 3, 4 and 5).

Table 2. Precision, Recall, F1 and Accuracy Scores of the five proposed models.

Model	Features	Class	Precision	Recall	F1	Accuracy
LRM	Bag of Words+TFIDF	Negative	0.76	0.73	0.74	75%
		Positive	0.74	0.77	0.75%	
SVM	Bag of Words+TFIDF	Negative	0.74	0.75	0.74	74%
		Positive	0.75	0.73	0.74%	
NBA	Bag of Words+TFIDF	Negative	0.74	0.77	0.75	75%
		Positive	0.76	0.72	0.74%	
RFC	Bag of Words+TFIDF	Negative	0.74	0.62	0.68	70%
		Positive	0.67	0.78	0.72%	
Bi-LSTM	Word2Vec	Negative	**0.84**	**0.86**	**0.85**	84%
		Positive	**0.85**	**0.83**	**0.84%**	

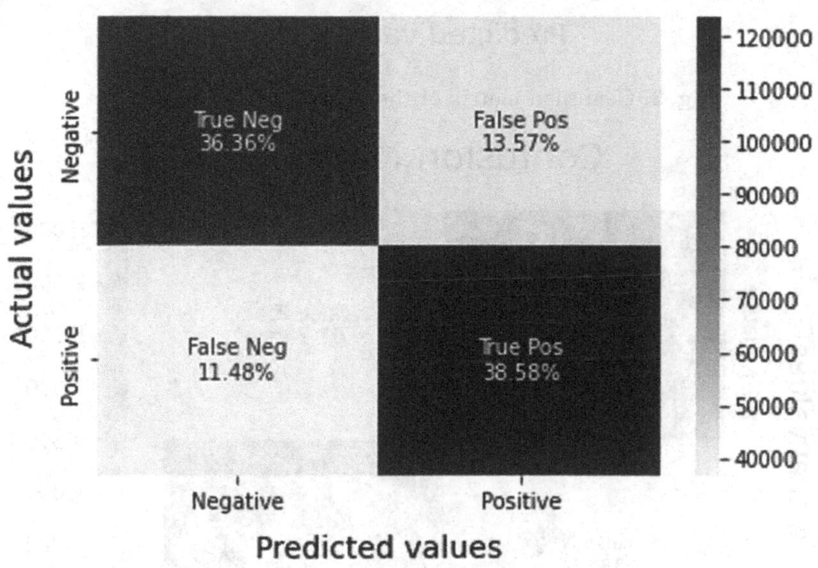

Fig. 1. Confusion matrix of the logistic regression model

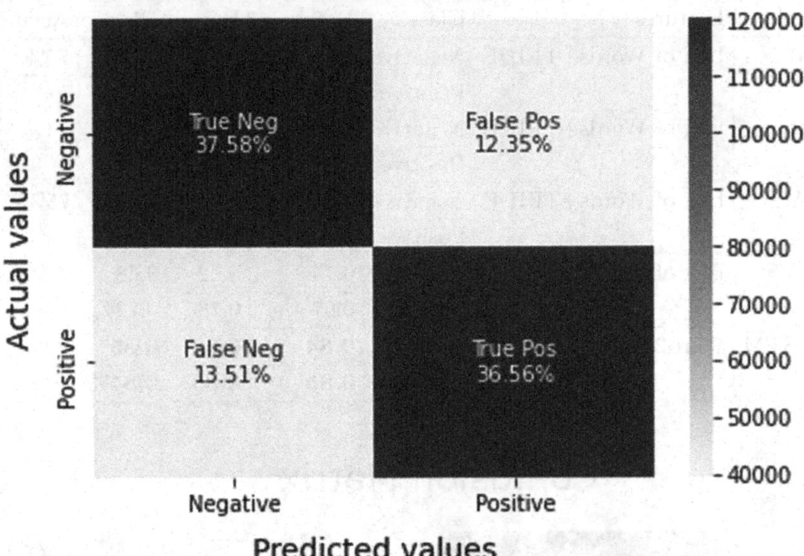

Fig. 2. Confusion matrix of the support vector machine

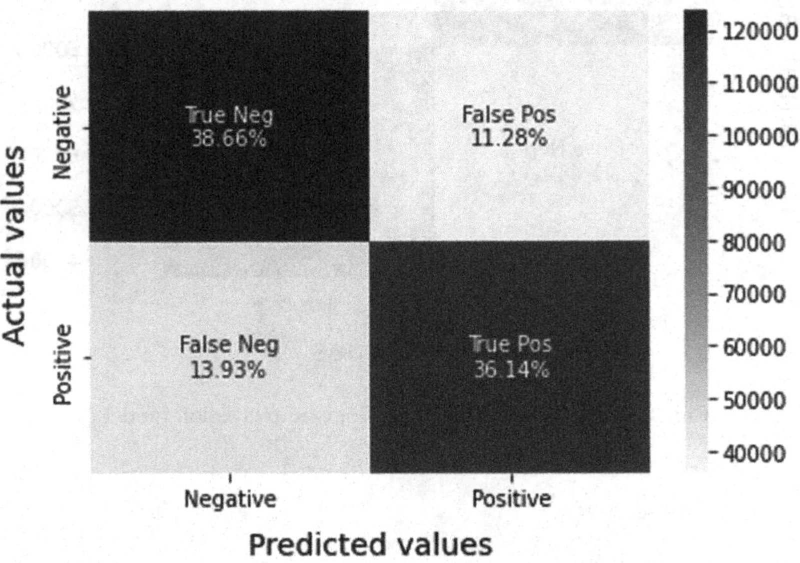

Fig. 3. Confusion matrix of the Naive Bayes algorithm

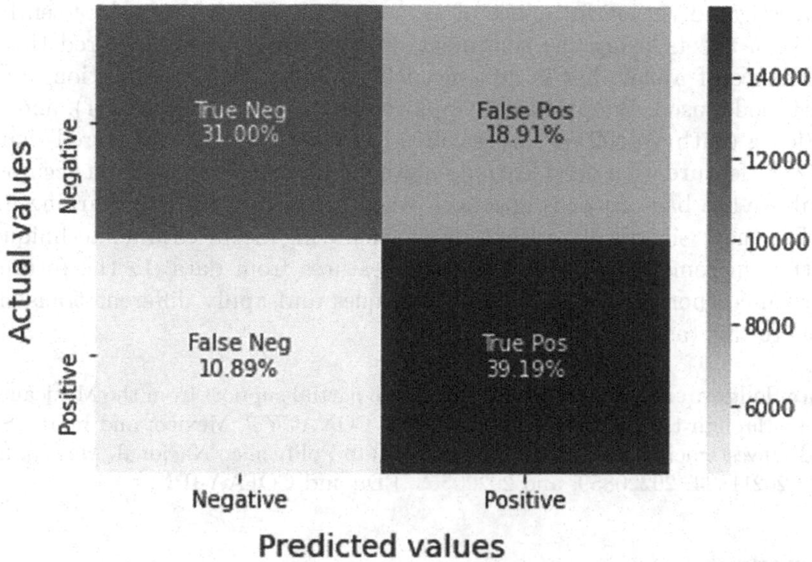

Fig. 4. Confusion matrix of the random forest classifier

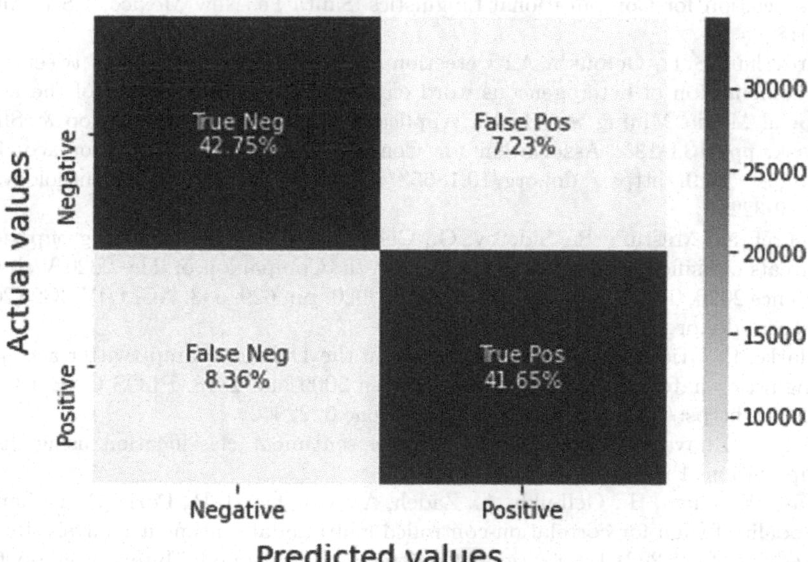

Fig. 5. Confusion matrix of the Bi-LSTM model

5 Conclusion

We investigated the performance of sequential models in the task of sentiment analysis of tweets using the sentiment140 dataset. It was discovered that the performance of a classifier is influenced by the feature representation and the type of model used. We primarily employed bag-of-word (with tf-idf), and word embedding (with Word2Vec) as features in this study, and discovered that the Word2Vec feature with deep learning method had an average gain in accuracy of 10% above the bag-of-words approach with traditional machine learning methods. The most significant advantage of employing deep learning techniques is that they incrementally learn high-level features from data. In the future, we plan to use other word embedding techniques and apply different transformer models to this task.

Acknowledgement. The work was done with partial support from the Mexican Government through the grant A1-S-47854 of the CONACYT, Mexico, and by the Secretaría de Investigación y Posgrado of the Instituto Politécnico Nacional, Mexico, under Grants 20211884, 20220859, and 20220553, EDI; and COFAA-IPN.

References

1. Aroyehun, S.T., Gelbukh, A.: Aggression detection in social media: using deep neural networks, data augmentation, and pseudo labeling. In: Proceedings of the First Workshop on Trolling, Aggression and Cyberbullying (TRAC-2018), pp. 90–97. Association for Computational Linguistics, Santa Fe, New Mexico, USA, August 2018
2. Aroyehun, S.T., Gelbukh, A.: Detection of adverse drug reaction in tweets using a combination of heterogeneous word embeddings. In: Proceedings of the Fourth Social Media Mining for Health Applications (#SMM4H) Workshop & Shared Task, pp. 133–135. Association for Computational Linguistics, Florence, Italy, August 2019. https://doi.org/10.18653/v1/W19-3224, https://aclanthology.org/W19-3224
3. Ashraf, N., Mustafa, R., Sidorov, G., Gelbukh, A.F.: Individual vs. group violent threats classification in online discussions. In: Companion of The 2020 Web Conference 2020, Taipei, Taiwan, 20–24 April 2020, pp. 629–633. ACM/IW3C2 (2020). https://doi.org/10.1145/3366424.3385778
4. Clarke, I., Grieve, J.: Stylistic variation on the Donald Trump twitter account: a linguistic analysis of tweets posted between 2009 and 2018. PLOS ONE **14**, 1–27 (2019). https://doi.org/10.1371/journal.pone.0222062
5. Go, A., Bhayani, R., Huang, L.: Twitter sentiment classification using distant supervision. Processing 1–6 (2009)
6. Han, W., Chen, H., Gelbukh, A., Zadeh, A., Morency, L.P., Poria, S.: Bi-bimodal modality fusion for correlation-controlled multimodal sentiment analysis. In: Proceedings of the 2021 International Conference on Multimodal Interaction, pp. 6–15. ICMI 2021. Association for Computing Machinery, New York, NY, USA (2021)
7. Hernández-Castañeda, A., Calvo, H., Gelbukh, A., Flores, J.J.: Cross-domain deception detection using support vector networks. Soft Comput. **21**(3), 585–595 (2017). https://doi.org/10.1007/s00500-016-2409-2

8. Hoang, T.T., Ojo, O.E., Adebanji, O.O., Calvo, H., Gelbukh, A.: The combination of BERT and data oversampling for answer type prediction. In: CEUR Workshop Proceedings, vol. 3119. CEUR-WS (2022)
9. Kolesnikova, O., Gelbukh, A.: Supervised machine learning for predicting the meaning of verb-noun combinations in Spanish. In: MICAI (2010)
10. Kolesnikova, O., Gelbukh, A.: A study of lexical function detection with word2vec and supervised machine learning. J. Intell. Fuzzy Syst. **39** (2020)
11. Majumder, N., Poria, S., Hazarika, D., Mihalcea, R., Gelbukh, A., Cambria, E.: DialogueRNN: an attentive RNN for emotion detection in conversations. In: Proceedings of the AAAI Conference on Artificial Intelligence, vol. 33(01), pp. 6818–6825 (2019). https://doi.org/10.1609/aaai.v33i01.33016818
12. Mikolov, T., Chen, K., Corrado, G., Dean, J.: Efficient estimation of word representations in vector space. CoRR abs/1301.3781 (2013). http://dblp.uni-trier.de/db/journals/corr/corr1301.html#abs-1301-3781
13. Ojo, O.E., Gelbukh, A., Calvo, H., Adebanji, O.O.: Performance study of n-grams in the analysis of sentiments. J. Nigerian Soc. Phys. Sci. **3**(4), 477–483 (2021). https://doi.org/10.46481/jnsps.2021.201
14. Ojo, O.E., Gelbukh, A., Calvo, H., Adebanji, O.O., Sidorov, G.: Sentiment detection in economics texts. In: Advances in Computational Intelligence: 19th Mexican International Conference on Artificial Intelligence, MICAI 2020, Mexico City, Mexico, 12–17 October 2020, Proceedings, Part II, pp. 271–281. Springer-Verlag, Berlin, Heidelberg (2020). https://doi.org/10.1007/978-3-030-60887-3_24
15. Ojo, O.E., Hoang, T.T., Gelbukh, A., Calvo, H., Sidorov, G., Adebanji, O.O.: Automatic hate speech detection using CNN model and word embedding. Computación y Sistemas **26**(2) (2022)
16. Poria, S., Cambria, E., Gelbukh, A.: Deep convolutional neural network textual features and multiple kernel learning for utterance-level multimodal sentiment analysis. In: EMNLP (2015)
17. Salton, G., Buckley, C.: Term-weighting approaches in automatic text retrieval. Inf. Process. Manage. **24**(5), 513–523 (1988)
18. Schuster, M., Paliwal, K.: Bidirectional recurrent neural networks. IEEE Trans. Signal Process. **45**(11), 2673–2681 (1997). https://doi.org/10.1109/78.650093
19. Sidorov, G., et al.: Empirical study of machine learning based approach for opinion mining in tweets. In: Batyrshin, I., González Mendoza, M. (eds.) MICAI 2012. LNCS (LNAI), vol. 7629, pp. 1–14. Springer, Heidelberg (2013). https://doi.org/10.1007/978-3-642-37807-2_1
20. Sidorov, G., Velasquez, F., Stamatatos, E., Gelbukh, A., Chanona-Hernández, L.: Syntactic N-grams as machine learning features for natural language processing. Expert Syst. Appl. 41(3), 853–860 (2014). https://doi.org/10.1016/j.eswa.2013.08.015

Intelligent Applications and Robotics

Analysis of Procedural Generated Textures for Video Games Using a CycleGAN

Julia Alejandra Rodriguez-Abud(✉) and Andres Mendez-Vazquez(✉)

Department of Computer Science, CINVESTAV Guadalajara, Jalisco, Mexico
{julia.rodriguez,andres.mendez}@cinvestav.mx

Abstract. The creation of content for video games is a costly and time consuming task if done manually. Especially in modern times, the amount of content required to create a video game is expected to be much greater than in the past. Procedural Content Generation techniques can be used to alleviate this issue and allow the creation of more content with less input. The proposal in this work is to explore the use of Generative Adversarial Networks for video game textures to be developed by a computer, more specifically style-transfer with a CycleGAN. The generation experiments in this work use a variety of textures commonly used in video games such as sky-boxes and tiled images. In addition, the analysis performed has a usability perspective and an emotional one. The usability analysis detects any problems in the implementation. The affective/emotional analysis measures the players' evoked feelings and then cross-references the traditionally-generated and the computer-generated emotional result vectors $c = (V, A)$ (composed of valence and arousal). The results obtained show an emotional transfer between the vectors to be at minimum 26.53% and at best 91.23%. These results demonstrate that the performed experiments always had a successful emotional transfer.

Keywords: PCG · Procedural · Video games · Textures · Adversarial learning · GAN · CycleGAN

1 Introduction

Manually creating content for video games is an expensive and time-consuming task that can be optimized. Procedural Content Generation (PCG) [1] is an established method to create video game assets and content via algorithmic systems. It is an important part of the video game industry, as it allows for improvement and optimization in production pipelines [2]. PCG allows the art team to focus on other parts of the creative process by having the computer create some of the assets. It can be pursued by many methods such as heuristic algorithms [3], evolutionary algorithms [4], machine learning [5], deep learning [6], amongst others.

Many Machine Learning techniques require previously accumulated data to use as inputs and to be able to learn based on this information. When a game is

O. Pichardo Lagunas et al. (Eds.): MICAI 2022, LNAI 13613, pp. 239–251, 2022.
https://doi.org/10.1007/978-3-031-19496-2_18

in its beginning stages there may not be a lot of content to learn from because it has not been made yet. However, one of the prime reasons to pursue the training of a content generator is in fact to not have to produce all of the content [6].

This industry is an important part of the global economy and is one of the current spear-points for technological advancement. Video games have been made professionally since the 1970's and since then, their development costs have been mostly on the rise. Being roughly a tenfold rise in cost every ten years, even considering the inflation-adjustment [7]. One of the main reasons this increment has occurred, is the amount and caliber of the required video game content (assets including 3D, 2D, sound, code, story-script, gameplay etc.).

As studios hit practical caps on how much content can be generated and delivered, Procedural Content Generation (PCG) plays an important role when developers are producing a large amount of content. By implementing these algorithmic processes, the pipeline takes some of the weight off the manual work required by the development team.

In the realm of possible algorithmic solutions, there have been multiple proposals for how to approach PCG [1], including randomness, heuristics, evolutionary algorithms, machine learning and deep learning. Deep Learning [6] has brought new opportunities and advances, such as autoencoders (VAEs) [8], long short-term memory (LSM) [9] and generative adversarial networks (GANs) [10].

In this research the deep learning route is explored, as it is one of the newest proposals used to approach PCG. For this purpose, Cycle Generative Adversarial Networks (CycleGAN) were implemented to generate video game textures that were analyzed to identify usability problems and measured within an emotional perspective. This focus was chosen because although, there have been CycleGAN implementations in video game contexts [11] the analysis usually focuses on efficiency and quality. The specific objectives are the following three:

- Measure the emotional components (valence and arousal [12]) of the textures provided to and from the CycleGAN and compare them to find a direct correlation.
- Detect any usability problems with the generated content when implementing it in a game.
- Define the permutation in the video game pipeline process, so we are able to implement the GAN. Where in the production process will it be implemented? and if human intervention is required to the generated content?

The paper is organized as follows. In Sect. 2, related work is reviewed, explaining the concepts of Procedural Content Generation, GANs and more specifically the CycleGAN. In Sect. 3, the proposed methodology and the hypothesis are described. Section 4 shows the experiment which includes descriptions of the pre-trained model, the generation of content, the collection of emotional data and the data analysis. Finally, in Sect. 5 conclusions are given.

2 Related Work

2.1 Procedural Content Generation

Procedural Content Generation, PCG, is an established method for generating game assets through algorithmic systems. For procedural content generation, there have been multiple techniques [1] and methods [13] implemented over the years such as the use of fractals [14], noise [13], heuristics [3], artificial intelligence [15], machine learning [5], deep learning [6] and hybrid methods [16]. The first two are older methods, but with wider use. The rest fall under the artificial intelligence umbrella in terms of its multiple uses and approaches. [4] These approaches can be categorized into optimization, imitation, and innovation. This work focuses on the imitation approach for the transfer of style and emotion.

- **Optimization** refers to the tuning of values of the game for it to be the best it can be in whichever aspect.
- **Imitation** refers to the replication of what can and would be done by a human user.
- **Innovation** refers to the generation of interesting and complex elements, leaving behind the optimization aspect when generating content.

2.2 Generative Adversarial Networks

A Generative Adversarial Network (GAN), [10] is defined as a framework with an adversarial process between two models. The basics of a GAN consist of a Discriminator model that has the job of classifying real vs fake data, and a Generator model that is attempting and learning to create better counterfeits that the discriminator will classify as real. This process, applied multiple times, will result in both models improving in their respective jobs, with the Generator eventually becoming good enough to generate content that can pass as the original data.

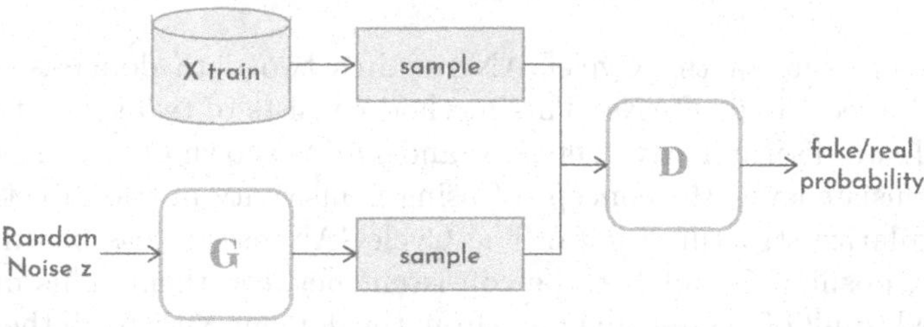

Fig. 1. Basic architecture of a GAN.

The architecture of these neural networks is shown in the Fig. 1, where the Generator output G(z) and a sample from the database X are fed into the Discriminator. The Discriminator wants to maximize the probability of assigning the correct label to the samples. The Generator wants to do the opposite, as it aims to minimize these probabilities. G generates samples by passing random noise through a multilayer perceptron. This MinMax game between these two models can be described with Eq. 1.

$$\underset{G}{\min}\underset{D}{\max} V(D,G) = \mathbb{E}_{x \sim p_{data}(x)}\left[\log D(x)\right] + \mathbb{E}_{z \sim p_z(z)}\left[\log(1 - D(G(z)))\right]. \tag{1}$$

$$\mathbb{E}_{x \sim p_x}\left[f(x)\right] = \int f(x)p(x)dx. \tag{2}$$

2.3 CycleGAN

The CycleGAN [17] model is used specifically for style transfer between two unpaired databases. This image-to-image translation has the goal of learning the mapping $G : X \rightarrow Y$ where the distribution of the images generated by $G(X)$ is indistinguishable from the distribution Y by using an adversarial loss, and vice versa within the $F(Y)$ and X distributions.

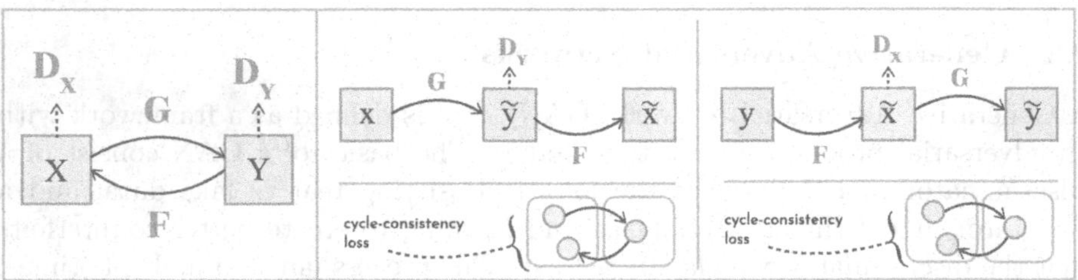

Fig. 2. Left) CycleGAN architecture consisting of two adversarial structures working together. **Center)** forward cycle-consistency loss $x \rightarrow G(x) \rightarrow F(G(x)) \approx \tilde{x}$ **Right)** backward cycle-consistency loss $y \rightarrow F(y) \rightarrow G(F(y)) \approx \tilde{y}$.

The architecture of the CycleGAN requires two data domains X and Y, which will be fed to our GANs. This method consists of two generative nets G and F, and two discriminative nets D_X and D_Y as shown on Fig. 2.

Cycle-consistency is the concept of using transitivity in two directions to be able to regularize structured data. The CycleGAN uses a loss based on cycle-consistency, pushing G and F to be consistent between them. This means that the expected result of passing an image from the domain X through the generator G, and then through the generator F, should be as close as possible to the original input. The comparison between the input and output of this process is what is needed to calculate the cycle-consistent loss, which will prevent the generators from contradicting each other. This type of GAN has proven to be a method with good results for style transfer between two unpaired sets of images as long as there are enough images to put in the given sets.

3 Proposed Approach

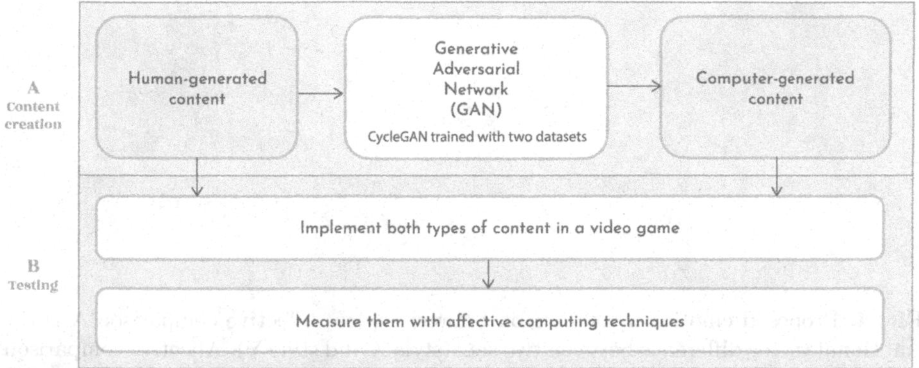

Fig. 3. Proposed methodology. The first part consists of obtaining two types of content by using a GAN. The second part implements those contents in a way that allows for their comparison and analysis.

The proposed approach of analyzing the usability and affectivity of the CycleGAN can be described by Fig. 3. The first stages focus on training our GANs and transferring the style into the video game content. The final stages consist of implementing and testing the content.

To start, one of the most important steps for this research is the training of a CycleGAN. This trained model can then be used whenever needed during the game production process. For this, two unpaired data-sets need to be selected/created with the original and the new style. Following this, the CycleGAN can be trained with both this data-sets. Next, the game textures need to be style transferred. The textures being a selection of Skyboxes and ground tiles. Therefore, the original textures of the video game scene will be collected, the required properties for each image are defined (such as the final resolution) and then passed through the pretrained CycleGAN. By the end of this stage there is a collection of video game textures in the original and the new style.

After the textures are generated, both types of content are implemented in a video game. A playable Minimum Viable Product [18] was designed. The needed minimum characteristics were defined to be implemented in the video game, enough to make it playable and give the capacity of detecting any usability problems. While not being a final product, it was designed to have sufficient elements to visualize a full production process. This minimum viable product was a simple racing game and was created in Unity3D. The last step for the implementation, makes sure that there are scenes with computer and traditionally generated content. It is imperative that the data provided can be implemented into a usable level. Thereupon some final tweaks can be made but are considered as permutations in the production process.

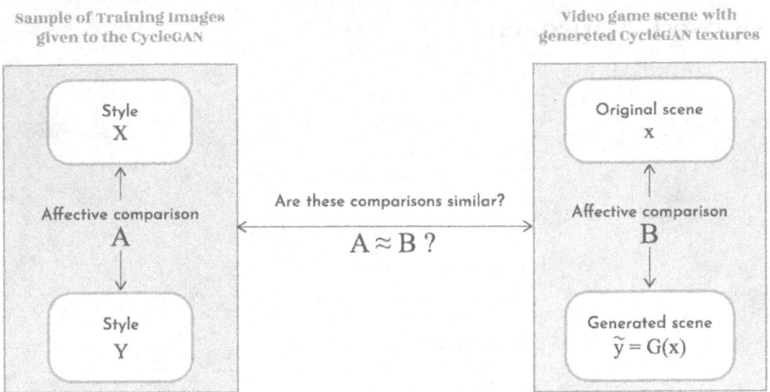

Fig. 4. Proposed emotional comparison between styles. Affective comparison A is the emotional vector difference between two sets (style X and style Y). Affective comparison B is the emotional vector difference between the "original scene" (textures in style X) and the "generated scene" (transfer of the textures into style Y).

The last analysis to make is the affective/emotional results of our content. A self-assessment [19] survey was implemented to collect the evoked feelings of the users. This was done through the selection of two basic emotional components, valence and arousal. The image groups required to find the correlation in Fig. 4 were: Original style training images, new style training images, original style video game scene and new style video game scene.

Then, collected data was analyzed to find this correlation. The relation of the valence and the arousal between the two styles in the CycleGAN style transfer training should have been maintained between the input and the output of said trained model. In other words, the emotional response of the user to our generated content should be similar to the emotional response to the training images in the desired style.

4 Experimental Results

4.1 CycleGAN Training Details

For this exercise we used four pretrained models from the PyTorch implementation of CycleGAN[1]. The training classes and their sizes that were used in those pretrained models can be seen in Fig. 5.

With these pretrained models new content was generated. This was done by feeding them with a set of game textures. Several equirectangular sky images were selected from the "ALLSKY"[2]. We chose 12 images to test the CycleGAN,

[1] https://github.com/junyanz/pytorch-CycleGAN-and-pix2pix.
[2] "AllSky - 220+ Sky/Skybox Set" catalogue at https://assetstore.unity.com.

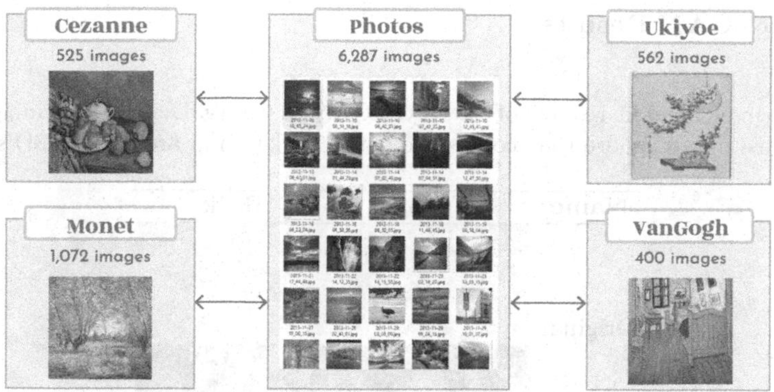

Fig. 5. Trainings performed between datasets for the CycleGAN. **1)** Cezanne ⇔ Photos. **2)** Monet ⇔ Photos. **3)** Ukiyoe ⇔ Photos. **4)** VanGogh ⇔ Photos.

the selection of which was determined by considering aspects such as hue, brightness, level of detail and amount of clouds. Some of the selected images can be seen in the first column of the Table 1.

Table 1. Results of using some of the selected equirectangle skybox images as input with the pretrained CycleGAN models. The first column shows the selected sky images, and the following columns show the results of passing them through each of the four pretrained style models: Cezanne, Monet, Ukiyoe and VanGogh.

Original	Cezanne	Monet	Ukiyoe	VanGogh

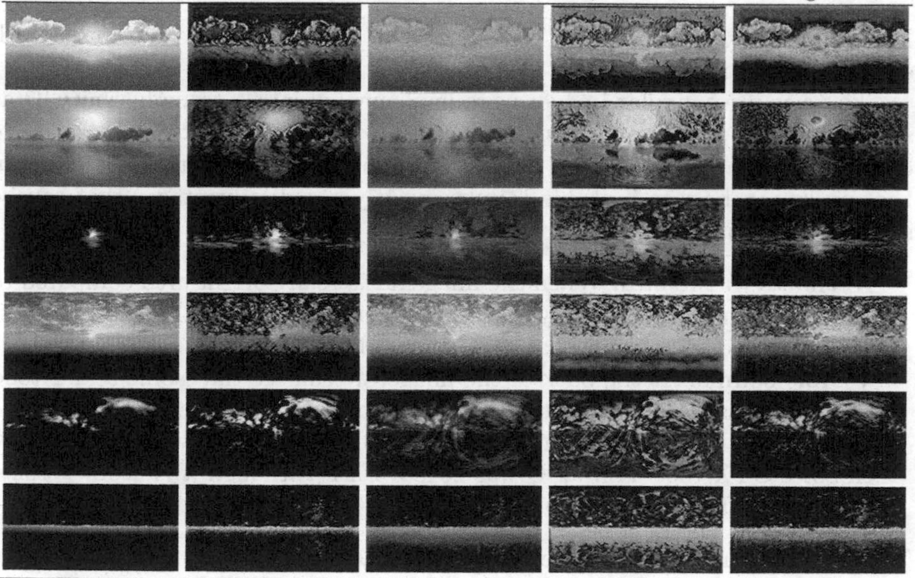

4.2 CycleGAN Results

Table 2. Implemented results of the CycleGAN in Unity3D. The sky images were implemented into a sphere that covers the entire background area of the 3D scene.

Name	Front	Back
Original		
Cezanne		
Monet		
Ukiyoe		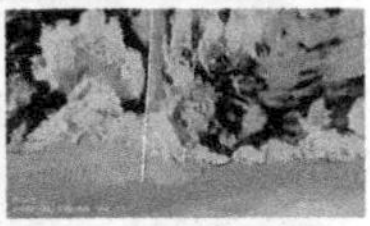
Vangogh	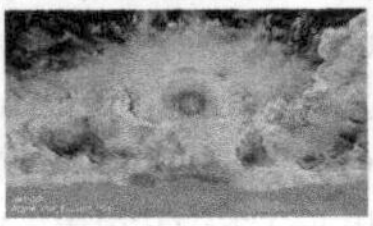	

The results shown in the Table 1 are images of 2048×1024 and were used with each of the pretrained models.

These equirectangular images were implemented into a scene in Unity3D as skyboxes [20]. Additionally, a small algorithm was used to extract the average color of our image and apply it as fog to produce a more natural look. Some of the results can be seen in Table 2. Subsequently, the disadvantages that can be seen in the testing of this experiment are:

- **Artifacts in the sun.** When the image has a really bright area compared to the rest of the image, the CycleGAN tends to produce results with artifacts around it and to not give that area enough brightness.
- **Visible seams.** At the back of the image, we can see that some seams tend to be very visible, breaking the illusion of continuity in the sky.
- **Image size.** The maximum size we were able to achieve with an NVIDIA GeForce GTX 1660 Ti Max-Q was 2048×1024. Although it is usable, a skybox double this size would be preferable.

The artifacts and the seams are problems that, although we would rather them not show up, are easily fixable by an artist in the development team. This fix would still be faster than creating/stylizing the images from zero. This makes style transfer with CycleGANs a feasible option for this type of texture in a video game production.

4.3 Emotional Data Collection

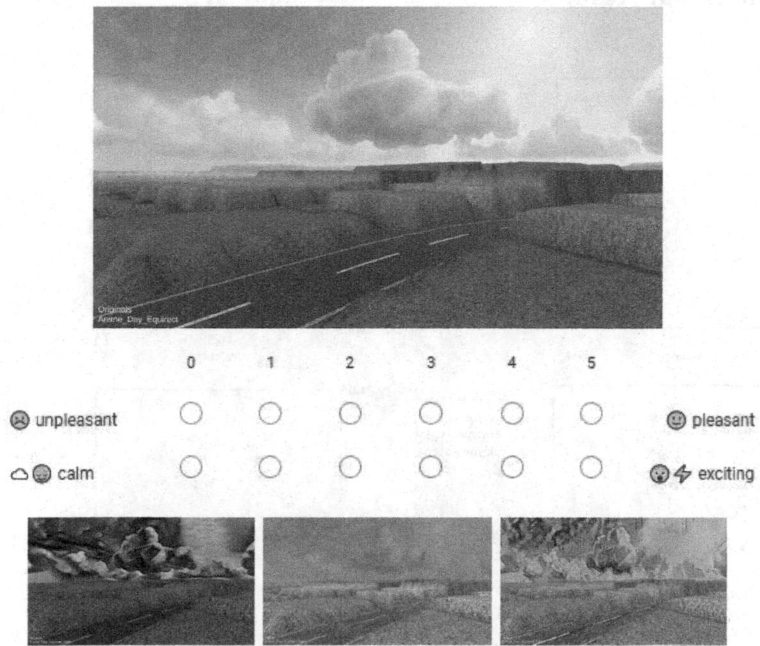

Fig. 6. Example of the survey question made to collect the emotional components data and some of the images shown during the survey. (From a total of 30 images to assess)

Another objective of this research is to carry out an affective/emotional analysis by cross-referencing human-generated content and computer-generated content. In the proposal section and in Fig. 4 we have mentioned that our hypothesis is that 'the relation of the valence and the arousal between the two styles should be maintained between the input and the output of said trained model'. Valence is the pleasantness level generated by an event. It ranges from positive to negative. Arousal or intensity, is the level of autonomic activation that an event creates. It can range from calm to excited.

This correlation is done 4 times between the styles in the pre-trained models: Original ⇔ Cezanne; Original ⇔ Monet; Original ⇔ Ukiyoe; Original ⇔ VanGogh. A total of 30 images were selected for the survey in which we have a sample of images used in the CycleGAN training and a group of images from the video game scene with textures before and after passing through the style transfer process. The question made to collect the emotional components data for each one of these images can be seen in Fig. 6.

The collected data was in the form of scalar values for the valence and the arousal components. These two selected components can be mapped in a plane and be described as vectors. This survey was answered by a total of 50 people in the age range of 22 to 55 years old, 66% males and 34% females.

4.4 Emotional Results

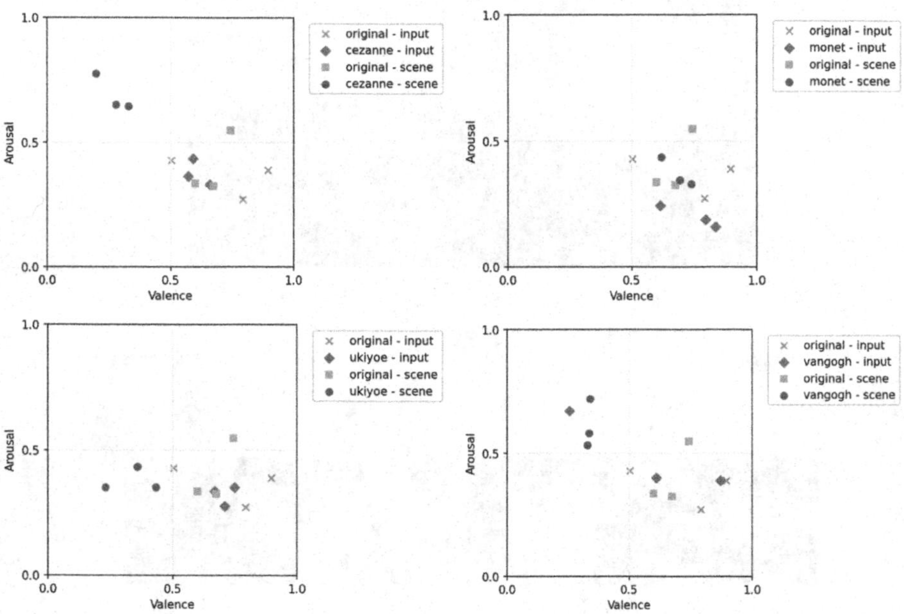

Fig. 7. Scatter plots showing the average emotional results of each image used in the survey. Each point represents the emotional vector (valence, arousal) of an image. The color/shape of these points represents the type-style.

The collected data was parsed into a data table where each image in the survey has the components of valence and arousal, as shown in Fig. 7. The value for each of the components is the arithmetic mean result of the answers given by the 50 users. To be able to visualize the final correlations, the images with the same type and style were collapsed.

The comparisons use the emotional vectors $e = (V, A)$, that have as components valence and arousal, which are shown in Table 3. This way, the comparison will be between $e_{input} = e_{inputStyle} - e_{inputOriginal}$ and $e_{scene} = e_{sceneStyle} - e_{sceneOriginal}$, where e_{input} represents the emotional change between the samples used to train the CycleGAN and e_{scene} represents the emotional change to the video game scene between the scene with original textures (prior to using the CycleGAN) and the one with generated textures.

Table 3. CycleGAN emotional results. Average results type-style.

Type	Style	Valence	Arousal
Input	Cezanne	0.608000	0.377333
Input	Monet	0.749333	0.197333
Input	Original	0.730667	0.362667
Input	Ukiyoe	0.708000	0.321333
Input	Vangogh	0.580000	0.486667
Scene	Cezanne	0.269333	0.690667
Scene	Monet	0.684000	0.369333
Scene	Original	0.673333	0.402667
Scene	Ukiyoe	0.341333	0.378667
Scene	Vangogh	0.334667	0.610667

All the calculated emotional vectors for each comparison between two styles can be seen in Table 4. There is an obvious correlation in each comparison. Although the valence and the arousal are not in the same magnitudes in the e_{input} as in the e_{scene}, they always change in the same direction. This means that if the input images have an increase in the valence, there will also be an increase in the valence of the video game scene. This would also be the case for the arousal component.

Table 4. CycleGAN emotional vector results compared side-to-side.

Style comparison	Type	e = (V,A)
Cezanne vs original	e_{input}	(−0.122667, 0.014666)
	e_{scene}	(−0.404000, 0.288000)
Monet vs original	e_{input}	(0.018666, −0.165334)
	e_{scene}	(0.010667, −0.033334)
Ukiyoe vs original	e_{input}	(−0.022667, −0.041334)
	e_{scene}	(−0.332000, −0.024000)
Vangogh vs original	e_{input}	(−0.150667, 0.124000)
	e_{scene}	(−0.338666, 0.208000)

With all these vectors set in place it can be defined that if the angle between any pair of vectors is 180°, it is going in the opposite direction and is considered to be doing the opposite of transferring the emotion. For the hypothesis to be valid the angle between the vectors would need to be between 0° (a 100% emotional transfer) and 90°(a 0% emotional transfer). The results of this Emotional Transfer percentage can be seen in Table 5.

Table 5. Emotional transfer percentage results.

Style comparison	Angle between e_{input} and e_{scene}	Emotional transfer percentage
Cezanne vs original	28.666°	68.15%
Monet vs original	11.303°	87.44%
Ukiyoe vs original	57.125°	36.53%
Vangogh vs original	7.897°	91.23%

5 Conclusions

In this paper, the study conducted had the objective of detecting the usability and emotional capabilities of doing style transfer with a CycleGAN.

The usability problems detected were mostly the seams, which can be corrected by the art team without much problem (but still with human intervention). Also, the large scale images used in this process require a powerful computer to process. A lower end gaming PC was used for this particular experiment only allowing for a maximum size of 2048 × 1024.

The emotional results were as expected for style transfer. The emotional components were swayed in the same direction by the training images and the generated ones. In our must successful experiment being the VanGogh style we got an emotional transfer of 91.23%. This makes using a CycleGAN a feasible option in an affective media such as video games, as it will behave emotionally as expected when implementing it doing this process.

The original contribution of this paper is the proposal and use of a self-assessment model to collect the emotional components of the input and output of a style transfer process. Furthermore, it provides a method of comparing this recollected data to fulfill the emotional transfer hypothesis.

In future work, the affective/emotional comparisons with other style transfer Neural Networks could be explored further to look into whether the emotional transfer accompanies other style transfer procedures.

Acknowledgments. This work was carried out with the support of CONACYT and the Centro de Investigacion y de Estudios Avanzados del Instituto Politecnico Nacional.

References

1. Stangl, R.: Procedural content generation: techniques and applications. In: ACM Proceedings (2017)
2. Chandler, H.M.: The Game Production Toolbox. Taylor and Francis, Milton Park (2020)
3. Silver, E.A., Victor, R., Vidal, V., de Werra, D.: A tutorial on heuristic methods. Eur. J. Oper. Res. **5**(3), 153–162 (1980)

4. Togelius, J., De Nardi, R., Lucas, S.M.: Towards automatic personalised content creation for racing games. In: Proceedings of the 2007 IEEE Symposium on Computational Intelligence and Games, CIG 2007, pp. 252–259 (2007)
5. Khalifa, A., Bontrager, P., Earle, S., Togelius, J.: PCGRL: procedural content generation via reinforcement learning. In: Proceedings of the 16th AAAI Conference on Artificial Intelligence and Interactive Digital Entertainment, AIIDE 2020, pp. 95–101 (2020)
6. Liu, J., Snodgrass, S., Khalifa, A., Risi, S., Yannakakis, G.N., Togelius, J.: Deep learning for procedural content generation. Neural Comput. Appl. **33**(1), 19–37 (2021)
7. Koster, R.: The cost of games, January 2018
8. Kingma, D.P., Welling, M.: Auto-encoding variational Bayes. In: 2nd International Conference on Learning Representations, ICLR 2014 - Conference Track Proceedings, pp. 1–14 (2014)
9. Hochreiter, S., Schmidhuber, J.: Long short-term memory. Neural Comput. **9**(8), 1735–1780 (1997)
10. Goodfellow, I.J., et al.: Generative adversarial networks. Commun. ACM **63**(11), 139–144 (2014)
11. Guo, X., et al.: Gan-based virtual-to-real image translation for urban scene semantic segmentation. Neurocomputing **394**, 127–135 (2020)
12. Kensinger, E.A., Schacter, D.L.: Processing emotional pictures and words: effects of valence and arousal. Cogn. Affect. Behav. Neurosci. **6**(2), 110–126 (2006)
13. Korn,O., Lee, N.: Game dynamics: best practices in procedural and dynamic game content generation. Game Dynamics: Best Practices in Procedural and Dynamic Game Content Generation, pp. 1–177 (2017). https://doi.org/10.1007/978-3-319-53088-8
14. Breting-García: Fractal geometry. Salem Press Encyclopedia of Science (2020)
15. Seidel, S., Berente, N., Lindberg, A., Lyytinen, K., Martinez, B., Nickerson, J.V.: Artificial intelligence and video game creation: a framework for the new logic of autonomous design. J. Digital Soc. Res. **2**(3), 126–157 (2020)
16. Togelius, J., Justinussen, T., Hartzen, A.: Compositional procedural content generation. In: Proceedings of the Third Workshop on Procedural Content Generation in Games, PCG 2012, pp. 1–4, New York, NY, USA. Association for Computing Machinery (2012)
17. Zhu, J.Y., Park, T., Isola, P., Efros, A.A.: Unpaired image-to-image translation using cycle-consistent adversarial networks. In: Proceedings of the IEEE International Conference on Computer Vision, pp. 2242–2251, October 2017
18. Lenarduzzi, V., Taibi, D.: MVP explained: a systematic mapping study on the definitions of minimal viable product. In: 2016 42th Euromicro Conference on Software Engineering and Advanced Applications (SEAA), pp. 112–119 (2016)
19. Bradley, M.M., Lang, P.J.: Measuring emotion: the self-assessment manikin and the semantic differential. J. Behav. Therapy Exp. Psychiatr. **25**(1), 49–59 (1994)
20. Prescott, S.: Games: breaking the game: the beauty of a gameworld's outer limits. The Lifted Brow, p. 30 (2014)

Vibration Analysis of an Industrial Motor with Autoencoder for Predictive Maintenance

Cristian Nuñez(✉), Roberto Moreno, Victor Benitez, and Jesus Pacheco

Universidad de Sonora, 83000 Hermosillo Son, Mexico
crisng100@gmail.com

Abstract. This paper describes the implementation of a vibration analysis in an industrial servo motor for anomaly detection. For this, a test bench was built with the purpose of simulating an industrial process. The vibration analysis was performed with an accelerometer which took the acceleration data from a running engine. For the detection of anomalies, an Autoencoder was used which was trained with samples of the normal operation of the motor in order to reconstruct a "normal operation" signal. Once the model was trained, the MAE (Mean Absolute Error) is used to see the differences between the analyzed signal and the one reconstructed by the Autoencoder, if the difference is greater than a threshold, the signal is classified as an anomaly. The proposed methodology represents an alternative to perform vibration analysis in rotative machines and can be used to conduct predictive maintenance in several industrial processes.

Keywords: Predictive maintenance · Artificial intelligence · Machine learning · Neural networks · Industry 4.0 · Anomaly detection · Autoenconder

1 Introduction

1.1 A Subsection Sample

The industry has evolved over time, this evolution can be easily seen thanks to the so-called "industrial revolutions". These revolutions have brought with them multiple technological advances that have allowed manufacturing to be increasingly efficient. But this has made the processes more complex, thus increasing the cost of maintenance on many occasions. These costs can represent 40% to 70% of the total production budget [1].

Industry 4.0 has allowed to know the status of all the variables in a process in real time, this allows to a better analysis of its operation and even predicts if a fault is going to occur at a certain time in the future. To analyze these variables, artificial intelligence can be used to create models that can identify failures or anomalies in the desired system. This is the basis of what is called predictive maintenance.

Predictive maintenance consists of applying various techniques to detect and regulate trends in the processes that can cause a future failure [2]. In order to predict when it will be necessary to apply maintenance on a machine, it is necessary to analyze its operation

O. Pichardo Lagunas et al. (Eds.): MICAI 2022, LNAI 13613, pp. 252–265, 2022.
https://doi.org/10.1007/978-3-031-19496-2_19

and be able to detect anomalies or failures. For that, there are many algorithms that can be used for this purpose, some of the most used are neural networks like [3] autoencoders.

Convolutional Autoencoders (CAE) are a variant of Convolutional Neural Networks (CNN) that are used as the tools for unsupervised learning. CAE have been widely used in images processing [4, 5], but in recent years, various authors have used as this technique to detect anomalies [6–8].

For this work, a test bench was designed and built to simulate an industrial manufacturing process. For this test bench, an industrial servo-type motor was used with its respective controller to move a linear guide, in addition to a robot with 4 degrees of freedom. The vibrations of the engine were analyzed using an artificial intelligence model to detect anomalies, in this way it can be estimated when some maintenance will be needed.

2 Background

Cyber-physical systems are those that are built to connect their physical part at the same time that they collaborate with computational tools to communicate information about their surroundings, such as data in real-time. These systems installed in the factories allow greater control of production [9, 10]. Cyber-physical systems have been a direct evolution of traditional embedded systems, where now systems, in addition to fulfilling a specific function, are also responsible for communicating their performance through data. This has allowed industries to push their processes to another level, as they now have greater knowledge of how the process is working and can make improvements as needed. And if the process is optimized, it translates into better products with higher quality [11].

Cyber-physical systems are the foundation of what is now Industry 4.0, as this revolution is built around these systems and this interaction between the physical and the cyber world. In support of other technologies such as the internet of things and artificial intelligence is that these systems can have a greater impact on the industry since on the one hand, these systems need to share information, then the fact that they are connected to the internet and services in the cloud is important. But, on the other hand, data analysis is another fundamental aspect, and it is where technologies such as big data and automated learning come in [10].

To be able to apply Predictive Maintenance to a system, some kind of analysis needs to be done on its performance. There are different artificial intelligence techniques that can be used to analyze the data coming from a manufacturing line, some of them and one of the most used ones are neural networks.

Neural networks are a type of architecture for creating algorithms that is inspired by the way neurons work in the human brain. The basic concept to be able to understand neural networks it's the neuron. The neuron is a mathematical function, it is composed of a set of inputs, a set of weights, a bias and an activation function. A neuron can be represented with the Eq. (1) [12].

$$T(x) = \alpha(\textstyle\sum_i W_i x_i + b) \tag{1}$$

where $\boldsymbol{x}$ is the series of inputs $x_1, x_2, \ldots, x_n$. $\boldsymbol{W}$ is a set of Weights and $\boldsymbol{b}$ is the bias. The activation function $\boldsymbol{\alpha}$, could be a sigmoid, ReLU, or any other function that can be used to ger an output. This way, neural networks can be explained as a group of neurons connected commonly in layers, with an input layer, one or multiple hidden layers and an output layer [12].

Artificial Neural Network that manages data with local correlations, reducing the training parameters. Uses convolutional filters instead of neurons that decrease the instances of the connection between layers [13]. CNN is commonly used for classification, object detection, and segmentation, but it can also be implemented on unsupervised activities [14].

A CAE is a type of neural network, specifically CNN, which is responsible for reconstructing input data to an output optimizing parameters to minimize the error when extracting characteristics [6, 12]. They are used primarily for image reconstruction but have also recently been used for anomaly detection. An example of a convolutional autoencoder with its layers is shown in the Fig. 1.

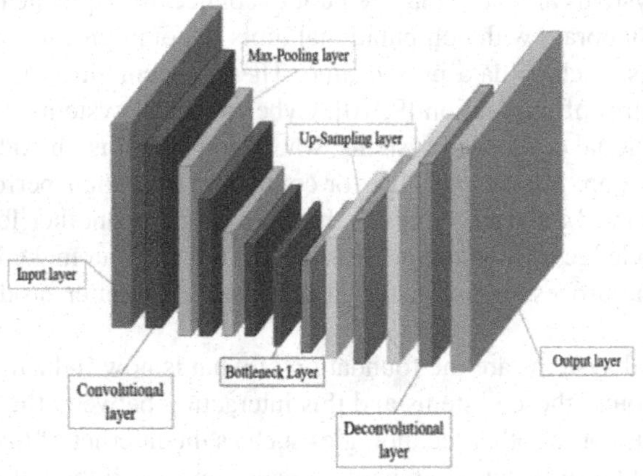

Fig. 1. Convolutional autoencoder illustration.

The events deviating from the normal patterns [15] are called anomaly detection. Those events can indicate incidents on the historical or the real-time data observation. This is also called outlier o novelty detection [16]. This technique focuses on finding when there are differences in the test data relative to the data that was used when training a model. These types of methods are normally used when the amount of "normal" data is a lot more abundant than the "abnormal" ones and it is necessary to find these anomalies or outliers.

There are different types of pattern recognition. The most common types are those that are responsible for classifying 2 or more classes, named two-class classification and multiclass classification respectively. In these types of classification, the information is already labeled with the classes, and this dataset is what is used to train the model that has to be able to distinguish between the classes. In anomaly detection, the so-called one-class classification is used, which consists of only one class (the most abundant) being used to train the model, and all the data that is different from these "normal" data will be "abnormal" or "anomalies" [16]. This work focused on the last type of recognition, since an Autoencoder is trained with the purpose of "learning" the normal operation of a motor, and consequently when reconstructing this training signal, it can distinguish when there are anomalies in the engine performance and some kind of maintenance can be applied to fix it. To test the autoencoder, some intentional data of "abnormal operation" is introduced to see its effectiveness.

Autoencoders are Symmetrical Neural Networks, which contains an encoder network and a decoder network. The encoder network maps the input data to a low-dimensional feature space, and the decoder network restores the data in the feature space to the input data [17]. These kinds of neural network have been used in anomaly detection, mainly due to its characteristic of being able to reconstruct a series of data, in such a way that it can learn how the behavior of a signal is. When learning the behavior of a dataset, the Autoencoder can detect when an input signal contains atypical values, which will be shown in the reconstruction that the network presents in the decoding phase.

The Mean Squared Error (MSE) is one of the most popular functions to estimate the performance of a statistic or machine learning model. This function calculates the difference or error between the real and the predicted values. Is widely used in regression models. In this work, this function is used to calculate the error between the prediction made by the convolutional autoencoder model, with the values of the real sensor.

The MSE is found by calculating the mean of the sum of the differences between the real and predicted values squared, as shown in Eq. (1) [18].

$$MSE = \frac{\sum_i^n (u_i - \widehat{u_i})^2}{n} \tag{2}$$

where u_i is the real value, $\hat{u}_i$ is the predicted value, and n is the number of samples.

The Mean Absolute Error (MAE) is the mean of the absolute error in the prediction, as shown in Eq. (2) [18].

$$MAE = \frac{\sum_i^n |u_i - \widehat{u_i}|}{n} \tag{3}$$

This function is used to determine the threshold of the model. Any value above this threshold will be marked as an anomaly.

3 Methodology

3.1 Materials and Test Bench Construction

In order to simulate a manufacturing environment, a test bench was built using different industrial components which were installed together to create a cyber-physical system capable of working continuously, just as it would be in a real industry. This system consists of a linear guide which will transport an object of a certain weight from one place to another which will be picked up by a robotic arm that will move it to another station. Thanks to this test bench, it will be possible to develop Cyber-physical applications and analyze their operation using Artificial Intelligence techniques, which can be easily replicated in the industry. For this work, we worked with an analysis of vibrations in the engine, this with the purpose of detecting and predicting failures to provide the line with some kind of predictive maintenance.

The test bench was built with the following materials:

- Industrial type servo motor
- Linear guide rail
- Robotic arm, 4 degrees of freedom
- PID control system with its controller and interface

For a better understanding of the test bench and its components, a diagram of the process flow is displayed in Fig. 2 and a 3D assembly is shown in Fig. 3.

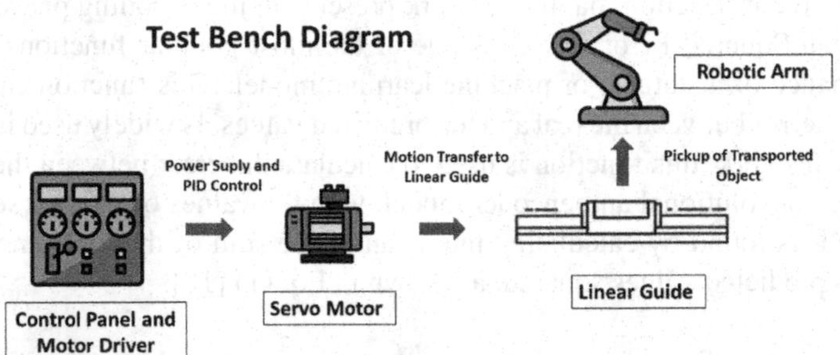

Fig. 2. Test bench diagram.

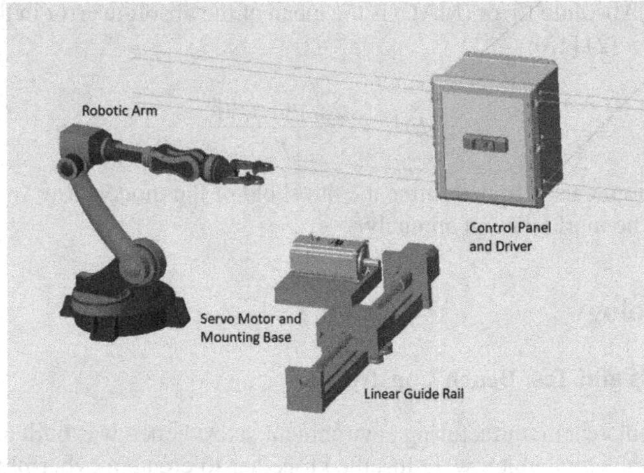

Fig. 3. Test bench 3D assembly.

For the construction of the system, some initial configurations were made to the servo motor using the Mint Workbench software. The motor works as an actuator to control the linear guide rail. The brand of the servo motor is Baldor, this motor has a power input and another for the communication with the driver.

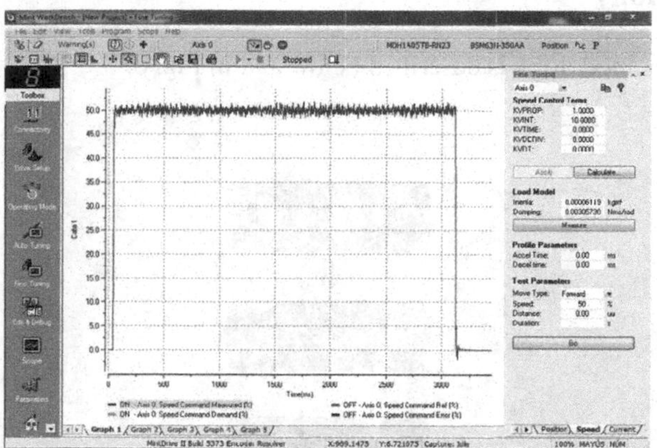

Fig. 4. Velocity fine tuning.

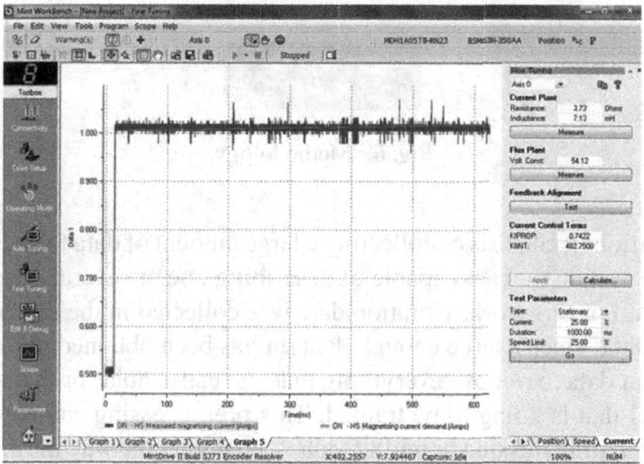

Fig. 5. Current fine tuning.

Through a software called Mint Workbench, the necessary configurations and adjustments were made to the servomotor. These adjustments consisted of the selection of the parameters of the servo according to its model, a BSM-63N-350AA. Once selected, an auto tuning was performed on the motor without load through an application that the same software offers. In order for the motor to work better, tests and adjustments (fine tuning) were made changing proportional, integral and derivative gain changes in speed and current, as seen in the Figs. 4 and 5. The goal of these adjustments is to provide the engine with the optimum performance increasing its power input, reducing the energy consumption and allowing it to have a longer life. It also reduces the unwanted vibrations, which is vital for this work.

4 Methodology

The proposed methodology is described below and in Fig. 6:

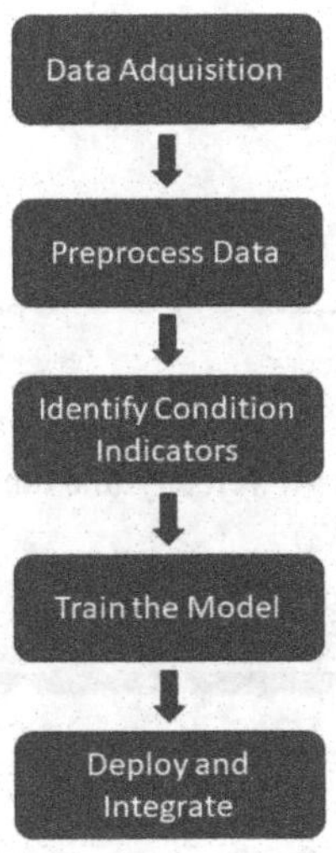

Fig. 6. Methodology.

- Data Acquisition: It consists of collecting a large amount of data from the sensors connected to the system that are capable of describing one or several operating variables in the system. For this work, vibration data was collected in the servo motor.
- Preprocess Data: Once a large enough data set has been obtained, the next phase is to work with that data to remove everything that can cause noise or that is not necessary for the model that is going to be trained. This preprocessing can consist of filtering the data, eliminating missing or outlier values, changing the way the data is displayed, etc.
- Identify Condition Indicators: The next phase consists of finding all those indicators that can describe the conditions of the system, for example those that separate a healthy running from an unhealthy one. This is to be able to separate the classes more easily. This step will help the model to find those anomalies in the operation of the motor
- Train the Model: Once the data and the indicators for the operating ranges of the system have been collected, one of the most important steps follows, training the artificial intelligence model that will help detect anomalies, classify them, or predict when the system can go from one state to another.

- Deploy and Integrate: The last step is to integrate the model in the system. This model can be installed in embedded systems or even in the cloud.

To collect the healthy and unhealthy data, an experiment was driven. In this experiment the servo motor was installed on a mounting base while it was running moving the linear guide. With the base firmly stablished, measurements were taken with samples of 140 values at a frequency of 10 Hz. It was decided to use this frequency due to the optimum functional range of the accelerometer, and after several tests with different frequencies, this was the option that gave better results. The 140 samples at a frequency of 10 Hz allows to have a small window of time where even the slightest anomalies can be detected. After a couple minutes of continuous operation, 100 samples were taken and labeled as "normal behavior", these samples will be used to train the Autoencoder. On the other hand, to simulate an abnormal behavior, some adjustments were made to the mounting base to produce some mechanical unbalance on the motor. These adjustments consisted of manually manipulate the mounting base in such a way that the engine had a very slight movement, making sure that the movement was "small" but that it could be identified by the autoencoder to differentiate it from the "normal operation" of the motor. Doing that, the motor will have different vibration as if it were working properly. The acceleration data with this scenario was labeled as "abnormal behavior". The "abnormal behavior" data was taken similarly as the healthy data, with also 100 samples to have a balanced dataset, although these samples will not really be used in training, only to validate the model. It was decided to use this small set of samples to determine if the autoencoder might be able to detect anomalies even with little training data.

5 Results

To analyze the vibrations of the motor, an adxl345 accelerometer was used to obtain the acceleration values in m/s2 in each of the 3 axes: X, Y and Z. These data were obtained using a capture frequency of 10 Hz. The accelerometer was installed on the motor in such a way that it was fixed, so it could only read data from the vibrations of the motor. Data were taken both for correct operation (see Fig. 7) and for abnormal or incorrect operation (see Fig. 8). The final dataset consisted of 200 samples with 140 points each. 100 samples for each condition.

For the samples shown in Fig. 7 and 8 it seems like the X axis is the most affected by the malfunction of the motor. However, not all the samples obtained show such a clear difference, so when working only with these data taken in the time domain, good results were not obtained when it came to detecting a malfunction. For this reason, the data was cleaned and then transformed to the frequency domain using the discrete Fourier transform (DFT). To make the conversion, the FFT (Fast Fourier Transform) algorithm was used, and also the amplitude was normalized. By observing the amplitude of the signal at different frequencies, it is easier to observe the differences between the states of the motor, which will facilitate the creation and training of the neural network. An example of the frequency amplitudes for motor conditions can be seen in Fig. 9.

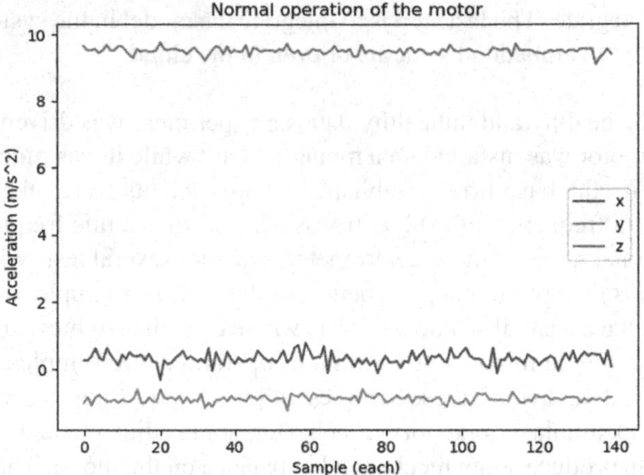

Fig. 7. Acceleration data of the motor with normal operation.

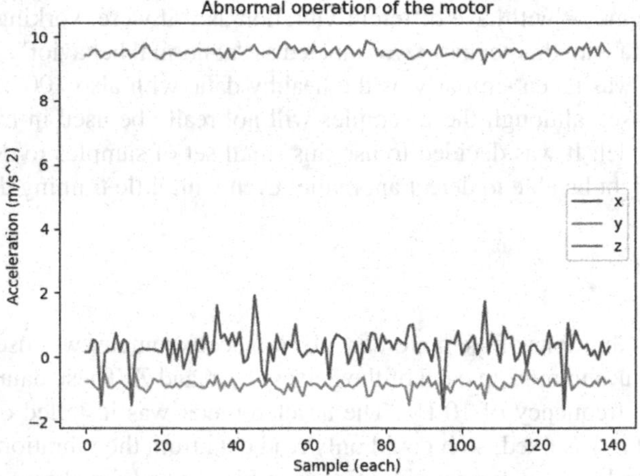

Fig. 8. Motor abnormal operation data.

When analyzing the three axes, it was determined that the X axis is the one that is most affected by the variations in the vibrations of the motor (in this experiment), and when working with it, it will allow to have better results.

Once the processed data was ready and the main axis was selected, the creation and training of the neural network continued, in this case using an Autoencoder. Only the 100 samples of engine vibrations with normal operation were used for training, so that the model only learned to reconstruct a correct signal. 80% of the data was used for training and 20% for evaluation. In this way, the reconstruction error could be compared, which should be greater for incorrect operation, by having higher frequency amplitude values, as observed before in Figs. 9.

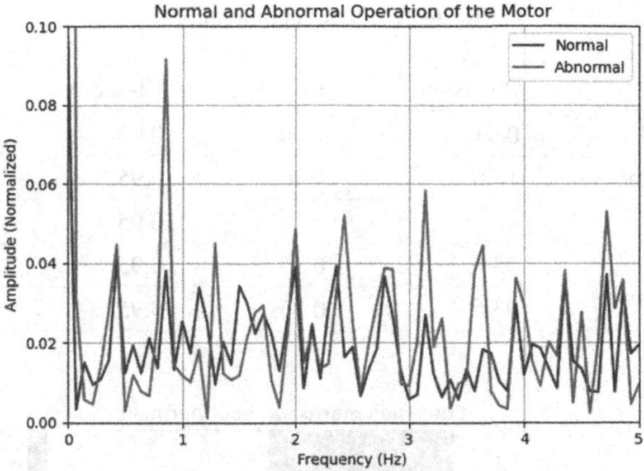

Fig. 9. Normal and abnormal X-ais operation in the frequency domain.

The Autoencoder model was created using 3 layers for the encoder and 3 layers for the decoder, as shown in Fig. 10. This Autoencoder was built in Python using the TensorFlow libraries. An Adam optimizer and MAE were used as loss criteria. For training and validation, some tools from scikit-learn were utilized. With various tests, it was observed that the best result was obtained when using 50 epochs for training. Once the model was trained, it was evaluated, this time using both engine conditions. The results of the evaluation can be seen in Table 1. In Fig. 11 it can be seen the confusion matrix of the model for a better visualization.

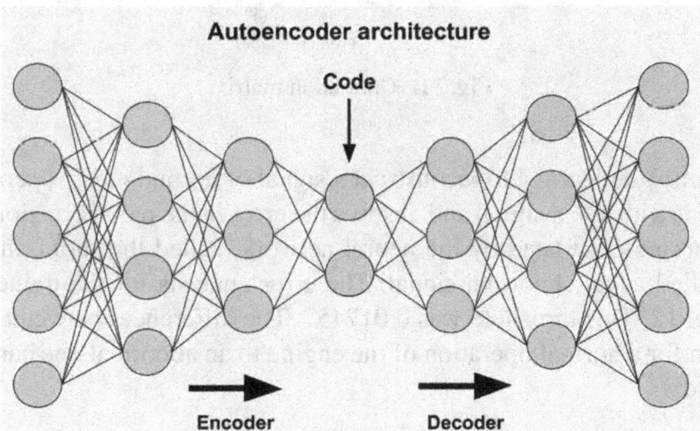

Fig. 10. Model's architecture.

Table 1. Classification report.

	Precision	Recall	F1-score	Support
Normal operation	0.91	1.00	0.95	21
Abnormal operation	1.00	0.90	0.95	20
Accuracy			0.95	41
Macro avg	0.96	0.95	0.95	41
Weighted avg	0.96	0.95	0.95	41

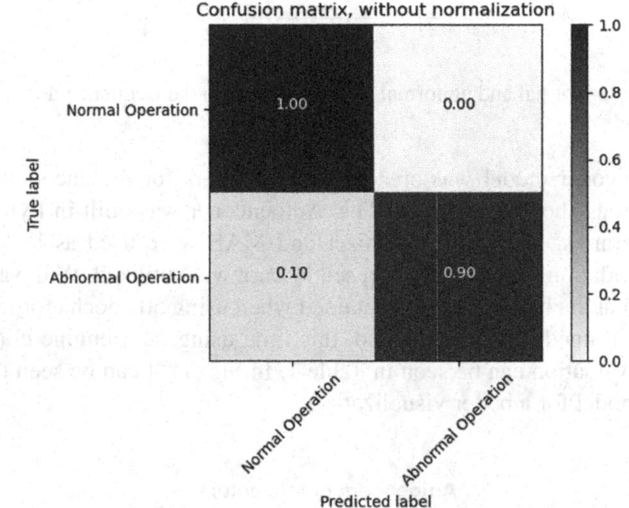

Fig. 11. Confusion matrix.

The Autoencoder learned to reconstruct a signal of normal motor operation in order to 41compare it with a real signal and observe the error in the reconstruction. If this error is greater than one calculated by the neural network, called threshold, then the signal will be classified as an abnormal signal. The error analysis for the trained model can be seen in Fig. 12. This threshold was 0.017457. The differences between the error of a reconstruction for a normal operation of the engine to an abnormal one can be observed in Figs. 13 and 14.

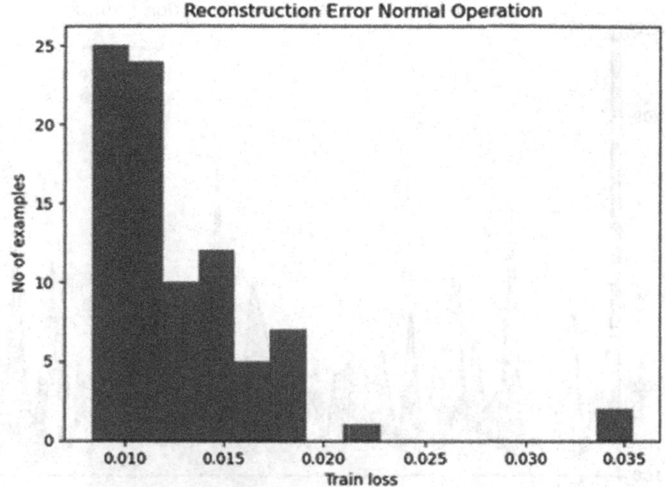

Reconstruction error threshold: 0.017457172

Fig. 12. Reconstruction error.

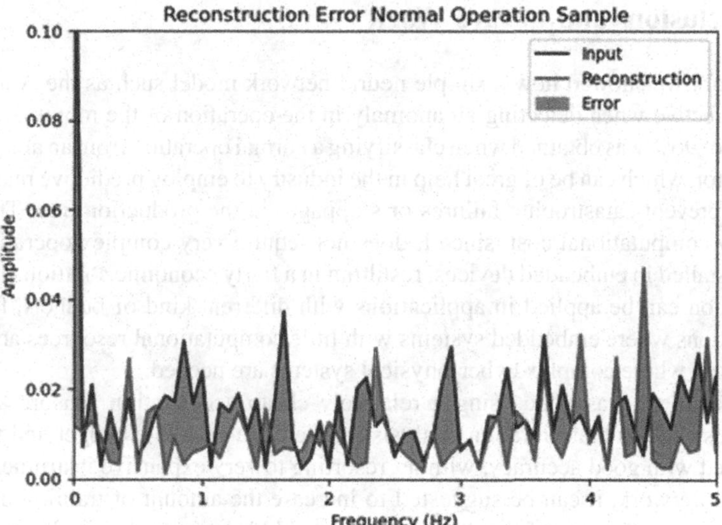

Fig. 13. Reconstruction for normal operation sample.

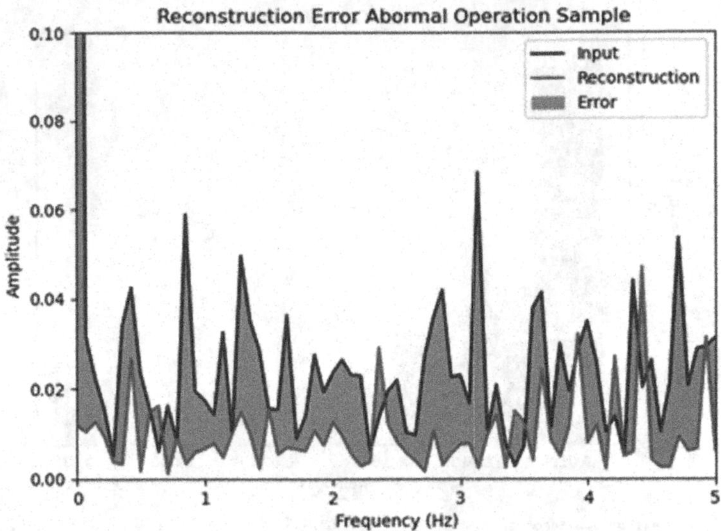

Fig. 14. Convolutional autoencoder example.

6 Conclusions and Future Work

In this work we showed how a simple neural network model such as the Autoencoder can be effective when detecting an anomaly in the operation of the motor. An average accuracy of 96% was obtained when classifying a normal operation from an abnormal one in the motor, which can be of great help in the industry to employ predictive maintenance and thus prevent catastrophic failures or stoppages in the production line. This model has a low computational cost, since it does not require very complex operations, so it can be installed in embedded devices, resulting in a fairly economic solution. Therefore, this solution can be applied in applications with different kind of budgets, from low-cost solutions where embedded systems with little computational resources are used, to applications where complex cyber-physical systems are needed.

This analysis was done using a relatively cheap acceleration sensor, which this method also shows that vibration analysis can be done on a low budget and faults can be detected with good accuracy, without resorting to very expensive instruments.

As future work, it can be suggested to increase the amount of training data, since surely the reconstruction of the Autoenconder could be more precise, also resulting in an increase in the accuracy of the model. Dimension reduction algorithms such as PCA or LDA could also be used, thus being able to work with the 3 axes at the same time and be able to have a more complete analysis.

References

1. Lemes, L.C., Hvam, L.: Maintenance costs in the process industry: a literature review. IEEE International Conference on Industrial Engineering and Engineering Management, pp. 1481–1485 (2019). https://doi.org/10.1109/IEEM44572.2019.8978559

2. Mobley, R.K., et al.: An Introduction to Predictive Maintenance Second Edition (2002)
3. Shao, H., Jiang, H., Zhao, H., Wang, F.: A novel deep autoencoder feature learning method for rotating machinery fault diagnosis. Mech. Syst. Signal Process. **95**, 187–204 (2017). https://doi.org/10.1016/j.ymssp.2017.03.034
4. Cheng, Z., Sun, H., Takeuchi, M., Katto, J.: Deep convolutional autoencoder-based lossy image compression. In: 2018 Picture Coding Symposium PCS 2018 – Proceedings, pp. 253–257 (2018). https://doi.org/10.1109/PCS.2018.8456308
5. Azarang, A., Manoochehri, H.E., Kehtarnavaz, N.: Convolutional autoencoder-based multi-spectral image fusion. IEEE Access. **7**, 35673–35683 (2019). https://doi.org/10.1109/ACCESS.2019.2905511
6. Al-Marridi, A.Z., Mohamed, A., Erbad, A.: Convolutional autoencoder approach for EEG compression and reconstruction in m-health systems. In: 2018 14th International Wireless Communication and Mobile Computing Conference IWCMC 2018, pp. 370–375 (2018). https://doi.org/10.1109/IWCMC.2018.8450511
7. Chow, J.K., Su, Z., Wu, J., Tan, P.S., Mao, X., Wang, Y.H.: Anomaly detection of defects on concrete structures with the convolutional autoencoder. Adv. Eng. Informat. **45**, 101105 (2020). https://doi.org/10.1016/J.AEI.2020.101105
8. Seyfioğlu, M.S., Özbayoğlu, A.M., Gürbüz, S.Z.: Deep convolutional autoencoder for radar-based classification of similar aided and unaided human activities. IEEE Trans. Aerosp. Electron. Syst. **54**, 1709–1723 (2018). https://doi.org/10.1109/TAES.2018.2799758
9. Marwedel, P.: Embedded System Design 433 (2021). https://doi.org/10.1007/978-3-030-60910-8
10. Ali, S., Al Balushi, T., Nadir, Z., Hussain, O.K.: Embedded systems security for cyber-physical systems. Stud. Comput. Intell. **768**, 115–140 (2018). https://doi.org/10.1007/978-3-319-75880-0_6
11. Choi, S., Kang, G., Jun, C., Lee, J.Y., Han, S.: Cyber-physical systems: a case study of development for manufacturing industry. Int. J. Comput. Appl. Technol. **55**, 289–297 (2017). https://doi.org/10.1504/IJCAT.2017.086018.4
12. Teuwen, J., Moriakov, N.: Convolutional neural networks. In: Handbook of Medical Image Computing and Computer Assisted Intervention, pp. 481–501. Academic Press (2019). https://doi.org/10.1016/B978-0-12-816176-0.00025-9
13. Canizo, M., Conde, A., Charramendicta, S., Minon, R., Cid-Fuentes, R.G., Onieva, E.: Implementation of a large-scale platform for cyber-physical system real-time monitoring. IEEE Access. **7**, 52455–52466 (2019). https://doi.org/10.1109/ACCESS.2019.2911979
14. Haselmann, M., Gruber, D.P., Tabatabai, P.: Anomaly detection using deep learning based image completion. In: Proceedings - 17th IEEE International Conference on Machine Learning and Applications, ICMLA 2018, pp. 1237–1242. Institute of Electrical and Electronics Engineers Inc. (2019). https://doi.org/10.1109/ICMLA.2018.00201
15. Ullah, W., et al.: Artificial Intelligence of Things-assisted two-stream neural network for anomaly detection in surveillance Big Video Data. Futur. Gener. Comput. Syst. **129**, 286–297 (2022). https://doi.org/10.1016/j.future.2021.10.033
16. Pimentel, M.A.F., Clifton, D.A., Clifton, L., Tarassenko, L.: A review of novelty detection (2014). https://doi.org/10.1016/j.sigpro.2013.12.026
17. Yoon, H.G., et al.: Interpolation and extrapolation between the magnetic chiral states using autoencoder. Comput. Phys. Commun. **272**, 108244 (2022). https://doi.org/10.1016/j.cpc.2021.108244
18. Qi, J., Du, J., Siniscalchi, S.M., Ma, X., Lee, C.H.: On mean absolute error for deep neural network based vector-to-vector regression. IEEE Signal Process. Lett. **27**, 1485–1489 (2020). https://doi.org/10.1109/LSP.2020.3016837

Modeling and Simulation of Swarm of Foraging Robots for Collecting Resources Using RAOI Behavior Policies

Erick Ordaz-Rivas and Luis Torres-Treviño(✉)

Facultad de Ingeniería Mecánica y Eléctrica, Universidad Autónoma de Nuevo León, Ave. Universidad S/N, Cd. Universitaria, 66455 San Nicolás de los Garza, Nuevo Leon, Mexico

luis.torrestrv@uanl.edu.mx

Abstract. In swarm robotics systems, each agent has too simple capabilities to perform complex tasks; however, working together arise self-organization and robustness that allow solutions to be found efficiently. An example of a study is the collection of objects; this is an important problem because it has several areas of investigation and potential applications. One of the main challenges is solving several essential subtasks in an emergent way, such as search, navigation, transport, location, and collection, that are associated with different environmental stimuli, which impact the swarm's performance when making decisions. In this work, we used the mathematical model of foraging robots, including physical parameters for its implementation in a swarm simulator. Through the simulator, the effect of the *RAOI* parameters is presented with different parametric configurations, environmental conditions, sizes in the swarm population, and multiple influence stimuli to solve a resource collection problem in an emergent way. The results are associated with different parametric configurations and are evaluated by various performance criteria.

Keywords: Foraging robots · Foraging task · RAOI polices · Swarm robotics · Emergent behavior

1 Introduction

Foraging is inspired by the behavior of ant colonies and is a widely studied scenario in swarm robotics [23]. Ants and other animal societies can efficiently exploit the task of gathering resources from food sources through local interactions between individuals [12]. In swarms of foraging robots, a specific area is defined as the "nest", and the objective is to collect the scattered resources in the environment and deposit them in the nest [1].

The use of foraging robot swarms has several potential applications and research areas [19]. Different models of collective behavior in swarm systems have been actively investigated due to their autonomy and robustness properties [2]. Each robot has individual behaviors that are too simple to perform assigned

O. Pichardo Lagunas et al. (Eds.): MICAI 2022, LNAI 13613, pp. 266–278, 2022.
https://doi.org/10.1007/978-3-031-19496-2_20

tasks, such as searching for resources. However, it is possible to achieve this problem with the collective behavior that emerges through local interaction with its neighbors and environment [8]. In this work, we developed a Python simulator of a foraging robot swarm for resource collection through *RAOI* (repulsion, attraction, orientation and influence) behavior policies [14], which provides exciting results in solving the problem. Although swarm behaviors using RAOI policies have already been reported in previous works [15], the effects of changes in the orientation parameter have not been fully explored, which are shown in the results. The simulator includes the dynamic model of each robot and considers possible sensor reading errors, outliers, and non-Gaussian noise.

2 Foraging Behavior

In foraging behavior, many robots R roam on a surface E that contains many objects O distributed in space. The objects are called food or resources that need to be collected and transported by a group of robots in a collection area defined as a "nest" N. The nest is an area on the surface E in which objects which are in unknown positions are deposited for robots in the environment. The goal is to collect as many objects as possible and transport them to the nest [6]. Potential applications of this task include search and rescue [3], hazardous waste clearance [7], demining [11], and planetary exploration [20].

The foraging problem applied to each robot in the swarm can be divided into two subtasks: a robot searches for objects in the environment or carries an object to take it to the nest. In Winfield [24], a cycle of four execution states was proposed to collect resources in multiagent systems: searching, grabbing, homing and deploying tasks of a robot in foraging. These subtasks performed by each robot can be facilitated by the interaction mechanisms and collaboration between neighbors and the environment [21].

One challenge in foraging is the collaboration between the members of the swarm; there must be some way that the robots can interact or communicate so that the decisions made by one robot are influenced by the decisions of the rest of the swarm [1]. Some ways to collaborate are through shared memory [22], with the direct exchange of information between robots [18] and local environmental changes [9].

Another challenge in foraging is discovering areas of interest, such as the location of objects and the nest. Even if a robot has already been to some area of interest in the past, it may forget how to get to the same point in the future due to a lack of global positioning [6]. Different approaches have been used to address this problem, such as particle swarm optimization [5], nature-inspired approaches [13], and machine learning (ML) approaches [10].

To face these challenges, the *RAOI* behavior rules are used in this work, based on the behavior model proposed by Couzin [4], which in turn uses the Reynolds congregation rules [17]. This model depends on four parameters, repulsion, attraction, orientation and influence, which significantly impact robot swarms' behavior when performing collaborative tasks [14]. A swarm behavior simulation platform was developed in Python, and performance criteria were established to test the effects of parameters on swarm behavior.

3 Swarm Features

3.1 Robot Mathematical Model

A swarm simulator with conditions as close as possible to reality was developed to test the effects of *RAOI* behavior rules on swarm behavior and performance. Each robot in the swarm is represented by a WMR (wheeled mobile robot) as shown in Fig. 1, in which the dynamics are described by a simplified model reported in [16], that considers DC motors as actuators on the wheels.

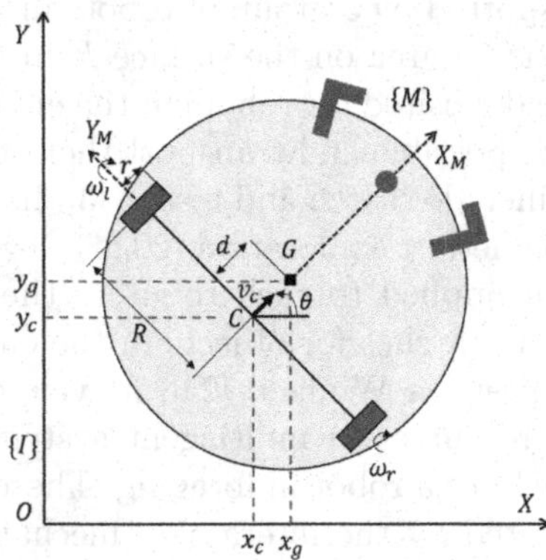

Fig. 1. Representation of each robot by a *WMR* with differential configuration.

$$\bar{M}\dot{\mathbf{v}} + \bar{H}(\mathbf{v}) = \bar{B}u \tag{1}$$

with $\bar{M} = M + BP_L^{-1}\Phi A^{-1}$, $\bar{H}(\mathbf{v}) = H(\mathbf{v}) + Z(\mathbf{v}) + BP_L^{-1}A^{-1}\mathbf{v}$, $\bar{B} = BP_L^{-1}P_s$,

$$M = \begin{bmatrix} m & 0 \\ 0 & I + md^2 \end{bmatrix}, \; H(\mathbf{v}) = \begin{bmatrix} -md\dot{\theta}^2 \\ mdv_c\dot{\theta} \end{bmatrix}, \; B = \begin{bmatrix} \frac{1}{r} & \frac{1}{r} \\ \frac{R}{r} & -\frac{R}{r} \end{bmatrix},$$

$$\Phi = \begin{bmatrix} \phi_{s,r} & 0 \\ 0 & \phi_{s,l} \end{bmatrix}, \; P_L = \begin{bmatrix} \rho_{L,r} & 0 \\ 0 & \rho_{L,l} \end{bmatrix}, \; P_s = \begin{bmatrix} \rho_{s,r} & 0 \\ 0 & \rho_{s,l} \end{bmatrix},$$

$$Z(\mathbf{v}) = \begin{bmatrix} \zeta_{r11} & \zeta_{r12} \\ \zeta_{r21} & \zeta_{r22} \end{bmatrix}\mathbf{v}, \; A = \begin{bmatrix} \frac{r}{2} & \frac{r}{2} \\ \frac{r}{2R} & -\frac{r}{2R} \end{bmatrix},$$

where m is the mass of *WMR*, d is the distance between the origin C of the mobile frame and the center of mass G, r is the radius of the wheels, R is the distance between the origin C of mobile frame and the wheel, $\dot{\theta}$ is the angular velocity of *WMR*, v_c is the linear velocity of *WMR*, $\mathbf{v} = [v_c \ w_c]^T$ is the vector of speeds of mobile frame, I is the inertia moment and $u = [u_r \ u_l]^T$ is the vector of voltage inputs for right and left DC motors, $\phi_{s,\imath}$, $\varrho_{L,\imath}$ and $\varrho_{s,\imath}$ are model coefficients of the DC motor, for $\imath = \{r, l\}$, given by

$$\phi_{s,\imath} = \frac{J_{m,\imath}}{\beta_\imath + \frac{\sigma_{T,\imath}\sigma_{emf,\imath}}{R_{a,i}}}, \ \rho_{L,\imath} = \frac{\frac{1}{\eta_\imath^2}}{\beta_\imath + \frac{\sigma_{T,\imath}\sigma_{emf,\imath}}{R_{a,\imath}}},$$

$$\rho_{s,\imath} = \frac{\frac{\sigma_{T,\imath}}{\eta_\imath \Upsilon_{a,\imath}}}{\beta_\imath + \frac{\sigma_{T,\imath}\sigma_{emf,\imath}}{R_{a,\imath}}},$$

where $J_{m,\imath}$ is the rotor and wheel inertia, $R_{a,\imath}$ is the armature resistance, $\sigma_{T,\imath}$ is the motor-torque constant, $\sigma_{emf,\imath}$ is the back *EMF* constant, $\eta_\imath$ is the gears reduction ratio, and $\beta_\imath$ is the actuator viscous friction constant.

3.2 Limitations of Sensory Capacity of Robots

Each simulated robot is inspired by the prototype presented in [15]. The robot has proximity sensors to calculate the distance with its neighbors, obstacles and boundaries and light sensors (*LDR*) to obtain the light information detected in the environment as an influence stimulus. They also incorporate a magnetometer so that each robot can know its orientation. In addition, they have a gripping mechanism activated by a servo motor to grab small objects.

Due to the limitations of the type of sensor, the robots can only detect the presence of neighbors and not their direction of movement, nor do they have direct communication between them. In addition, backward movements were restricted, so the robots can only turn on their axis and move forward.

3.3 Local Behavior Rules

The following behavior rules are explained based on the model presented in [14]. Diverse collective behaviors are exhibited in this model through three behavioral tendencies observed in social animals (repulsion, orientation, and attraction), represented by zones surrounding each individual, as shown in Fig. 2a. The closest zone to the robot is the zone of repulsion (*ZOR*) of radius r_r; if neighbors are detected within the *ZOR*, the robot tries to avoid them. The next zone is the zone of orientation (*ZOO*) of radius r_o; if neighbors are detected within *ZOO*, the robot tries to align itself in the same direction. The next zone is the zone of attraction (*ZOA*) of radius r_a; if neighbors are detected within the *ZOA*, the robot tries to approach them. The final zone is the zone of influence (*ZOI*) of radius r_i, which is superimposed on the other zones (Fig. 2b); if a stimulus by influence is perceived in the environment within *ZOI*, the robot tends to approach the influence source detected. By changing the values of the parameters

r_r, r_o, r_a, and r_i collective behaviors arise that adjust the swarm distribution or emphasize the task at hand.

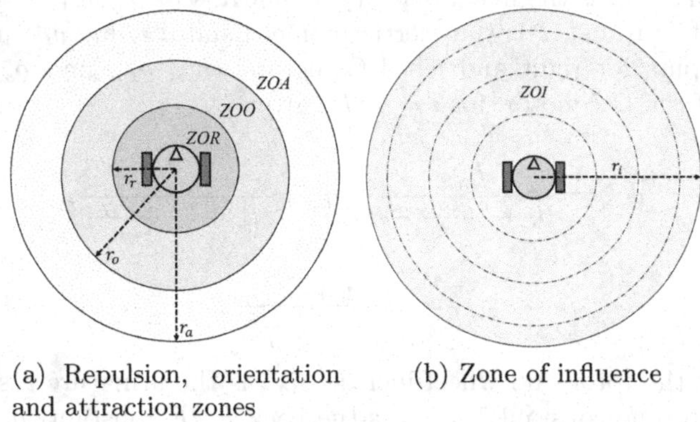

(a) Repulsion, orientation and attraction zones (b) Zone of influence

Fig. 2. Zones proposed for the swarm behavior model.

The direction of movement arises from interactions with neighbors and influence stimuli detected in *ZOR*, *ZOO*, *ZOA* and *ZOI*. Figure 3 shows the direction vector of each individual concerning the detected zone; where ν_i is the current direction vector of the robot, d_r is the direction of repulsion, d_o is the direction of orientation, d_a is the direction of attraction, d_ι is the direction of influence and $d_{\iota a}$ is the direction of attraction with active influence.

The gripping mechanism implemented in each i robot to transport objects has a sensor to detect its presence, granting the ability to perform search and delivery subtasks. Each subtask is associated with a state of the gripping mechanism ϱ_i. If no objects are found, the gripping mechanism will remain open $\varrho_i = 0$, allowing search behavior. If objects are found, the gripping mechanism will close $\varrho_i = 1$, allowing a delivery behavior. On the other hand, the magnetometer estimates the orientation and identifies the direction in which they are, whether search or delivery. Therefore, the states of the gripping mechanism and orientation are indicators that help each robot know the subtask to perform and are complemented by the *RAOI* rules.

Depending on the state of the gripping mechanism ϱ_i, each robot moves to the corresponding delivery or search zone, which are identified by an influence stimulus. The robots are placed in a random position within the nest, which corresponds to the delivery zone, heading towards the search zone until they find an object randomly placed within an area of influence to estimate their location. When an object is detected, the robot returns to the nest, which is also identified by an influence stimulus to calculate the drop point. Once the object is placed in the nest, the search process begins again. This process is described in Fig. 4 through a finite state diagram.

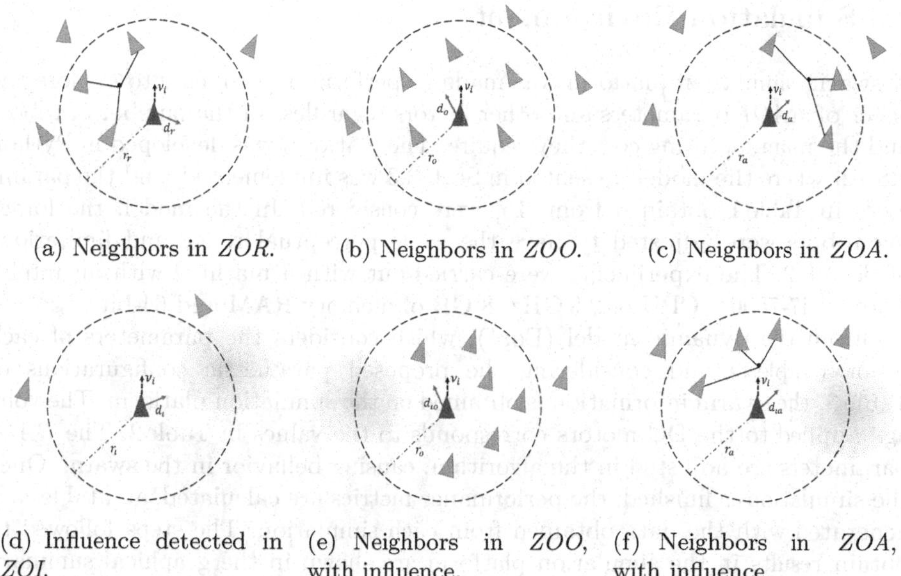

(a) Neighbors in *ZOR*. (b) Neighbors in *ZOO*. (c) Neighbors in *ZOA*.

(d) Influence detected in *ZOI*. (e) Neighbors in *ZOO*, with influence. (f) Neighbors in *ZOA*, with influence.

Fig. 3. Movement direction vectors concerning the active zone of the robot due to detected neighbors and influence.

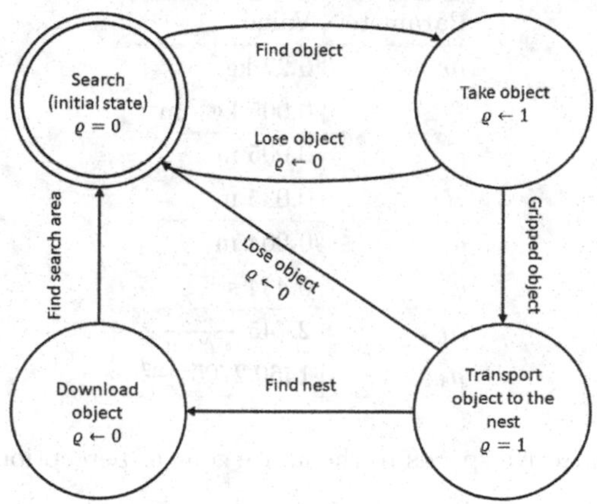

Fig. 4. Behavior states for object transport task.

4 Simulation Environment

A swarm simulation platform was made to perform experiments to explore the effect of *RAOI* parameters and other factors regardless of the number of robots and the manufacturing cost they require. The platform was developed in Python 3.8.12, where the model presented in Sect. 3.3 was implemented, and the parameters in Table 1 obtained from [15] were considered. In the model, the foraging robots were adjusted to have the same perceptual range and limitations of Sect. 3.2. The experiments were carried out with a machine with an Intel® Core™ i7-7500U CPU of 2.9 GHz, 8 GB of memory RAM and 64-bit.

From the dynamic model (Eq. 1), which considers the parameters of each robot (Table 1) and considering the proposed parametric configurations of Table 3, the swarm information is obtained on the simulation platform. The voltage applied to the DC motors corresponds to the values in Table 2. The *RAOI* parameters are adjusted in the algorithm, causing behavior in the swarm. Once the simulation is finished, the performance metrics are calculated, and tables are generated with the data obtained from each simulation. The steps followed to obtain results in the simulation platform are shown in the graphical summary of Fig. 5.

Table 1. Robot parameters.

Parameter	Value
m	0.22 kg
I	0.005 kg $\cdot$ m^2
r	0.005 m
R	0.035 m
d	0.004 m
$\phi_{s,i}$	0.434 s
$\rho_{L,i}$	2.745 $\frac{rad}{s \cdot N-m}$
$\rho_{s,i}$	1460.2705 $\frac{rad}{s \cdot V}$

Table 2. Respective speeds to the active zone of perception (see Fig. 2).

Zone	Speed (m/s)	Applied voltage (v)
Repulsion	0.08	2.8
Attraction	0.2	4.2
Orientation	0.1	3
Influence	0.1–0.2	3–4.2

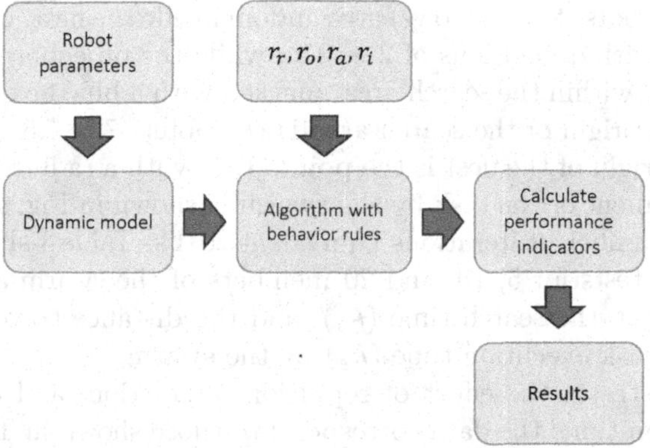

Fig. 5. Simulation graphical summary.

5 Results

Simulations were performed in a 10×10 m test arena with different population sizes (5, 10, and 20 robots). For each experiment, three replicates were performed, where each robot in the swarm has the same value of $RAOI$ parameters. The initial

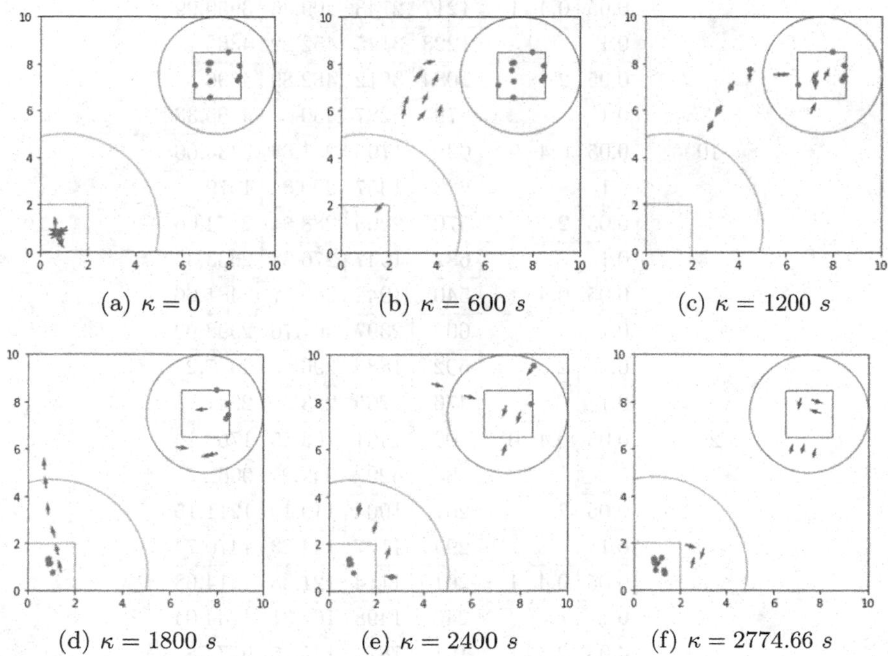

(a) $\kappa = 0$ (b) $\kappa = 600$ s (c) $\kappa = 1200$ s

(d) $\kappa = 1800$ s (e) $\kappa = 2400$ s (f) $\kappa = 2774.66$ s

Fig. 6. Swarm simulation of 10 robots performing an resource collecting task with $r_r = 0.05$, $r_a = 0.2$ and $r_o = 0.2$

position of the robots (black arrows) are random inside the nest, which are marked with a red box with dimensions of 2 × 2 m; while the objects (green circles) are randomly placed within the search area, marked with a blue box with dimensions of 2 × 2 m. The origin of the search area is the point (7.5, 7.5) with a radius of 2 m, while the origin of the nest is the point (1, 1) with a radius of 4 m.

The development of the task by the swarm is shown in Fig. 6, where κ corresponds to the number of iterations equivalent to 1 s. Table 3 shows the average result of all the tests for 5, 10, and 20 members of the swarm and includes the delivery time (κ_d), the search time (κ_s), and the distance traveled (δ) for each robot, also the task execution time (κ_e) by the swarm.

Figure 7 illustrates the effect of repulsion, attraction, and orientation concerning execution time; the data correspond to those shown in Table 3. Through these data, we can see an important relationship between the behavior of the

Table 3. Average results of the resource collecting task

Robots	r_r	r_a	r_o	κ_d	κ_s	δ	κ_e
5	0.05	0.4	0.2	1150	1765	310.24	2914.8
	0.1			1145	2396	372.74	3541.31
	0.05	2		1302	3970	558.82	5271.66
	0.1			1316	2576	422.51	3891.66
	0.05	0.4	1	1217	2743	409.36	3959.99
	0.1			1223	3145	452.22	4368
	0.05	2		1084	3612	482.89	4696
	0.1			878	3287	430	4165.33
10	0.05	0.4	0.2	639	1795	251.84	2434.66
	0.1			623	1357	209.3	1979
	0.05	2		570	2205	288.54	2774.66
	0.1			687	1947	276.38	2633.33
	0.05	0.4	1	540	1942	249.17	2481.66
	0.1			602	2397	304.76	2998.99
	0.05	2		502	1885	296	2387.2
	0.1			476	1765	283	2241
20	0.05	0.4	0.2	302	1461	163.55	1763.14
	0.1			284	622	94.02	906.27
	0.05	2		207	1004	119.19	1211.15
	0.1			294	1177	144.63	1470.74
	0.05	0.4	1	201	1114	121.33	1314.68
	0.1			246	1498	164.31	1744.04
	0.05	2		191	787	145.15	977.78
	0.1			209	787	149	995.57

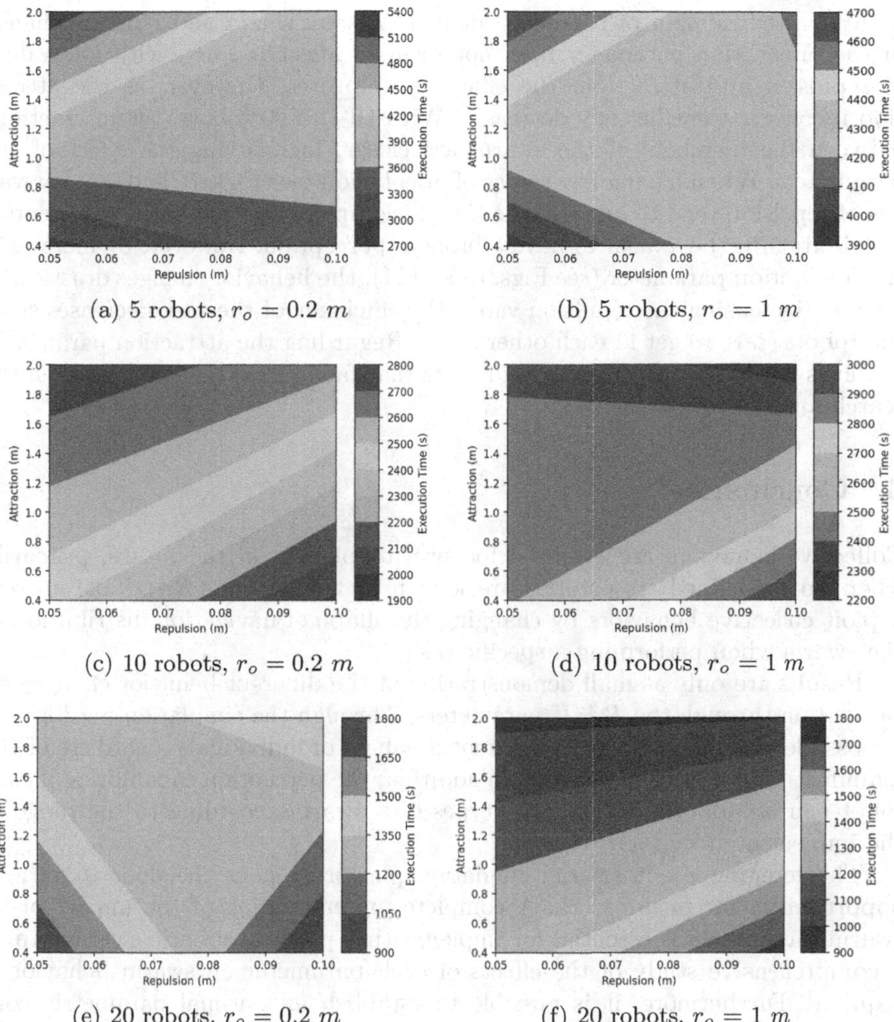

(a) 5 robots, $r_o = 0.2\ m$

(b) 5 robots, $r_o = 1\ m$

(c) 10 robots, $r_o = 0.2\ m$

(d) 10 robots, $r_o = 1\ m$

(e) 20 robots, $r_o = 0.2\ m$

(f) 20 robots, $r_o = 1\ m$

Fig. 7. Repulsion and attraction effect on the execution time for resource collecting task. The blue areas represent that the swarm takes less time to finish the task. (Color figure online)

swarm and the *RAOI* parameters, which can improve task performance. Based on these relationships, parameters can be established to decrease the time to complete the task and avoid selecting parameters that increase it.

The change of *RAOI* parameters allows the robots to move in groups or be autonomous when transporting and depositing the objects in an emergent way. When the swarm moves in a group, it is possible to facilitate the location of the search and delivery areas to reduce time and distances traveled, which in turn allows a saving of battery and resources of the robot.

When the number of robots is equal to 5 (see Figs. 7a and 7b), the change in the orientation parameter does not seem to affect it since, with low values of repulsion and attraction, the efficiency improves. However, as the attraction increases, the efficiency decreases. With 10 and 20 robots, the interactions between the members of the swarm are closer, intensifying the effect of the parameters. When having low values of orientation (see Figs. 7c and 7e), low values of repulsion tend to increase the time to complete the task since it prevents a distribution in the swarm to have a broader perception. However, by increasing the orientation parameter (see Figs. 7d and 7f), the behavior changes drastically; now, by increasing the repulsion value, the efficiency of the task decreases since the robots start to get in each other's way. Regarding the attraction parameter, it allows the formation of chains of robots that facilitate navigation between the search and delivery areas.

6 Conclusion

Collective behaviors are essential for swarm robotics in the future, primarily when no predefined trajectories are known in the system. *RAOI* parameters exploit collective behaviors by changing the shape of navigation distribution of the swarm when performing a specific task.

Results are only a small demonstration of the different behavior changes we can obtain through the *RAOI* parameters. Through the simulation platform, it is possible to experiment with different numbers of individuals regardless of the manufacturing cost of each robot. In addition, the perception capabilities of each robot can be adapted to the prototypes of a swarm according to the range of the implemented sensors.

The foraging robot swarm simulation platform opens the door to various opportunities for future work. A complete understanding of the impact of all swarm parameters is essential for implementing physical robotic swarms; thus, a comprehensive study of the effects of each parameter on swarm behavior is required. Furthermore, it is possible to establish an optimal parametric configuration using multi-objective optimization approaches to improve task performance against various evaluation criteria. Finally, with a task partitioning approach, it is possible to improve the efficiency of diverse complex processes based on multiple influence stimuli.

References

1. Bayındır, L.: A review of swarm robotics tasks. Neurocomputing **172**, 292–321 (2016)
2. Brambilla, M., Ferrante, E., Birattari, M., Dorigo, M.: Swarm robotics: a review from the swarm engineering perspective. Swarm Intell. **7**(1), 1–41 (2013)
3. Couceiro, M.: An overview of swarm robotics for search and rescue applications. Artif. Intell. Concepts Methodol. Tools Appl. 1522–1561 (2017). https://doi.org/10.4018/978-1-5225-1759-7.ch061

4. Couzin, I.D., Krause, J., James, R., Ruxton, G.D., Franks, N.R.: Collective memory and spatial sorting in animal groups. J. Theor. Biol. **218**(1), 1–11 (2002)
5. Dadgar, M., Jafari, S., Hamzeh, A.: A PSO-based multi-robot cooperation method for target searching in unknown environments. Neurocomputing **177**, 62–74 (2016)
6. Efremov, M.A., Kholod, I.I.: Swarm robotics foraging approaches. In: 2020 IEEE Conference of Russian Young Researchers in Electrical and Electronic Engineering (EIConRus), pp. 299–304. IEEE (2020)
7. Falker, J., Zeitlin, N., Leucht, K., Stolleis, K.: Autonomous navigation, dynamic path and work flow planning in multi-agent robotic swarms project. Technical report (2015)
8. Florea, A., Buiu, C.: An Overview of Swarm Robotics, pp. 58–69. IGI Global (2020). https://doi.org/10.4018/978-1-7998-1754-3.ch003. ISBN 9781799817550
9. Hamann, H., Wörn, H.: An analytical and spatial model of foraging in a swarm of robots. In: Şahin, E., Spears, W.M., Winfield, A.F.T. (eds.) SR 2006. LNCS, vol. 4433, pp. 43–55. Springer, Heidelberg (2007). https://doi.org/10.1007/978-3-540-71541-2_4
10. Hüttenrauch, M., Šošić, A., Neumann, G.: Guided deep reinforcement learning for swarm systems. arXiv preprint arXiv:1709.06011 (2017)
11. Kumar, V., Sahin, F.: Cognitive maps in swarm robots for the mine detection application. In: SMC 2003 Conference Proceedings. 2003 IEEE International Conference on Systems, Man and Cybernetics. Conference Theme-System Security and Assurance (Cat. No. 03CH37483), vol. 4, pp. 3364–3369. IEEE (2003)
12. Lee, J.H., Ahn, C.W., An, J.: A honey bee swarm-inspired cooperation algorithm for foraging swarm robots: an empirical analysis. In: 2013 IEEE/ASME International Conference on Advanced Intelligent Mechatronics, pp. 489–493. IEEE (2013)
13. Li, S., et al.: Particle robotics based on statistical mechanics of loosely coupled components. Nature **567**(7748), 361–365 (2019)
14. Ordaz-Rivas, E., Rodriguez-Liñan, A., Aguilera-Ruíz, M., Torres-Treviño, L.: Collective tasks for a flock of robots using influence factor. J. Intell. Robot. Syst. **94**(2), 439–453 (2018). https://doi.org/10.1007/s10846-018-0941-2
15. Ordaz-Rivas, E., Rodriguez-Liñan, A., Torres-Treviño, L.: Autonomous foraging with a pack of robots based on repulsion, attraction and influence. Auton. Robot. **45**(6), 919–935 (2021). https://doi.org/10.1007/s10514-021-09994-5
16. Ordaz-Rivas, E., Rodriguez-Liñan, A., Torres-Treviño, L.: Flock of robots with self-cooperation for prey-predator task. J. Intell. Robot. Syst. **101**(2), 1–16 (2021). https://doi.org/10.1007/s10846-020-01283-0
17. Reynolds, C.W.: Flocks, herds and schools: a distributed behavioral model. In: Proceedings of the 14th Annual Conference on Computer Graphics and Interactive Techniques, pp. 25–34 (1987)
18. Rybski, P.E., Larson, A., Veeraraghavan, H., LaPoint, M., Gini, M.: Communication strategies in multi-robot search and retrieval: experiences with MinDART. In: Distributed Autonomous Robotic Systems, vol. 6, pp. 317–326. Springer (2007). https://doi.org/10.1007/978-4-431-35873-2_31
19. Schranz, M., Umlauft, M., Sende, M., Elmenreich, W.: Swarm robotic behaviors and current applications. Front. Robot. AI **7**, 36 (2020)
20. St-Onge, D., et al.: Planetary exploration with robot teams: implementing higher autonomy with swarm intelligence. IEEE Robot. Autom. Mag. **27**(2), 159–168 (2019). https://doi.org/10.1109/MRA.2019.2940413
21. Tang, Q., Ding, L., Yu, F., Zhang, Y., Li, Y., Tu, H.: Swarm robots search for multiple targets based on an improved grouping strategy. IEEE/ACM Trans. Comput. Biol. Bioinf. **15**(6), 1943–1950 (2017)

22. Vaughan, R.T., Støy, K., Sukhatme, G.S., Matarić, M.J.: Blazing a trail: insect-inspired resource transportation by a robot team. In: Distributed Autonomous Robotic Systems, vol. 4, pp. 111–120. Springer (2000). https://doi.org/10.1007/978-4-431-67919-6_11
23. Verlekar, H., Joshi, K.: Ant & bee inspired foraging swarm robots using computer vision. In: 2017 International Conference on Electrical, Electronics, Communication, Computer, and Optimization Techniques (ICEECCOT), pp. 191–195. IEEE (2017)
24. Winfield, A.F.T.: Foraging robots. In: Meyers, R. (ed.) Encyclopedia of Complexity and Systems Science, pp. 3682–3700. Springer, New York (2009). https://doi.org/10.1007/978-0-387-30440-3_217

Data-Driven Adaptive Force Control for a Novel Soft-Robot Based on Ultrasonic Atomization

Isaias Campos-Torres[1], Josué Gómez[2(✉)], and Arturo Baltazar[1]

[1] Centro de Investigación y de Estudios Avanzados del Instituto Politécnico Nacional Unidad Saltillo, Ramos Arizpe, Mexico
{isaias.campos,arturo.baltazar}@cinvestav.edu.mx

[2] Facultad de Ingeniería de la Universidad Autónoma de Coahuila, Arteaga, Mexico
jogomezc@uadec.edu.mx

Abstract. Soft robots present a different approach to rigid robots in the way they can interact with a rigid surface and their adaptability to work under unstructured environments. In most cases, flexible robots are equipped with pneumatic and hydraulic actuators that are bulky for small-scale soft robotic applications. In this work, an alternative option for rapid actuation of a mini soft- robot using an ultrasonic atomizer and a heater to accelerate the phase change of ethanol from liquid to gas is proposed. The resulting force is a nonlinear phenomenon that imposes limitation for a traditional model-based control algorithm. To overcome that, we developed a data-driven control which does not require a model and works with minimum information of the input and output signals from the nonlinear system. The controller is designed using a neuro-fuzzy network with an adaptive stage to compensate uncertainties of the system. The system is experimentally tested and incorporated in the proposed soft robot. The results show that the developed soft robot-fuzzy controller system can reach a reference force −0.2 N with minimum error using the proposed actuation based on atomization.

Keywords: Atomization · Soft-robot · Data-driven control · Artificial neuro-fuzzy network · Force control

1 Introduction

In contrast to traditional robots, soft robotics has become a wide field of study for advantages such as task adaptability, interaction with rigid surfaces, and safe human interaction just to mention a few (see [1] and [14]). These advantages are specially noticeable for robot tasks in non-structured environments and fragile object manipulation. The use of a flexible robot for force control could guarantee a soft contact in comparison to conventional rigid robots due to their compliance properties. Soft robots are generally manufactured from elastomer material, which is flexible and adjustable. However, force control is a challenging problem due to high non-linearities and uncertainties during mechanical contact.

O. Pichardo Lagunas et al. (Eds.): MICAI 2022, LNAI 13613, pp. 279–290, 2022.
https://doi.org/10.1007/978-3-031-19496-2_21

Actuation is a main research area in soft robotics, where the most implemented techniques are the pneumatic and hydraulic actuation. In the case of pneumatic actuation, a inner chamber of the soft robot is filled with compressed air, this provides fast responses and large deformations [10,13,15,16]. A similar approach is the hydraulic actuation where the chamber is filled with a pressurized liquid [9]. This generates large forces at relative low input pressures, but with slow response time. Despite the advantages presented by these methods, the main drawback of these methods is the bulky power sources used. This is specially relevant for a small soft robot. In this work, to miniaturize the actuation system dimensions, a new actuator based on atomization is presented. Atomization is a process to break liquids into a mist of micro-droplets. There are many methods to achieve the atomization including nozzle atomization where the liquid is pushed with air into a conical nozzle to generate the droplets [7]. Recently atomization through piezoelectric materials that vibrate when an electric field is applied forcing the superficial fluid to pass through a mesh has been studied [2]. The mist generated by this process is not in a gas phase. However, if we expose it to a hot surface, it should vaporize by evaporation which can exert pressure if we have a closed-system (the elastomer chamber in our case). In which case, the temperatures needed to achieve a pressure change inside the chamber are far below the liquid boiling point.

Force control using the proposed actuation system is a highly nonlinear phenomena contaminated with vibration induced noise. Therefore a traditional model-based actuation control will fail. In this work an intelligent model-free control based on a Neuro-Fuzzy Network (NFN) to regulate the force contact of the conceived mini soft-robot is developed. The proposed NFN is used to compensate the uncertainties and nonlinearities in the controller. The proposed methodology is based on a Data-Driven Model and Control (DDMC) where the robotic system is approximated online without any requirement of the mathematical model using only the input and output signals association. MFAC (Model Free Adaptive Control) is computed by an equivalent dynamic linearization from data dynamic system. This simplifies the global identification of a nonlinear plant to operate an online closed-loop system, see for instance [5,6]. The DDMC for a nonlinear system becomes in an alternative online identification method under the concept of the CFDL (Compact From Dynamic Linearization). The PPD (Pseudo Partial Derivative) is the time-varying parameter from the CFDL to approximate a Data-Driven Model (DDM) only using the input and output signals relationship for a Single-Input Single-Output (SISO) system. So that, PPD parameter computes the closed-loop control for a nonlinear system using minimum information. That means, a non-rigorous mathematical computation is needed in comparison to traditional methods such as Control Based on Analytical Model (CBAM). In contrast, CBAM requires complete information from the system, for example, physical and mechanical parameters to approximate a nonlinear model. On the contrary, a DDMC needs only a minimum information to estimate the system dynamics, [11] and [12].

The principle of the PPD and DDMC can be extended to the force control in robotic application as mentioned below. A grasping control in a contact mechanism applying an NFN to regulate the force signal using only the principle of DDMC considering the input and output relationship to estimate the dynamic of system response was studied in [19]. In [17] an industrial system of soft contact in an end-effector neglecting the mathematical model is discussed. The controller design was based on the input and output signals information using an NFN. A force control of a soft contact ultrasonic sensor mounted on a robot end-effector was developed in [3]. The proposed adaptive controller was based on an NFN with a learning algorithm using a stochastic gradient to compensate the non-linearities and noise in the measurements.

The innovation of this work is the development of a mini soft-robot with unidirectional displacements that uses a novel prototype of soft actuation based on atomization and controlled by an NFN data-based controller. The objectives of this research are: first, to integrate a mini soft-robot and soft actuation system; second, to implement the system in a closed-loop force control; and third, to develop a force neuro-fuzzy control under the concept of DDMC.

The structure of this paper is: Sect. 2 describes the soft actuation and robot design, Sect. 3 presents the NFN control, Sect. 4 shows the experimental results, and finally, Sect. 5 gives the conclusions of this research work.

2 Actuation and Soft-Robot Design

This section presents the operating principle of the ultrasonic atomization, rapid actuator design and mini soft-robot development.

2.1 Ultrasonic Atomization

The principle of the ultrasonic atomization is based on the phenomena of high frequency vibrations produced by a piezoelectric meshed disk that comes into contact with a liquid to produce a mist. The piezoelectric is attached to a metallic mesh with micro-holes over its surface, hence, micro-droplets are dispersed when the piezoelectric is activated by an electrical source Fig. 1(a),(b). The piezoelectric ring vibrates forcing the liquid to pass through the micro-holes of the mesh forming micro-droplets Fig. 1(c). The result is a conical mist flow with concentrated droplets at the center. These types of ultrasonic atomizers can be found in apparatus such as mist humidifiers and portable nebulizers. The atomized liquid does not generate enough pressure to use it in actuation applications. To generate pressure, a change phase transition is required to evaporate the mist which is done by the contact of the mist's micro-droplets to a heater. Our proposed design of a novel rapid actuation for mini soft-robot is based on liquid vaporization by atomization and heating below the boiling point to generate actuation as discussed in [9].

Thus, a heater was designed to induce the phase state change below boiling point of the liquid ethanol used in the experiments. The time for the phase change transition observed was nominally instantaneous. The optimal frequency to vibrate the mesh was found approximately at 110 kHz, where the displacements are maximized at the center of the mesh, see [4] and [8] for a numerical analysis. The applied voltage was found nearly linear to the atomization rate.

Based on the principle of ultrasonic atomization, a new design for rapid actuation optimizing the heater contact area for a mini soft-robot application is described below.

2.2 Rapid Actuator Design

The ultrasonic atomizer has a diameter of 20 mm and a thickness of ≈1 mm. A driver board with a variable input voltage from 3.7–12 V supplies a maximum voltage of 70 V and a frequency of 113 kHz. Thus, the atomizer produces a mist of micro-droplets by the supplied voltage into vibrating mesh. The proposed heater was designed with a spiral shape to increase the contact area of the mist. The atomizer is mounted directly over the liquid to produce a mist of micro-droplets which at contact with the heater evaporate at 35 °C, thus, reducing the ethanol boiling point (78.6 °C). Ethanol gas exerts enough pressure to displace the mini soft-robot, Fig. 2(a) depicts a schematic representation of the rapid actuation system.

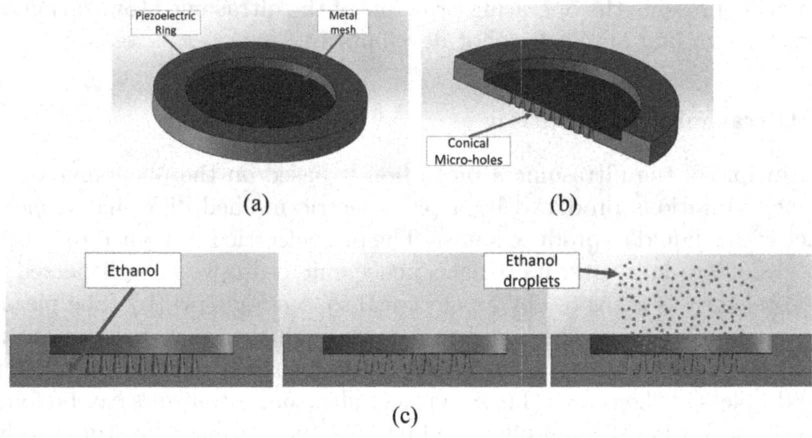

Fig. 1. Principle of the ultrasonic atomization: a) atomizer components: piezoelectric ring and metal mesh, b) cross sectional view of the atomizer and c) ethanol micro-droplets dispersion.

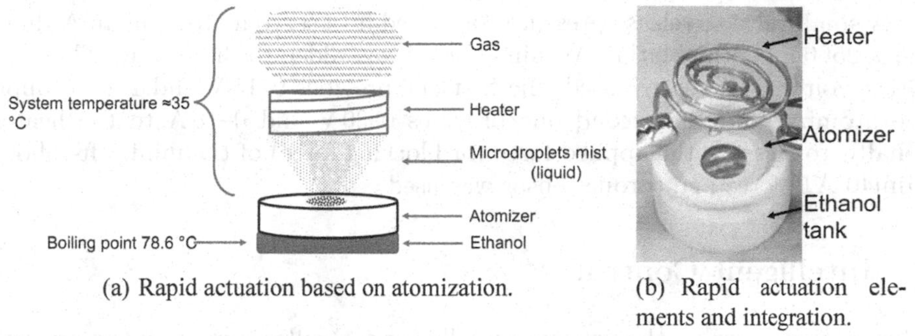

(a) Rapid actuation based on atomization.

(b) Rapid actuation elements and integration.

Fig. 2. Schematic representation of the rapid actuation system based on a liquid-gas phase state change.

The ethanol tank was designed using Solid Works and manufactured in a 3D printer. The heater was built with a Nicromel-Cr20Ni80 wire. The total height of the actuation system is 22 mm, that includes the atomizer, heater and the ethanol tank. Figure 2(b) shows the elements and prototype of the rapid actuation system.

2.3 Mini Soft-Robot Design

The mold of the robot was designed using Solid Works and manufactured in a 3D printer using Polylactic Acid (PLA) as printing material. A elastomer Ecoflex-0050 solution was poured into the printed mold, while a vacuum chamber was used at 550 mmHg during 20 min to prevent bubble formation in the elastomer. Once the Ecoflex-0050 solution was cured, the actuation system in Fig. 2(b) was sealed inside of the mini-soft robot case. Figure 3(a) and (b) show a comparison between initial robot position and actuated robot position. The total height of the robot is 40 mm and its displacement during the actuation is 13 mm, which is about 32.5 % of the total height.

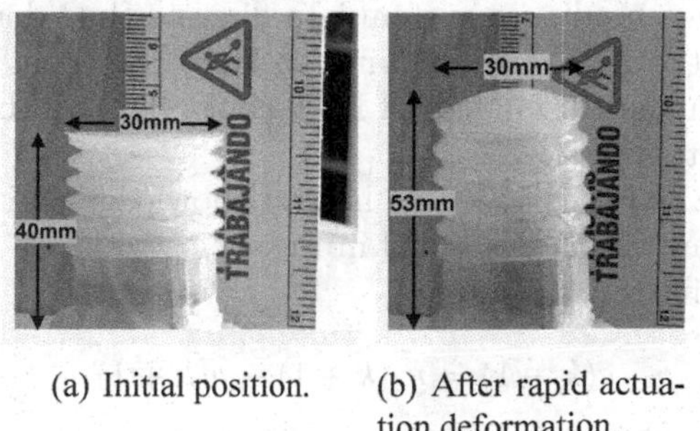

(a) Initial position.

(b) After rapid actuation deformation.

Fig. 3. Results and comparison of the mini soft-robot displacements.

A small valve to release pressure controlled by a servo motor and an Arduino mega 2560 using the Matlab Arduino library was added to the system. Thus, two direct voltage sources are used, the first one provides 0–15 V and 1 A to supply the atomizer and the second one provides 0–30 V and 0–10 A to the heater. Finally, to measure the applied force (or blocking force) of the mini soft-robot a Mini40 ATI force and torque sensor was used.

3 Intelligent Control

This section describes the proposed intelligent controller inspired by an artificial NFN considering the soft-robotic system as a nonlinear discrete-time control plant.

Remark 1. *where the SISO system* $\hat{\Phi}(k) = \frac{\Delta y(k+1)}{\Delta u(k)}$ *denotes the input signal (angle position of the release valve) and output signal (force signal) of the system; hence, the representation of the ideal system* $\Phi^*(k)$ *is given by:*

$$\Phi^*(k) = \hat{\Phi}(k) + \epsilon(k) \tag{1}$$

where $\epsilon(k)$ is the estimation error. Therefore, the following assumptions should be satisfied for the control law.

Assumption 1. *The robotic system is considered Lipschitz and a positive constant* L *exists that defines the direct relationship between the input-output* $\| y(k+1) \| \leq L \| u(k) \|$. *That means, a change in the force signal imposes a change in the pressure level in the robotic system.*

Assumption 2. *The output of the robotic system is observable, i.e.,* $y(k+1) = \hat{\Phi}(k)u(k)\ \forall k > 0$. *It is possible to estimate the equivalent model of the robotic system from the measured force signals.*

An artificial NFN is characterized by an adaptive stage based on human experience and the intuitive initial set of parameters. The adaptation stage adjusts its parameters using the descending gradient technique. The NFN considers the plant as an unknown nonlinear system in a discrete-time domain. Therefore, to control the plant, the NFN only requires to know the input and output signals of the system. A further discussion of NFN controllers can be found in [18] and literature referred there.

The structure of NFN is based on human knowledge and an intuitive initialization of its parameters as described in Fig. 4.

The error is defined as

$$e(k+1) = y_d(k+1) - y(k+1) \tag{2}$$

where $y(k+1)$ is the current force and $y_d(k+1)$ is the desired force.

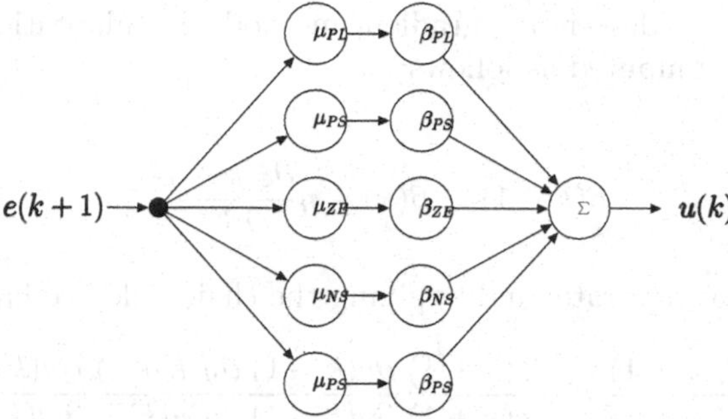

Fig. 4. NFN architecture.

3.1 Neuro-Fuzzy Architecture

NFN structure has 4 layers and 5 nodes.

- Layer 1. This layer is the input to the artificial neural network $e(k+1)$, and the signal is transferred to each node in the next layer.
- Layer 2. This layer contains the membership functions. Each node in this layer is a membership function corresponding to the design of the linguistic variables. The output of each node is calculated as follows:

$$\phi(k) = \mu(e(k)) \tag{3}$$

- Layer 3. This layer is the adaptation stage where the parameters $\beta(k+1)$ are adjusted.
- Layer 4. This layer is the output of the NFN:

$$O(k) = \sum_{i=1}^{N} \phi(k)\beta(k) \tag{4}$$

where N represents the number of linguistic variables.

3.2 Adaptation Algorithm

An adaptive technique based on the descending gradient method is proposed to adjust the NFN parameters. First, an objective function is defined to achieve the optimal value of the network parameters. The parameters are adjusted in terms of the control error at each time step through a quadratic function $\xi(k+1)$:

$$\xi(k+1) = \frac{1}{2}e^2(k+1) \tag{5}$$

According to the descending gradient method, the adaptation of the parameters $\beta(k+1)$ is computed as follows:

$$\beta(k+1) = \beta(k) - \eta \frac{\partial \xi(k+1)}{\partial \beta(k)} \tag{6}$$

where η is the learning rate; and applying the chain rule, we have:

$$\begin{aligned} \frac{\partial \xi(k+1)}{\partial \beta(k)} &= \frac{\partial \xi(k+1)}{\partial e(k+1)} \frac{\partial e(k+1)}{\partial y(k+1)} \frac{\partial y(k+1)}{\partial u(k)} \frac{\partial u(k)}{\partial O(k)} \\ &= e(k+1)[-1]\hat{\Phi}(k)\mu(e(k)) \end{aligned} \tag{7}$$

when substituting (7) in (6) is found the adaptation law

$$\beta(k+1) = \beta(k) + \eta e(k+1)\hat{\Phi}(k)\mu(e(k)) \tag{8}$$

and the control law is:

$$u(k) = \mu(e(k))\beta(k) \tag{9}$$

4 Experimental Results

Figure 5 shows the closed-loop system, the equivalent model is approximated under the concept of the DDMC taking the online measurements from the force sensor and the position angle of the release valve, which are considered as the output and input signals of the mini soft-robot. Once, the PPD $\hat{\Phi}(k)$ approximates the system dynamics, the control law in (9) and the adaptation in (8) are computed to reach the desired force and the control error converges close to zero.

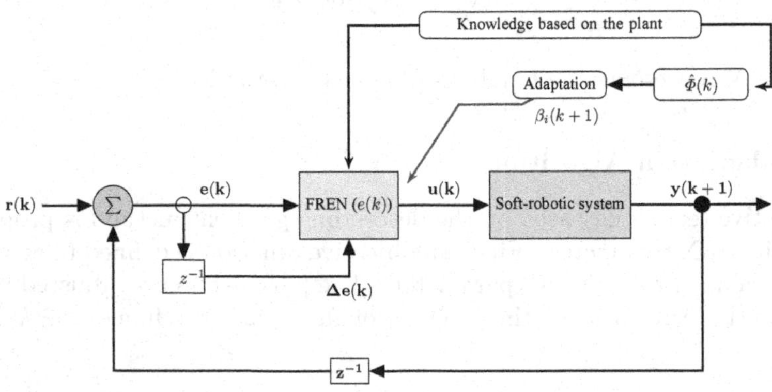

Fig. 5. Control-loop block diagram.

Figure 6(a) shows the experimental and Fig. 6(b) depicts the bock diagram of the control system for the soft robot. The information exchange among the ultrasonic atomizer, the force sensor, and the release valve is done using Matlab 2018a.

Therefore, the linguistic variables are μ_i : P_L is positive large, P_S is positive small, Z_E is zero, N_S is negative small and N_L es negative large. Figure 7(a) shows the membership function design and Table 1 shows the control setting parameters.

Table 1. Control setting parameters values.

Parameters	Value
$\beta_{PL}(0)$	1
$\beta_{NL}(0)$	0.5
$\beta_{ZE}(0)$	0
$\beta_{NS}(0)$	−0.5
$\beta_{NL}(0)$	1
η	0.01

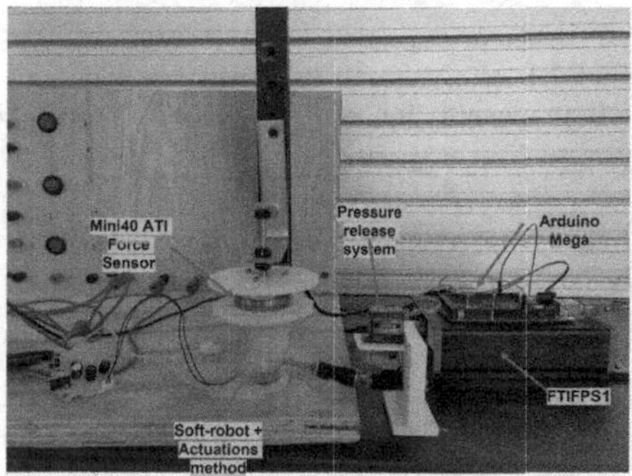

(a) Experimental setup.

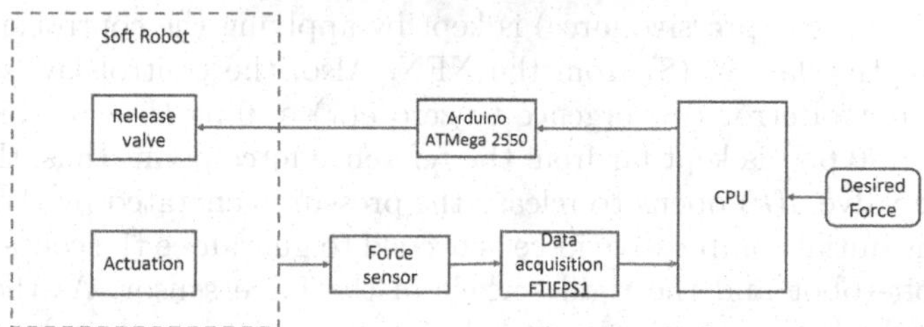

(b) Experimental setup diagram for soft robotic system signals.

Fig. 6. a) Description of the experimental setup and b) the block diagram of the plant for the robotic system.

IF-THEN rules are established by the input function $e(k+1)$ and the control signal $u(k)$ as follows:

- IF $e(k+1)$ Is positive large (P_L), THEN $u(k)$ Is positive large (P_L),
- IF $e(k+1)$ is positive small (P_S), THEN $u(k)$ is positive small (P_S),
- IF $e(k+1)$ is zero (Z_E), THEN $u(k)$ Is Zero (Z_E),
- IF $e(k+1)$ is negative small (N_S), THEN $u(k)$ Is negative small (N_S),
- IF $e(k+1)$ is negative large (N_L), THEN $u(k)$ Is negative large (N_L).

Figure 7(a) depicts the design of the membership function according to the force loads generated by the mini soft-robot over a rigid surface and user experience. Figure 7(b) shows the adaptive parameter $\beta(k+1)$ of the NFN regarding the adaptive law in (8).

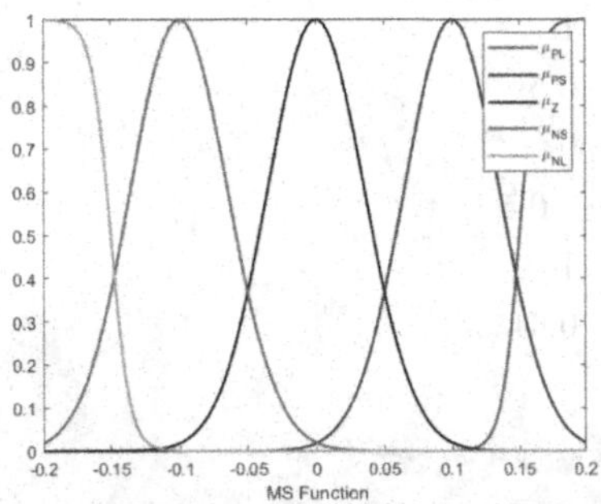

(a) Membership function design for soft robotic system $\mu(e(k))$.

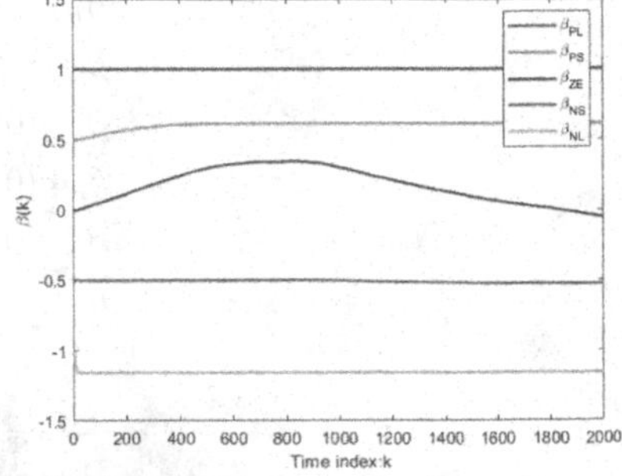

(b) Adaptive parameters $\beta(k+1)$.

Fig. 7. a) Membership function design represents the second layer; and b) adaptive parameters that represent the third layer of the NFN.

Figure 8 shows the evolution of the force signal from the initial condition to the reference signal $y_d(k+1) = -0.2$N. The control signal $u(k)$ represents the demand in the position angle of the valve to the pressure released inside of the mini soft-robot. Therefore, a reference force value of -0.2N (negative value indicates a compressive force) is kept by applying the control signal in (9) and the adaptive law in (8) from the NFN. Also, the control law successfully allows the control error convergence to zero $e(k) \approx 0$ as $k \to \infty$. Initially, the force signal (-0.6N) is kept far from the reference force point, thus, the position angle of the valve $u(k)$ opens to release the pressure generated by the actuation system. This initial compressive force is needed to guarantee the contact between the mini soft-robot and the rigid surface of the force sensor. As the reference point is reached, the position angle of the valve closes to regulate the force signal exerted by the robot over the rigid surface. At the end of the experiment, the actuation system generates enough pressure to maintain the reference and the position angle of the valve opens. As is demonstrated in Fig. 8, the force reference is reached due to the robustness of the control law against the noise signal generated by the release valve.

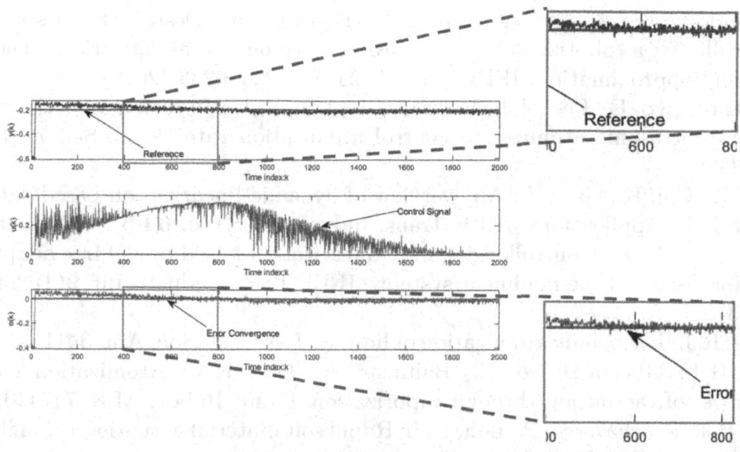

Fig. 8. Experimental results for the force control of the soft robotic system; where $y(k)$ and $u(k)$ are the output and input of the system respectively, and $e(k)$ is the control error.

5 Conclusions

In this paper a small soft actuated robotic system was presented. This is built with an atomizer and a heater to generate micro-droplets of ethanol below their boiling point which generate enough pressure to displace a soft-robot. The heater design and nebulizer integrate a compact actuation apparatus. The novel actuation system was tested on the developed mini soft-robot manufactured in our laboratory. A DDMC using an NFN as a force control was developed to validated the performance and applicability of the soft actuation. Experimental tests on the robot established the correctness of the proposed closed-loop force control. As a future work, an improved intelligent control with stability analysis for a mini soft-robot with more degrees-of-freedom that can overcome uncertainties, and non-linearities of more challenging force-reference environments will be studied. That should include an analysis of speed, acceleration and jerk. Additionally, we are working on a compact mini soft-robot where all components: power source, actuator, heater and release valve will be integrated into a single unit.

Acknowledgments. This work was supported by a grant from CONACyT through project CB-286907 that included a post doctoral fellowship for Josue Gomez.

References

1. Amend, J.R., Brown, E., Rodenberg, N., Jaeger, H.M., Lipson, H.: A positive pressure universal gripper based on the jamming of granular material. IEEE Trans. Rob. **28**(2), 341–350 (2012)
2. Anandharamakrishnan, C.: Spray-freeze-drying of coffee. In: Caffeinated and Cocoa Based Beverages, pp. 337–366. Elsevier (2019)

3. Facundo-Flores, L., Treesatayapun, C., Baltazar, A.: Design of a pose and force controller for a robotized ultrasonic probe based on neural networks and stochastic gradient approximation. IEEE Sens. J. **21**(5), 6224–6233 (2020)
4. Guerra-Bravo, E., Lee, H.J., Baltazar, A., Loh, K.J.: Vibration analysis of a piezoelectric ultrasonic atomizer to control atomization rate. Appl. Sci. **11**(18), 8350 (2021)
5. Hou, Z., Chi, R., Gao, H.: An overview of dynamic-linearization-based data-driven control and applications. IEEE Trans. Industr. Electron. **64**(5), 4076–4090 (2016)
6. Hou, Z., Zhu, Y.: Controller-dynamic-linearization-based model free adaptive control for discrete-time nonlinear systems. IEEE Trans. Industr. Inf. **9**(4), 2301–2309 (2013)
7. Lang, R.J.: Ultrasonic atomization of liquids. J. Acoust. Soc. Am. **34**(1), 6–8 (1962)
8. Lee, H.J., Guerra-Bravo, E., Baltazar, A., Loh, K.J.: Atomization control to improve soft actuation through vaporization. Front. Robot. AI **8**, 747440 (2021)
9. Lee, H.J., Prachaseree, P., Loh, K.J.: Rapid soft material actuation through droplet evaporation. Soft Rob. **8**(5), 555–563 (2021)
10. Li, Y., Cao, Y., Jia, F.: A neural network based dynamic control method for soft pneumatic actuator with symmetrical chambers. In: Actuators, vol. 10, p. 112. Multidisciplinary Digital Publishing Institute (2021)
11. Liu, H., Cheng, Q., Xiao, J., Hao, L.: Data-driven optimal tracking control for SMA actuated systems with prescribed performance via reinforcement learning. Mech. Syst. Signal Process. **177**, 109191 (2022)
12. Liu, H., Cheng, Q., Xiao, J., Hao, L.: Performance-based data-driven optimal tracking control of shape memory alloy actuated manipulator through reinforcement learning. Eng. Appl. Artif. Intell. **114**, 105060 (2022)
13. Mosadegh, B., et al.: Pneumatic networks for soft robotics that actuate rapidly. Adv. Func. Mater. **24**(15), 2163–2170 (2014)
14. Polygerinos, P., Wang, Z., Galloway, K.C., Wood, R.J., Walsh, C.J.: Soft robotic glove for combined assistance and at-home rehabilitation. Robot. Auton. Syst. **73**, 135–143 (2015)
15. Shepherd, R.F., et al.: Multigait soft robot. Proc. Natl. Acad. Sci. **108**(51), 20400–20403 (2011)
16. Suzumori, K., Endo, S., Kanda, T., Kato, N., Suzuki, H.: A bending pneumatic rubber actuator realizing soft-bodied manta swimming robot. In: Proceedings 2007 IEEE International Conference on Robotics and Automation, pp. 4975–4980. IEEE (2007)
17. Treesatayapun, C.: Fuzzy rules emulated discrete-time controller based on plant's input-output association. J. Control Autom. Electr. Syst. **30**(6), 902–910 (2019)
18. Treesatayapun, C., Uatrongjit, S.: Adaptive controller with fuzzy rules emulated structure and its applications. Eng. Appl. Artif. Intell. **18**(5), 603–615 (2005)
19. Treesatayapun, C.: Adaptive control based on if-then rules for grasping force regulation with unknown contact mechanism. Robot. Comput.-Integr. Manufact. **30**(1), 11–18 (2014)

Data-driven-modelling and Control for a Class of Discrete-Time Robotic System Using an Adaptive Tuning for Pseudo Jacobian Matrix Algorithm

Josué Gómez[1(✉)], América Morales[2], Chidentree Treesatayapun[2], and Rodrigo Muñiz[1]

[1] Facultad de Ingeniería de la Universidad Autónoma de Coahuila, Arteaga, Mexico
jogomezc@uadec.edu.mx

[2] Centro de Investigación y de Estudios Avanzados del Instituto Politécnico Nacional Unidad Saltillo, Ramos Arizpe, Mexico

Abstract. This paper proposes a data-driven modelling for a nonlinear discrete-time MIMO system in a robotic application, using a redundant robot for a trajectory tracking control of the end-effector. The Pseudo Jacobian Matrix computes an online equivalent model for the robotic system taking into account only two parameters tuning; the step parameter scales the estimation error and the weight parameter guarantees the estimation. The Lyapunov analysis based on a quadratic function in terms of the estimation error validates the setting parameters of the step parameter. A neuro-fuzzy network strcucture is used to adapt the step parameter considering the estimation error as input in oder to improve the identification of the Jacobian matrix during suddenly changes and uncertienties in the system. Besides, a novel control law is proposed for a trajectory tracking control based on a future function of the position error. The simulation results demonstrated the proposed data-driven model and control scheme for a redundant robot.

Keywords: Data-driven model · Pseudo jacobian matrix · Artificial neuro-fuzzy network · Step parameter · Control law design

1 Introduction

Advances in industrial instrumentation systems have been increasing remarkably in recent years, developing precise sensors and actuators for automation systems, [1]. In turn, advances in software and hardware design permit a better processing, storage and communication of instant information. Currently, robotic systems are equipped with online data communication technology, which allows Model Free Adaptive Control (MFAC) to be implemented only using the input and output signals of the system to perform position tasks, see [6] and [7]. From the data-driven control point of view, manipulator robots are considered as a nonlinear discrete-time Multi-Inputs and Multi-Outputs (MIMO) systems, see for instance [10]. The Pseudo Jacobian Matrix (PJM) algorithm becomes in a versatil option for position control in the task space of the end-effector,

O. Pichardo Lagunas et al. (Eds.): MICAI 2022, LNAI 13613, pp. 291–302, 2022.
https://doi.org/10.1007/978-3-031-19496-2_22

including redundant and no redundant robots [5]. Moreover, as is mentioned by [8], the only requirement to apply DDC (Data-Driven Control) is the association between the input and output signals of a robotic plant. On the previous researches, [2,3] and [4] demonstrated the data-driven control for a redundant robot using an estimated Jacobian matrix based on the concept of the PJM algorithms for real experiments.

The data-driven model of a robotic system is estimated by the PJM algorithm. This algorithm approximates the Jacobian matrix by the end-effector velocity observation and the estimation error tracking. Moreover, PJM algorithm only requires tuning two parameters to approximate the Jacobian matrix; the step parameter scales the estimation error and the weight parameter guarantees the estimation. However, both parameters remain constant during the Jacobian matrix estimation and the closed-loop control. Therefore, the step and weight parameters become impractical against suddenly changes, nonlinearities and uncertainties in the system. As well, the end-effector control and the Jacobian matrix computation for manipulator robots are time-varying and unrepeatable for each experiment and position task. As consequence, the step parameter should be tuned according to each end-effector axies coordinate demand.

The innovations of this research are: (a) the adaptation of the step parameter of the PJM algorithm using the estimation error as an input into a neuro-fuzzy artificial network, (b) the setting values for the step parameter are determined by the Lyapunov stability analysis in terms of the estimation error ans (c) the adaptive step parameter is able to detect disturbances and uncertienties during the online model estimation. In contrast, the model approximation using a fixed step parameter becomes vulnerable during suddenly changes in the system. The adaptive step parameter reduces the estimation error, and it allows a high identification of the Jacobian matrix during a kinematic control of the end-effector. This approach was applied to the academic platform KUKA youBot with 8° of freedom (dof); integrated by 3 dof in a mobile platform and 5 dof in a robotic arm. The joint configuration space of the robot is the Cartesian product $SE(2) \times \mathbb{T}^5$. In addition, a novel control law is approached to validate the performance of the PJM algorithm with adaptive step parameter.

The structure of this paper is: Sect. 2 describes the data-driven model approach, the Sect. 3 presents the control law proposal, Sect. 4 shows the results, and Sect. 5 gives the conclusions of the research.

2 Data-driven Model for Discrete-Time System

The position of the robot end-effector is defined in terms of the joints positions in continuous time

$$\chi(t) = f(q(t)) \tag{1}$$

where $\chi(t) \in \mathbb{R}^m$ is the robot's end-effector position, and $q(t) \in \mathbb{R}^n$ is the robot's joints positions. The velocity of the end-effector is

$$\dot{\chi}(t) = J_A^*(t)\dot{q}(t) \tag{2}$$

where $J_A^*(t) = \frac{\partial \chi(t)}{\partial q(t)} \in \mathbb{R}^{m \times n}$ is the ideal Jacobian matrix, and $\dot{q}(t)$ is the velocity of the joints. By this paper the system is working within discrete time domain, then the end-effector velocity (2) is approximated by

$$\frac{\chi(k+1)-\chi(k)}{T_s} = J_A^*(k)\frac{q(k)-q(k-1)}{T_s} \tag{3}$$

where T_s is the sampling time, $\nu(k+1) = \frac{\chi(k+1)-\chi(k)}{T_s}$ is the end-effector velocity, and $\omega(k) = \frac{q(k)-q(k-1)}{T_s}$ is the joints' velocities. For a first order kinematic control the Jacobian matrix $J_A^*(k)$ represents the model of the robot. The following assumption is required for the robot controller design.

Assumption 1. *The robotic system is Lipschitz and exists a positive constant L that defines the direct relationship between system input-output* $\parallel \nu(k+1) \parallel \leq L \parallel \omega(k) \parallel$. *That means, a bounded change of the output respect to a bounded change in the input.*

The representation of the ideal Jacobian matrix approach $J_A^*(k)$ is

$$J_A^*(k) = \hat{J}_A(k) + \epsilon(k) \tag{4}$$

where $\hat{J}_A(k)$ is the Jacobian matrix coming from an estimation method, and $\epsilon(k)$ is the estimation error. The position of robot's end-effector is in function of the joints' positions. The Jacobian matrix is approximated in discrete-time by the relationship of the output/input signals considering (2) in continuous time

$$J_A^*(t) = \frac{\partial\chi(t)}{\partial q(t)} \approx \frac{\Delta\chi(k+1)}{\Delta q(k)} \tag{5}$$

then, the approximation in (5) can be written in discrete-time as

$$\hat{J}_A(k) = \frac{\nu(k+1)}{\omega(k)} \tag{6}$$

the structure of the Jacobian matrix is

$$\hat{J}_A(k) = \begin{bmatrix} \hat{J}_{A_{x1}}(k) \cdots\cdots \hat{J}_{A_{xn}}(k) \\ \hat{J}_{A_{y1}}(k) \cdots\cdots \hat{J}_{A_{yn}}(k) \\ \hat{J}_{A_{z1}}(k) \cdots\cdots \hat{J}_{A_{zn}}(k) \end{bmatrix} \in \mathbb{R}^{3\times n} \tag{7}$$

where n is equal to the number of robot dof and the system is considered as a MIMO system. The second assumption is established for the data driven model and control.

Assumption 2. *The output is observable, i.e.,* $\nu(k+1) = \hat{J}_A(k)\omega(k)\ \forall k > 0$. *It is possible to identify the equivalent model of the system from the measured output signals.*

The Jacobian matrix is approximated by the adaptive PJM algorithm, see for instance [?]. The updated estimated Jacobina matrix is

$$\hat{J}_A(k+1) = \hat{J}_A(k) + \frac{\eta\left[J_A^*(k)\omega(k) - \hat{J}_A(k)\omega(k)\right]\omega^T(k)}{\mu + \parallel \omega(k) \parallel^2} \tag{8}$$

where $\mu \in \mathbb{R}^+$ is a weight parameter and $\eta \in \mathbb{R}^+$ is a step parameter.

2.1 Equivalent Model Stability Analysis

This section looks for the Lyapunov stability analysis of the equivalent model based on PJM algorithm in (8). The updated estimation error is

$$\epsilon(k+1) = J_A^*(k+1) - \hat{J}_A(k+1) \tag{9}$$

and $J_A^*(k+1) = J_A^*(k)$, for the ideal Jacobian matrix the estimation error is going to be zero $\epsilon(k) = 0$ when $k \to \infty$, and the updated estimated Jacobian matrix is

$$\hat{J}_A(k+1) = \hat{J}_A(k) + \Theta_k \parallel \omega(k) \parallel^2 \epsilon(k) \tag{10}$$

where

$$\Theta_k = \frac{\eta}{\mu + \parallel \omega \parallel^2} > 0, \in \mathbb{R}^+ \tag{11}$$

when replacing (10) in the updated estimation error matrix in (9) the error estimation matrix is

$$\begin{aligned} \epsilon(k+1) &= J_A^*(k+1) - \hat{J}_A(k+1) \\ &= J_A^*(k) - \hat{J}_A(k) - \Theta_k \parallel \omega(k) \parallel^2 \epsilon(k) \\ &= \epsilon(k) - \epsilon(k)\Theta_k \parallel \omega(k) \parallel^2 \end{aligned} \tag{12}$$

now it is possible to obtain the change in the estimation error

$$\begin{aligned} \epsilon(k+1) - \epsilon(k) &= -\epsilon(k)\Theta_k \parallel \omega(k) \parallel^2 \\ \Delta\epsilon(k+1) &= -\epsilon(k)\Theta_k \parallel \omega(k) \parallel^2 \end{aligned} \tag{13}$$

Theorem 1. *If the MIMO system in (6) is observable and Lipschitz, then $\epsilon(k) \approx 0$, and $\hat{J}_A(k) \approx J_A^*(k)$ when PJM algorithm is applied.*

Proof. Considering the following discrete Lyapunov function

$$V_{\text{sys}}(k+1) = \frac{1}{2}\epsilon(k+1)\epsilon^T(k+1) \tag{14}$$

the change in the Lyapunov function is

$$\Delta V_{\text{sys}}(k+1) = V_{\text{sys}}(k+1) - V_{\text{sys}}(k) \tag{15}$$

the change in the Lyapunov function in terms of the estimation error $\Delta\epsilon(k+1)$ is

$$\Delta V_{\text{sys}}(k+1) = \Delta\epsilon(k+1)\left[\epsilon(k) + \frac{1}{2}\Delta\epsilon(k+1)\right]^T \tag{16}$$

substituting the estimation error from (13) in the change in Lyapunov function

$$\Delta V_{\text{sys}}(k+1) = -\epsilon(k)\epsilon^T\Theta_k \parallel \omega(k) \parallel^2 \left[1 - \frac{1}{2}\Theta_k \parallel \omega(k) \parallel^2\right] \tag{17}$$

the Lyapunov condition is $V_{sys}(k+1) > 0$ and $\Delta V_{sys}(k+1) < 0$, then from (17) the next inequality should satisfy

$$\Phi_k = 1 - \frac{1}{2}\frac{\eta \parallel \omega(k) \parallel^2}{\mu + \parallel \omega(k) \parallel^2} > 0, \in \mathbb{R}^+ \tag{18}$$

Remark 1. *The upper and lower bounded velocities are determined according to the actuators saturation to avoid possible mechanical damages into the robot. At the beginning, the estimation error is far from zero and the control signals are close to the saturation values.*

Therefore, when $k \to \infty$ then $\omega(k) \approx 0$ the stability condition Φ_k is satisfied according to (18). The value of saturation actutor $\omega_{sat}(k)$ depends directly on the robot physical condition. However, to avoid damages into the KUKA youBot actuators the operating range of the revolute joints is $\omega(k)_{sat} = \pm 0.6\frac{rad}{sec}$. From (18) the next inequality should satisfy

$$2(\mu + \parallel \omega_{sat}(k) \parallel^2) > \parallel \omega_{sat}(k) \parallel^2 \eta \tag{19}$$

Then, $\Phi_k \leq \Upsilon$, where Υ is the upper bounded constant, when $\Phi_k(||\omega_{sat}(k)||, \eta_{\text{Max}})$, hence (17) becomes:

$$\Delta V_{sys}(k+1) \leq -||\epsilon(k)||^2 \Theta_k \parallel \omega(k) \parallel^2 \Phi_k \tag{20}$$

Therefore, $V_{sys}(k+1) > 0$ and $\Delta V_{sys}(k+1) < 0$, when (19) is fulfilled and $\mu > 0$, moreover $\epsilon(k) \approx 0$, *i.e.* $J^*_A(k)\hat{J}^\dagger_A(k) \approx I$ as $k \to \infty$. ■

2.2 Neuro-fuzzy Network and Adaptive Step Parameter

In this section the varying step parameter $\eta_i(k)$ is designed according to a neuro-fuzzy network and let's consider only adaptation for each axis, where the i-th axis corresponding to x, y and z axes, respectively.

The estimation error $\epsilon_i(k)$ is the input to the artificial neuro-fuzzy network to tune the online step parameter $\eta_i(k)$. The artificial neuro-fuzzy network consists of the Fuzzy Rules Emulated Network (FREN) structure; their main characteristics are the online adaptation and the reasoning ability, proposed by [9]. The architecture of FREN can be seen in Fig. 1.

The structure of FERN is as follows:

Layer 1: The estimation error $\epsilon_i(k)$ is the input of this layer which is sent to each node in the next layer directly.

Layer 2: This is called input membership function layer. Each node in this layer contains a membership function corresponding to one linguistic variable. The output at the jth node of this layer is calculated by ϕ_{ij} as

$$\phi_{ij} = \mu_{ij}(\epsilon_i) \tag{21}$$

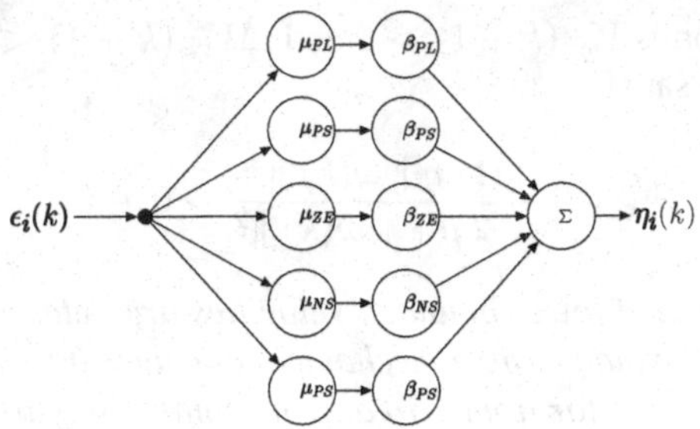

Fig. 1. Artificial Neural Network architecture.

where μ_{ij} denotes the membership function at the jth node ($j = 1, 2, ..., N$) of the ith axis. The five membership functions are: PL is positive large, PS is positive small, ZE is zero, NS is negative small, and NL is negative large.

Layer 3: This layer may be considered as a defuzzification step. It is called the linear consequence (LC) layer, where the parameters β_{ij} are selected by the experince to the robotic system.

Layer 4: This is the output of the artificial neuro-fuzzy network and is calculated as

$$\eta_i(k) = \sum_{j=1}^{N} \beta_{ij}\phi_{ij} \tag{22}$$

where N represents the number of linguistic variables.

The generalized rules for the realtionship among the function $\epsilon_i(k)$ and the adaptive step parameter η_i are:

1. IF $\epsilon_i(k)$ is Positive Large (PL), THEN $\eta_i(k)$ is Positive Large (PL),
2. IF $\epsilon_i(k)$ is Positive Small (PS), THEN $\eta_i(k)$ is Positive Small (PS),
3. IF $\epsilon_i(k)$ is Zero (ZE), THEN $\eta_i(k)$ is Zero (ZE),
4. IF ϵ_i is Negative Large (NL), THEN η_i is Negative Large (NL),
5. IF $\epsilon_i(k)$ is Negative Small (NS), THEN $\eta_i(k)$ is Negative Small (NS).

Accordingly, the values of the membership functions ϕ_{ij} are from 0 to 1 and the β_{ij} parameters are positive. Therefore, the selection of the β_{ij} parameters is possible regarding the performance of the step parameter η_x, η_y and η_z. The maximum value of β_{ij} is determined by the maximum value of $\eta_{ij} = 7.55$ regarding (19) for $\mu = 1$, hence $\beta ij = \eta_i \phi_{ij}^{-1}$. As a result, the lower and the upper bounded constants for the βi values are as follows:

$$0 < \beta_{ij} < 7.55 \tag{23}$$

The five rules are designed according to the system stability analysis through Theorem 1 and (19). The parameters β_{xj}, β_{yj} and β_{zj} in Table 1 are setting according to the guidelines demonstrated in through the conditions in (23).

Table 1. Value of β_{ij} parameters.

Parameters	Value
β_{PL}	7
β_{NL}	5
β_{ZE}	3.5
β_{NS}	2
β_{NL}	1

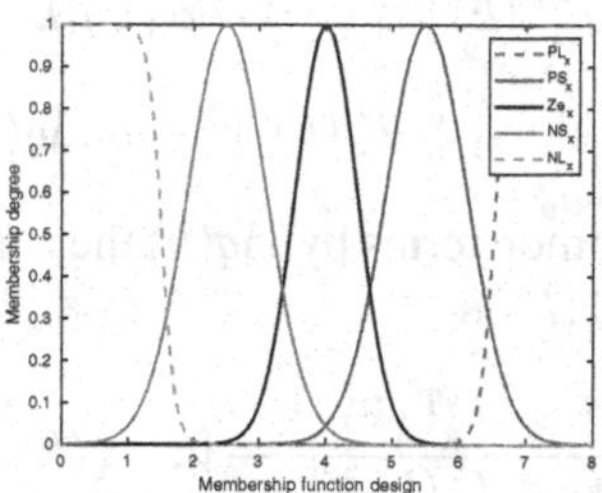

Fig. 2. The 5 membership functions designed in terms of η stability conditions.

3 Control Law

In this section the control law is designed according to the estimated Jacobian matrix. The error is defined as

$$e(k+1) = \chi(k+1) - \chi_d(k+1) \tag{24}$$

where $\chi(k+1)$ is the current position of the end-effector and $\chi_d(k+1)$ is the desired position. The controller design considers the future error function as

$$s(k+1) = \alpha_1 e(k+1) + \alpha_2 e(k) \tag{25}$$

where α_1 and α_2 are positive constants. The position of the robot's end-effector is

$$\begin{aligned} \chi(k+1) &= \chi(k) + \bar{J}_A(k)\omega(k) \\ &= \chi(k) + T_s\hat{J}_A(k)\omega(k) + T_s\epsilon(k)\omega(k) \end{aligned} \tag{26}$$

where $\bar{J}_A(k) = J_A^*(k)T_s$ includes the ideal Jacobian matrix and the sampling time. Then, from (4) the ideal Jacobian is $J_A^*(k) = \hat{J}_A(k) + \epsilon(k)$. Substituting the current position (26) in the control error (24)

$$\begin{aligned} e(k+1) &= \chi(k) + \bar{J}_A(k)\omega(k) - \chi_d(k+1) \\ &= \chi(k) + J_A^*(k)\Delta q(k) - \chi_d(k+1) \end{aligned} \tag{27}$$

equally, the future error function can be written in terms of the control error

$$\begin{aligned} s(k+1) = &\alpha_1 \left[\chi(k) + J_A^*(k)\Delta q(k) - \chi_d(k+1)\right] \\ &+ \alpha_2 e(k) \end{aligned} \tag{28}$$

considering the next cost function

$$\xi_c(k+1) = \frac{1}{2} \parallel s(k+1) \parallel^2 + \frac{1}{2}\rho \parallel \Delta q(k) \parallel^2 \tag{29}$$

where ρ is a positive constant value, and differentiating the cost function $\xi_c(k+1)$ with respect to $\Delta q(k)$ in (29), it is possible to find the optimal value of the cost function when $\dfrac{\partial \xi_c(k+1)}{\partial \Delta q(k)} = 0$

$$\begin{aligned} \frac{\partial \xi_c(k+1)}{\partial \Delta q(k)} =& J_A^{*T}(k) \left[\alpha_1 \chi(k) - \alpha_1 \chi_d(k+1) + \alpha_2 e(k)\right] \\ &+ \left[\alpha_1 \parallel J_A^{*}(k) \parallel^2 + \rho\right] \Delta q(k) = 0 \end{aligned} \tag{30}$$

simplifying and grouping common terms by $\Delta q(k)$ the controller is in terms of the ideal Jacobian matrix modelling $J_A^{*}(k)$ is

$$\begin{aligned} \Delta q(k) =& -\frac{J_A^{*T}(k)}{\alpha_1 \parallel J_A^{*}(k) \parallel^2 + \rho}[\alpha_1(\chi(k) - \chi_d(k+1)) \\ &+ \alpha_2 e(k)] \end{aligned} \tag{31}$$

assuming that the equivalent model $\hat{J}_A(k)$ is approximated to the ideal Jacobian $J_A^{*}(k)$, and substituting the desired position $\chi_d(k+1) = \chi_d(k) + \Delta\chi_d(k+1)$. The control law is established by

$$\Delta q(k) = -\hat{J}_A^{T}(k) \frac{1}{\alpha_1 \|\hat{J}_A(k)\|^2 + \rho} \left[\alpha^* e(k) - \alpha_1 \Delta\chi_d(k+1)\right] \tag{32}$$

wherer $\alpha^* = \alpha_1 + \alpha_2$. Besides, for a first order kinematic control through $\omega(k)$ as a control signal, the end-effector Cartesian velocity $\nu(k+1)$ must reach the desired velocity of the end-effector while $\nu(k+1) \to \nu_d(k+1)$. The control law in (32) is

$$\omega(k) = -\hat{J}_A^{\dagger}(k) C_k u(k) \tag{33}$$

where C_k is a diagonal matrix with gains, and $u(k)$ is the control law as follows

$$u(k) = \left[\alpha^* e(k) - \alpha_1 \nu_d(k+1)\right] \tag{34}$$

the control law $u(k)$ in (34) is designed at velocity level, and α^* is a design parameter to scale the convergence rate. The robot control is based on the adjustment gains for each robot axis independently of each other. Considering the dynamic system from the equivalent Jacobian matrix, $\hat{J}_A(k)$ is defined in (8). Hence, the control design uses the i-th row of the Jacobian matrix as follow: $\hat{J}_{A_x}(k) = \frac{\nu_x(k+1)}{\omega_n(k)}$, $\hat{J}_{A_y}(k) = \frac{\nu_y(k+1)}{\omega_n(k)}$, and $\hat{J}_{A_z}(k) = \frac{\nu_z(k+1)}{\omega_n(k)}$. In this way C_k is a diagonal matrix

$$C_k = \begin{bmatrix} C_{kx} & 0 & 0 \\ 0 & C_{ky} & 0 \\ 0 & 0 & C_{kz} \end{bmatrix} \in \mathbb{R}^{3\times 3} \tag{35}$$

which contains the gains according to the end-effector axis

$$C_{ki} = \frac{1}{\alpha_1 \|\hat{J}_{A_i}(k)\|^2 + \rho_i} \tag{36}$$

where $\rho_i > 0$. The inverse kinematics determines the joint parameters that involves the end-effector desired position. The pseudo inverse Jacobian matrix $\hat{J}_A^\dagger(k)$ is

$$\hat{J}_A^\dagger(k) = \hat{J}_A^T(k) \left[\hat{J}_A(k) \hat{J}_A^T(k) + \xi I \right]^{-1} \tag{37}$$

where $\hat{J}_A^\dagger(k)$ is built with the PJM and FREN algorithms, and $\xi = 0.01$ is the damping factor. The updated joints' positions are

$$q(k+1) = q(k) + \omega(k) T_s \tag{38}$$

the signal in (38) allows end-effector update to reach the desired position.

4 Results

Figure 3(a) depicts the simulation results for a tracking trajectory control of the end-effector, applying the PJM algorithm in (8) with adaptive step $\eta_i(k)$ parameters by FREN (22) and the proposed control law in (33) and (34). Figure 3(a) shows a circular trajectory of the end-effector expressed by:

$$\begin{aligned} \chi_{xd}(k+1) &= 1 + 0.15 \sin\left(\tfrac{4\pi k}{kmax}\right) \\ \chi_{yd}(k+1) &= 0.15 \cos\left(\tfrac{4\pi k}{kmax}\right) \\ \chi_{zd}(k+1) &= 0.5 \end{aligned} \tag{39}$$

The conditions of the simulation are in Table 2 regarding the condition in (19) and the control laws in (34).

Figure 3(b) shows the control errors convergence in the 3 axes, where the proposed control law remedies the convergence successfully. Figure 3(c) depicts the 2 prismatic

Table 2. Parameters setting for robot model and control.

Parameters	Values
μ	1
α_1	2.5
α_2	0.85
ρ_x	0.65
ρ_y	0.65
ρ_z	0.5
ξ	0.01

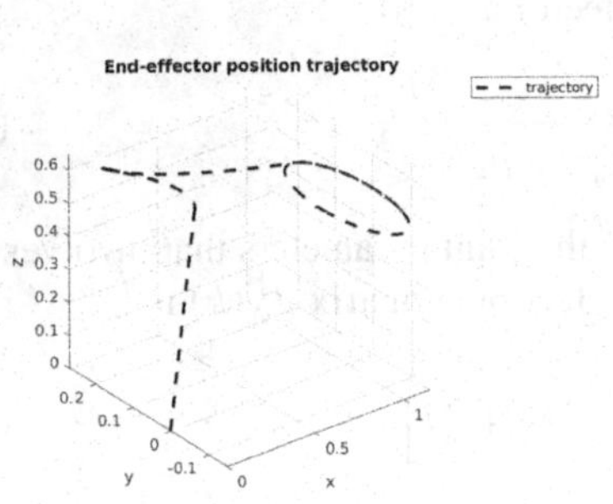

(a) End-effector position trajectory the x, y and z directions tracking control.

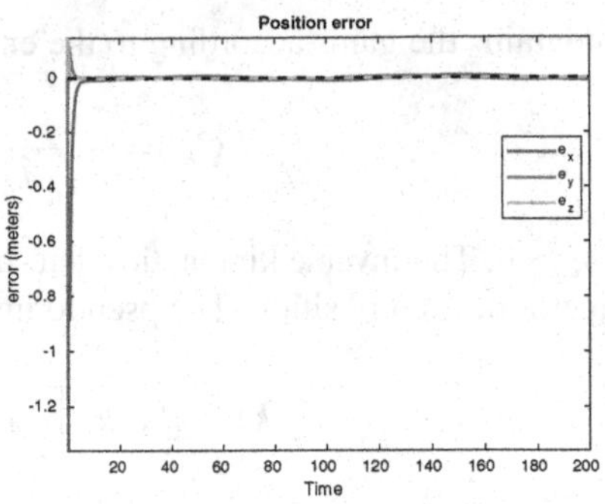

(b) Control position error in x, y and z.

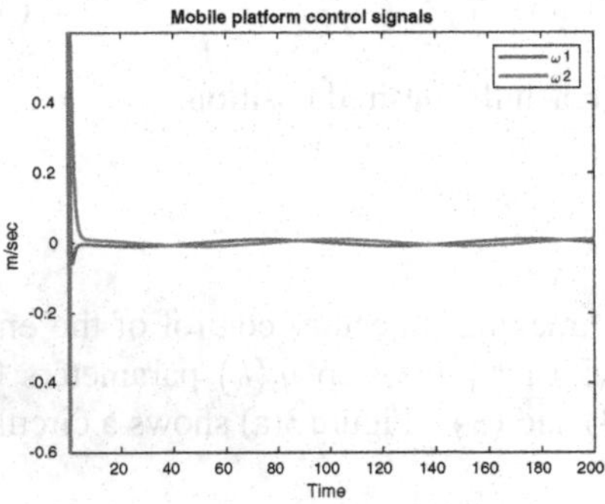

(c) Performance of the control signal for prismatic joints $\omega_1(k)$ and $\omega_2(k)$ of the mobile platform.

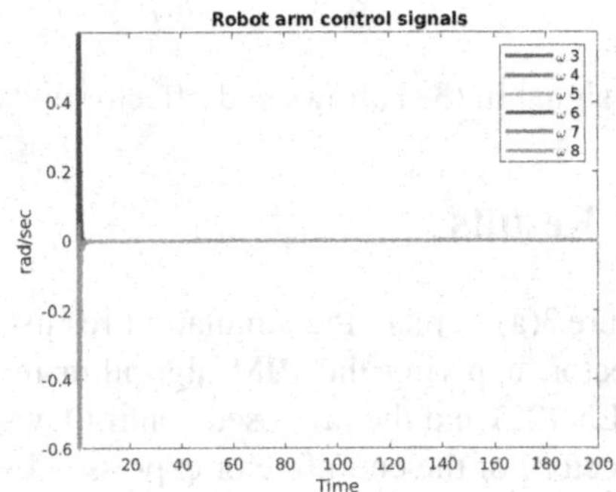

(d) Performance of the control signal for revolute joints: revolute joint of the mobile platform $\omega_3(k)$, and from $\omega_4(k)$ to $\omega_8(k)$ of the robotic arm.

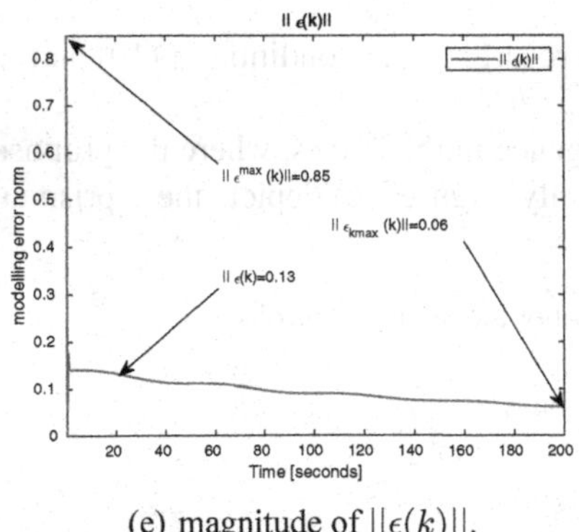

(e) magnitude of $||\epsilon(k)||$.

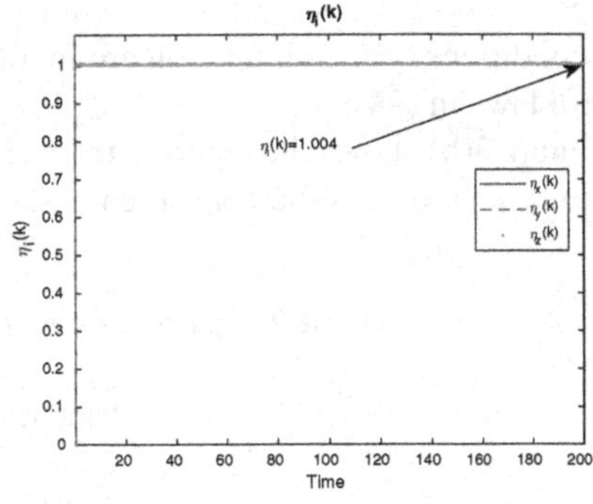

(f) The adaptation of the step parameters $\eta_i(k)$.

Fig. 3. Results for the tracking control: (a) end-effector position, (b) control error, (c) prismatic joints, (d) revolute joints, (e) magnitude of $||\epsilon(k)||$, and (f) adaptive step parameter η_i(k).

joints velocities, where is easily observed the circular trajectory in the mobile platform in order to follow the desired trajectory for the end-effector. The revolute joints velocities are considered smooth in Fig. 3(d), and also it is should be noted that the boundaries values of the actuators are $\omega_{\text{rev}} \pm 0.6\frac{rad}{sec}$. Figure 3(e) represents the magnitude of the estimation error $||\epsilon(k)||$ for the direct relationship between the ideal and estimated Jacobina matrix $P_k = J_A^*(k)\hat{J}_A^\dagger(k) \approx I$ where $||\epsilon(k)|| \to 0$ during $k \to \infty$. Therefore, the maximum order of the estiamtion error occurs at the beginning of the Jacobian estimation $||\epsilon^{\max}(k)|| = 0.85$, as the Jacobian matrix is estimated by the PJM algorithm using FREN for the step parameter, the magnitude of the estimation error is descending to $||\epsilon_{\text{kmax}}(k)|| = 0.06$. Finally, Fig. 3(f) depicts the adaptation of the step parameter $\eta_i(k)$, where the β_{ij} in (23) and the membership function in Fig. 2 are designed according to characteristics of the robot.

Regarding the stability condition in (19) the next inequality needs to be satisfies $\eta_i(k) < 7.55$, then the *Theorem 1* is dissatisfied when the step parameter is constant $\eta = 9$, hence this value neglects the inequality in (19). Therefore, the control-loop system is unstable for $\epsilon(k) \neq 0$ and $e(k) \neq 0$ during $k \to \infty$ as is appreciated in Fig. 4 (a) and (b), respectively. In this strict case, the Lyapunov stability condition in (20) is unfulfilled.

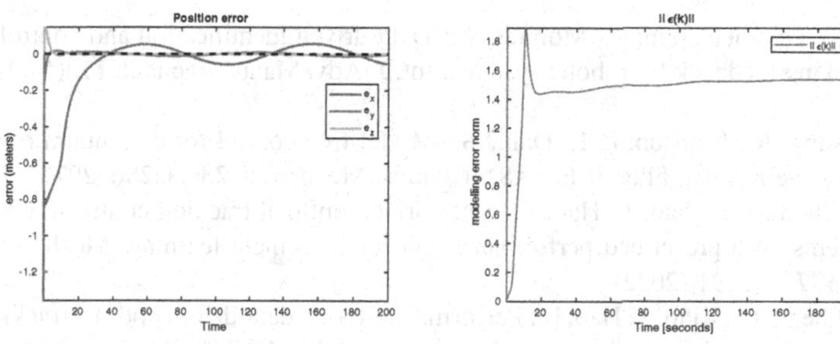

(a) Unstable case for the position error in the x, y and z directions.

(b) Unstable case for the estimation error.

Fig. 4. Unstable case conditions.

5 Conclusions

The data-driven model was tested for a 8 dof redundant robot from the academic platform KUKA youBot. The PJM algorithm only requires to know the input and output signals of the robot to approximate the Jacobian matrix. Also, it only needs to tune 2 parameters; the step and the weight parameter simplifying the computation of the Jacobian matrix. The Lyapunov stability analysis of the system was determined to set the step parameters values. Once, this setting parameters are known, FREN strcucture is used to adapt the step parameter considering the estimation error as input. The simulation results demonstrated the performance of the adaptive step parameter during the trajectory tracking of the end-effector to reduce the estimation and control error, satisfactorily. It allows a better identification of the Jacobian matrix during a kinematic control of the end-effector. The magnitude of the estimation error decreased to 0.06, that means 94% of the Jacobian matrix approximation. In addition, the proposed control law based in a future function of the error was validated by the simulation. This controller allowed the robot end-effector to robustness the performance of trajectory tracking for position task. As a future work, a more challenge simulations will tested and the closed-loop approach will be validated in an experimental setup.

Acknowledgments. The authors thank to the Facultad de Ingeniería de la Universidad Autónoma de Coahuila.

References

1. Bolton, W.: Instrumentation and control systems. Newnes (2021)
2. Gómez, J., Treesatayapun, C., Morales, A.: Free model task space controller based on adaptive gain for robot manipulator using Jacobian estimation. In: Batyrshin, I., Martínez-Villaseñor, M.L., Ponce Espinosa, H.E. (eds.) MICAI 2018. LNCS (LNAI), vol. 11289, pp. 264–275. Springer, Cham (2018). https://doi.org/10.1007/978-3-030-04497-8_22
3. Gómez, J., Treesatayapun, C., Morales, A.: Multi-inputs and multi-outputs equivalent model based on data driven controller for a robotic system. IFAC-PapersOnLine **53**(2), 9784–9789 (2020)
4. Gómez, J., Treesatayapun, C., Morales, A.: Data-driven identification and control based on optic tracking feedback for robotic systems. Int. J. Adv. Manuf. Technol. **113**(5), 1485–1503 (2021)
5. Li, M., Kang, R., Branson, D.T., Dai, J.S.: Model-free control for continuum robots based on an adaptive Kalman filter. IEEE/ASME Trans. Mechatron. **23**(1), 286–297 (2018)
6. Liu, H., Cheng, Q., Xiao, J., Hao, L.: Data-driven optimal tracking control for SMA actuated systems with prescribed performance via reinforcement learning. Mech. Syst. Signal Process. **177**, 109191 (2022)
7. Liu, H., Cheng, Q., Xiao, J., Hao, L.: Performance-based data-driven optimal tracking control of shape memory alloy actuated manipulator through reinforcement learning. Eng. Appl. Artif. Intell. **114**, 105060 (2022)
8. Treesatayapun, C.: Fuzzy rules emulated discrete-time controller based on plant's input-output association. J. Control, Autom. Electr. Syst. **30**(6), 902–910 (2019)
9. Treesatayapun, C., Uatrongjit, S.: Adaptive controller with fuzzy rules emulated structure and its applications. Eng. Appl. Artif. Intell. **18**(5), 603–615 (2005)
10. Zen, Z., Cao, R., Hou, Z.: MIMO model free adaptive control of two degree of freedom manipulator. In: 2018 IEEE 7th Data Driven Control and Learning Systems Conference (DDCLS), pp. 693–697. IEEE (2018)

Retrieval-based Statistical Chatbot in a Scientometric Domain

Victor Lopez-Rodriguez and Hector G. Ceballos(✉)

Tecnologico de Monterrey, Monterrey, Mexico
ceballos@tec.mx
https://www.tec.mx/

Abstract. The scope of this research work is to integrate a statistical ontology model of scientometric indicators in a chatbot. Building a chatbot requires the use of Natural Language Processing (NLP) as a capability for recognizing users' intent and extracting entities from users' questions. We proposed a method for recognizing the requested indicator and transforming the question expressed in natural language into a query to the semantic model. The chatbot and the ontology model represent a novel framework that can answer questions about Scientometric Indicators. The chatbot is evaluated in terms of Goal Completion Rate (GCR). It measures how many questions the chatbot answered correctly and identifies intent and entity extraction correctly. The second evaluation approach of the chatbot is a survey that focuses on usability, the strictness of language variations, chatbot comprehension, correlation in chatbot responses, and user satisfaction.

Keywords: Chatbot · Statistical ontology · Natural language processing · Scientometric indicators

1 Introduction

A chatbot is a machine conversation system that interacts with human users via natural conversational language [1]. Chatbots are increasing their appearance in several environments related to software interaction with humans. This software is used to perform tasks such as quickly responding to users, informing them, helping them purchase products, and providing better service to customers [2]. Common chatbots' applications are Frequently Asked Questions (FAQ), Customer Support, and helping users obtain fast answers to their questions. The chatbot creates strength in the methodology by implementing several Natural Language Processing techniques that allow the user to feel a one-to-one conversation. One of the best advantages of using a chatbot is creating context in a conversation. Comparing the chatbot against other alternatives such as Online Query or Dashboards, the conversation agent can use the conversation history, including questions and answers, to create a context and have a fluent conversation with correct responses.

Supported by organization x.

O. Pichardo Lagunas et al. (Eds.): MICAI 2022, LNAI 13613, pp. 303–315, 2022.
https://doi.org/10.1007/978-3-031-19496-2_23

The chatbot domain is about Scientometric Indicators. The term scientometrics was coined by Vassily V. Nalimov in the 1960s and referred to the science of measuring and analyzing science, such as a discipline's structure, growth, change, and interrelations [3]. Scientometric analysis studies the quantitative areas of the process of science, science policy, and communication in science by having a focus on the measure of authors, articles, journals, and institutions by understanding citations related to them [4].

Reviewing the state of the art, we found a relevant research work that present the use of a chatbot for solving a specific task. Baby [8] presented a chatbot using Natural Language Processing techniques to understand and extract key information on user requests. The chatbot was connected to a web application for home automation and performed several tasks such as fan or light controlling and other electrical appliances. In our research work, a chatbot approach is to fully understand the request and create a context to have better insight for answers.

The main research question of this work relies on how a retrieval-based chatbot can be used along with an ontology model as a knowledge-base to answer questions in natural language in the Scientometric Indicator domain. We stated the following specific research questions to design the methodology: How to fully understand users' intents related to scientometric indicators? Which important keywords does the chatbot need to recognize to perform the tasks? If there is not enough information to answer the question, how will the chatbot converse to create a context to gather the needed data?

The objective of this research work is apply an ontology model that allows the chatbot to understand and classify the user's input to extract the correct information and answer the question correctly. The goal is to propose and design a scalable chatbot that can be used in the future in other academic areas or industries.

The chatbot will be validated in terms of completeness. Completeness refers to a specific set of indicators in which the chatbot recognizes and answers correctly. Time validation is a subject of study in performance; unfortunately, previous work does not exist that we can use to compare the new development in this research work.

This research work consists of 4 Sections including the introduction. Methodology is presented in Sect. 2. In Sect. 3 results are shown along its discussion. Finally, in Sect. 4, we present conclusions and future work.

2 Methodology

The strategy that the chatbot follows is a retrieval-based approach. For this research work, we will extend the work proposed in [5] which a semantic modeling of scientometric indicators using the ontology Statistical Data and Metadata (SDMX) is proposed. This ontology contains a set of scientometric indicators stored in a graph database in Neo4j. It is an updatable ontology model and will provide a quick access for retrieving information in our proposed chatbot.

Our chatbot is classified in the closed domain of Scientometric Indicators. It is a task-based chatbot whose main task is to answer questions related to the mentioned domain. In order to answer the questions, the chatbot will follow a retrieval-based strategy that will use the ontology model to dig into data and return values in the form of answers.

2.1 Natural Language Processing

This section of the methodology will analyze the natural language questions that the users may ask to the Chatbot. As one of the initial steps, some frequently asked questions were retrieved in order to understand their characteristics and patterns.

After we analyze this information, we decided to define a classification that will allow us to detect the intention of the question and prepare the process to answer it. The complexity of questions depends on the number of indicator values recovered and the type of calculations applied for generating the answer. Depending on the complexity of the question, the categories are described as follow:

- Low Complexity: Simple questions with a direct answer, i.e. a single indicator value is required for answering.
- Medium Complexity: Questions that require calculations such as sum, average, difference or further analysis, i.e. two or more indicator values are recovered and combined for providing a new value.
- High Complexity: Questions that require machine learning models for prediction, i.e. multiple indicator values are recovered and a series of expected values are generated.

We also add the greeting and none intent. Greeting intent will be used to identify when the user wants to start a conversation in the chatbot and the None intent is empty at purpose because we can identify questions out of the domain.

2.2 Intent Classificaiton and Entity Extraction

In this step of the methodology we will identify the intention of the question and extract relevant information from it to be able to answer it. An intent can be represented as a task or action the user wants to perform, it can be considered as a purpose or goal. An entity can be defined as words or phrases inside the utterance that describe important information of the intent. We proposed the following entities:

- Indicador: Entity created for finding Scientometric Indicator names.
- Lugar: Entity created for finding a school, set of schools, or referring to Tecnologico de Monterrey that considers all the schools.

- Objecto: Entity created for obtaining the “thing” that we are looking for in medium complexity intentions.
- Tiempo: Entity created for finding years or time related words.
- Tipo Indicador: Entity created for finding if the Scientometric Indicator refers to annual or quinquenial type.

2.3 Data Labeling

The next step is to label entities in all the utterances in each intent type as shown in Table 1. With the intent classification and entities labeling, we are ready for training the model.

Table 1. Intent and Entities labeling

Intent	Uterrance examples	Indicador	Lugar	Objeto	Tiempo	Tipo indicador
Greeting	Hola	NA	NA	NA	NA	NA
Low Complexity	Cuántos SNIS hay en el Tec en el 2019?	SNIS	Tec	NA	2019	NA
Medium Complexity	Cuál ha sido el año con el menor número de SNIS?	SNIS	NA	Año	NA	NA
High Complexity	Cuál citas habrá en el 2025?	citas	NA	citas	2025	NA
None	Empty	NA	NA	NA	NA	NA

2.4 Model Training

We choose to use an Artificial Intelligence service from Azure Cognitive Service called Language Understanding (Luis). This service applies custom machine learning intelligence to user's conventional natural language text to predict the meaning or pull out relevant information. One of the reasons for choosing this approach is the integration with the Chatbot framework of Azure.

The next step of the process is to train the model. Training is performed in Luis AI service and is done iteratively. We start by randomly selecting 5 utterances with different classification of intents and already having the entities labeling done in the previous step. We train the model and make some tests to observe the accuracy of correct identification and extraction. We continue doing this step iteratively until we reach the 50 utterances including several variations to the questions to achieve a better result.

2.5 Scientometric Indicator Identification

In this methodology process, we will use the intent identification and entities extraction of the natural language question to identify the Scientometric Indicator that the user wants an answer about. The first part is to obtain descriptive information of the Scientometric Indicators and we will obtain this by querying the ontology model as shown in Fig. 1.

"match(n:ns0__DataSet) return n.rdfs__label as entities, n.rdfs__comment as dataset"

Fig. 1. Query for obtaining Scientometric Indicators Dataset labels and description.

By matching all the nodes of type dataset and return all the rdf:labels and comments of the dataset that will allow us to make a knowledge base of Indicators for the Chatbot. The result of the query will be transformed from a json data type to a dictionary to be able to use it in a further process. The knowledge base of True Scientometric Indicators is shown in the following list and it contains the description of the Indicator and relevant tags extracted from the label node property.

- annual publications scopus-tec datase: ['publication', 'annual']
- annual school publications dataset: ['school', 'publication', 'annual']
- quinquennial school publication dataset: ['quinquennial', 'school', 'publication']
- quinquennial school cites dataset: ['quinquennial', 'school', 'cite']
- annual school document cites dataset: ['cite', 'school', 'annual']
- researchers dataset: ['researcher', 'annual']
- posdocs dataset: ['posdoc', 'annual']
- quinquennial publications dataset: ['quinquennial', 'publication']
- quinquennial cites dataset: ['quinquennial', 'cite']
- document cites dataset: ['quinquennial', 'cite']

Suppose we have the following natural language question: How many publications were made in the quinquenium ending in 2021?, by sending this question to Luis AI service, it will return the following response.

- topIntent: Low Complexity
- entities: indicador: 'publicaciones', tipo indicador: 'quinquenales', tiempo: '2021', Lugar: "

In order to identify the correct Scientometric Indicator to which the natural language question is referring, we will work with both sets. Our approach for a correct identification is to use the set theory.

- Equal Sets: When elements (labels) are the same members of True Scientometric Indicator and Tags Sets. Also called super sets.
- Proper Subset: When elements (labels) from Tag Set are included in the True Scientometric Indicator Set elements but still have other elements missing to be a Super Set.
- None equal Sets: Both sets have difference elements.

The result of matching the indicator of the mentioned question is having an equal set with the quinquennial publications dataset indicator.

2.6 Natural Language Transformation into Cypher Query

In this last step of the methodology, we will use the intent identification provided by Luis AI service. Depending on the complexity intention, there is an structured query ready with some parameters to fulfill with the entities extracted from the natural language question. Our approach for this chatbot will only focus in the low complexity intention. We define the following parameters to fullfil the query structure:

- uri_observation: Uses the following URI (https://www.tec.mx/ontos/observation/) defined in our ontology model for querying Scientometric Indicator observations.
- dataset_name: This value is obtained from the True Scientometric Indicator Set in which the descriptive value is selected by matching with the Exact Indicator key.
- time: Numerical value obtained after comparing with Time Knowledge-base, if the indicator is of type annual we will only use a year. However, if it is quinquennial, we will use the range period of year-(year-5).
- school: If the label school is in our tags, the structure changes and we add the condition by obtaining the value of the entity Lugar.
- indicators_property: This value is obtained from the Measure knowledge base by matching the Exact Indicator key.

After filling up all the values of our parameters, we run the following query in Fig. 2.

```
  if 'school' in tags:
      query = ("match(n:ns0__Observation) " +
              "where n.uri = " + uri_observation + dataset_name + "/" + time + "/" +
str(entities.get('lugar')) + "/count' "
              "return n."+indicators_property+" as result " )
  else:
      query = ("match(n:ns0__Observation) " +
              "where n.uri = " + uri_observation + dataset_name + "/" + time + "/count' "
              "return n."+indicators_property+" as result " )


  return query
```

Fig. 2. Natural language question into cypher query.

2.7 Chatbot Deployment

The first step to start building the Chatbot for Scientometric Indicator is to use a tool provided from the Azure Bot Service called Bot Framework Composer. The chatbot runs through a flow diagram in which two main concepts are Dialog and Triggers. Dialogs are a central concept in the SDK, providing ways to manage a long-running conversation with the user. It performs a task that can represent part of or a complete conversational thread, and it can span just one turn or many and span a short or long time-period [6]. Dialog triggers handle dialog specific events that are related to the life-cycle of the dialog [7].

We built and integrated our Scientometric Indicator Chatbot with the ontology model in this section. We built a Scientometric Indicator API (SI API) that enables communication between the Chatbot Framework in Azure and the ontology model in Neo4j. An architectural diagram of the main components is shown in Fig. 3.

The Scientometric Indicator API was created in python language using the flask framework for a faster development. The goal of the API is to connect the several components such as the ontology model in Neo4j, the chatbot framework and the Luis AI service for intent identification and entities extraction.

The process of hosting the chatbot for the testing period was achieved using Google Sites for sharing the Chatbot with the users.

3 Results and Discussion

In this section we shown the results by testing the chatbot with users from the Research Office at Tecnologico de Monterrey. For this evaluation we host the Scientometric Indicator Chatbot in the web and make it available for the users for testing. The users had 3 weeks for testing several natural language questions to the Chatbot and at the end evaluate it with a survey that will contain the following questions with answers from 1 to 5. 1 meaning Few Knowledge or Deficient and 5 meaning Expert or Excellent depending on the type of question.

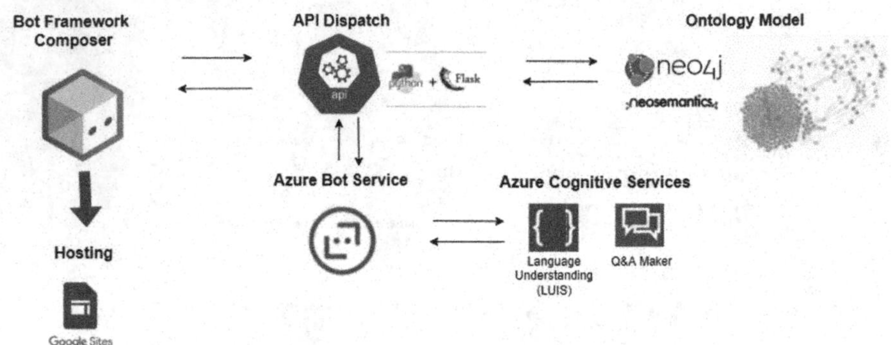

Fig. 3. Architectural diagram

- User's email
- User's knowledge about Scientometric Indicators
- Usability: Ease of use and time required for the Chatbot to answer the questions.
- Strictness: Ability from the chatbot to understand language variations.
- Comprehension: Ability from the chatbot to understand the question and answer respect the relevant information.
- Correlation: Relevance of the questions according to the context of the question.
- Satisfaction: User's feeling with the Chatbot and it's future.
- Comments or Feedback

Along with this survey, we will log all the users' interactions with the chatbot. With this logs we will evaluate the following metrics:

- Structure of the Conversation: Number of users and Total Conversations.
- Goal Completion Rate: Number of times chatbot answered correctly, number of correct intention detected, correct indicator detected and correct entity extraction.
- Bot Response Time: Comparison between the time took to answer a question of the chatbot and the actual process.

3.1 Goal Completion Rate

A total of 11 users participated in this test in which they made 35 different questions about Scientometric Indicators to the Chatbot. Whenever the users asked the chatbot, relevant information such as the date-time, user, top intent, exact indicator, comments, answer, and list of possible indicators were retrieved and stored in the ontology model. This section will evaluate the Goal Completion Rate (GCR) in terms of answers, intent detection, entity extraction, and scientometric indicators identification.

The first evaluation is the GCR of the correct intention detection. Intent detection is a great resource for correctly retrieving the scientometric indicator value. In Table 2 we can observe that 21 questions were identified as Low Complexity intention. Users made 6 questions of Medium complexity and finally, 8 questions were identified with the None and Greeting intentions. The GCR evaluates how many intentions were correctly identified by the chatbot. In Fig. 4 we can observe that 25 intentions, that represent 71.42% from the total questions, were identified correctly.

Table 2. Intent identification

	Intent	Number of questions	Correct intent
1	Low Complexity	21	21
2	Medium Complexity	6	3
3	Greeting	7	0
4	None	1	1

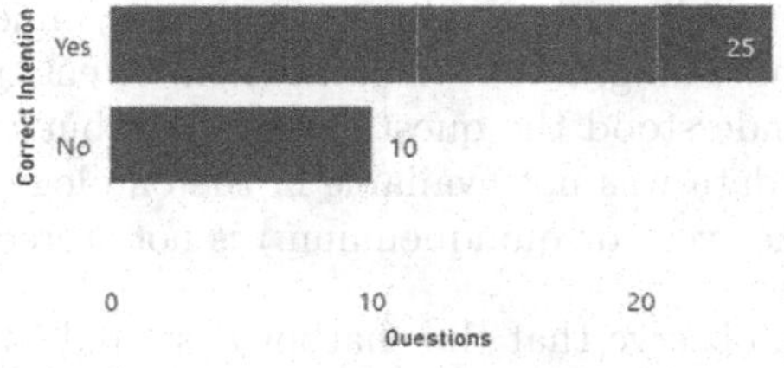

Fig. 4. Goal completion rate: correct intention

This result means that the training helped a lot in terms of variances in the questions due to complexity. Obtaining this result allowed the chatbot to understand what process to follow to answer the question correctly.

The second evaluation consists of assessing the GCR of the correct identification of scientometric indicators. In Fig. 5 we can observe that the chatbot identified the scientometric indicator correctly in 17 questions made by the users. This outcome represents 48.6% of the total questions.

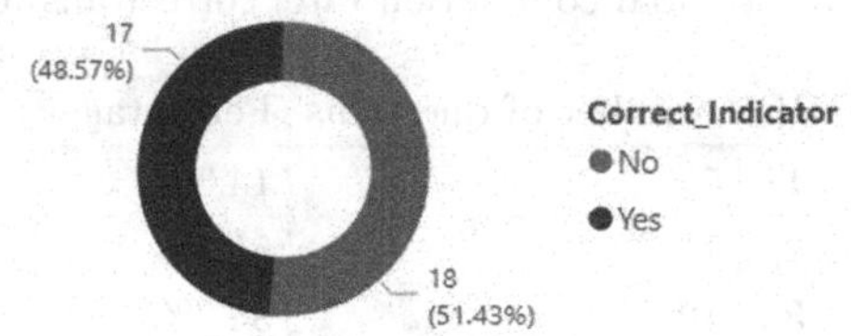

Fig. 5. Goal completion rate: correct indicator

The next evaluation is about the GCR from entity extraction. Entity extraction allows us to find relevant data for retrieving the scientometric indicator value more precisely. In Table 3 we can observe that 23 questions entities were extracted correctly and it represents 65.71% from all the question.

Table 3. Entity extraction

	Number of questions	Correct entity
1	23	Yes
2	12	No

We can state that the chatbot correctly identifies these entities in 65.71% of the questions due to differences in asking questions and missing required data.

In order to evaluate the GCR for correct answers from the chatbot to the questions, we need to establish the following categories.

- 1: Answered correctly with the required value
- 2: Answered incorrectly with a value or could not understand the question due to indicator matching, intent identification, or entity extraction.
- 3: The chatbot understood the question correctly but could not answer the question because data was not available in the ontology. In other words, the value for that time (year or quinquennium) is not stored in the ontology.

In Table 4 we can observe that the chatbot answered 14.3% of the questions correctly with a proper value from the ontology. In the other case, the chatbot could not answer 51.4% of the questions because it could not understand the question properly due to indicator matching or entity extraction. In the last case, the chatbot answered 34.3% correctly because it understood the question, but unfortunately, the value in the period was not uploaded for this test.

With the previous results, we decided to group categories 1 and 3 because the chatbot understood the question and answered correctly according to the values stored in our ontology due to the problem nature. The results are shown in Fig. 6 and state that the chatbot answered correctly 48.6% of the questions from the test evaluation while 51.4% were answered incorrectly.

Table 4. Goal completion rate: correct answer

ID	Number of questions	Percentage
1	5	14.3%
2	18	51.4%
3	12	34.3%

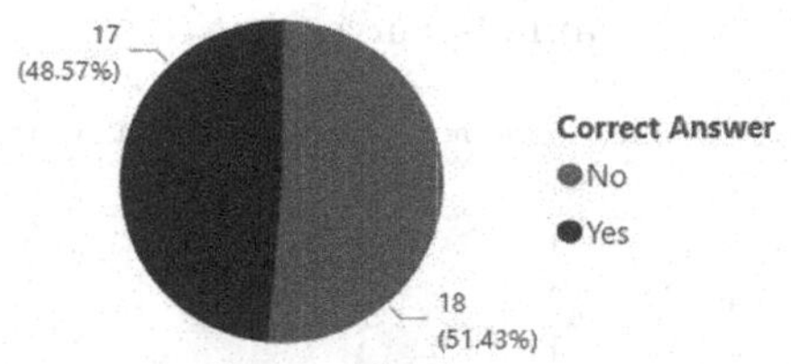

Fig. 6. Goal completion rate: correct answer

From this evaluation approach, we can state that every time the chatbot correctly identified the scientometric indicator, it answered the question correctly. It is essential to state that the chatbot only had one round of training and obtained reasonable goal completion rates.

Our research highlights the approach of defining three types of complexities for intention identification by obtaining a good result in the evaluation. However, this only represents a part of the process of interpreting the question correctly. There can be several issues like not extracting the correct entities and not filtering the desired value or not having the value stored in the model. Issues can be solved by adding more training steps to the model.

Bot Response Time. We extracted the chatbot's time to answer the questions and calculated the average from the testing log data. The chatbot took approximately 1.5 s to answer a question of scientometric indicators, and the actual process takes approximately 10 s to retrieve the answer.

3.2 Survey Evaluation

This evaluation consists of a survey in which users submitted their responses after testing the chatbot. The survey contained questions about metrics such as user confidence in their knowledge about scientometric indicators at Tecnologico de Monterrey, chatbot usability, strictness in language variations, chatbot comprehension, correlated replies from the chatbot, and users' satisfaction over the chatbot. The response was available from 1 to 5, 1 meaning low, and 5 refers to a high level. We had 11 users from the Research Office at Tecnologico de Monterrey who participated in the survey, and the replies are shown in Table 5.

Table 5. Survey data

User	User confidence	Usability	Strictness	Comprehension	Correlation	Satisfaction
1	4	4	1	1	1	1
2	5	3	1	1	1	1
3	4	4	3	3	3	4
4	4	4	1	1	1	1
5	4	1	1	1	1	3
6	5	4	1	1	1	1
7	3	4	3	3	3	3
8	4	4	3	4	4	4
Avg	4.2	3.5	1.75	1.87	1.87	2.25

This result was expected because the chatbot was trained with only a language format and the questions made during the testing period had different language variations in the questions. We decided only to briefly explain the chatbot and not provide sample questions not to produce bias in the users. Users tested the chatbot without any experience, which provoked several misunderstandings in the way of asking questions.

Finally, we also consider that these results would have improved if more training steps were added to the model to increase the chatbot's capacity to understand questions. We found much feedback from this evaluation approach that will allow us to improve the chatbot.

4 Conclusion

The main research questions stated in this research was proven correct. This research demonstrated that a chatbot could be used along with a statistical ontology model that extends SDMX to correctly answer any given questions about Scientometric Indicators. We can state that the specific objectives have been met, and the research questions were answered during the development of this research work.

The Natural Language Process allowed us to answer the research question of how the chatbot talks with the user to create a context for gathering data when there is not enough information to answer the question. The chatbot needs to identify the question's intention and extract the entities needed to understand the question and provide a correct response. It allows us to answer the research question on which essential keywords the chatbot must recognize to perform the task.

The chatbot answered correctly in almost 50% of the questions made to it. We can conclude that we met the goal of applying an ontology model that allowed the chatbot to understand and classify the user's input to extract the correct information of the question and provide a correct answer. The chatbot development knowledge was designed to create context during the conversation where information was needed to understand the user's question. It allows us to meet the objective of proposing and designing a scalable chatbot that creates a context for missing information for answering a question that can be used in other academic areas or industries.

Many different features and developments, also considered opportunity areas, have been left for the future. This research work can be considered the initial step for using the statistical ontology model and the chatbot in the Research Office at Tecnologico de Monterrey. Future work will concern with the following aspects:

- It will be interesting to add medium and high complexity knowledge to the chatbot in the future. Having a feature of using aggregation functions in time intervals and using stored information to forecast the number of cites in a particular year using machine learning models can lead to a very intelligent chatbot.
- Improve the training in Luis AI service to achieve higher results in Goal Completion Rate in answering the questions correctly, correctly identifying scientometric indicators and correct entity extraction.
- In the chatbot deployment, we can improve the usability by using thumbnail cards during the conversation to guide the user in building the question according to the knowledge, context, and stored data in the ontology model. This feature will help in having fewer questions with missing entities.

Acknowledgements. We thank Tecnologico de Monterrey and CONACyT for the financial support.

References

1. Shawar, B.A., Atwell, E.S.: Using corpora in machine-learning chatbot systems. Int. J. Corpus Linguist. **10**(4), 489–516 (2005)
2. Albayrak, N., Özdemir, A., Zeydan, E.: An overview of artificial intelligence based chatbots and an example chatbot application on Proceedings, pp. 1–4. IEEE(2018)
3. Hood, W., Wilson, C.: The literature of bibliometrics, scientometrics, and informetrics. Scientometrics **52**(2), 291 (2001)
4. Zakka, W., Lim, N.H.A., Chau, M.: A scientometric review of geopolymer concrete. J. Clean. Prod. **280**, 124353 (2021)
5. Lopez-Rodriguez, V., Ceballos, H.: Modeling scientometric indicators using a statistical data ontology. J. Big Data **9**(1), 1–17 (2022)
6. Dialogs library. http://docs.microsoft.com/en-us/azure/bot-service/bot-builder-concept-dialog?view=azure-bot-service-4.0. Accessed 27 Mar 2020
7. Events and triggers in adaptive dialogs - reference guide. http://docs.microsoft.com/en-us/azure/bot-service/adaptive-dialog/adaptive-dialog-prebuilt-triggers?view=azure-bot-service-4.0. Accessed 27 Mar 2020
8. Baby, C., Khan, F., Swathi, J.N.: Home automation using IoT and a chatbot using natural language processing. In: 2017 Innovations in Power and Advanced Computing Technologies (i-PACT) on Proceedings, pp. 1–6. IEEE (2017)
9. Chen, Z., Lu, Y., Nieminen, M., Lucero, A.: Creating a chatbot for and with migrants: chatbot personality drives co-design activities. In: 2020 ACM Designing Interactive Systems Conference on Proceedings, Eindhoven, Netherlands, pp. 219–230. Association for Computing Machinery (2020)

Red Light/Green Light: A Lightweight Algorithm for, Possibly, Fraudulent Online Behavior Change Detection

Vitali Herrera-Semenets[1], Raudel Hernández-León[1], Lázaro Bustio-Martínez[2(✉)], and Jan van den Berg[3]

[1] Advanced Technologies Application Center (CENATAV). 7a ♯ 21406, Playa, C.P. 12200, Havana, Cuba
{herrera,rhernandez}@cenatav.co.cu

[2] Universidad Iberoamericana, DEII, Prolongación Paseo de Reforma 880, 01219 CDMX, Mexico
lazaro.bustio@ibero.mx

[3] Intelligent Systems Department, Delft University of Technology, Mekelweg 4, 2628, CD Delft, The Netherlands
j.vandenberg@tudelft.nl

Abstract. Telecommunications services have become a constant in people's lives. This has inspired fraudsters to carry out malicious activities causing economic losses to people and companies. Early detection of signs that suggest the possible occurrence of malicious activity would allow analysts to act in time and avoid unintended consequences. Modeling the behavior of users could identify when a significant change takes place. Following this idea, an algorithm for online behavior change detection in telecommunication services is proposed in this paper. The experimental results show that the new algorithm can identify behavioral changes related to unforeseen events.

Keywords: Online data processing · Behavior changes · Anomaly detection · Concept drift · Cybersecurity · Multimodal data analysis

1 Introduction

Today telecommunications are essential for people and companies: in other words, the more users are connected to telecommunication services, the greater the communication possibilities and needs. Telephony-related telecommunications services carry a large volume of call, message and data traffic every day. Such services can be used to monetize third party services, also in unintended ways [7]. In this sense, telephony can become a very profitable environment for fraud schemes.

There are common techniques that fraudsters often use, such as: malicious software (malware) and the phone call scams [7]. Malware that infects mobile

O. Pichardo Lagunas et al. (Eds.): MICAI 2022, LNAI 13613, pp. 316–327, 2022.
https://doi.org/10.1007/978-3-031-19496-2_24

phones may initiate phone calls or send short messages stealthily. Although many of such techniques are known, the number and diversity of these continues growing. Fraudulent techniques are becoming increasingly difficult to track and investigate due to their frequency, their layers of anonymity, and their global nature.

To deal with the latter shortcoming, a lightweight algorithm for online behavior change detection in telecommunication services is proposed in this paper. The algorithm is designed to process large data streams, while updating the behavior of each user in real-time without requiring large computing resources. The experimental results, show that the new algorithm can identify behavioral changes related to unforeseen events (such as losing the phone, texts or calls not made by the user, among others) that, in some cases, can be linked to malicious activities. In addition, a case study on SMS messaging is presented, which shows the feasibility of using the proposed algorithm in real-world scenarios.

The remainder of this paper is structured as follows. Related works are described in Sect. 2. The proposed algorithm is introduced in Sect. 3. In Sect. 4, the experimental results are discussed. Then, in Sect. 5, a case study on real SMS messages dataset is presented. Finally, the obtained conclusions are outlined in Sect. 6.

2 Related Work

To date, there is a wide variety of classification algorithms proposed for the detection of malicious activities in telecommunications services. Specifically, this work focuses on anomaly-based algorithms.

Anomaly-based algorithms first identify normal behavior and look for variations in behavior that represent an anomaly. Generally, the normal behavior is identified using an unlabeled training collection consisting of historical information. Then, the normal behavior defined can be compared to the current behavior in order to determine if significant changes occur that may indicate an anomaly. These algorithms have some advantages: (1) subtle changes in the subscribers behavior can be detected, and (2) a prior domain knowledge is not required, which allows to identify new unknown malicious activities. On the other hand, a common drawback is: (1) certain anomalies are associated with normal behaviors (increase of false positives).

The drawback mentioned above is usually related to the fact that a user changes his behavior and starts behaving differently than he did originally. In such cases, it cannot be determined if this behavior change is related to fraud, but at least it can be accepted as suspicious, which may result into false positives. Fraudulent user behavior changes are characterized by a potentially high number of user action changes related to sending SMS messages, calls, among others, within a short period of time [3].

Some algorithms based on profiling human social behaviors have been proposed to detect anomalies. Stolfo et al. [10] introduce an algorithm that models behavioral profiles based on user cliques, Hellinger distance, and cumulative distributions for email users. SMSBotHunter is an anomaly detection approach that uses a one-class classification to detect SMS botnets on mobile devices [2].

Anomaly detection in mobile phone networks has been addressed in several works. For example, calling activities have been analyzed to detect fraud on mobile phones [6], as well as the mobility patterns of mobile devices have been profiled to detect cloning attacks [12]. With the rise of smartphones, a growing number of malware has been identified on these devices. This fact has led to the proposal of various approaches to detect mobile malware that work by profiling the behavior of normal applications [13].

A large portion of anomaly-based algorithms are designed to be used offline, since the high dimensionality and volume of the data negatively affects the efficiency of conventional approaches, such as algorithms based on distance, density and clustering [1]. Although there are proposals that allow a more efficient processing of large volumes of data, these are designed to be used in distributed environments that require large computing resources [11]. However, there are "lighter" proposals designed for the online detection of behavior changes such as the algorithm proposed by Shaeiri et al. [8]. This algorithm have a time complexity, in the worst case, of $\mathcal{O}(N * M)$, where N is the number of users and M is the amount of phone numbers that have interacted with the user, which makes it the most efficient of the algorithms analyzed in this section.

In general, from the algorithms described in this section, at least two issues can be identified. One of them is the generation of multiple alarms, where each alarm does not have the same level of importance for the analyst. The other issue is the benefit of timely alarms. Fraud must be detected as soon as possible and the algorithm used must reflect it. The benefit of a timely alarm can often be quantified. In telecommunications services fraud detection scenarios, the cost of delaying an alarm can have a negative effect on the economy of a company or a user.

The algorithm proposed in this work addresses both issues. In addition, it is designed to be applied in scenarios that do not have large computing resources, so its efficiency, in terms of time complexity, is a fundamental aspect to be considered.

3 Red Light/Green Light Algorithm

The Red Light/Green Light (RLGL) algorithm proposed in this paper has its name based on the popular children's game of the same name [5].

The RLGL algorithm analyzes the daily behavior of each user and checks for any significant change that suggest anomalous behavior. To do this, it is analyzed how the user's behavior has been at different times of the day and compares it with the historical profile of the user. If the probability that the user performs an action, be it sending an SMS message or making a call at some point in the day, increases above a defined threshold, it is considered a change in behavior and is reported.

Algorithm 1: RLGL($r, th, detect, minNumRec$)

```
   Input: r: new record, th: threshold increase, detect: anomaly detection enabled,
          minNumRec: minimum number of records
   Output: changeAlert: alert of detected changes
1  currentday = -1
2  activeUsers = [ ]
3  usersHistory, tmpUsersHistory = Hash_Table()
4  if detect == True then
5  |   usersHistory, tmpUsersHistory = Load_Profiles()
6  while !stopSignal do
7  |   if detect == True then
8  |   |   if r.Date.weekDay != currentDay then
9  |   |   |   currentday = r.Date.weekDay
10 |   |   |   foreach userNumber in activeUsers do
11 |   |   |   |   changeList = Analyze_Behavior(usersHistory[userNumber],
   |   |   |   |   tmpUsersHistory[userNumber], th, minNumRec)
12 |   |   |   |   if changeList != Empty then
13 |   |   |   |   |   changeAlert = ChangeAlert(userNumber,anomaliesList,Date())
14 |   |   |   |   |   ThrowAlert(changeAlert)
15 |   |   |   activeUsers = [ ]
16 |   |   |   tmpUsersHistory = usersHistory
17 |   |   activeUsers.Add(r.userNnumber)
18 |   if usersHistory.hasKey(r.userNnumber) then
19 |   |   usersHistory[r.userNnumber].Update_Statistics(r)
20 |   else
21 |   |   usersHistory[r.userNnumber] = NewUser().Update_Statistics(r)
22 Save_Profiles(usersHistory)
```

The RLGL algorithm requires some input parameters to be defined. As it is shown in Algorithm 1, the input parameter *detect* will indicate if the algorithm is going to be executed in anomaly detection mode ($detect = True$), or if it is only going to model the behaviors of the users ($detect = False$). The latter is recommended for the initial execution of the algorithm, since by having previous users profiles, it is possible to reduce false positives in the anomaly detection mode. In this way, the algorithm can model the behaviors of the users, by updating their statistics, for a suitable period of time (see lines 18–21 in Algorithm 1). The time defined for modeling the behavior of the users must be in correspondence with the context where the algorithm is applied. When it is decided to finish the previous process, a stop signal is sent (see line 6 in Algorithm 1). Next, it saves the modeled profiles of each user and ends its execution (see line 22 in Algorithm 1).

The *Update_Statistics* method consists of updating the count of actions performed by a user based on the time range of the day in which the new record r originated (see lines 19 and 21 in Algorithm 1). For this, a full day is divided into four 6-h time ranges. Each time range is associated with a different part of the day: (0:00–5:59) early morning, (6:00–11:59) morning, (12: 00–17:59) afternoon and (18:00–23:59) evening. Thus, if a user sends an SMS at 6:30, the algorithm updates the statistics of said user by increasing the number of SMS sent in the time range (6:00–11:59) and the total number of SMS sent.

When the anomaly detection mode is activated, the algorithm proceeds to load the previously modeled user profiles in two hash tables: *usersHistory* and

Algorithm 2: Analyze_Behavior(*currentP, historicalP, pDay, th, minNumRec*)

Input: *currentP*: current user profile, *historicalP*: historical user profile, *th*: threshold increase, *minNumRec*: minimum number of records
Output: *changeList*: list of detected changes

```
1 anomalies = [ ]
2 if currentP.totalRecords > minNumRec then
3     foreach timeRange in range(0,4) do
4         P(current) = currentP.timeRange[timeRange] / currentP.totalRecords
5         P(historical) = historicalP.timeRange[timeRange] / historicalP.totalRecords
6         changeTh = P(historical) + th
7         if P(current) > changeTh then
8             changeList.Add(Change(timeRange, P(current), changeTh))
9 return changeList
```

tmpusersHistory (the latter is a temporary copy of the first (see lines 4–5 in Algorithm 1)). The hash table *usersHistory* will continue to be updated during the day, while the temporary copy *tmpusersHistory* remains unchanged and will serve as a historical profile for behavioral analysis. However, as the algorithm is running online, new user records could arrive that have not been considered during the behavior modeling process. In this case, the input parameter *minNumRec* is included, which defines the minimum number of records that a user must generate so that the algorithm can perform the behavior analysis. A record stores information (source number, destination number, date, etc.) about an action performed by the user, be it making a call, sending an SMS message, among others.

Since the RLGL algorithm analyzes the daily behavior of each user, it must recognize when it is time to analyze users behaviors. To do this, it checks if the day of the week present in the date of the new record is different from the one stored in the *currentDay* variable. If yes, it suggests that the new record already belongs to a new day. Therefore, the *currentDay* variable is updated (see line 9 in Algorithm 1) and the behavior analysis of each user is performed (see lines 10–14 in Algorithm 1).

A small number of records may not be sufficient to define the historical behavior of a user. Therefore, the first step of the behavioral analysis algorithm is to check if the number of records generated by the user exceeds the *minNumRec* variable (see line 2 in Algorithm 2). This step ensures that each user has at least a minimum number of records defining the historical profile, which guarantees a better behavioral analysis.

If the above condition is satisfied, for each time range of the day, the probability that a user generates a record is computed (see lines 3–8 in Algorithm 2). Note that the current probability and the historical probability are computed (see lines 4 and 5 in Algorithm 2). The probability is given by the number of records generated in a time range over the total number of records generated. The threshold *changeTh*, which will indicate when a change in behavior occurs, is given by the sum of the historical probability and a coefficient *th* defined by the analyst (see line 6 in Algorithm 2).

To determine if there is a behavior change in the evaluated time range, it is checked whether the current probability exceeds the computed threshold (see lines 7–8 in Algorithm 2). If this condition is satisfied, it means that there has been an increase in the number of user-generated records indicating a change in user behavior. If so, a behavior change alert is created and added to the list of detected changes to be reported (see line 8 in Algorithm 2). After analyzing each time range, the list of detected changes *changeList* is returned (see line 9 in Algorithm 2).

If any change in the analyzed user behavior is detected, an alert with the necessary information is created and reported (see lines 12–14 in Algorithm 1).

After analyzing each user that has been active in the previous day, some variables are reset (see lines 15 and 16 in Algorithm 1) and the statistics of the users during the current day begin to be updated.

The algorithm proposed in this work is considered "lightweight", not only because of its heuristics, but also by its time complexity. The proposed algorithm iterates over each active user, with a time complexity of $\mathcal{O}(N)$, and gets the user profile from a Hash Table, which has a computational complexity of $\mathcal{O}(1)$. Therefore, when applying the sum rule, the time complexity that defines the RLGL algorithm would be $\mathcal{O}(N)$, which makes it more efficient than the proposals analyzed in the previous section.

4 Experimental Results

To evaluate the proposed algorithm, an unlabeled phone calls data sets (13035 records) were used. Such data set is the result of the mobile phones usage, collected through monitoring devices of 27 users during a 5-month study [4]. The first three months were used to model user behavior and the last two months were used to detect behavioral changes. The experiments were conducted on a PC equipped with a 3.2 GHz Intel Quad-Core processor, 8 GB of RAM memory running Ubuntu 18.04 OS.

4.1 Experiments on Phone Calls

In the phone call data set, during the initial three months, there were some users that only made between 10 and 30 calls, which is a low number of calls, compared to those performed by the rest of the users. This fact can cause false positives, since if the user makes two or three calls during a day, the probability of said user can increase considerably and can be reported as a change in behavior. To avoid this type of situation, the RLGL algorithm allows defining a parameter for a minimum number of records to be considered to analyze a user ($minNumRec = 90$).

The experimental results are shown only for the threshold increase parameter $th = 0.02$. This threshold is enough to analyze the behavior of the proposed algorithm during the experiments. Using a smaller threshold would increase the number of behavioral changes detected, an opposite effect would be obtained by increasing the threshold.

After applying the RLGL algorithm on the phone call data set, using the threshold increase parameter $th = 0.02$, 6 users with behavioral changes were detected. The Table 1 shows the users with identified behavior changes, as well as the time range, the date and the day that it represents in the five months processed (being day 0 on 2/9/2010 and day 145 on 30/1/2011).

Table 1. Behavioral changes detected in the phone calls data set.

Time range	Date	Day	User
Evening	17/12/2010	101	19
Early morning	1/1/2011	116	13
Early morning	1/1/2011	116	8
Early morning	1/1/2011	116	10
Evening	8/1/2011	123	
Afternoon	8/1/2011	123	22
Afternoon	11/1/2011	126	26

Figure 1a shows the daily behavior of the user 19 during the five months of registered calls. Note that the first 90 days are associated with the 3 months used to model the user behavior. Although during that time, two days were recorded with more than 40 calls made at the evening, in general, this user does not make more than 20 calls in that time range. Therefore, the behavior change highlighted with a red circle in Fig. 1a is due to the user making 41 calls during the evening. In this sense, the probability of making calls for the user 19 at the evening increases above the threshold, which represents a behavior change.

The probability that user 13 will make a call in the early morning is very low. As shown in Fig. 1b, the highest number of calls that user 13 made in the early morning were 2. In this sense, the behavior change detected (highlighted in a red circle in Fig. 1b) is related to 12 calls made in the early morning, which increased the probability of making a call in that time range above the threshold. A similar case can be seen in Fig. 1c where user 8, with only 3 calls recorded in the early morning history, made 42 calls in a single early morning.

Figure 1d shows, highlighted with a red circle, the two behavioral changes that were detected for the user 10. The first one occurred when the user made 11 calls at the early morning. This figure represents more than 5 times the maximum number of calls made by user 10 in a single early morning. As can be seen in Fig. 1d, the second change in behavior occurred at the evening making 26 calls, when user 10 usually made no more than 5 calls at night. Both events represent a considerable increase in the probability of making calls at the corresponding times, which is why they are identified as behavioral changes.

The user 22 had a behavior change similar to user 19 discussed above. As shown in Fig. 1e, during the behavioral modeling, two days were recorded with 8 or more calls in the afternoon. However, in general, the user does not make more

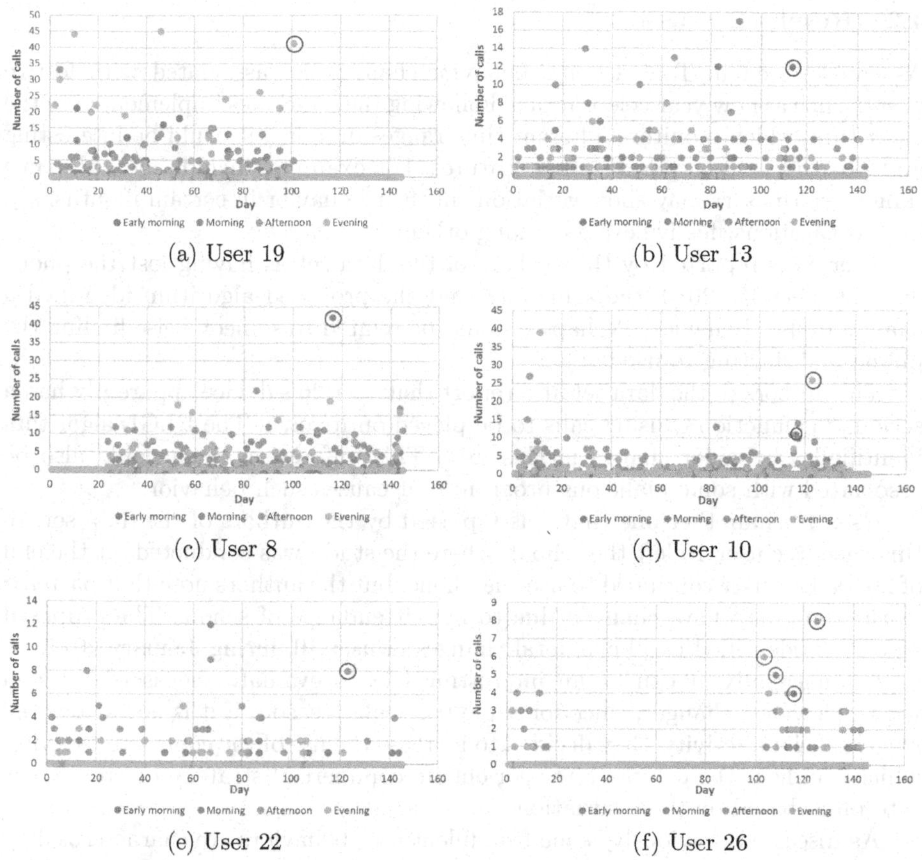

(a) User 19 (b) User 13

(c) User 8 (d) User 10

(e) User 22 (f) User 26

Fig. 1. Number of calls performed each day by users 19, 13, 8, 10, 22 and 26. (Color figure online)

than 4 calls in the afternoons. For this reason, a behavior change is identified when making 8 calls in a single afternoon (see Fig. 1e, red circle).

The user 26 is an example of users who made few calls during the three months of behavioral modeling. In Fig. 1f, it can be seen that in the first month the user 26 did not exceed 30 calls in total, and the remaining two months did not make any calls. As RLGL is an online algorithm, it is capable of constantly modeling user behavior and when the user exceeds the number of calls established in the *minNumRec* parameter, the user behavior is analyzed. That is why in some cases, such as those highlighted with a green circle in Fig. 1f which could turn out to be anomalies, a behavioral analysis is not performed, since at that time the number of calls does not exceed the value of the parameter *minNumRec*. On the other hand, when the user makes 8 calls in a single afternoon (see Fig. 1f, red circle), the *minNumRec* value is reached, which is why its behavior is analyzed detecting a change.

4.2 Results Discussion

As can be seen in Table 1 some behavior changes are associated with festive events such as new year celebrations. Following the heuristics implemented in the algorithm, which monitors different time ranges in a day, it could be interesting and positive to incorporate other features. For example, include monthly time ranges, since users may show variations in their behavior in certain months, say due to vacations, festive events among others.

User 19 is reported by the authors of the data set as having lost the phone on December 17, 2010, the same day that the proposed algorithm identified a change in user behavior. Perhaps it could be related to someone else finding the phone and starting to use it.

The authors of the data set also report that user 26's device apparently had a serious malfunction causing calls to be placed on its own. The RLGL algorithm identified a behavior change in this user. This unforeseen event could also be associated with some malicious program that causes such behavior.

User 10 is another one that was reported by the authors of the data set. In this case, the user 10 left the school, where the study was conducted, at the end of 2010. This user continued to use the phone, but the authors note that patterns in the data may have changed due to non-attendance of school. The proposed algorithm identified two behavioral changes in user 10 during January 2011.

Commercially, it can be an interesting fact to evaluate the users detected with behavioral changes, since for some particular reason, if it is not associated with malicious activity, they decided to increase the use of the contracted service, which can help the company to reorient its commercial strategy or create new rate plans based on these situations.

As discussed previously, some fraudulent user behaviors are characterized by the unexpectedly high values of call counts or SMS messages within a period. As can be seen from the results achieved, the proposed algorithm can identify behaviors similar to those that describe a fraudulent behavior. At the fist stage, we cannot determine if these behavior changes were exactly fraud, but we can accept them as suspicious behaviors.

5 A Case Study on Real SMS Messages Dataset

The performance and behavior of the RLGL algorithm have been verified and validated by a Mexican telecommunications company (named hereafter as "TC") in a real scenario[1]. Following the same experimental design described in Sect. 4, five months of SMS data were collected, hereby obtaining a dataset composed of 21772546 records. Each record contains the source and destination number, as well as the date that the SMS message was sent. From the dataset created, three

[1] Due to privacy and commercial policies of the telecommunication company, names, data, and other information that could lead to a personal or commercial information leakage are not offered. This was guaranteed by a Statement of Confidentiality signed between the research authors and TC.

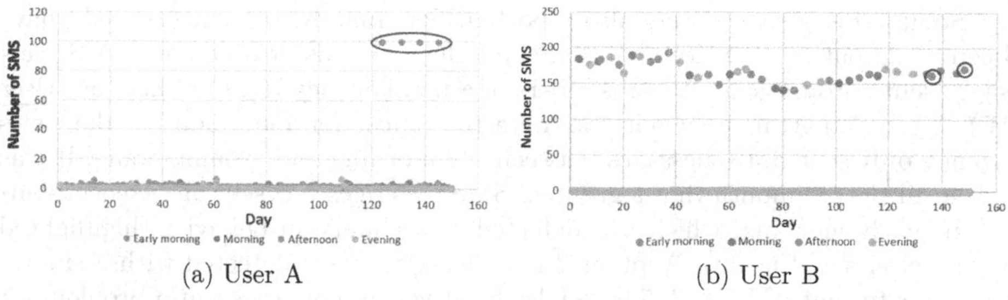

(a) User A (b) User B

Fig. 2. Number of SMS messages sent each day by two users.

months (13963527 records) were used as baseline for modeling user's behavior. The other two months (7809019 records) were used to detect changes that deviate from the baseline. Also, the parameters $minNumRec$ and th got the same values as used in the experiments reported in Sect. 4, 90 and 0.02 respectively.

In this case study, the RLGL algorithm detected a behavioral change by a user (referred here as "User A") on the 124th day, where User A sent 100 SMS messages to several cellphone numbers in a range of $xxx - xxx - 0000$ to $xxx - xxx - 0099$. All these SMS messages were sent in the early morning (at 03:00 am), which contrasts with the historical behavior of this user. In day 131, User A sent others 100 SMS messages, but this time, the targets were moved to other 100 cellphones number in the range $xxx - xxx - 0100$ to $xxx - xxx0199$. This behavior was repeated four times every seven days after the 124th day. Figure 2a shows the behavior of User A during the five months evaluated, and the behavior changes detected are highlighted with a red oval.

Considering the behavioral change detected by the RLGL algorithm, the security analysts conducted a detailed study of the behavior of User A. This study determined that User A was not a bot, but a legitimate user that kept a normal historical behavior. Apparently, before the 124th day, User A's device was infected by malware that sent 100 SMS at 03 : 00 am to 100 different users. This behavior is repeated periodically every seven days at the same hour. Furthermore, the SMS sent contain a fraudulent URL inviting the victims to access a supposed Facebook address to update their credentials. In this way, the fraudsters can obtain personal information from users who enter their credentials on the URL suggested in the SMS message. This can be seen as a typical case of scam or Phishing [9].

The RLGL algorithm identified 123 other users with behavior similar to that of User A. After examining each of the reported users, security analysts concluded that their devices were infested with the same malware as User A.

Another 18 users were also identified with specific behavior changes, that is, a notable increase in the probability of sending SMS messages at a certain time (mainly at the evening and at the early morning). These cases only occurred on a single day, which is why security analysts determined that they may be normal behaviors associated with some personal event.

Some false positives were also reported. Fortunately, these cases could have been ruled out by security analysts, since they were associated with SMS messages sent automatically to subscribers of a news agency (referred here as "User B"). This change in behavior was detected since, for four months, the news agency only sent SMS messages between the morning and evening hours. It was not until the 5th month that a group of SMS messages was sent on two occasions at the early morning, which was detected as a change in behavior (highlighted in red circles in Fig. 2b). Another 7 news agencies were detected with a similar behavior to that of User B. These false positives do not represent a problem for security analysts, since they have identified these, and other, news agencies and can filter their SMS, so that they will not be processed by the RLGL algorithm.

The RLGL algorithm processed a data flow associated with 5 months of SMS messaging without showing any deterioration in its performance, in terms of efficiency. A large part of the users identified with a behavior change were verified by security analysts, who concluded that they were related to a malicious activity. In addition, another group of users with behavioral changes not associated with malicious activities, also was detected. However, this phenomenon is known to security analysts, so the related false positives can be filtered out to unnecessary detection by the RLGL algorithm.

6 Conclusions

A new algorithm for online behavior changes detection was presented in this work. Its linear time complexity makes it an efficient algorithm, with a feasible use in scenarios with low computing resources, and lighter than other proposals reported in the literature.

Although the detection of a behavioral change does not necessarily imply a malicious activity, the alarms provided by the RLGL algorithm facilitate the investigative work of security analysts. The experimental results show that RLGL detects behavioral changes related to festive events that, fortunately, can be ruled out by security analysts. In addition, RLGL also detected unforeseen events that, given their nature, could be linked to some malicious activity. A sample of them is the case study presented, where the RLGL algorithm identified 124 users who carried out a malicious activity associated with a scam or Phishing.

In future work, it is intended to incorporate other variables to the modeling of user behavior. The challenge is to do this without negatively affecting the efficiency of the algorithm, as well as its time complexity.

Acknowledgement. This research was supported by the Universidad Iberoamericana (Ibero) and the Institute of Applied Research and Technology (InIAT) by the project "Detection of phishing attacks in electronic messages using Artificial Intelligence techniques."

References

1. Ahmed, M., Mahmood, A.N., Hu, J.: A survey of network anomaly detection techniques. J. Netw. Comput. Appl. **60**, 19–31 (2016)
2. Faghihi, F., Abadi, M., Tajoddin, A.: Smsbothunter: a novel anomaly detection technique to detect SMS botnets. In: 2018 15th International ISC (Iranian Society of Cryptology) Conference on Information Security and Cryptology (ISCISC), pp. 1–6. IEEE (2018)
3. Kilinc, H.H.: A case study on fraudulent user behaviors in the telecommunication network. Electrica **21**(1), 74–85 (2021)
4. McDiarmid, A., Bell, S., Irvine, J., Banford, J.: Nodobo: detailed mobile phone usage dataset (2013). Unpublished paper, accessed http://nodobo.com/papers/iet-el.pdf on pp. 9–21
5. Nakamura, T., Munekata, N., Nakamura, F., Ono, T., Matsubara, H.: Universal game based on traditional children's outdoor games. In: Anacleto, J.C., Fels, S., Graham, N., Kapralos, B., Saif El-Nasr, M., Stanley, K. (eds.) ICEC 2011. LNCS, vol. 6972, pp. 59–64. Springer, Heidelberg (2011). https://doi.org/10.1007/978-3-642-24500-8_7
6. Peng, L., Lin, R.: Fraud phone calls analysis based on label propagation community detection algorithm. In: 2018 IEEE World Congress on Services (SERVICES), pp. 23–24. IEEE (2018)
7. Sahin, M., Francillon, A.: Understanding and detecting international revenue share fraud. In: Proceeding of the Network and Distributed System Security Symposium (NDSS 2021), Reston, VA. The Internet Society (2021)
8. Shaeiri, Z., Kazemitabar, J., Bijani, S., Talebi, M.: Behavior-based online anomaly detection for a nationwide short message service. J. AI Data Mining **7**(2), 239–247 (2019)
9. Sonowal, G.: Introduction to Phishing. In: Phishing and Communication Channels, pp. 1–24. Apress, Berkeley, CA (2022). https://doi.org/10.1007/978-1-4842-7744-7_1
10. Stolfo, S.J., Hershkop, S., Hu, C.W., Li, W.J., Nimeskern, O., Wang, K.: Behavior-based modeling and its application to email analysis. ACM Trans. Internet Technol. (TOIT) **6**(2), 187–221 (2006)
11. Thudumu, S., Branch, P., Jin, J., Singh, J.J.: A comprehensive survey of anomaly detection techniques for high dimensional big data. J. Big Data **7**(1), 1–30 (2020). https://doi.org/10.1186/s40537-020-00320-x
12. Ullah, F., Naeem, M.R., Mostarda, L., Shah, S.A.: Clone detection in 5g-enabled social IoT system using graph semantics and deep learning model. Int J. Mach. Learn. Cybernet. **12**, 3115–3127 (2021)
13. Yu, B., Fang, Y., Yang, Q., Tang, Y., Liu, L.: A survey of malware behavior description and analysis. Front. Inf. Technol. Electron. Eng. **19**(5), 583–603 (2018). https://doi.org/10.1631/FITEE.1601745

Machine Learning Model of Digital Transformation Index for Mexican Households

Alfredo García, Vladimir Salazar, and Hiram Ponce(✉)

Facultad de Ingeniería, Universidad Panamericana, Augusto Rodin 498, 03920 Ciudad de México, Mexico
{0252444,0203685,hponce}@up.edu.mx

Abstract. Digital transformation refers to the change in all aspects of human society by the adoption of digital technologies. Different methodologies and measurements have been proposed to determine the level of digital transformation in regions or countries. In this work, we propose the creation of a digital transformation index for Mexican households using machine learning models for digital transformation measurement analysis and estimation. We include three dimensions in terms of the information and communication technologies infrastructure, availability of services, and usage. We also use a public dataset from the Mexican government to build and train three machine learning models. Experimental results validate that our methodology can deliver a digital transformation measurement using machine learning models consistently with 84% of accuracy and 84% of F1-score. We also prototype a simple web application using the best machine learning model found. We anticipate that measuring the digital transformation in companies, governments, and households allows better decisions in business intelligence and public policy.

Keywords: K-means · Artificial intelligence · Decision trees · Support vector machines · Digital transformation

1 Introduction

The digital ecosystem creates a virtuous circle with the economy and certain indicators of well-being in our society. The Inter-American Development Bank (IDB) [13] has indicated that an average increase of 10% in broadband penetration in the countries of Latin America and the Caribbean (LAC) causes an increase of 3.19% of the gross domestic product (GDP) and 2.61% of productivity, while generating more than 67,000 direct jobs. The drivers of the digital economy are based on the digital infrastructure (e.g., Internet access), the accelerated adoption of applications and digital services, and digital skills to use them [3].

O. Pichardo Lagunas et al. (Eds.): MICAI 2022, LNAI 13613, pp. 328–338, 2022.
https://doi.org/10.1007/978-3-031-19496-2_25

Digital transformation is understood as the change in all aspects of human society by the adoption of digital technologies. Then, it is relevant to determine the level of development or evolution of the digital economy in regions or countries. In 2016, the World Bank proposed the Digital Adoption Index [8] aiming to measure the relationship between the digital economy of households in a country and the economic performance (measured by GDP). Also, the Inter-American Development Bank published a document entitled “Digital Economy in Latin America and the Caribbean” [13]. It proposes the Application Economy Index which measures the broadband ecosystem, as well as the social and economic characteristics of the population. In total, it includes 66 variables to compare the countries of Latin America and the Organisation for Economic Co-operation and Development. In addition, the United Nations Organization, through the United Nations Conference on Trade and Development, published a report on the digital economy [11] which addresses various aspects of the measurement and adoption of the digital economy around the world.

Other efforts to measure digital transformation have been proposed. For example, the Digital Transformation Index [12], proposed by Dell, is a global benchmark that indicates the state of digital transformation of companies around the world and how they are performing in this digital age. Erns & Young's research proposed the EY Digital Transformation Index [9] that aims not only to examine respondents' knowledge of new technologies from various regions of the world, but also their subjective opinion, such as possible fears or enthusiasm about the advancement of technology and digitization in various areas. The European Commission proposed the Digital Economy and Society Index [4] which measures key aspects of connectivity, human capital (population), integration into the digital economy, digital public services, and information and communication technologies (ICT) research and development. The World Economic Forum proposed the Networked Readiness Index [1] to evaluate 139 economies that measures the capacity of countries to take advantage of ICT to increase competitiveness and well-being.

This work proposes the creation of a Digital Transformation Index for Mexican households using machine learning models for digital transformation measurement analysis and estimation. The Digital Transformation Index for Mexican housing includes three dimensions: (i) the availability of equipment and terminal devices (infrastructure), (ii) the accessibility to connectivity services, and (iii) the use of applications and digital services. For this purpose, we use a dataset from the National Survey on Availability and Use of Information Technologies in Households (ENDUTIH) from the National Institute of Statistic and Geography (INEGI) [7].

Many of the indexes in the literature are designed by econometrics and statistical analysis. Until now, there are very few works in the literature that report the use of machine learning models for estimating the digital transformation. In this regard, we anticipate that the use machine learning models can provide an accurate estimation of the digital transformation, but also they can be used for the analysis of the features importance in the digital transformation in developing countries, e.g. Mexico, so those can be further influence on the digital transformation policies.

The rest of the paper is organized as follows. Section 2 presents the proposal, including the foundation, the dataset preparation, and the building and training models. Section 3 describes the experimental results and discussion. Lastly, Sect. 4 concludes the paper.

2 Methodology

The general methodology implemented in our proposal includes six steps as shown in Fig. 1. Our goal is to design a Digital Transformation Index for Mexican households using machine learning models to estimate the level of digital transformation ('low', 'medium', 'high') for each of the 32 states of the country. To do that, we propose to use a Digital Transformation Index that includes three dimensions: (i) the availability of equipment and terminal devices (infrastructure), (ii) the accessibility to connectivity services, and (iii) the use of applications and digital services. We prepare and use the ENDUTIH dataset, and three machine learning models are built and trained: support vector machines, decision trees, and K-means clustering. The model are validated and, lastly, we implement a simple application for data visualization and analysis.

First, an overview of the existed frameworks for digital transformation measurement is presented, then the workflow adopted in this work (Fig. 1) is described.

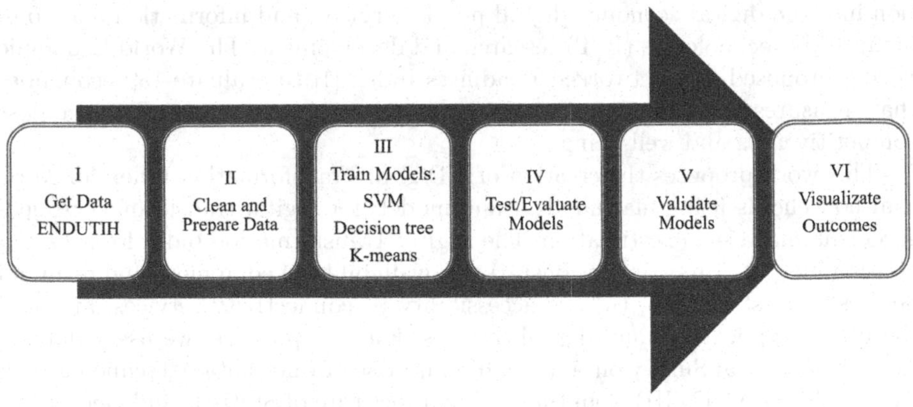

Fig. 1. Workflow of our proposal.

2.1 Methodologies for Digital Transformation Measurement

In the framework proposed by Rumana Bukht and Richard Heeks [3], the authors propose methodological aspects to define and measure various aspects of the digital economy. The identification of certain levels of development or evolution of the digital economy is relevant, starting from infrastructure aspects, such as telecommunications networks, to greater adoption, such as electronic commerce and other digitized services that even use algorithms; as shown in Fig. 2. This framework is relevant to our proposal because it allows us to identify the progress of digital transformation in Mexican households. For example, the availability of broadband infrastructure at home does not carry the same weight as carrying out financial transactions using the Internet.

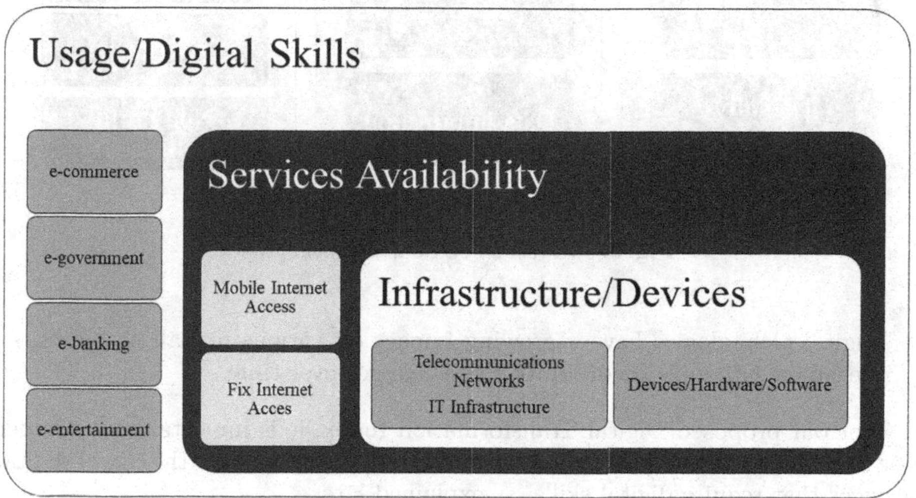

Fig. 2. Framework modified from Bukht and Heeks (2017) [3].

The framework proposed by the International Monetary Fund (IMF) [10] distinguishes that people, households, companies, and governments are agents of the digital transformation and, at the same time, they are beneficiaries of the digital economy. Figure 3 summarizes the notions of the IMF that identifies the nature of the digital transformation (i.e., how it does), the products provided (i.e., what are the outcomes), and the actors who participate in this transformation.

From the above, common aspects are identified:

- Digital transformation can be measured considering: the availability of ICT infrastructure and devices (basic level); the provision of services that enable the digital economy, such as connectivity and broadband services (medium level); and the use of digital applications and services that require digital skills (high level), such as e-commerce, online financial transactions, e-government, among others.
- The evolution of the digital economy is a dynamic process, where new applications (sometimes more sophisticated) of new technologies are generated over time. Therefore, adjustments to the indices have been observed over time.

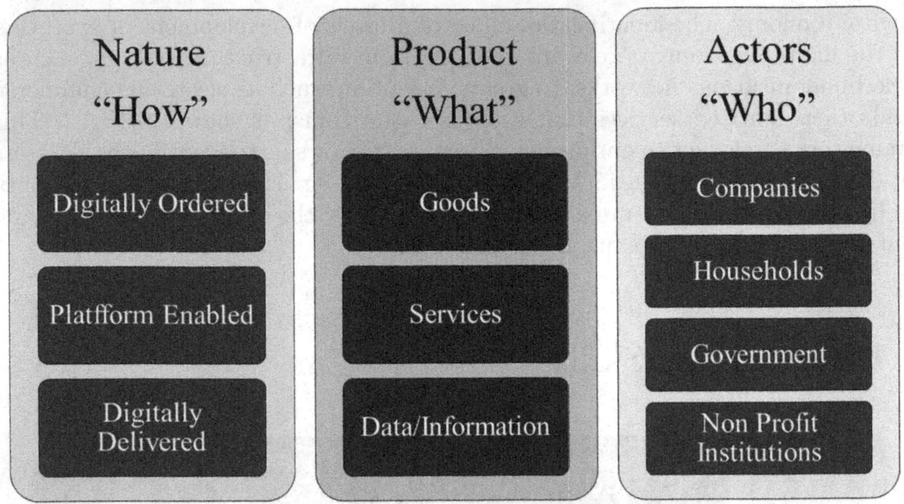

Fig. 3. IMF scheme, adapted from [10].

– Digital technologies have a growing impact on various human activities, so measurements must incorporate these changes over time.

For our proposed Digital Transformation Index, it is important to consider not only the infrastructure and availability of devices, but also the use of digital services that require digital skills, as explained later.

2.2 Data Preparation

The data comes from the ENDUTIH[1], published by INEGI [7], a survey for the generation of statistics on the availability and use of ICT. The ENDUTIH dataset is a probabilistic household survey with representative data and its results could be generalized to the entire population with a certain level of reliability. The database aggregates information from five editions of the ENDUTIH, from 2015 to 2020. It includes both ICT user variables and variables related to ICT availability in households. The information contained in the dataset was provided by a person in the household (randomly selected) who describes his/her own experience in the use of ICT. The units of analysis are households and individuals, and information is collected from people with an age of six or older, who reside permanently in private homes located in the national territory.

The dataset is comprised of twenty one numerical variables that ranges from 0 to 1, and distributed in the three dimensions, as shown in Table 1.

We pre-processed the dataset as follows. Some variables that are not directly related to digital transformation were eliminated, for example, variables related to sound broadcasting and free television. It was checked that all the records of

[1] https://bit.ift.org.mx/BitWebApp/descargaArchivos.xhtml.

Table 1. Data set features.

No	Variable	Dimension
1	TV_DIG	Infrastructure/Devices
2	TEL_MOVIL	Infrastructure/Devices
3	CONSOLA_V	Infrastructure/Devices
4	COMPUTADORA	Infrastructure/Devices
5	CELULAR	Infrastructure/Devices
6	CEL_SMART	Infrastructure/Devices
7	CEL_INT_WIFI	Services Availability
8	CEL_INT_DATOS	Services Availability
9	INTERNET_HOG	Services Availability
10	INT_COMPU	Services Availability
11	INT_SMART	Services Availability
12	INT_TV	Services Availability
13	INT_OTROS	Services Availability
14	USUARIOS_INTERNET_P	Usage/Digital Skills
15	COMPRAS_INT	Usage/Digital Skills
16	PAGOS_INT	Usage/Digital Skills
17	GOBIERNO	Usage/Digital Skills
18	OBT_INF	Usage/Digital Skills
19	ENTRET	Usage/Digital Skills
20	COMUNICAR	Usage/Digital Skills
21	CONT_AV	Usage/Digital Skills

the variables were complete. In this regard, no empty features were identified. The data comes from the 31 states of the country. Each one has data for five years, from 2015 to 2020 in a percentage format. We converted the percentage in decimal format values.

We then labeled the data, since the ENDUTIH dataset is not prepared for digital transformation measurement. To do so, we manually labeled the dataset using the high-level rules proposed by the World Bank in the Digital Adoption Index [8]. The data were labeled according to the levels: 'low', 'medium', and 'high'.

2.3 Building and Training Models

In this work, we propose to use two supervised learning methods: Support Vector Machines (SVM) and Decision Trees (DT). For training the models, we split the data into 70% for training and 30% for testing. We implement grid search for hyper-parameters tuning in both models, as depicted in Table 2. Then, a 5-fold cross-validation was conducted using the training set, and the best model was evaluated using the testing set.

Table 2. Hyper-parameters tuned in the models using grid search.

Hyper-parameter	Value
Criterion	Entropy
Max Depth	5
Max Features	15
Splitter	Random

Furthermore, we use K-means clustering to automatically find three groups of data resembling the three levels of digital transformation. This model is proposed here to determine how close our manual labeling was done in comparison with an automatic clustering.

Support Vector Machines [2] is a type of machine learning algorithm originally proposed for multi-class classification problems. The idea behind the method is to compute the most suitable separable support using the kernel trick in non-separable data.

Decision Trees [6] method is a type of supervised machine learning where the data is continuously split according to a certain parameter including two entities: decision nodes and leaves.

K-Means Clustering is an unsupervised learning algorithm [5] which groups the unlabeled dataset into different clusters. Here K defines the number of predefined clusters that need to be created in the process.

2.4 Test and Evaluation Models

We evaluate the performance of the supervised models using four metrics: accuracy (1), precision (2), recall (3), and F1-score (4); where, TP are the true positive, TN are the true negative, FP are the false positive, and FN are the false negative.

$$accuracy = \frac{TP + TN}{TP + TN + FP + FN} \tag{1}$$

$$precision = \frac{TP}{TP + FP} \tag{2}$$

$$recall = \frac{TP}{TP + FN} \tag{3}$$

$$F\text{-}score = 2 \times \frac{precision \times recall}{precision + recall} \tag{4}$$

Accuracy measures the total number of true positives in the whole testing data; precision is the ratio of the true positives and true negatives, and the total number of samples; recall is the ratio of true positives to all positives in the ground truth; and F1-score metric uses a combination of precision and recall. High F1-score means high precision as well as high recall.

2.5 Visualization

The best model is chosen based on the evaluation criteria. We implement the best model into a simple application in which the user is able to change the values of the features and to get the estimation for the level of digital transformation. The implementation was done in Gradio and Python, and hosted in a web server.

3 Experimental Results and Discussion

We evaluate the performance of both models, as summarized in Table 3 and Table 4. As shown, the SVM model has 86% of accuracy, 87% of precision, 82% of recall, and 84% of F1-score. The DT model performs 84% of accuracy, 82% of precision, 89% of recall, and 84% of F1-score. Figure 4 shows the best DT model found in this work.

Table 3. Evaluation metrics of the SVM model.

	Precision	Recall	f1-score	Support
High	0.88	0.70	0.78	10
Medium	0.83	0.93	0.88	27
Low	0.91	0.83	0.87	12
Accuracy			0.86	49
Macro avg	0.87	0.82	0.84	49
Weighted avg	0.86	0.86	0.86	49

Then, we clustered the dataset using the K-means method. In this case, we obtained 81% of accuracy between the manual labeling and the automatic clustering using K-means. We found interesting that the labeling done by the K-means was very similar to the manual labeling.

In this case, both models performs similarly in terms of the F1-score, a useful metric to evaluate unbalanced data, such as the present one. Thus, we select the SVM model as the best model found in terms of the slightly higher accuracy

Table 4. Evaluation metrics of the DT model.

	Precision	Recall	f1-score	Support
High	0.83	1.00	0.91	10
Medium	0.95	0.74	0.83	27
Low	0.69	0.92	0.79	12
Accuracy			0.84	49
Macro avg	0.82	0.89	0.84	49
Weighted avg	0.86	0.84	0.84	49

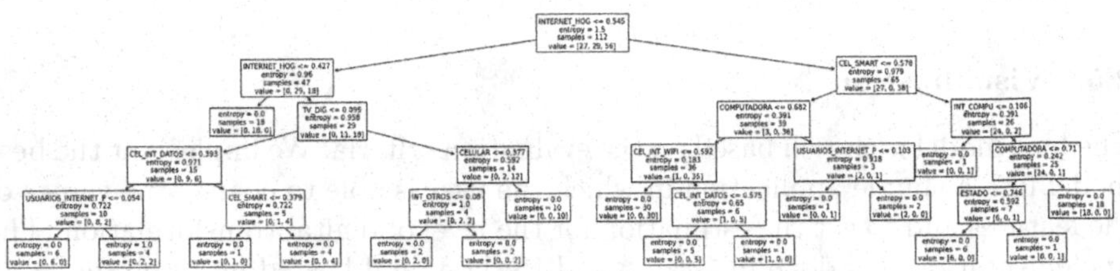

Fig. 4. The best DT model.

over the DT model. Figure 5 shows an excerpt of the Gradio application developed for digital transformation measurement using the SVM model. The application can be accessed at: https://huggingface.co/spaces/ML-Project/Digital-Transformation-Index.

Digital Transformation Index

TV DIGITAL
0
TELÉFONO MÓVIL
0
CONSOLA DE VIDEOJUEGOS
0
COMPUTADORA
0
CELULAR
0
SMARTPHONE
0
CELULAR CON INTERNET DE WIFI
0
CELULAR CON INTERNET DE DATOS
0
INTERNET EN EL HOGAR
0

DIGITAL TRANSFORMATION INDEX
DTI: Bajo
Avisar

Fig. 5. Digital transformation measurement application using the SVM model.

The application can be used for analyzing the estimations on the digital transformation adopted by a National state. This would be very useful for estimating the most influential or sensible features in the digital transformation and how policies might be shaped in order to reach a certain level of digital transformation.

To this end, we consider that our methodology is able to estimate the level of digital transformation using machine learning methods, specifically with the SVM model. This is the first attempt for including machine learning in estimating the digital transformation in Mexican households, so we can validate that our methodology is consistent and valid. However, this study is preliminary in the sense that there are no so many data available. Also, we manually labeled the data using high-level rules adopted from a methodology of the World Bank, and other approaches for labeling might be considered.

4 Conclusions

In this work, we proposed a digital transformation measurement in Mexican households using machine learning models, i.e. SVM. For this, we used the ENDUTIH dataset that is a collection of data from the Mexican government about the ICT infrastructure, services and uses in Mexican households. We got inspiration from the methodology of the World Bank to manually label the data, so that the machine learning models could be built and trained.

Moreover, a digital transformation measurement in households would support the following aspects: (a) investment, because it would make it possible to identify investment opportunity areas for telecommunications operators; (b) connectivity policy because it can help target government connectivity subsidies or potential social coverage funds to deliver connectivity to households; (c) business intelligence, because it would allow application and content companies to identify which are the entities with the greatest potential for users.

So, we anticipate that the use machine learning models can provide an accurate estimation of the digital transformation, but also they can be used for the analysis of the features importance in the digital transformation in developing countries, e.g. Mexico, so those can be further influence on the digital transformation policies.

Future work could be done so that the K-means model obtains more shaped clusters. Also, it is proposed to use some methods such as Bayesian networks to analyze the correlation of the variables involved in the models. In future examples that fall into a certain category (using the predictive models), it would be relevant to evaluate the degree of precision as a metric.

References

1. Baller, S., Dutta, S., Lanvin, B.: The Global Information Technology Report 2016. Innovating in the Digital Economy. World Economic Forum, 91–93 route de la Capite, CH-1223 Cologny/Geneva, Switzerland (2016)

2. Betancourt, G.A.: Las máquinas de soporte vectorial (svms). Scientia Et Technica (2005). https://www.redalyc.org/articulo.oa?id=84911698014
3. Bukht, R., Heeks, R.: Defining, conceptualising and measuring the digital economy. Dev. Inform. **1**(68), 10–11 (2017)
4. Commission, E.: Digital economy and society index (desi) 2021 (2021). https://digital-strategy.ec.europa.eu/en/policies/desi. Accessed 11 June 2022
5. Heras, J.M.: Clustering (agrupamiento), k-means con ejemplos en python (2020). https://www.iartificial.net/clustering-agrupamiento-kmeans-ejemplos-en-python/. Accessed 11 June 2022
6. IBM: What is a decision tree? https://www.ibm.com/topics/decision-trees. Accessed 11 June 2022
7. INEGI: Nota sobre el cambio metodológico de la ENDUTIH (2020). https://www.inegi.org.mx/contenidos/programas/dutih/2020/doc/nota_tecnica_endutih_2020.pdf. Accessed 11 June 2022
8. Mishra, D., et al.: Digital Dividens, chap. Overview. The World Bank, 1818 H Street NW, Washington DC 20433 (2016)
9. Poland, E.: Digital transformation index (2020). https://www.ey.com/en_pl/technology/digital-transformation-index. Accessed 11 June 2020
10. Reinsdorf, M., Quirós, G., Group, S.: Measuring the digital economy. Policy Papers, pp. 9–11 (2018)
11. Sirimanne, S.N.: Digital economy report 2019. In: Value Creation and Capture: Implications for Developing Countries. 300 East 42nd Street, New York, New York 10017, USA (2019)
12. Technologies, D.: Measuring digital transformation progress around the world (2018). https://www.dell.com/en-us/dt/perspectives/digital-transformation-index.htm#scroll=off. Accessed 11 June 2022
13. Zaballos, A.G., Rodríguez, E.I.: Economía digital en América Latina y el Caribe. Situación actual y recomendaciones. Banco Interamericano de Desarrollo, 1300 New York Avenue, N.W. Washington, D.C. 20577 (2017)

Credit Risk Models in the Mexican Context Using Machine Learning

Ana Lilia López, Estefanía López, and Hiram Ponce(✉)

Facultad de Ingeniería, Universidad Panamericana, Augusto Rodin 498, 03920 Ciudad de México, Mexico
{0253687,0142136,hponce}@up.edu.mx

Abstract. The Default Rate is related to the period of the economic cycle in which they are observed, during expansion periods of the economy the default rate tends to be lower. But in contraction periods, the default rate tends to increase and this could be a risk for the stability of a country's economy. Therefore, it is important to monitor the perspective of the economy in case it is expected to decrease or have abrupt movements. This work aims to identify the economic variables that determine the default rate of the Mexican Financial System and to find a machine learning model that forecasts the default rate. For this, we aggregate a dataset based on three official Mexican sources that compile data from 2013 to 2022, including the COVID-19 pandemic time frame. Then, we propose the analysis using two machine learning models. After the analysis, the results confirm that the artificial neural networks model shows better predictive power for the default rate values. We also implement an easy to use web application to estimate the default rate based on three simple variables. We anticipate this work might help on estimating the default rate and might impact on the strategic policies in the Mexican economy.

Keywords: Machine learning · Linear regression · Artificial neural networks · Credit risk · Mexican financial system

1 Introduction

The financial crises that the Mexican Financial System has faced, have caused significant changes in the way banking does business. Some Financial Institutions have improved their management tools and have been strengthened to have a broader view of risks.

As we experience financial crises, we learn more about how to manage credit portfolios and it is reflected in financial management. For example in 1970 the origins of portfolio risk was created and in 1990 credit scoring techniques became popular using data mining models and mathematical statistical techniques [7].

O. Pichardo Lagunas et al. (Eds.): MICAI 2022, LNAI 13613, pp. 339–347, 2022.
https://doi.org/10.1007/978-3-031-19496-2_26

The analysis of the different types of risks faced by the Financial System is important in order to guarantee its sustainability and the development of the economy. In terms of credit risk, it is relevant to study the probability of default because it reflects the behavior of clients and their delinquency; since it is an issue that affects the country's banking situation, monitoring the default rate and estimating its future behavior helps to evaluate the potential risk of lending money to consumers and mitigate the losses caused by the non-performing portfolio.

The Default Rate is related to the period of the economic cycle in which they are observed, during expansion periods of the economy the default rate tends to be lower, and in contraction periods the default rate tends to increase [8]. At this moment, and after the crisis caused by the COVID-19 pandemic, we have much more information to analyze the Mexican Banking System and recognize possible vulnerabilities it may have. Therefore, the current work is focused on identifying the economic variables that determine the default rate of the Mexican Financial System and that help as early warning indicators of changes in the economy.

Due to the uncertainty of how the default rate of the Mexican Financial System will behave, and in case of adverse scenarios of the economy, it would have a negative impact on the financial health of the Banks, it is planned to perform a Multiple Linear Regression Model and an Artificial Neural Networks in order to obtain a model that adjusts the behavior of default rates (delinquency) of the Mexican Financial System according to the economic variables that turn out to be significant for credit delinquency and thus be able to make estimates of future default rates according to the projections of macroeconomic variables (GDP, interest rates, exchanges rates, etc.) as it has done in the study of Neural Networks and Credit Risk Assessment but with data from Mexico [9].

This work aims to determine a model that describes the pattern of the default rates in the Mexican context and can forecast the behavior of future default rates in the context of projected economic scenarios, considering different macroeconomic variables as input. In order for the Mexican Financial System to have an early warning indicator that allows it to make appropriate decisions in case of adverse economic scenarios and to have a better risk management, seeking an approach that helps the vulnerability reduction strategy.

To do so, we use the aggregation of three public data sets from the Mexican financial system. Then, we propose using an artificial neural network and compare it with a multivariate linear regression model. After the building and evaluation analysis, we found that the neural network model is able to estimate the default rate. Lastly, we implement an easy to use application for predicting the level of the default rate of the Mexican financial system.

The rest of the paper is organized as follows. Section 2 summarizes the related work. Section 3 proposes the methodology of our work. Section 4 shows the results. Lastly, Sect. 5 concludes the paper.

2 Related Work

In the work of Perez et al. [9], the authors conducted a research project on risk classification in credit portfolios by applying neural network methodology. This work shows the application of neural networks to the quantification of credit risk. The objective of the analysis is to find some relationships for certain groups of the population, according to their particular characteristics and in Arrieta et al. [1], the authors apply a study that tries to find a model to predict the performance of a stock in the market. This study compares the results of statistical, econometric and artificial neural network models. Evidence was obtained in favor of the use of econometric and artificial neural network models built from principal components that allow to achieve daily stock predictions.

Both works were inspirational for the study conducted, however, the first work is based on data from Colombia and the second one focuses on the prediction of the price of a share. So our study contributes to the study of the prediction of the Default Rate with data specifically from Mexico.

3 Methodology

In this work, we propose to use a standard workflow of machine learning that comprises four main steps: (a) data collection, (b) data preparation, (c) building models, and (d) evaluation of models. Details are presented next.

3.1 Dataset Description

For this work, we aggregate data from three different sources. The target value is retrieved from the public dataset of the National Bank and Stock Commission (CNBV) namely the Default Rate "SH_SOCAPS_202104" of the Mexican Financial System [3]. The target value:

- **IMOR or Default Rate:** from January 2013 to December 2021.

We also retrieved data of economic variables in Mexico from the INEGI [5]:

- **GDP:** history series is available from January 1980 to April 2022.
- **Inflation:** there is a historical series from January 1970 to March 2022.
- **Unemployment rate:** there is a historical series from January 2005 to March 2022.

Lastly, the data of economic variables in Mexico from the National Bank (BANXICO) [2], including:

- **TIIE to 28 days:** consider a monthly time series from March 1995 to April 2022.
- **TIIE to 91 days:** consider a monthly time series from January 1997 to April 2022.

- **CETES to 28 days:** consider a monthly time series from September 1982 to April 2022.
- **CETES to 91 days:** consider a monthly time series from January 1980 to April 2022.
- **CETES to 182 days:** consider a monthly time series from September 1984 to April 2022.
- **CETES to 364 days:** consider a monthly time series from November 1990 to April 2022.
- **BONO 3A:** Three-year bond, consider a monthly time series from January 2000 to April 2022.
- **FIX:** Exchange rate Pesos per dollar U.S. dollar from March 1995 to March 2022.
- **TC EUR:** Exchange rate Pesos per Euro from January 2000 to March 2022.

For consistency, although some variables have more in-depth historical information, the information has been standardized to use data from January 2013 through March 2022. Due to the nature of the data we have, which is a series of historical data, it was decided to group the data at different levels, obtaining the data at the monthly and quarterly levels, and obtaining the annual increases versus the same period of a previous year.

3.2 Data Pre-processing

To group the data at different period levels, as GDP is reported quarterly, we obtain the monthly series through a linear interpolation. Thus, the trend of quarterly observations, month by month, are completed.

If T_i is the observation value in the quarterly period i, and T_{i+3} is the observation value of the next quarterly period, then, the interpolated intermediate values are as (1). Subsequently, from the monthly GDP series, the percentage of change of GDP is obtained.

$$\begin{aligned} T_{i+1} &= T_i + 1/3(T_{i+3} - T_i) \\ T_{i+2} &= T_i + 2/3(T_{i+3} - T_i) \end{aligned} \tag{1}$$

On the other hand, to obtain the quarterly data, the average of the quarter is considered as the quarterly data and the quarterly increase percentage is obtained as the quarterly increase of the original series, that is, of the monthly series.

For data pre-processing, we split the macroeconomic variables and rates at monthly and quarterly levels. Once we have this partitioning, we divide the data in small time windows for the training and test sets. Here we would like to use the training set to predict the next months. We repeat this procedure for quarterly and annual data.

In case the series has null values, the imputation technique implemented is to assign the value of the mean to the missing numerical data. A standardization scaling of the data is also performed to prevent that a variable, like the GDP, dominates more over others.

3.3 Building Models

In this work, we propose to use an artificial neural network model for forecasting the level of the default rate. In addition, we compare this model against a multiple linear regression that acts like the baseline model.

Multiple Linear Regression. It is a supervised model that allows to relate a set of independent variables X_i that are observable with a dependent variable Y, plus a random term E, through a linear equation. The dependent variable is assumed to have a linear relationship with respect to the set of independent variables, and (2) holds. Where, $\beta_0, \beta_1, \ldots, \beta_p$ are the regression coefficients for the independent variables $x_1, x_2, \ldots, x_p$ [4].

$$Y = \beta_0 + \beta_1 x_1 + ... + \beta_n x_p + \varepsilon \tag{2}$$

Considering the above, we fit a regression model and draw the actual values and the predictions.

Artificial Neural Networks. It behaves like a neuron of the human brain, as shown in the representation of Fig. 1. This technique is a subset of the machine learning methods that is implemented for complex nonlinear models. Therefore, we have considered this tool for the prediction of the series that we consider in our macro model [6].

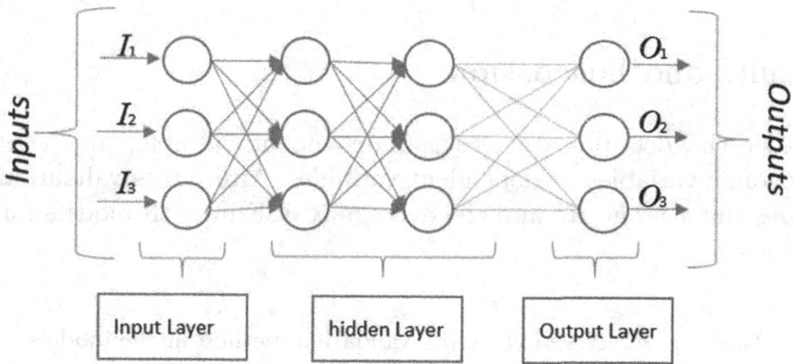

Fig. 1. Example of an artificial neural network.

The distribution of neurons within the network is carried out forming levels or layers, with a certain number of these neurons in each of them. From their location within the network, three types of layers can be distinguished (see Fig. 1):

- *Input:* it is the layer that directly receives the information coming from the external sources of the network.

- *Hidden:* they are internal to the network and do not have direct contact with the external environment. The number of hidden levels can be between zero and a high number. Neurons in the hidden layers can be interconnected in different ways, which determines, along with their number, the different topologies of neural networks.
- *Outputs:* transfer information from the network to the outside.

3.4 Model Validation

The available data were divided into 80% of training set and 20% of test set. In order to achieve a more accurate estimation, the validation strategy based on re-sampling and cross-validation is used to fit and evaluate the model repeatedly, using each time different subsets created from the training data and obtaining at each repetition an estimate of the error. In this work, we use a 5-fold cross-validation on the training set.

The evaluation metrics implemented in this work are the coefficient of determination R^2 (3) and the root mean square error RMSE (4); where, y_i is the target value, $\hat{y}_i$ is the estimated value, $\bar{y}_i$ is the mean of the target value, and n is the total number of samples.

$$R^2 = 1 - \frac{\sum_i (y_i - \hat{y}_i)^2}{\sum_i (y_i - \bar{y})^2} \tag{3}$$

$$RMSE = \sqrt{\frac{\sum_i (y_i - \hat{y}_i)^2}{n}} \tag{4}$$

4 Results and Discussion

We consider the default rate as the independent variable, and the different macroeconomic variables as dependent variables. After cross validation, Table 1 summarizes the average R^2 and the average RMSE in both models for training and testing.

Table 1. Results of the cross-validation method in the models.

Model	Train R^2	Test R^2	Train RMSE	Test RMSE
Linear regression	0.9645	0.9479	0.1466	0.1285
Neural network	0.9995	0.9499	0.0020	0.0186

The variables that were statistically significant and showed a good level of goodness of fit was used as independent variables. In this case, these variables are: the annual change in the quarterly 91-day TIIE, the annual change in the quarterly FIX, and the annual change in quarterly GDP.

From the results obtained above, the linear regression model performed with 0.1285 of RMSE and 0.9479 of R^2, while the neural network performed 0.0186 of RMSE and 0.9499 of R^2. These values validate that the neural network model performs slightly better for estimating the default rate. Figure 2 shows the behavior of the linear regression model versus the neural network model. Figure 3 shows the Monte Carlo simulation using both models.

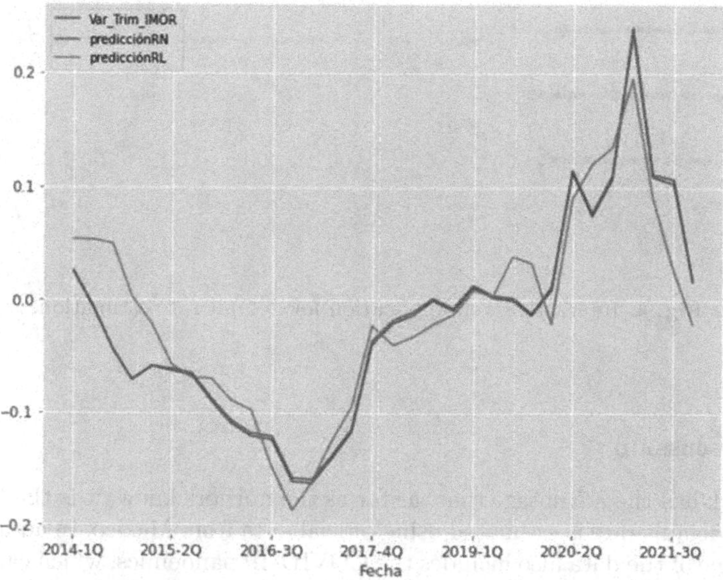

Fig. 2. Behavior of the machine learning models, linear regression (blue) and neural network (green), and the default rate value (red). (Color figure online)

				Neural Network Estimation		Linear Multiple Regression Estimation	
	TIIE 91	FIX	PIB	tasa_mora_est_RN	tasa_mora_estimada	tasa_mora_est_RL	tasa_mora_estimada_RL
0.50	0.049682	0.062375	0.011010	-0.015816	4.763450	-0.012657	4.778740
0.75	0.274599	0.127682	0.048070	0.023701	4.954712	0.044479	5.055276
0.90	0.460028	0.186992	0.085985	0.070678	5.182084	0.101794	5.332685
0.95	0.562732	0.225147	0.104844	0.098809	5.318235	0.125236	5.446141
0.99	0.775204	0.298896	0.137103	0.152623	5.578696	0.161764	5.622940

Fig. 3. Comparison of estimation with neural network vs linear regression.

4.1 Implementation

We also created an interactive web application on Gradio in Python, so that users can interact with the variables of TIIE 91 days, exchange rate with the dollar FIX, and depending on the forecasts of the macroeconomic variables can estimate the level of the default rate of the Mexican financial system. Figure 4 shows the web application with the three independent variables and the output response. It is possible to interact with the application at: https://huggingface.co/spaces/Ani1712full/Estimacion_tasa_morosidad.

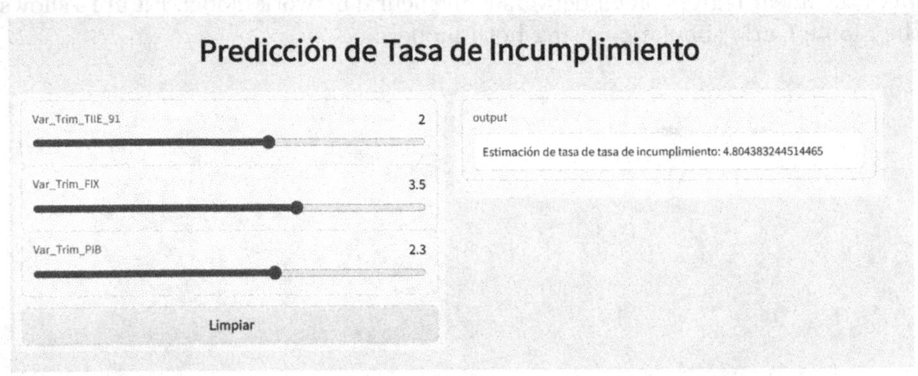

Fig. 4. Interactive web application for default rate estimation.

4.2 Discussion

This work has the advantage that, as far as the authors know, it is the first time that the default rate is estimated using official data from Mexico. In addition, the time frame of the data also includes the COVID-19 pandemics, which can be very informative nowadays. As limitation of this work, the analysis was performed with the default rate at a global level and it is not possible to observe the behavior of this variable at the loan portfolio level.

From the results, we can proved that it is possible to estimate the default rate in Mexico using a machine learning model with high predictive power.

In the following table, the .50 percentile can be seen as the mean value, while data greater than .50 are conservative predictions which indicate there could be a higher percentage of risk.

5 Conclusions

The objective of this project was to determine a model that describes the pattern of the default rates of the Mexican financial system for forecasting the behavior of future default rates according to the projected economic scenarios, to have an early warning indicator that allows it to make appropriate decisions in case of adverse economic scenarios. For which, we developed two machine learning models: the multiple linear regression model and the neural network model.

The results of the neural network model as well as the results of the multiple linear regression model show a good fit to the data and a good performance in

RMSE and R^2. In addition, it is concluded that neural networks are better to predict the default rate of the Mexican financial system. It generates confidence for the elaboration of strategies to minimize the expected risk, allows to generate models in a practical and easy way, and shows greater performance at the time of execution.

Given that this work carried out with official information from the CNBV, BANXICO and INEGI, we consider that one of the users of the interactive application could be the CNBV since they have the capacity to make tactical decisions in adverse economic scenarios to help mitigate the negative effects on default rates, just as they made decisions in the COVID-19 pandemic.

For future work, it is proposed to do a back-testing on the neural network model. It is also proposed to analyze at the portfolio level of the Mexican financial system such as: mortgages, credit card, consumer, corporate, developers, etc. And it is not ruled out to continue testing other machine learning models.

References

1. Arrieta Bechara, J., Torres Cruz, J., Velásquez Ceballos, H.: Predicciones de modelos econométricos y redes neuronales: El caso de la acción de suraminv. semestre económico, vol. 12, no. 25. Semestre Económico (2009)
2. BANXICO: Banxico: Sistema de información económica. https://www.banxico.org.mx/SieInternet/
3. CNBV: Cnbv: Portafolio de información. https://portafolioinfo.cnbv.gob.mx/portafolioinformacion/forms/allitems.aspx
4. Hu, Y., Yu, S., Qi, X., Zheng, W., Wang, Q., Yao, H.: An overview of multiple linear regression model and its application. Zhonghua yu Fang yi xue za zhi [Chin. J. Prevent. Med.] **53**(6), 653–656 (2019)
5. INEGI: Inegi: Banco de información económica. https://www.inegi.org.mx/sistemas/bie/
6. Matich, D.J.: Redes neuronales: Conceptos básicos y aplicaciones. Universidad Tecnológica Nacional, México, vol. 41, pp. 12–16 (2001)
7. Morales, I.R.: Un modelo de calificaciÓn estadÍstica para una instituciÓn mexicana especializada en microcrÉditos. In: 3er Simposio Internacional de Investigación en Ciencias Económicas, Administrativas y Contables - Sociedad y Desarrollo (2013)
8. Ntiamoah, E.B., Oteng, E., Opoku, B., Siaw, A.: Loan default rate and its impact on profitability in financial institutions. Res. J. Finance Account. **5**(14), 67–72 (2014)
9. Pérez Ramírez, F.O., Fernández Castaño, H.: Las redes neuronales y la evaluación del riesgo de crédito. Revista Ingenierías Universidad de Medellín **6**(10), 77–91 (2007)

Ventilator Pressure Prediction Using a Regularized Regression Model

Amaury Arellano, Erick Bustamante, Carlos Garza, and Hiram Ponce[✉]

Facultad de Ingeniería, Universidad Panamericana, Augusto Rodin 498, 03920 Ciudad de México, Mexico
{0253685,0253695,0252780,hponce}@up.edu.mx

Abstract. The mechanical ventilation is one of the most frequent methods used in Intensive Care Units (ICUs) to improve the breathing of patients. During the early days of the COVID-19 pandemic, the use of mechanical ventilators has been crucial. In this work, we propose to build a Lasso regression model based on lung simulators for predicting the airway pressure in the respiratory circuit of ventilators while breathing. We model the whole breathing process in two separate states. After that, we analyze the feature importance in the regression model to better understand the ventilator pressure prediction. We anticipate this model would help improving the patient's health and overcoming the cost barrier of new methods for mechanical ventilators.

Keywords: Mechanical ventilation · Airway pressure · Simulators · Lasso regression · Machine learning

1 Introduction

The mechanical ventilation is one of the most frequent methods used in Intensive Care Units (ICUs) in order to decrease the work of breathing of patients until patient improve enough to no longer need it, among other different diseases. During COVID 19 Pandemic, mechanical ventilation has been fundamental to assist infected patients [2].

Even though mechanical ventilation has been in place for decades on ICUs are many challenges to face as to have an efficient control of mechanical ventilator and to prevent ventilator-induced lung injury (VILI) [2]. Nonetheless, developing VILI not only depends of the ventilator, there are more things to consider as the lungs medical condition of the patient. The baseline patient characteristics make that the trained clinicians have to constant monitoring thus in order to make more efficient the process. Given the highly manual process of mechanical ventilation, it is desirable to have data-driven control methods that can better track prescribed pressure targets and are robust to variations of the patient's lung. [6].

O. Pichardo Lagunas et al. (Eds.): MICAI 2022, LNAI 13613, pp. 348–355, 2022.
https://doi.org/10.1007/978-3-031-19496-2_27

Motivated by this potential to improve patient health, we studied the lung data simulated by the Google Brain team in order to develop a machine learning model for pressure prediction. Previous works tackle this task with deep learning models [4] and [7] but this models lack of interpretability.

In this work, we propose a much simpler model with a better understand of the prediction. For this, we build a regularized regression model for both high predictability of the ventilator pressure prediction and the interpretability of the features involved.

The rest of the paper is as follows. Section 2 summarizes the related work. Section 3 presents the details of the proposal. Section 4 shows the experimentation. Section 5 summarizes the experimental results and discussion. Lastly, Sect. 6 concludes the paper.

2 Related Work

In 1994, the work in [5] studied how different configurations of the mechanical ventilator are linked with a lower mortality. Predicting survival on patients requiring mechanical ventilation. This work is focused on the patient characteristics as predictive variables.

Further work is related on how machine learning and artificial intelligence can help to produce a better ventilator management. In Kuo et al. [4], the authors developed an artificial neural network for predicting successful extubation in mechanically ventilated patients. As well as in other studies, this work relays on the patient previous studies and deceases in order to predict the treatment success.

More work related with ventilators and other diseases is studied like in Chen et al. [1] in which this work mainly discusses the treatment of obstructive sleep apnea syndrome with a positive pressure ventilator based on artificial intelligence processor in order to identify when the patient is having an apnea episode and alert to the medical personal.

The previous work has as a common objective to predict the treatment success on patients, having as input variables the patient medical conditions. In the current work, our objective is slightly different, because we aim to predict the correct operation of mechanical ventilators.

3 Description of the Proposal

We propose to implement the workflow shown in Fig. 1. It comprises of four main steps: data collection (data set), data preparation (exploratory analysis and feature extraction), building models (train the models), and evaluation of models (test the models and re-design of the training). Details are presented next.

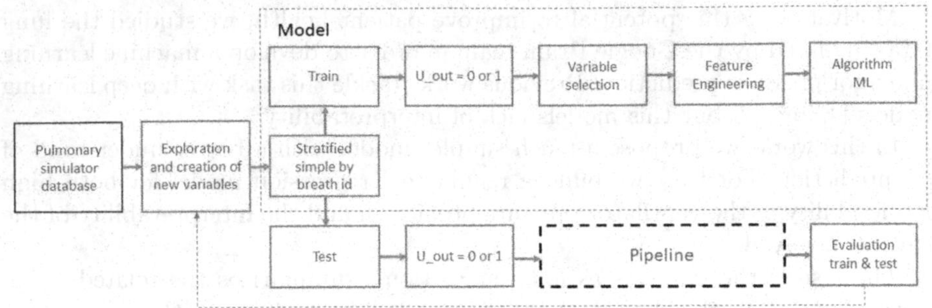

Fig. 1. Workflow implemented in this problem.

3.1 Dataset Description

The ventilator data used in this work is a public dataset from Google Brain (the original data is available in Kaggle[1]). The data set was produced using a modified open-source ventilator connected to an artificial bellows test lung via a respiratory circuit. In the Fig. 2 the setup is illustrated, with the two control inputs highlighted in green and the state variable (airway pressure) to predict in blue. The first control input is a continuous variable from 0 to 100 representing the percentage the inspiratory solenoid valve is open to let air into the lung (i.e., 0 is completely closed and no air is let in and 100 is completely open). The second control input is a binary variable representing whether the exploratory valve is open (1) or closed (0) to let air out.

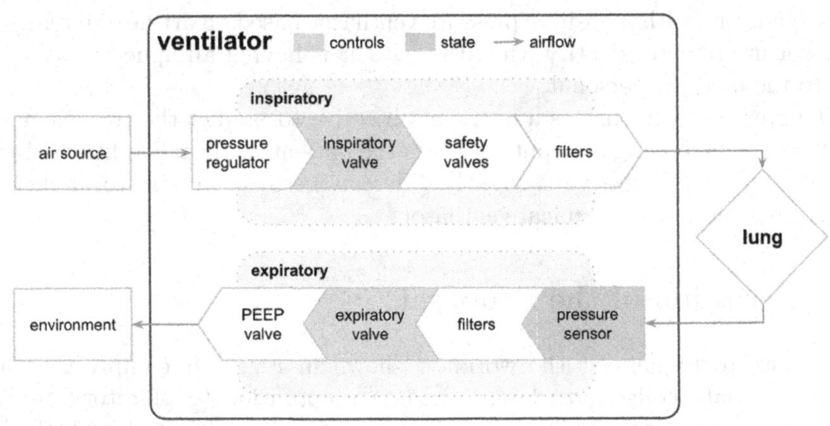

Fig. 2. Ventilator process scheme.

[1] https://www.kaggle.com/competitions/ventilator-pressure-prediction/data.

Each time series represents an approximately 3-second breath. The files are organized such that each row is a time step in a breath and gives the two control signals, the resulting airway pressure, and relevant attributes of the lung, described in Fig. 1.

Table 1. Attributes in the time series.

Name	Description	Type
id	Globally-unique time step identifier across an entire file	ID
breath_id	Globally-unique time step for breaths	ID
R	Lung attribute indicating how restricted the airway is (in cmH2O-L-S)	Integer
C	Lung attribute indicating how compliant the lung is (in mL/cmH2O)	Float
time_step	Actual time stamp	Float
u_in	Control input for the inspiratory solenoid valve	Float
u_out	Control input for the exploratory solenoid valve	Binary
pressure	Airway pressure measured in the respiratory circuit in cmH2O	Target

3.2 Exploratory Data Analysis

According to the above dataset description, the model should predict the pressure, based on one of the variables presented. In this case, the target variable is given by the 'pressure' variable.

In order to find certain patterns in the data, an analysis of pressure distribution with respect to time was performed. This analysis shows that there is a change in the distribution when the variable 'u_out' takes different values. This can be seen in Fig. 3.

Since there are two distributions, we propose to build one model when the variable 'u_out' = 1 and another when 'u_out' = 0. This will help us to find different patterns for each one.

Once these two populations to be modeled were defined, it was decided to create extract some features in order to obtain prior information on each observation. The following features were extracted:

- **u_in_cumsum** - cumulative sum of inspiratory solenoid valve control input
- **u_in_sh2** - control of the inspiratory solenoid valve observed two positions below
- **RC** - concatenation of R and C

We also calculated the correlation matrix in order to explore the possible linear relations. The matrix can be seen in Fig. 4.

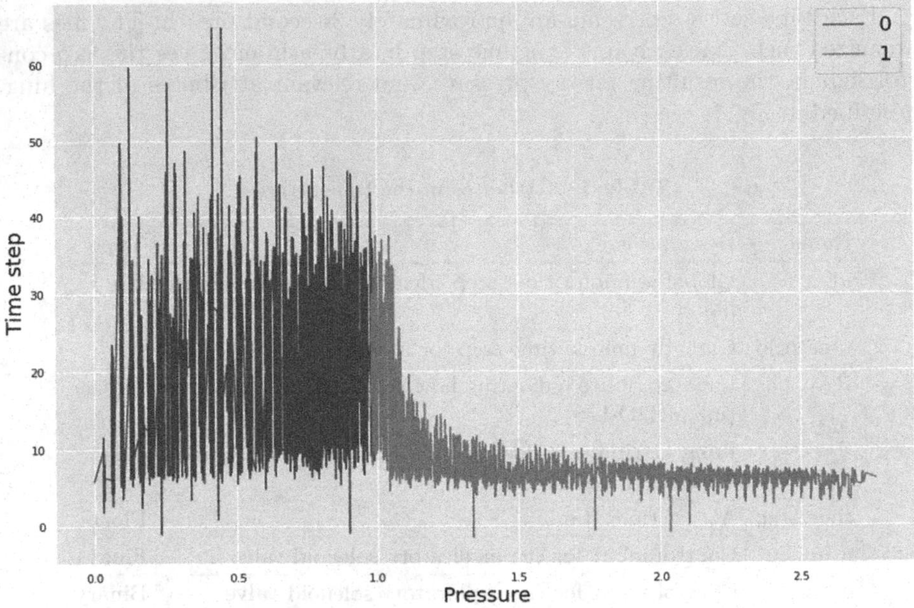

Fig. 3. Distribution pressure when changing 'u_out'.

	R	C	time_step	u_in	u_out	pressure
R	1.00	-0.10	-0.01	-0.15	-0.01	0.02
C	-0.10	1.00	0.00	0.15	0.00	-0.04
time_step	-0.01	0.00	1.00	-0.35	0.84	-0.52
u_in	-0.15	0.15	-0.35	1.00	-0.42	0.31
u_out	-0.01	0.00	0.84	-0.42	1.00	-0.61
pressure	0.02	-0.04	-0.52	0.31	-0.61	1.00

Fig. 4. Correlation matrix.

3.3 Building Models

This section aims to explain how the models have been developed. First, the extracted features are created to obtain information before each observation, as described above. Second, training and test samples are obtained by stratifying 'breath_id'. Third, splitting is performed when 'u_out' is 0 or 1. Finally, a model is trained based on the loss metric MSE (1), where y_i^p is the estimated pressure value. In this work we discussed the use of mean absolute error (MAE) and mean squared error (MSE), for the nature of the data analyzed we need a loss function that prevents extreme estimations. As the pressure variable is continuous and we need to assure that the model has not extreme pressure estimations, we decided to use MSE as loss function, the formula is described below and the effect of the squared error magnifies an extreme estimation.

$$MSE = \frac{1}{n}\sum_{i=1}^{n}(y_i - y_i^p)^2 \tag{1}$$

In this work we explored three models aiming to reduce the MSE loss function. The first model explored is a Lasso regression [8], we tried to use this model because of the simplicity of the estimators and also to take advantage of the regularization techniques for the feature selection process because the parameters could be zero. We have the hypothesis that the relation between pressure and the attributes studied is linear, as we can see in the correlation matrix some features correlated to pressure. The second approach explored is a neural network [3], this choice was based on the predictive power of the algorithm and also because we have a reduced number of variables and it could help to reduce the time involved on training the model, also we decided to use neural networks because of previous work that we find in Kuo et al. [4] in which this approach is used to predict successful extubation. The last model is random forest [3]. We explore this approach because in other studies it is able to recognize a set of characteristics on the patients to predict the success of the treatment, one example of this is Chen et al. [1] where the approach is to find inconsistencies on the correct ventilator operation. We have a similar hypothesis in this study, that we could determine a set of rules in order to predict the malfunction of a mechanical ventilator.

4 Experimentation

In order to be able to predict as accurately as possible, a series of experiments were carried out where different models were tested with different hyperparameters, using grid-search. These experiments are described as follow:

1. As mentioned, in order to generate the test and training set, we stratify by 'breath_id' and select only 70% for training and 30% for testing.
2. The feature selection was done based on a random forest with $max\_depth = 6$ and $n\_estimators = 100$.
3. Three models were tested as follow:
   (a) Neuronal Network: $reduce\_n\_components : [4, 6, 8, 9]$, $hidden\_layers' : [(10, 10), (25, 25)]$, $model\_activation : [identity, logistic, tanh, relu]$
   (b) Lasso regression: $\lambda : [0.1, 0.5, 0.8, 1]$
   (c) Random Forest: $nEstimators : [50, 100, 150]$, $maxDepth : [None, 4, 5, 6]$
4. After an evaluation, a proper selection of the model was made.

All the experiments were done in Python using the scikit-learn library.

5 Results and Discussion

Table 2 summarizes the results of the predictive power of the three models in terms of the MSE. Notice that these models are built using the best hyper-parameters found with grid-search, as explained earlier.

Table 2. MSE results of the models.

Model	MSE, 'u_out'=0	MSE, 'u_out'=1
Neural networks	30.32	10.97
Lasso Regression	53.12	30.12
Random Forest	18.65	2.52

From Table 2, we validated that Lasso regression is the best model for the dataset. In this regard, we proceeded to determine the covariate weights of the Lasso regression model with $\lambda = 1$, as shown in Table 3, so we can explain the features involved.

Table 3. Covariate weights of the Lasso regression model.

Covariates	Weights, 'u_out' = 0	Weights, 'u_out' = 1
time_step	5.3214	−3.2428
u_in_cumsum	0.0158	0.0013
C	−0.130	−0.0102
u_in_sh2	0.1588	0.4994
RC	0.0012	0.0001
u_in	−0.0839	−0.3120

From Table 3, we can observe that 'time_step' has the highest magnitude weight for the prediction in both states. Thus, we validate that the pressure depends mainly on time, something that had already been observed previously (see Fig. 3). This leads us to think that we should include new information that considers this time factor, that is, variables that give us previous information of the observation.

On the other hand, we observe that the weight of the covariate 'RC' is very close to 0. This indicates that it has very little predictive power, it practically does not play an important role in the regression. We could mix RC with another variable, in case we do not want to lose that information, or remove it from the regression.

6 Conclusions

In this work, we proposed a simple machine learning model for predicting the ventilator pressure, and to use it for better understanding on this specific domain. To do so, we explored different approaches, from the exploratory analysis we found that a split on the data was necessary because there is a completely different behaviour depending on the state of the control 'u_out'. Then, we found that the better way to solve the problem was the simplest model, to say the Lasso regression model with a regularization coefficient $\lambda = 1$. Lastly, we found that the time step is the most relevant feature in the model, while the RC factor (a combination between the restrictive airway and the compliant of the lung) is the least important one.

For future work, we suggest considering variables concerning to patient's characteristics, food habits, and other variables from related studies. This would make models be more accurate. Also, it would help to predict the patient's treatment as well as the correct operation of the mechanical ventilator.

References

1. Chen, Z., Zhao, Z., Zhang, Z.: Obstructive sleep apnea syndrome treated using a positive pressure ventilator based on artificial intelligence processor. Healthcare Eng. **2021**(Article ID 5683433), 10 (2021)
2. Wunsch, H.: Mechanical ventilation in COVID-19: interpreting the current epidemiology. Am. J. Respir. Crit. Care Med. **202**(1), 1–4 (2020)
3. James, G., Witten, D., Hastie, T., Tibshirani, R.: An Introduction to Statistical Learning. STS, vol. 103. Springer, New York (2013). https://doi.org/10.1007/978-1-4614-7138-7
4. Kuo, H.J., Chiu, H.W., et al.: Improvement in the prediction of ventilator weaning outcomes by an artificial neural network in a medical ICU. Respiratory Care **60**(11), 1560–1569 (2015)
5. Nava, S., Rubini, F., Zanotti, E., et al.: Survival and prediction of successful ventilator weaning in COPD patients requiring mechanical ventilation for more than 21 days. Eur. Respir. J. **1994**(7), 1645–1652 (1994)
6. Rittayamai, N., Katsios, C.M., et al.: Pressure-controlled vs volume controlled ventilation in acute respiratory failure: a physiology-based narrative and systematic review. Chest **148**(2), 340–355 (2015)
7. Suo, D., Zhang, C., et al.: Machine learning for mechanical ventilation control. CoRR abs/2102.06779 (2021)
8. Tibshirant, R.: Regression shrinkage and selection vi lasso. J. R. Satist. Soc. B **1996**(59), 267–288 (1996)

An Intelligent Human Activity Recognizer for Visually Impaired People Using VGG-SVM Model

Rabeeya Saleem[1(✉)], Tauqir Ahmad[1], Muhammad Aslam[1], and A. M. Martinez-Enriquez[2]

[1] Department of Computer Science, UET Lahore, Lahore, Pakistan
rabeeyasaleem160@gmail.com
[2] Department of CS, CINVESTAV, Mexico City, Mexico
{tauqir_ahmad,maslam}@uet.edu.pk

Abstract. With the advancement of artificial intelligence and computer vision, assistive devices for visually impaired people is an active research area for the last decade. People with visual disabilities face challenges in the detection and recognition of various human actions which leads to a lack of confidence and constant dependency while performing daily routine activities. The objective of this research is to recognize and classify different human actions based on the position and posture of their body. In this research, captured video is processed for human pose estimation by extraction of 2D body skeleton using OpenPose method. The extracted body points further to the process for feature extraction using pre-trained VGG-19 CNN which classifies the human actions using an SVM classifier. Furthermore, the proposed method integrates with a voice-enabled feature to deliver instructions on classified human activities. The proposed deep learning method is to train and test using three different dataset (a) Weizmann dataset for gesture based human actions, (b) Kinetics dataset for interaction based human actions and (c) CK+ dataset for behaviour based human actions. The accuracy for classification of different human actions reached to 93.08%, 95.03%, and 93.12% and the F1 score reached 93.59%, 95.19% and 93.66%, respectively. These results indicate the significance of proposed method for the assistance of visually impaired people.

Keywords: Human Action Recognition (HAR) · VGG-19 · OpenPose · Support Vector Machine (SVM) · Visually Impaired People

1 Introduction

According to published statistics of the Vision Health Initiative (VHI), it was estimate that more than 253 million people suffer because of visual disability. Furthermore, 36 million people are entirely blind, while 217 million have impaired eyesight [1] In addition to this, as per reporting from World Health Organization

O. Pichardo Lagunas et al. (Eds.): MICAI 2022, LNAI 13613, pp. 356–368, 2022.
https://doi.org/10.1007/978-3-031-19496-2_28

(2021), 2.2 billion people are categorized as visually impaired that are unable to visualize surrounding environment [2]. For a person, who need to perform their routine task independently, analyze the surrounding environment, gather information about person, their orientation and predict the activities perform by other [11]. To visualize the surrounding environment and capture this information, normal people depends on their visual sense barely on the hearing or tactile ones. However, independent orientation is difficult for the blind or visually impaired due to insufficient contextual information obtained through audio and sensory medium [25].

Human activity recognition (HAR) is a challenging task belonging to computer vision that provides recognition of various activities in complex interactions without verbal communication. With the increasing trends of computer vision and deep learning techniques, researcher are working for detection and recognition of various activities to facilitate people having visual disability [19]. Recognition of human activities provide the sense of confidence and safer lifestyle for blind to understand behavior of other people lead to enhance person to person interaction. Activity recognition with sensors [13,26] and smart devices [8] are very common and available for assistance as various benchmarks applications are available. However, these systems rely on collecting data from sensors installed on the devices and user needs to wear these devices that are uncomfortable in practical.

Intelligent vision based systems are better alternative to overcome such challenges as user are not required to carry or wear any device all the time. Detection and recognition of human poses using from images or video stream is one of the popular framework with integration of advance intelligent technology [10]. Human poses impart remarkable success in human activity recognition, and researchers are widely using them in this problem these days. The concept is beneficial in various tasks such as HAR [22], content extraction and spatio-temporal features [5,20] using various deep learning technique because these are much efficient in dealing with images. Currently, the recognition of various human activities focus on to extract features using neural network methods and classifier that provide more appropriate and accurate classification of human activities more effectively and efficiently.

The main contribution of this research is to propose human pose estimation and activity recognition system that overcome the challenges arise due to wearable device. The system takes video input, extract the frame that contains person. If there exist person in video frames, human joints are labeled for 2D body skeleton through OpenPose technique which extract the features of detected person. The extracted features are then processed to classify the human activities by applying support vector machine (SVM) based on extracted features.

The rest of this paper is structured as: Sect. 2 discuss the literature of relevant research papers. Section 3 contains the description about dataset and their characteristics. Section 4 relevant to detail of proposed methodology, architecture and models applied for human action recognition. Experimental results have been discussed in Sect. 5. Finally, the Sect. 6 conclude the research work with some future direction.

2 Related Work

People having visual disabilities are unable to detect and recognize human activities and their behaviour to analyze and understand their intention. Due to increasing rate of crimes and abnormalities of various human actions, people having visual disability needs some assistance to recognize and predict objective of people around them [23]. Hidden Markov Model (HMM) methods have been widely employed as recognition techniques in the past due to their ability to decode temporal patterns [14]. However, deep learning techniques have stimulated the interest of researchers due to their capacity to automatically extract features and learn deep pattern structures.

With an betterment of local dependency and scaling in-variance, the deep learning algorithms are highly capable and efficient to extract features from images or video stream and classification based on these features. Ronao and Cho [28] presented a novel CNN architecture to extract complicated features by exploiting a convolutional neural network on human action dataset using raw signals and temporal characteristics of Fast Fourier Transformed signals [30]. However, these techniques for HAR require a significant degree of feature engineering and data preprocessing, which entails time for processing and application specificity. For human action recognition, a multi-input CNN-GRU classifier for HAR has been proposed [9]. The presented model's architecture includes the use of various sized convolutional filters (i.e. 3, 7, 11) capable of capturing diverse temporal dependencies in data. Also, the method can extract features automatically on the raw dataset. The performances of these systems are better and significant for uni modal sensors. However, the main problem is detecting and recognising actions by combining multi-modal sensors such as smart watches, stretch sensors, and wearable devices.

Human action recognition based on skeletons and their activities majorly focused on feature maps are divided into two categories based on feature extraction methods. The most important deep learning approaches are spatiotemporal networks and two-stream networks [7]. Recognition of human activities using vision sensors is a difficult problem due to fluctuations in lighting conditions and complex movements during sports, fitness workouts and routine activities [23]. An automatic human pose estimation proposed to extract the human body posture from images using entropy markov model which marked different body points to minimize the possibility of in-correction. The extracted features are then processed to classify complex human activities. The results from these methods are promising for limited human activities and face challenge of taking times while classification of human activities due to multidimensional cues.

To identify the single person and their interactive activities, researcher has proposed a deep learning based framework that extract human key-points using Mask R-CNN, and LSTM to capture temporal information for classification of these activities [24]. Furthermore, the proposed study is more relevant to safety and security for the purpose of surveillance, which would then be effective and advantageous while serving society with balanced lifestyle. However, the system is limited for accurate and fast classification due to lack of deep learning classification methods for activity recognition.

Coherent motion descriptors of moving objects using optical flow have gained a lot of attention in recent studies about violence detection and human crowd analysis. In [27], the researcher concentrated on the difficulty of identifying human activity by using optical flow histograms in both horizontal and vertical dimensions as action descriptors. Although it is an effective method for action recognition, it requires specialised hardware, making it computationally expensive. To recognize distant activities in video frame, optical flow method uses either histogram of the orientation or histogram of the magnitude of optical flow to represent an activity. It certainly works for a few rare circumstances, such as jogging in public or travelling in the other direction, among other things. However, the limitation exist while selection of histogram in different scenario for different functionalities.

To overcome these challenges while recognition and classification of human activities, the main goal of this research is to classify human activities while extraction of 2D skeleton data of detected human from captured video stream. For this purpose, image frames after pre-processing processed through OpenPose method for extraction of body pose joint. The information of human body joint are then processed to generate a feature vector for training of VGG-19 Convolutional method. In addition, the system classify the human activities through SVM classification method that predict the human activities in video. Finally, the classified activities are then communicate to visually impaired people while understanding human behavior around them.

3 Intelligent Vision-Eye for Blind

People having visual disability are unable to analyze the activities of other people while performing their daily routine activities. The detection and recognition of various human activities are challenging task through computer vision techniques. The proposed solution for visually impaired people takes the video input captured through camera which process to detect the existence of human in it using Yolov5 object detection method. The system after detection of human presence are processed through four major phases: A) The extraction of human body joints to extract features of 2D body skeleton using OpenPose library. B) The extracted features are then map to feature vector that is used for the training of VGG-19 method. C) The classification of human activities into their relevant class using support vector machine (SVM) classification method for effective and accurate activity classification. D) Finally, the extracted outcome from activity recognition module is converted into speech command to deliver information to visually impaired people as demonstrated in Fig. 1.

3.1 Proposed Solution

In this section, we explain the details of human action recognition and classification into various classes using OpenPose with VGG-19 method. The processing of video for accurate results of action classification include various modules as discussed below.

Data Pre-processing The dataset collected for detection of various human activities are processed to extract the foreground features and improve frame data. The input frame captured by the given video sequence, which is originally RGB format. The step by step process of video pre-processing enhance its features to overcome the hidden observation challenges using computer vision techniques.

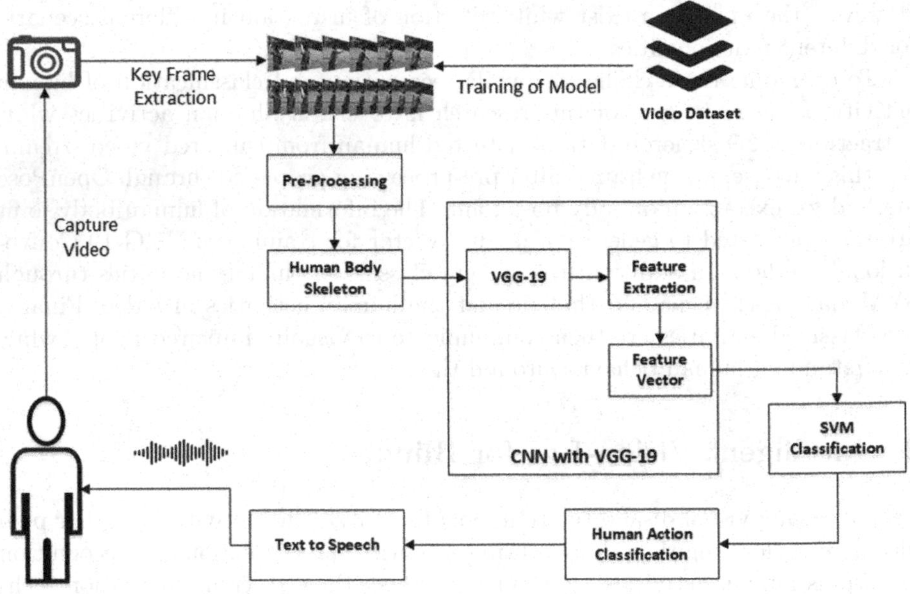

Fig. 1. Proposed architecture for human action recognition

The steps of pre-processing enhance the visualization ability and flexible to feature extraction from video frame. The designed approach first enhances image frames before transforming them into Hue saturation-intensity (HSI) colour space. In RGB colour space, the HSI transformation is executed after each colour channel's contrast stretching [29]. After color differentiation from video frames, there is need to remove extra noise using Gaussian function to apply blur effect and remove noise. The min-max normalisation is employed to stabilise the convergence of the loss functions.

The pre-processed video frame processed to detect the human object in moving clips. The frames contain human object are process further otherwise remove for detection and recognition of human action. For this purpose, deep learning methods based on yolov4 [31] detect the various object in video stream and remove those frames that didn't detect human objects. Yolov4 include cross-iteration batch normalization (CBN) and pan aggregation network which detect the human object in more accurate and efficient manner.

Extract Human Body Skeleton. The processed video frame after pre-processing techniques extract the human body skeleton using 2D pose estimation model called OpenPose [4] which provide potential to a computer to analyze and understand human action in videos. Using openpose library, the computer have ability to extract 2D skeleton of human body indicating 25 different points in different area. Figure shows the extraction of human body skeleton and indicate 25 different point that provide the information of body position in video. In Fig. 2, (a) the system extract the video frame contain the human body for human body joints that classify human actions for the assistance of visually impaired people. In (b) and (c), figure indicates the mapping of 2D body skeleton joints that processed using deep learning feature extraction techniques for appropriate classification.

(a) Image Frame Extraction

(b) OpenPose 2D Body Joints

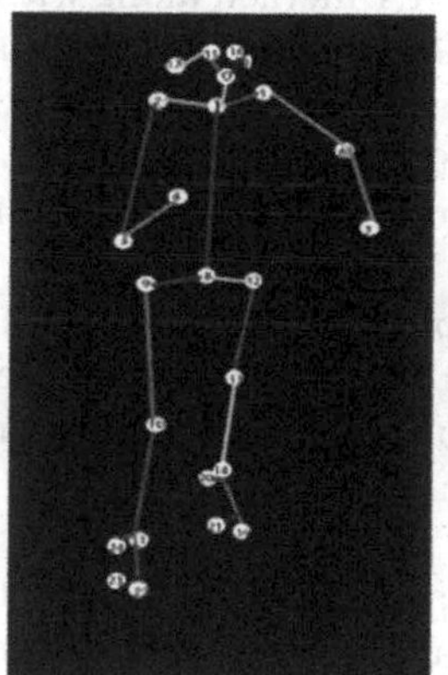

(c) Human Body Skeleton

Fig. 2. Extraction of 2D human body skeleton from video frames

Deep Feature Extraction for Activity Recognition. To extract spatio-temporal features of human skeleton, ten body joints including shoulder left, shoulder center, shoulder right, spine base, knee left, hip right, ankle left, hip left, ankle right, and knee right. Out of these 25 joints label provided by OpenPose, these ten were selected because these joints are presumably more relevant to the types of activities for recognition. The extracted joints position used to calculate the angle and displacement between joints. The average of the difference between two joint are used for calculating the angle values. The process of feature extraction from captured video using convolutional neural network. The working of VGG-19 CNN discuss below.

The VGG-19 convolutional neural network was implemented, and the model parameters were fine-tuned based on the model training and testing results. VGG-19 extracted low-level and high-level imaging features layer by layer, eventually achieving image classification and satisfying the recognition accuracy standards. It contains six main structures, each of which is mainly composed of multiple connected convolutional layers and full-connected layers. The size of the convolutional kernel is 3×3, and the input size is $224 \times 224 \times 3$. It is preferable to come up with traditional convolution because it employs an alternating structure of numerous convolutional layers and non-linear activation layers. The layer structure can better extract image features, apply Max-pooling for downsampling, and change the linear unit (ReLU) as the activation function, that is, choose the greatest value in the image area as the pooled value of the region, which improves anti-distortion ability.

Action Classification. In this section, the extracted feature from VGG-19 CNN method along with labeled dataset is used to train deep learning model for classification of human actions. Instead of the eliminated layer for classification using CNN, support vector machine classifier has been employed to predict the human activity label that supposed as machine learning classifier method while providing good results in comparison with other types of classifier.

While SVM training, hyperplanes in a high-dimensional space are produced to divide the training dataset into multiple classes. If the training data subset is not linearly separable, the data is sent to a new vector space using a kernel function SVM. SVM works well with big training datasets and produces accurate and effective results.

Despite the fact that SVM was originally designed for binary classification, it has been successfully extended to multi-class classification issues. The fundamental technique is to divide the multi-class problem into multiple bi-class problems and then integrate the outputs of all the sub-binary classifiers to generate a sample's final class prediction.

Text to Speech Instructions. To provide the extracted information to those having visual disability, an interactive communication environment integrated with vision based human activity recognition. People having visual disability need speech based interaction because they are unable to read textual information as an accessibility features to interact.

In this modules, text generated in natural language is then passed to speech generation module that translate the extracted text into speech using google text-to-speech (TTS) API. It has ability to convert textual information into speech output in different languages. The text is analysed and converted into audio waves which is then hear by user through headset. Text to Speech conversion takes two types of input: raw text and Speech Synthesis Markup Language (SSML)-formatted data. It allows to convert the arbitrary strings, words, and sentences in sequence of audio wave format for effective and interactive communication.

4 Dataset Description

In this research, approximately 30 different routine human activities are classified belonging to three major categories as following: I) Gesture level, II) Interactive level and III) Behaviour level as shown in Fig. 3. The dataset for training purpose are collected from various publicly available dataset. The Table 1 indicate the list the of different actions based on categories of gestures, interaction and behaviour of detected human.

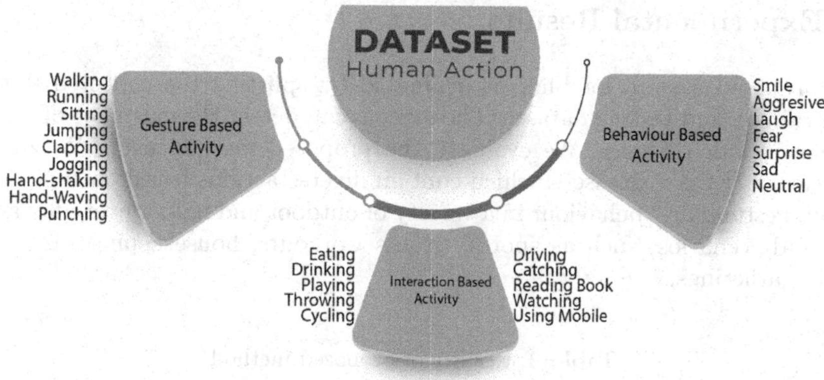

Fig. 3. Different classes of dataset for HAR

Table 1. Human action dataset description and features

Gestures based actions	Interaction based actions	Behaviour based actions
Walking	Easting	Smile
Running	Drinking	Aggressive
Sitting	Playing	Laugh
Jumping	Throwing	Fear
Clapping	Cycling	Surprise
Jogging	Driving	Sad
Hand-Shaking	Catching	Neutral
Hand Waving	Reading Book	
Punching	Watching	
	Using Mobile	

- For Detection of Gesture Based Human Activities
  To detect and recognize human gesture, we have used Weizmann dataset [12] for training and evaluation purpose. It includes various gesture activities i.e. walking towards, walking away, running toward, running away, jumping, sitting down, standing, jogging, hand clapping, hand shaking, one hand waving, both hands waving and punching.
- For Detection of Interaction Based Human Activities
  For the detection and recognition of human action using kinetics dataset [15] contains various activity including some event i.e. eating, drinking, playing, throwing, cycling, driving, catching, reading book, using mobile-phone, and watching.
- For Detection of Behaviour Based Human Activities
  For the detection and recognition of human action based on their facial expression, CK+ dataset [18]. The data include major expressions i.e. aggressive, smile, laugh, fear, surprise, sad and neutral.

5 Experimental Results

The proposed system for blind is evaluated by splitting the collected dataset into training and testing dataset. The system can detect the existence of human actions in video frames. We evaluate the proposed method using Weizmann, Kinetics, and CK+ datasets, which contain diverse actions based on their interaction, gesture, and behaviour in a variety of outdoor and indoor everyday activities and scenarios, such as sports, fitness workouts, housekeeping tasks, and public gatherings.

Table 2. Results of proposed method

Category of human action	Dataset	Accuracy	Precision	Recall	F1-Score
Gesture	Weizmann dataset	93.08	96.93	90.47	93.59
Interaction	Kinetics	95.03	96.47	93.93	95.18
Behaviour	CK+	93.12	95.05	92.30	93.66

F1-score, recall, precision, and accuracy are the performance measures employed in this study. Accuracy ratio is the proportion of correctly identified samples to the total number of samples. Activities can be classified as True Positives (TP) and True Negatives (TN) when they are classified correctly and as False Negatives (FN) and False Positives (FP) when they are wrongly classified.

To evaluate the deep learning convolutional method for extraction of features and then classification it into human action, experiments are performed using Kinetics, CK+ and Weizmann datasets. Table 2 shows the result of human action classification methods using three different datasets. The results after performing training and testing activities indicate that the proposed method for classification of human action provide significant visualization for people having visually disabled people.

Table 3. Comparison of proposed method with existing method for Weizmann dataset

Model	Accuracy	F1-Score
CNN [16]	95.8	96.47
CNN-LSTM [3]	–	96.39
VGG-19+SVM (Proposed)	93.08	93.59

Table 4. Comparison of proposed method with existing method for Kinetics dataset

Model	Accuracy	F1-Score
CNN [21]	93.32	–
CNN-LSTM [30]	91.08	–
VGG-19+SVM (Proposed)	95.03	95.18

Table 5. Comparison of proposed method with existing method for CK+ dataset

Model	Accuracy	F1-score
CNN [17]	95.90	91.66
CNN-LSTM [6]	98.13	92.76
VGG-19+SVM (Proposed)	93.12	93.66

Furthermore, the overall outcomes of our strategy are fairly excellent with a 97.9% accuracy, 95.05% precision, 98.9% recall and 96.9% F1 score. Models are compared based on the accuracy and F1-score values with existing models. The results for the comparisons of proposed method with existing methods on different datasets are presented in table below. Table 3 shows the comparison of proposed method with existing one's for classification of gesture based human actions using weizmann dataset. In Table 4, there is comparison of proposed method with existing for interaction of human using kinetics dataset which include video clips of human interaction. Finally, Table 5 come up with comparison of behaviour based human activities through CK+ dataset.

6 Conclusion

With the advancement of technology and computer vision assistance, people having visual disability face challenges while detection and recognition of human activities in their daily routine task. In this paper, the proposed research is to detect human from video stream, extract their body position, classify their actions and convey the extracted human activities to user using deep learning methods. The system takes the video stream which can be a real time video or captured video stream. This video content is then processed to extract meaningful information by extracting the 2D human body skeleton using OpenPose. The extracted joints are then processing using pre-trained VGG-19 CNN method for extraction of human features. These extracted features are used to classify different human body actions using SVM classifier that classify more accurately. Finally, the information from classified human actions convey to user using text to speech methods because visually disable people are unable to read screen.

In this research, we proposed an effective deep learning method based on VGG-19 CNN and SVM for detection and recognition of human activities. The training and testing of proposed method achieved using weizmann, kinetics and CK+ datasets for gesture, interaction and behaviour based actions respectively. The performance of proposed method is evaluated by testing it pre-defined evaluation metrics i.e. accuracy, precision, recall and F1-score. These computational results indicate the significant accuracy on various human activities which can enhance confidence and interaction level for blinds without any dependency. In addition to this, a comparison of proposed method with existing methods in different human actions provide remarkable consequences for general adaptation. The future direction of proposed research is detect multiple actions in a video frames for violent event detection and crowd analysis that facilitate to visually impaired people.

Acknowledgements. This research with project id 16499 is funded by the National Research Program for Universities (NRPU), Higher Education Commission (HEC), Islamabad, Pakistan.

References

1. Fast facts of common eye disorders, June 2020. https://www.cdc.gov/visionhealth/basics/ced/fastfacts.htm
2. Vision impairment and blindness (2022). https://www.who.int/news-room/fact-sheets/detail/blindness-and-visual-impairment
3. Aparna, R., Chitralekha, C., Chaudhari, S.: Comparative study of CNN, VGG16 with LSTM and VGG16 with bidirectional LSTM using kitchen activity dataset. In: 2021 Fifth International Conference on I-SMAC (IoT in Social, Mobile, Analytics and Cloud)(I-SMAC), pp. 836–843. IEEE (2021)
4. Cao, Z., Simon, T., Wei, S.E., Sheikh, Y.: Realtime multi-person 2D pose estimation using part affinity fields. In: Proceedings of the IEEE Conference on Computer Vision and Pattern Recognition, pp. 7291–7299 (2017)
5. Dai, C., Liu, X., Lai, J.: Human action recognition using two-stream attention based LSTM networks. Appl. Soft Comput. **86**, 105820 (2020)
6. Debnath, T., Reza, M., Rahman, A., Beheshti, A., Band, S.S., Alinejad-Rokny, H., et al.: Four-layer convnet to facial emotion recognition with minimal epochs and the significance of data diversity. Sci. Rep. **12**(1), 1–18 (2022)

7. Deep, S., Zheng, X.: Leveraging CNN and transfer learning for vision-based human activity recognition. In: 2019 29th International Telecommunication Networks and Applications Conference (ITNAC), pp. 1–4. IEEE (2019)
8. Dirgová Luptáková, I., Kubovčík, M., Pospíchal, J.: Wearable sensor-based human activity recognition with transformer model. Sensors **22**(5), 1911 (2022)
9. Dua, N., Singh, S.N., Semwal, V.B.: Multi-input CNN-GRU based human activity recognition using wearable sensors. Computing **103**(7), 1461–1478 (2021)
10. Ehatisham-Ul-Haq, M., Javed, A., Azam, M.A., Malik, H.M., Irtaza, A., Lee, I.H., Mahmood, M.T.: Robust human activity recognition using multimodal feature-level fusion. IEEE Access **7**, 60736–60751 (2019)
11. Gamache, S., Routhier, F., Morales, E., Vandersmissen, M.H., Boucher, N.: Mapping review of accessible pedestrian infrastructures for individuals with physical disabilities. Disabil. Rehabil. Assistive Technol. **14**(4), 410–422 (2019)
12. Gorelick, L., Blank, M., Shechtman, E., Irani, M., Basri, R.: Actions as space-time shapes. Trans. Pattern Anal. Mach. Intell. **29**(12), 2247–2253 (2007)
13. Hao, Z., Zhang, D., Dang, X., Liu, G., Bai, Y.: Wi-CAS: a contactless method for continuous indoor human activity sensing using Wi-Fi devices. Sensors **21**(24), 8404 (2021)
14. Jalal, A., Kamal, S., Kim, D.: A depth video-based human detection and activity recognition using multi-features and embedded hidden markov models for health care monitoring systems (2017)
15. Kay, W., et al.: The kinetics human action video dataset. arXiv preprint arXiv:1705.06950 (2017)
16. Khan, M.A., Zhang, Y.D., Khan, S.A., Attique, M., Rehman, A., Seo, S.: A resource conscious human action recognition framework using 26-layered deep convolutional neural network. Multimedia Tools Appl. **80**(28), 35827–35849 (2021)
17. Kim, H., Lee, S., Jung, H.: Human activity recognition by using convolutional neural network. Int. J. Electr. Comput. Eng. **9**(6), 5270 (2019)
18. Lucey, P., Cohn, J.F., Kanade, T., Saragih, J., Ambadar, Z., Matthews, I.: The extended Cohn-Kanade dataset (CK+): A complete dataset for action unit and emotion-specified expression. In: 2010 IEEE Computer Society Conference on Computer Vision and Pattern Recognition-Workshops, pp. 94–101. IEEE (2010)
19. Mmereki, W., Jamisola, R.S., Mpoeleng, D., Petso, T.: YOLOv3-based human activity recognition as viewed from a moving high-altitude aerial camera. In: 2021 7th International Conference on Automation, Robotics and Applications (ICARA), pp. 241–246. IEEE (2021)
20. Muhammad, K., et al.: Human action recognition using attention based LSTM network with dilated CNN features. Future Gener. Comput. Syst. **125**, 820–830 (2021)
21. Mutegeki, R., Han, D.S.: A CNN-LSTM approach to human activity recognition. In: 2020 International Conference on Artificial Intelligence in Information and Communication (ICAIIC), pp. 362–366. IEEE (2020)
22. Nadeem, A., Jalal, A., Kim, K.: Human actions tracking and recognition based on body parts detection via artificial neural network. In: 2020 3rd International Conference on Advancements in Computational Sciences (ICACS), pp. 1–6. IEEE (2020)
23. Nadeem, A., Jalal, A., Kim, K.: Automatic human posture estimation for sport activity recognition with robust body parts detection and entropy Markov model. Multimedia Tools Appl. **80**(14), 21465–21498 (2021)
24. Naik, A.J., Gopalakrishna, M.: Deep-violence: individual person violent activity detection in video. Multimedia Tools Appl. **80**(12), 18365–18380 (2021)

25. Paré, S., Bleau, M., Djerourou, I., Malotaux, V., Kupers, R., Ptito, M.: Spatial navigation with horizontally spatialized sounds in early and late blind individuals. PloS ONE **16**(2), e0247448 (2021)
26. Pham, C., et al.: SensCapsNet: deep neural network for non-obtrusive sensing based human activity recognition. IEEE Access **8**, 86934–86946 (2020)
27. Rodríguez-Moreno, I., Martínez-Otzeta, J.M., Sierra, B., Rodriguez, I., Jauregi, E.: Video activity recognition: state-of-the-art. Sensors **19**(14), 3160 (2019)
28. Ronao, C.A., Cho, S.B.: Human activity recognition with smartphone sensors using deep learning neural networks. Expert Syst. Appl. **59**, 235–244 (2016)
29. Sun, H., et al.: Color correction and repair of haze images under hue-saturation-intensity color space and machine learning (2021)
30. Wan, S., Qi, L., Xu, X., Tong, C., Gu, Z.: Deep learning models for real-time human activity recognition with smartphones. Mob. Netw. Appl. **25**(2), 743–755 (2020)
31. Wu, D., Lv, S., Jiang, M., Song, H.: Using channel pruning-based YOLO v4 deep learning algorithm for the real-time and accurate detection of apple flowers in natural environments. Comput. Electron. Agric. **178**, 105742 (2020)

Takagi-Sugeno Type Neuro Fuzzy System Model Based Fault Diagnostic in Photovoltaic System

Moulay Rachid Douiri(✉) and Noureddine Aouzale

Department of Applied Physics, Faculty of Science and Technology, Cadi Ayyad University, Marrakesh, Morocco
douirirachid@hotmail.com

Abstract. Exposing photovoltaic installations to the outdoors for a long time leads to various breakdowns. Accurate and quantitative diagnosis of defect severity is vital for decision-making given the cost of defect removal. In this paper, a *Takagi-Sugeno* type neuro-fuzzy approach for the detection, identification and location of faults in solar photovoltaic systems is proposed. Then, an algorithm for optimizing the structure of the neuro-fuzzy model is developed, in order to improve the convergence capacity, resolve the influence of random parameters on the predictive performances, and to reduce both the number of synaptic weights and membership functions. This approach accurately detects, identifies and locates photovoltaic faults based on measurements of fault current, photovoltaic voltage, irradiance level, temperature and weather. Various fault scenarios are experimentally verified and validated in a large-scale solar photovoltaic power plant in order to demonstrate the efficiency and accuracy of the proposed approach.

Keywords: Fault diagnostic · Neuro-fuzzy · Optimisation · Photovoltaic system

1 Introduction

A photovoltaic system can be subjected, during its operation, to various faults and anomalies leading to a drop in the performance of the system and even to the total unavailability of the system. All these unfavorable consequences will obviously reduce the productivity of the installation, and therefore reduce the profit of the installation, not to mention the maintenance cost to restore the system to normal [1, 2]. For instance, experimental analyses have shown that the insufficient protection of bypass diodes can lead to the overheating of shaded PV cells [3, 4]. Several authors have thus developed simulation and modeling approaches to better understand the effect of shadows on photovoltaic installations [5, 6]. Despite these considerable contributions, the observed behavior of real photovoltaic systems suggests a need to improve the description of the impact of these shadows [7, 8]. Indeed, more accurate models have been shown to improve the PV power production forecast, allow the optimal design of PV installations, and improve the simulation reliability of fault detection methods [9, 10]. Currently, the techniques most used by researchers to diagnose photovoltaic installation faults are based on the analysis of the resulting *I-V* characteristic [11], image and output signal analysis [12],

O. Pichardo Lagunas et al. (Eds.): MICAI 2022, LNAI 13613, pp. 369–381, 2022.
https://doi.org/10.1007/978-3-031-19496-2_29

real-time difference detection [13], artificial intelligence [14], etc. [15] uses the dynamic time window approach and the kernel density estimation method to develop a fault diagnosis technique based on data from the dynamic modeling of photovoltaic installations. [16] it develops a recurrent neural network to locate the six types of relevant defects and estimate the severity of each defect, based on daily measurements. Another method [17] uses intelligent variable predictive models and *I-V* curves to diagnose PV string faults. A method of metaheuristic optimization is used by [18] as to identify, locate and diagnose the defects of photovoltaic string under non-uniform meteorological conditions. [19] presents an adaptive neuro-fuzzy Inference System to predict and classify different PV defects. An approach was proposed by [12] using a deep learning algorithm to diagnose two types of failures in PV installations named the hot-spot and hot substring. In this work, an optimized neuro-fuzzy *Takagi-Sugeno* approach for the detection, location and identification of PV string defects is proposed. The optimization algorithm improves the convergence capacity, resolves the influence of random parameters on the predictive performance, and reduces both the number of synaptic weights and the membership functions. This approach ensures an accurate photovoltaic fault diagnosis based on measurements of fault current, PV voltage, irradiance level, temperature and weather conditions. Various fault scenarios are experimentally verified and validated in a large-scale solar photovoltaic power plant to demonstrate the efficiency and accuracy of the proposed approach.

This paper consists of the following sections: Sect. 1 presents the photovoltaic model for unshaded and shaded conditions; Sect. 2 introduces the diagnostic PV system based on the NF system model; in Sect. 3, the optimization of the NF model is proposed, in Sect. 4, the effectiveness of the proposed approach is validated by three scenarios; the last Section presents the conclusion.

2 PV Model for Unshaded and Shaded Conditions

2.1 PV Cell Model for Unshaded Conditions

The single diode model describes the PV cell behavior for unshaded conditions. The relationship between cell current I and cell voltage V is given by the following equation:

$$I = I_{ph} - I_0\left[\exp(\frac{V + IR_s}{V_t}) - 1\right] - \frac{V + IR_s}{R_p} \tag{1}$$

R_s: series resistance related to the conductive losses, R_p: parallel resistance defined for modeling the distributed losses. I_0: inverse saturation current, and V_t: thermal voltage. I_{ph}: photogenerated current given by Eq. (2):

$$I_{ph} = I_{phTi} = \left[I_{sc-STC} + (C_{Ti}(T_c - T_{STC}))\right]\frac{G_i}{G_{STC}} \tag{2}$$

I_{phTi}: photogenerated current for the unshaded condition, G_i: incident irradiance, C_{Ti}: thermal current coefficient, T_c: cell temperature. $I_{sc\text{-}STC}$, T_{STC}, and G_{STC} are nominal values for the standard test condition (STC) (25 °C and 1000 W/m^2).

The PV model for unshaded conditions is well known in PV system studies. However, PV installations usually require a more detailed analysis owing to the effects of shadows and other external factors.

2.2 PV Cell Model for Completely Shaded Conditions

Completely shaded photovoltaic cells can be obliged to move current in reverse bias [11]. Thus, a negative voltage can appear at the photovoltaic cell terminals and the unsafe reverse current tends to increase. According to *Herrmann et al.* in [20], free electrons inside of the *p-n* material gain enough energy for colliding with atoms and separate other electrons from their corresponding atoms [20]. After each collision, each new free electron is able to cause similar collisions thus leading to a sudden current multiplication or avalanching breakdown condition. Reference [11] explains this current multiplication effect (Eq. (3)) by modeling shaded photovoltaic cells using a non-lineal multiplier factor $M(V_d)$, which is associated with the parallel resistor current as illustrated in Fig. 1 [11]. In Eq. (3), *k*: fraction of avalanche breakdown current, V_b: breakdown voltage, *n*: avalanche breakdown exponent.

$$I = I_{ph} - I_0\left[\exp(\frac{V + IR_s}{V_t}) - 1\right] - \frac{V + IR_s}{R_p}\left[1 + k\left(\frac{V + IR_s}{V_b}\right)^{-n}\right] \quad (3)$$

This avalanche breakdown that occurs in reverse bias is harmful to PV cells because the risk of structural failure increases. Manufacturers thus use bypass diodes to prevent the occurrence of this dangerous operation condition in PV modules. However, despite the use of bypass diodes, reverse bias cells can still carry current and hot-spots can thus arise [20].

3 Neuro Fuzzy System Model Based Diagnostic PV System

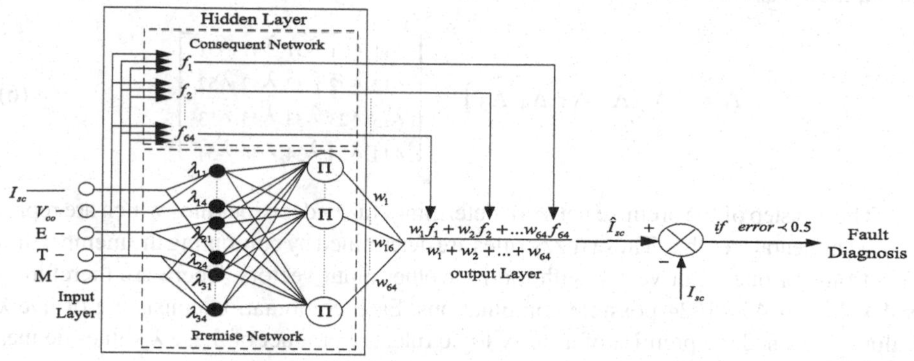

Fig. 1. Neuro-fuzzy architecture

Our approach focuses on the detection of fault states in photovoltaic systems using the *Takagi-Sugeno* type neuro-fuzzy model (see Fig. 1). The NF approach is executed in a series-parallel interconnect circuit, and the entire PV array is fully dynamic during partial shading conditions. The designed neuro-fuzzy system contains five inputs and one output. The five input variables are short circuit current (I_{sc}), PV voltage (V_{pv}),

Irradiance (E), temperature (T) and weather (M). The output variable of the model is the default state of the PV system.

The hidden layer receives the sampled data for the five input vectors. The latter consists of a premise and consequent network (see Fig. 1) constituting a set of weight factors w_i which uses the vectors of each input to implement the whole Eq. (8), thus, its output is a set of function values f_k. The specificities of these two networks are described as follows [21]:

$$f_k = c_k^0 + c_k^1 x_1 + c_k^2 x_2 + \ldots + c_k^m x_m \tag{4}$$

${c_k}^i$: linear coefficients for k^{th} subsystem, x_i: i^{th} input to the model, m: total inputs number.

The premise network aims to partition the input space, in fact, each of the five input vectors their samples are associated into four membership functions (MF) of *Gaussian* type defined as [22]:

$$\lambda_{in} = \exp\left(-\frac{(x_i - \mu_{in})^2}{(\sigma_{in})^2}\right) \tag{5}$$

λ_{in}: value of nth membership functions for the ith input variable, μ_{in} ($n = 1$ to 4): corresponding mean value, σ_{in}: spread factor of the nth *Gaussian* function.

Each value of μ and σ defines a fuzzy band, the four bands are associated with a linguistic label as follows: *HIGH (H)* for $n = 1$, *MEDIUM HIGH (MH)* for $n = 2$, *MEDIUM LOW (ML)* for $n = 3$; and *LOW (L)* for $n = 4$. Hence, this results in 20 *Gaussian* functions for the five input vectors of the neuro fuzzy system, which yields 12 numeric values in the range near 0 to 1 for each set of sampled input values grouped into a matrix as follows:

$$\Lambda = \left[\Lambda_1\ \Lambda_2\ \Lambda_3\ \Lambda_4\ \Lambda_5\right] = \begin{bmatrix} \lambda_{11} & \lambda_{21} & \lambda_{31} & \lambda_{41} & \lambda_{51} \\ \lambda_{12} & \lambda_{22} & \lambda_{32} & \lambda_{42} & \lambda_{52} \\ \lambda_{13} & \lambda_{23} & \lambda_{33} & \lambda_{43} & \lambda_{53} \\ \lambda_{14} & \lambda_{24} & \lambda_{34} & \lambda_{44} & \lambda_{54} \end{bmatrix} \tag{6}$$

The 2nd step of the premise network determines fuzzy decision rules which are represented as neural weights. These fuzzy rules are determined by combining the membership functions for one input vector with the four other input vectors. There are therefore 4 x 4 x 4 x 4 x 4 = 1024 possible combinations. Each combination consisting of five λ values, is named the premise of a fuzzy logic rule, the product of these λ values defines a neural weight as follows:

$$w_r = (\lambda_{1a}) \times (\lambda_{2b}) \times (\lambda_{3c}) \times (\lambda_{4d}) \times (\lambda_{5e}) \tag{7}$$

a, *b*, and *c*: index fuzzy band associated, r (1 to 1024): the rth weighting factor out of 1024 in total.

The consequent network calculate a set of linear equations using the sampled data set of input vectors (Eq. (6)) expressed in vector form as [23]:

$$F = \begin{bmatrix} f_1 \\ f_2 \\ . \\ . \\ f_{1024} \end{bmatrix} = C \begin{bmatrix} I_{pv} \\ V \\ E \\ T \\ M \end{bmatrix} \tag{8}$$

$$C = \begin{bmatrix} C_1 \\ C_2 \\ . \\ . \\ C_{1024} \end{bmatrix} = \begin{bmatrix} c_0^1 & c_1^1 & c_2^1 & c_3^1 & c_4^1 & c_5^1 \\ c_0^2 & c_1^2 & c_2^2 & c_3^2 & c_4^2 & c_5^2 \\ . & . & . & . & . & . \\ . & . & . & . & . & . \\ c_0^{1024} & c_1^{1024} & c_2^{1024} & c_3^{1024} & c_4^{1024} & c_5^{1024} \end{bmatrix} \tag{9}$$

C is a 1024×6 tall matrix containing 6144 parameter coefficients.

The output layer contains 1024 premise network neural weights and 1024 consequent network functions f_r, are multiplied to estimate the photovoltaic current, and then compared with the input current of the neuro-fuzzy system to determine the fault state of the photovoltaic system. The expression for the estimated photovoltaic current I_{pv} is given as follows [23]:

$$\hat{I}_{pv} = \frac{w_1 f_1 + w_2 f_2 + \ldots w_{64} f_{64}}{w_1 + w_2 + \ldots + w_{64}} = \frac{\Phi\Gamma}{\Omega} \tag{10}$$

Γ is a column vector grouping all the 6144 parameter coefficients of the 1024 f_r functions given as follows:

$$\Gamma = \left[c_0^1\, c_1^1\, c_2^1\, c_3^1\, c_0^2\, c_1^2 \ldots c_5^{1024} \right]^t \tag{11}$$

$\Omega = \sum_{n=1}^{1024} w_n$ designates the sum of all neural weights, and Φ is a 1 x 6144 row $n = 1$ vector grouping the products between the samples of the input vectors and the corresponding neural weights is expressed as follows:

$$\Phi = \left[w_1 I_{pv}\; w_1 V_{pv}\; w_1 E\; w_1 T\; w_1 M\; w_1\; w_2 I_{pv}\; w_2 V_{pv}\; w_2 E\; w_2 T\; w_2 M\; w_2 \ldots w_{64} \right] \tag{12}$$

4 Model Structure Optimization

The model described above has a total number of 1048 components: 20 membership functions and 1024 fuzzy rules. Some of these components may be redundant, so this structure may not be the optimum. Furthermore, for 20 membership functions there are 40 membership functions parameters (μ and σ). Thus, the design of the optimal NF system suggests looking for a combination with a reduced number of sets of fuzzy rules, membership functions, and sets of membership function parameters.

4.1 Selecting Valid Fuzzy Rules

A set of fuzzy rules corresponds to the combination of different membership functions from different inputs. As shown in Fig. 2, a rule structure diagram is used to represent all rules for the PV model. One can see that each membership function of the 1st input variable (photovoltaic current) has a connection with each membership function of the 2end input variable (PV voltage). Similarly, each membership function of the PV voltage has a link with the membership functions of the insulation. Each membership function of the latter is connected to the membership functions of the temperature. Then, each temperature membership function is connected to weather membership functions. Finally, each membership function of the weather is reconnected to the membership functions of the photovoltaic current, to form a closed path. In total there are 80 connections - links as presented in Tables 1, 2, 3, 4 and 5.

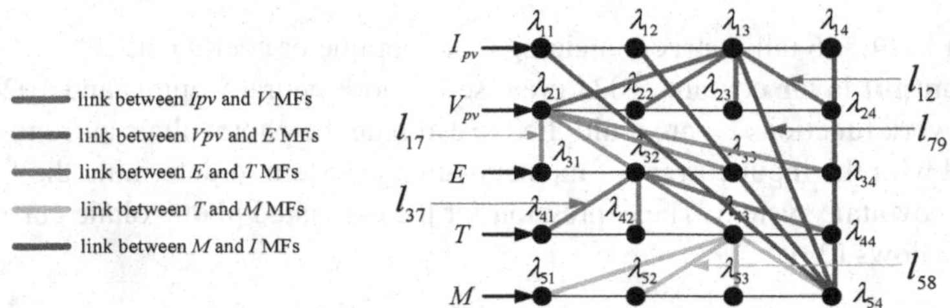

Fig. 2. Fuzzy rules link topology for the PV model.

Each 3 of these links are related by a rule by tracing through the closed path that starts and ends at the same membership functions of each input. For instance, λ_{14}, λ_{24}, λ_{34}, λ_{44}, and λ_{54} form the 1024th fuzzy rule, and this involves five links, l16, l32, l48, l64 and l80. Thus, all fuzzy rules are determined by a set of links which are grouped in a vector expressed by:

$$L_l = \left[l_1 \; l_2 \ldots l_{80} \right] \tag{13}$$

Initially, neural link values are randomly and manually set between 0 and 1 and then iteratively estimated. A fuzzy rule becomes inactive if only one of the 3 neural links has a value strictly less than 0.01. Therefore, the corresponding weighting factor is set to zero and will not be taken into account during the neuro-fuzzy model training process of predicting the output values of the photovoltaic current. Using this set of weighting factors allows the neuro-fuzzy system to reduce the number of links to 80 links instead of 1024 fuzzy rules.

Table 1. Link between MFs of I_{pv} and V_{pv}.

		Vpv			
		λ_{21}	λ_{22}	λ_{23}	λ_{24}
I_{pv}	λ_{11}	l_1	l_2	l_3	l_4
	λ_{12}	l_5	l_6	l_7	l_8
	λ_{13}	l_9	l_{10}	l_{11}	l_{12}
	λ_{14}	l_{13}	l_{14}	l_{15}	l_{16}

Table 2. Link between MFs of V_{pv} and E.

		E			
		λ_{31}	λ_{32}	λ_{33}	λ_{34}
V_{pv}	λ_{21}	l_{17}	l_{18}	l_{19}	l_{20}
	λ_{22}	l_{21}	l_{22}	l_{23}	l_{24}
	λ_{23}	l_{25}	l_{26}	l_{27}	l_{28}
	λ_{24}	l_{29}	l_{30}	l_{31}	l_{32}

Table 3. Link between MFs of E and T.

		T			
		λ_{41}	λ_{42}	λ_{43}	λ_{44}
E	λ_{31}	l_{33}	l_{34}	l_{35}	l_{36}
	λ_{32}	l_{37}	l_{38}	l_{39}	l_{40}
	λ_{33}	l_{41}	l_{42}	l_{43}	l_{44}
	λ_{34}	l_{45}	l_{46}	l_{47}	l_{48}

Table 4. Link between MFs of T and M.

		M			
		λ_{51}	λ_{52}	λ_{53}	λ_{54}
T	λ_{41}	l_{49}	l_{50}	l_{51}	l_{52}
	λ_{42}	l_{53}	l_{54}	l_{55}	l_{56}
	λ_{43}	l_{57}	l_{58}	l_{59}	l_{60}
	λ_{44}	l_{61}	l_{62}	l_{63}	l_{64}

Table 5. Link between MFs of M and I_{pv}.

		Ipv			
		λ_{11}	λ_{12}	λ_{13}	λ_{14}
M	λ_{51}	l_{65}	l_{66}	l_{67}	l_{68}
	λ_{52}	l_{69}	l_{70}	l_{71}	l_{72}
	λ_{53}	l_{73}	l_{74}	l_{75}	l_{76}
	λ_{54}	l_{77}	l_{78}	l_{79}	l_{80}

4.2 Selecting Active MFs

Another set of neural weights W_{ij} is made to store the active membership functions information, it is given by:

$$W = \begin{bmatrix} w_{11} & w_{21} & w_{31} & w_{41} & w_{51} \\ w_{12} & w_{22} & w_{32} & w_{42} & w_{52} \\ w_{13} & w_{23} & w_{33} & w_{43} & w_{53} \\ w_{14} & w_{24} & w_{34} & w_{44} & w_{54} \end{bmatrix} \quad (14)$$

Each element of the matrix W (value fixed between 0 and 1) indicates if the corresponding linguistic label is active, or not. e.g., if w_{23} is less than 0.01, the 3rd membership function for PV voltage input is disabled and its fuzzy value, λ_{23} is not taken into account in the neural weights computation w_r. Fuzzy rule selection, membership functions, and fuzzy rules are enabled and disabled accordingly. Additionally, two special scenarios can lead to further rule elimination; the first is that some active rules are linked to all invalid membership functions, which means that they can be deleted. The second is that for links among weights, there may be two or more closed paths along which the same valid membership functions occur. In this case, only one of the associated rules is kept while the others are deleted.

5 Experimental Results

Table 6 shows the specifications of the *JAP6 60- 255/3BB* polycrystalline silicon under standard condition (STC). Various meteorological conditions are applied to the photovoltaic modules for learning, training and testing of the neuro-fuzzy model.

Table 6. Parameters of photovoltaic module.

Parameter	Value
Maximum rate power/W	255
Open circuit voltage/V	37.87
Short circuit current/A	8.7
Operating voltage at maximum power/V	31.68
Operating current at maximum power/A	8.05

Table 7 presents the specifications of the developed neuro-fuzzy model. The computation time to run the system is 34 s.

Table 7. Specifications of the developed neuro-fuzzy system.

Parameter	Value and Depiction
FIS Configuration	*Takagi-Sugeno* type
Initial FIS for training	Grid Partition
No. of MFs/type	MFs = 2/*Gaussmf*
Output MF	Linear
Inputs	5
Outputs	1
Optimization method	Hybrid
Number of fuzzy rules	80
No. of epochs	170

5.1 Failure Scenarios

The efficiency of the photovoltaic system has a close relationship with the various faults such as hot spot, abnormal aging and short-circuit fault which are comparable to that of the photovoltaic shading fault. In order to analyze the quantitative results under different shading faults, experimental fault tests on photovoltaic output characteristics with various scenarios were carried out. As a result, the developed neuro fuzzy approach has been effectively applied to quantify the severity of photovoltaic defects mentioned above.

The fault severity diagnosis experiment is performed on three typical shaded faults as illustrated in Fig. 3. The *X*, *Y* and *Z* scenario shades a PV cell, a PV cell column and a PV cell row respectively. By analyzing the three scenarios, we find that scenario *X* represents the least weak fault, on the other hand in scenario *Z*, the by-pass diode in parallel will light up and the sub-chain will be short-circuited to avoid the hot-spot effect, which will result in a more severe fault than scenario *Y*.

The evaluation of the seriousness of the defect is quantified by the mean deviation rate (RMSE) expressed as follows:

$$RMSE = \frac{\sqrt{\frac{1}{n}\sum_{i=1}^{n}\left(P - P_i'\right)^2}}{P_{max} - P_{min}} \times 100 \tag{15}$$

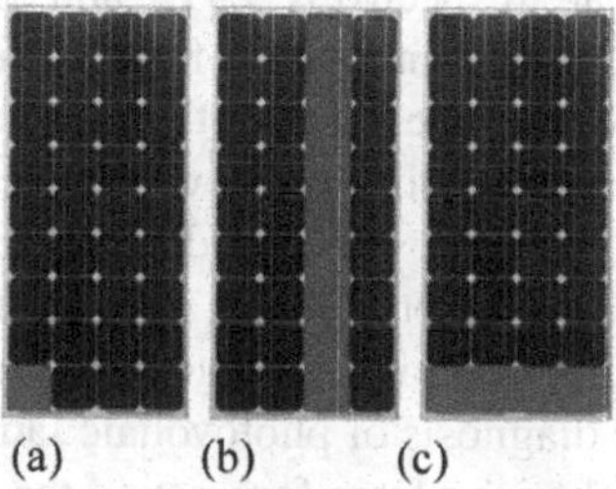

(a) (b) (c)

Fig. 3. Modules affected by a shading fault (a) scenario *X*; (b) scenario *Y*; (c) scenario *Z*.

5.2 Photovoltaic Fault Diagnosis Results

The real-time diagnostic results of the *X*, *Y* and *Z* failure scenarios were carried out over a week under different types of weather.

Within 24 h (day 1), the fault diagnosis results in the three scenarios *X*, *Y* and *Z* are shown in Fig. 4. Figure 4(a) shows that the estimated PV current of fault state in scenario *X* is close to that of normal state, and the value of the mean deviation rate is 8.33%. Therefore, no need to eliminate the fault for scenario *X*, since shading of a single PV cell will cause a slight decrease in electricity production.

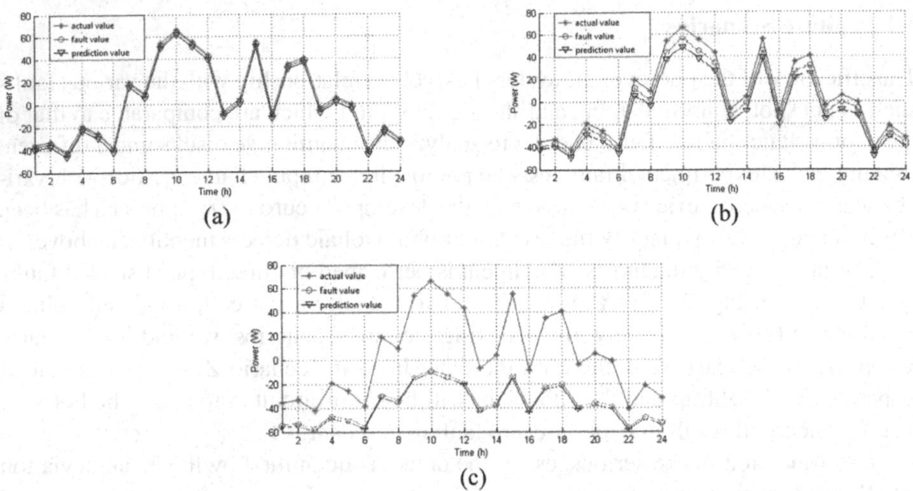

Fig. 4. Experimental diagnostic test of various scenarios over time on day 1. (a) scenario *X*. (b) scenario *Y*. (c) scenario *Z*.

On the other hand, the estimated output photovoltaic current deviations between the normal state and the fault state in the scenarios *X*, *Y* and *Z* are visible, as illustrated in Figs. 4(b) and Fig. 4(c). The calculation shows that the fault mean deviation rate values of the two scenarios *Y* and *Z* are respectively 9.41% and 61.17%, which are visible and serious, hence the need to urgently eliminate the fault in time to both scenarios *Y* and *Z*.

The results obtained prove that the value of the mean deviation rate increases with the severity of the photovoltaic shading fault, which is a quantitative, effective and precise characteristic for fault diagnosis. In addition, the neuro fuzzy approach also accurately estimates the PV energy production under different fault states and under various meteorological conditions, which validates the effectiveness of our applied NF approach for the quantitative diagnosis of photovoltaic faults.

According to the results obtained from forecasting the three weather types *A*, *B* and *C*, it can be concluded that the forecasting performance of weather type *C* is inferior to that of the other two weather types. In order to validate the approach proposed for the detection and efficient quantification of defects in the type of weather 3. The experimental diagnostic tests of the scenario *X*, *Y* and *Z* are given in Fig. 5. The calculation shows that the mean deviation rate of the 3 scenarios are respectively 09.13%, 37.68% and 62.09%. The experimental test results show that defects and their quantification in time type 3 can be diagnosed efficiently and quickly using the proposed neuro fuzzy approach. It is noted that it is urgently necessary to eliminate the fault in advance of scenario *Z*.

According to different types of weather, the severity of different photovoltaic shading faults can be effectively quantified. The mean deviation rate values of real-time diagnostic results in scenarios *Y* and *Z* are relatively considerable under various types of weather time, in this case the shading fault is visible and the PV modules working in fault states. In addition, the mean deviation rate defect of the same severity under weather types 1 and 2 are in a relatively close interval, but which is different from that of weather type 3. Therefore, the model is insensitive when the weather varies between type 1 to type 2.

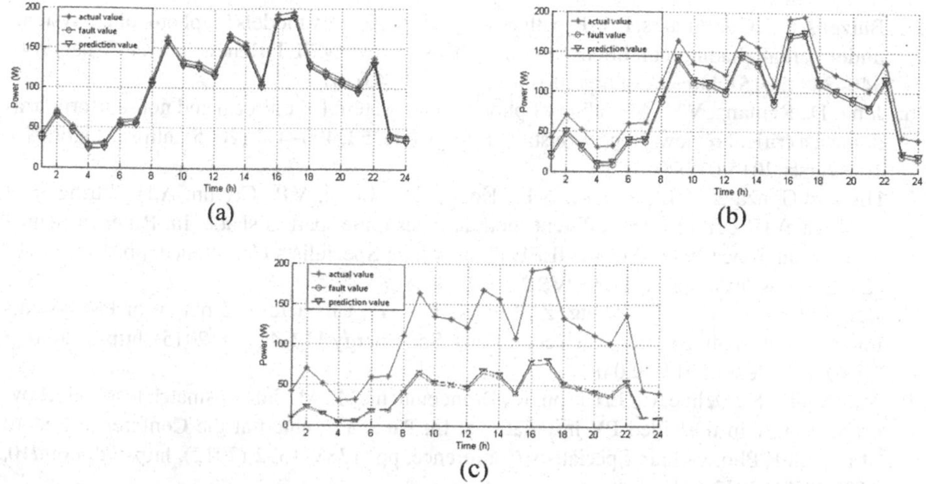

(a) (b) (c)

Fig. 5. Experimental diagnostic test of various scenarios over time on day 63. (a) scenario *X*. (b) scenario *Y*. (c) scenario *Z*.

6 Conclusion

The proposed fault detection, identification and location algorithm for a photovoltaic system is based on a new optimized neuro-fuzzy hybrid model, applied to improve the convergence ability, solve the influence of random parameters on the performance of predictive shading faults. The results of the experimental tests successfully demonstrate the ability and efficiency of the proposed approach in the precise and quantitative diagnosis of the severity of shading faults, which guarantees safe, stable and economical operation of the electrical network, while building a reasonable and effective database for the intelligent operation and maintenance of the photovoltaic system.

References

1. Toledo, O.M., Oliveira Filho, D., Diniz, A.S.A.C., Martins, J.H., Vale, M.H.M.: Methodology for evaluation of grid-tie connection of distributed energy resources - case study with photovoltaic and energy storage. IEEE Trans. Power Syst. **28**(2), 1132–1139 (2013). https://doi.org/10.1109/TPWRS.2012.2207971
2. Brooks, A.E., Cormode, D., Cronin, A.D., Kam-Lum, E.: PV system power loss and module damage due to partial shade and bypass diode failure depend on cell behavior in reverse bias. In: Paper Presented at the 2015 IEEE 42nd Photovoltaic Specialist Conference, PVSC 2015 (2015). https://doi.org/10.1109/PVSC.2015.7356290
3. Bressan, M., El Basri, Y., Galeano, A.G., Alonso, C.: A shadow fault detection method based on the standard error analysis of I-V curves. Renew. Energy **99**, 1181–1190 (2016). https://doi.org/10.1016/j.renene.2016.08.028
4. Daliento, S., Di Napoli, F., Guerriero, P., d'Alessandro, V.: A modified bypass circuit for improved hot spot reliability of solar panels subject to partial shading. Sol. Energy **134**, 211–218 (2016). https://doi.org/10.1016/j.solener.2016.05.001

5. Batzelis, E.I., Georgilakis, P.S., Papathanassiou, S.A.: Energy models for photovoltaic systems under partial shading conditions: a comprehensive review. IET Renew. Power Gener. **9**(4), 340–349 (2015). https://doi.org/10.1049/iet-rpg.2014.0207
6. Jena, D., Ramana, V.V.: Modeling of photovoltaic system for uniform and non-uniform irradiance: a critical review. Renew. Sustain. Energy Rev. **52**, 400–417 (2015). https://doi.org/10.1016/j.rser.2015.07.079
7. Hidalgo-Gonzalez, P.L., Brooks, A.E., Kopp, E.S., Lonij, V.P., Cronin, A.D.: String-level (kW-scale) IV curves from different module types under partial shade. In: Paper Presented at the Conference Record of the IEEE Photovoltaic Specialists Conference, pp. 1442–1447 (2012). https://doi.org/10.1109/PVSC.2012.6317868
8. Bai, J., Cao, Y., Hao, Y., Zhang, Z., Liu, S., Cao, F.: Characteristic output of PV systems under partial shading or mismatch conditions. Sol. Energy **112**, 41–54 (2015). https://doi.org/10.1016/j.solener.2014.09.048
9. MacAlpine, S., Deline, C., Erickson, R., Brandemuehl, M.: Module mismatch loss and recoverable power in unshaded PV installations. In: Paper Presented at the Conference Record of the IEEE Photovoltaic Specialists Conference, pp. 1388–1392 (2012). https://doi.org/10.1109/PVSC.2012.6317858
10. Daliento, S., et al.: Monitoring, diagnosis, and power forecasting for photovoltaic fields: a review. Int. J. Photoenergy 2017 (2017). https://doi.org/10.1155/2017/1356851
11. Li, B., Delpha, C., Migan-Dubois, A., Diallo, D.: Fault diagnosis of photovoltaic panels using full I-V characteristics and machine learning techniques. Energy Convers. Manag. **248**, 114785 (2021). https://doi.org/10.1016/j.enconman.2021.114785
12. Haidari, P., Hajiahmad, A., Jafari, A., Nasiri, A.: Deep learning-based model for fault classification in solar modules using infrared images. Sustain. Energy Technol. Assess. **52**, 102110 (2022). https://doi.org/10.1016/j.seta.2022.102110
13. Iqbal, M.S., Niazi, Y.A.K., Khan, U.A., Lee, B.: Real-time fault detection system for large scale grid integrated solar photovoltaic power plants. Int. J. Electr. Power Energy Syst. **130**, 10690 (2021). https://doi.org/10.1016/j.ijepes.2021.106902
14. Voutsinas, S., Karolidis, D., Voyiatzis, I., Samarakou, M.: Development of a multi-output feed-forward neural network for fault detection in photovoltaic systems. Energy Rep. **8**, 33–42 (2022). https://doi.org/10.1016/j.egyr.2022.06.107
15. Ying, S., et al.: Dynamic probability modeling of photovoltaic strings and its application in fault diagnosis. Energy Rep. **8**, 6270–6279 (2022). https://doi.org/10.1016/j.egyr.2022.04.072
16. Van Gompel, J., Spina, D., Develder, C.: Satellite based fault diagnosis of photovoltaic systems using recurrent neural networks. Appl. Energy **305**, 117874 (2022). https://doi.org/10.1016/j.apenergy.2021.117874
17. Liu, Y., et al.: Intelligent fault diagnosis of photovoltaic array based on variable predictive models and I-V curves. Sol. Energy **237**, 340–351 (2022). https://doi.org/10.1016/j.solener.2022.03.062
18. Das, S., Hazra, A., Basu, M.: Metaheuristic optimization based fault diagnosis strategy for solar photovoltaic systems under non-uniform irradiance. Renewable Energy **118**, 452–467 (2018). https://doi.org/10.1016/j.renene.2017.10.053
19. Abbas, M., Zhang, D.: A smart fault detection approach for PV modules using adaptive neuro-fuzzy inference framework. Energy Rep. **7**, 2962–2975 (2021). https://doi.org/10.1016/j.egyr.2021.04.059
20. Herrmann, W., Wiesner, W., Vaassen, W.: Hot spot investigations on PV modules - new concepts for a test standard and consequences for module design with respect to bypass diodes. In: Paper Presented at the Conference Record of the IEEE Photovoltaic Specialists Conference, pp. 1129–1132 (1997)
21. Douiri, S.M., El Bernoussi, S.: An ant algorithm for the sum coloring problem. Int. J. Appl. Math. Stat. **27**(3), 102–110 (2012)

22. Douiri, M.R., Cherkaoui, M.: Comparative study of various artificial intelligence approaches applied to direct torque control of induction motor drives. Front. Energy **7**(4), 456–467 (2013). https://doi.org/10.1007/s11708-013-0264-8
23. Douiri, M.R.: A predictive model for solar photovoltaic power based on computational intelligence technique. Arab. J. Sci. Eng. **44**(8), 6923–6940 (2019). https://doi.org/10.1007/s13369-019-03725-w

Author Index

Printed in the United States
by Baker & Taylor Publisher Services